CLINICAL STUDIES IN CHILDHOOD PSYCHOSES

Clinical Studies
in
Childhood Psychoses

25 Years in Collaborative Treatment and Research
The Langley Porter Children's Service

Edited by

S. A. Szurek, M.D.
Director, The Children's Service, The Langley Porter
Neuropsychiatric Institute
Professor of Psychiatry, University of California
School of Medicine (San Francisco)

and

I. N. Berlin, M.D.
Professor of Psychiatry and Pediatrics
Head, Division of Child Psychiatry, University of Washington
School of Medicine (Seattle)

BRUNNER/MAZEL • New York
BUTTERWORTHS • London

Introduction

TOWARDS A BREAKTHROUGH

These clinical studies in childhood psychoses covering 25 years of experimental work in treatment, training, as well as research at the Langley Porter's Children's Service are brought together in a volume which not only presents S. A. Szurek's work and influence but honors this pioneer. It touches off in me competitive admiration, and the wish to accompany a critical evaluation of his work with a self-evaluation of my own research concerning psychotic children, covering approximately the same length of time. Briefly, as I think back to my beginning interests at the Southard School in Topeka, I recall my attempts to find a middle ground between what then seemed to be the leading but extreme opposite approaches in focus, in interest, in methodological procedure, and in treatment outlook. Lauretta Bender and her associates stressed the biological aspects and the maturational lag, while S. A. Szurek stressed the environmental impact, the interpersonal, the parent-child interaction, as he investigated the etiology of childhood psychosis. In my own work I turned away from the search for the causes of the illness and stressed the study of the causes of cure, focusing on the need to understand one-to-one psychotherapeutic interaction based on psychoanalytically-oriented treatment procedures.

These last 25 years were extremely productive years in the study of childhood psychosis even though much of our productivity suffered from the fact that we were like small medieval guilds, keeping their secrets of productivity. The students identified with the master teacher, continued his tradition, and found it difficult to accept the secrets of the other guilds. Szurek's search for truth is evident in this volume. The authors caution us convincingly about the need to never let that search be hampered by institutional needs. He

knows, as we all do, how difficult it is to carry out our research, our therapeutic work, without institutional strength and yet how that very same institutional strength may make that reflective research island into a fortress of
mere dogmatic conviction and vested interest.

As I review the work of Szurek and Berlin and their collaborators, many
of them now leading figures in various psychiatric centers, I find that they
deal with familiar and challenging problems with rare honesty and erudition.
I find in this volume, attitudes which are close to my heart, encouragement to
enter the psychotic world of the child, to study his environment, and to try to
penetrate the forest of etiological issues, so that we may find some harvest
of insight, the possibility of therapeutic success. We can experience with the
writers the relationship of investment to failure, the training problems, many
of us have lived through. It is heartening to be reminded that our colleagues
are actually brothers-in-arms, that there are bridges between our different
islands.

It was fascinating for me to see how Szurek, Berlin and their colleagues
have approximately the same results that others have. They describe vividly
some of the clinical issues, the need to broaden the technical and theoretical
armamentarium. They graphically illustrate that a good many of the clinical,
therapeutic and research procedures are not different in basic nature. The
editors have in this volume allowed us to see eye to eye with them, to see that
we can actually learn from each other and adapt our views to clinical realities.

I am enthused about the fact that this book does not try to achieve artificial
unity as we see in premature textbooks or in superficial primers. Rather, it
requires of us that we ourselves work through with the authors again and
again, the questions, the methods, the changing views of 25 years of earnest
creative work.

There is a willingness on the part of Szurek to be playful with his ideas,
through creative variations on a number of basic themes characteristic for
him, for Berlin and for their collaborators.

These pages emphasize and illustrate a need for historic perspective, a
special interest in the interaction between child and parents, a stress of ward
management and milieu treatment, a careful consideration of statistical
analysis and a constant searching review of the several hundred children who
were treated at Langley Porter. There is also emphasis on the training of
young residents, their countertransference problems and suggestions as to
their training. Finally, there is a willingness to include the individual case
study and to courageously describe not only the successes but also failures. I
found the case histories vivid and moving accounts of the human drama in
psychotherapy of psychotic children and their parents.

Szurek and Berlin have reinforced my convictions that the work with psychotic children requires strange mixtures of attitudes which seem to be incompatible. The writings illustrate compassion for the child and the family; endless commitment to treatment; a wish to struggle for the vital support from the institution in order to carry on the work; a willingness to maintain theoretical and therapeutic views which are not always immediately accepted by those who hold to the more conventional approaches. I feel in consonance with their emphasis on the capacity not to be overcommited to a system of treatment or a basic philosophy. This permits the ability to allow research, an objective search for truth, to be a dominant theme in all one's activities. I find Szurek and Berlin's clinical concerns manifested in richly detailed accounts of their work stimulating to my thinking and very important to the development of students and young professionals working with severely disturbed children and their parents.

This volume demonstrates how one can combine compassionate commitment and objective research; how one can stand up under constant social pressures, lack of support and lack of funding, and still maintain playful reflection on the issues of one's work; how one can create an organization which will give students an opportunity to combine compassion with objectivity, empathy with the wish to count and to account, to develop exact research methodology, to question evidence even if it seems to be satisfactory. Szurek's and Berlin's book, and Szurek's influence on his collaborators reflected in this book, are proof that clinical work can be creative research. This work presents an example of synthesis between individuality, the staying with one's core convictions and mutuality, the capacity to build bridges to other individuals, other centers. Perhaps the next 25 years of the study of childhood psychosis, the intensive treatment of these children and their families—thanks to individuals like Szurek—will bring the breakthrough in the treatment of psychotic children. This volume, for many years to come, will be a visible milestone in our conquest of this illness.

RUDOLF EKSTEIN, PH.D.
Director, Childhood Psychosis Project
Reiss-Davis Child Study Center

CONTENTS

ix

Section III
Some Current Clinical Issues 85

Section IV
Clinical Research 189

Section V
Sexual Problems with Psychotic Children in Treatment 479

Section VI
Therapeutic Experiences with Psychotic Children and Their Families 509

CONTRIBUTORS

BERLIN, I. N., M.D., Professor of Psychiatry and Pediatrics, and Head, Division of Child Psychiatry, University of Washington School of Medicine, Seattle; formerly, Associate Clinical Professor of Psychiatry, University of California School of Medicine, San Francisco, and Co-ordinator of Training, Children's Service, Langley Porter Neuropsychiatric Institute, San Francisco.

BLOCK, JACK, Ph.D., Professor of Psychology, University of California, Berkeley; formerly, Research Psychologist, Langley Porter Neuropsychiatric Institute.

BLOCK, JEANNE H., Ph.D., Research Psychologist, Institute of Human Development, University of California, Berkeley; formerly, Research Psychologist, Palo Alto Medical Research Foundation, Palo Alto, California.

BOATMAN, MALETA J., M.D., Assistant Professor of Psychiatry, University of California School of Medicine, San Francisco, and Assistant Director, Children's Service, Langley Porter Neuropsychiatric Institute.

BOMBERG, DOROTHY, M.A., Psychologist in private practice in Oakland, California; formerly, Research Psychologist, Langley Porter Neuropsychiatric Institute.

BRUNSTETTER, RICHARD W., M.D., Professor of Psychiatry, and Director of Child Psychiatry, Tulane University School of Medicine, New Orleans; formerly, Associate Clinical Professor of Psychiatry, University of California School of Medicine, San Francisco, and Supervising Psychiatrist, Children's Service, Langley Porter Neuropsychiatric Institute.

CHRIST, ADOLPH, M.D., Associate Professor of Psychiatry, and Director of Children's Inpatient Service, Downstate Medical School, State University of New York, Brooklyn; formerly, Assistant Professor of Psychiatry and Director of Psychiatric Day Care Service for Children, University of Washington School of Medicine, Seattle.

ETEMAD, JACQUELINE G., M.D., Clinical Instructor of Psychiatry, University of California School of Medicine, San Francisco, and Supervising Psychiatrist, Children's Service, Langley Porter Neuropsychiatric Institute.

GIANASCOL, ALFRED, M.D., Presently in private practice in Monterey, California; formerly, Professor of Child Psychiatry, University of Pennsylvania Medical School and University of Pennsylvania Postgraduate School of Education, and Assistant Clinical Professor of Psychiatry, University of California School of Medicine, San Francisco.

JEFFRESS, MARY, M.S.W., Field Instructor and Supervisor, University of California School of Social Welfare, Berkeley, and Supervising Psychiatric Social Worker, Langley Porter Neuropsychiatric Institute.

LANGDELL, JOHN I., M.D., Associate Clinical Professor of Psychiatry, University of California School of Medicine, San Francisco, and Supervising Psychiatrist, Children's Service, Langley Porter Neuropsychiatric Institute.

MEJIA, BERTA, R.N., B.S., Associate Specialist, Department of Psychiatry, University of California School of Medicine, San Francisco.

METCALF, AUBREY, M.D., Assistant Clinical Professor of Psychiatry, University of California School of Medicine, San Francisco, and Supervising Psychiatrist, Children's Service, Langley Porter Neuropsychiatric Institute.

MILLER, DALE, M.A., Educational Psychologist and Associate Research Specialist, Department of Psychiatry, University of California School of Medicine, San Francisco.

MORRISON, DELMONT, Ph.D., Associate Clinical Professor of Medical Psychology, University of California School of Medicine, San Francisco, and Coordinator of Clinical Psychology Training Program, Langley Porter Neuropsychiatric Institute.

PATTERSON, VIRGINIA, M.A., Assistant Clinical Professor of Medical Psychology, University of California School of Medicine, San Francisco, and Senior Psychologist, Langley Porter Neuropsychiatric Institute.

PHILIPS, IRVING, M.D., Clinical Professor of Psychiatry, University of California School of Medicine, San Francisco, and Supervising Psychiatrist, Children's Service, Langley Porter Neuropsychiatric Institute.

SCHULKIN, FRANK R., M.D., Instructor in Psychology, University of San Francisco, and Fellow, Center for Training in Community Psychiatry, University of California, Berkeley, and in private practice in San Francisco; formerly, Senior Resident, Children's Service, Langley Porter Neuropsychiatric Institute.

SUSSELMAN, SAMUEL, M.D., Associate Clinical Professor of Psychiatry, University of California School of Medicine, San Francisco, and Supervising Psychiatrist, Children's Service, Langley Porter Neuropsychiatric Institute.

SZUREK, S. A., M.D., Professor of Psychiatry, University of California School of Medicine, San Francisco, and Director, Children's Service, Langley Porter Neuropsychiatric Institute.

WALD, ROBERT D., M.D., Assistant Clinical Professor of Psychiatry, University of California School of Medicine, San Francisco, and in private practice in San Francisco.

WALKER, J. FRED, M.D., Clinical Instructor of Psychiatry, University of California School of Medicine, San Francisco, and Supervising Psychiatrist, Children's Service, Langley Porter Neuropsychiatric Institute, and in private practice in Kent, California.

YANDELL, WILSON, M.D., Lecturer, School of Education, and Consultant to the School Psychology and Teacher Training Programs, University of California, Berkeley; formerly, Assistant Clinical Professor of Psychiatry, University of California School of Medicine, San Francisco.

YEAGER, C. L., M.D., Professor in Residence, Department of Psychiatry, University of California School of Medicine, San Francisco, and Senior Psychiatrist, Langley Porter Neuropsychiatric Institute.

ACKNOWLEDGMENTS

We are grateful to Jessimai Strange, Amy Dobbyn, Mary Weiss and Vicki Carney for their suggestions, great patience and tender loving care of our work during the many revisions of the manuscripts for this volume.

PREFACE

This book has been a labor of love for this editor (I. N. B.) and the contributors, to whom S. A. Szurek has been teacher and mentor during his distinguished career in Child Psychiatry at the Langley Porter Neuropsychiatric Institute. We welcomed this opportunity to honor Dr. Szurek by compiling a volume of his work and ours which we hoped would embody the spirit and the unique venture in learning which he has shared with so many students and colleagues through the years.

Dr. Szurek's attitudes towards teaching were embodied in his request to all of us as students. Did we want to participate in the effort to understand the nature of conflicts in and between parents which would affect the child? Those students who undertook this effort came to observe carefully, to understand and to work psychotherapeutically with psychotic children and their parents, and to collate the data and psychotherapeutic experiences for further learning and research. Students and colleagues alike were caught up in the enthusiasm for observing and recording clinical work precisely and gathering data to test the hypothesis that one of the major factors, if not the most important one, in the etiology and treatment of childhood psychosis is the result of severe intrapsychic conflicts in and between parents. To investigate how such conflicts affected the child, we worked to discover prognostic signs which related to improvement in the child and those which indicated that difficult life events would lead to severe increase in conflicts in and between some parents which would adversely affect our child patients.

As an early and long time collaborator of Dr. Szurek's, I was puzzled for awhile by the reactions of some colleagues outside the Langley Porter Children's Service. Some seemed to feel that Dr. Szurek "brainwashed" his students and associates to accept his point of view and follow his plan for testing these hypotheses. Later, I recognized how difficult it would be for outsiders to understand the excitement generated by being invited to join this outstanding scientist, theoretician, clinician and teacher in collaborative research and treatment efforts. He offered each of us the opportunity to vigilantly scrutinize one's own work and to design and carry out studies to assess a hypothesis critically, in concert with one's own colleagues and Dr. Szurek. This is a difficult opportunity to turn down for scientifically trained and research oriented students, who in the spirit of science, do not fear, but welcome the opportunity to learn from open examination and criticism of their work with colleagues.

Faculty, trainees and staff of the Langley Porter Children's Service have actively participated in collaborative gathering of data and in testing how particular interventions affect family equilibrium and the psychosis in the child. Such opportunities in participant learning of clinical scientific method are rare.

This volume reflects data gathering efforts from over 250 cases treated on the Children's Service, plus efforts to examine various parameters of that data, to give our readers an historical perspective of our own learning. We publish a number of case histories in this volume to accede to requests from colleagues, nationwide, to describe in detail a process rarely written about, simultaneous psychotherapy with seriously disturbed children and their parents. Readers will note from some of the detail presented of the psychotherapeutic work the difficulties of adequately describing this process.

The long chapter which describes our effort to work with a child and his parents for ten years illustrates both the problems and the process of simultaneous psychotherapy. The other long chapter, "Attachment and Psychotic Detachment," represents Dr. Szurek's effort to place into perspective data from child development research and Bowlby's new theoretical ideas and examination of data, as they relate to our own clinical therapeutic work and research with psychotic children and their families. The chapter, "Clinical Work and Clinical Research as Scientific Inquiry," is our reaction to the eloquent description of clinical research in medicine by Alvan Feinstein which epitomized many of the same principles which have guided our work.

In this volume, Dr. Szurek's students and colleagues honor him as a teacher and a behavioral scientist whose rigorous thinking, uncompromising standards and integrity have inspired us all. We believe his contributions in this book clearly reflect his attitudes and his unparalleled clinical acumen recognized by all of us in Child Psychiatry throughout the English speaking world.

For me personally, this book represents an opportunity to show my respect and to express my gratitude to Stan Szurek in the only tangible way acceptable to him, in clinical writing. My effort has been to record my experiences and what I've come to learn from them, for others to examine as critically as Dr. Szurek has inspired us to examine our own work and his.

IRVING N. BERLIN, M.D.

Section I

INTRODUCTORY SECTION

"Psychoses of Childhood, Retrospect and Prospect" selectively views past and present work in the field with psychotic children. The chapter examines current points of view and projects from them the possibility of prevention of serious disorders of infancy and childhood.

"Playfulness, Creativity and Schisis" looks at the origins of the capacity to play and to be creative as well as the malintegrative splitting of the personality in psychosis from the critical vantage point of inter- and intrapersonal dynamics in the family. A metaphorical examination of the experience of Oedipus is the vehicle for this examination.

1

1

Psychoses of Childhood, Retrospect and Prospect

I. N. Berlin, M.D.

and

S. A. Szurek, M.D.

Historically, childhood psychoses when first described by DeSanctis as Dementia Praecox or Dementia Praecocissima was recognized by him as being related to a variety of possible etiological factors and was sometimes associated with mental retardation or idiocy. DeSanctis had seen cured instances and believed the disease or disorder could be reversed. A chapter in this volume is a translation of those portions of his 1906 publication that describe his experience with instances of juvenile psychoses. Nosologically, he places the variety of symptom complexes he describes under one name; however, he also highlights by precise clinical observations examples of various conditions. Such close and exact observation is at the heart of both good therapy and good clinical research (9).

The editors' biological background and training have given them deep appreciation of the role of detailed observations as the first step in naturalistic investigations. From these experiences, hypotheses are formulated and then tested in further clinical therapeutic work and observational experience. Such a procedure of theory building and testing is the appropriate scientific method not only for clinical science but very probably also for other social sciences. Essentially, the testing of such hypotheses that guide *experimental* therapeutic maneuvers are the clinical equivalents of laboratory experiments. We would thus see developmental psychology, psychiatry, and psychoanalysis as basic behavioral sciences within an encompassing biological framework. The senior editor (S.A.S.) long ago wrote a mimeographed syllabus for medical students in an effort to integrate the phenomena seen in clinical psychiatry into biologically based science.

Freud, with his earlier training in neuroanatomy and neurology, made an effort to provide his theoretical formulations with a biological base. His theoretical formulations were, of course, derived from his experience in working with patients with the therapeutic method that he named psychoanalysis. His effort to do so was made with the then current biological and physicalist theories with which, however, he was never fully satisfied. He recognized that further advances in biological and particularly biochemical science would be necessary before it would be possible to supply a sounder scientific basis for his psychological theories. These latter theories were sufficiently supported by his clinical observations of his patients' behavior both before and after his therapeutic maneuvers. Thus, his basic contributions regarding unconscious mental processes, repression, the impact of early infant and childhood experiences on the development of personality and the tripartite division of the psyche into id, ego and super ego, were all evolved from the most detailed and repeated observations of patients. He sought to understand and explain patients' illnesses and their symptom components by building and testing his hypotheses through subsequent psychoanalytic treatment of each particular disorder. Freud's emphasis on early childhood experiences as the critical factor in neuroses and probably psychoses led to the first clinical efforts to apply a systematic treatment method to children (14). Thus, Anna Freud, Melanie Klein, and August Aichhorn were among those who pioneered the development of a variety of psychoanalytic treatment methods for neuroses of childhood (13, 17, 1). Some of their colleagues, co-workers, and students have continued the work in psychoses of childhood.

In the early 1900's, Lightner Witmer, a psychologist at the University of Pennsylvania, developed the first psychological clinic in the United States. (One of the first elegant and classical case histories of his treatment of a psychotic child is reprinted in this volume.) Witmer was an acute and astute observer. From his observations, he developed his theories about the underlying psychopathology, essentially interpersonal environmental factors, and the rationale for his successful treatment of several psychotic children through efforts at altering the environmental stimuli in therapy, leading the child to a new adaptation (25).

The concept of early infantile autism as first described by Kanner in the later 1930's was influenced by Adolph Myers' holistic view of mental disease. All factors must be considered to understand etiology. Thus, Kanner early discussed an inborn factor as etiologic to infantile autism but his case histories clearly considered environmental factors, especially parental characteristics (16). Later Kanner and Eisenberg stated that although "emotional refrigeration that has been the common lot of autistic children" because of parents' characteristics is important in the development of the syndrome, it is not sufficient in itself to result in the appearance of autism (10). Bender, Silver, Fish, Chess, Birch, Thomas, and others have described the neurophysiological, maturational and neuro-developmental aspects of childhood psychoses based on their clinical observations and subsequent clinical research. Much of their work was inspired by Schilder's classical studies of neurointegrative processes in adults (2, 24, 11, 12, 7, 23). Goldfarb described a mixture of developmental neurophysiologic and environmental factors in childhood psychoses (15). Mahler, a psychoanalyst, describes two variants of infantile psychoses, each related to a critical period of ego development and both related to environmental factors and the relationship to the mother (19). Of all investigators, Bettelheim most firmly adheres to the concept of psychogenic etiology of childhood psychoses. He has documented his experience and his position in a scholarly publication which covers the gamut of research in autism (3).

Current investigations into the etiology of childhood psychoses involve genetic, biochemical, neurophysiologic, environmental and developmental areas of research. Some of the genetic, biochemical and neurophysiologic research has begun to demonstrate the reciprocal relationship between these factors and the environmental-developmental factors in determining a total result. Thus, environmental stress may possibly activate genetic potentials for disease, or as some experiments have shown, environmental stress at a critical developmental period may alter the size, weight, and number of brain cells. There is growing evidence for a reciprocal and interdependent relationship between some of these factors. Currently, the genetic factors are the least well delineated. However, in light of current research, some genetic factors need to be considered as being eventually demonstrable in some patients. We now begin to regard all mental disorders as being multicausal in etiology. The precise contributions of various factors vary in each instance. Their manifestations are always behavioral. Thus, the research of Craviotto and Birch (8), and Pasamanick and Knoblock (20) integrates nutritional factors which result in protein deficiency in infancy and early childhood with other environmental stresses in poverty (premature birth and maternal depression resulting in reduced maternal nurturance and sensory-motor stimulation, etc.) as being possibly etiologic to some varieties of childhood psychoses.

The exciting research in infant and child development and some of the animal experiments to isolate developmental variables points to the need for adequate "sensory stimulation" coupled with responsive nurturance during the critical first few days and months of the infant's life as crucial in determining learning capacities, and developing social and adaptive functions, especially the capacity to relate to parent figures. Sanders, Lipsett and others have revealed that important learning experiences may so alter the infant's behavior that after a few months the patterns may become stable (21, 18). They then appear to be the result of genetic or neurophysiologic disorders rather than early experiences. As Lipsett and co-workers have shown, effective learning experiences in the first three days of life lead to more rapid learning in later infancy (18). Sanders and co-workers have described irreversible maladaptive learning due to lack of response to the newborn's needs on the part of caretakers (22). In psychosis and neurosis of childhood, learning very likely occurs in a relatively non-interactive and nonfacilitating environment and leads to some irreversible patterns of behavior.

Brazelton and other investigators point to a wide variety of cultural differences in infant handling and mother-infant interaction which may be etiologic to "culturally" determined passivity or activity as well as suspiciousness, etc. (5). Certainly, maturational lags due to malnutrition and maternal depression common to poverty in many cultures leads to infant apathy on a neurobiochemical basis (i.e., fewer and smaller brain cells, smaller stature, slower learning) related to protein and vitamin deficiencies. A poorly nourished mother, depressed or not, cannot respond quickly to an infant's signals and needs because of decades of nutritionally caused tiredness resulting in apathy. Affective and cognitive development are thus seriously affected by interpersonal and neurobiochemical influences early in life. We would also view maternal post partum depression as not always resulting in total deprivation. Mother's slowness to respond on a nutritional or psychological basis or her tense and anxious responses to an infant's behavior might be less tender, gentle, or adapted to the child's signals of distress or altered physiological state. Such mother-child transactions might result in interfering with developing affective responsiveness in the infant. In our experience, such qualitative differences of mother's capacity to interact with the infant may result in the infant's apathy toward mother and in the eventual disturbance or lack of attachment as described by Bowlby. The data indicates that in such a chain of events, the motivation of the child regarding contact with the human environment is affected.

We have been most excited by the work of Bowlby on infant-mother attachment (4). We feel the thrust of his work, its integration of biological research with primates and other animals with human developmental research in early mother-child interactions, has great value in helping to explain some of the clinical phenomena we have noted in normal development and in neuroses, anti-social reactions and psychoses of childhood.

We are encouraged by the data from child development research which begins to help explain certain phenomena that we and others have related in detailed clinical work and have described in the case histories and clinical research chapters in this volume. From our experience we would caution that sometimes father, not mother, provides the actual nurturance to the infant. More important, the conflicts of both parents and the troubles between them affect the caregiver's capacity to nurture and respond with sensitivity to the infant.

From much of present research and from many clinical studies, there are important implications for prevention of and very early intervention in severe psychological disorders of childhood. Our own clinical data support investigative work that shows that maternal depression may result from many causes and may be primarily due to intrapsychic conflicts or to external environmental stresses and the inevitable intrapsychic reactions to them. Maternal depression very early in the infant's life leads to distortion of normal attachment with frequent severe behavioral consequences.

Early recognition of maternal depression prior to a child's birth may permit its treatment. Such treatment, when effective, represents optimum prevention (6). Data also indicate that helping a depressed mother as a result of continued clinical observation of mother-child relations in the critical early days and months of the infant's life is also effective primary prevention of severe psychopathology in infancy. Work with a depressed mother to help her relate more easily with the infant by means of a developmentally based task oriented educative approach facilitates treatment of the mother's depression as she becomes a more effective and responsive parent. At the same time the infant's potentially serious behavior disorder usually responds rapidly to behavior changes in the mother. Again, if the intervention is early enough, we have effective primary prevention, somewhat later amelioration of the infant's disturbance becomes secondary prevention and might prevent the more serious disturbances from occurring later in childhood.

With investigators and clinicians who are concerned with prevention, we see the possibility that early detection of problems in attachment can lead to more rapid remediation by working through the parent figures and may bring about the reversal or amelioration of the psychotic process.

We view the work presented in this volume as a continuous effort not only to treat such serious disorders more effectively, but also to elucidate the data from our clinical work and investigations that can be and have been utilized to recognize the early signs of disorder. Hopefully, we can begin to isolate those variables which give us a still better understanding not only of psychoses but also of less severe disorders in form but often almost equally prognostically grave when occurring in infancy and early childhood. We believe these clinical data will bring us closer to early therapeutic intervention and eventually closer to preventing psychoses and other severe psychological disorders of childhood.

REFERENCES

1. AICHHORN, A. *Wayward Youth*. New York: Viking Press, 1935.
2. BENDER, L. The Concept of Plasticity in Childhood Schizophrenia. In: Hoch, D.A. and Zubin, U. (Eds.), *Psychopathology of Schizophrenia*. New York: Grune & Stratton, 1966.
3. BETTELHEIM, B. *The Empty Fortress*. New York: The Free Press, 1967.
4. BOWLBY, J. *Attachment and Loss*. Vol. I, *Attachment*. New York: Basic Books, 1969.
5. BRAZELTON, T. B. Observations of the Neonate. *J. Amer. Acad. Child Psychiat.*, 1962, 1, 38-58.
6. CALL, J. D. Interlocking Affective Freeze Between An Autistic Child and His "As If" Mother. *J. Amer. Acad. Child Psychiat.*, 1963, 2 (2) 319-344.
7. CHESS, T. A., THOMAS, A., BIRCH, H. Characteristics of the Individual Child's Behavioral Responses to the Environment. *Amer. J. Orthopsychiat.*, 1959, 29, 791-802.
8. CRAVIOTTO, J., BIRCH, H. G., et al. Nutrition, Growth and Neurointegrative Development: An Experimental and Ecologic Study. *Pediatric Monograph Supplement*, 1966, 38, 31a.
9. DE SANCTIS, S. On Some Varieties of Dementia Praecox. *This Volume*.
10. EISENBERG, L., KANNER, L. Early Infantile Autism. 1943-1955. *Amer. J. Orthopsychiat.*, 1956, 26, 556-566.
11. FISH, B. Longitudinal Observations of Biological Deviations in a Schizophrenic Infant. *Amer. J. Psychiat.*, 1959, 116 25-31.
12. FISH, B. Involvement of the Central Nervous System in Infants with Schizophrenia. *Amer. Arch. Neurol.*, 1960, 2, 115-122.
13. FREUD, A. *The Psychoanalytic Treatment of Children*. London: Imago Publication, Co., 1946.
14. FREUD, S. *Collected Papers*. Standard Edition. London: Hogarth Press, 1953.
15. GOLDFARB, W. *Childhood Schizophrenia*. Cambridge, Mass.: Harvard University Press, 1961.
16. KANNER, L. Autistic Disturbances of Affective Contact. *Nervous Child.*, 1943, 2, 217-250.
17. Klein, M. *The Psycho-Analysis of Children*. London: Hogarth Press, 1932.
18. LIPSETT, L. P. Learning Processes of Human Newborns. *Merrill-Palmer Quart.*, 1966, 12, 45-71.
19. MAHLER, M. On Childhood Psychosis and Schizophrenia: Autistic and Symbiotic Infantile Psychosis. *Psychoanalytic Study of the Child*. Vol. VII, p. 286. New York; International Univ. Press, 1952.
20. PASAMANICK, B. and KNOBLOCK, H. Early Feeding and Birth Difficulties in Childhood Schizophrenia: An Explanatory Note. *J. Psychol.*, 1963, 56, 73-77.
21. SANDER, L.W. Issues in Mother-Child Interaction. *J. Amer. Acad. Child Psychiat.*, 1963, 1, 141-166.

22. SANDER, L.W. and et al. Early Mother-Infant Interaction and 24 Hour Patterns of Activity and Sleep. *J. Amer. Acad. Child Psychiat.*, 1970, 9, 104-123.

23. SCHILDER, PAUL. *The Image and Appearance of the Human Body.* New York: Internat. Univ. Press, 1950.

24. SILVER, A. and GABRIEL, H. P. The Association of Schizophrenia in Childhood with Primitive Postural Responses and Decreased Muscle Tone. *Developmental Med. and Child Neurol.*, 1964, 6, 495-497.

25. WITMER, L. Orthogenic Cases XIV Don: A Curable Case of Arrested Development Due to Fear Psychosis and the Result of Shock in a Three-Year-Old Infant. *Psychol. Clinic.*, 1919-22, 13, 97-111. (And *This Volume.*)

2

Playfulness, Creativity and Schisis

S. A. Szurek, M.D.

SCIENCE CREATES ETHICS

In J. Bronowski's *Science and Human Values* (3) you will recognize this work as the source of the form of my hope for this meeting. This English mathematician, scientist, playwright and author writes eloquently there of "The Creative Mind," of "The Habit of Truth" (of the scientist and artist alike) and of "The Sense of Human Dignity." I should like to review with you just a little of the profound thoughtfulness of his argument.

Among other things, he wishes to correct the error even more often heard in this nucleonic age—the error that science is responsible for creating and loosing upon the human race this foulest of its Frankensteins, and for turning the entire earth into a potential abattoir. He points out that, contrariwise, it is out of more than 400 years of the scientists' practice of their craft that our present values and ethics are.derived and are transforming the world.

Truth—being the drive at the center of science, not as a dogma, but as the only process by which created concepts can be tested by their conformity with explored fact—truth gives birth to the rest of this ethic; namely, independence in observation and thought; love of originality and therefore of dissent; but dissent not as an end in itself but as a mark of freedom. Bronowski finds the society of scientists powerful in their oddly virtuous ways of working. Scientists—despite individual human weakness—he states, in their work do not make wild claims, do not cheat, do not try to persuade at any cost, do not appeal either to prejudice or to authority. They are often frank about their ignorance; their disputes are fairly de-

Presidential Address delivered at the 1959 Annual Meeting of the American Orthopsychiatric Association.

corous; they do not confuse what is being argued with race, politics, sex or age; and they listen patiently to the young and to the old, who both know everything.

"In a world," he says, "in which state and dogma seem always either to threaten or to cajole, the body of scientists is trained to avoid and organized to resist every form of persuasion but the fact."

Science can pursue the exploration of truth only by confronting the work of one man with that of another, grafting each on each, and it cannot survive without justice and due honor and respect between man and man. Therefore, science has had to create these values in societies where they did not exist. These values deriving from its method have formed those who practice science into a stable, incorruptible and living society, into "a community into which everyone is welcome freely to speak, to be heard and to be contradicted." In it men make no distinction between ends and means. With fact as the only test of truth there is no justification for the smallest self-deception even about the minute detail, for suppressing a scruple about the means infects the man and his ends.

The stability of this society—unlike that of any based on dogma—continues despite complete transformations of its theories from one century to the next, from one year, or even from one day, to the next. "The whole structure of science has been changed, yet no one has been either disgraced or deposed. Through all the changes of science, the society of scientists is flexible and single-minded together and evolves and rights itself." Scientists, neither moralists nor revolutionaries, practicing their crafts modestly and steadfastly, letting the values implicit in the manner of their working speak for themselves, have thus "slowly remade the minds of men." And then when slavery ceased to be a matter of course, "and empires crumbled, men asked for the rights of man and for government by consent." Thus speaks Bronowski.

PERVERSION OF CREATIVE IDEAS

In contrast to this, W. J. Brown, a member of Parliament, wrote vividly in 1947 of what has happened and can happen to the most creative of ideas when they become incarnate in an organization—whether political, social, or religious—and, I would add, perhaps sometimes even scientific. In an article entitled "Imprisoned Ideas" (4), he asserts that the most fundamental categorization of men is into "Servants of the Spirit" and "Prisoners of the Organization." He thinks that the idea, the inspiration, originating in the internal world of the spirit, must incarnate in an organization just as the human spirit must incarnate in a body. Then the idea having embodied itself in an organization, the organization—itself needing to survive—proceeds to pervert the idea, often into its opposite, and in effect slay the idea which gave it birth.

He gives many reasons, now well known, for the pressure upon an organization to develop a self-interest disconnected from, foreign, and even inimical to the idea upon which it was formed. It is then obvious why heresy is condemned and suppressed, why what was conceived as a vehicle of a new and higher truth becomes a prison for the souls of men; and then, men murder each other for the love of God and the thing becomes its opposite. He reviews how both leaders and the rank-and-file members become prisoners of the organization even without conscious infidelity to the great idea; how the organization retreats from the idea; how it deteriorates as it grows because, as he says, "In this world the devil walks and it is necessary sometimes to hold a candle to the devil." Or, on the other hand, to fight the devil with the devil's weapons seems inescapable to the disciples but it is practically catastrophic. For then, the disciples, the servants of God, descending to the devil's level are, as leaders, no longer the men they were.

The deeper moral of all this, according to Brown, is that our attitude towards organization as such, needs to be—even while being members of it—one of partial detachment towards it; of knowing that we have no abiding place in it; of being "weekly tenants, not long lease holders"; of accepting no commitments that would prevent our leaving it when circumstances make this necessary; of regarding all loyalties to organization as *tentative* and *provisional*.

CONFLICT AND SCHISIS ALMOST UBIQUITOUS

Brown's general dramatic portrayal of the dilemmas implicit in the history of organizations serves to emphasize again the fact that in the present development of man conflict and schisis are widely prevalent in his social living and, as we can add, in his internal, subjective processes as well. In fact, we are so impressed with its ubiquity in our professional and personal lives that some of our current theories of personality development and of human behavior are based upon the assumption that repression, that is, conflict—in contrast to orderly, harmonious subordination, or better ordering of actions into an effective, timely sequence—that conflict is an essential dynamic of normal growth and psychological functioning. Then suggestions such as those of Bronowski seem too idealistic to be possibly true and achievable, or may serve to give us only a temporary surcease from the threats and guilts of the atomic age, rather than as a step toward,

or encouragement to, further clarifying our often confused ways of thinking about human behavior.

A more recent warning of the danger to the contemporary American's initiative, integrity and creativeness but now from a pervasive, *cooperative* ethic subtly seducing him into even an *inner* conformity comes from William H. Whyte in *The Organization Man* (31). If and when this ethic invades every aspect of his life, deprecates individual differences of temperament, interest, taste, preference and even of ability, and when it increases his fears of openly expressing them and of indulging them, it contributes powerfully to conflict, to neurosis and schisis.

OBSERVATIONS FROM CLINICAL WORK

As I have listened to patients I have become more and more impressed with the frequency with which their deepest and most persistent anxiety is about impulses which are purely self-assertive. I do not mean by self-assertive the rebellious or defiantly hostile thoughts and impulses—although these may be condensations of the assertive and of the anxious impulses, and such condensations and displacements may appear in awareness as precursors to the more simply self-assertive statements. By self-assertive, I also do *not* mean those feelings of self-glorification which are part of a total attitude that includes derogation of others. I mean something of the kind of impulse a child expresses when, at the final mastery of a new skill, he delightedly shouts, "Look at me, Mom!" And, of course, I mean a child who has previously experienced the undiluted pleasure of his parent in the growth and development of his unique spontaneous interests; in his discoveries during playful explorations of his body's maturing capacities; in his explorations of the nonpersonal world around him, living and nonliving; in his contented, restful, contemplative and solitary fantasies and pursuits which enlarge his inner world and his sense of self—a self which is uncoerced by anxieties that he must always think, feel and do as others or else be strange, different and hence inferior; or that in everything he keep up with an externally imposed time schedule rather than in rhythm with his own biological processes.

By "undiluted pleasure of his parent" I do not mean the tense, driving approbation of a parent who seeks compensations for his own discontents in the achievements of his child toward which he has pushed and driven him. I mean the pleasure of a parent whose satisfactions in his own life are sufficient for him, so that his pleasure in his child's growth is undiluted and untainted by any of the manifold results of conflict. Such a child and such a parent at such times have no need beyond the deep content of the moment of such learning, growth and integration. There is then little or no need to denigrate oneself or anyone else, nor to equal or surpass some envied competitor, nor to redress some sense of inferiority to another child in some other respect.

By this detour to the child and his parent I have also indicated at least a major source and origin of the anxiety of the patients I mentioned. For it is frequently the case, if therapeutic resolution of such anxieties occurs, that such patients can then vividly recall a host of experiences with their parents primarily, but with others as well, in which not only was there no undiluted pleasure evident in the parent's reaction, but on the contrary, there followed some warning or admonition about "pride going before a fall." It is no mystery then that such patients are rarely able to experience full pleasure in their actual achievements, that they often even murmur something belittling of themselves when others praise them, and that they seem deeply convinced of the genuineness of their so-called modesty and virtuous humility. Some of them are even stirred to suspicion and distrust at quite friendly and genuine overtures and compliments.

CREATIVE PLAYFULNESS WITH IDEAS

There is, of course, much more to this complex of such conflictful attitudes. But this aspect struck me particularly as the kind of distortion of human psychological functioning and behavior which perhaps lies quite pervasively at the root of some of the most difficult obstacles to human creativity and playfulness—a playfulness which in the adult, I think, is akin to, or allied to, creativity. By creativity I do not mean *merely* those relatively rare moments in human history when we tend to pinpoint someone's achievement or idea which is subsequently acclaimed as a turning point of great consequence to humanity—"moments" which perhaps never occurred as moments in any case. I mean by creativity the kind of solving of our everyday problems which brings with it a sense of fullness of living, a keen and vivid satisfaction from any activity and an exuberant eagerness for every variety of possible nondestructive experience in every phase of our finite lives. By this I do not imply absence of all anxiety and frustration. But if anxiety remains only a signal for closer self-scrutiny and scrutiny of the situation, then the frustrations may be less frequently those of the most destructive kind, those which are self-imposed and self-induced. In this sense, the playfulness, the creativity I speak of, is synonymous with integration or, as more of us would perhaps prefer to call it, with mental health. In this sense, too, human creativity would be contrasted with schisis, with the splitting, the cleavages and divisions in our energy which result from conflict.

In these days when the sciences called basic—often rather invidiously contrasted to careful, systematic, clinical therapeutic work with patients —when these basic sciences are expected eventually if not almost momentarily to bring the solution to many of our still unsolved problems in human behavioral disorders, in these days to equate conflict and schisis and to hint thereby that at least some of the psychoses might also be still included among the reactions to events in our living with others of our kind requires some temerity.

This is particularly so when we hear from the biochemists and psychopharmacologists (12) new information about neurohormones, catecholamines, steroids, serotonin, ceruloplasmin, taraxein, about the effects of psychotomimetic substances and about an increasing host of drugs we call tranquilizing; when we hear from chemists like our guest tonight, Dr. Linus Pauling, how neatly the genetic and the pathophysiological mechanisms of some diseases like sickle-cell anemia can be demonstrated through understanding of the relevant molecular structures and behavior and how conditions like phenylpyruvic oligophrenia can be elucidated in similar molecular terms (20); and when neuroanatomists and neurophysiologists among others advance our knowledge of the details of the integrative function of the nervous system (11) in further explorations of the pattern of cerebral and cortical functioning, of the role of mesodiencephalic activating reticular substance and of the limbic system and so on. Yet until the biochemist does come along with a solution to more of the syndromes which remain still in the domain of our clinical responsibility, it seems important— while keeping a close eye on the work of the biochemist—that we *not* desert our own methods of work and study, which can be further developed (28), for ways and means which are still clearly not here.

MAN'S ECOLOGY—MAN

I have read Iago Galdston's recent statement (9) that physiological medicine interested in the normal functioning of the body as differentiated from clinical specialities oriented toward cure of disease, and human ecological science underlying public health practices have together conquered such diseases as have become less frequent and rare and that, with this, some medical specialities have "died."

Since the basic goal of orthopsychiatric disciplines, it seems to me, is to work in such a way that professional service will become unnecessary to more and more individual patients, we cannot but welcome and work towards any developments which would result in more creative, more playful and more kindly living for more human beings. However, even if physiological medicine does eventually conquer some of those severe disorders we call the psychoses—there is much in human ecology quite germane to orthopsychiatric way of thought. There is therefore a good deal for us and for future generations of members of this Association to learn about, and to contribute to, the science of relation of relations—as Iago Galdston partly defines ecology. For it is becoming more and more obvious with each passing decade of this century, in which the world has shrunken more quickly than in any other, that man's relation to himself and to others of his kind remains as his chief problem and difficulty.

I said his relation to himself and to others *remains* his chief problem because it seems probably true that this has been one of his difficult problems ever since he acquired his human characteristics biologically. And then, perhaps in about the past five to ten thousand years—or, in only two to four hundred generations—man has developed to his present state of dominance over the rest of nature primarily by the changes he has progressively wrought in the *human* environment of the developing child in each successive generation (30). It is unnecessary here to review the factors in this development, such as his highly retentive and plastic brain, his sensitiveness, the slow maturation of the young, his gregariousness and progressive development of his art of communicating his mode of behavior and of his thought through speech and script, not only to his living kin but to subsequent generations. It is only important that we remind ourselves that all this has occurred in a relatively brief period of time, biologically speaking, and hence this development of man is in all probability primarily a matter of his cumulative learning from his own experience and from that of his fellows, rather than the result of genetic variations in his hereditary constitution (13). But now that man has covered his planet with his kin by his capacity to adapt to nature, to procreate, and by his great interest in, and increasing capacity to travel—and now has even the yearning to travel beyond his own globe—he has progressively found *himself* as perhaps the most important factor in his environment which he needs now to adapt to better, in the next phase of his development, than he has done in the past.

When one begins to ponder whether and how man might conceivably learn something useful to his further development, and not merely to his survival, one may be first tempted to soliloquize with Goethe's Faust thus (10):

> I have studied, alas! Philosophy,
> And Jurisprudence, and Medicine too,
> And saddest of all, Theology,

With ardent labour, through and through!
And here I stick, as wise, poor fool,
As when my steps first turned to school.

. . . .

To no idol of scruple or doubt do I grovel,
I know no fear of Hell or of Devil.
But joy is a stranger to my seclusion.
I hug to my heart no fond illusion,
As that I know aught worth the knowing,
Or men could better, my wisdom showing.

. . . .

So I've turned me to magic in my need,
If haply spirit-power and speech
May many a hidden mystery teach,
That I with bitter labour so
No more need say what I do not know;
That I the mighty inmost tether
May know, that binds the world together;
All germs, all forces that lifewards struggle;
And with vain words no longer juggle.

With the hope that one shall not "with vain words juggle," one might consider—and play with—the oedipus concept or situation which clearly, to me, is part of man's ecology. Many students have considered this concept from many points of view, bringing to bear upon it rich observational data from many cultures and from knowledge of the phylogenetic past of man as a species related to, and differentiated from, his relatives among the anthropoid primates and the hominids. One of these, as you know, is my colleague tonight on this platform, Dr. Weston LaBarre, who has written a lively and deeply informative discourse on "The Human Animal." (16)

OEDIPUS AND HIS PARENTS

This concept and the situation in the human family to which it refers has in classical theory, I think, been emphasized generally more from the point of view of Oedipus himself. I know, of course, that Freud himself considered the role of the parents. Nevertheless, even though more of us in this field are, and probably always were, quite aware of the fact that all three persons of the trinity or triangle influenced each other, it may not be amiss to review again a few aspects of this well-known, or better-known, problem. It is relevant, too, to the genesis of schisis—and to the destruction of play and creativity and humor in some of the senses to which I previously referred.

It was probably never quite accurate to say to myself—as I did years ago—that in the classical notion all three members, but particularly Oedipus, appeared to be at least passive, or rather helpless, victims. They seemed to be victims overwhelmed by an inevitable fate in the form of forces either internal to the organism as residues from a phylogenetic past, or external, those of continuing necessity on which the existence of the family and hence that of culture rested—or of both.

I see no need here to discuss either the possibility of a genetically transmitted interruption—in the first decade of life—of the full development of human sexual reproductive capacity, or the incest taboo (1). What I wish, however, to underline again is the variety of some additional components, to my mind not always sufficiently emphasized, of the total problem contributed to the family situation by the sometimes deep and severe conflicts and their compromise solutions of one, or perhaps more frequently, of both parents and of their surrogates in later life (6, 14, 27). And this is not at all to deny the contribution to the problem from the side of Oedipus himself and from his maturing sensual and sexual responsiveness.

There are now many reports (22, 23, 24, 29), and very probably still more clinical experiential data in the hands of students of family troubles, to make very probable a few, perhaps limited, generalizations. For example, we know fairly well by now at least some of the circumstances in which many of the sudden, severe, episodic excitements of hospitalized psychotic patients of all ages occur. These excitements, at least sometimes, appear on close study in the context of a triangular situation of the patient and two staff members who are in some unresolved conflict with respect to each other although apparently only in theoretical disagreement about the patient. The fact that such excitements can just as suddenly subside, sometimes within 3 to 48 hours, after some resolution of the conflict between the two staff members, recalls similar experiences of workers in psychiatric clinics for children (or for adults) when parents (or spouses) were also in concomitant therapy. In short, the "patient," whether chronologically also a child or not, often lived through a period of change in the intensity of his conflict under certain clearly identifiable conditions. Such intensifications of his conflict—whether manifested primarily through impulsively self-destructive behavior against others, or through an increase of predominantly self-stultifying neurotic symptoms—tended to occur either: 1) when he could in effect "induce" two current parental surrogates, who were susceptible, to fight each other in some degree or manner about him; or 2) if he could seem passively but vicariously to participate in their mutual —and apparently exclusive—struggle, as in for example some "primal" scenes; or 3) when he was caught more or less innocently between them.

I still recall N. Lionel Blitzsten's phrase for such situations. He was fond of saying about such moments, "Yes! Let's *you* and *he* fight about me!"

Somewhat parenthetically, the memory is perhaps still vivid in the minds of many members of this Association of the variety of clinical practice adopted by the clinic team to meet this problem of the parent who needed to bring the child patient to the clinic. Such a parent also often insisted on talking to someone, on asking questions, on begging or demanding advice. This parent was—and perhaps still is—more often the mother although fathers appear occasionally. In any case it has become evident to more—but perhaps not to all—students of such problems that in many, if not in all, of these interviews with such parents, it did not seem at all enough merely to listen to these parents, nor to answer their obviously elementary and reasonable questions, nor even to yield to temptations to play the omnipotently omniscient expert and only to give them the advice they begged, or righteously and apparently rightfully demanded.

In these now enlightened days of well-developed clinic teamwork, it is now only an amusing evidence of the darkness of those ages of ten, fifteen or twenty years ago that the obviously more important therapist of the child patient required that some lowly clinic teammate—as I have heard it expressed—"hold such a parent at bay," perhaps "educate" him in proper principles of child rearing, and by every available stratagem help to keep pure and uncontaminated the situation in the playroom. Somewhat a little more seriously, it appeared to me in that dim past when the ideal of psychoanalytic "passivity" and essential "permissiveness" was so difficult and conflict-producing for some of us to maintain amid somewhat dangerously flying objects and other events of destruction in these primitive play therapy rooms (25)—it appeared to me then that there were problems and conflicts not only in the souls of those primordial therapists but difficulties between those aboriginal clinic teammates as well. Nowadays, with all the roles of, and the relations between, the various disciplines represented on the team so clearly settled in the form of an egalitarian democracy, it is quite easy to see that those ancient conflicts and defensive solutions concerning skill, prestige and hierarchical structure of the staff added their quota of obfuscating tensions and quite obviously interfered with the perception of any clear and distinct ideas about Oedipus and his situation.

Still more seriously, it is by now rather evident, to some survivors of such internecine strife in the staff, that childhood neurosis of whatever form and at whatever age it comes to clinical attention is probably best understood as an adaptation to parental neurosis. This is no news to this modern audience, and may even seem, as I think George Bernard Shaw would have said it, a discovery by research of what always had been obvious. Whether therapy with parents is, or can be, undertaken concomitantly by collaborating teammates, or by the therapist of Oedipus himself, is decided by those factors in the individual clinical situation which need no review just here. But when such therapy is undertaken and fortunately does progress there is no dearth of evidence for two processes: 1) that each parent shows some degree of failure in resolving during the vicissitudes of his own early and later life the oedipus situation with his own parents; and 2) that this failure is quite regularly found related *both* to the difficulty with his own child and, what is equally important, to his child's difficulty with him. In sum, what could not remain integrated in the parent's personality because of *his* experience is not available to facilitate the integrated development of his child.

This last statement has many implications—only a few of which can be made explicit here—which are important for the conception of schisis. I should like first to restate the problem thus: The unresolved oedipus conflict of both parents, intensified by whatever discontents their current reality arouses, constitutes the important and variable factors in the total dynamics and economics which contribute to, if they do not generate, the child's conflict. Included among other of their current discontents—i.e., those external to the family—would be any which arise from the genetic endowment of their child's sex, health, developmental anomalies, intelligence, beauty, and such resemblances to others, or the timing of his birth, which aggravate specific and individual aspects of their pre-existing conflicts.

Some of these pre-existing, unresolved parental conflicts often interfere with full, or continuing, genital mutuality between the parents. A rather common effort at solving the discontent in adult living of one or both parents is a regressive tendency to relive with, or through, the child some aspect of their own usually unconscious oedipal conflict. This is often rationalized as essential for the child's immature and dependent needs and as a protection against the partly projected, and partly actual cruelty or indifference of the other parent. Such a relation between one parent and the child has the effect of more or less excluding the other parent as the devil in the piece. Then both such a parent and the child are bound together, caught in a mutual sadomasochistic net of guilty satisfactions and the ever-threatening loss of these partial satisfactions.

ORIGINS OF SADOMASOCHISTIC TRANSFORMATIONS

The threat of loss of such satisfactions comes from several sources. In the first place, the other parent, frightened and resenting the exclusion, may retaliate in various ways against both the child and the first parent, both of whom may need him still. Then the child inevitably grows at least in size and sexual maturity—that is, biochemical, reproductive capacity— which brings varying degrees of feared preference for libidinal trans- actions with coevals. Guilty rage on the part of each, the child and the parent, and retaliatory anxieties at such threatened rupture of the sado- masochistic mutual parasitism are inevitable. Uneasy lies the head that would wear a crown, and attempts to reign under the banner of apparent divine grace but actually through fomenting divisions and rivalries in the subjugated subjects. And this is true not only for such a child, who may use exaggerations of his helplessness to bring one or both of such parents to heel, but it is equally true of a masochistically cruel parent who cries to the child, "After all I've sacrificed for you!" and "You don't love me!" to the other parent. In such enslavements—if not in all—it is difficult to distinguish which is the masochist and which is the sadist; which one, the dictator and which one, the slave. Kamiat's aphorism that every dictator is slavish and every slave dictatorial seems very apt (15). In this context I recall another of Lionel Blitzsten's statements, namely, that every masochist has limits beyond which it *really* hurts. Every sadist, on the other hand, fears revenge, rebellion, and loss both of his sadistic pleasure and his own passive masochistic longings.

The most important implication of all such complications in the oedipal triangle for the present thesis is that the repression of any particular identifiable or describable sensual impulse of the child after its appear- ance in his maturation follows as a consequence of similar repressions of the parent or parents.

In other words, if any sensual impulse of what we call the primary narcissism of the child repeatedly encounters early in life an affective, unconscious, but reactive conflictful tension of the person upon whose parental behavior the child depends biologically for satisfaction of all, and later of most, of his needs, there begin those changes we call re- pression. The subsequent and inevitable return of the repressed sensu- ality, however, comes in a sadomasochistically distorted form. The original libidinous, sensual, impulse of any erogenous zone, interrupted and un- satisfied because of the anxious tension of the child reacting to the anxious tension of the parent, is distorted in form by the fusion with the anxiety and the resulting rage. Eventually all three elements—libidinous impulse, anxiety, and rage—thus fused are even more dangerous and pressing. Meeting then with even greater anxious guilty, disgusted and even revengeful parental tension, these now irrepressible impulses of the child, distorted by the fusion, arouse in him even greater anxiety, in effect a further increase of the repressive forces. This whole complex of re-pressed impulses but particularly the original libidinous impulse itself is ungratifiable, or relatively so, in any simple activity either within oneself or with others. Ungratifiable impulses are now the insatiable longings of a secondary narcissim of a dissociated human character.

I have for some years now found it useful to consider the processes of learning and of repression as essentially opposite, contradictory and mutu-ally exclusive. Depending on describable variables of such situations and their repetitions instead of satisfying learning (7) we find: the stulti-fications, the affective stupidities, the positive avoidances, the fascinated aversions or the mislearnings—that is, the condensations and displace-ments—which are characteristic of psychological disorder or schisis. These changes may affect specific impulses and certain situations only, or perhaps always also to some extent the general affective, instinctive spontaneity of the human organism. The consequent displaced, distorted intensification of drives we have already touched upon. Here then it is important to learn and to distinguish the egocentric but integrated quality of the impulse expressing the *undistorted* drive characteristic of the human organism and expressive of its simple organic need on the one hand, from the desperate, insatiable intensity of the same drive which has been already sadomasoch-istically transformed—and which is now sometimes unrecognizably com-plicated—in some still earlier experience on the other.

It therefore appears to me an error to assume that for normal, inte-grated development repression is essential. It seems simpler to distinguish the diametrically *opposite* effects of progressively integrated development of learning and of repression and its consequent distortion and schisis. This appears true even if the two, repression and thorough learning, may and do coexist in the same personality. The degree and extent of both, and with respect to which specific organic processes either learning or repression has occurred during previous development, then determine the total balance of integration and of psychopathology.

Among the most fundamental consequences of the processes of repres-sion, distortion and fixation, of such division, splitting or schisis in the energy of the human organism partly against its own impulses, is the varying degree of disturbance of its biologic rhythms. The basic drives rooted in the biochemical processes—whatever specific names we may give them from the organs or functions involved or from the directions and forms of the whole organism's activity—the basic drives in these circum-stances lose their usual cycle of tension and release in satisfying action appropriate to, and characteristic of, the individual person's state of devel-opment.

SCHISIS AND DUALISTIC MALDEVELOPMENT

The periodicity of integrated behavior and functioning—which is so characteristic of many young children and some older persons who from more fortunate earlier experience are spontaneous, direct and wholeheartedly genuine in expressing the whole gamut of human states of feelings—is transformed into a prolongation and increase of perverted drive, and simultaneously a much diminished capacity for the full release of complete gratification. This obsessiveness affects both the instinctive, the directly sensual *and* the intellectual, the logically deliberate, components of mental life. As Lancelot Law Whyte (30) states it in characterizing the dualism implicit in the European tradition of Western man in the past 2,000 years:

> . . . it matters little whether the aim is union with God or woman, the ecstasy of the pursuit of unity or truth, or power or pleasure— the sustained intensity and lack of satisfaction proves the European stamp. The European soul never truly loses itself in God; the mind never finds ultimate truth; power is never secure; pleasure never satisfies. Bewitched by these illusory aims which appear to promise the absolute, man is led away from the proper rhythm of the organic processes to chase an elusive ecstasy. Morbid religiosity, hyperintellectualism, deliberate sensuality and cold ambition are some of the variants of the dissociated personality's attempt to escape its own division.

Another aspect of all this is the ambivalent attitude not only toward love, sex and sensuality, but also towards all authority, competence and learning. That all these are involved in the schisis is not surprising, since all these aspects of living are affected in the childhood situation. Authority is then rarely seen clearly as special competence and a particular responsibility which one can progressively acquire through steady learning. All three are conceived, experienced, desired and despaired of as absolute power which might compensate for, reduce or eliminate the inner, constantly lurking sense of impotence from one's own self-frustrations. Hence a constant fear of, and rebelliousness against, all authority or competence makes satisfying learning in collaborative effort with teachers difficult if not impossible—yet constantly the object of strenuous striving. On the other hand, any exercise of competence by oneself is similarly fantasied as a dangerously placed omnipotent authority whose omniscience is absolutely essential and clearly and obviously impossible.

POSTULATE OF INTEGRATIVE DEVELOPMENT AS BASIC

I have spoken much of conflict, of schisis. I wish space would permit me to speak at equal length of unity, of integration. I wish I could review with you in detail the encouragement I experienced at reading *The Next Development of Man* by Lancelot Law Whyte (30)—an encouragement to the notions I had learned in my primary biological training. I have in mind in particular the ideas of Child (5) and Coghill and Herrick (11): about the organism as a unity in, and polarized against, its environment as a hierarchically organized pattern in protoplasm; some of the findings and ideas of Coghill of the *secondary* individuation of organs, systems and particular skills within the total integrated pattern in development; and of the basically similar ideas of Herrick regarding the integrating function of the central nervous system in all motile organisms.

In particular I would have stressed Whyte's historical analysis of the origin, the factors and the effects upon the entire human race of the schisis in European and Western man, as well as of his scientific development. I would have emphasized more such efforts as those of Northrop (17, 18, 19) and of Siu (21) to search for a unification or blending of Western and Eastern modes of thought and living, of Zen and of Tao and of Buddhism's Nirvana as practical and practiced methods of reducing or eliminating the strain of conflict.

But most especially I wish I could have discussed in greater detail Whyte's suggestions: why contemporary thought needs to embrace a basic unitary form to free itself, to transform itself, out of its preoccupation with dualisms which can never explain integration; why taking Goethe's suggestion to convert the problem of integration into a postulate would help to resolve the dilemma.

Since all this is impossible, I wish to bring you only a few of Whyte's own words (30). He says:

> For more than two thousand years thought has mainly relied on methods of thought which assume that the apparent confusion of natural processes must be reduced to order by analyzing from every process component parts which are permanent and unchanging. From long habit thought tends to beg the question, and to assume the necessity of this demand for static parts as the ultimate elements of structure. The structure of an organism has then to be regarded as an assembly of parts, and the fact of integration, being denied at the start, becomes an insoluble problem.

He goes on:

> This difficulty must sooner or later be resolved by a more general scientific method reconciling two sets of facts: those which have been successfully described in terms of independent and relatively static atoms, tissues, or organs and their changing relations, and those other facts connected with the development of organic form which are covered by the term integration.

He emphasizes that the development of organic form must be treated as a special case of the development of form in general, including inorganic form, and states the postulate thus:

> Process consists in the development of form when circumstances permit. This fact must be represented in the general form of natural law and does not require explanation.

And this he calls the unitary postulate and method in contrast to the analytic method which assumes the existence of static, permanent, component parts. Since this postulate undercuts assumptions implicit in much of the thought of recent centuries, and since the postulate of the development of form implies in the universal process as displaying the asymmetry between earlier and later states, all philosophical and scientific terms have to be reconsidered. Further he asserts that:

> [as] long as integration remains merely an unsolved problem of analytical thought, it is impossible to discover the reason for the partial failure of integration in civilized man. But if the tendency of systems to develop their characteristic forms is treated as the expression of a normal property of natural processes, then it may be possible to find the reason for its failure in particular cases. Our approach to the diagnosis of contemporary man therefore takes the following shape: We assume that the tendency to develop form is universal, that organic integration is an expression of this general tendency, that the development of society is a process continuous with organic nature and the animal world, and that the partial failure of integration in contemporary civilized man is a process requiring special explanation.

He is fully aware of many dangers in the use of such a system of thought, particularly of the tendency to neglect the complexity of fact. Hence he recognizes the need to guard against crude oversimplifications. The central principle needs to be "one which invites caution, always stimulates consideration of the complementary thesis, and denies the ultimate validity of all sharp categories." The more serious dangers of misinterpreting a philosophy of development as an optimistic doctrine of moral progress, and of the acclamation of the principle as a guarantee of what each individual chooses to understand by progress, he thinks are avoided by a concept of development which denies permanence and permits no flattering of the individual as a conscious subject because it is too austere to encourage runaway optimism in those who understand it.

All such considerations suggest the need for reconsidering our theories of human personality, of personality development, of personality disorder.

It may be that when such theoretical work, taking account of all accumulating knowledge about man, is done, we may see some of the dualisms in our current thought—between facts and theories of physics and chemistry and biology on the one hand, and those of psychology, the social sciences and anthropology on the other—fade and dissolve into a unitary conception.

LEARNING AND INTEGRATIVE BEHAVIOR

The conceptions of the past which call attention to the current, the actual, divisions in the personality of many now living human beings may then be recognized as the inevitable results of human history on this planet thus far. When the physiochemical processes of the human organism expressing themselves as drives in its behavior are recognized as aspects of the animal to be integrated into the person, rather than as enemies of the person and of society and as such to be condemned, suppressed and repressed by a conscience which as Whyte says is negative; when such unitary development and functioning is facilitated, the divisions of the personality will and do fade. Again as Whyte says, "Integrity supersedes conscience."

Then it may become clear to more and more persons that in any walk of life, but especially as parent—or more particularly in our own small field as therapist—one's aim is to behave in such wise that one may facilitate in oneself, and hence in others, continuous discriminative learning—learning how to act in conformity with *all* the circumstances of the present in the light of relevant past experience. For it is often the apparently trivial detail (8) and difference in a situation—otherwise similar to old ones—which remains unnoticed by many, which may give the clue to modifying one's ideas and behavior enough to make for a wholly creative act—an act which may transform the situation and oneself simultaneously into a more integrated and satisfying unity. And such experiences rarely fail to bring with them still further development within the finite limits of one's world and of one's life. This does not mean that one shall attain heaven on earth, nor very probably altogether avoid the hell of self-deception and frustration. But it may mean that perhaps one's life may be less liable to the dizzy oscillations between the blind ecstatic optimisms and the equally blind profound, depressive pessimisms of schisis. One may then, perhaps, live more creatively as a more integrated and continually developing person as long as circumstances permit life to continue.

REFERENCES

1. BARRY, MAURICE, JR., and JOHNSON, ADELAIDE M. The incest barrier. *Psychoanal. Quart.*, 1958, 27, 485-500.
2. BRONOWSKI, J. *The Common Sense of Science.* Cambridge, Mass.: Harvard Univ. Press, 1955.
3. BRONOWSKI, J. *Science and Human Values.* New York: Julian Messner, 1958.
4. BROWN, W. J. Imprisoned ideas. *Spectator*, Sept. 19, 1947.
5. CHILD, C. M. *The Physiological Foundations of Behavior.* New York: Holt, 1924.
6. DEVEREUX, GEORGE. Why Oedipus killed Laius. *Int. J. Psychoanal.*, 1953, 34, 132-141.
7. DOLLARD, JOHN, and MILLER, NEAL E. *Personality and Psychotherapy.* New York: McGraw-Hill, 1950.
8. FREUD, SIGMUND. The Moses of Michelangelo. *Collected Papers*, Vol. 4, London: Hogarth Press and Institute of Psycho-Analysis, 1948. Pp. 257-287.
9. GALDSTON, IAGO. The birth and death of specialties. *J.A.M.A.*, 1958, 167, 2056-2061.
10. GOETHE, J. W. *Faust.* Parts I and II. Translated by Albert G. Lathan; edited by Ernest Rhys. Everyman's Library No. 335, Dutton, New York; and J. M. Gent, London, 1908.
11. HERRICK, CHARLES J. *The Evolution of Human Behavior.* Austin: Univ. of Texas, 1956.
12. HIMWICH, HAROLD E. Psychopharmacologic drugs. *Science*, 1958, 127, 59-72.
13. JACKSON, DON. *A Critique of the Literature of the Genetics of Schizophrenia.* New York: Basic Books, 1959.
14. JOHNSON, ADELAIDE, et al. Studies in schizophrenia at the Mayo Clinic. *Psychiatry*, 1956, 19, 137-148.
15. KAMIAT, ARNOLD H. *Social Forces in Personality Stunting.* Cambridge, Mass.: Sci-Art Publishers, 1939.
16. LABARRE, WESTON. *The Human Animal.* Chicago: Univ. of Chicago Press, 1954.
17. NORTHROP, F. S. C. *The Logic of the Sciences and the Humanities.* New York: Macmillan, 1947.
18. NORTHROP, F. S. C. *The Meeting of the East and West.* New York: Macmillan, 1946.
19. NORTHROP, F. S. C. *The Taming of the Nations.* New York: Macmillan, 1952.
20. PAULING, LINUS. The molecular basis of genetics. *Am. J. Psychiatry*, 1956, 113, 492-495.
21. SIU, R. G. H. *The Tao of Science.* Technology Press, Mass. Institute of Technology, and John Wiley, New York, 1957.
22. SPERLING, MELITTA. The role of the mother in psychosomatic disorders in children. *Psychosom. Med.*, 1949, 11, 377-385.
23. STANTON, ALFRED H., and SCHWARTZ, MORRIS S. The management of a type of institutional participation in mental illness. *Psychiatry*, 1949, 12, 13-26.
24. STANTON, ALFRED H., and SCHWARTZ, MORRIS S. Observations on dissociation as social participation. *Ibid.*, 339-354.
25. SZUREK, S. A., and BERLIN, I. N. Elements of psychotherapeutics with the schizophrenic child and his parents. *Psychiatry*, 1956, 19, 1-10.

26. SZUREK, S. A. Childhood schizophrenia: Psychotic episodes and psychotic maldevelopment. *Am. J. Orthopsychiatry*, 1956, 26, 519-543.
27. SZUREK, S. A. Concerning sexual disorders of parents and children. *J. Nerv. Ment. Dis.*, 1954, 120, 369-378.
28. SZUREK, S. A. *Roots of Psychoanalysis and Psychotherapy.* Springfield, Ill.: Charles C. Thomas, 1958.
29. TIETZE, TRUDE. A study of mothers of schizophrenic patients. *Psychiatry*, 1949, 12, 55-65.
30. WHYTE, LANCELOT LAW. *The next development of man.* New York: Holt, 1948.
31. WHYTE, WILLIAM H., JR. *The organization man.* Garden City, New York: Doubleday, 1957.

Section II

HISTORICAL ASPECTS

From the earliest efforts to classify psychosis of childhood by De Sanctis in 1906 to the earliest American attempts to systematically treat psychosis in young children by Witmer, there are important lessons applicable to present day treatment of psychosis of childhood. Our colleague, Gianascol, reviews many of the psychodynamic approaches to childhood schizophrenia important to understanding current investigations and psychotherapeutic work.

3

On Some Varieties of Dementia Praecox[1]

Professor Sante De Sanctis

EDITOR'S NOTE:

When this translation of perhaps the first reference in the psychiatric literature to the psychotic disorders of childhood was planned and completed it was considered by the present editors to be the first complete rendition into English. However, its publication was delayed by the inevitable problems of gathering, preparing, and editing all the other manuscripts for this volume.

In this interval of several years duration a complete English translation of the contribution of Dr. De Sanctis by Maria-Livia Osborn appeared as the first paper in Chapter XXII, entitled "Three Historic Papers," in *Modern Perspectives in International Child Psychiatry*, John G. Howells, Editor, pp. 590-609, Brunner/Mazel, Inc., 1971.

In view of this last named publication the translator of the present version, Mrs. Mary Jeffress, M.S.W., agreed with the editors of this volume that its readers' interest in some historical aspects might be best served by including here only those portions of the translation relevant to the general subject of the book, namely the psychoses of childhood. Therefore, selections of the entire De Sanctis paper, here omitted, concern the author's discussion of nosological problems, not entirely solved in Kraepelin's formulation of his concept of dementia praecox. These omitted selections include those numbered in the Osborn translation as follows:

All of I, III, and introductory paragraph of V.

---

[1] This paper by Sante De Sanctis, "Sopra alcune varieta della demenza precoce," was published in *Rivista Sperimentale di Freniatria*, Vol. 32, 1906, pp. 141-165, and has been literally translated by Mary Jeffress, M.S.W. (A. J. Gianascol, M.D., and Anna Mallardi Corbascio, Ph.D. collaborated in this work.)

PREMATURE DEMENTIA

Every conscientious contribution to the nosography of dementia praecox may therefore prove to be useful and is not to be despised. My study of some clinical cases in the institutes under my direction and in my private practice gives me the opportunity to make some comments.

The first problem which has particularly interested me is the relation between dementia praecox and mental deficiency.

Schule[2] speaks of "hebephrenic imbecility," grouping under this title those cases of youthful insanity which end in imbecility, as well as those cases of youthful insanity which are complicated with imbecility. He observes that true hebephrenia sometimes does not rise above a fundamental idiocy and that some hebephrenics end in imbecility (though not in dementia, to be sure!).

This acute observation of Schule would seem at first glance to generate confusion, but we may recognize its value—in spite of its lack of precision —if we call to mind an opinion of Morel's.[3] He called to our attention that *dementia in certain cases is nothing but the final outcome of a foetal evolution, the seed of which has been carried by the adolescent since birth.* It is a meaningful coincidence that it was Morel who gave the name of démence précoce to the *premature dementia* which during puberty sometimes strikes the children of alcoholics and insane persons.

Tolouse[4] revived the ingenious view of Morel when he affirmed that puberty is the boundary between congenital and acquired psychic weaknesses or insanity, so that Toulouse considered dementia praecox of puberty an idiocy of the congenitally predestined individual.

But many psychiatrists have long affirmed, and without reservation, that the weak and the imbecilic (mental deficients) at the time of puberty undergo a deterioration in their mental condition. This observation had not escaped Esquirol and those others who had described primary dementia, hereditary insanity, hebephrenia, heboidophrenia, moral insanity, and the various psychic disturbances that accompany and follow puberty.

Finzi and Vedrani[5] pointed out the "relative frequency" with which imbeciles and idiots at about the time of puberty (a little earlier, or at times later,) present symptoms of dementia praecox. Finzi himself had

---

[2] Schule. Clinical Psychiatry (Italian translation). "Imbecillita ebefrenica."

[3] Traité des maladies mentales, Paris, 1860.

[4] Toulouse: Classification des maladies mentales, in *Revue de Psychiatrie*, February 1900. See also S. De Sanctis: On the classification of psychopathy, *Rivista sperimentale di Freniatria*, 1902. *Atti del Congresso Freniatrico di Ancona* of 1901.

[5] Finzi and Vedrani, Contributo alla dottrina della demenza precoce, *Riv. Sper. di Freniatria*, 1902.

already noted that a demenza precocissima (very precocious dementia) could constitute a form of mental deficiency.

Several years ago I[6] spoke of "progressive mental deficiency." This term referred to the phenomenon, repeatedly observed by me, that mentally deficient children, cerebroplegics, as well as those without paralyses (epileptics apart), manifest, as they grow older, an increasingly accentuated mental decline (with educational arrest and regression) despite suitable medico-pedagogic treatment. Certainly this phenomenon was observed more frequently among the patients of the institutes for deficients and abnormals than among those in the elementary schools, a fact which was recently noted by Cramer.[7]

I do not feel like insisting on the term and on the concept of progressive mental deficiency. It would even appear to me idle to discuss the prejudgement of Toulouse, that is, whether a mental weakening which occurs at the time of puberty is by definition mental deficiency.[8]

In my opinion, if we wish to avoid academic discussion, one must on the one hand respect the classical concept of mental deficiency given to us by Esquirol, and one must, on the other hand, not doubt the independent existence of a psychosis which develops during the pubertal period and which today we call "dementia praecox."

However, more recently I had the occasion to observe another interesting fact, namely, that *among the mentally deficient children one could find some with a type of mentality truly insane (that is with a dementia praecox mentality).*[9] I could not, however, state at that time whether in these cases one dealt with individual psychopathic varieties or with true dementia praecox, which given the age of the patient, I called *dementia praecocissima*. The fact remained and its importance was not diminished by its implications.

---

[6] S. De Sanctis: Sui criteri e i metodi per la educabililtà dei deficienti, reported to the Psychiatric Congress of Ancona, 1901. In *Rivista sperimentale di Freniatria*, 1902.

[7] A. Cramer: Entwickelungsjahre und Gesetzgebung, 1902.

[8] Bourneville (C. R. de Bicetre, 1897) calls idiots also the weak mentalities that occur at the beginning of puberty at 13 or 14 years, following pathological processes in the brain. This is the accidental acquired idiocy of Esquirol. Perhaps it would be better to speak in such cases of dementias (following traumas or inflammatory processes of the meninges and of the brain, tumors, or other).

[9] S. De Sanctis: Su alcuni tipi di mentalita inferiore communication at V. International Congress of Psychology. See also *Annali della R. Clinica psichiatrica di Roma*, 1905.

EXISTENCE OF PRE-PUBERTAL DEMENTIA PRAECOX

Given these observations two distinct questions faced us: (1) If dementia praecox can occur among mental deficients, then how does it occur and when does it occur? (2) *Does a pre-pubertal dementia praecox exist, that is, a dementia which can be called praecocissima because of the time of onset?*

Another question was suggested to me by another kind of observation. The authors that follow the views of Kraepelin, and Kraepelin himself have admitted that dementia praecox is not always a pubertal or juvenile psychosis, but that, on the contrary, it can appear beyond 30 years and even to the age of 40-45 and more years, especially the paranoid form.[10]

CHILDHOOD SIGNS OF DEMENTIA PRAECOX

A last question, which we need to distinguish from the previous ones just mentioned, but which, after all, is part of them, regards the *childhood of those with dementia praecox.* It is admitted that hebephrenia, like the other forms of dementia praecox, may appear in subjects that were, up to that point, intelligent and completely normal; but *I have collected certain curious facts which raise serious doubts about the alleged normal mentality of those who become victims of dementia praecox, and which make us ask whether in the childhood of these individuals one may not frequently find signs that reveal their destiny.* This problem may bear upon the etiology of dementia praecox.

In summary, I wish to discuss these clinical-nosographical problems about dementia praecox:

1. Does a *dementia praecox subsequens or comitans* (subsequent or concomitant with mental deficiency) exist?

2. Does a *dementia praecocissima* (of childhood) exist?

3. Does a *dementia praecox retardata* exist? (Later I shall explain why I prefer the term *retardata* (delayed) to *tardiva* (late), the first term which would come to mind.)

4. Does dementia praecox in both *subsequens or comitans* and in the *retarded* form have *premonitory signs at an early age?*

In this brief prefatory note I do not pretend to have definitive answers for such questions, but I do propose to summarize concisely my clinical experiences with these ideas and so invite psychiatrists to gather the facts

---

[10] The case of A. Pick (Ueber primare Demenz bei Erwachsenen in *Prager medezin Wochensche*, N. 32, 1904). Even more famous is the case of Schroeder in which dementia praecox apparently began at the age of 59! (cited by Kraepelin).

required for a solution to these problems—*Dementia praecox subsequens* or *comitans*.[11]

Thus I provisionally describe the precocious dementia which appears in mentally defective individuals, the so-called mentally deficient (idiots, imbeciles, the slow, deficients). Perhaps not all the psychiatrists are convinced, as I am, of the great frequency of this type; but nevertheless, this type is so easily observed that it would not deserve such attention if various psychiatrists did not persist in confusing the dementia praecox of mental deficients with those periods of agitation that are characteristic of idiots and imbeciles, or with the psychopathologic states, the episodes of delirium, melancholia, etc., of the so-called degenerates. It is in the name of that clarity which clinical forms must attain that I insist on provisionally describing such cases as cases of *dementia praecox subsequens* or *comitans*. In reality, this variety is very frequent; in a few months and in a restricted field of observation (that is, outside of a mental hospital), six cases have come to me, each of which I have studied closely over a long period. I am now convinced that *in the prognosis of mentally deficient educable children, dementia praecox must be considered as a serious possibility.*

PROGNOSIS OF DEMENTIA PRAECOX IN MENTALLY DEFICIENT CHILDREN

Here is what I conclude from my personal experience with this clinical variety:

a) Dementia praecox *subsequens* or *comitans* is a fairly common variety which occurs more in the female than in the male. Of my last six cases, four were of the female sex.

b) In my six cases, it appeared between the twelfth and the twentieth year.

c) The immediate apparent causes were, in one case, a febrile sickness; in another, exhaustion (surmenage) (?); in two, more or less intense emotions (fear, terror); in the remaining two cases, any precipitating cause escaped completely.

d) In only one of the six cases was the antecedent mental deficiency serious; in the remaining four cases, the degree of deficiency was moderate. One of the female patients learned without special pedagogical methods to read and write well, and even to acquire the elements of a foreign language (see reported case). The other five cases completed the

---

11 Professor Tamburini would suggest calling this form *dementia praecox phrenasthenica*. See discussion in my paper at the *E. Accademia di Roma*, January 28, 1906.

first three elementary grades. In all cases, however, a deficient mentality had been noted by the family and by the physician from the time of early childhood. *However, based on my experience, I can affirm that patients with serious mental deficiency are less disposed than the others to dementia praecox.*

e) All six cases exhibited forms of mental deficiency without paralysis; but among cases observed by me on a different occasion there were two in which the original mental defect was accompanied by epileptic attacks.

f) The symptoms with which the dementia praecox announced itself in my six cases were, in order of frequency, the following: strangeness of character and capriciousness; apathy; depressed mood; scruples; negativism; hallucinations; and agitations. In only one of the six cases was there marked catatonia.

AGE OF BEGINNING DETERIORATION

In general in the mental deficients who develop dementia praecox, the intellectual deterioration begins in the eleventh or twelfth year or sometimes later and proceeds at least for some months or even years progressively, to the extent that it becomes necessary to suspend any pedagogical treatment. The most serious cases—those which in general fall under the observation of the psychiatrist—have the characteristics of the hebephrenic or paranoid form; but many cases have the characteristics of simple dementia and for this reason pass unobserved. In some of these cases the intellectual decline was so placid I was led, in 1901, to the concept of "educational regression."[12] Rereading what Kahlbaum had written on heboidi forms and some other cases I found in the literature (Diem, Cramer, Monod) called simple dementia or frusta, I found a complete resemblance between these and some of my cases of educational regression.[13]

It seems unnecessary to report all the six cases more recently observed by me. I shall report only one of them as a sample illustrative of the clinical variety that I am describing.

Typical Case—S.A., Age 17

Although the family history is not entirely free of neurosis, six sisters and two brothers of the patient enjoy good physical and mental health.

---

[12] See my report to the Psychiatric Congress of Ancona already cited, 1901.

[13] I say some; and above I said that the term educational regression was suggested to me in part by the cases of which I speak, just because the *educationally regressed* can be determined not only by the *decline*, now placid, now tumultuous, of *intelligence, coinciding with the time of puberty*, but also by epileptic forms, by the environmental influence, by precocious intoxication, and by other causes unknown to us.

The patient had no incidence of disease in early or late childhood, but both her family and teachers had recognized her intellectual deficiency in her early years. She was inactive, had little capacity for attention, had a weak memory, and despite her perfect physical development was regarded by everyone as defective. Her character was normal; she studied willingly, so much so that with much effort she succeeded in completing all the elementary courses and finished two grades beyond that, and she was also able to learn a little of the French language.

We should note, however, that she completed all her studies in private religious schools[14] and several times repeated the same classes. Her first Communion marked the beginning of her scruples and sadness, although she maintained a correct demeanor until she was sixteen. Then, as her scruples became aggravated, A. began to show marked changes of character, diminution of affection towards her parents, a spirit of contradiction, indocility, extravagant ideas, and, as expressed by her mother, "strange ideas."

On some days the patient refused even to eat, giving the reason that she wanted to mortify her senses. The spring and summer of 1905 passed fairly well, but in August of that year A. became very restless, strange, and contradictory to excess. In September when I saw her for the first time, I was unaware of her history, and I diagnosed her as a common case of dementia praecox. On the 3rd of October she was admitted to my hospital, and on the 26th of the same month she was transferred to a sanatorium because she had become agitated, strange, at every moment changeable in mood and wishes, and obstinately refusing to eat or to leave her room.

Here in brief are the patient's most obvious symptoms observed in my hospital and in the sanatorium between the 10th of October and the 20th of November:

Subject well-developed, brunette-type, well-proportioned, 162 centimeters in height, her weight 51 kg., her thyroid gland under-developed[15]; presenting a sharp, facial assymetry, both anatomical and functional (the right side of her face moves more than the left); physiological functions regular, except on some days she has had bad breath, constipation, and sleepless nights. No

---

[14] Translator's note: In Italy children in religious schools are tutored if they are having learning difficulties.

[15] One should note this detail. In another case of hebephrenia which I have mentioned elsewhere, one had an enlarged thyroid and had symptoms of hyperthyroidism. However, any further significance escapes us. In the case which I here describe, the use of thyroid tablets had no effect.

alteration of muscle strength with active or passive movements, nor of reflexes or sensation.

From the mental point of view her silly behavior, her movements, her affective instability and nonsense were particularly surprising. Periodically, she is very agitated, she breaks things and threatens to commit suicide, wants to run away, and does not stop smiling and grimacing. In periods of calm, she either laughs or cries, or keeps an obstinate silence, or expresses absurd ideas, or speaks words without sense, or assumes statuesque postures and grotesque affected poses. At certain times her negativism becomes extreme. For many days she refuses food, becomes mute, and even refuses to urinate, so that several times she was catheterized.

In the patient's speech I noted frequent associations of assonance, rhyme, foulness of speech, neologisms, echolalia, verbigerations, confusion of words without sense (Wortsalat)—symptoms that have their counterparts in her writings. Here is an example of her speech:

> "And I am sure that all the Saints in Heaven will assist me and will make me in the end a novice of the Sacrament, and there should not be locomotives, or carriages, or horses. But everybody must walk with their legs. By day or night one must never rest, but I would not want anyone drunk or badly behaved, lazy, vagabond, but that all shall work with the sweat of his brow, and the vines must be all thrown in the fire, in short all burned and the grain not even, etc. . . . in short, they should all be controlled or they should all eat equally as in an institution."

On other occasions the patient, with much laughing, said:

> "Sel . . . selleri . . . Buoni i selleri. I shall do it, you shall do it, they shall do it. Beautiful French . . . ne pa, papa, Napoleon, tiger, ferocious beasts . . . No, no, no . . . "

In this passage the superficial associations of assonance are abundant. And even more characteristic are her writings. Here is one of her letters:

> "My dear D. M.
> "Do me the pleasure of sending me a half onion, because instead of being called Assunta, I am called Addolorata (Our Lady in Sorrow); therefore, do me the kindness of sending me also the tears of the Madonna."

And in another letter written in very bad French to her relatives, she adds as postscript these words: "But only say to the Archpriest of Santa Maria to change his name to Lucifer, or rather they should call him in another manner, which frightens me."

The patient expresses the most absurd ideas imaginable. Her condition is plainly one of dementia. All told during the three months I had her under observation I found in her all the mental symptoms of a dementia praecox.

DEMENTIA PRAECOCISSIMA

Those that have written about *hebephrenia, heboidophrenia, simple dementia* or *primary dementia,* etc., have not considered the possibility that such illnesses could occur many years before the period of puberty. Stecker did not consider it, nor did Kahlbaum, Fink, Clouston, Bevan-Lewis, Ball, Mairet, Spitzka, and Marro. Seppilli[16] claimed that the psychoses of puberty were rare even between the twelfth and fourteenth years. We should remember, however, *that the so-called moral insanity* (acquired after a trauma, or an illness, or an emotional condition) has also been observed in children. The statistics of Bertschinger also provide cases of *dementia praecox at ten years,* although no one can say that *dementia praecocissima* has a literature. Kraepelin limits himself to the observation that *certain* conditions of psychic weakness in early childhood must be regarded as manifestations of *hebephrenia.* He compares certain catatonic disorders of idiots to those which appear in the final stages of dementia praecox and recalls apropos of this, the opinion of Masoin. Weygandt warns that the occurrence of dementia praecox before puberty is still open to question.

CURABILITY OF DEMENTIA PRAECOX

In my work about "Some Types of Inferior Mentality," quoted later, I said: "I am certain that in childhood mental insufficiency (mental deficiency) is frequently characterized by the mental symptomatology of heboido and hebephrenia . . . I doubt that this is a different clinical entity, or variety of mental deficiency." I reaffirm these words, but I must add something. It appeared probably to me then, as I have stated, that the insane type constitutes simply one type of mentality in mental deficiency. One must admit with much caution that in infancy and in childhood there are other causes of true intellectual deficit apart from those which determine mental deficiency. My opinion was strengthened by the fact that children of the insane type could at times derive improvement from medical-pedagogical treatment as do mentally deficient children, whose deficiency was of a different mental sort. But today I ask myself, no one could indeed rule out that mental defectives (of the insane type) have (true) dementia

---

16 Seppilli: Delle psicosi della puberta. Of the psychoses of puberty. *Atti del V. Congresso della Societa Freniatrica Italiana* in Siena, 1886.

praecox because of the single fact that they can improve. Using this unique fact of the curability-educability (therapeutic criteria), I begged the question. I used to believe that all forms and varieties of dementia praecox were incurable. Now I believe that some children regarded as mentally deficient, who present clearly insane mentality, not only have improved but can be cured. *This suggests that these are not cases of mental deficiency with insanity (psychosis), but true cases of dementia praecox,* because, apart from symptomatology, *it is more reasonable to believe in recovery from an attack of dementia praecox than to believe in recovery from mental deficiency,* which if you want to be precise, should not be thought of as an active disease process but rather as a final result of a process.

OTHER PHYCHOSES IN CHILDREN

Thus, I certainly do not claim that all mental defectives with insanity have dementia praecox. Moreover, I would like to add that *one must not confuse with dementia praecox other psychoses which are not very rare in children from five to eight years of age and which usually recover.* (These other psychoses) which I have observed include hysterical dream-like states, certain forms of strange deliria, which resemble paranoia in miniature, the hallucinatory psychoses. Thus one can observe in children, for example, the epileptic dementia, which is not at all rare.

DEMENTIA PRAECOCISSIMA

I only use the diagnoses of *dementia praecocissima* when (the children) exhibit the classical symptomatology of dementia praecox. I exclude it (using only a diagnosis of insanity) when the child since early infancy showed symptoms of dementia praecox along with concomitant somatic phenomena *(paresis, spasms, defective development, etc.)* which makes one think of a pre- or post-natal cerebroplegia (brain damage). I cannot exclude, however *hereditary syphilis from the diagnosis of dementia praecocissima.* It is curious that many of my cases of dementia praecocissima were born to syphilitic parents and had the so-called *ocular syphilitic stigmata.* But I do not intend now to enter into details. It is enough for me to establish the *fact* that there is in childhood a *form of dementia praecox* that I called *dementia praecocissima,* in which the prognosis is not always so grave as that of dementia praecox in young people and in adults, but which, like certain forms of *heboidophrenia of Kahlbaum,* may be at times curable.

A few months ago I explained my views to a German colleague, and I learned that he too had *observed dementia praecox in children who later were cured,* and that a very interesting case of a similar kind had occurred to Professor Binzwanger of Jena.

Typical Case—D. Flavio, Aged 10 (observed in 1899)

Father choleric, impulsive but healthy. Paternal uncles irritable and of little regular conduct; mother chronic cough, maternal grandfather alcoholic and brutal, maternal great-aunt insane.

Flavio was born at term with spontaneous birth, had the eruption of teeth early; the first tooth appeared at four months and dentition was complete during the first year of age. He began to walk at three years. He was delayed in the development of articulate speech. He began to pronounce words well only at five years. Ever since childhood, he has been of irritable character, but he went to school and profited from it. Now he has finished the second elementary class. His father notes, however, that for the past two years Flavio's character has become increasingly strange, so that now he has changed so much they are no longer able to keep him disciplined. He refused everything, and for that reason they brought him to me.

Boy well-developed, a little pale, a brachycephalic head, wide face, with nose a little flattened. Weight 26.500 kg.; height 126 cm., with some degenerative signs. State of general nutrition poor. Respiratory function weak. Flavio was subject to frequent bronchitis, he has a healthy heart, but suffers from palpitation of the heart, especially at night. He has very little appetite. He sweats in an extraordinary manner at night, in winter as well as in summer. He habitually sleeps soundly but has frequent night terrors. He tosses much in his sleep. Trophic condition of muscles regular. Reflexes superficially lively; knee jerks normal. Passive and active movements regular. The small movements of the fingers, upon request, are all possible, but one needs time and patience to get the patient to perform; for the most part, he is distracted or likes to joke. Muscular strength regular. Sight A.D.V.=1/3, A.S.V.=1/2, distinguishes well by name the colors green, red, and yellow. Hyperesthesia of the retina with tearing reflex. Traucoma localized at the conjunctive tarsae. Skin sensation normal; strong tolerance to pain provoked with mechanical stimulus. Easily satiated little appetite.

His attention is prompt and of sufficient duration, except when he is occupied in play. Often he becomes fixed in contemplating objects and asks many questions in regard to them. Memory fair, musical memory is very good; his father says that "he has a good ear." He can add and subtract numbers up to 1000; he finds multiplication very difficult. He reads fairly well but writes very badly. He is afraid of darkness but does not seem afraid of other things. His emotions of anger are frequent and quick, erotic emotions do not appear. No sense of pity; Flavio is cruel to animals, shows emotion (physically) rather strongly and cries and laughs with extreme facility; but sensibility is very obtuse. He does not feel affection for anyone. His spasmodic laugh is peculiar, bursts out occasionally with the greatest facility, provoked by one word or one rather strong impression. Asked with insistency why he laughs so loudly and endlessly, he either does not answer or says "Who knows?" His mood is habitually gay, but above all, variable. His behavior is silly, without motive, postures are grotesque; he grimaces, has affectations in walking and in greeting. Childish curiosity. Tends toward solitude and to drink alcoholic beverages. He doesn't like to play games with other children, flees from company, and prefers to remain in idleness and make grimaces alone. His sense of imitation is much developed, he imitates the physiognomy and gestures of others. He does not like cleanliness, is disorderly, unstable. In school he behaves as one who does not understand the reason for things; however, he shows good memory, and when it seems that he has not understood anything the teacher has explained, it is surprising to hear him repeat what the teacher has said or read. From time to time he has an inane expression; he laughs, repeats endless times a gesture or any movement, he moves, he contorts, makes faces with his mouth and with his eyes; and all this without the least reason in the world. His father adds that often in the house he repeats for many minutes the same word; and sometimes this repetition of the same word is accompanied by stereotyped head and hand movements (stereotypes with verbigerations).

On certain days he displays a very sharp spirit of contradiction and even refuses to eat.

Recently I was able to gather from this patient, whom I have not seen since 1899, some news of great interest. Flavio in these last six years has changed much. He continued for about two years to show himself as described above, and his father was desolate over this; but then, his father said, "He became more serious." He has put him to work and finally, now that he is fifteen years old, he earns 5 lire per week.

IMPROVEMENTS OF PATIENTS

The improvement of the patient is neither due to pedagogy nor to medicine of any kind. It came about little by little during the period of pre-puberty, after the condition of deficiency and insanity as his father had described had lasted about six years. I cannot at all ascertain that recovery may follow this improvement. It is probably that Flavio may retain a certain amount of intellectual deficit.

DIAGNOSIS OF DEMENTIA PRAECOCISSIMA

The *diagnosis of dementia praecocissima* does not seem to be doubtful in the case described above. The reasons are as follows: (1) The condition did not manifest itself in early or late infancy, when mental deficiency usually appears, but only in childhood; (2) The condition appeared without apparent causes and without concomitant symptoms involving sensory or motor behavior; (3) The condition presented the common symptoms of *dementia praecox;* (4) The condition had a well-defined course as true disease processes have and which mental deficiency does not usually have. In summary, I have observed at least five of these cases that I believe I could distinguish from cases of mental deficiency with insanity only. I was unable to observe in all five the decline of the dementia syndrome in puberty that I have described in the above patient.

I now want to refer to one of the cases in which one is *uncertain whether one deals with dementia praecocissima or only with mental deficiency with insanity.*

Doubtful Case: G. M., 6 years old (observed in 1899).

The paternal grandfather killed himself for love at age 55. Father immoral; liar, dissembler, very sensual, of very irregular conduct; has never loved his son Giuseppe. A paternal great-aunt died in a mental hospital, a paternal great-uncle was considered half insane. His paternal uncles had irregular conduct and were all erotic. The mother is deficient, vain, very fond of festivities and pleasures, jealous of her husband. A sister is well developed physically and rather beautiful; therefore she is loved by her parents. G. was delivered with forceps (at term). He suffered much during suckling; also later on he often lacked necessary nutrition. Maltreated as a baby, he had many traumas. He always wet the bed, and his aunt states that this habit is due to the fact that the mother never trained him as she should have. There is a suspicion of congenital syphilis. He always showed himself incapable of learning and therefore was dismissed from all the schools to which he had been admitted. In the winter of 1899 he was received in my school for poor, deficient children. He is a child normally developed physically, a brunette, weight 17.600 kgs., height 107 centimeters. Hands stumpy, fingers short, nails small; low forehead, straight black hair with abnormal vortex of the scalp; small eyeballs, iris dark, face slightly asymmetrical, teeth with anomalies of form and position.

The state of G.'s general nutrition is very poor; respiration was regular, his heart was healthy. Nocturnal enuresis. Sleeps habitually soundly. G. presented stenosis of the left nostril because of a deviated nasal septum; cartilaginous crest of the same nostril, nasal catarrh.

Superficial reflexes sluggish, deep reflexes normal, pupillary reflexes normal, trophic conditions of muscles normal. Slight hypotonia of the lower limbs. Alternating strabismus is noted. The movements of the face, tongue, neck, trunk, upper limbs (at request) were impossible to examine on account of the mental state of the child; it does not seem, however, that there were important anomalies. His motor ability is little developed. G. always needs the help of someone in everything. The muscular strength of his hands seems normal. G. has habits among which is the sucking of his fingers. Sight and hearing normal. Sensitivity of touch normally developed. Sensitivity to pain (skin and mucous membranes) with mechanical stimuli is dull. Voracity in eating.

His attention is little developed. There is torpor and mobility. Memory is weak. He has no capacity to calculate. The capacity for emotion is very slight; no demonstration of affection towards his parents; no liking for companions. Mood habitually hostile or effusive, always very changeable, countenance silly. An extraordinary tendency to contradiction. Suggestibility paradoxical. G. has attacks of absolute mutism that last many days. Many times he has refused to urinate and to take food. Many times also he has been discovered eating some piece of bread which he kept in his pockets when he thought he was not observed. Here are the fundamental traits of his character: Indocility, negativism, and when he is in school, he keeps himself mute, solitary. Occasionally with the slightest stimulation he becomes very impulsive. He has a stereotyped smile that stays with him even when he is overcome by impulsive behavior.

To a superficial eye these would look like idiotic stigmata, but they are not so, because returning home in the evening G. comes out of his mutism, tells what he has seen and heard in school. Therefore, it is easy to rule out that the behavior of G. may be the product of pathological timidity. G. is not timid; rather, he is insensitive and impulsive.

. After three months during which his condition remained unchanged, he was dismissed from the school, and I have not been able to hear any further news from him.

In this case the *diagnosis is doubtful* because the control of the course of the illness escaped us and we do not know anything concerning the beginning of the illness. The presence then of alternating strabismus and slight paraplegia makes us suspect one of the many simulated forms of cerebroplegia. Certainly in G. M. one finds at least a type of insane mentality.

And finally a question (which is based upon what I have said about dementia retardata): *Has dementia praecox, in general, premonitory signs in the early years of life?*

According to my experience I should reply: very often.

I have had at my disposition only a small amount of material, but nevertheless I have become convinced that the history of patients with dementia praecox is never or hardly ever negative. Not only their heredity is tainted most of the time (it is admitted that 75% and even more have obvious hereditary predisposition), but these patients attracted attention for changes of character, or intellectual deficiency, or episodes of excitement, or of depression, etc. Whenever a case is presented to me of a youth that may exhibit hallucinations, confusion, excitement, and whose syndrome does not offer any other means for excluding dementia proecox, I believe it is valid to exclude it if he has a perfectly negative personal and family history.

I had already reached these convictions from my personal clinical observations when I reread the chapter on dementia praecox in the seventh edition of Kraepelin. I was surprised to discover that Kraepelin acknowledged certain psychopathological phenomena as antecedents of dementia praecox: timidity, strangeness, bigotism, affected behavior, irritability, and intellectual weakness; and he reports also observations analogous to those made by Schroeder.

THOSE DESTINED TO DEMENTIA PRAECOX

Furthermore, when we leaf through the literature of dementia praecox, we are struck by the need for distinguishing between two forms of this psychosis. There is the sort made up of individuals, completely normal and intelligent, who become acutely ill with dementia praecox at an age that varies between the 20th and 45th years. There is the second sort made up of predestined individuals who already in adolescence and in the dawn of youth are struck by melancholy, by hallucinations, and by psychomotor excitement. In the grip of these tumultuous symptoms (dementia simplex) these patients run their course heading toward precocious intellectual decline, as if nature had endowed them with a cerebral organization and structure devoid of resistance.

In this second category we find those individuals, *the mental deficients,* who are destined to *dementia praecox.*

Is this clinical distinction logical? Let us look at the pathogenic hypotheses that have been advanced for dementia praecox. To tell the truth there are not many plausible ones, but the hypothesis of Kraepelin (auto-intoxication from abnormal internal secretions of the sexual glands)[17] does not seem to be without evidence.

Kraepelin, indeed, intends a hypothetical relation between dementia praecox and the sexual function, in a very broad way, because he believes that auto-intoxication would be capable of provoking the cerebral process of dementia praecox whenever the genital glands enter into activity—puberty, menstruation, pregnancy, climacteric. Under these various circumstances the glandular activities are not so different. Thus it would be hard to understand how a brain, having withstood the physiological storm of puberty without deleterious consequences, would be affected deleteriously by pregnancy or the climacteric when cerebral development is complete and has occurred normally (sound brains).

In any case, the question is why such auto-intoxication should affect normal individuals as well as originally defective individuals. Is the generally acknowledged fact of the high frequency of infirmities among the dementia praecox patients a mere coincidence?

PREDISPOSITION OF BRAIN STRUCTURE TO DEMENTIA PRAECOX

But let us turn to pathological anatomy. In the various forms of dementia praecox, besides easily detectable alterations found in the brains of the amentias or of the melancholy (Kiernan, 1877, and all the recent authors: Nissl, Deny, Voisin, Ballet, Hoch, Meyer, et al.), besides unspecific chemical alteration of blood (Deny, Lhermitte and Camus, W. Prout, et al.), morphological and structural modifications of the cerebral cortex have been found of more value, like hypoplasia, atrophy, deviations of development, specifically localized in the deeper cortical layers, especially in the associative areas, or cellular atrophy and degeneration (Dunton, Alzheimer, Lugaro, Klippel and Lhermitte). It seems, therefore, difficult to explain certain structural alterations and certain specific localizations without *postulating a definite predisposition* in the brain structure of *patients with dementia praecox.*

It is more logical to consider dementia praecox a psychosis with a single pathogenesis and a single etiology that strikes in various degrees and with differing rapidity the developing organism.

---

[17] I have observed a typical case of dementia praecox in which from time to time the thyroid gland visibly swelled, and I have observed three cases also of classical dementia praecox, in which the development of the thyroid gland was very slight.

PREMONITORY SIGNS OF DEMENTIA PRAECOX IN CHILDHOOD

Individuals with dementia praecox may become ill even late, to pay, as it were, at a later date their constitutional debt, but they do not cease to be predestined, and the signs of their destiny may be found upon careful inquiry even in their childhood. How many times the epileptic attack due to congenital cerebral illness appears late in individuals who are destined to epilepsy; in epileptics in which the attacks began only at 25 or 30 years of age there were found at autopsy traces of prenatal encephalitis or porencephaly and microgyria. But in these cases before the attack would fully occur the *congenital illness* was revealed by other signs: slight motor phenomena, abnormalities of character, defective mentality, etc.

It is not conceivable that true dementia praecox may erupt in the constitutionally healthy organism completely developed and integrated. Psychiatric nosography would profit by a re-examination of those reports of dementia praecox described in the fourth or fifth decade of life in patients previously mentally balanced and robust, as well as those patients reported to have regained all their lost intellectual strength.

Kraepelin himself cannot explain how a psychic organism which had developed regularly and vigorously until adult life suddenly could without apparent cause stop in its development and often disintegrate. He adds that not even the most grave hereditary disposition could explain this extraordinary fact to us. And then? . . . We are dealing with nosography; the syndrome is not enough to determine a classification. Why not consider that in such cases one is dealing with a psychosis other than dementia praecox?

I think that the introduction of the term dementia praecox in psychiatry has been of incalculable utility, but only if by dementia praecox one means a psychosis linked to constitutional predisposition and to states of mental development which from their beginning and from their nature are truly demented, and therefore of invariably serious prognosis. Mental weakening must be real and therefore lasting, not only apparent, as is that of amentia, or of the hallucinatory form, or of nervous exhaustion. [18]

---

[18] Naturally the characteristics of the variety which I have here called "very precocious dementia" could be, in part, different from those of the common dementia praecox.

4

What I Did with Don

Lightner Witmer

HISTORICAL INTRODUCTION

BY A. J. GIANASCOL, M.D.

Lightner Witmer, Ph.D., a psychologist, is mentioned in histories of psychiatry and psychology, if at all, for having established in 1896 at the University of Pennsylvania, the first psychological clinic for maladjusted children.

As Sarason and Gladwyn (5) point out, however, Dr. Witmer may be considered a pioneer in child psychiatry because of his other contributions. He was, for example, one of the first to explicitly differentiate between childhood psychosis and mental deficiency. He also used psychotherapy to test his diagnostic impressions by reducing the degree of retardation due to emotional factors.

Earlier efforts had been made with the mentally deficient, particularly following the report of Itard (3), summarizing his five years of intensive efforts with Victor, the "wild boy" of Aveyron. Victor was found at an age estimated between 10 and 12 years in 1799 running on all fours in a French forest, apparently a feral child.

Itard initially believed that mental defectives were uneducable. Initially he considered Victor not to be mentally deficient. Instead he felt Victor's condition was due to environmental deprivation and therefore amenable to educative efforts.

As Witmer (10) pointed out, however, Itard proved himself wrong twice, first by demonstrating that Victor was actually mentally deficient, and second, by accomplishing some habit training in Victor, Itard demonstrated that he was educable to some degree. Thus his initial prejudice that the mentally deficient are not educable did not hold entirely.

Itard's pupil, Seguin, a French psychiatrist, continued Itard's enthusiasm and approach in the education and training of the mentally retarded, and when he came to the United States in 1848 he was influential in giving impetus to the movement in this country for the development of facilities for the education of the mentally retarded.

When Witmer opened his clinic in 1896, psychological tests were limited to association tests and sensory-motor measurements used by the experimental psychologists in their evaluations of individual differences. These tests and form boards devised by Seguin and Witmer comprised the total armementarium. It wasn't until 1904 that Binet, a French psychologist, and Simon, a French psychiatrist, devised intelligence tests. These were modified by them several times in the following years and translated into English by Goddard in 1910. In 1911, Stern defined the intelligence quotient as the ratio of mental age to chronological age (MA/CA). The Stanford-Binet, Terman's revision in 1916 of Binet's tests, led to the widespread use of intelligence testing in the United States,

Psychiatric knowledge at the time Witmer began his clinic was largely preoccupied with nosology. For example, in 1896, the year Witmer opened his clinic, the fifth edition of Kraepelin's *Textbook of Psychiatry* was published in which Kraepelin's final formulation of dementia praecox was presented, a classification which persisted in the official APA nomenclature up to the publication of the APA *Diagnostic and Statistical Manual of Mental Disorders* in 1952.

Following Kraepelin's classification and introduction of the term dementia praecox, the history of the study of psychoses in children became the history of various dementias, such as De Sanctis's description beginning in 1906 (1) of dementia praecocissima, and Heller's description in 1908 of dementia infantilis (2).

With the publication of Bleuler's *Textbook of Psychiatry* in 1911, the term schizophrenia, which he introduced, began to supersede dementia praecox in publications.

In 1929 Kasanin and Kaufman (4) commented that psychoses in children were relatively rare in their report which included six cases of childhood schizophrenia from all children seen over a 3-year period at the Boston Psychopathic Hospital. In 1933, Dr. Richmond (8), relating her experience at St. Elizabeths Hospital in Washington, D.C., noted how often children diagnosed as mental defectives may be schizophrenic.

The next year, Dr. Potter (7) at the Psychiatric Institute of New York reported six cases of schizophrenia in children. He noted their superficial resemblance to mental defective children, adding that if one studied

carefully patients in institutions for the mentally deficient, childhood schizophrenia might not be considered so rare.

The problems involved in differentiating schizophrenic children from
mentally defective children were examined more closely, and in 1937 Piotrowski's paper (6) appeared on the use of psychological tests in the differential diagnosis of schizophrenia and mental deficiency in children.

It is evident, therefore, that Witmer's early case descriptions anteceded
developments in child psychiatry by several decades.

The case report reprinted here was first published in *The Ladies Home
Journal* in April 1919. Later, in 1920, it was reprinted in the *Psychological
Clinic* (9), a journal founded by Witmer, in which he described many
"orthogenic" cases. In his introduction to this article as it appeared in the
Psychological Clinic, Witmer raised the question as to the nature of feeble-
mindedness. He maintained that there were two types of feeblemindedness:
the first due to congenital defects, for example, the Mongoloid child, and the
second he termed "arrested development," a condition he ascribed to the
same causes which produced insanity in an adult. He maintained that in
some of the latter cases the "psychosis", as he termed it, could be cured
completely if treatment began early enough. This psychotherapeutic optimism
was a landmark during an era when more nihilistic attitudes prevailed.

Witmer also noted that a child may be both feebleminded and insane
and he described such cases in his journal.

Witmer's description of clinical material without technical jargon is
refreshing for its vivid, direct style.

His claim that the following case proves that a child with arrested
development amounting to feeblemindedness may be cured and the child
restored to normal mentality is a surprisingly modern account of therapy
with a schizophrenic child.

WHAT I DID WITH DON*

He was five years old last July, and so I entered him the following
autumn in a near-by school, where he is the youngest of a group of first-
grade children. His teacher says that he reads better than any of them
and, except that he is poor in handwork, she considers him as competent
as the other children.

"Terence," said he to his pal, the gardener, who was taking him to

---

* Originally printed in the *Ladies' Home Journal*, Volume 36, No. 4, pp. 51-,
122, 123, April 1919.

Reprinted by special permission of the *Ladies' Home Journal.* Copyright
1919. The Curtis Publishing Company.

school the first day, "don't call me Donnie when we get near the school; don't call me Donnie or Don; call me Donald, which is right."

I saw Donald for the first time when he was two years and seven months old. His father carried him into my office, and deposited him, a soulless lump, upon the couch. He sat there with the stolidity of a Buddhist image, absorbed in the inspection of a card which he held in his pudgy hands, as regardless of his father and mother as of the new objects about him. While his gaze moved over the card, he scratched the back of it gently and incessantly with his finger nails. At times he gritted his teeth; and then again he made a crooning, humming sound with which it is his habit to lull himself to sleep.

He paid no attention to a rattle, to a bright-colored ball or to a picture book which I held before him, but every effort to remove the card from his hands he resisted. His face, already crimson, became empurpled. His physiognomy took on an expression of angry hostility; and I retreated before the approaching storm, leaving him again to his absorption in the card.

"He is fond of music," his mother said; but the liveliest strains of the talking machine were powerless to distract him from his chosen preoccupation. In the months to come I was to discover that by preference he would sit or lie in bed for hours, looking attentively at the object which he happened to be holding in his hands. It appeared to be persistent, concentrated attention, that most difficult and valuable of mental powers to cultivate.

From two to six years the child has the flitting attention of a monkey. "How do you select your monkeys for training?" a trainer of animals was once asked.

"I hold a lighted match before them," he replied, "and pick out as the easiest to train those that look longest at the burning match."

Donald would look at nothing but his card. One could not guess what lay behind those dull blue eyes. Was it interest, or only emptiness of mind —the dreamy listlessness with which the corner loafer looks at the passing world?

"What are those abrasions about the mouth and ears?" I asked.

"When he gets angry," his mother said, "he will scratch and tear at them."

"What else can he do?" I asked, not venturing to break in upon this obstinate immobility by trying to get him to perform the simple task which might, perchance, reveal some hidden mental ability.

"Can he walk?"

"A little, but he only began about two months ago," she replied. "Until

he was over two years old he hadn't even crawled; and he only learned
to crawl by his nurse taking hold of his knees and advancing them one
after the other."

As the flower blooms, the fish swims or the bird flies, so the child
crawls, walks and talks. It is the unfolding of his own instinctive impulses.
But this child had to be taught to crawl and to walk, and even yet he
could only toddle about uncertainly. If he fell upon his face he would lie
helplessly crying with his nose to the floor. Either he did not have the
strength to change his position, or he did not know how, or he was
unwilling to make the effort.

He never uttered a word spontaneously, and he could repeat at command only a few words like "Kitty," "Mamma"—eight words in all. His
understanding of language seemed to be limited to pointing to his head,
eyes, ears and nose when these words were spoken. Even a chimpanzee
of the same age as this boy, if brought up in human surroundings, will
give evidence of understanding more of spoken language than this boy
did. He could not feed himself. A much younger child can hold a cup or
a spoon, but this boy could not even close his lips upon a cup when it
was offered to him. He was still in diapers, and weeks were to pass before
he could be safely clothed like the normal boy of two years and a half.

At two years and seven months Donald was doing no more than many
a child does at twelve months, no more than every child should do at
fifteen months. No one who saw him needed to consult an expert before
deciding that he was subnormal. You had only to look at the large head
—"top-heavy Bill" one of his teachers called him—the fat red face, the
expressionless eyes and the helpless body, to arrive instantly at the conviction that "this child is feeble-minded."

And feeble-minded I thought him—of such low grade that I refused
at first to accept him for educational treatment in my school. With reluctance I finally yielded to the parents' pleas. He was the youngest child I
had ever accepted for psychological treatment, and apparently the most
hopeless.

The expert, like the parent, bases his opinion on the child's appearance,
behavior and history. But even more important than these is the *"attempt
to teach."* In doubtful cases I do not like to express an opinion until after
I have observed the results of attempting to teach the child something new.
This can often be done at the first examination, but I could not even
begin to teach Donald.

"I should like to see him walk," I said. But when he was lifted from
the couch, put upon his feet and made to walk, he burst into a paroxysm
of rage. His eyes became bloodshot; even his gums bled. When he was

put back upon the couch he returned to his contemplative absorption in the card. Offered a block, he made no effort to take it. He even closed his eyes, as though the very sight of it and me were more than he could endure.

When I took the card away, so as to secure his undivided attention, he had another paroxysm of rage. From this, however, I derived a little hope, for passion and rage may be an expression of strength. The child at least had energy at his disposal. His violent resistance evidenced resolute determination. Obstinate children are better material for training than the overpliant sort. I looked at him, sitting impassive, but always bolt upright, and this, too, I thought an encouraging sign.

"He is a very easy child to neglect," one of my teachers entered in her report soon after he came to school. "If you let him alone he will sit or lie in bed for hours and give no trouble. It is only when you try to do something with him, to dress him, or bathe him, even at times to feed him, that the trouble begins."

It takes some time and care to adjust a child to new surroundings, so I considered it no great misfortune that Donnie promptly got the measles. For a couple of weeks it was necessary to isolate him in the care of a trained nurse. This probably helped to make him less resistant to strangers. Perhaps there also awoke within his soul some responsive feeling of gratification when the soothing hand of the nurse or the doctor brought him relief from his distress of body. One month after Donnie's arrival I began his education.

"What to do" and "How to do it" are two puzzling questions confronting teacher and parent at every turn. To answer the first question is to present the aims of education. In the early years of education the three R's are the chief objective. The answer to the second question, "How to do it," will determine our method of procedure.

Educational aims and practice are commonly the outcome of theory. For example, an interesting and important theory of recent origin is the Montessori method. It aims to develop a child's natural abilities. It also has a theory of educational practice. It emphasizes and, in the opinion of many, relies exclusively upon appealing to the child's natural inclinations and desires. Deprecating the use of constraint and force, it throws the reins over the neck of the horse. Several children have been brought to me for examination and educational treatment who were nearly ruined by too close adherence to this supposed Montessori method.

I hold that constraint and liberty have equal value. At one time constraint, at another liberty, will bring the best results. The wise employment of constraint and force calls for greater intelligence and judgment on the part of the teacher and parent than the leaving of the child free to work out his own salvation and development.

I try to approach the problem of educating a child like Donald without any preferred theory. More than twenty years of experience has led me to see that there is some good in most theories. A few are fit only for the scrap heap. One guiding principle, however, has stood the test of time and use: "The first task of teacher and parent is to gain and hold the child's attention by giving him something he *can* do, and after that, something he can't do"—this in general is my method.

My educational aim is to develop attention by choosing tasks which develop it. Whether a child be one year of age, or two years, or six, whether he be in high school or college, the guiding principle of the educator should be to gain and hold attention first, and then to cultivate concentration, alertness, persistence and endurance, all of these being attributes of attention.

For the rest, I feel my way. I watch the child to discover what he does with interest and with ease, and from here I get him to take a step forward in the direction best calculated to bring him to what I am aiming at, "the next higher level of attention." Montessori provides the child with stimulating objects—her didactic material—and leaves it with the child to make the next step forward. This is doubtless an acceptable procedure; but suppose the child refuses to take a step in any direction. He must be shoved.

To shove a child in the direction you want him to go is easy if the child is pliant and submissive. If he is a fighter like Donnie, and if, like him, he has no desires except to be let alone, the development of attention and the enforcement of obedience must go hand in hand.

When you have a trout on a hook at the end of a thin line, the only way to land him is to play him. He is lively and vigorous. He has desires which conflict with yours. If you use too much force you will break the line. If you use skill, yielding and yet constraining, you will in time get him into your basket. In this way the skillful teacher "plays" the child. The hook of attention is attached to the line of obedience, and then she watches the child's every move to insure his advance in the required direction. Shall she coax or force him? On the lee shore of this question many a gallant educational craft lies shipwrecked.

You can coax most children, some of the time at least, by appealing to their interests and desires, even as the hunter entices the deer to come within gunshot by appealing to its curiosity. But some children can't be coaxed, any more than you can wheedle a trout into your basket.

For example, take Donald. He did not have a keen desire even for food.

He would not eat prunes, apparently because he disliked their appearance, and so they had to be mixed with his cereal in order to get him to eat them. He would not drink milk or water from a transparent glass. It must be offered to him in a cup. In the early days, indeed, he declined to drink water at all, and got his only liquid in the shape of milk or soup.

He declined to accept a sugarplum offered as a reward of merit; and if you took away the object he so fondly clapsed in his hands, and then yielded to his ragings and returned it to him, he would very likely throw it violently across the room. He disliked to be dressed. He disliked to be taken out of bed and put on the floor. He disliked to be taken for a walk.

All these things aroused angry resistance; and in his passion he went so far as to do himself bodily injury; but as long as Donald held something in his hand there was peace and quiet.

"What to do with him?" He could not be bathed and dressed in this happy state of calm contemplation. Take away what he held and his hands went up to his ears and mouth, tearing at them till they bled. Tell him to keep his hands down, they went up just the same; perhaps he only scratched himself a little more strenuously. Put mittens on him, as his former nurse did, and he still went through the motions.

Smack his hands, anger and passion intensified the violence of his resistance. The only thing to do was to hold his hands. Could he be compelled to keep them down after they were released? The historic battle lasted for an hour and a half. His hands were held while his teacher spoke to him from time to time: "If I let your hands go, will you keep them down?"

He raged, he stormed, he grew apoplectic, but the hands were firmly held. At every lull in the storm they were released, and up they went again. In the end he gave in. Ninety minutes showed remarkable endurance, determination and consistency of purpose, qualities which might be successfully employed in his educational development later.

Never again did Donnie hold out for so long on this or any other issue. My records show that though he raged at intervals during the ensuing twelve months, the longest period of resistance lasted for ten minutes only. He had learned his lesson. There was an inevitable persistence that would outlast his own. He might as well give in first as last.

Obedience may be enforced by punishment, by suggestion and threat, or by impression. Of all these the most effective is impression—to get home to the child the impression of a will stronger than his own, and, above all, the impression of its inevitableness. This struggle of opposing wills begins soon after the child is born; and my experience shows that no child is too young or too feeble-minded to know when his will has prevailed, and to profit by it.

The next lesson which the child must learn is to give attention. Many times each day the teacher admonishes her class: "Pay attention." But how is the child to learn to pay attention? How shall we compel him to give attention if he refuses it? The drillmaster commands "Attention!" and expects from his squad of soldiers an obedient alertness to concentrate upon the execution of his command. Behind the drillmaster's command is the threat of punishment for disobedience; in the last resort, even the threat of death. But how may we oppose successfully the conflicting impulses and desires of a little child? How awaken the child's interest in something in which he is not yet interested? This is the real problem of beginning an education.

I took my form board—a tray of eleven blocks of different shapes, each block fitting into a recess of the same shape from which it can be easily removed and then replaced. A four-year-old child is able on the first trial to replace every block, He does it slowly, perhaps, and with many errors, but he corrects his errors and finally succeeds. His method of solving the new problem set him by the form board may reveal to the observing psychologist many of the child's abilities and defects.

As children increase in years they replace the blocks with greater speed, precision and dexterity, but even twenty-five per cent of three-year-old children can successfully replace the blocks without instruction. Many normal children of two years and a half, and even older children, may fail to get all the blocks in place, and some may not succeed with a single block; but very few normal children over two years of age will be unable at least to pick up a block and try to do something with it.

When the form board was put before Donnie, he made not the slightest effort to obey the order to replace the blocks. I put a block in his hand and guided it to the proper recess. Quickly I picked the block out, put it in his hand again and said: "Put it back." He instantly replaced it. A dozen times I repeated this performance. His movements increased in accuracy and speed. Thus I proved to my gratification: (1) That he could be made to obey a command; (2) that he had sufficient control over the movements of his hand and arm to hold the block and adjust it into place; (3) that he was able to see the space, giving to the task sufficient concentration of attention to accomplish what he had undertaken; (4) that he had enough persistence to repeat a task over and over again; and (5) that he learned something from each performance as was shown by improvement in speed and accuracy.

I then repeated the experiment with a second block, obtaining a like result. I was now able to proceed to the real test of his capacity for educational development. I took out both blocks, leaving two spaces empty, and handed him first one and then the other. I was amazed to find that even on the first trial he put the right block in the right space. I also observed that for the first time he showed a little interest in the performance.

On the fourth day of training, when six recesses were exposed, he put in two blocks successfully; then he became obstinate and dropped the block on the bed, dragged it across the board and finally put it in the wrong recess. At length, after much urging, he had four blocks in place, but he persistently refused to do anything with the other two. On the fourteenth day, however, he reached for the board as soon as he saw it, fell to work immediately and put nine blocks away correctly. On the next day, with all the spaces exposed, he put away the eleven blocks in one minute and fifteen seconds. Thus, fifteen days after his first lessons began, he was doing the form board as well as the average four-year-old.

Observing that his interest increased with the difficulty of the task I set him, I decided to try him with my cylinder test. This is a modification of the Montessori cylinders, but it is more difficult than any of the Montessori material, combining the three sets of cylinders into one. I call it an "intelligence" test, and it is of sufficient difficulty to make it a useful test with college students. Donnie mastered this test in thirteen days. He showed from the beginning the greatest interest and avidity for it. He would reject the form board and hold his hand out eagerly for the cylinder.

As soon as he had learned to do the cylinders, I picked up a large capital letter B made of wood and, giving it to him, said: "Donald, this is B. Put B on the chair." When he had done this I said: "Give me B." In this way I taught him to pick the letter B out of a jumble of six other letters. In the afternoon of the same day he appeared to have forgotten it, but the next day he learned to pick out three letters from a confused pile of six, and he was able to name the letter B.

On the day following, exactly one month after his training had begun, a very satisfactory test showed that he had retained the three letters he had learned the day before, and he was able in addition to learn three more letters. One month later he could pick out and name all the letters of the alphabet, the capital wooden letters as well as the capital and small letters printed very large in a child's pictorial alphabet book. He was now doing work which six-year-old children are just about able to do in the first school year.

From the results of this "attempt to teach" I discovered that Donald had an aptitude for recognizing, remembering and discriminating forms. Teachers are advised to select their material and methods so as to appeal to the child's interests. In the beginning Donald gave no evidence of having the slightest interest in form. This interest developed only under compulsion, though it was undoubtedly founded upon the fact that he learned easily what some children learn only with effort. He was, withal, very human. He always chose the easy way. To fill a board with thirty-six pegs bored him. Monotonous and easy tasks still bore him.

We never could get him to take an interest in the Montessori buttoning and lacing frames, and even now he will never dress himself if he can get somebody else to do it for him. He learned to like the form board, cylinders and letters because this work was relatively easy for him. He had a natural aptitude for form discrimination, a tenacious memory and that greatest endowment of the human being, intelligence. To use his natural abilities gave him pleasure and excited interest. We were always able to carry him along more quickly in the direction indicated by his natural abilities; thus he learned his letters in half the time it took him to distinguish and name colors.

The quick change from distaste to liking was characteristic of Donald. He hated to walk. At times he was dragged outdoors, screaming and raging. At times he was enticed to walk by trundling ahead of him a moving wagon; for, like other children, Donald was interested in motion, and this one interest alone we did not have to draw out or cultivate.

One day he was kept outdoors twenty minutes, howling all the time, and only stopped when he was taken upstairs and put to bed. A week later he went outdoors with eagerness, and walked about poking a stick here and there into the ground, or picking up stray objects, until he was made to sit down and rest. Then he howled because he was not allowed to keep on walking.

He could say so few words when he came, and was so slow learning, that I was not sure he would ever learn to talk. Asked to say "shoe," he would make a sound like "h-m?" with a rising inflection, as though he had not quite heard the word, but would be delighted to oblige you if you would only say it again and a little plainer.

After you had repeated the same word fifty times, always getting the same response, you lost confidence in his desire and ability to please. He learned the word "shoe" when his teacher, tossing his shoe in the air, said with great gusto each time she caught it "shoe!" This amused him, but it took ten minutes to get him to follow suit. When he finally gave the word he mimicked her exact tone.

In the same way I taught him to give the sound of V, at which he balked for a long time. It was only because he was amused at the way in which I elongated the sound, that he was finally induced to imitate it.

Soon he was learning words rapidly, and at the end of the second month, his initial vocabulary of eight words had increased to one hundred and fourteen. With sixty-three of these words he had some association evidencing at least a partial understanding. He early showed that his intelligence was not defective. He had been taught to "kiss the pretty lady" on the back of a magazine. In the fifth week when he was given the magazine without the picture of the lady, and was told to "kiss the pretty lady," he turned over the pages, but, not finding the picture, hesitated. When the picture was returned to the magazine, he recognized it and kissed it.

After he had been with us three months he began to name objects: "It's a spoon;" "It's a shoe," "It's a lady." His sense of humor could always be appealed to. He learned to grunt like a pig, to gobble like a turkey, and even formal lessons were often enlivened by grunts and gobbles. If some parts of his education were accompanied by tears, other parts won smiles, and awoke his full, rich laughter.

After the second month of formal training and the third month of his stay with us, Donald went to Nova Scotia for the summer. There, by the seaside, he was given a month of full enjoyment, the chance to adjust himself to the new environment and the opportunity to learn through natural and spontaneous reaction to people and things. He was now picking up many new words, the names of those about him, and even an occasional sentence. To the question, "Who are you?" he was taught to answer "I'm Sunny Don," and to "How do you feel?" to reply "I feel happy." "A new Donald," a teacher reports, "went to the seashore, a Donald clear-eyed and cleanskinned, alert, with a disposition as good as it was determined."

To carry forward my plan of training his powers of attention and discrimination, I began to teach him numbers up to four by holding up one or more fingers. At the same time he was taught to put the three large wooden letters, C, A and T, together, and then to pick and spell CAT and DOG when the whole six letters were jumbled together. Next the words were printed on paper, and he was taught to see, spell and read as separate words such sentences as "I see a man," "A cat can see a dog." Before three months had elapsed, and after only five months of formal training in all, I made the crucial test, putting a primer into his hand for the first time. Haltingly, to be sure, but like a normal child just beginning in the first grade, he read the sentence: "A man can see a dog."

One day, just a year after Donald came to the school, his parents visited him. He walked into the room and, carefully coached beforehand, he greeted them: "How do you do, mother?" "How do you do, father?" Otherwise his behavior was spontaneous and wholly childlike. With the delight which he always took in showing off, he said his pieces: "Little Bo-Peep," "Little Boy Blue" and Stevenson's "Bed in Summer." His delivery was amusingly solemn, his articulation perfect and his intonation reproduced the exact tones of those who had taught him.

He read for his father and mother three pages from his primer. He spelled words like jump and John, and he gave the four separate sounds of jump. He put together a jig-saw puzzle of fifteen pieces. He strung beads, picking out each color upon demand. He put together twelve sliced animals, saying each time, "That's a bear," "That's a kangaroo," and so forth, enlisting his mother's cooperation by: "Will mother put the kangaroo together? Will mother put the elephant together?" Playing with blocks, he built up a house, tumbling it down and then turning to his father with: "Will father build a house?"

In one year he had arrived at this level of performance from a condition so abnormal that when of his own accord he looked through and around a picture frame at his teacher it was considered an event worth recording.

Five months later Donald was four years old, and another summer at the seashore brought him by the following autumn to a stage of general development where I was willing for the first time to consider him normal, lifting from the hearts of his parents the heavy burden of a diagnosis of feeble-mindedness.

Having stirred to activity all the mental abilities which I considered essential to the normal child, our work was directed to developing him in an all-around way. I did not push his reading in the second year as I had done in the first. Attempting to teach him phonic analysis as this is employed in language work, I made up my mind that he was not ready for it. Primarily I was not interested in having him read, write and cipher efficiently. I was interested only in arousing his latent capacity to do this work. I had no desire to produce an unbalanced monster.

In the past year and a half only I could easily have carried him on to second-grade work, but his general abilities would still have remained far behind those of a first-grade pupil. I used his natural ability to distinguish form in order to develop his powers of attention, and carried him far beyond the average child of his age in reading. But in all this the training of attention was my chief concern because I thought this essential for the development of his powers of observation, self-control and responsiveness to all the stimuli of a child's environment.

It was necessary now to let time and steady training humanize him, so we gave him what conspired to make him a normal, laughing, playful child, ready to work at times, but always preferring to play. In the further carrying out of this plan I entered him last autumn in a small private day school, where he is in the first grade. His class is now reading a little book which Donald finished reading a year and a half ago, but he is learning from the class and his teacher far more important things than what the "Little Red Hen" did. He is beginning to adjust himself to the everyday world of children and adults in which he lives and must play his part.

If I began my work without a theory and without understanding Donnie's mental status, I am far from that position now. I have unraveled much of the mystery, and I find the understanding of this one child of important value in interpreting the behavior and progress of other normal children. I believe that Donnie was at the start dominated by fear, which plays still an important role in his behavior. His concentration on the card was in the nature of a defensive reaction. He disliked to get out of bed because he was afraid to get out of bed. He disliked to walk and talk because he was afraid—perhaps of failure.

It was noted on one occasion that when taken outdoors he would not stop screaming even after he had been put on the back of a pony. I know now that this was the worst thing that could have been done to him. Donnie is afraid of all animals. He takes kindly, however, to little creatures and has often alarmed his teachers by bringing them caterpillars and worms.

One day Donnie, while seated at a table playing with a train of cars, had his attention called to the fact that a little gray kitten was in the room. He was mortally afraid of it, so he would not turn his head to look, but kept moving the train back and forth, saying "Puff! Puff!" in the same absorbed concentration which was characteristic of him at the beginning. He was ignoring the kitten just as he used to ignore people he disliked by closing his eyes when they came into the room.

He was afraid to look down a well, he was afraid of a doll, of a soft rubber ball, of a balloon, a loaf of bread, a spinning top. He was afraid to go on a sailboat the first time, but the second time he went with joy. He took a fearful pleasure in trains, for he loved them as moving things, and yet they terrified him. He would say: "Let us go to town in the three trolleys;" but when you asked him why he would rather go in the trolleys than in a train he would never tell you.

He has never verbally admitted that he is afraid of anything. "Won't hurt you," he very early exclaimed whenever he was frightened by anything; and this was one of his first spontaneous reflections. "Don't have to pat the pony," he would reiterate during the many weeks required to get him to overcome his fear of the school pet. The effort to take him out driving in a little pony cart, which it was thought would entertain him, only succeeded after a period of two months. But then, as was usual with him, he couldn't get enough of driving behind the pony.

Even yet he is afraid. "I like dogs," he declared lately, as he started on his way to school. "Nice kind dogs which don't bite," he added thoughtfully. Nevertheless, he managed unobtrusively to place his companion between himself and every dog. "I like to pat dogs," he boasted, but when one appeared unexpectedly he excused himself tactfully: "I don't like them that color."

So, while Donnie is fearful, he is not a coward. He is doing his best to overcome his fears, and he has worked out his own method of doing this. He had no fear of dark or of the supernatural.

Fears and desires are the two greatest motive forces of mankind. No problem is more perplexing and none so absolutely fundamental as the proper treatment of fears and desires so that these motive forces may excite the actions desired. As I understand Donnie now, he had no desires, but many fears. We compelled him to do those things which he feared. As soon as he had done the fearful thing, the fear, in many instances, disappeared and desire took its place. Donnie is now afraid chiefly of what surprises him.

Donnie's obstinacy measured the intensity of his fear, but in part it measured also the intensity of his desires. Always, from the very beginning, Donnie has known just what he wanted. Never was there any wobbly uncertainty of choice. He either desired it or he didn't desire it. This, to my mind, is a strong and valuable trait of character if you can turn it to the right use.

The desire for possession gives rise perhaps to his keenest pleasure. He held on to his card, not only because it enabled him to ignore the fearful things of the world about him, but he held on to it because here was something "all his own." Not until recently has he been willing to share any of his possessions with others. For a long time he not only clung passionately to his own possessions, but appropriated the playthings of all the other children as well, so much so that his room was known as the "Robber's Den." He is now so far advanced on the road to generosity that he will give away his second-best toy.

He has always shown the same concentration of attention which he showed at the beginning. One day recently he wore to school a necktie which he had borrowed from the gardener, Terence. The teacher could do nothing with him that day because he persistently explored the attributes of his new possession. He met Terence, who came to take him home, with the matured fruit of his morning's work: "Terry, can you see the top of *your* necktie?"

His first craze was for automobiles, and then for sailboats, bicycles, trains and cars—anything that moved. As he learned to talk, he went through the magazines. "It's an automobile, see the automobile," he kept reiterating. When he grew fond of excursions abroad, "Are we going out, Agnes?" he would say, "Agnes, are we going out?" a thousand times until he threatened to drive his nurse to distraction. No child can have a better endowment for future accomplishment later than this power of persistent concentration.

Donnie's traits of character are therefore positive traits. He has a definite array of abilities, keen desires, self-dependence. Even from the first he preferred to walk alone, though in constant fear of falling, rather than hold someone's hand. He only sought the hand if a terrifying object came in view. With strong desires and fears, strong likes and dislikes, Donnie has an equal capacity for happiness and great unhappiness, for success and failure. He can be sweet-tempered or angry and resentful. His emotional balance is easily disturbed, and he still requires very careful handling.

Of the causes of Donnie's mental condition when he came to us, and which led several experts to diagnose him as feeble-minded, I cannot be sure. He had an illness after birth, which I now believe left his brain so devitalized that it permitted fear to gain the upper hand over desire. Of one thing I am certain: If Donnie had not been given the painstaking and expert training to which we subjected him he would by now have fallen into a state of irremediable feeble-mindedness.

REFERENCES

1. DE SANCTIS, S. Sopra alcume varieta della demenza precoce. *Rivista sperimentale di freniatria*, 1906, 32, 165. See Chapter 3 this volume.
2. HELLER, T. About dementia infantilis, translated by Wilfred C. Hulse, *Journal of Nervous & Mental Disorders*, 1954, 119, 471-477. Originally appeared in the 5th (Schluss-) Heft, 37. Band, pages 661-667, *Zeitschrift fuer Kinderforschung*, Berlin: Julius Springer Verlag, 1930.
3. ITARD, J. M. G. *The Wild Boy of Aveyron*. Translated by G. and M. Humphrey, New York: Appleton-Century, 1932.
4. KASANIN, J. and KAUFMAN, M. R. A study of the functional psychoses in childhood. *American Journal of Psychiatry*, 1929, 86, 307-384.
5. MASLAND, R. L., SARASON, S. B. and GLADWYN, T. *Mental subnormality*. New York: Basic Books, 1958. (See chapter XVII.)
6. PIOTROWSKI, Z. A. A comparison of congenitally defective children with schizophrenic children in regard to personality structure and intelligence type. *Proceedings of the American Association of Mental Deficiency*, 1937, 61, 78-90.

7. POTTER, H. W. Schizophrenia in children. *American Journal of Psychiatry,* 1933, 89, 1253-1270.
8. RICHMOND, W. The dementia praecox child. *American Journal of Psychiatry,* 1932, 88, 1153-1159.
9. WITMER, L. Orthogenic cases, XIV—Don: A curable case of arrested development due to a fear psychosis the result of shock in a three-year-old infant. *Psychological Clinic,* 1920, 13, 97-111.
10. WITMER, L. What is meant by retardation? *The Psychological Clinic,* 1910, 4, 121-131.

5

Psychodynamic Approaches to Childhood Schizophrenia: A Review

A. J. Gianascol, M.D.

The increased number of children reported as having schizophrenic reactions of childhood seems related more to their recognition than to an actual increase in their incidence. The studies of these children have similarly multiplied. This paper reviews the development of psychodynamic approaches to these disorders and summarizes the Langley Porter Institute studies of schizophrenic children and their parents. Within the development, pertinent references are made to child psychiatry and its background.

CHILD PSYCHIATRY DURING THE NINETEENTH CENTURY

Itard, in France, made the first major psychiatric contribution to the study of children with his attempt to train a mentally defective feral child at the close of the 18th century, when his colleague Pinel was freeing mental patients from their chains. Seguin, Itard's pupil, came to the United States in 1848 and encouraged the development of facilities for the retarded. He became superintendent of the first training school for mentally defective children, a school named for a later superintendent, Dr. Fernald (70). The intelligence tests developed in France by Binet and Simon from 1900 to 1908 were adapted by Goddard (47) in 1910 for American use.

The first psychological clinic for maladjusted children was opened at the University of Pennsylvania in 1896 by Dr. Lightner Witmer, a psychologist interested in retarded children. Witmer (98) distinguished mental

Reprinted from: *J. of Nervous and Mental Disease*, 1963, 137(4), 336-348. Adapted from a paper presented at the Annual Meeting of the California Medical Association, Section on Psychiatry and Neurology, San Francisco, April, 1962.

deficiency caused by congenital defects of the central nervous system from that caused by severe emotional disturbances, which he maintained might be cured if treatment were begun early. He described his therapy of a boy who initially appeared defective. His paper, first published in the Ladies' Home Journal (99), is a surprisingly modern, untechnical account of the therapy of a schizophrenic child. A few excerpts follow:

"I saw Donald for the first time when he was two years and seven months old. His father carried him into my office, and deposited him, a soulless lump, upon the couch. He sat there with the stolidity of a Buddhist image, absorbed in the inspection of a card which he held in his pudgy hands, as regardless of his father and mother as of the new objects about him. While his gaze moved over the card, he scratched the back of it gently and incessantly with his finger nails. At times he gritted his teeth; and then again he made a crooning, humming sound with which it is his habit to lull himself to sleep. . . .

"What are those abrasions about the mouth and ears?" I asked.

"When he gets angry," his mother said, "he will scratch and tear at them."

"What else can he do?" I asked, not venturing to break in upon this obstinate immobility by trying to get him to perform the simple task which might, perchance, reveal some hidden mental ability.

"Can he walk?"

"A little, but he only began about two months ago," she replied. "Until he was over two years old he hadn't even crawled; and he only learned to crawl by his nurse taking hold of his knees and advancing them one after the other . . . . "

"He never uttered a word spontaneously, and he could repeat at command only a few words like "Kitty," "Mamma"—eight words in all. His understanding of language seemed to be limited to pointing to his head, eyes, ears and nose when these words were spoken. Even a chimpanzee of the same age as this boy, if brought up in human surroundings, will give evidence of understanding more of spoken language than this boy did. He could not feed himself. A much younger child can hold a cup or a spoon, but this boy could not even close his lips upon a cup when it was offered to him. He was still in diapers, and weeks were to pass before he could be safely clothed like the normal boy of two years and a half . . . .

"In this way [as a fisherman plays with a trout hooked on a thin line] the skillful teacher 'plays' the child. The hook of attention is attached to insure his advance in the required direction. Shall she coax or force him? On the line of obedience, and then she watches the child's every move to the lee shore of this question many a gallant educational craft lies ship-wrecked . . . .

"He declined to accept a sugarplum offered as a reward of merit; and if you took away the object he so fondly clapsed in his hands, and then yielded to his ragings and returned it to him, he would very likely throw it violently across the room. He disliked to be dressed. He disliked to be taken out of bed and put on the floor. He disliked to be taken for a walk . . . .

"All these things aroused angry resistance; and in his passion he went so far as to do himself bodily injury, but as long as Donald held something in his hand there was peace and quiet . . . .

"What to do with him? He could not be bathed and dressed in this happy state of calm contemplation. Take away what he held and his hands went up to his ears and mouth, tearing at them till they bled. Tell him to keep his hands down, they went up just the same; perhaps he only scratched himself a little more strenuously. Put mittens on him, as his former nurse did, and he still went through the motions . . . .

"Smack his hands, anger and passion intensified the violence of his re-sistance. The only thing to do was to hold his hands. Could he be compelled to keep them down after they were released? The historic battle lasted for an hour and a half. His hands were held while his teacher spoke to him from time to time. "If I let your hands go, will you keep them down?" . . .

"He raged, he stormed, he grew apoplectic, but the hands were firmly held. At every lull in the storm they were released, and up they went again. In the end he gave in. Ninety minutes showed remarkable endur-ance, determination and consistency of purpose, qualities which might be successfully employed in his educational development later . . . .

"He could say so few words when he came, and was so slow learning, that I was not sure he would ever learn to talk. Asked to say 'shoe' he would make a sound like 'h-m?' with a rising inflection, as though he had not quite heard the word, but would be delighted to oblige you if you would only say it again and a little plainer . . . .

"After you had repeated the same word fifty times, always getting the same response, you lost confidence in his desire and ability to please. He learned the word "shoe" when his teacher, tossing his shoe in the air, said with great gusto each time he caught it "shoe!" This amused him, but it took ten minutes to get him to follow suit. When he finally gave the word he mimicked the exact tone . . . . "

The boy at five years entered the first grade, functioning fairly well and reading better than his classmates. Witmer also described children who were both feeble-minded and insane. Although his efforts went unnoticed, they remain a historical landmark.

At the close of the 19th century, when Witmer was opening his clinic, Kraepelin (13) united various syndromes, including Morel's *demence precoce,* Kahlbaum's *catatonia,* and Hecker's *hebephrenia,* under the term *dementia praecox.* He considered it a genetically determined organic or metabolic disease. He did not describe childhood forms, but traced 3.5 per cent of his cases back to childhood. Kraepelin (28) reported recovery in 13 per cent of catatonic patients and eight per cent of hebephrenic patients, a statistic not disputed by his critics and at odds perhaps with his prognostic pessimism.

Rubinstein's review (82) of American literature before 1900 summarizes the scanty references to insanity in children. The nosology and concepts were pre-Kraepelinian, with few descriptions of mental disorders in children.

1900-1910: The Decade of Childhood Dementias, and the Development of Psychodynamic Psychiatry

Under Kraepelin's influence, several dementias of childhood were described. In 1905, De Sanctis (29, 30) reported three children, six, seven and ten years old, with childhood forms of dementia praecox which he termed *dementia praecocissima.* Like Witmer, he noted the difficulties in distinguishing these children from psychotic mental defectives and emphasized the therapeutic criteria in the differentiation, saying, ". . . it is more reasonable to admit the recovery of an attack of dementia praecox, than the recovery of a true mental deficiency . . . " (30).

The same year Heller (52), a remedial teacher working with feeble-minded children, applied the term *dementia infantilis* to six children with mental deterioration without neurological abnormalities. The condition was characterized by onset at age three or four years and a rapid regression to complete "dementia" in nine months. In 1930 (51), he alluded to data about 28 children with dementia infantilis and added follow-up observations with no mention of any positive signs suggesting neurological disease. His data, although scanty, suggest he may have been describing a form of childhood schizophrenia.

Corberi considered dementia praecocissima a prepubertal form of dementia praecox (23) and distinguished it from the dementias of infants and children caused by organic brain disease such as juvenile paresis, tuberous sclerosis, cerebral "scleroses" and the cerebral lipoidoses. He classified dementia infantilis as a form of familial amaurotic idiocy without amaurosis (23, 24). His initial report (25) included four case summaries; two children whose symptoms he felt warranted the clinical diagnosis of dementia infantilis. Each had a neuropathological diagnosis of amaurotic idiocy established by bilateral frontal lobe biopsy confirmed later by autopsy. The third child, a psychotic epileptic whose brain biopsy was not definitive, was diagnosed clinically by Corberi as having "cerebral sclerosis" as was the fourth patient, an adolescent psychotic epileptic who did not undergo brain biopsy.

Malamud (75) has reiterated recently that degenerative diseases like the late infantile forms of amaurotic idiocy without amaurosis may initially be confused with schizophrenic reactions of childhood.

At the time of Kraepelin's formulation of dementia praecox, Freud (36, 37, 39, 42, 43) initiated a new era of investigation into the psychology of children and into parental attitudes as determinants of psychopathology. His influence soon pervaded this country through the work of White, Brill and Jelliffe. White in 1919 emphasized (97) Freud's theory of infantile sexuality, especially the ways parental attitudes may disrupt the child's psychological development. He sagely observed that not heredity but the child's early experience with parents who have the same personality defects might account for his abnormality.

Even now, the Achilles heel of a study purporting to demonstrate a genetic basis for behavior may be its failure to eliminate experiential factors. Kallmann's (59) comparison of the frequency of schizophrenia in co-twins of schizophrenic nonidentical (15 per cent) and identical (86 per cent) twins does not establish a genetic basis for schizophrenia because it does not eliminate prenatal, natal and particularly postnatal factors which might account for the findings. Lorenz's (69) studies of imprinting underscore the influence of early experience upon behavior that has been considered genetically determined. He noted that the crucial period for imprinting goslings was limited to the first few hours after hatching— hence emphasizing the importance of the timing of experiential factors on analyses of subsequent behavior.

Freud's study of experiential factors gave impetus to the study of the psychopathological basis for mental disorder. In 1908 Freud treated a phobic five-year-old boy (35), by making recommendations to the father that were based on the father's records and reports of the child's behavior. He described (41) in 1911 the diary of a patient with dementia praecox and the psychology of such mechanisms as projection and the formation of delusions, but (38) considered schizophrenia inaccessible to psychoanalytic cure. Later he tempered this dictum, perhaps because of Federn's (33) psychoanalytically oriented therapy of schizophrenics.

Bleuler, director of the Burgholzli Clinic in Zurich, and his assistant

Jung became interested in Freud's work and in 1907 Jung proposed (58) that dementia praecox might be psychogenic, although he considered somatic or metabolic factors also important. He described emotionally charged conflictual ideas which may be repressed by the term "complex."

G. Stanley Hall, a pioneer in American child psychology, invited Freud and Jung to lecture at Clark University in 1909 along with Meyer, and Freud (40) summarized the development of psychoanalysis and his theories. Jung (57) presented his experimental studies of associations, including a word-association test given to 24 families, and noted that the conflicts of children resembled those of their parents. His anticipation of some basic concepts of child psychiatry is best expressed in his words:

"It is not the good and pious precepts, nor is it any inculcation of pedagogic truths that have a moulding influence upon the character of the developing child, but what most influences him is the peculiarly affective state which is totally unknown to his parents and educators. The concealed discord between the parents, the secret worry, the repressed hidden wishes, all these produce in the individual a certain affective state with its objective signs which slowly but surely, though unconsciously, works its way into the child's mind, producing therein the same conditions and hence the same reactions to external stimuli. We know that association with mournful and melancholic persons will depress us, too. A restless and nervous individual infects his surroundings with unrest and dissatisfaction, a grumbler with his discontent, etc. If grownup persons are so sensitive to such surrounding influences we certainly ought to expect more of this in the child whose mind is as soft and plastic as wax. The father and mother impress deeply into the child's mind the seal of their personality, the more sensitive and mouldable the child the deeper is the impression. Thus even things that are never spoken about are reflected in the child (57)."

Meyer objected to the prognostic pessimism of Kraepelin's "dementia praecox" and its organic implications. He considered mental illness as a reaction to life situations, stressing the role of experience in the genesis of the disorders. Because he went further than Freud or Jung in considering schizophrenia as a psychogenic disorder, it would be of interest to quote briefly from Meyer's presentation at Clark University (76).

"We owe to our European guests, Professor Freud and Dr. Jung, the demonstration that what is at work in the centre of the stage is a complex or group of complexes consisting of insufficiently balanced experiences in various ways modified by symbolism. Their ingenious interpretations have made possible a remarkable clearing up of many otherwise perplexing products of morbid fancy in ways the discussion of which, no doubt I had better leave to their lectures.

"Yet, if I interpret their accounts correctly, the reason why only few persons create these complexes and few yet develop them to a disastrous form and often to a deterioration, is mainly left to heredity or finally to toxines, whereas I would prefer to adhere to my attempts to define the responsible factors as far as possible . . . in terms of untimely evocation of instincts and longings, and ensuing habit-conflicts with their effects on the balance of the person, and, on the sum total of mental metabolism and actual doings and on the capacity for regulations in emergencies (76)."

SCHIZOPHRENIA

In 1911 Bleuler (15) proposed the concept of the group of schizophrenias to replace Kraepelin's dementia praecox, since these illnesses neither always began precociously nor always led to deterioration. His optimism stemmed in part from his experience (14, 16) with severely disturbed and long-hospitalized schizophrenic patients who at times improved dramatically with therapy; he saw that the prognosis might be more related to the psychotherapeutic efforts than to the diagnosis.

The *schisis*, Bleuler emphasized, was between *thinking* and *feeling*. The characteristic disturbances of each function he termed the diagnostic primary symptoms, which he attributed to a genetically determined brain pathology. Under the influence of Jung, he considered that the secondary symptoms such as delusions, illusions and hallucinations were psychologically determined by the patient's complexes. He described five per cent of such disorders as beginning in childhood, although he did not distinguish childhood forms.

At the opening ceremonies of the Phipps Clinic in 1913 Bleuler (at the invitation of Meyer) presented a paper, "Autistic Thinking" (12), in which he substituted the term *autistic* for his earlier term *dereistic* to describe the schizophrenic thought disturbance. At the same clinic 21 years later Kanner described the syndrome of early infantile *autism* (61).

Early Psychodynamic Formulations of Adult Schizophrenia

One of the first to report the psychoanalytic treatment of schizophrenia was Coriat, who in 1917 described improvement in five patients (26).

In 1925, Sullivan (85) stated that in schizophrenic patients "the life situation determines the prognoses . . . [and] serious mental difficulties pertain chiefly to contact with others." From his observations of some of the parental attitudes involved, Sullivan concluded that "the matter of wretched adjustment of one parent to another, and of one or both to the conventional pattern to which they strive to conform, grows more and more important as we try to understand the subsequent disaster to the off-spring." Sullivan developed his ideas, a hybrid of those of Freud, Meyer and White, into his interpersonal theory of psychiatry and his psycho-therapeutic approach to schizophrenia (84). Sullivan, however, did not believe that a schizophrenic illness could occur in a preschool child (86).

In 1929 Brill (21) reviewed his encouraging experience with the psycho-therapy of schizophrenic patients based on psychoanalytic techniques. He acknowledged that he was undaunted by Freud's prognostic pessimism, which was not in keeping with his own earlier experience with schizophrenics at Bleuler's clinic and in the United States.

The following year Zilboorg reported (101) the analysis of a schizo-phrenic patient and tentatively formulated the importance of "a repressive, usually strict parental ideal combined with early traumatic stimulations of sexual life." He further elaborated his approach and formulation in later papers (102, 103).

Fromm-Reichmann, influenced by Sullivan, developed a psychoanalytic psychotherapy for adult and adolescent schizophrenic patients and intro-duced the concept of the "schizophrenogenic mother" (45, 46). Subsequent psychogenetic hypotheses and psychotherapeutic approaches to adolescent and adult forms of schizophrenia have been concisely reviewed by Bellak and Blaustein (3, 4).

Thus early workers such as White, Jung, Meyer, Sullivan, Brill, Klein and Zilboorg implicated parental psychopathology in the genesis of ado-lescent and adult schizophrenia. Their impressions of the parents were gleaned from the psychotherapy of the patient and from occasional con-tacts with the parents, usually related to efforts to obtain histories. During the 1920s and early 1930s, when psychotherapeutic approaches to adult schizophrenia were developing, as were psychiatric facilities and techniques for children, childhood and schizophrenia came to be considered rare and its study lagged.

The Recognition of Childhood Schizophrenia

In 1926 Brill (20) briefly described four psychotic or prepsychotic children and noted the relationship between their behavior and environ-mental factors, particularly parental attitudes. He followed Freud's model of treating children through a parent (35). Hart (50) briefly described in 1927 a seven-year-old psychotic child. Kasanin and Kaufman (64) in 1929 reported 21 children who were diagnosed as having dementia praecox. They commented on its rarity in children and described two cases of propf-hebephrenia—cases of mental deficiency with superimposed childhood psychosis. They noted that some patients had "unusually difficult family situations which beyond doubt served as important etiologic factors," and they mentioned the relevance of other environmental stresses. None of these patients had an unequivocal onset before puberty (or the age of 12) and today they would not be classified as childhood schizophrenics. Kasanin and coworkers (63) studied in 1934 the records of 45 adult schizophrenics for whom there were adequate historical data about early development. They found evidence of "overprotective mothers" (a term introduced by Levy), also of some "overprotective" fathers and in many cases the father's attitudes significantly contributed to the mother's pathogenic behavior.

Hug-Hellmuth (54) first used play with children as a substitute for the technique of free association as used with adults; it became part of the subsequent development of child analysis by Anna Freud (34) and Melanie Klein (67). Klein soon applied child analysis to childhood schizophrenics and in 1930 she presented her analysis of a schizophrenic boy, proposing that one task of child analysis would be the discovery and cure of childhood psychoses (66).

Richmond (81) recognized, by 1932, that dementia praecox could begin in early childhood, adding that both teachers and the child guidance clinic staff were becoming increasingly aware of children with normal intelligence who functioned at a retarded level because of learning difficulties and behavioral problems. These children might therefore be misdiagnosed as mentally defective rather than schizophrenic.

The following year Potter (78) reported six cases of childhood schizophrenia with onset before the age of ten. He elaborated diagnostic criteria for childhood schizophrenia, limiting the diagnosis to prepubertal children. He characterized the mothers as "dominant and overprotective" and the fathers as "submissive." His findings and studies were confirmed and elaborated by Despert (31). Potter observed that schizophrenic children superficially resembled mental defectives and stated that childhood schizophrenia might not be considered rare if careful study was made of children in institutions for the mentally deficient.

In 1937 Lutz (72) reviewed the world literature, using ten as the upper age for classifying the illness as childhood schizophrenia, and concluded that only 14 of 60 reported cases were unequivocal. He added six cases from his own experience. The same year Piotrowski (77) described the use of psychometric and projective psychological tests in the differential diagnosis of childhood schizophrenia and mental deficiency.

In 1941 Bradley's book (19) appeared, the first book devoted to childhood schizophrenia. Bradley reviewed the knowledge of childhood schizophrenia and discussed the symptoms, course and diagnosis, but with little attempt to formulate psychodynamic factors.

Childhood Schizophrenia, 1941 to the Present

The studies of Bender and her coworkers at Bellevue since 1934 and her publications since 1942 have been unsurpassed in their clinical observations of schizophrenic children.

Bender's (6) inferences about etiology and treatment and her descriptions reflected the concepts of Schilder concerning body image and the development of maturational patterns, psychoanalytic contributions, particularly those of Klein (66, 67), and the influence of Gestalt psychology on her study of perceptual motor integration (i.e., the Bender-Gestalt visual motor test). Bender's development of play techniques (8) included the use of puppets (9) and of children's art (5) as diagnostic and therapeutic adjuncts.

Although Bender initially (7) described childhood schizophrenia as an encephalopathy, she later omitted this term, perhaps because there has been no demonstrable neuropathology in schizophrenic children or adults. The significance of the "soft neurological signs" she described, such as motility disturbance and vasovegetative changes, needs careful appraisal, particularly in the absence of neuropathology. The twirling of a schizophrenic child may be understandable in psychological terms as an autistic sensual experience and the vasomotor changes may be psychophysiological phenomena.

More recently Bender (6) concluded, "No child can develop schizophrenia unless predisposed by heredity; the psychosis is precipitated by a physiological crisis; the pattern of a psychosis and its defense mechanisms are determined by environmental and psychological factors." Of the children studied, 40 per cent had one parent with "definite or suggestive diagnosis of schizophrenia in the record," and ten per cent had "both parents with such a recorded or suggested diagnosis." Initially she emphasized somatic treatment methods such as electroconvulsive therapy, but the results were not particularly encouraging (6). Studies by other investigators (22) revealed that the schizophrenic children who initially improved after electroconvulsive therapy later worsened.

Bender later (6) increasingly mentioned the use of psychotherapeutic approaches to children, "of the kind which stimulates neurotic formation and does not break it down," and advocated treatment of the parents (6), particularly in groups, to help them understand their problems in dealing with their children. Her approach to parents reflected her view that the child's disorder produced psychological problems in the parents. She did not feel that the parental psychological disturbances were of etiologic importance.

Kanner (60) in 1943 described a syndrome which he later termed *early infantile autism* (61), a syndrome characterized by the onset during the first year of infancy of " . . . a profound withdrawal from contact with people, an obsessive desire for the preservation of sameness, a skillful and even affectionate relation to objects, the retention of an intelligent and pensive physiognomy, and either mutism or the kind of language which does not seem intended to serve the purpose of interpersonal communication" (62). Initially hesitant, Kanner later concluded it was an early form of childhood schizophrenia (62).

Eisenberg and Kanner (32) considered that the pathognomonic primary features in early infantile autism were the children's extreme self-isolation and obsessive insistence on the preservation of sameness. They described the parents of such children as intelligent, sophisticated "successfully autistic adults" who provided an atmosphere of "emotional refrigeration" for the child (32), but they did not find the high incidence of parental schizophrenic psychosis reported by Bender, and the children came from a homogeneous socioeconomic background, a discrepancy so far unexplained. They considered the role of a genetic predisposition to this syndrome because of its onset "from the very beginning of life" (60) but also allowed for the role of experiential factors (32). They did not elaborate any therapeutic approach to the child and parents.

Mahler (73, 74) differentiated in 1949 a *symbiotic psychosis* from the autistic psychosis described by Kanner because of its later onset, between the ages of two and five—a period described as involving the infant's differentiation of its body and self image from that of its mother. She considered the symptomatology a protest by the infant against any separation from the mother and emphasized the role of the mother's emotional disturbance in the genesis of the syndrome without eliminating the possibility of genetic factors.

The same year Rank (79) used the less specific term *atypical development* to describe these severe emotional disorders of childhood. She emphasized the severe emotional deprivation such children experience and described the emotional disturbances found in the mothers, as well as the ways their disturbances were heightened by the father.

Bergman and Escalona (10) in 1949 reported briefly on four psychotic children and a fifth, probably psychotic, ranging from 2.8 months to seven years of age, who from an early age displayed an unusual sensitivity to various sensory stimuli like light, sound or color. They postulated that the child's "thin protective barrier" to these stimuli might stem from similar defects in the mother or from genetic factors.

Reichard and Tillman (80) in 1950 reviewed the literature concerned with parental and intrafamilial pathology in the development of adult and childhood schizophrenia, finding 66 cases with details about parent-child relationships and adding 13 of their own cases. They noted that prior investigators had concentrated on the mother (49, 61, 63, 96) with the father's role occasionally sketched from her description, and they commented on the unreliability of the initial history as a basis for reconstruction of the psychogenesis of the disorder. Their review of the 79 families revealed 76 per cent with a "dominant mother," 13 per cent with an "overly rejecting mother" and 63 per cent with "covertly rejecting put apparently overprotective" mothers, whereas only 15 per cent had "domineering, sadistic and rejecting" fathers. They concluded that the parent-child relationships of schizophrenics differed from those of neurotics in severity rather than pattern; that despite a disturbed family background, schizophrenia sometimes did not develop because a "rescue parent" entered the family situation; and that a disturbed substitute parent may be a factor in the disease.

A significant contribution to the study of intrafamilial psychodynamics occurred with the development of collaborative therapy during the 1930s in child guidance clinics (27, 48, 71, 95). Collaborative or concomitant psychotherapy involves the individual psychotherapy of the emotionally disturbed child and one or both parents.

Szurek, Johnson and Falstein (88) in 1942 explicitly encouraged the use of collaborative psychotherapy by psychiatrists, particularly in severely distorted family disturbances and applied it to the problem of school phobias (56) and the study of acting-out children (55).

Since 1946 the Children's Service of Langley Porter Institute under the direction of Dr. Szurek has tested through collaborative therapy of the child and each parent the hypothesis that childhood schizophrenia is due to the experience of the child with its parents or other significant adults or both. The selection of this treatment method is not meant to imply that to treat all three members is better than to use other methods like separation of the child from the parents, as advocated by Bettelheim (11). It is premature to evaluate treatment methodologies for childhood schizophrenia, since adequate statistics are unavailable. Most reports deal with the individual convictions of therapists as based on their experience and are not fully documented.

Others who have begun to study the intrafamilial pathology in these children include Kaufman and colleagues (65), who in 1957 emphasized the role of both parents in the genesis of the child's disorder, and Lidz (68), who in the same year emphasized the role of the father in the families, as did Bowen et al. (18) in 1959. Johnson (2) and her coworkers also developed collaborative psychotherapy as a method of intensive study in schizophrenia, reporting similar findings. Other recent studies corroborating the hypothesis include those of Bateson, Jackson and coworkers (1).

To date, we have studied over 203 schizophrenic children; 139 children and their parents have undertaken collaborative therapy, the majority for periods ranging up to four years, with fewer continuing for periods up to eight years.

Details of our application procedures, intake policies, studies and evaluation of the children (17, 87) and the nature of our psychotherapeutic work (91, 93) have been previously described, as have the problems involved in training a staff in collaborative psychotherapy (94).

Our outpatient treatment program consists of individual weekly interviews with each parent and weekly play sessions with the child. The most disturbed children may be considered for inpatient treatment or a day-care program which involves at least three hours of play therapy a week and weekly interviews with each parent. The contributions to the program by nurses, technicians, school teacher, occupational and recreational therapists have been described elsewhere (17, 89, 90, 92). We have offered several families an increased frequency of therapeutic sessions, but limitations of staff time preclude extension of this practice.

Parents who inquire about services for their child are given an appointment with a psychiatric social worker who strives in the initial meeting to understand with the parents their concerns about their child and to review with them both the nature and availability of our services and the available alternatives within the community. If psychiatric staff time is available—and the parents wish to proceed—three or four weekly outpatient visits for the child and each parent are scheduled with a child psychiatrist. During this time, the study of the child includes a physical and neurological examination, complete blood count, urinalysis, chest x-ray, electroencephalogram, and psychological testing. Occasionally, for research purposes psychological testing of each parent is carried out.

The goals of the brief service include our attempt to understand with the parents the current crisis and to see whatever resolution is possible. The psychiatrist is alert to the parents' expression of their feelings about the relationship between their emotional difficulties and those of their child, particularly since the social stigma of mental illness tends to increase the unconscious as well as conscious guilt feelings. He attempts to understand with the parents any innuendoes concerning their self-blame or their anticipation of blame by the therapist.

The therapist may comment that he is sure they have done nothing consciously which could produce the kinds of difficulty their child is having, and even if they were aware of their emotional problems they did not know that such difficulties would result in the disturbance of their child. The therapist might then state his conviction that the most helpful way for them to understand and resolve their difficulties is through individual psychotherapy for all three, a recommendation based on our experience that the child's difficulties are related to problems of the parents. If they do not wish to commence such a therapeutic program, he helps them with whatever course they elect. It is understood that their decision is respected, nor will their present choice influence the staff's willingness to undertake therapy at a later date if the parents decide to reapply.

Elaboration and description of the psychotherapeutic approach termed "conflict reductive" (91) has previously been elaborated by Szurek and his coworkers (87, 93). Nor will the general symptomatology and clinical course of childhood schizophrenia be elaborated, since our experience (17, 91, 93) has been similar to that of others (7, 32, 44, 53).

In our series 12 per cent of the children have one parent and in several instances two parents who have been unequivocally psychotic as documented by hospitalization in a mental institution; with several exceptions the diagnosis has been a schizophrenic reaction. Although the majority of the parents seemed initially to be making a satisfactory adjustment, they have rather often expressed in therapy experiences which represent either "larval" psychotic episodes or more chronic thoughts and feelings sometimes described as typical of "borderline or ambulatory schizophrenias." Kanner's description of the parents of autistic children as "successfully autistic adults" is understandable to us as is the rubric "schizoid personality." These generalizations, however, may lead to possible misinterpretation and misunderstanding.

In our experience each parent of the child with a disorder severe enough to be termed childhood schizophrenia manifests severe intrapsychic conflicts anteceding the development of the child's disorder. We find no consistent pattern to support the notion of a "schizophrenogenic" mother or father. It is the duration and depth of each parent's psychopathology, and the intensification of their conflicts through intercurrent stresses that involve the child, which seem most significant in the genesis of the child's disorder. The child's psychological resiliency and rigidity become understandable in the context of his development and experience in the family.

Szurek (93) has described the disorder of the psychotic child as representing both its identification with, and the futile rebellion against, the disorder of each parent. Similarly the healthy aspects of the child's personality correlate with the integrative experiences with the parents. The child's symptoms often represent caricatures of parental personality traits. These traits include both intellectual and emotional disturbances which in their more severe form are found in the schizophrenic reactions. Illustrative case histories have been described in previous reports (17, 91, 93).

The thought disturbances of these parents may include denial, blocking, disturbances of associations such as vague tangential associations, isolation, intellectualization, externalization and projection. The affective disturbances include ambivalence, lability of affect, or seeming apathy and a schisis between thought and feeling which may be termed "inappropriate affect." These mechanisms may be considered as defenses against an underlying pervasive anxiety triggered by the parents' inability to tolerate either close, tender, sensual impulses or aggressive impulses. These parents manifest a deep-rooted distrust and derogation of themselves and others which lead to basic distortions and disruptions of their human relationships. The parental personality traits may become apparent only in the course of prolonged psychotherapy. Although all parents do not show all the mechanisms, the symptoms of their child represent the hybrid expression of those present in the parents.

The gradients of psychopathology usually found in these families range in a spectrum from the parents at one end, where their integrative capacities usually predominate, through the other children in the family manifesting varying degrees of schizoid distortions, to the other end of the spectrum with the florid symptomatology of the schizophrenic child.

Often, without seeing the child, we can predict from our initial interview with the parents the degree of psychopathology in the child. These intuitive hunches open a vista for further development of clinical research to test our hypothesis.

A contribution to understanding the psychogenesis of the severe emotional disorders are the studies of Wynne and Singer (100), who were able to predict the presence of schizophrenic illness in young adults by blind studies of the projective tests of parents of nonschizophrenic and schizophrenic young adults. They concluded that the type of schizophrenic reaction could also be predicted from the data of the parents' psychological tests.

Similarly, Singer (83) studied the projective psychological tests of the parents of five schizophrenic and five neurotic children studied and treated in our clinic. On the basis of her formulations of psychological characteristics in these parents, she then studied the projective tests of 30 additional sets of parents of children in our clinic. The group included 15 pairs whose child was schizophrenic and 15 whose child was neurotic. She was able to predict blindly the nature of the disturbance in the child in 24 of the 30 families.

Such highly significant and independent confirmation of our clinical hunches gives further impetus to our studies of the parental psychopathology and the modes of family interaction through which the disorders arise.

REFERENCES

1. BATESON, G., JACKSON, D. D., HALEY, J. and WEAKLAND, J. Toward a theory of schizophrenia. *Behav. Sci.*, 1:251-264, 1956.
2. BECKERT, P. G. S., ROBINSON, D. B., FRAZIER, S. H., STEINHILBER, R. M., DUNCAN, G. M., ESTES, H. R., LITTEN, E. M., GRATTAN, R. T., LORTON, W. L., WILLIAMS, G. E. and JOHNSON, A. M. The significance of exogenous traumata in the genesis of schizophrenia. *Psychiatry*, 19: 137-142, 1956.
3. BELLAK, L. and BLAUSTEIN, A. B. General psychotherapy, group therapy, and allied methods. In Bellak, L., ed. *Schizophrenia: A Review of the Syndrome*, pp. 337-396. Logos Press, New York, 1958.
4. BELLAK, L. and BLAUSTEIN, A. B. Psychoanalytic aspects of schizophrenia. In Bellak, L., ed. *Schizophrenia: A Review of the Syndrome*, pp. 279-335. Logos Press, New York, 1958.
5. BENDER, L. Art and therapy in the mental disturbances of children. J. Nerv. Ment. Dis., 86: 249-263, 1937.
6. BENDER, L. Childhood schizophrenia. *Psychiat. Quart.*, 27:663-681, 1953.
7. BENDER, L. Childhood schizophrenia: Clinical study of 100 schizophrenic children. *Amer. J. Orthopsychiat.*, 17:40-56, 1947.
8. BENDER, L. and WOLTMAN, A. G. Play and psychotherapy. *Nerv. Child*, 1:17-42, 1941.
9. BENDER, L. and WOLTMAN, A. G. The use of puppet shows as a psychotherapeutic method for behavior problems in children. *Amer. J. Orthopsychiat.*, 6:341-354, 1936.
10. BERGMAN, P. and ESCALONA, S. K. Unusual sensitivities in very young children. *Psychoanal. Study Child*, 3-4:333-352, 1949.
11. BETTELHEIM, B. Schizophrenia as a reaction to extreme situations. *Amer. J. Orthopsychiat.*, 26:507-518, 1956.
12. BLEULER, E. Autistic thinking. *Amer. J. Insanity*, 69:873-886, 1913.
13. BLEULER, E. (trans. by Joseph Zinken). *Dementia Praecox or the Group of Schizophrenias*, pp. 3-6. International Universities Press, New York, 1950.
14. BLEULER, E. (trans. by Joseph Zinken). *Dementia Praecox or the Group of Schizophrenias*, pp. 471-489. International Universities Press, New York, 1950.
15. BLEULER, E. (trans. by A. A. Brill). *Textbook of Psychiatry*, pp. vii and 372-444. Macmillan, New York, 1924.
16. BLEULER, M. Eugene Bleuler's conception of schizophrenia: An historical sketch. *Bull. Isaac Ray Med. Libr.*, 1:47-60, 1953.
17. BOATMAN, M. J. and SZUREK, S. A. A clinical study of childhood schizophrenia. In Jackson, D. D., ed. *The Etiology of Schizophrenia*, pp. 389-440. Basic Books, New York, 1960.

18. BOWEN, M., DYSINGER, R. H. and BASAMANIA, B. The role of the father in families with a schizophrenic patient. *Amer. J. Psychiat.*, 115:1017-1020, 1959.
19. BRADLEY, C. *Schizophrenia in Childhood.* Macmillan, New York, 1941.
20. BRILL, A. A. Psychotic children: Treatment and prophylaxis. *Amer. J. Psychiat.*, 82:357-364, 1926.
21. BRILL, A. A. Schizophrenia and psychotherapy. *Amer. J. Psychiat.*, 86:519-541, 1929.
22. CLARDY, E. R. A study of the development and course of schizophrenia in children. *Psychiat. Quart.*, 25:81-90, 1951.
23. CORBERI, G. Dem. Praecoc., D. Infantilis, phrenasthenia aparetico aphas. tard. und vorübergehende psychopathische Geistesstorungen der Praepubertat. Zbl. Neurol. Psychiat., 63:821-822, 1932. (A German abstract by Zingerle of CORBERI, G. Dementia praecocissima, dementia infantilis, phrenasthenia aparetico, aphasica tardiva e stati psicopatici prepuberali transitori. *Infanzia Anorm.*, 3:201-211, 1930.)
24. CORBERI, G. Infantile familiare Demenz. Z. Kinderheilk., 21:368, 1927-1928. (A German abstract by Siemerling of CORBERI, G. Regressio mentis infanto-juvenilis, forma dementia infantilis familiaris. *Riv. Pat. Nerv. Ment.*, 32:301-318, 1927.)
25. CORBERI, G. Sindromi di regressione mentale infanto-giovanile. *Riv. Pat. Nerv. Ment.*, 31:6-45, 1926.
26. CORIAT, I. H. The treatment of dementia praecox by psychoanalysis: A preliminary report. *J. Abnorm. Psychol.*, 12:326-330, 1917.
27. DAWLEY, A. Trends in therapy: Inter-related movement of parent and child in therapy with children. *Amer. J. Orthopsychiat.*, 9:748-754, 1939.
28. DEFENDORF, A. Ross. *Clinical Psychiatry, A Text-Book for Students and Physicians*, p. 200. Macmillan, New York, 1904. (Abstracted and adapted from the sixth German edition of Kraepelin's *Lehrbuch der Psychiatrie.*)
29. DE SANCTIS, S. Dementia praecocissima catatonica oder Katatonie des frueheren Kindesalters? *Folia Neuro-Biologica*, 2:9-12, 1908.
30. DE SANCTIS, S. Sopra alcune varieta della demenza precoce. *Riv. Sper. Freniat.*, 32:141-165, 1906.
31. DESPERT, J. L. Schizophrenia in children. *Psychiat. Quart.*, 12:366-371, 1938.
32. EISENBERG, L. and KANNER, L. Early infantile autism, 1943-1955. *Amer. J. Orthopsychiat.*, 26:556-566, 1956.
33. FEDERN, P. *Ego Psychology and the Psychoses.* Basic Books, New York, 1952.
34. FREUD, A. Introduction to the technique of child analysis. *Nerv. Ment. Dis. Monogr. Ser.*, 48, 1928.
35. FREUD, S. Analysis of a phobia in a five year old boy. *Collected Papers*, Volume 3, pp. 149-289. Hogarth, London, 1946.
36. FREUD, S. The defence neuro-psychoses, *Collected Papers*, Volume 1, pp. 59-75. Hogarth, London, 1948.
37. FREUD, S. The interpretation of dreams. In Brill, A. A. ed. & trans. *The Basic Writings of Sigmund Freud*, pp. 181-467. Modern Library, Random House, New York, 1938.
38. FREUD, S. On narcissism: An introduction. *Collected Papers*, Volume 4, pp. 30-59. Hogarth, London, 1948.
39. FREUD, S. and BREUER, J. On the psychical mechanism of hysterical

phenomena. *Collected Papers*, Volume 1, pp. 24-41. Hogarth, London, 1948.

40. FREUD, S. (trans. by H. W. Chase). The origin and development of psychoanalysis. *Amer. J. Psychol.*, 21:181-218, 1910.
41. FREUD, S. Psycho-analytic notes upon an autobiographical account of a case of paranoia (dementia paranoides). *Collected Papers*, Volume 3, pp. 390-470. Hogarth, London, 1948.
42. FREUD, S. Psychopathology of everyday life. In Brill, A. A., ed. & trans. *The Basic Writings of Sigmund Freud*, pp. 35-178. Modern Library, Random House, New York, 1938.
43. FREUD, S. Three contributions to the theory of sex. In Brill, A. A., ed. & trans. *The Basic Writings of Sigmund Freud*, pp. 553-629. Modern Library, Random House, New York, 1938.
44. FRIEDMAN, S. W. Diagnostic criteria in childhood schizophrenia: Review of some major trends in the literature. *Bull. Menninger Clin.*, 18:41-51, 1954.
45. FROMM-REICHMANN, F. Notes on the development of treatment of schizophrenics by psychoanalytic psychotherapy. *Psychiatry*, 11:263-273, 1948.
46. FROMM-REICHMANN, F. Psychotherapy of schizophrenia. *Amer. J. Psychiat.*, 111:410-419, 1954.
47. GODDARD, H. H. A measuring scale for intelligence. *Training School*, 6:146-154, 1910.
48. GREIG, A. B. The problem of the parent in child analysis. *Psychiatry*, 3:539-543, 1940.
49. HAJDU-GIMES, L. Contributions to the etiology of schizophrenia. *Psychoanal. Rev.*, 27:421-438, 1940.
50. HART, H. H. Psychosis in a child aged 7 years. *Arch. Neurol. Psychiat.*, 18:584-587, 1927.
51. HELLER, T. Uber Dementia Infantilis. Z. Kinderforsch., 37:661-667, 1930 (Hulse, W. C., trans. About dementia infantilis. *J. Nerv. Ment. Dis.*, 119: 471-477, 1954).
52. HELLER, T. Uber Dementia Infantilis. Z. Erforsch. Behandl., 1 Heft 1908. (Cited in reference 51, page 474.)
53. HIRSCHBERG, J. C. and BRYANT, K. N. Problems in the differential diagnosis of childhood schizophrenia. *A. Res. Nerv. Ment. Dis. Proc.*, 34:454-461, 1954.
54. HUG-HELLMUTH, H. VON. On the technique of child-analysis. *Int. J. Psychoanal.* 2:287-305, 1921.
55. JOHNSON, A. M. and SZUREK, S. A. The genesis of antisocial acting out in children and adults. *Psychoanal. Quart.*, 21:323-343, 1952.
56. JOHNSON, A. M., FALSTEIN, E. I., SZUREK, S. A. and SVENDSEN, M. School phobia. *Amer. J. Orthopsychiat.*, 11:702-711, 1941.
57. JUNG, C. G. The association method. *Amer. J. Psychol.*, 21:219-267, 1970.
58. JUNG, C. G. (trans. by F. Peterson and A. A. Brill). *The Psychology of Dementia Praecox*, pp. 32, 88, 89. Nervous and Mental Disease Pub. Co., New York, 1909.
59. KALLMANN, F. The genetic theory of schizophrenia. *Amer. J. Psychiat.*, 103:309-322, 1946.
60. KANNER, L. Autistic disturbances of affective contact. *Nerv. Child*, 2:217-250, 1943.
61. KANNER, L. Early infantile autism. *J. Pediat.*, 25:211-217, 1944.
62. KANNER, L. Problems of nosology and psychodynamics of early infantile autism. *Amer. J. Orthopsychiat.*, 19:416-426, 1949.

63. KASANIN, J., KNIGHT, E. and SAGE, P. The parent-child relationship in schizophrenia: I. Over-protection-rejection. *J. Nerv. Ment. Dis.*, 79:249-263, 1934.
64. KASANIN, J. and KAUFMAN, M. R. A study of the functional psychoses in childhood. *Amer. J. Psychiat.*, 86:307-384, 1929.
65. KAUFMAN, I., ROSENBLUM, E., HEIMS, L. and WILLER, L. Childhood schizophrenia: Treatment of children and parents. *Amer. J. Orthopsychiat.*, 27:683-690, 1957.
66. KLEIN, M. The importance of symbol formation in the development of the ego. *Int. J. Psychoanal.* 11:24-39, 1930.
67. KLEIN, M. *The Psychoanalysis of Children.* Hogarth, London, 1932.
68. LIDZ, T., CORNELISON, A. R., FLECK, S. and TERRY, D. The intrafamilial environment of the schizophrenic patient: I. The father. *Psychiatry*, 20:329-342, 1957.
69. LORENZ, K. Z. Der Kumpan in der Umwelt des Vogels. *J. Ornith.*, 83:137-213, 1935.
70. LOWERY, L. G., Psychiatry for children: A brief history of developments. *Amer. J. Psychiat.*, 101:375-388, 1944.
71. LOWERY, L. G. Trends in therapy: Evolution, status and trends. *Amer. J. Orthopsychiat.*, 9:669-706, 1939.
72. LUTZ, J. Uber die Schizophrenie im Kindesalter, *Schweiz. Arch. Neurol. Psychiat.*, 39:335-372, 1937; 40:141-163, 1937.
73. MAHLER, M., ROSS, J. R. and DE FRIES, Z. Clinical studies in benign and malignant cases of childhood psychosis. *Amer. J. Orthopsychiat.*, 19:295-305, 1949.
74. MAHLER, M. On childhood psychosis and schizophrenia: Autistic and symbiotic psychoses. *Psychoanal. Study Child*, 7:286-305, 1952.
75. MALAMUD, N. Heller's disease and childhood schizophrenia. *Amer. J. Psychiat.*, 116:215-218, 1959.
76. MEYER, A. The dynamic interpretation of dementia praecox. *Amer. J. Psychol.*, 21:385-403, 1910.
77. PIOTROWSKI, Z. A. A comparison of congenitally defective children with schizophrenic children in regard to personality structure and intelligence type. *Proc. Amer. A. Ment. Deficiency*, 61:78-90, 1937.
78. POTTER, H. W. Schizophrenia in children. *Amer. J. Psychiat.*, 89:1253-1270, 1933.
79. RANK, B. Adaptation of the psychoanalytic technique for the treatment of young children with atypical development. *Amer. J. Orthopsychiat.*, 19:130-139, 1949.
80. REICHARD, S. and TILLMAN, C. Patterns of parent-child relationships in schizophrenia. *Psychiatry*, 13:247-257, 1950.
81. RICHMOND, W. The dementia praecox child. *Amer. J. Psychiat.*, 88:1153-1159, 1932.
82. RUBINSTEIN, E. A. Childhood mental disease in America: A review of the literature before 1900. *Amer. J. Orthopsychiat.*, 18:314-321, 1948.
83. SINGER, M. T. Personal communication, 1962.
84. SULLIVAN, H. S. Conceptions of modern psychiatry. *Psychiatry*, 3:1-117, 1940.
85. SULLIVAN, H. S. Peculiarity of thought in schizophrenia. *Amer. J. Psychiat.*, 82:21-86, 1925.
86. SULLIVAN, H. S. Research in schizophrenia. *Amer. J. Psychiat.*, 86:553-567, 1929.
87. SZUREK, S. A. An attitude towards (child) psychiatry. Part II. *Quart. J. Child Behavior*, 1:36-54, 1949. Also in S. A. Szurek and I. N. Berlin

(Eds.), *Training in Therapeutic Work with Children*. Palo Alto: Science and Behavior Books, 1967, pp. 1-116.

88. SZUREK, S. A., JOHNSON, A. and FALSTEIN, E. Collaborative psychotherapy of parent-child problems. *Amer. J. Orthopsychiat.*, 12:511-516, 1942. Also in S. A. Szurek and I. N. Berlin (Eds.), *Training in Therapeutic Work with Children*. Palo Alto: Science and Behavior Books, 1967, pp. 162-169.

89. SZUREK, S. A. A descriptive study of the program of the Langley Porter Clinic, Children's In-Patient Service. In Reid, J. H. and Hagan, H. R. *Residential Treatment of Emotionally Disturbed Children*, pp. 200-221. Child Welfare League of America, New York, 1951.

90. SZUREK, S. A. Dynamics of staff interaction in hospital psychiatric treatment of children. *Amer. J. Orthopsychiat.*, 17:652-664, 1947. Also in S. A. Szurek, I. N. Berlin and M. J. Boatman (Eds.), *Inpatient Care for the Psychotic Child*. Palo Alto: Science and Behavior Books, 1971, pp. 138-145.

91. SZUREK, S. A. and BERLIN, I. N. Elements of psychotherapeutics with a schizophrenic child and his parents. *Psychiatry*, 19:1-9, 1956. See Chapter 9 in this volume.

92. SZUREK, S. A. The family and the staff in hospital psychiatric therapy of children. *Amer. J. Orthopsychiat.*, 21:597-611, 1951. Also in S. A. Szurek, I. N. Berlin and M. J. Boatman (Eds.), *Inpatient Care for the Psychotic Child*. Palo Alto: Science and Behavior Books, 1971, pp. 264-279.

93. SZUREK, S. A. Psychotic episodes and psychotic maldevelopment. *Amer. J. Orthopsychiat.*, 26:519-543, 1956. Also in S. A. Szurek, I. N. Berlin and M. J. Boatman (Eds.), *Inpatient Care for the Psychotic Child*. Palo Alto: Science and Behavior Books, 1971, pp. 92-119.

94. SZUREK, S. A. Remarks on training for psychotherapy. *Amer. J. Orthopsychiat.*, 19:36-51, 1949. Also in S. A. Szurek and I. N. Berlin (Eds.), *Training in Therapeutic Work with Children*. Palo Alto: Science and Behavior Books, 1967, pp. 216-233.

95. SZUREK, S. A. Some problems of collaborative therapy. *A.A.P.S.W. News Letter*, 9:1-7, 1940.

96. TIETZE, T. A study of mothers of schizophrenic patients. *Psychiatry*, 12:55-65, 1949.

97. WHITE, W. A. *The Mental Hygiene of Childhood*, pp. 7-11, 134, 138. Little, Brown, Boston, 1919.

98. WITMER, L. Orthogenic Cases: XIV. Don: A curable case of arrested development due to a fear psychosis the result of shock in a three-year-old infant. *Psychol. Clinic*, 13:97-111, 1920.

99. WITMER, L. What I did with Don. *Ladies' Home Journal*, 36:55, 122, 123, 1919. See Chapter 4 in this volume.

100. WYNNE, L. C. and SINGER, M. T. Thought disorder in the family relations of schizophrenics. *A.M.A. Arch. Gen. Psychiat.*, 9:191-198, 1963.

101. ZILBOORG, G. Affective reintegration in the schizophrenias. *Arch. Neurol. Psychiat.*, 24:335-347, 1930.

102. ZILBOORG, G. Ambulatory schizophrenias. *Psychiatry*, 4:149-155, 1941.

103. ZILBOORG, G. The problem of ambulatory schizophrenias. *Amer. J. Psychiat.*, 113:519-525, 1956.

Section III

SOME CURRENT CLINICAL ISSUES

The papers on Blame reflect current problems of concern to child mental health workers in many countries. So often the press and even some colleagues view the inclusion of parents in the treatment process as blaming the parents. Similarly, discussions of the dynamics of the etiology of childhood psychosis which includes all the environmental factors—especially the important caretakers of the child, the parents—is also sometimes viewed not as a scientific view of the variables of possible etiologic significance to a disease but as placing blame on those who unwittingly become part of a process because they are there and thus involved.

"Depressive Reactions of Childhood . . . " reviews a seldom discussed or described—but very important—group of serious disorders of childhood and adolescence.

In "Elements of Psychotherapeutics . . . " we examine general issues related to simultaneous psychotherapeutic work with Child and Parents. This paper presents some early findings and issues which stem from this method of work.

"The Unique Role of the Child Psychiatry Trainee . . ." defines some of the opportunities and problems inherent in collaborative psychotherapy in an in-patient unit. When all child mental health professionals and housekeeping personnel are viewed as important contributors to the milieu therapy program, role definition and professional expertise require careful examination and delineation for effective collaboration to occur.

"A Milieu Treatment Program . . ." details how such a program evolves and how its continued growth depends on critical evaluations and resulting implications for new ways of working suggested by all personnel.

85

6

The Problem of Blame in Therapy with Parents and Their Children

This is even worse than I feared.

S. A. Szurek, M.D.

and

I. N. Berlin, M.D.

THE PROBLEM

For over thirty years, to the knowledge of one of the present writers, efforts at therapy with parents as well as with their children have been repeatedly regarded by some psychiatrists and sometimes by members of related disciplines as evidence that therapists so engaged, or suggesting therapy for parents, *blamed* the parents for the disorder of their child. A treatise, "In Defense of Mothers" (9), was written. Articles, even in recent times, attacking the conception as destructive to the parents of especially psychotic children have appeared (11, 12, 13). Statements in published, professional literature described such practices of a clinic as forcing or coercing parents to submit to therapy, or implied (4) that this was so.

As just one example of such published opinion on this question is the following: The writer regards ". . . psychogenesis as an inadequate and *pernicious* hypothesis" (of childhood autism) (italics ours) (13). He adds that ". . . the damage and torment . . . wrought upon parents whose lives and hopes have already been shattered by their child's illness is not easy to imagine nor pleasant to contemplate. To add a heavy burden of shame and guilt to the distress of people whose hopes, social life, finances, well-being and feelings of worth have been all but destroyed seems heartless and inconsiderate in the extreme."

Bruno Bettelheim (1) makes a very cogent reply to the above quoted comments. Since the etiology of autism, psychogenic or any other, has not yet been definitely established, Bettelheim states, "To make them [parents]

87

guilty will only add to the misery of all and help no one." Further, even
". . . if it turned out one day that the parents' contribution is indeed crucial,
they did as they did because they could not help themselves to do otherwise"
(1) (p. 404). For further discussion of both Rimland's and Bettelheim's
ideas by the present writer, see References (17, 18).

Another example—this one somewhat more oblique—is taken from a well-
written monograph on group therapy of autistic children by a psychologist
and a psychiatric social worker who had at least one child psychiatrist as a
consultant to the work of the team. In a chapter on group work with parents,
one finds (4) (p. 90) the following statements:

"It frequently happened that a mother had had what she considered an
unhappy experience with a clinic in which *she felt that she had been forced
to accept therapy* for herself and her husband *in order to have her child
accepted for therapy*. Often, though they had complied, *they had at best
simply brought their bodies to the treatment sessions and felt that nothing
had happened. At worst they had come away with a harassed and indignant
feeling that they had been blamed for their child's illness. The effect of
this was once very ably expressed by one of the most articulate mothers* in
a discussion which compared the organization of the parents of the mentally
retarded and their activities for obtaining services to the lack of organization of the parents of the mentally ill; she said, *'When we go to psychiatrists
and they make us feel that we are to blame for our children's illness, our
shame and guilt immobilize us.'*

"*As for the problems of the parents, particularly the parents of the psychotic children, it is sometimes difficult to determine to what degree the
parents' problem caused the child's or the child's problems caused the parents'.* As one mother put it, 'One cannot live several years with this kind
of child without having problems.' *Since there seems to be considerable
evidence for suspecting an organic basis, particularly in childhood autism,
manifesting itself as it usually does in the early infancy, the frequent reaction
of the mother as the one who has been rejected seems valid.*"

All italics in the above quotation are ours. The report of the mother's
statements about her feelings are commented upon below. At this point, the
reader will note particularly the italicized sentences in the second paragraph
which are statements of the authors of the book. Their experience with psychotic children and their parents seems much less in number and in duration
than those of clinicians who have reported twenty or more years of their
work (1, 7). (Also see Chapters 14-17, 28, 30, 32, 33 in this volume.)

Nevertheless, they find it ". . . difficult to determine . . . etc," and say
that "Since there seems to be considerable evidence for suspecting an organic
basis . . . the reaction of the mother as one who has been rejected seems

where did those quotes come from?

valid." They give no other "evidence" for the organic basis other than that
". . . particularly in childhood autism, manifesting itself as it usually does
in the early infancy. . . ."

It is also quite possible that in the face of the self-blame of mothers of
psychotic children (even when indicated by denial or any other indirect *tails you lose.*
manner) may be found by many clinicians so difficult a problem to deal
with, that the question of possible etiology may be altogether avoided as
one way to deal with it. However, it has repeatedly become clear to some
of the therapists at this clinic most experienced with such families that
such intense self-blame of mothers particularly is rooted in her sense of
ineffectualness in caring for the continually crying and "fussing" infant or *"he was a good baby."*
child. It is perhaps the hope of those who avoid the question of "cause"
may also reduce this sense of failure as a woman—if only the ineffectualness
of mothering can be reduced. Perhaps this may at times be in a measure
reduced by such emphasis. Whether it can be reduced sufficiently (or in a
sufficient number of such mothers) unless they gain a more thorough understanding of the difficulties which occurred earlier in her child's life in the
process is a possibility which must be considered.

The complex clinical spectrum of childhood psychosis is the subject of
separate chapters in this volume (Chapters 13-16, 18) as well as dealt with
at length by Bettelheim (1) and Goldfarb (7). All this is reminiscent of
Rimland's speculations (13) based primarily on a review of the literature and
little if any *direct* clinical experience with psychotic children and their parents.
[See also discussion in Ref (17).] In short, there is no consideration of
alternative hypotheses for etiology to the fact that the onset in a proportion
of the psychoses of childhood is in early infancy.

On the other hand, there is no question about the accuracy of the former
statement as representing the expression of the feelings of the mother to
whom the reference is made. The staff of the Children's Service of the
Langley Porter Neuropsychiatric Institute during its 24 years of experience
in working with parents of such children has heard exactly the same expressions from such parents many, many times. In some of these instances
similar statements have been heard from such parents about psychiatrists
who had had clinical contact with the family prior to that of the clinic
staff. In a number of these instances the staff had knowledge of these
psychiatrists' attitudes and often knew fairly well the distortion about them
in such statements of the parents.

In even a greater number of such instances, such statements of parents
were made about the clinic staff itself, when therapy at Langley Porter
had continued for a sufficiently long time to make it possible for such
parents to be more frank in therapeutic sessions about these aspects of

their attitudes towards the work. If the work continued long enough and with a therapist experienced enough, such negative feelings were expressed repeatedly not only about the staff's "coercion" about their participation in the work. Negative feelings were expressed also about many other aspects of the program: about bringing children back to the clinic from home on time; about wishing to leave them with the staff over week-ends when no staff was assigned to increase the staff-patient ratio during week-days; about not having enough attention for their child from the staff— particularly when they themselves paid more attention when on the ward to these other children than to their own child; about supplying their child with better fitting clothes or with spending money; about various aspects of their own therapist's clothing, appearance, manner, way of speaking, or his not speaking enough or too much; about his subservience to other members of the staff; about his lack of concern about their child's health, or his over-concern about it. In short, about any aspect of their relations to the work: their reluctance and feeling "forced" to travel long distances to and from the clinic—even though they had been told at the outset this might be difficult and had been encouraged to consider seeking service closer to their home or to consider moving closer to the clinic; about paying their fees, especially when their management of their own other financial affairs were disorderly, or on the other hand, insisting on paying higher fees than they could afford; and so on *ad infinitum*.

Parenthethically it needs to be noted that the work with both the psychotic child and his parents is often and frequently unremittingly so frustrating that resentment, anger and discouragement is not infrequently experienced not only by the beginning psychotherapists but also by many milieu staff of the ward. Such reactions of staff may then be experienced by the parents as being "blamed" for burdening the staff with their difficulties and manifested in a severely disordered child.

When the therapist knew that the parents *had been offered* the opportunity to begin the work or to seek help elsewhere with full readiness of the staff to accept either of these decisions, he had clear evidence that their sense of being "coerced" was projection of some internal sense of "coercion" from feelings of danger about their own impulses. If he could either wait quietly for their subsequent associations, some indications of such dangers might at least in time be forthcoming within their own living. If the parents continued to accuse and press their complaints without such progression in the work, some comment that they had undertaken the work with the clinical staff of their own free will and hence their work could be similarly terminated (despite the recommendation to the contrary from the therapist) they often experienced some relief of their tension, and sometimes become tearfully touched. Some of the parents, thus reminded, could then either (less frequently) withdraw from therapy with their child, or could then go on to examine other sources of such "coercion" in aspects of their lives unrelated to the work with the therapist and clinic staff.

Of course, another aspect or source of the parents' experience of being blamed even by the invitation to participate in the work of therapy is quite frequently eventually traced—in those parents who persist in the work—to sources in their own experience with their own parents during *ecch !* their own childhood. This is the fact that they project ("transfer") onto the therapist and staff that they often felt hated, coerced in a retaliatory way by their own parents. It is almost commonplace in our experience that such transference reactions which occur even early in the work of being coerced are part of their own often easily recollected experience of being greatly deprived of affection. Parents hurt by both humiliation and/or severe physical punishment during their own early years of life are made to feel guilty if they verbalize any feelings and objections to the treatment they received. Bateson described this process for the adult patient as a "double bind" (to us another term for the dilemma experienced in severe conflict); it seems to us that the same could be said for parents placed in this dilemma with their own parents.

It is clear that a central aspect of this whole problem is intimately and intricately connected with the terminology used to describe the situation. In short, what *names* are used to describe observations and mutual study *with* the parents of the events in the life of their child are critically important for accurate definition, and for clear thought and reasoning, i.e., for analysis and elaboration of working hypotheses.

DISTINCTION BETWEEN "BLAME" AND SELF-ASSESSMENT IN THERAPY

The word "blame" implies a failure due to moral defect, sin, or a failure in the performance of a responsibility evoking censure, ostracism or other punishment. Such a term or name for an event, or a sequence of events, which carries with it a *proscription,* and a *prescription* for action about the behavior so named can hardly be expected to be useful. That is, it is unlikely to foster scientific inquiry, and thus further the possibility of increasing knowledge and discovery of effective ways of reducing difficult problems in the behavior of all persons involved. The reason for this is that implying guilt, or possibly increasing the sense of guilt, by such implications leads to a disorganizing anxiety, to an impulse either to deny or to submit to the "accusation." Neither impulse, or both in alternation, is a helpful, internal psychological climate for detailed recall of all the facts of the episode or of their thorough assessment.

In contrast to this reaction of blame and its consequences, is the reaction of critical (but not self-destructive) self-assessment. As a response or reaction, to a failure or to relative ineffectiveness of one's own activity in achieving its goal or purpose, this latter evaluation of results and of the methods used can be sharply differentiated. This manner of evaluation is not concerned with assigning blame, guilt and punishment. It is directed:

1) to examine the unfavorable results of an activity to its sources;

2) to study these sources for possible modification so that errors, or previously unanticipated negative effects, are removed or reduced;

3) to consider and plan new and experimental methods so that more effective ways to achieve desired ends and goals are obtained. All this is followed by a still closer evaluative study of the new method and its further development and refinement that is evaluated only by its effectiveness.

In this attitude of problem solving, little or no energy and time are wasted in self-recrimination and its numerous and various psychopathological consequences, such as some obscure sense of contemptuous self-pity. Instead, both the energy and the time are utilized for the repetitive and continuous solution to problems—which, of course, are always with us.

Perhaps another technical point of procedure is important to add at this juncture. It is often of considerable advantage to the therapeutic process that the parent be early and constantly encouraged to express promptly any sense of being blamed during any moment during a therapeutic session. The complementary aspect of this is the therapist's alertness to any even slight *non-verbal* sign or evidence of discomfort, of uneasiness, and so forth, on the part of parent and to inquire about it promptly.

Of course, this requires a similar alertness on the therapist's part to his own behavior, to nuances of his verbal expression, to his appearance, etc., and to their affective meaning, their sources and their quality. It requires also that he has the freedom to acknowledge them at least to himself and, if technically advantageous to the therapeutic process, to the patient. This latter is particularly important to help the patient enhance *his* discrimination of *what* he perceives accurately about the therapist and his *affective* reaction to such perception of the actuality of the events perceived. There is then a greater probability that the patient himself, or the therapist—or both—may identify something in the therapist's behavior which evoked the parents' reaction of being blamed.

Further exploration of whether the bit of the therapist's behavior was or was not even a slight indication of a countertransference problem of

But 119 : "We need to explore some of the reasons for the all too frequent + persistent phenomena of blaming parents seen in our clinics + in special schools."

See also 702

117-21 gives many examples of blame, from this very clinic!

his (from some unresolved experience of earlier life—which will be discussed more fully later), or whether it had no such source but was idiosyncratically reacted to by the parent from his past may then be revealed. At times with some parents the train of associations by the parent (especially in the last instance) may at least begin to unravel its sources in experiences with people earlier in his life.

MISUSES OF THE WORD "BLAME"

but cf. same authors' use of "blame" on 117 ff.

An experience some years ago in this regard is but an illustration of a very commonly occurring difficulty. A scientific writer for a newspaper somewhat proudly sent a clipping of his published report to the author of a paper on the subject of therapy with parents that the author had delivered at a scientific, professional organization's meeting. The newspaper article was well written and accurately portrayed the non-judgmental tone and description in the paper of the parents' troubled ways of living; in short, their behavioral disorder. However, the included headline which ran across all seven or eight columns, and for which the science writer was obviously not responsible, read, "PSYCHIATRIST BLAMES PARENTS."

A sequel to this event also illustrates the pervasiveness of the difficulty in the ranks of the professionals' own use of language in a similar way. The author of the aforementioned scientific paper had occasion to tell the aforementioned incident to a colleague who was studying journalistic practices with regard to reporting the activities of the medical and psychiatric professions. The colleague, rather mature, and trained scientifically to an extent above the average, upon hearing the tale and especially the headline, "PSYCHIATRIST BLAMES PARENTS," promptly replied, "Well, don't you?"

Et tu, Brute!

One wonders whether such readiness among even relatively well-trained professionals to jump to the conclusion here indicated may not stem from still unresolved conflicts that make it so easy to blame patients for the obstacles to progress in therapy and hence to see blaming in a colleague of the latter's patients.

ecch!

As a much more recent example of such journalistic usage is the following: as a subhead placed at the side of several paragraphs of an article in a Sunday newspaper magazine section describing the practices of an emergency children's psychiatric service of a general hospital, one reads, "Psychiatrists blamed parents for mental illness in their children." Note that quotation marks are included in the subhead. These quotation marks may have been placed there by the headline writer. They imply that it was a statement of the young psychiatrist featured in the article by the reporter. This young psychiatrist's photographs—an attractive young woman described as one who "recently completed her fourth year of residency—where she has become part-time supervisor of psychiatric residents"—together with a child patient (presumably psychotic) appeared twice: once on the front page, in color, of the magazine section and a second time as a full page picture in the course of the article.

There are in the body of the article along the subhead several direct quotations from presumably the director of the Psychiatric Institute of which the children's service is a part, who is mentioned by name and from the young psychiatrist previously mentioned. The quotation marks around the subhead seem to imply that it is a direct quotation from one of these child psychiatrists. However, close reading of the article itself reveals that there are three paragraphs *between* the direct quotations which are *not* marked off by quotation marks. The first of these reads: "Not long ago, many psychiatrists *blamed* parents for mental illness in their children. This kind of *rigidity* is softening." (Quotation marks and italics, ours.)

Wow! we are uptight!

The implication that one of the psychiatrists, particularly the young woman featured and described in glowing terms, is the source of the statement is further strengthened by the following and concluding paragraphs of the article, some of which *are* indicated as direct quotations. (Quotation marks are given as in the article.)

> Some scientists are investigating the possibility that schizophrenia is based on a biochemical disturbance. Others are exploring the possibility that schizophrenia—which accounts for more than half the mental illness in the nation—might be a state of dreaming during waking hours caused by a brain disorder.
>
> Pinpoint that disorder, some experts suggest, and it might respond to drug therapy.
>
> "If somebody can find a magic pill—fine! But there are no final answers yet," says Dr. .... (resident), who is concerned for parents who feel guilty because their children are emotionally disturbed.
>
> "The main thing is this: Are parents willing to try and do things differently to prevent problems from building up again?
>
> "We are not interested in judging people here. If someone asks for help, we aren't going to say 'you did wrong.'
>
> "What we do is ask 'what's the problem and what can we do about it?' "

Since the present writers have known the director mentioned in this article and his attitudes about parents and their children for a good number of years, it seemed to us rather doubtful that he would have much, if any, impulse to attribute to "many psychiatrists" the attitude that they blamed parents for the mental disorder of their children—particularly in the destructive sense previously discussed. Still, one would be left uncertain as to whether it is another example of the insufficient, journalistic discrimination on the part of the reporter and headline writer of the meaning of the words, or whether the distinction was not ever sufficiently made clear to them by professionals regarding the concepts used by experienced psychotherapists in their work. However, correspondence (10) with the director mentioned in the article clarified this. He writes, in part, " . . . in the interview with Dr. .... (resident), the fact of psychiatrists 'blaming parents' or 'not blaming parents' never was mentioned and is not a quotation."

Words such as "blame" are but one instance of a very pervasive tendency in the behavioral sciences in general, and perhaps in psychiatry in particular, to use words of common usage with their frequent moralistic, legalistic and judgmental connotations. Such words and the attitudes they express evoke strong feelings of praise or condemnation to describe problem situations which require study. Ordinary everyday speech, the common parlance, of which much journalistic writing is not altogether free, is of course infused with just such terms and connotations.

SOME SOURCES OF THE PROBLEMATIC USE OF LANGUAGE

Such widespread problematic tendencies in the use of language are understandable. They are the results and legacies of the contexts of the earliest years of childhood rearing in which language was originally learned. These childhood contexts almost inevitably include the learning of all the "do's" and "don'ts," the "shoulds" and "should nots," the "oughts" and "ought nots," and the "musts" and "must nots," with the accompanying rewards and penalties, or the consequences of deprivations. The language that the child heard and learned as part of such behavioral transactions with adult authorities expressed the peremptory imperatives—not only as to actions, but also as to feelings and thoughts. Subsequent use of this language in ordinary daily social relations, in which self-regard and invidious comparisons with others is so often overtly and covertly a central issue, reinforces this moralistic aspect of thought, speech, and emotional reaction with respect to one's own behavior as well as to that of others.

PROBLEM IN SCIENCE

This heritage of judgment in the sense of condemnation or approval, or tendencies to coercion by censure, ostracism and other punishments, to achieve control and conformity in interpersonal relations is what many, if not most of us bring to the scientific study of human behavior—that of others as well as that of our own. To free our scientific effort of such *prejudicial* connotations in making observations and descriptions of the phenomena and events in the subject matter of our science, namely human behavior, requires an unremitting, alert, discriminative effort and, often very lengthy, practice in our speech, writing and discourse with one another. It is possible that even in a whole life time of such work one may not be entirely successful in this endeavor.

It may be recalled in this connection how many centuries it took the natural sciences of physics and chemistry to free themselves of animistic, mythological projections onto nonpersonal phenomena and events in order to create and recreate a technical terminology and language suitable for scientific inquiry and experimentation; that is, a language free of implications of gods, angels, devils, spirits, of forces and other personalized projections of the impulses to action of man himself. It is also a matter of well known history against what persistent, vigorous, and at times vicious opposition this effort needed to be directed. We are still not altogether free from such opposition in biological science; for example, with respect to the theory of evolution; or to the advantages of sex education of preadolescent children; and there are other examples. When this history is recalled, then it may be somewhat more comprehensible what the much younger science of psychiatry and the behavioral sciences in general are struggling with at present.

One might ponder, too, the fact that *perhaps* it may be somewhat easier for the human being to be "more objective about a rock (16), a wind, a light, or an atom. This may be particularly so if these are not an immediate danger to his physical integrity or survival. In short, it may be easier to be less pejorative and hence less fearful of retaliation about such inanimate objects than about other human beings. This may be especially true if his experience with such other persons has been in a great measure destructive. In the latter instances, fear of potential danger from such another person with a consequent welter of impulses of defensive self-protectiveness, of readiness to flee, to submit, to retaliatory attack and so forth, may becloud his capacity to observe dispassionately, to speak and to think quite clearly about any experience involving such other persons.

In view of all these considerations, it is possible to say that to use the word "blame" in this context is an *unwarranted misuse of the term*. That is, it is unwarranted to say that a psychotherapist blames the parents of an emotionally disturbed or mentally disordered child when he offers all three of them an opportunity for therapy. Psychotherapeutic work for such parents is an opportunity for them to study, to analyze with the therapist the details of their life together and with their child to discover any possible disorder or disturbance of their own. Such study, when sufficiently prolonged, adequately collaborative and meticulously thorough, has generally revealed to such parents and to their therapist that each of them generally brings to the intrafamilial life some emotional difficulty. Emotional difficulties of this sort often have their origins not only in unresolved frustrations of the premarital past but also in their recent, or current present life probably outside of the family. These extrafamilial difficulties inevitably affect negatively in some measure their intrafamilial life together with each other—in spite of any of their integrative efforts to reduce them. The tensions of such extrafamilial difficulties, with similar inevitability, destructively influence their child in the direction of disorder, or of conflictful maldevelopment. The child's disturbance may of course arise additionally from his own experience of unsolved, or insufficiently solved difficulties in maturational (non-personal) processes and in development.

It needs to be emphasized here for further clarity that the terms "maturational processes" and "development" in the last sentence are meant to follow what the writers consider an increasing conceptual distinction being made by child psychiatrists. By maturation is meant all those processes of primarily morphological and physiological growth as principally determined by genic factors (or perhaps prenatal influences). Biologists tend to term them the "environmentally stable" characteristics of an organism—i.e., relatively uninfluenced in their appearance and changes with age by events external to the organism. On the other hand, development is here used to denote those primarily behavioral (and affectively toned tendencies towards behavior or personality traits) characteristic of a child which arise, or result, from his *experience* with the environment.

In child psychiatry this is more often considered the human environment (particularly the parents or others in the family although not exclusively so). Strictly speaking, experience with the non-human, and non-living aspects of the environment would also be here included. Again, biologists more recently tend to refer to such characters of organisms as "environmentally labile."

For the sake of completeness it needs to be added that such modern biological conceptions no longer make such sharp, dichotomous distinctions as are implied in the older terminologies which used concepts such as "innate" or "acquired" or "nature" *versus* "nurture". Their tendency now is toward a conception of a *continuum* of all organismic characters (whether morphological, physiological or behavioral) between these extremes which on adequate study can be considered more or less strictly environmentally stable or environmentally labile with a graded series between them. Such biological concepts are congruent with our own concepts, especially as they refer to critical developmental periods and organizing factors in development both embryologically and postnatally. This is especially true in early maturation and development of the brain and its functions which also relate to various environmental factors, nutritionally in terms of sensorimotor stimulation, emotional and motivational development, and the deprivational syndrome described by Goldfarb, Spitz, and Caldwell (2, 3, 7, 8, 14, 15).

It is for these reasons that individual psychotherapeutic work with each of the parents, in addition to direct work with their child, is considered the most likely to be useful in a fundamental way. Such therapeutic work is directed not merely to identify the pathologic, distorting compromise solutions to their individual conflicts. Its prime purpose is for each of them to achieve a *resolution* of the conflicts that then results in a new attitude *and* a new behavior towards oneself and those to whom one is emotionally related.

Thus to say that offering therapy to parents is a form of blame is wholly inapplicable. It does not define the situation accurately; and more, it purports to connote attitudes and purposes which are absent. In short, it confounds instead of clarifying the inquiry.

It has sometimes been said by psychiatrists that to recommend or to do psychotherapy with parents carries with it the danger of "making them guilty" when presumably they are innocent of any "wrongdoing" with respect to their child. The conception of the nature of psychological therapy implied in such admonitions seems strange. As a matter of fact, it is the obverse of the one held by most experienced therapists. That is, therapy is designed to *relieve* existing guilt *and the reasons for it,* rather than to create guilt.

All this is not to deny that some sense of being blamed, or considered hopeless may have been experienced by parents as the consequence of the *avoidance* by either psychotherapists or staffs of clinics, hospital or residential treatment centers to undertake what is clearly an arduous task with a psychotic child or with his family.

Such events may even occur in those clinic staffs where only the more experienced, the senior staff, despite the expected difficulties in such work, are themselves free of such tendencies to avoid engagement in the work in which they know that prognosis is grave or very problematical. It does happen when junior members of the staff or relatively inexperienced trainees have in a treatment review, a continuous case seminar, or in individual supervisory hours with such senior staff have heard from the latter about the need for acceptance of a family's rejection of the offer of therapeutic work. Such acceptance is a necessary measure to help the family experience complete freedom from external coercion or "pressure".

Some such junior or inexperienced staff have been observed to use such discussions to jump to the conclusion that they had then "the freedom" to discharge the patient and family rather prematurely. By "prematurely" is here meant not giving the family sufficient time to absorb and digest such interpretative comments and work through sufficiently *their* conflict about continuing until they achieve an inner decision they felt was their *own*, uncomplicated by anxieties of the reaction of the therapist or staff to whichever decision they made.

SOURCES OF SENSE OF BLAME IN THERAPY

Nevertheless, also in view of all these considerations, other aspects of this problem of "blame" require review. For example, it is not surprising that many beginning trainees in such centers have found, and still find, it difficult not to accept the ambivalent reactions of parents as an indication that coercion *did* and *does* indeed form a part of the regular staff's suggestion that there is a potential advantage to the whole family from the inclusion of parents in the therapeutic program. There are a number of reasons for this difficulty of trainees. Particularly during their very beginning of training in psychotherapy they may have either little clear notion of therapeutic processes, especially of the task of the patient as distinct from the task of the therapist (20). Or, they may enter the career training program in child psychiatry with some beginning conception and skill in therapy based upon a number of apparently conflicting (and to him still confusing) theories of psychopathology and of therapy. In any case, their previous experience has generally included work with adults who are miserable and who seek help and relief for this misery from a therapist; and this is true more often than is perhaps the case with parents (particularly fathers) who bring their child as *the* patient. Such adults who come without a child and for their own emotional turmoil at least overtly more often make some effort to work with even the inexperienced therapists for perhaps longer periods.

Parenthetically it may be noted here that some parents who have experienced some of the benefits of their own therapeutic work may re-experience a sense of blame when they observe some improvement in their child's disorder. Such resurgence of parents' sense of blame has been observed to occur particularly when the reduction of the child's disorder approaches the degree which might make trial of continued therapeutic work in the outpatient service concomitant with the child spending more time at home than in the hospital.

In such instances it has been often quite clear that the parents' own conflictful disorder has not been reduced sufficiently to contemplate such a change without still considerable anxiety. The reluctance to consider the change because of such anxiety then serves to revive the original sense of self-blame, at times to an intense degree.

This greater apparent willingness of adults, who come to therapy more clearly for relief of their own discomfort, to accept the therapist, are at least less troublesome, if not in some measure soothingly reassuring to the beginner's uncertainty about his skill. But if a parent more readily expresses ambivalence or even rejection of the need for therapy for himself, the beginner reacts with discomfort, doubt about his skill and seeks relief in considering the staff's more convinced attitude about the parent's neurotic involvement in their child's disorder as being coercive in an *authoritarian* way.

Hence the beginner's preference for being needed by a patient who wants his service, rather than being "attacked" by a parent who accuses him of "blaming" him, is rooted in his wish to remain at least noncoercive in his therapeutic work and thus less shaken in his professional self-regard.

Furthermore, it is probably a rare therapist of experience with such families who indirectly, and often quite directly, has not heard similar accusations from parents engaged in such an endeavor. That these accusations occurred at certain difficult periods in the work of such parents with their therapists did not always make it any easier to help them, i.e., the parents, resolve the underlying conflict of their feelings. It is also not unlikely that trainees, or even therapists of some greater experience, have found it not only difficult to maintain therapeutic behavior at such moments or periods because of essentially counter-transference problems.

TRANSFERENCE-COUNTERTRANSFERENCE "JAMS"

There are, of course, several aspects to the underlying, conflictful roots to any therapist's countertransference difficulties in such work. Only a few can be mentioned here. The writers hope that by "countertransference" they will be understood by the reader as meaning only those of the therapist's conflicts that interfere with his optimally effective contribution to the work of the patient himself.

As mentioned previously, a beginner, uncertain about his skill and his grasp of his own task and ashamed or fearful about it, has, therefore, a greater need to feel that he is a "potent" doctor and a "successful" one with each patient no matter how severe the patient's disorder. He needs this early, soon and more continuously than a therapist who is more experienced.

If, as is very often if not generally the case, the patient is in need of persistent, firmly repetitious encouragements to persist in *his* part of the work in spite of recurrent, despairing hopelessness from failures to achieve clarification from his own review of a problem out loud; if as a result of such helplessness the patient silently, or more explicitly, requests or even demands that the therapist either help him, or *do* something for him that only he himself can do (as supplying the associated thoughts, memories, or the verbal expressions of the fearful obstacles only he experiences and is aware of); then it is just at these times that the inexperienced therapist finds himself in more or less insuperable difficulty. His previous efforts with the patient seem ineffective and hence may be "wrong"—although he may have been "right" but it has been derogated or even ridiculed by the patient. If the patient in his derogating, self-impatience expresses this feeling, as he often does directly or indirectly, about the therapist's competence, then the situation is ripe for at least feelings, if not actual intimations of mutual "self-blame" and "blame" of the other for the impasse.

The variations on this general theme of what has been named "transference-countertransference jams" are legion. But their general effect on both patient and therapist may be one of a sense of dangerous rise in mutual hostility, distrust, and, in effect, accusations and counter accusations that are repetitious for both of impotent rages experienced in destructive episodes with persons outside of the therapeutic situation and generally, earlier in the life of each of them.

Of course, such episodes may not reach such direct, simple and explicit expression in the therapeutic situation on the part of either. There may instead supervene a subtle estrangement between them instead of a strengthening of what Ralph Greenson (6) has called "the working alliance." The patient expresses his part of this estrangement in longer silences, in partial and tangential expression of all of his thoughts, feelings and sensations. These are impossible for the therapist, therefore, to understand much less follow closely. He may become "bored" and preoccupied with his own reactive tensions and less capable of the necessary "evenly hovering attentiveness" to the patient's speech and non-verbal expressions and hence he is less able to note and observe the sequence of events, and so on. There occur other processes that lead to further complicated, mutual obfuscations as to the actual experience of each of them.

It is easily imaginable how such episodes are the more readily evoked if the patient originally brings to the therapeutic situation a schizoid way of living with great distrust, with a great fear of enslaving attachment to anyone and yet with an intense need of affective contact, as well as with enormous retaliatory anxieties about his own hostile impulses which seem the only protection he has against probable "hurts" to his own tenuous and vulnerable self-regard.

The nature of unconscious processes also needs to be clearly understood by the therapist if he is to reduce, or to avoid for himself, such impasses, such transference-countertransference jams first with himself and hence with his patient. This understanding can come primarily from his own personal analysis, from his supervisors' assistance in his therapeutic work with *his* own patients and finally, thereafter from his own continuing and interminable self-analysis during the remainder of his more independent professional work following "completion" of his training. During this latter period a good number of therapists, who have completed their initial formal training experience, find it useful periodically to return for additional periods of personal analysis, or at the very least for consultative discussions with more experienced colleagues about such episodes of difficulty in their work with particular patients.

Space here precludes any exhaustive, extended discussion of the nature of those aspects of these unconscious processes important to these impasses. However, a few of these aspects may be here noted.

One of these is the speed and intensity of the condensed, conflictfully distorted feelings which erupt seemingly "out of context," or to what seems a minor or "irrelevant" point in the discussion, or to some aspect of the therapists' behavior, appearance, tone of voice, etc. The speed or intensity of the patient's (or the therapist's) reaction may become obvious only much later in the work. At first there may be contrariwise only a *slowing* of overt response, or even a "blankness" period following it, and no recall of the fleeting (often very hostile, murderous or on the other hand embarrassing, affectionate, and tender) impulses, which preceded it.

Such "welding" of conflictful impulses with anxiety and the resulting rage followed by their prompt repression are signs to the experienced therapist of the emergence, however momentary, of the pathology that both the patient and he are searching for as occurring in the here and now of the therapeutic situation. They are also signs to the therapist that perhaps some intervention (or non-intervention) of his may have been premature although possibly quite accurate. Hence, such moments—which become this clear only much later in the work—are "forgotten" (repressed), cannot be recalled and hence unconscious.

Mystery and obscurity about what happened or is happening during and after such moments pervades the situation for both patient and therapist. The patient feels a very disagreeable helplessness and implies, or directly expresses, a need or a desperate demand that the therapist say something or do something to bring him relief. The inexperienced therapist reacts with similar disagreeable tension and helplessness not only in response to the patient's demand but even more from his *own* self expectation that he "do something" competent "like a real doctor."

The experienced therapist recognizes such episodes as some obscure, very brief emergence of some aspect of the transference and the defense against it. He knows that neither the patient nor he understands, nor does he expect to understand it. He *does* however know that if the work does continue, such episodes will recur in a variety of ways, and that with their repetition they may slowly become more understandable to him as the patient becomes less anxious about the therapist reacting as he does toward his own impulses. Imperturbably he waits. The patient reacts to this attitude of the therapist, at least at one level, with some relief and may continue—while perhaps protesting the uselessness of the effort and the work, and so on.

In short in the latter situation neither the patient nor the therapist finds a caricatured, monstrously dangerous, mirror image of himself in the other's reaction or behavior. This however is not infrequently the case in the former situation of the less experienced therapist and his patient. But it may also be true that such countertransference behavior on the part of therapists may have contributed to a resulting feeling on the part of parents—or others—that they were justified in their suspicions that they were indeed being "blamed."

The intensity of confusing feelings in such situations on the part of both patient and therapist is difficult to convey convincingly unless one has experienced them. It is not surprising that such periods in therapy lead at times not only to abrupt terminations of the work but also to what in all probability may have been mutual paranoid solutions to these periods of impasse. Such accusations of therapists by parents are not limited to those parents who are at the beginning of the work overtly rather reluctant, ambivalent or fearful of agreeing to begin it. It also occurs quite frequently with parents who begin the work with evident and stated eagerness or relief that they too would be offered an opportunity for amelioration of *their* troubled feelings.

To the experienced therapist such developments are not limited only to therapeutic work with persons who first come to a psychotherapeutic clinician because of some intolerable turmoil of their child. In short, they are also common, if not ubiquitous, in the course of the work with individual persons who are either unmarried and without children, or come primarily because of complaints which appear unrelated to difficulties within their families. The intensity of such reactions is also not surprising to him when he glimpses, or has had considerable evidence in the course of therapeutic work with the family, of the degree of severity of the conflictful tension resulting from a serious, chronic disorder of living within each of several members of the family and between them.

CONCERNING REDUCTION OF SENSE OF BLAME

One of the present writers has already written previously of some of these problems and of the efforts needed to reduce the possibility, of the intensity, of the parental reactions of being blamed in such circumstances (19). When the therapist is free of countertransference turmoil in himself, it is often then fairly clear that the feeling of being blamed, or more generally, coerced in the therapeutic situation proceeds, or is an aspect of, the parent blaming himself for his own thoughts, feelings and actions. These actions may be ones either of omission or of commission which are contrary to his own ethics. His uncomfortable feeling of guilt about them leads to his sense of being coerced to do otherwise. If the disagreeable feeling of guilt is denied as present in one's own feelings or is repressed, it then is often, if not generally, projected onto someone else, often a person in authority such as a therapist who often is experienced as an authority—rather than a collaborator.

The drive of the patient is to relieve himself of guilty anxiety which is unsuccessful till the conflictful tensions *and their behavioral compromise solutions* are *reduced* and *resolved* and *a new solution in behavior is achieved.* The misperception under these circumstances that the blame or coercion proceeds from the therapist is clearly classifiable as an instance or aspect of the more general process of the projections onto the therapist of the phenomena of transference. A preexisting, or even ancient, conflict is experienced in the *present of the therapeutic situation.* The self-critical feelings of the parent—a residue of his identification with his own parents—is experienced as proceeding from the therapist.

In the successful instances of therapeutic work, such projections onto the therapist are often the first steps in the working through. Subsequent to such projections and accusations by the patient of the therapist, the patient sooner or later recalls similar feelings in situations with *other* people *outside* the therapeutic situation both in his current and his past life. Eventually with the recall and delineation of enough detail of such episodes of extra-therapeutic, interpersonal conflictful tension, the patient may begin slowly to consider and eventually to recognize his *own* contributions, or even provocations, to such events in which he *was* blamed, or *blamed himself* or both.

Similar analysis of the events *in* the therapeutic situation are also, of course, equally, and probably even more important, and may be the most helpful part of the work of therapy. Such insights, of course, may be, and indeed often are, evanescent. They appear as endless repetitions of the same theme in a variety of ways. In other words, this sequence of the process, i.e., of projection, of its analysis, of development of some insight, of the loss of this insight in another crisis is a uniform occurrence in the ongoing work of therapy. Such repetitions are technically known as part of the process of "working through." Of course such self-blame and projections of being blamed, which are often also partly correct perceptions, also occur between the parents, and between them and their child.

Also in the more successful instances of such therapeutic work with parents, the therapist learns that with each episode of at least some and temporary conflict reduction in either child or parent or in both there appears on the part of each a new way of solving the problems of living together. Such new ways of living together are, of course, more satisfying to both the child and his parents. In short, the therapist observes some aspects of more integrated family behavior. Such developments may occur more frequently and earlier in the therapeutic work especially in families in whom the disorder of the child is less severe, and less long standing than that of childhood psychosis. These episodes may at first be brief and transitory. But they may become eventually with increasingly frequent successful outcomes a more common way of life.

Such more successful outcomes are in all probability related to a number of factors. Among them are: 1) the *degree of severity and duration* of the disorder of child and parents at the beginning of the work; 2) the *frequency of the sessions;* 3) the *duration of the work;* 4) the *skill* and *experience* of the *therapist*; 5) the resulting *quality* of the mutual labor of patient and therapist in the *therapeutic situation;* 6) the occurrence, or the absence, of stressful, or even catastrophic, *events in the family* beyond their control, or in part precipitated by their disorder occurring during the period of therapy, and 7) the *therapeutic, or obverse,* character of events in the milieu of the *hospital situation* if the child is in residence, and the like.

In addition to the factors just mentioned, the use by the therapist of opportunities to define and delineate with parent and child particularly clear and recurrent situations between them may enhance whatever problem solving capacities they possess. This is apt to occur especially when energy is freed from its previous binding in self-defeating, conflictful, vicious cycles for problem solving, intellectual work by reduction of conflictful tension even in moderate degrees and in the early stages of the process. Even transient and slight successes in the direction of a less conflict-laden way

of mutual living can be very useful. They may be recalled by the therapist
to the patient later during periods of recurrence of intrafamilial, mutually
maladaptive, behavior.

Such repeated recollections by the therapist at times of resurgence of
mutual discouragement, depression or apathetic withdrawal of parents and
child from each other may at times, or at least eventually, have a marked
potentiating effect on the therapeutic process. This is the more likely to
be true if such recollections of success are made with appropriate and
precise timing. For example, such maneuvers are more likely to be effective
if they are made after sufficient reduction of his current tension by the
patient's ventilation; or, if they are part of an enlightening or elucidating,
reconstructive, interpretative comment about the current episode of conflictful resurgence and as a contrast to it.

It is relevant here, however, to mention somewhat parenthetically that a
good many parents who witness the persistent effort of the staff in all
spheres of the child's living—in short their "all-out" effort—at times re-
experience some wish that they could be a child again. Perhaps then, *they
too* might receive the same kind of care their child is receiving from the
total milieu staff. There occur then to them memories of periods in their
own childhood wishing for such considerate, and in effect the tender, kind
of relationships which were not then available to them. There are, too,
those parents who in a way could be described as suffering in addition to
the internalized conflicts from the repetitive sense of failure in dealings as
a parent with his own child. Such a sense of failure appears to stem from
both his difficulty in understanding his child's behavior, and hence, unable
to respond to it—especially to the paradoxical, symptomatically unresponsive aspects of his child's activity. At such times a circularity between
parent and child interactions follows that appears endless and insoluble to
such a parent.

The repetition of similarities of the conflictful trends in the recurrent
episodes in addition to the previous occurrence of successful solving of
what the patient may again experience as a hopelessly endless and unmodifiable maelstrom may have several results. The current episode of difficulty,
whether with spouse, or with child, or with both, may be lifted from the
whirlpool of what seems to the patient as the evidence of unchanging and
overwhelming, global inadequacy and hopeless inferiority as a more understandable discrete episode. Each such episode may then with *sufficient
repetitions* become to the patient a recognizable piece of experience with
an identifiable beginning in external events and his internal reactions to
these events. These recognitions and understandings themselves may arouse
in the patient increased feelings of the manageability of such episodes and

of some slight hope. The memory of the previously experienced, specific, successful solution may enhance these feelings. The possibility of returning to the more constructive mode in some aspect of the current crisis may occur to the patient himself, or it may be pointed out to him by the therapist. There may be also other discernible and describable effects in different patients, or in the same patient at different times in the course of therapy.

The aforementioned use by the therapist of instances of the parents' more integrated and successful behavior in situations *outside* of the family circle, or *within* his family generally, and *with the child* particularly, needs further exploration. The further delineation of this aspect of the therapist's activity in the therapeutic situation may then lend more emphasis to its potential for increasing the effectiveness of the therapeutic work.

It is a great advantage and probably necessary, of course, for the therapist to comprehend that any serious and long-standing difficulty which an adult may experience in contributing as a parent to the integrated development of his child at various stages of the child's maturation are the results of malintegrative experiences of that parent's past life that are often exacerbated by current stresses. If as a result of clinical therapeutic experience the therapist knows this, he can then be prepared for a number of aspects of the task before him. He will then be ready to recognize that sufficient time and *repetition* of such sessions will be required for him *first* to attain a grasp of the details of current living within the family. Only then can he begin in his own mind gradually to untangle the web of the effects of the past from the exacerbating current stresses of his patient's life. He will generally withhold definitive assessments of his patient's difficulties until he has explored as far as possible *with* his patient all the details of the sequence of events in any current episode brought to the interview by the patient.

If the patient's collaboration can be, or has been, achieved for such exploration, the therapist will not hesitate to point to, and inquire about, any aspect or detail of the sequence of the episode which remains unclear or uncertain to him. This may result either in the patient's filling in such gaps, or in a mutual recognition that these gaps are at the moment incomprehensible to both and require further, future attention. If such explorations are conducted with an attitude that fuller recapitulation of such events may lead to better mutual understanding of what "went wrong" and when; if the patient experiences from the therapist none of the blame, derision and contempt *he* (the patient) feels during the exposure of some failure or incompetence; the patient then, at least in time, may be progressively encouraged to participate in such a task.

Arduous though efforts in such a direction may be for both patient and therapist, and repeatedly interrupted though such work may be by setbacks of recurrent tension and reluctance from discouragement on the part of the patient, the progressive clarification of the patient's characteristic tendencies, conflictful *and* integrated, and often of their sources and roots in past and/or in present events is rewarding. From such repetitive clarifications, both patient and therapist become clearer of the actual reasons in his past *and* current experiences and behavior for the patient's underlying, or overt, self-recriminations.

Some of the general aspects of the disorder of living of the patient may come more fully into view in the study of the details of each episode. They form a complex web in the patient's guilty tension. He may be unable to fulfill compensatory *over*commitments with consequent anxieties about hurried, and harried, incomplete or inadequate performance. He may avoid tasks he has never fully mastered. His lack of, or inability, to plan with some foresight may lead to his failure to remember to perform in a timely sequence important necessities for himself and family. Together with these difficulties he may experience anxieties and fears about his own physical welfare because of self-neglect.

The disorganizing impatience of the parent, his irritation and self-derogation resulting from such behavior, not only lead to further compounding of his own emotional disorder and to contribution to the disorganizing hurts, irritation, retaliatory resentments on the part of others in the family. But such reactions also lead to his intense impatient, destructive criticism of others' failures, delays or incompetence. All this returns in full circle to abysmal self-contempt, intense feelings of inferiority and global hopelessness—and not infrequently to both.

Estrangement between Parents

A frequent result and accompaniment of such vicious circles of intense, conflictful tension are transient episodes, or more prolonged periods, of emotional estrangement not only between the parents, but also some measure of alienation between them and their child. An often equally destructive variation of the estrangement may occur between child and either one of the parents and a period of a more ambivalently "close" relation of the child to the *other* parent. In some families the parent who is excluded from the "close" parent-child dyad may vary from one period to another. These "couplings" change generally for eventually understandable reasons. Another describable variation of such estrangements within a family is a centrifugal one: that is, with each member of the triad feeling and behaving in an ambivalently alienated way from the other two.

However, to return to and focus upon the emotional estrangement between the two parents—whatever the relations of each, or of both, are to their child—it is of importance to note several particular aspects of this "divorce". One of these, of course, is the reduction, disappearance, or worse, a sado-masochistic transformation of their sexual relation and satisfaction. Some measure of, or complete, frigidity on the part of the wife is a frequent occurrence. Either episodes, or more enduring periods, of impotence on the part of the husband often specifically only in contact with his wife may appear. Impulses toward, or actual occurrences of, infidelity are then almost inevitable on the part of either, or of both marital partners.

One may add here that it is not at all uncharacteristic, in our experience, for parents of psychotic children to have had little if any mutually satisfying sexual experience with one another. There have also been seen parents in our clinic who have had no sexual relations with each other at all for a good many years. Paradoxically, too, in such families it may be the occasion for increased turmoil and more emotional disruption between the marital partners when one or the other begins to feel enough better about himself as a result of therapeutic work sooner than his spouse and begins to desire and express this desire for sexual contact to his mate.

Such maldevelopments of sexual relations between the mates generally are either centrally connected, or an added impetus, to further deteriorations of the behavior of each toward the other. Mutual courtesy, tenderness, and consideration for the other's wishes, preferences, tastes, health and welfare decrease or practically disappear. In their place justified or unjustified suspicions and fears of the other's motivations, guilty resentments and revengefulness readily flare upon even relatively slight provocations. One is tempted to the analogy with impersonal *allergens* and say that over the years each parent, each mate (as well as the child) becomes psychologically "allergic" to a word, a phrase, a tone of voice, an incipient act, etc., of the other parent. Then, either insomnia, depressive moods, intensification of somatic illness with reduced capacity of each to perform adequately his or her own familial function, or furious quarrels with mutual recriminations occur more frequently or continue for long periods.

Under such circumstances, precise and adequate communications about mutual, and even essential family plans or necessities suffer, decrease or even disappear. These miscommunications almost inevitably bring in their train an endless variety of disappointments, if not disasters, even regarding family finances, and hence a host of consequent troubles in family living. The effect of such mounting crises, or smouldering mutual withdrawals between the parents upon the child's development, learning, and general eagerness for living within and outside his family, varies with the qualities, frequency, intensity, and duration of these tensions, and with his phase of maturation and other factors.

In all these conditions, guilt, self-blame, and self-derogation are central concomitants in each member of the family, whether experienced consciously or whether unconsciously projected upon one or both of others in the triad. Reconciliations are difficult and occur less and less frequently. Some impulse to express regret for *only* his, or her, *own* action or contribution to the estrangement on the part of one parent (or child) appearing some time after the last destructive transaction with the other, may succumb to, or be delayed by, a conflicting impulse. This conflicting impulse is one of combined hurt pride, still active revengefulness, and (con)fused with a self-abasing acceptance of the entire blame for the episode that requires pleading for "forgiveness." Whatever solid and genuine self-respect exists cannot survive such an impulse to be carried out into masochistic action.

The confusing, self-abasing aspects of the impulse (opposing the impulse to make some conciliatory gesture or effort at restitution) can be with often *great* effort—or as a result of progressively effective therapeutic work —discriminated from a guilt-relieving wish necessary to restore *one's own* self-regard by acknowledging simply and aloud to the other one's shame and regret for the hostile-destructive aspects of *one's own behavior*. Such discrimination altogether *avoids* any assumption of blame for the other's revengefully hurtful action in the original destructive transaction. This latter impulse, thus clarified from the previous confusion, then seeks no "forgiveness," nor even expects any prompt reconciliation. The act has one and only one purpose: to do something for one's own inner comfort; to end one's own distress from one's own outraged and raging ethical conscience. To achieve this purpose, no act of another person can in any way be durably useful or effective.

Another complication we have witnessed in some families occurs when the disorder of two of the triad—generally one parent and the child— improves in some more permanent degree. The other parent under these circumstancs may then become much more disturbed. This last mentioned member of the triad then may express his disturbance with anger that he is the one who is "blamed" for the disorder of the child since the other two have been able to benefit from their therapeutic work. He may even very angrily accuse the therapist of not helping him to achieve the kind of integrated capacity for mutually satisfying living attained by the child and his spouse. There occurs as part of such an accusation that the therapist does not wish to help although he could if he so wished.

In some such instances the latter spouse—who has for a variety of reasons which may be idiosyncratic often for him—may disrupt the total therapeutic effort of the staff. On the other hand, we have seen in a few instances of this sort (perhaps with a greater skill on the part of the therapist than in the previously described situation) that such a parent has been helped to examine more closely the processes by which the other two members of his family have achieved the amelioration of their disorder. In this case the parent lagging in his therapeutic progress has then been able to become more sharply aware of his own anxieties and the consequent fears about committing himself more fully to the same process with consequent gain for himself.

But even when such internal discrimination *is* achieved and the impulse *is freed* from conflict to make it possible to carry it out in action, it may not end the estrangement and restore emotional harmony with the other person. It frequently happens that the response of the other person [who may be still at, or near, the peak of his (or her) guiltily revengeful hurt] is one of blaming, accusing self-justification. This response also frequently then *reevokes* the traumatic effect of the original destructive transaction in the first person who makes the conciliatory effort. Following the release of *his* tension, the second person may reach in time an emotional state in which a conciliatory approach to the first person may then be possible. If this approach is actually made by the second person, the first person who made the first conciliatory effort may again be in an unresponsive phase of his own turmoil for the previously described reasons.

Thus, approaches by each to the other may fall in the "refractory periods" of his partner's turmoil. The time consumed, or the repetitions of these cycles that perpetuate the estrangement between "the combatants," before an actual reduction of conflict tension within each of them and between them, or an actual reconciliation, eventually supervenes could be examined for the factors responsible. They can, however, to the initiated and experienced therapists, be perhaps readily imagined. Before such ending of estrangement actually occurs, one is reminded of "ships passing in the night."

During such periods of active estrangement, the accompanying or resulting insistent demands for help, or for impossible performance, from spouse, child or therapist, then reach a pitch of intensity that may be hardly believable to those not intimately aware of all details of any one episode of the disorder and the cumulative effect of any one episode upon the next.

REINTEGRATIVE PROCESSES

If, however, time, frequency of sessions, and skill of the therapist in the sense previously indicated are not greatly wanting, at least slowly some elements of a more fully understood episode may be the crucial point for attentive examination by parent and therapist that could reduce, if not reverse, the destructiveness of what is otherwise an inevitable cycle or spiral toward another crisis. Such points might be the delineation by the therapist (and at times by the patient) of the need for some of the following: the need for more accurate planning of what can be done in a period of time on the basis of actual time studies, i.e., of what time is needed for unhurried, thorough performance of each task; of the advantages of using memory aids, of notes, calendars and lists of tasks to be done; of the necessity of informing oneself more adequately, or of refreshing one's information, about ways of doing things (e.g., of studying a map or recipe) and about new problems; of the usefulness of experimental practicing of methods not yet mastered; of exploring ancient, or current, reasons for anxiety and fear about physical health; of the reassuring effect of consulting a physician early in the development of a discomfort or somatic symptom; of learning from one's own personal experience of the calming and satisfying effect of adequate nutrition, rest and exercise, etc.; of the satisfaction resulting from closer attention to fiscal matters or to the arithmetic involved; of the importance of one's appearance to one's poise and self-regard; and for scrutiny of many other matters like the former, i.e., all those elements which contribute to one's comfort, self-care, self-consideration and hence to one's own self-respect.

When such attention of the therapist is regularly directed to the possible improvement, if not alleviation, of the roots of his difficulties, with here and there a successful, or partially successful outcome, and these too are noted and acknowledged by the therapist, then the patient's destructive spiral of tension about himself may be slowed and hopefully eventually be reversed. When in fortunate circumstances his self-regard may be thus increased in a more positive direction, he may then inevitably be better able to consider the welfare of spouse and child as important to him as his own. As he begins to blame himself less for incompetence in his daily life, which he has reduced and transformed into competent, satisfying behavior, he blames others less. He can be more sturdily and firmly encouraging to *them* as he continues doing himself all he can to reduce or resolve difficulties and tensions of his own and thus those of others in his family.

Of course, what has been just emphasized as the very individual and personal difficulties of such a patient who is a parent does not in any way exclude similar analysis and similar attention from the therapist of any specific, comprehensible and identifiable difficulty such a parent may have with his child and, probably, with the spouse. Opportunities for possible reduction of such other-centered difficulties may be identified early or in the course of the work about the matters already discussed. Now and then a question from the therapist about some nodal point in an event involving the child or spouse may lead to a suggestion by patient, or therapist, of an alternative way of behaving that may be more useful.

It needs to be remembered, however, that such alternatives are more likely of success if they are consonant with the parent's own deeper personal and individual wish and interest, and if they do not make demands upon him too great for him to make in any given state of his own emotional equilibrium. Also, it must be borne in mind that such alternatives are the more likely to be effectively attempted and to become a more durable way of dealing with such problems when the parent himself has gained the previously mentioned benefits from his own efforts about his own behavior. In short, when he has less reason to *blame* himself, he then also blames others—those of his family and the therapist—less. He is then, naturally, less likely to *mis*interpret an inquiry from the therapist for simple information as a suspicious accusation. In short, he will be much less likely to *feel* blamed.

If eventually the balance of the parent's satisfactions with himself, or herself, over his self-discontent increases more durably, the therapist will then witness all those changes he has worked for with the parent. It goes almost without saying that similar work and similar results achieved with the other parent and with the child would enhance the progress of all three.

REFERENCES

1. BETTELHEIM, B. *The Empty Fortress: Infantile Autism and the Birth of the Self.* The Free Press, New York, 1967, p. 484.
2. CALDWELL, BETTYE, M. The effect of psychosocial deprivation on human development in infants. *Merrill Palmer Quarterly,* 16:260-277, 1970.
3. CALDWELL, BETTYE M. The usefulness of the critical period hypothesis in the study of filiative behavior. *Merrill Palmer Quarterly,* 8:229-242, 1962.
4. COFFEY, H. S. and WIENER, L. L. *Group Treatment of Autistic Children.* Prentice-Hall, Inc., Englewood Cliffs, New Jersey, 1967, p. 90.
5. DUNGAN, E. Coping is a serious game. *San Francisco Sunday Examiner And Chronicle.* July 26, 1970. California Living Magazine Section, pp. 22-24.
6. GREENSON, R. R. and WEXLER, M. The non-transference relationship in the psychoanalytic situation. *Inter'l. J. Psychoanal.* 50:27-39, 1969.
7. GOLDFARB, W. Emotional and intellectual consequences of psychologic deprivation in infancy: A revaluation. *Psychopathology of Childhood.* Eds. Hoch and Zubin, New York. Grune and Stratton, 1955, pp. 105-111. Vol. 10.

8. GOLDFARB, W. The effects of early institutional care on adolescent personality. *J. Experimental Educ.*, 12(2):106-129, 1943.
9. KANNER, L. *In Defence of Mothers. How to Bring up Children in Spite of the More Zealous Psychologists.* Charles C Thomas, Springfield, Illinois, p. 167, 1941.
10. KHLENTZOS, M. T., M.D. Personal communication.
11. KYSAR, J. E. Reactions of professionals to disturbed children and their parents. *Arch. Gen. Psych.*, 19(5):562-570, 1968.
12. KYSAR, J. E. The two camps in child psychiatry: A report from a psychiatrist father of an autistic and retarded child. *Am. J. Psych.*, 125(1): 103-109, July 1968.
13. RIMLAND, B. The syndrome and its implication for a neural theory of behavior. *Infantile Autism.* Appleton-Century-Crofts, Div. of Meredith Publishing Co., New York, pp. 65, 282, 1964.
14. SPITZ, R. A. Hospitalism. *Psychoanalytic Study of the Child I.* International University Press, New York, pp. 54-74, 1945.
15. SPITZ, R. A. Hospitalism: A follow-up report. *Psychoanalytic Study of the Child II.* International University Press, pp. 113-117, 1946.
16. STANDEN, A. *Science is a Sacred Cow.* Dutton, New York, p. 221, 1950.
17. SZUREK, S. A. A child psychiatrist's comments on therapy of schizophrenia. *Inpatient Care for the Psychotic Child.* The Langley Porter Neuropsychiatric Institute Child Psychiatry Series. Eds. Szurek, S. A., Berlin, I. N. and Boatman, M. J. Science and Behavior Books, Inc., Vol. 5, Palo Alto, California, p. 298, 1971.
18. SZUREK, S. A. Review of "The Empty Fortress: Infantile Autism and the Birth of the Self," by Bruno Bettelheim. *Social Service Review*, 42:241-251, June 1968.
19. SZUREK, S. A. Some lessons from efforts at psychotherapy with parents. *Am. J. Psych.*, 109:296-302, 1952. Also *Training in Therapeutic Work with Children.* The Langley Porter Child Psychiatry Series, Eds. Szurek, S. A., and Berlin, I. N. Science and Behavior Books, Inc., Vol. 2, Palo Alto, California, p. 300, 1967.
20. SZUREK, S. A. *The Roots of Psychoanalysis and Psychotherapy.* Charles C Thomas, Springfield, Illinois, p. 134, 1958. (See especially Part II; Chapters 2 and 3, pp. 58-77.)

7

Parental Blame: An Obstacle in Psychotherapeutic Work with Schizophrenic Children and Their Families

This seems to have been written by a couple of other guys!

I. N. Berlin, M.D.

and

S. A. Szurek, M.D.

INTRODUCTION

Overidentification with the child and resentment of parents has been a frequent and common feature in most psychotherapeutic work with children. Fred Allen (1), over 30 years ago, initiated a therapeutic method still prevalent in this country which emphasizes treating the child and counseling parents to facilitate and understand the treatment. It may well be said that the classical psychoanalytical method of treating only the child and trying to prevent parental interferences with the analysis reflects a similar bias, so clearly delineated by Melanie Klein (8). These positions are taken despite the theoretical understanding that most psychopathology results from conflictful relations between parent and child during psycho-sexual development (8, 6). Thus, the work of Melita Sperling (11) on simultaneous analysis of mother and child and Hilde Bruch's (4) work with families in psychoanalysis of psychosomatic disorders of childhood are significant early departures in child analysis.

Not until after World War II, with the growth of child guidance clinics influenced by Meyer (10) and Healy (7), did the concern with families become reflected in the work of Szurek and Johnson (12), Almena Dawley (5), etc. and result gradually in more systematic inclusion of parents in the treatment process.

It is perhaps not coincidental that the increased recognition of disturb-ances of childhood reflected the wide concern over psychiatric disabilities in the war. Thus increased numbers of facilities were developed to diagnose and treat children's disorders. Concern with disturbed children made it easier and perhaps necessary to seek out someone to blame rather than to examine the many root causes in the increasing intrapersonal troubles in our families and in society with their effects on individuals. Thus, books and papers on momism, passive fathers, aggressive mothers, etc. became widespread. Simple cause and effect relations are easiest to make plausible since multifactorial causes require self searching and critical evaluation not easily written about in the popular press.

Parents who felt blamed turned to the easiest target available and blamed schools in whose care they had placed their children. Teachers, faced with insurmountable problems with disturbed and disturbing children, in addition to a crushing population flow to the cities, in turn blamed parents or the unresponsive system. Someone has to be blamed or else we need to look carefully for causes and remedies—no easy tasks for either mental health practitioners or well-trained researchers.

SOCIO-CULTURAL ASPECTS OF PARENTAL BLAME

In our experience with children and parents from the poverty population, the very serious impact of poverty resulting in helplessness, prolonged mal-nutrition, chronic depression, apathy and unsuccessful periodic efforts to escape these effects have profound impact on psychic and interpersonal problems. Thus the chronic withdrawal, indifference and apathy often coupled with the child's non-learning is frequently ascribed to the parents' not caring about the child. Similar inference is made with regard to the hyperactive, angry, destructive and non-learning behavior of other children from the same socio-economic circumstances. It is difficult for professional persons to ascribe these behaviors of children not only to intrapsychic factors but also to the socio-cultural setting of poverty over several gener-ations mediated through desperately unhappy, depressed and deprived parents who for generations saw no future for themselves as adults or their children other than a life of poverty.

We don't like to be reminded that such conditions exist and that we as fellow human beings have some accountability for their perpetuation.

CASE VIGNETTE NO. 1

Thus, in one instance a mute, withdrawn 4½ year old referred to us from a Head Start program appeared like a classically autistic child. The mother of this child had four other young children. She also seemed withdrawn, apathetic, non-communicative and hostile. It was difficult for our middle-class professional staff to relate to the mother. Only when the child began to cling to a nurse, play a bit, and react to a good deal of age-appropriate stimulation in play and in preschool with increased alertness and efforts to say a few words did the staff feel less angry at "the rejecting mother." They then included her in the ward activities with her child. To their amazement in the course of two months, Mother also began to blossom as she learned to play with children and was given some clearly defined tasks in teaching another child picture recognition and vocabulary building through some learning games. As one of us has described elsewhere (3), the concomitant changes in child and mother were striking, and Mother was more able to be nurturant and to play with her own child and later to work effectively as a Head Start aide. Mother's evident strengths appeared only as she was involved and helped to pleasurably play, teach, and learn, and thus feel effective as a person.

CASE VIGNETTE NO. 2

In another instance a 6 year old girl who was mute, starved, and cachectic, self destructive, i.e., scratching and tearing at herself, was brought to us by the court. Mother was a very poor woman from the same generational matrix of poverty. She was frequently drunk and left the child locked up alone without food in the house. Repeated complaints of neighbors in the housing project finally caused protective social services to act. When the mother visited her child the staff was very hostile toward this "terrible" mother. They could not understand why the child clung to this obviously "unconcerned" mother with such desperation.

The court workers were also angry because this mother refused to relinquish the child for adoption, foster care, etc., and the court proceedings would be necessary. Most of the professionals could not see the moments of tenderness between mother and child nor understand mother's needs to hold onto the child as one way of gaining some attention and concern from others, even through hostility.

David Looff in his book, *Appalachia's Children* (9), describes the impact of generations of poverty on families which bring about stereotyped roles of infantilization of children to bind them to the extended family, the only comfort for both mother and child in a hostile, depriving and frightening world. These children's subsequent learning problems and failures to become effective in any way also leads to blaming the absent drunken fathers and the infantilizing, depressed mothers who try to keep the brood close to them.

Thus the socio-economic factors of poverty, starvation, malnutrition, unemployment and consequent hopeless-helpless feelings which require social action to correct appear as overwhelming to us to begin to resolve, as the instance of childhood psychosis with its burdens of treatment. In these instances it is easier to blame individual parents for their children's plight than to look to the root causes that require more systematic and programmatic analysis and working through of both socio-economic and therapeutic problems to some beginning resolution.

BLAME IN PSYCHOTHERAPEUTIC WORK

Many of us who do simultaneous psychotherapeutic work with children and parents could examine the myriad of factors possibly etiologic to a child's severe disturbances. We found that where *each* parent's internal conflicts resulted in apparent great ungratifiable needs for "nurturance" and "closeness" with their spouse that these compromise solutions to neurotic conflict and resulting needs often preclude mutual fulfillment. Clinically we have noted in some parents an apparent insatiable need, or perhaps demand for, "nurturance" which reflects a sense of helplessness about doing things for themselves. Such helplessness often occurs in areas where the parent has never been helped to learn, or has only partly learned, to be self sufficient and effective on his own behalf. Thus, in treatment a guilty rage or revengeful feeling toward the spouse may reflect the helplessness felt when one needs to do these things for oneself, has not learned how to begin to do them and therefore expects them to be done by the spouse and is fearful of, or feels shameful about, overtly expressing the need. At other times there is evident anxiety about the desire or need for nurturance with denial of it and loss of feelings of affection for the spouse and estrangement. Often there is no conscious awareness of the looking for nurturance or wanting to be taken care of.

In these several instances the effect may be an irritable overreaction, coldness, blaming the child, and other conflicted feelings in response to the child's requests or demands. This lack of understanding and empathy with the child may lead to feelings of guilt and ambivalent appeasement or unclear judgments about what to permit, limit, encourage, or discourage. The resulting uncertainties may lead to perplexity in living for both parents and child. Thus often both parents had little capacity for nurturance and ability to recognize and respond to a child's developmental needs. Blame was clearly not a relevant issue. Even in those instances of child abuse that we saw there was clear evidence of severe personality disturbance and conflict with its origins in the parents' childhood. Thus the behavioral consequences of these conflicts, and not malice, accounted for the trauma to the child.

PSYCHOLOGICAL ISSUES IN BLAME

Many of us began to describe etiology of childhood disorders in terms of many factors—parental conflicts from their childhood which could not have been relieved by marriage, but the relief of which is more or less unconsciously expected or hoped for. Thus fulfillment of the hope that one spouse could supply the needs of another was further frustrated by needs of each spouse to be responsible for his or her part of the division of labor necessary in marriage. Intercurrent life events which overwhelmed parents, such as death in the family, loss of job, severe illness occuring at birth of a child or during critical developmental periods, severe individual genetic differences in body habitus and sensory motor differences may make parents' habitual modes of communication difficult for the child to comprehend and vice versa. Thus, a very bright, highly sensitive and alert infant with small body habitus might feel out of tune with large vigorous parents who communicate through physical and nonverbal means.

Particular and unusual sensitivities in infants may not be responded to by parents whose experiences with their own parents preclude being sensitive to their infant's unusual needs, such as extra sensitivity to noise or light. Sometimes unusual physical mobility in a very vigorous, large infant may exhaust his intellectually-oriented parents. These physiologic differences which require particular parental attention, if not responded to, may result in mutual alienation. The concept of parent-child fit makes a good deal of sense. Further, the circular problems between child and parents can only continue and escalate if not dealt with by outside help.

A few of our retrospective therapeutic studies have also provided prospective information which confirms other observations when a family, in treatment because of a psychotic child, has a new infant. In several instances both parents, but especially the mother, describe how much more tender and aware they are of the infant's needs and how responsive and loving they feel toward the new infant, as if it were their first. Increased tenderness and closeness between parents was also described by each parent. Each parent could describe both resolution of some of their own conflicts and in some instances the absence of external pressures like absence of father due to war or death of a parent near the birth of the disturbed infant.

We need to explore some of the reasons for the all too frequent and persistent phenomena of blaming parents seen in our clinics and in special schools. Work with difficult and disturbed and severely retarded children often results in angry blame of parents because the retarded and troubled children are so frustrating and difficult to help.

COUNTERTRANSFERENCE ISSUES IN BLAME

From some of our own experiences some elucidation of these attitudes may become possible. One of the present writers (Berlin) can vividly recall the first severely psychotic five year old child with whom he worked. His sense of helplessness in trying to understand the etiology of the illness and what was needed of him to begin a therapeutic experience with the child was constantly frustrated by the child's silent aggression, destructive and often assaultive behavior. He was also working with the father; another therapist saw the mother. The father was an angry, demanding person who caustically demanded that the therapist give his child medication or at least electroshock like they did for adults. Neither E.C.T. nor any of the antipsychotic drugs then available had been proved helpful to children. The therapist tried to explain this to him. Father's derisive, angry comments about what a poor doctor the therapist was and what a sorry clinic milieu program we had and his recurrent questions about why they should continue this farcical treatment left the therapist defensive, angry and impotently unable to work therapeutically with either child or father. It was only during a supervisory session as the therapist bitterly described how furious and helpless the father's angry, derisive comments made him feel that the supervisor's empathic question of who else came to mind at such a moment brought the therapist to blurt out, "my father when I did not please him." Thus, slowly the countertransference feelings which interfered with a more objective understanding of this father were reduced and permitted the therapist to become aware of the father's helpless, hopeless, and very sad feelings which underlaid the angry demands. As the therapist was able to empathize with these feelings and, when appropriate, describe his own reaction to the father's angry demands, often a sense of paralysis and feelings of not being able to help him help his child, then the father was more accurately able to describe his love, aspirations, and anger toward the child and toward Mother who had been severely depressed at the child's birth.

Simultaneously the therapist was able to deal with the child's hostile, destructive behavior with gentle restraint and by encouraging play with clay and toys while he held him loosely. The child always carried with him a plastic dragon. The therapist built many clay dragons and encouraged the child to build his own clay model of the plastic dragon. His many tries at imitating the therapist's dragon usually ended with the child destroying the therapist's model. The child's first spontaneous words, "I made it," occurred after he successfully built his own giant clay dragon. In retrospect, the therapist stopped hating and blaming Father for his child's illness when the therapist understood his own countertransference problems and the feelings of frustration and helplessness which both father and son engendered in the therapist. He could then see beneath them the enormous hurt, pain, and hopelessness which they both felt as nothing changed to alter the conflicts in their lives.

Subsequent experiences with very angry, bitter parents whose severely psychotic children have changed little in psychotherapy lead us to feel their demands that we initiate other forms of treatment or agree with them that their child is hopeless and should be placed elsewhere must be dealt with quite realistically. Thus, we do not hastily agree with them as if we also want to be rid of them as bad parents, but instead we seriously and empathically explore the impact of such a child on their lives and mode of living. At the same time we express our convictions that while perhaps our work could be fruitful, we are quite willing to consider transfer to another institution and do all we can to facilitate the process. In the serious consideration of parents' needs and the slowness of therapy, many parents become less angry and as one said, "for the first time I feel you don't blame me and are considering my human needs."

REDUCTION OF SELF BLAME

One of the therapeutic goals is to help parents both blame themselves less and feel less criticized by others. As they learn to use their therapy to reduce their obstacles to integrative living with themselves, that is, to realize their own desires, they are able to reduce the obstacles to living with their spouse. Subsequently they also eventually learn to parent their children more effectively. Our serious consideration of their reality needs often makes it possible for them to plan, when they wish it, for needed vacations from their children or periods of rest and later, more vigorous return to therapeutic work.

Experiences with Teaching Retarded Children and Issues of Blame

Our subsequent experiences in consulting with teachers of severely retarded and disturbed children confirmed time and again how easy it was for the teacher to blame parents for the children who were so difficult to reach and work with effectively. It was also clear that the parents' recurrent anger at teachers for lack of change in their children which would make living with them easier, resulted from their conflicted feelings about the child, themselves, and their spouse. Often their self blame and blame of spouse reflected the hopeless, helpless feelings and conflicts in each parent and between parents which were difficult to resolve. It was therefore impossible to evolve more integrative patterns of behavior with their child or between themselves as parents. Most often they were unable to work out the firm discipline required to reduce chaos at home. Teachers often found their own anger and helpless feelings augmented by the parents' rage at them. Thus, teachers found it difficult to apply their knowledge to help parents work with their children in learning and evolving more socially adaptive behaviors to making living together easier.

INCREASED COMPETENCE OF PARENT AND CHILD—REDUCED
BLAME AND BLAMING

We found that we could gradually help teachers comprehend the parental dilemmas and reasons for their feelings and behavior (3). Teachers would then begin to examine together with parents where they could take tiny steps to help a child learn and to reinforce more cooperative behavior. The need for realistic tiny increments and small attainable goals had to be carefully and repeatedly explained to the parents until their cooperation could be elicited. Parents could then be helped to understand the importance of staying close to their child and slowly, despite the frustration, helping an 8 or 9 year old to dress himself rather than more expeditiously doing it for him. Each garment the child learns to put on by himself is a step nearer to self care and self sufficiency.

In one instance a teacher helped a twelve year old girl with an IQ of 60 learn to set the table. It took 20 days of dividing the task into small steps, rewarding each success and ignoring failures. When her mother saw her set the table in school she was incredulous. There had been no expectations of her at home at all. Simultaneous with this successful learning, some of this girl's hitting out at other children in school decreased. At home mother and teacher collaborated to devise ways of breaking down each task into increments of learning. Thus teaching Anne to make beds, vacuum the house, etc. became possible. It made Anne the recipient of frequent praise from all the family. Living at home became more tranquil as her temper tantrums were reduced because she looked and behaved as if she were more satisfied with herself and a valued member of the family.

As changes in behavior slowly did occur, parents, feeling a part of the effort to help their child, were more readily able to recognize and support small changes in their child and work with teachers toward their common goals. In a number of instances such collaboration of teachers and parents on the child's behalf required home demonstrations by teachers which helped parents to carry out the program more effectively. With each shift in the child, teachers and parents felt more competent as the child became more effective and progressed in learning and more socially acceptable behavior, to the child's own obvious delight. In these instances both blame of parents and of teachers with the child as the victim is decreasingly evident. This is especially true when the adults are also helped to anticipate the repetitious regressions and occasional behavior reversals that are part of the learning process.

PROFESSIONAL OMNIPOTENCE: A FACTOR IN PARENTAL BLAME

Parental blame has several other implications as it is voiced by professionals working with very difficult children. Not only are the therapist's unresolved angers toward the therapist's own parents mobilized by the unrelieved frustrations of daily work without much hope for success, but his sense of competence is severely threatened. Each new child provides a challenge and, despite contrary evidence, we hope that we may succeed again with a severely disturbed child. Thus we feel and tell parents we hope to succeed where others failed. In all of us, the threat to such everpresent feelings of needing to accomplish the impossible may endanger our self esteem and the expectations others have had for us since childhood. When we face failure we need to find someone to blame and relieve us of the intolerable feelings of inadequacy. Only as we recognize and face our human needs and our human capacities can we empathize with parents who are faced with these difficult children for many years. Only then do we recognize the escalation of problem behavior contributed to by both child and parent in an unrelieved, intolerable living together. Often rather than working toward gradual, incremental changes and the unremitting hard work required in psychotherapy or education, we continue desperately to hope for magical change, that is, sudden giant steps resulting from our interpretive maneuvers. We thus encourage parents in much the same way that they have been encouraged by other medical and educational advisors that maturation, changes from one therapist or from one center to another will produce the hoped-for sudden and magical change. Such professional attitudes usually will not clarify and bring to the parents' awareness the nature of their own intrapersonal conflictful attitudes, those attitudes which, when resolved with further therapeutic work, make it possible for parents to begin to fulfill their total parental commitment in the difficult work.

Such learning in the parents, the child, and the therapist is often experienced at first as an impossible global task, a task which is unclear, especially with regard to where to begin, without prior experience. Therapeutic work gradually enhances the capacity to become more like "oneself" than the person has previously dared to be. Thus, in therapeutic work any inhibition of learning ways of exploring a problem for possible new solutions arouses anxiety which tends to obstruct such a learning process. As the anxiety and conflict which reduces new learning, problem solving, or freedom to explore is gradually reduced (especially with therapeutically oriented supervisory help) the "patient" makes efforts at trial or practice solutions to problems, until in the therapeutic situation slowly greater freedom and new learning actually begins to be possible. Then growing up in the sense of enhanced competence and greater freedom to find new solutions and in fact be one's own person with a new and often hoped for, but not previously attained, sense of self regard begins to evolve.

THERAPEUTIC COLLABORATION AND REDUCTION OF MUTUAL BLAMING

Parents from poverty levels require of the professional both understanding of the generational effects of poverty and how efforts at persistent therapeutic collaboration enhance the parent's sense of effectiveness as a person and parent. These mutual efforts, difficult for both parent and professional mental health worker, increase the sense of efficacy of both parties. There then is less parental blame by the professional and less anger by the parent.

The professional's continued efforts to be aware of and to reduce countertransference problems make it more likely that he can be helpful to parents, especially to help them through their own work in therapy, and with their child to enhance their sense of competence and self regard.

The therapist's openness and honesty with the parents help them to greater self awareness and understanding of their child. The attitudinal and behavioral changes in the adults which encourage and help support change in the child requires a forthright, therapeutic collaboration. The therapist must be willing to help the parents assess current reality and the prognosis for the child's improvement. It is clear that parents as well as professionals require models to identify with to encourage change. Thus the professional who learns from his teacher's attitudes toward him can often provide a model for his patients.

We have noted that the most hostile and difficult parents are those who have little else in their lives in which to find pleasure, satisfaction and a sense of personal effectiveness. Such hostility, we have come to learn, comes from self hatred or low self regard generated by conflicts begun with his own parents whose own low self regard and hostility are in a variety of ways transmitted to their child. The impact of poverty and generational conflict on self esteem is enormous.

Thus, anyone else's competence and clear self regard may evoke endless anxiety, conflict, and reactive anxiety. Such reaction is often seen as compensating arrogance and hostility. The efforts to justify such attitudes take many forms of derogating others. It makes for many therapeutic problems for young therapists.

The need of parents to go from one center or authority to another in a never-ending quest for an answer to the child's problems often mirrors the fact that no professionals have both faced them gently with the truth about their child's problems and prognosis and at the same time offered to help them begin the enormous job of collaborative work. Collaboration must be designed to reduce their own problems so they are able, nondestructively, to help reduce the disturbance or disability of their spouse and/or their child. An honest statement about the long period of work that needs to be undertaken is a prerequisite for such collaboration. Further reassessments in the course of the work and realistic re-evaluation with clear and compassionate attention to the parents' need for rest and recreation because of their stresses of living with a disturbed child, increases the family's capacity to face—without guilt, self blame or feeling of blame from others—their own needs and to work them out realistically. Under these conditions, parents express their surprise that there is little opposition from their disturbed child to the parents' attending both to their own needs and to the long-term work.

SUMMARY

Thus, the phenomenon of parental blame must be understood and dealt with as in part reality based, in part socially determined, and in part a projection of the guilt and self blame arising from internalized conflicts and unrealizable self expectations which have arisen from past experiences with others. The psychotherapist's task is to help the parents achieve their previously unrealizable self expectations by reducing conflict and providing opportunities for new learning which result in greater competence and effectiveness in living. The child thus is freed to learn from the therapeutic endeavors, the changing attitudes and behaviors of the parents and his own experience. The therapist, by his honest efforts to effect a collaboration with the parents, permits his own as well as the parents' past experience to be modified on behalf of the growth toward healthy and competent parents, child and therapist.

REFERENCES

1. ALLEN, F. H. *Psychotherapy with Children.* New York: W. W. Norton & Co., 1942.
2. BERLIN, I. N. Consultation and special education. In I. Philips (Ed.), *Prevention and Treatment of Mental Retardation.* New York: Basic Books, Inc., 1966. Pp. 270-293.
3. BERLIN, I. N. The emotional and learning problems of the socially and culturally deprived child. *Ment. Hyg.,* 1966, 50:340-347.
4. BRUCH, H. and POWAINE, G. Obesity in Childhood, V: The family frame of obese children. *Psychosomatic Med.,* 1940, 2:141.
5. DAWLEY, A. Interrelated movements of parents and child in therapy with children. *Amer. J. Orthopsychiatry,* 1939, 9:748-754.
6. FREUD, S. The development of the libido and the sexual organizations. In James Strachey (Ed.), *The Complete Introductory Lectures on Psychoanalysis.* New York: W. W. Norton & Company, Inc., 1966. Pp. 320-338.
7. HEALY, W. The child guidance clinic: Birth and growth. In L. G. Lowery (Ed.), *Orthopsychiatry 1923-1948: Retrospect and Prospect.* New York: AOA, 1948. Pp. 14-49.
8. KLEIN, M. The psychoanalytic play technique: Its history and significance. In M. Klein (Ed.), *New Directions in Psychoanalysis.* New York: Basic Books, 1955.
9. LOOFF, D. *Appalachia's Children.* Lexington: University of Kentucky Press, 1971. Pp. 185.
10. MEYER, A. Birth and development of the mental hygiene movement. *Ment. Hyg.,* 1935, 19:29.
11. SPERLING, M. The handling of mothers of children with psychosomatic disorders. *Psychosomatic Med.,* 1949, 11:315.
12. SZUREK, S. A., JOHNSON, A. M. and FALSTEIN, E. I. Collaborative psychiatric therapy of parent-child problems. *Amer. J. Orthopsychiatry,* 1942, 12:511-516.

8

Depressive Reactions of Childhood and Adolescence

John Langdell, M.D.

INTRODUCTION

It is a rare occasion when one makes an official diagnosis of a depressive reaction of childhood, even though the most common of psychiatric complaints is depressed affect, and child psychiatrists are quite aware that children are not immune to feelings of depression. One reason for the rarity of depressive diagnoses may be that our official diagnostic code book does not provide for appropriate diagnostic categories of childhood psychopathology. Further, the depressive aspects of a child's disorder may go unrecognized because the depressive reactions of childhood and adolescence are so protean in nature and so seldom resemble adult diagnostic models. When such depressions are recognized, they may be viewed as symptoms rather than as basic diagnostic entities.

Psychotic children are seen whose anguished affect and self-punishing self-destructive behavior form a predominant feature of their symptomatology. Such children are usually classified as having schizophrenia of childhood because there is no more specific diagnostic category. Markedly low self-esteem and recurrent turning of hostile impulses against the self would lead one to think in terms of depressive dynamics. One would diagnose depression on seeing such a clinical picture in an adult patient. It is sometimes clinically difficult to distinguish severe autistic withdrawal from the depressed affect and apathy of a severely maternally-deprived depressed child.

It is important that we recognize depressive reactions in childhood and understand their etiology in order to treat more effectively or, better yet, prevent the development of such depressive reactions. Although psychiatric etiology is always multifactorial, childhood depressive reactions are usually related to severe and prolonged lack of nurturant mothering and/or loss of self-

127

esteem, depending on the developmental stage. Since object loss and loss of self-esteem are also important predisposing and precipitating components of adult depressions, a clearer understanding of the role of childhood experiences as antecedents for adult depressive reactions may make possible a clearer understanding of the psychodynamics of the adult disorder and make preventative work possible in the future. There have been a number of studies in which statistically significant associations were found between childhood experiences of bereavement and subsequent adult depressive reactions (6, 10, 20, 25) and suicides (21, 28, 29). Other authors have questioned whether there is a simple relationship between childhood bereavement and adult depressive reactions (27, 31, 38, 51).

In spite of the infrequency of the diagnosis of depressions in childhood, there has been a time-honored recognition in the literature of the existence of depressive reactions in children. Such references can be traced back historically long before Kraepelin. There are many publications which consider the existence or non-existence of manic-depressive reactions in childhood (1, 4, 5, 7, 13, 14, 17, 22, 30, 33, 34, 39, 40, 47, 50, 53, 19).

From antiquity to the present day there have been numerous observations of an association between early object loss and depressive reactions. Such connections were noted long before modern researchers found a characteristic past history of predisposing childhood bereavement preceding a more recent precipitating object loss or loss of self-esteem in depressive reactions of adult life. There were ancient observations on the importance of mothering long before Spitz's demonstration of how childhood depressive reactions may be directly related to loss of a nurturant mothering person in anaclitic depression (partial emotional deprivation) (59, 60) or lack of such nurturance in hospitalism (total emotional deprivation) (57, 58, 61). It seems there is a basic human need for a mothering nurturance beyond the mere provision of physical care and nutrition. This has been demonstrated even in animal research with primates and other mammals (32, 36, 41, 42, 48, 49, 55). The life-or-death importance of the need for such mothering is seen most dramatically when failure to thrive leads to death despite excellent medical care in hospitalism. It seems that just as *loss* of a mothering person can lead to depression, the persistent *lack* of such mothering in an infant can lead even to death. The more precise and subtle aspects of attachment behavior are under current study by various investigators, most notably Bowlby (8, 9).

ANIMAL EXPERIMENTAL STUDIES

There have been a number of studies of animals in which experiments under controlled laboratory conditions have strengthened the human clinical evidence that childhood deprivation or bereavement experiences have an influence on later depressive conditions (32, 36, 41, 48, 49, 55, 42).

Most convincing are recent experiments showing that even brief separation of the rhesus monkey mother from her infant produces long term effects on the young monkey's behavior that can be measured as long as two years later. In behavioral observations and testing up to two years later the previously separated infants were still less active than the controls and differed significantly in a number of other measures of behavior (36).

In this study the young monkey's response to maternal deprivation resembled the human sequence of protest-despair-detachment as described by Bowlby [except for the absence of detachment behavior with the exception of the observation of frequent tantrums when the mother was first returned]. The monkey's initial response to removal of the mother was an increase in "whoo" calling followed by decreased locomotor and play activity, remnants of which behavior persisted for two years. The follow-up testing showed a quantitative difference between the groups which had experienced 6 days and 13 days of maternal separation, and an even more profound long-term effect was noted in monkeys subjected to two separate losses of their mothers for periods of 6 days each.

Individual differences between monkeys were also studied and it was noted that the response to maternal deprivation was related in part to the nature of the mother-infant relationship both before and after the separation period. There was a tendency for more distress after separation to occur in monkey infants who had been rejected most by their mothers and who had played the greatest relative role in maintaining proximity. A sex difference was also noted, the mean distress index of male infants being higher throughout the experiment.

Attempts to demonstrate suicidal behavior in animal experiments have been inconclusive (54).

HISTORICAL ASPECTS OF DEPRESSION

The diagnostic spectrum of depression will be discussed further in clinical and dynamic terms after a historical review which may serve to introduce the subject. Ancient observations serve more than academic historical interest because they represent data from individuals who can be assumed to be free from the taint of any particular modern psychological bias.

The earliest literary reference to adult depression is found in the myth of Bellerophon in the "Iliad". The description of the depressive reaction of Bellerophon indicates ancient awareness of the importance of bereavement, loss of self-esteem, and loss of bodily function in the dynamic etiology of

depression. Following the loss of his children and his fall from the winged
horse Pegasus (which injury left him blind and lame) Bellerophon wandered grief stricken and lonely "avoiding the paths of men and died
miserably" (11).

The earliest literary reference to a depressive type reaction of childhood
that the present author has discovered was an account by the monk
Salambine of the barbaric experiments of the Holy Roman Emperor, Frederick II about 1220 A.D. (52)

> He wanted to find out what kind of speech and what manner of
> speech children would have when they grew up if they spoke to no one
> beforehand. So he bade foster mothers and nurses to suckle the children,
> to bathe and wash them, but in no way to prattle with them or to
> speak to them, for he wanted to learn whether they would speak
> the Hebrew language, which was the oldest, or Greek, or Latin, or
> Arabic, or perhaps the language of their parents, of whom they had
> been born. But he labored in vain, because the children all died.
> For they could not live without the petting and the joyful faces
> and loving words of their foster mothers. And so the songs are called
> "swaddling songs" which a woman sings while she is rocking the
> cradle, to put a child to sleep, and without them a child sleeps badly
> and has no rest.

A contrary result was reported in an amazingly similar experiment at an
even earlier date. Herodotus in the Fifth Century B.C. described an
experiment in which two children were reported to have been subjected
to maternal deprivation and to deprivation of speech and were not described as dying or becoming depressed (35). These early precursors of
the experimental method thus presaged the continuing controversies of
science. According to Herodotus' history the experiment was conducted by
the Egyptian King, Psammetichos (664-610 B.C.), who attempted to determine "what men had come into being first."

> Taking two new-born children belonging to persons of the common
> sort he gave them to a shepherd to bring up at the place where his
> flocks were . . . charging him namely that no man should utter any
> word in their presence, and that they should be placed by them-
> selves in a room where none might come, and at the proper time he
> should bring to them she-goats, and when he had satisfied them with
> milk he should do for them whatever else was needed. These things
> Psammetichos did and gave him this charge wishing to hear what
> word the children would let break forth first, after they had ceased
> from wailing without sense. And accordingly so it came to pass: for
> after a space of two years had gone by, during which the shepherd

went on acting so, at length when he opened the door and entered, both the children fell before him in entreaty and uttered the word *bekos* . . .

As the word *bekos* was repeated constantly by the children, the shepherd brought them to King Psammetichos who heard them say the word and "began to inquire what nation of men named anything *bekos*." On finding the word to be the Phrygian name of bread, he concluded that the Phrygians must be a more ancient people than the Egyptians (35).

Herodotus refers with skepticism to an alternate version in which, "Psammetichos cut out the tongues of certain women and then caused the children to live with these women" (35). We may in turn be skeptical of various aspects of these accounts. For example, our observations of the development of speech in normal children as well as of the appearance of speech in mute psychotic children during psychotherapy indicates that there is a critical need for continuous feed-back of sounds and words from adults or other children for human speech to develop. With such observations in mind, one wonders if the word "bekos" might have been an attempt of the children to imitate the sound of their foster mother, a she-goat.

Both of these experiments antedated by centuries the time usually considered as the beginning of the scientific experimental method. It is surprising that the basic logical assumption of both experiments was a principle of evolution, to be discovered much later, namely, the principle that "ontogeny recapitulates phylogeny."

A few examples of later historical accounts of the adverse effects of lack of mothering follow.

In 1760 a Spanish Bishop observed:

"En la Casa de Niños Expositos el niño se va poniendo triste y muchos de ellos mueren de tristeza" (57).

(In the foundling home the child becomes sad and many of them die of sadness) (my translation).

In 1767, Dr. George Armstrong, who founded the first pediatric dispensary in England, explained the dangers of hospitalizing children and separating them from their parents. He stated:

"If you take a sick child from its parent or nurse, you break its heart immediately" (57).

In 1937 Dr. David Levy wrote of "primary affect hunger" and spoke of a deficiency disease analogous to vitamin deficiency if a child received an insufficient supply of mothering (45).

In 1933 at Bellevue Hospital, at Dr. Bakwin's urging, there was a concerted effort to supply tender loving nursing care to infants in the hospital which resulted in a drop in the infant mortality rate from more than 30% to 10% (2, 3). This statistical demonstration of the life saving nature of "tender loving care" occurred in those days before antibiotics. Since there was no other change in the medical management, no other factors than increased attention could account for the change in mortality.

In 1915, a study of 10 infant asylums in the United States had shown 100% mortality of infants in their first two years (16).

In 1946, Rene Spitz wrote of the clinical syndromes of "anaclitic depression" and "hospitalism", which may be considered forms of depressive reactions of early life as well as prototypes of depressions in later life (59, 60, 57, 58, 61).

A DESCRIPTION OF DEPRESSION IN ADULTS

Depression was recognized by Hippocrates as a clinical entity, which he called melancholia because depression was then considered to be the result of an excess of black bile. If only the mechanism of depression were that simple, our discussion could be complete at this point.

Depressive reactions result from multifactorial life experiences including object loss and loss of self-esteem that culminate with specific trauma into depressive episodes. In the adult there is usually historical material indicating such pre-disposing and precipitating factors as well as prior decompensation or depressive equivalents. We have all experienced some degree of depression and know how it feels.

Depression is easier to describe than to define. It involves melancholic, "blue" feelings, and a general psychomotor slowing down with retardation of thought and action. This affective state is accompanied by obsessive thoughts of low esteem and self-hate including suicidal ruminations. The end result of a depression may be suicide.

Depression is the opposite of mania, which is characterized by pseudo-elated feelings, a flight of ideas, pressure of speech, and hyperactivity. Anyone who has had to deny the demands of a manic patient knows how quickly the "elated" good humor can turn into destructive rage. There may be periodic alternation of manic and depressive manifestations.

In his classical essay "Mourning and Melancholia," Freud described the mental features of melancholia as follows: "A profoundly painful dejection, abrogation of interest in the outside world, loss of the capacity to love, inhibition of all activity, and a lowering of the self-regarding feelings to a degree that finds utterances in self-reproaches and self-revilings, and culminates in a delusional expectation of punishment."

Freud pointed out that mourning the loss of a loved person is similar to melancholia. The basic difference between grief and melancholia is that self-esteem is less seriously affected in grief. Freud stated that the fall in self-esteem is absent in grief. In brief, mourning is the reaction to the loss of a loved one while melancholia or depression is the result of loss of self-esteem (26).

A depression may be precipitated by such events as loss of a close inter-personal relationship, loss of prestige, loss of a job, loss of money, loss of one's possessions, failure to achieve an aspiration, loss of health particularly with chronic debilitating disease, or loss of a body part. There is a charac-teristic response of self-blame in individuals subject to depression in contrast to a paranoid person's tendency to project blame on others.

Depressive symptoms include hopeless feelings about the future, vague physical complaints, feelings of tiredness (which are unrelated to physical exertion), insomnia, loss of appetite and weight, sad appearance, slowing down of physical movements, constipation, and sometimes impotence in men and amenorrhea in women. The individual becomes preoccupied with thoughts and feelings of self-blame, and suicidal thoughts. A vicious cycle develops as the depressed person does less and less for himself and others and feels increasingly inadequate and low in self-esteem.

It is not surprising that many depressed patients are undiagnosed because so many of these symptoms suggest physical disease. The physician who responds to the patient's complaints only by laboratory tests to rule out physical disease may lower the individual's self-esteem further when he finally reports "there is nothing wrong with you."

The dynamics of a depression involve the turning of hostile aggression inward against the self in reaction to loss of self-esteem. In psychoanalytic terms, the ego punishes itself to ward off superego or parental punishment.

Kraepelin, the great categorizer in psychiatry, gave a clinical example to emphasize his view of the relative unimportance of psychogenic factors which actually better illustrates the precipitating power of a seemingly minor life event (43). His description is of a woman who had three attacks of depression. The depressions were all precipitated by losses of love objects. The first followed the death of her husband. The next depression followed the death of her dog. Her final and most severe depressive epi-sode came after the death of a pet dove. When Kraepelin observed these clinical facts he was apparently puzzled by the quantitative discrepancy in the responses to these varied precipitating causes. He seemed unable to consider how each loss symbolized not only the loss of a loved one, but also cumulative feelings about previous losses. Since the patient was growing older and approaching death, each loss also symbolized a progressive loss of meaning and purpose in her life. This is, admittedly, a simplification. A more detailed history would probably show additional multifactorial relationships.

In summary, the classical signs of an adult depression include retardation of mental and physical activity, insomnia, feelings of depression, apathy, worthlessness, and nihilism, as well as suicidal preoccupations. Physiological symptoms of depression include anorexia, constipation, and slowed physical movement. Although physical, physiological, hormonal, and genetic factors play an important role in depressive reactions, a detailed review of the somatic aspect of depression is beyond the scope of this writing.

DEPRESSIONS IN CHILDHOOD

Depression in childhood differs from depression in adult life, and the clinical picture of a childhood depression varies with the age or the developmental level of the child (18, 23, 62). In a small infant, one can observe eating and sleeping disturbances, colic, crying, and head-banging. On observation the mother will usually be noted to be seriously depressed and anxious as well. The infant reacts to loss of emotionally appropriate responsiveness or decreased nurturance by the mother with a depressive reaction with one or more of the above features depending on the degree and duration of the loss of mothering.

At a later stage of infancy one may see withdrawal, apathy, and regression in the severely emotionally deprived child. In emotionally deprived children the reactions may range from behavior disorders of apathy to hyperactivity and from mild intellectual impairment to death. In contrast, non-deprived children may merely play peek-a-boo to master their less profound anxiety about absence of mother.

Gross lack of mothering and general sensory deprivation leads to severe impairment. Sensory deprivation occurs in a non-responsive and non-reactive environment that fails to acknowledge the infant's cues, signals, and needs. In some instances there may be a lack of reciprocity in interactions between the infant and mothering adult.

An older child who is depressed will seem unhappy, whine, have temper tantrums, disobey, be truant, run away from home, be accident prone, be beaten up by other children, and may show self-destructive behavior; considers himself bad, evil, unacceptable, feels inferior, ugly, and sinful. This condition has been described as an "evil self-image." A child is so dependent on his parents that he may be more comfortable considering himself bad rather than acknowledging the harsh treatment by his parents from early years, which his parents explain as necessary because he is so evil. He may thus be reinforced in his denial of any "badness" on the part of his parents. The early roots of depression usually are deprivation of mothering and anxiety due to frequent or prolonged separation. Harsh superego pressures (the incorporation of adults' frequent blaming or proclaiming the child bad) may pre-dispose to the more profound self-blame and the self-derogatory, self-incriminating aspects one observes in adult depressions.

ADOLESCENT DEPRESSIVE REACTIONS

In adolescence the previously mentioned denial mechanism may be reversed with overt hostility expressed toward parents and destructive acting out against the environment. In the adolescent period ordinarily depression appears in the form of boredom and restlessness. The teenager may hide his tender feelings. The denial of such emotions is a characteristic dynamism used by adolescents. One may see a smiling depression with "cool" affect or clowning behavior. The adolescent characteristically cannot stand to be alone. Teenagers use the phonograph, TV, radio, telephone, drug usage, and parties to provide escape from "loneliness" and feeling dependent and depressed. Such "loneliness" is related to dislike of the self, which may lead to frenzied social activity to escape from self awareness. An adolescent girl added a P.S. to her suicide note saying "I cannot stand to live with myself."

Fatigue, hypochondriasis, and bodily preoccupations are frequent medical symptoms of depression in adolescence. A typical depressed teenager may complain of difficulty in concentration. A formerly excellent student may spend long hours trying to study without accomplishing anything. He may give up and fail scholastically and be accused of "laziness" because his depression is unrecognized. Attempts to run away from the self and to run away from psychiatric treatment are characteristic. A desperate "love affair" which breaks up may predispose to suicidal gestures. An alarming number of depressed adolescents commit suicide. Although suicide is rare before adolescence, in the teenage group it is a significant cause of death (44).

SUICIDE IN CHILDHOOD

Although suicide is rare in early childhood, it is the fifth cause of death in the 15 to 19 age group. Adolescents make 12% of all suicide attempts. Although more girl teenagers attempt suicide, boys are ten times as successful in killing themselves (62). Because suicidal boys are so efficient in killing themselves they are more rarely seen in psychiatric hospitals. In addition, the high incidence of auto accidents among boys may be in part due to self-destructive behavior. Accidents form the leading cause of death in this age group as well as in childhood.

Many suicidal attempts are "manipulations" directed against the parents as pleas for caring behavior as much as revenge. The following fantasy is frequent: "You will be sorry when I'm dead. You'll see how badly you treated me."

Other dynamisms of suicide include a dramatic call for help, a wish for a peaceful nirvana state as a release from painful anxiety, a desire to join a dead parent or other loved one, a reaction to hallucinatory commands.

Observations of certain Indian children in boarding schools as well as of the very poor black adolescents and white adolescents suggest that depressive reactions and suicidal behavior may be related to feelings of hopelessness of ever being competent or "making it" in a society where their parents in a poverty environment are seen as failures. Self-esteem is low as a consequence of lack of resources which might help them experience some success as well as the lack of adult models of success in society.

THE SUICIDAL PREOCCUPATIONS OF TOM SAWYER

Mark Twain has given us a good description of childhood melancholia in writing of the suicidal preoccupations of Tom Sawyer. This description of early adolescent thoughts seems so realistic that the author must certainly have been writing from personal experience.

Both Tom Sawyer and his author had experienced childhood bereavement. Since Tom lived with his Aunt Polly, we may assume he had experienced a separation or loss by death of both parents. There is no father in the household. Mark Twain's own father died when Twain was twelve. The family had moved because of the father's business failure when the author was four.

Tom's first suicidal fantasy occurred after "withdrawal of love" when he was unjustly punished by his aunt. Feeling hurt and deprived he reacted by thinking of death as a way to evoke tender feelings. He first thought of dying from sickness and then looked at the river with thoughts of drowning. He ended with a wish that he could die without discomfort.

The second suicidal fantasy followed a loss of love object when his girl friend, Becky Thatcher, had become engaged to him and then rejected his engagement token (a brass doorknob) when she learned by Tom's Freudian slip of the tongue that he had been engaged before. Tom ran away to the woods, with his "soul steeped with melancholy" and thought enviously of a boy who had recently died. He thought how Becky would be sorry when it was too late. Ah, if he could only die temporarily! He thought hopefully of a more reversible separation by running away to be a clown, a soldier, an Indian, or a pirate. He finally decided to be a pirate, and he was able to act out this fantasy by running off with his friends to an island to play pirate. The boys were assumed to be drowned, and Aunt Polly and Becky and the whole town mourned the loss of the boys. The climax occurred when the boys attended their own funeral.

Being aware of such dynamics, a fellow psychiatrist once managed to shock a patient out of a suicidal impulse by saying, "Remember this, you won't be around to read about it in the newspaper."

A DIAGNOSTIC SPECTRUM OF DEPRESSION ILLUSTRATED BY PERSONAL CLINICAL OBSERVATIONS

Marasmic-Anaclitic Depression Type

An infant in the hospital was dying of severe diarrhea in spite of nursing care, blood transfusions and intravenous fluids. The infant responded dramatically and recovered after the mother was allowed to hold her dying child. The mother had previously been prohibited from even visiting her child because of rigid rules at that time in the hospital communicable disease unit.

Autistic Type

A one and one-half year old, mute, withdrawn boy was unresponsive to humans and was preoccupied only with observing his fingers before his face. As the youngest child on the ward he received a great deal of "tender loving care" from the nurses. In six months, he became responsive and began to develop speech. Although he appeared clearly autistic on admission, his withdrawn behavior cleared up and the boy did not revert to autism even though his mother removed him and herself from therapy.

Marasmic Type

Only one marasmic patient has been seen on our child psychiatry ward. This child was admitted to the ward at the age of three and one half on an emergency basis because of serious failure to thrive. She had lost weight from 27 pounds to 18 pounds in the preceding three months. This small, weak, malnourished girl had a worried and depressed facial expression with an occasional grotesque smiling grimace. Her facial expression combined with a mannerism of constantly wringing her hands gave the child an appearance of a miniature adult with an agitated depression.

The parents had consulted a number of professionals in the preceding two years including several pediatricians, a psychiatrist, a college psychology department, a pediatrics department in a university medical center. The girl had even spent a month in a state psychiatric hospital. The parents were perplexed by the number of diagnoses they were given, which included deafness, mental deficiency, and autism.

The general medical history was unusual only in delayed motor development. The child held her head up at three months, sat at eight months, said "mama" and "dada" at one year, and did not walk alone until 20 months.

A more detailed chronological history of family events revealed a series of losses, separations, and a home environment reeking with mourning, melancholia, loneliness, isolation, and emotional distance. The father was a hard driving, tense, high-pressure salesman who gave little emotional support to a lonely and depressed mother. The father's work took him away from home more and more, and led the family to move when the child was six months old. In flying to their new home the child developed an upper respiratory infection with otitis media which was aggravated by the airplane trip. The previously placid child was quite fussy, and the mother was depressed and lonely because she knew no one in the new community, and the father's work kept him away from home. A few months after the move, the mother's mother died unexpectedly from pneumonia. On the anniversary of the death the maternal grandfather of the child came to stay in the home because he was still mourning and could not bear to be alone. There was little communication because the child's mother had never been close to her father. There was even a language barrier. This arrangement did not fulfill her need for companionship. The grandfather stayed in the same room as the child, who developed a serious sleep disturbance being awake and fussy most of the night. In two months the child had regressed so much that the pediatrician who had followed her decided she must be deaf and retarded. She was not interested in play and no longer vocalized.

When the girl was two years and nine months old the parents went on a trip and were away three days. (This was the only separation from the mother to that time.) On their return they found the girl quite disturbed. She had developed symptoms of breath holding (which alternated with hyperventilation), teeth grinding, crossing her eyes, and biting her hands. The symptoms were so extreme that she was admitted to a state hospital where she became worse. She did not seem to recognize her parents, which was seen as an abnormality rather than the usual reaction of children who are disturbed by separation. In the hospital, splints were placed on her arms to prevent hand biting. When the splints were removed, she had the mannerism of hand wringing so prominent on her admission to our ward. She would not use her hands otherwise.

In the five months she was on the children's ward, an attempt was made to provide tender loving care. Even with such efforts she responded only partially and had ups and downs of weight and also had periods of not walking. The parents were engaged in individual psychotherapy, which was interrupted by changes of therapists when the first therapist completed his period of training. The parents moved to another state where the father had an opportunity for advancement. Follow through was not possible. The child eventually entered an institution for mental retardation.

SELF-DESTRUCTIVE CHILDREN

Only one suicide has occurred on our ward when an extremely hostile, negativistic, aggressive, biting and scratching, provocative, eight year old girl drank cleaning solution from a toilet bowl. This may have represented delinquent, defiant, acting out behavior more than simply self-destruction or depression.

One child developed a cataract by poking repeatedly at his eye. Two boys attempted "self-castration" (one apparently identifying with a step-father with hypospadias, the other possibly having identified with a favored sister as a result of an ineffective father in a household of dominant females and the patient's rivalry with a more favored sister).

One head-banging child managed over a period of years on the ward to cause severe brain damage in spite of constant efforts by the staff to prevent this. His self-destructive activity started at age six when he witnessed the death of his grandfather from a heart attack. Apparently blaming himself, the boy beat his head against the wall when he was left at home while the family rushed off to the hospital. His feelings of loss were compounded when his father also died not long after this episode. Loss of important parental figures without much chance to mourn or be succored since mother was herself very depressed and isolated seemed an important aspect of his disorder.

A post-encephalitic child increased her self-destructive behavior when the previously mentioned boy left the ward. In spite of attentive protective nursing, she managed to knock out her front teeth, smash her nose, and develop cauliflower ears in addition to repeatedly inflicting less severe bruises and lacerations on herself and constantly biting and hitting nurses. Although her father was very effective in restraining her physically on her visits home, he occasionally lost his self-control and beat her. The mother was completely unable to restrain this self-destructive child or protect herself. The girl became quite self-destructive after kicking her mother in the stomach and causing an abortion. She gradually improved but continued to be very assaultive by biting, scratching, and hitting others as well as turning her aggression against herself.

In four such self-destructive children, I have observed a family constellation of a physically violent, punitive father and a mother who would stand by helplessly paralyzed and smiling grimly while her child beat his head against the wall or hit himself. I worked psychotherapeutically with one mother who vividly described how she would silently pray to God to give her the strength to stand her child's self-punishment. These mothers all had a characteristic smile which masked their feelings of despair.

I am sure these children are confused by their two parents' diametrically opposite behavior and one can only sympathize with the parents' extreme despair shown by the mother's helpless withdrawal from the child or the father's desperate punishing behavior when confronted by their violent and self-destructive child. The genesis of the child's parents' behavior can often be tied to unresolved unconscious conflicts, which result in circular, unsatisfactory, interpersonal relationships and their behavioral consequences.

The dynamics of depression in these cases may be considered to include "identification with the aggressor" father resulting in self-punishment as an attempt to elicit a response from the withdrawn helplessly detached mother, who is paralyzed in her responsiveness by her own conflicts about nondestructive expression of anger and self-assertion. This is of course an assumption with no direct verbal behavioral confirmation from the patient.

Such children are reassured and gradually improve in behavior when therapists and nurses patiently and persistently prevent self-injury, and thus act in ways that enhance the child's feeling of being loved. These children relax when one actively restrains them from self-destruction, making clear that one will not permit their self-destructive act. Such children are then gradually able to enjoy the physical closeness they crave but cannot allow themselves to seek directly.

It is very difficult working with such self-destructive children but gratifying to see them improve. One such child who was on the ward for six years was finally not self-destructive at all. For many months she would stand at the door of the ward, greeting and threatening everyone who entered with her right hand filled with saliva and her left hand stuck in the door jam, in an effort to trick staff members into injuring her fingers. The fact that she did not manage to lose any fingers attests to the great agility and carefulness of the staff. (The staff was particularly careful as a result of experience with another child who had lost part of a finger by similar behavior.) Her depressive reaction had increased each year as the addition of a new younger sibling displaced her increasingly further from her mother's already meager ability to provide emotionally sustaining interactions that were age appropriate and mutually satisfying.

DEPRESSIONS IN ADOLESCENCE

The author has worked therapeutically with three suicidal boys under the age of fourteen who had certain features in common. One had made two suicidal attempts by attempting to hang himself. In each case there was a close tie to a mother who was ambitious, controlling, and who had high hopes for her child's achievement. The mother in each case was strongly tied emotionally to the boy because of absence of the father. One of the fathers had died, one had divorced and left when the boy was four, and the third father was in the home but was quite involved in his work and was away most nights, and was also emotionally detached from mother and child. This last mentioned father was alcoholic, and the boy stole champagne and drank himself unconscious when his mother threatened divorce. By the age of twenty this particular boy had become a heroin addict and was arrested for smuggling drugs across the border from Mexico. The latter boy had a school disability, the previously mentioned two were A students who experienced feelings of failure when they got B's. One of the suicide attempts mentioned above followed a straight A report card which made the boy feel he was unworthy of such good grades. Later he had feelings of depersonalization and self-doubts. He felt he could not be sure whether two and two really equaled four even though he was earning A's in advanced mathematics. Although this boy improved with psychotherapy, he had a later depressive reaction requiring hospitalization when his mother died of cancer.

In working with this mother in concomitant psychotherapy it had been found that she herself had made a suicide attempt a year before and also had suspected that her own father had died by suicide. Statistics show that depression and suicide tend to run in families, but such familial suicidal behavior may be learned rather than inherited in nature.

DEPRESSIVE EQUIVALENTS IN PSYCHOSOMATIC ILLNESSES

A number of clinical conditions have been considered as depressive equivalents (24, 56). Some examples include aggressive behavior (12), headache (46), hyperkinesis (63), and poor school performance (37). Many other clinical situations may be equivalents to depressions as well as expressing other conflict states. Some of these may be described in the following ways.

In anorexia nervosa a depressed teenage girl may commit suicide by starving herself to death.

Obesity may be a depressive equivalent in which there is a vicious cycle of low self-esteem, depressed feeling, increased eating, and increasingly low self-esteem (44).

Other psychosomatic illnesses have been described as manifesting depressive symbolism.

In asthma a depressive aspect is implicit in the analogy of the bronchial constriction symbolizing a suppressed cry for mother.

In arthritis the body symbolism has been dramatically described as repressed grief causing "weeping into the joints."

Since eczema occurs typically on the flexor surfaces, it has been considered symbolic of a wish to embrace and has been treated successfully by providing cuddling and "tender loving care." The eczema makes the child repulsive to the mother and she responds with lack of cuddling, so a vicious cycle of interpersonal repulsion and withdrawal occurs.

In the case of frequent colds the weeping of mucous membranes may be somatization of depressed affect.

The self-hurtful aspects of depression may take the form of accident proneness which may be a form of partial or even successful suicide. Head banging is an overt depressive, self-destructive activity. Teeth grinding may represent depressive aggression turned to the self. (There is the classic example of a man cured of night teeth grinding by hypnosis who then tried to strangle his wife.)

There may be various physiological reactions to separation. It has been noted that schizophrenic children on a psychiatric ward may seem indifferent to their parents' leaving them. In some such children acetone was found in their urine which seemed to be related to mourning behavior expressed as failure to eat and drink which caused dehydration and acidosis and consequently the appearance of urinary acetone. One child with periodontal disease had spikes in his white blood count repeatedly on separation from his parents on the ward following weekends home. This seemed related to the grief reaction to separation from the parents. No physical cause was found except the dental condition.

PRACTICAL APPLICATIONS

Awareness of depressive etiology in childhood makes it possible to prevent or modify depressions by certain practical interventions. Some examples follow:

In placing a child for adoption it is well to place the child with adoptive parents as early as possible. It was once commonplace to keep babies in hospitals for one year for psychological testing and for observation to rule out mental deficiency. After such a year of hospitalization, mental retardation was frequent as a result of "hospitalism."

The provision of rooming-in service in obstetric services can provide early mothering to the child and an opportunity for the mother to learn to deal with her baby in a hospital setting where she can feel more secure in the presence of concerned and attuned professionals and can be helped with her uncertainties.

It is important that elective surgery be scheduled for the optimal time developmentally. Emergency surgery should be done as medically indicated plus providing "psychological first aid." The basic principle is to prepare the child to know what to expect and to provide continued presence of the mother after surgery. It is unfortunately still a frequent practice to deceive children by not letting them know about surgery in advance, and strict hospital visiting hours may keep mothers away.

Maternal bereavement predisposes to adult depression. It is good preventive medicine wherever and whenever possible to make sure that every child has an adequate mother or mother substitute and to provide help to young mothers stressed by bereavement so they may involve themselves more with their infants to their mutual gratification.

Mentally defective children who are raised at home have been found to be more physically active and to have IQ's that are about 30% higher than retarded children hospitalized early (15). Therefore, it is preferable to keep retarded children at home if at all possible even when it seems likely that it will be necessary to hospitalize them eventually.

One may expect to find signs of depression with any somatic illness. The doctor-patient relationship or other supportive relationships can provide needed emotional support during a difficult period.

In the course of psychotherapy one may anticipate a patient's over-reaction to change of appointment or a vacation of the therapist which reactivates feelings of rejection or abandonment. Awareness and discussion of the patient's feelings of this sort may lead to insight and reduction of disturbance and disability in similar associated depressive dynamisms. The general application of such principles as the above may in the long run have an impact on enhancing public mental health that extends far beyond the psychiatric influence of direct work with individual patients.

SUMMARY

An infant's response to loss of maternal nurturance is the prototype of a mourning or grief reaction and (in embryological analogy) forms a primordial anlage for depressive reactions of later life. We have probably all experienced to some extent the protest-despair-detachment reactions observed when infants are separated from their mothers. Such reactions may be re-experienced in later life around the death or departure of loved ones or in contemplation of one's own death.

The prototype for the loss of self-esteem so typical of melancholia or depression in adults may be observed in a child's repeated and hostile reaction to loss of parental approval when the parents' disapproval is incorporated to become lack of self-approval or loss of self-esteem.

Such experiences of object loss and lowered self-esteem in childhood may predispose to depressive reactions in later life which are precipitated by personal object loss or loss of self-esteem which may be experienced when the extent of one's achievements fails to reach the level of one's aspirations.

The clinical form of a depressive reaction varies considerably with age and the developmental differences between infancy, childhood, adolescence, and adulthood.

The form and magnitude of a depressive reaction is also dependent on the bodily substrate and there are important reciprocal influences between somatic factors and interpersonal relations such as loss or withdrawal of love objects and intrapersonal conflicts which lead to lowered self-esteem. The overlapping interrelationships of intrapersonal, interpersonal, and somatic factors may be represented by three overlapping circles with arrows going both ways between each to emphasize mutual reciprocal influences. This is analogous to a color wheel in the shape of a Boolean algebra Venn Diagram to indicate variations in the depressive diagnostic spectrum. Important physiological factors involved in depressive reactions include hormonal effects, electrolyte balance, electrochemical aspects of neural synapse transmission, genetic influences, and the effects of certain drugs which may produce or relieve depressive symptoms by acting on one or more of these sites.

There is clinical and statistical evidence that childhood experiences of parental loss may have profound effects even to the extent of death in the severe loss of maternal nurturance seen in hospitalism. There is also clinical and statistical evidence that such childhood experiences may predispose to depression and suicide in adult life. There are animal experimental findings supporting such clinical evidence in recent work with monkeys in which it has been demonstrated that even brief separation from the mother may produce measurable long term behavioral changes which bear some resemblance to human depressive reactions.

Awareness of the importance of experiential factors in predisposing to

THE DIAGNOSTIC SPECTRUM OF DEPRESSIVE REACTIONS
REPRESENTED IN THE FORM OF A BOOLEAN ALGEBRA VENN DIAGRAM
ANALOGOUS TO A COLOR WHEEL.

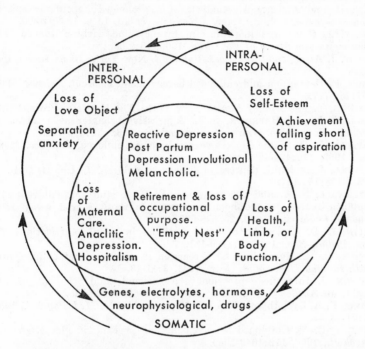

The overlapping circles indicate the interrelationships of the interpersonal, intrapersonal, and somatic components of depression. The arrows indicate the reciprocal influences between interpersonal, intrapersonal, and somatic factors.

and precipitating depressive reactions provides the opportunity to make effective prophylactic or preventative and therapeutic interventions in certain life situations.

REFERENCES

1. ANTHONY, J. and SCOTT, P. Manic-depressive psychosis in childhood. *Child Psychology and Psychiatry*, 1960, 1:53-72.
2. BAKWIN, H. Emotional deprivation in infants. *J. Pediatrics*, 1940, 35:512-521.
3. BAKWIN, H. Loneliness in infants. *American Journal of Diseases of Children*, 1942, 63:30-40.
4. BARRETT, A. M. Manic-depressive psychoses in childhood. *Int. Clin.*, 1931, 3(41):205-217.

5. BARTON-HALL, M. Our present knowledge about manic-depressive states in childhood. *Nerv. Child.*, 1952, 9:319-325.

6. BECK, A. T., SETHI, B. B. and TUTHILL, R. W. Childhood bereavement and adult depression. *Arch. Gen. Psychiat.*, 1963, 9:295-302.

7. BERES, D. and ALPERT, A. Analysis of a prolonged hypomanic episode in a five-year-old child. *Amer. J. Orthopsychiat.*, 1940, 10:794-800.

8. BOWLBY, J. Grief and mourning in infancy and early childhood. *The Psychoanalytic Study of the Child*, 1960, 15:9-53.

9. BOWLBY, J. *Attachment and Loss. Volume I.* New York: Basic Books, Inc., 1969.

10. BROWN, F. Depression and childhood bereavement. *J. Ment. Science*, 1961, 107:754-777.

11. BULFINCH, T. *The Age of Fables.* New York: The Heritage Press, 1942.

12. BURKS, H. L. and HARRISON, S. L. Aggressive behavior as a means of avoiding depression. *Am. J. Orthopsychiat.*, 1962, 32:416-422.

13. CAMPBELL, J. D. Manic-depressive psychoses in children. *J. Nerv. Ment. Dis.*, 1952, 116:424-439.

14. CAMPBELL, J. D. Manic-depressive disease in children. *J. Am. Med. Assn.*, 1955, 158:154-157.

15. CENTERWALL, S. A. and CENTERWALL, W. R. A study of children with Mongolism reared in the home compared to those reared away from the home. *Pediatrics*, 1960, 25:678-685.

16. CHAPIN, H. D. A plea for accurate statistics in infants' institutions. *Tr. Am. Pediat. Soc.*, 1915, 27:180-181.

17. CRONICK, C. H. Manic-depressive reaction in an 8-year-old child. *Quart. Bull. Indiana Univ. Med. Cent.*, 1941, 3:11-13.

18. DAVIDSON, J. Infantile depression in a "normal child." *Journal of The American Academy of Child Psychiatry*, 1968, 7:522-535.

19. DELMAS, F. A. Cyclothymia in a boy 16-years-old. *Am. Med. Psychol.*, 1937, 95:71-75.

20. DENNEHY, C. M. Childhood bereavement and psychiatric illness. *Brit. J. Psychiat.*, 1966, 112:1049-1069.

21. DORPAT, T. L., JACKSON, J. J. and RIPLEY, H. S. Broken homes and attempted and completed suicide. *Arch. Gen. Psychiat.*, 1965, 12:213-216.

22. DUSSIK, K. T. Manic-depressive psychosis in an 11-year-old child coupled with hereditary endocrine taint. *Psychiat. Neurol. Wehnsehr.*, 1934, 36: 305.

23. ENGEL, G. L. and REICHSMAN, F. Spontaneous and experimentally induced depression in an infant with a gastric fistula. *J. Amer. Psychoanal. Assn.*, 1956, 4:428-452.

24. EWALT, J. R. Somatic equivalents of depression. *Texas State Journal of Medicine*, 1964, 60:654-658.

25. FORREST, A. D., FRASER, R. H. and PRIEST, R. G. Environmental factors in depressive illness. *Brit. J. Psychiat.*, 1965, 111:243-253.

26. FREUD, S. Mourning and melancholia. In *Collected Papers*, Vol. IV. London: Hogarth, 1946.

27. GRANVILLE-GROSSMAN, K. L. The early environment in affective disorder. In A. Coppen and A. Walk (Eds.), *Recent Developments in Affective Disorders*: A Symposium. Special Publication No. 2, British Journal of Psychiatry, London: Headly and Brothers, 1967. Pp. 65-79.

28. GREER, S. The relationship between parental loss and attempted suicide: A control study. *British Journal of Psychiatry*, 1964, 110:698-705.

29. GREER, S. Parental loss and attempted suicide: A further report. *British Journal of Psychiatry*, 1966, 112:465-470.

30. GREGORY, M. S. A case of manic-depressive psychosis in a child. *J. Nerv. Dis.*, 1914, 41:41-44.
31. GREGORY, I. Studies of parental deprivation in psychiatric patients. *Am. J. Psychiat.*, 1958, 115:432-442.
32. HARLOW, H. F. and SUOMI, S. J. Induced psychopathology in monkeys. *Engineering and Science*, 1970, 33:8-14.
33. HARMS, E. The problem of depressive and manic sickness in childhood. *Nerv. Child.*, 1952, 9:310-316.
34. HARMS, E. Differential pattern of manic-depressive disease in childhood. *Nerv. Child.*, 1952, 9:326-356.
35. HERODOTUS. An account of Egypt. *The Harvard Classics*, New York: P. F. Collier and Son, 1910, 33:7-8.
36. HINDE, R. A. and SPENCER-BOOTH, Y. Effects of brief separation from mother on Rhesus monkeys. *Science*, 1971, 173:111-118.
37. HOLLON, T. H. Poor school performance as symptom of masked depression in children and adolescents. *Amer. J. Psychother.*, 1970, 25:258-263.
38. HUDGENS, R. W., MORRISON, J. R., and BARCHHA, R. G. Life events and onset of primary affective disorders. *Arch. Gen. Psychiat.*, 1967, 16:134-145.
39. JANOTA, O. On manifestations of manic-depressive psychosis in childhood. *Neurol. Psychiat. Ces.*, 1948, 10:1-12.
40. KASANIN, J. The affective psychoses in children. *Amer. J. Psychiat.*, 1931, 10:897-926.
41. KAUFMAN, I. C. and ROSENBLUM, L. A. Depression in infant monkeys separated from their mothers. *Science*, 1967, 155:1030-1031.
42. KAUFMAN, I. C. and ROSENBLUM, L. A. The reaction to separation in infant monkeys; anaclitic depression and conservation-withdrawal. *Psychosom. Med.*, 1967, 29:648-675.
43. KRAEPELIN, E. Manic-depressive insanity and paranoia. Livingstone, Edinburgh, 1921, as cited by Arieti, S. in *American Handbook of Psychiatry*. New York: Basic Books, 1959. P. 437.
44. LANGDELL, J. I. A psychiatric approach to obesity in childhood and adolescence. In S. A. Szurek and I. N. Berlin (Eds.), *The Langley Porter Child Psychiatry Series*. Palo Alto: Science and Behavior Books, Inc., 1968, Vol. 3:118-128.
45. LEVY, D. M. Primary affect hunger. *Amer. J. Psychiatry*, 1937, 94:643-652.
46. LING, W., OFTEDAL, G. and WEINBERG, W. Depressive illness in childhood presenting as severe headache. *Am. J. Dis. Child.*, 1970, 120:122-124.
47. MCHARG, J. F. Mania in childhood. *A. M. A. Arch. Neurol. Psychiat.*, 1954, 72:531-539.
48. MCKINNEY, W. T. and BUNNEY, W. E., JR. Animal model of depression. *Arch. Gen. Psychiat.*, 1969, 21:240-248.
49. MCKINNEY, W. T., JR., SUOMI, S. J. and HARLOW, H. F. Depression in primates. *American Journal of Psychiatry*, 1971, 127:1313-1320.
50. MORISON, T. C. Case of mania in a child six years old. *J. Psychol. Med.*, 1948, 1:317.
51. PITTS, F. N., JR., MEYER, J., BROOKS, M., ET AL. Adult psychiatric illness assessed for childhood parental loss and psychiatric illness in family members—a study of 748 patients and 250 controls. *Am. J. Psychiat.*, 1965, 121:i-x.
52. SALIMBENE OF PARMA. The Emperor Frederich II. In *The Portable Medieval Reader*. Ross, J. B. and McLaughlin, M. M. (Eds.). New York: The Viking Press, 1949. Pp. 366-367.

53. SCHACHTER, M. The cyclothymic states in the prepubescent child. *Nerv. Child.*, 1952, 9:357-362.
54. SCHAEFER, H. H. Can a mouse commit suicide? In E. S. Schneidman (Ed.), *Essays in Self-Destruction.* New York: Science House Inc., 1967. Pp. 494-509.
55. SENAY, E. C. Toward an animal model of depression. A study of separation behavior in dogs. *J. Psychiat. Res.*, 1966, 4:65-71.
56. SPERLING, M. Equivalents of depression in children. *J. Hillside Hospital*, 1959, 8:138-148.
57. SPITZ, R. A. Hospitalism. *The Psychoanalytic Study of the Child*, 1945, 1:53-74.
58. SPITZ, R. A. Hospitalism, A follow up report. *The Psychoanalytic Study of the Child*, 1946, 2:113-117.
59. SPITZ, R. A. Anaclitic depression. *Psychoanalytic Study of the Child.* New York: Int. Univ. Press, 1946, 2:313-342.
60. SPITZ, R. A. *The First Year of Life.* New York: International Universities Press, 1965. Pp. 268-277.
61. SPITZ, R. A. *The First Year of Life.* New York: International Universities Press, 1965. Pp. 277-284.
62. TOOLAN, J. M. Depression in children and adolescents. *Am. J. Orthopsychiat.*, 1962, 32:404-415.
63. ZRULL, J. P., ET AL. Hyperkinetic syndrome: The role of depression. *Child Psychiatry and Human Development*, 1970, 1:33-40.

9

Elements of Psychotherapeutics with the Schizophrenic Child and His Parents

S. A. Szurek, M.D.
and
I. N. Berlin, M.D.

The therapeutic approach of the Children's Service of the Langley Porter Clinic to those severe mental disorders known as schizophrenia, autism, psychosis, and atypical development is based on the hypothesis that these disorders are entirely psychogenic (6, 7, 8). The approach consists of simultaneous psychotherapeutic work with the child and both parents— a method which permits research into the psychopathology and etiology of the disorder, and also provides a therapeutic test of the psychogenic hypothesis.

EVALUATION OF HYPOTHESIS ON ETIOLOGY AND PSYCHOPATHOLOGY OF CHILDHOOD PSYCHOSES

Before we describe our experiences with such therapy, we should like to sum up, all too briefly, the ideas on etiology and psychopathology and the general therapeutic principles which have grown out of nine years of staff experience with over one hundred families in which the disorder of the child either was episodic or was a continuous psychotic maldevelopment (9). These ideas are based both on Freud's concepts and on the ideas advanced by more recent students (9) of the psychopathology of the schizophrenic disorder. They may be briefly outlined as follows.

Reprinted from Szurek, S. A. & Berlin, I. N. Elements of Psychotherapeutics with the Schizophrenic Child and His Parents. *Psychiatry: Journal for the Study of Interpersonal Processes*, 1956, 19(1).

In these disorders, repression of sensual or libidinal impulses—particularly of the earliest pregenital phases of development—arising from continuing incorporation and introjection of, identification with, and futile rebellion against, the disorder of both parents, is much more severe and more generalized than in the milder disorders known as the transference neuroses. This quantitatively greater degree of repression results in a dynamic state with the following describable aspects:

(1) An extremely tenacious libidinous fixation, rather than regression, of the sensual impulses of many modalities and zones characteristic of this period of life, but especially of the oral impulses. Irregular regression, however, does occur in the episodic form of the disorder.

(2) An extreme sadomasochistic distortion of these sensual impulses.

(3) A strong tendency for these distorted impulses to break through into overt action.

(4) The use of a disproportionate amount of the organism's energy in such self-defeating conflicts, leaving less energy available for the progressive learning of skills which maturation makes possible. Such learning is, of course, necessary for the independent seeking and obtaining of satisfactions of biologically essential urges.

In other words, integration, the executive ego organization, is weak. Since survival demands that the ego defend itself against the dangers of the destructively distorted libidinous impulses, the clinical picture is predominantly one of a negativistic attitude—a self-prohibition of the child's own drives, and, hence, of impulses toward contact with others.

Thus the overt withdrawal is the consequence of these internal psychodynamics, since impulses for contact imply inevitable repetition of previously experienced frustrations and disappointments. Frustration is inevitable for at least two reasons: First, the child internalizes the obstacles to, and the fears of, the satisfaction of these impulses for contact with other persons. Second, since the child can express his impulses for sensual contact only in the distorted form of revengeful or self-destructive behavior, retaliation from others is as inevitable as from the self.

Simultaneous therapeutic work with the child and his parents has, we believe, a number of advantages. For example, it may make it possible to achieve results in a shorter time than would be required for therapy with the child alone—a possibility which we have not critically tested, however. We have also experimented with having one therapist work with the entire family, a procedure undertaken because of various considerations, including shortage of time and the obstacles to unambivalent collaboration among different therapists working with a single family. We now feel that this can be a rewarding training experience, and offer it to all psychiatric fellows in training.

We have found progressively more parents willing to undertake such simultaneous psychotherapeutic work with us; some are eager, with a sense of an opportunity to resolve some of their own personality problems, as well as with a hope that the family as a whole will achieve an easier life in the future. Of course, even with the initially eager parents, problems of therapy implicit in transference and resistance inevitably appear.

THERAPY WITH THE PSYCHOTIC CHILD

The therapist's self-awareness, his attention to his internal processes—which does not interfere with, and in fact is consonant with, his equal attention to the patient—is his chief tool in work with schizophrenic children who are mute, autistic, regressed, or sadomasochistically aggressive. Freud first described the evenly hovering attentiveness of the therapist as essential in the psychoanalytic—that is, the *conflict-reductive*—process, as differentiated from any other efforts in therapy, such as those directed toward symptoms. Such attentiveness, refined if possible, is the essence of work with schizophrenic children as well as with their parents. This attentiveness can be described as both vigilant and relaxed: depending on what is therapeutically indicated, it may be a readiness to restrain destructive behavior; or it may be an 'active' inaction, as in silent, 'accepting,' 'permissive' behavior, which may be at once observing and interpretive. Relaxed attentiveness will permit, with repetition and in time, accurate observation of all details in every sequence of behavior, whether manifested in speech, sound, movement, or in any observable visceral changes. Such careful, regular observation of all details in every sequence of behavior and of any variations in a given pattern of behavior eventually may make sequences understandable to the therapist. Holt (2) has said, "A wish is a motor set to action," and has noted that close, careful, sequential study of action, even in the absence of speech, may elucidate motivation, which is the essence of psychological study. Moreover, close observation of persons with mental disorder can reveal *conflicting* motivation, which is the goal of psychotherapeutic work. It is thus that behavior heretofore regarded as unexpected, sudden, and without warning may eventually become predictable and capable of being anticipated; this has been the case with some of those patients with whom we have worked for three or more years.

The importance of the use of physical restraint to prevent action disintegrative to the patient's welfare and to the progress of therapy has been noted by Pious (4), Wexler (10, 11), Rosen (5), Knight (3), and others in their work with adult and adolescent schizophrenic patients. Our experience with psychotic children corroborates this observation. We feel that it is essential in the initial phases of work with children to prevent any revengefully destructive or masochistically libidinal behavior which would lead to guilt, fear of retaliation, massive anxiety about the consequences of the behavior, and further defiance. It should be noted, of course, that some children show no inclination to hostile, aggressive behavior; or, even though they may show it with some adults, do not do so in the therapeutic situation.

We wish to emphasize that restraint which proceeds from any impulse of the therapist of revenge for being hurt—which would be suppressive, a mere demonstration of greater power, or mere domination—would not be therapeutically effective. The restraint which is therapeutically effective is that restraint which is always clearly adapted to the actual reality of the patient's behavior at the moment, and of such quality that it does not interfere with further therapy. In short, its purpose is only to help the patient to learn to discriminate between internal conflict and the external reality of the therapeutic situation, and to learn how impulses may be expressed nondestructively. Parenthetically, the therapist's readiness to behave with a firmness which is free from any secondary narcissism reduces the chances of his being hurt and guilty and thus adds to his greater ease and attentiveness. Such ease contributes to the effectiveness of the therapeutic process in still another way. The schizophrenic is particularly sensitive to any ambivalent tensions in another person. In such situations the patient tends to project one or another aspect—superego or id impulses—of his own conflicts. He then tends to become frightened, to resist, and thus to get involved in a circular way in any such countertransference elements, or unresolved conflicts, of the therapist's reactions, even though these reactions in a way have nothing to do with the patient or with the mutual purpose of the therapeutic work.

If the child's hostile, aggressive behavior is prevented or adequately restrained, he usually appears relieved. He then often settles into some regressive sensual, usually oral, activity, such as sucking on a bottle, or rocking peacefully and singing, or contentedly rubbing various parts of his own body, often with guarded looks at the therapist to see if he will become uneasy and interrupt such self-gratification. After sufficient self-gratification of this sort, the child will often begin to play with the toys in the therapy room.

Thus the child identifies with the behavior of the therapist who, with little or no anxiety, attends to the expression of all of the child's impulses, prevents destructive behavior, and permits sensual self-gratification. Progressively resolving his conflicts, the child slowly learns to restrain himself. This usually comes about only after many repetitions of destructive behavior which, during the progress of therapy, is generally found to be secondary to the child's self-frustration and to his anxiety about his distorted impulses. He also learns to attend sooner to his own impulses, and finds that they can be experienced in the therapist's presence at first in self-absorbed self-gratification, later in play or in speech. Energy thus gradually released from conflict is freed for learning, and not merely used in blind, unreasoning identification with the therapist. The child begins to learn, with whatever genetically given capacities he has, from his unique developmental history and particular current life situations, with progressively greater freedom from retaliatory anxiety, and hence, with greater spontaneity and creativity.

We wish to emphasize that this initial phase—in which prevention of destructive acting-out in the therapeutic situation *may* be characteristic— is *only* a first step. It is an essential step which makes possible the subsequent, more thoroughly systematic process of working through the details of the conflict solutions of the patient—which is often the only kind of work done with the milder, transference-neurotic disorder. The following is an example of this sequence in therapy.

> The patient was a silent, alternately fearful and assaultive eight-year-old boy. At various times, he had made every effort to destroy clothes —his own and the staff's—to break eyeglasses of the staff, to set fires, and to jam locks, plumbing, and electrical fixtures. He had once cut his own penis. For many therapeutic hours he engaged in outbursts which necessitated physical restraint to quiet him down. After each period of effective restraint, he would rock contentedly and hum to himself. After eleven months of such repetitive behavior, the therapist learned the signs of incipient anxiously hostile, aggressive behavior, and a word would prevent the boy's eruption into action in the previously unexpected, lightning-like way. The boy would rock and hum for a while and then go on to engage in play or building activities. As these hostile eruptions continued to be anticipated, the boy began, when he felt tense, to seek out members of the regular nursing staff who knew how to work with him, or, if they were not around, the therapist on the ward. Gradually, as his destructive behavior decreased, his attitude in his work in therapy and on the ward changed markedly. There were increasingly shorter regressions to the previous behavior.

While aggressive, hostile behavior often occurs as the initial phase in therapy, some children are at first inactive and withdrawn, but later engage in destructive acting-out, as shown by the following example.

The patient was an almost silent, frozen-faced four-year-old boy. At home he destroyed all household furniture not bolted down, and repeatedly tried to poke his mother's eyes out and to assault his little sister. He spent the first several treatment hours in silent, isolated, immobile contemplation of the toys. As he tentatively touched the toys, the therapist named them. Hours later the child hesitatingly repeated the name of each toy after the therapist.

Following an hour in which the patient made the first tentative physical contact with the therapist, he hurled all of the blocks and toys at the therapist. This was halted by the therapist, who firmly held the child until he relaxed. On release, the boy halfheartedly threw a few more blocks at the therapist, and was again restrained for a few moments.

In the next few hours the child had screaming, kicking tantrums at the end of each hour when not permitted to take the toys back to the ward. The therapist would sit quietly with him and restrain him only when it appeared that he might injure himself. After a short time the therapist would firmly lead him to the ward, and on each occasion the boy relaxed. These tantrums diminished in intensity during the next four sessions. Then during one hour the child picked up a toy plane and began hesitatingly to fly it. At the therapist's motor noises he began to zoom the plane. Several hours later he began one day to drop the plane; the therapist's vocal "crash—bang" seemed to reduce the patient's anxiety and thus to encourage increased vigor and pleasure in the crashing to the therapist's accompanying sounds. Following this hour the boy said for the first time at the ward door, "Goodbye, Dr. B, see you later."

Work with the withdrawn, isolated, mute, and regressed schizophrenic child for us consists of all efforts which help the child to find that the autism is no longer necessary as a defensively revengeful reaction to dealing with inner and outer frustration. Betz (1) describes the process as "breaking through the autistic barrier." We prefer to say that the barrier gradually dissolves through the therapist's efforts at 'being with' the child—his efforts to become attuned to, and to understand what the impulses of the child are, however he expresses them. After sufficiently long experience with the child, when the therapist feels that he is beginning to understand the unexpressed or indirectly expressed impulses, he actively, vocally demonstrates to the self-absorbed, indifferent child his attentiveness and efforts to understand and follow the child. The therapist may offer tentative speculations about the feelings of the child, and now and then the child's reactions may confirm the therapist's guesses. These speculations, when correct, may indicate to the child a way out of his own circular impasses.

The following excerpts from case histories are illustrative of these processes—the ways in which the therapist can initially try simply to become attuned to the child, and later on can offer tentative speculations about the child's feelings.

When the therapist joined in the throaty growl of a five-year-old schizophrenic girl, she moved close to him for the first time. The growling together went on for parts of many hours, the girl participating in a way which was at first half-frightened and angry, and later joyful.

The patient was a schizophrenic boy, mute except for frequent apparently meaningless noises. During an hour with the boy, the therapist began to rock in unison with him, trying at the same time to imitate closely his anxious vocalizations. As the therapist did so, he recognized for the first time how close the boy's noises were to words such as *yes*, *no*, and *maybe*. In succeeding hours, as the therapist matched these words to the boy's vocalizations, the boy would occasionally seem to confirm the accuracy of the therapist's guesses by sudden, hearty, relieved laughter, followed by bodily relaxation and contented humming. This mute boy finally began to say words to a tutor and to his parents, to mouth words with the therapist, and to nod first tentative and later vigorous assent or dissent in response to the therapist's associations to all the nonverbal clues during the hours. In recent months he has begun to whisper, "Yes," when the therapist has accurately expressed his feelings verbally.

The patient, a silent, adolescent schizophrenic girl, was often sexually exhibitionistic in a tense and bizarre way. She was slovenly in appearance, untidy about toilet habits and about her menstrual flow, and given to occasional eating of garbage. After many therapeutic hours during which she was completely withdrawn, she began to lift her skirts, touch the therapist's foot, and occasionally giggle. The therapist eventually expressed to her his speculations about her wishes to grow up—wishes which were defiant and yet fearful—to have close, warm sexual experiences, and thus to have some sense of being equal to her own biological maturity. He also suggested that whenever she felt frightened and disappointed about these wishes, this resulted in biting, sucking, devouring impulses during her clouded, isolated, almost fugue-like episodes. After many of these tentatively offered interpretations at timely moments, a change appeared in her behavior. Instead of engaging in sudden outbursts of murderous fury, or immobile standing for hours on one foot, she became more spontaneous and responsive, and began to talk and to take greater care of herself. Eventually, this slovenly appearing girl became quite fastidious about her appearance. Finally, after four and one-half years of hospitalization, she was able to return home to school and eventually to marry. We have recently learned that she has become pregnant.

COUNTERTRANSFERENCE PROBLEMS

The therapist's own internal interferences with his full attention—that is, his conflicts—which sometimes occur in response to the withdrawal and self-absorption of the child, may be reacted to by the child with characteristic symptomatic behavior. Sometimes a sudden outburst of sadomasochistic fury is followed by a sulky, withdrawn look-what-you-made-me-do expression on the child's countenance. After such experiences the therapist recognizes earlier his contribution to the 'sudden outburst.'

> For example, on one occasion momentary self-preoccupation by the therapist resulted in the child patient's promptly sweeping all the finger-paint jars to the floor, spattering both child and therapist with the paint. The therapist immediately expressed regret for his lapse and annoyance that the patient had to react in such a way, and at this the frozen-faced child became a wildly weeping one. When the therapist, starting to clean up the mess alone, invited the child to help make things right, the child became calmer and eagerly worked at the cleaning in a more integrated fashion than anyone had previously observed her behave.

While so far we have discussed treatment in terms of the therapist, we would also like to say a word about the ward personnel. For the ward nurse, 'being with' the child patient means attending to him in all his activities; offering him nonsexual body contact and cuddling, so long as he, not the nurse, needs it; and standing by during periods of calm self-absorption and self-gratification. She offers contact after disappointments, during times of revengefully anxious isolation, and during periods when the child is anxiously rocking, twirling objects in his hands, or masturbating. She attempts always to recognize quickly the unspoken disappointments and the frustrating situations, so that the child may be helped through them to some more successful solution. An essential part of her work is helping the child with the minute details of self-care day after day, month after month, until he achieves satisfaction from being able to care for himself and from beginning to participate in school and ward activities.

As the child begins to experience satisfactions from doing things for himself, he seems to have fewer of the silent disappointments and frustrations which result in withdrawal or in tantrums directed toward himself or others. Greater ego integration results from the child's learning of skills; he becomes more self-reliant, and the ambivalent dependency and the dangerous vulnerability to inevitable disappointments are reduced. As he feels better, safer, and prouder of his own abilities, one might say that his primary narcissism is increased and he is able to live and learn to live with others.

A few staff members who have worked with these patients for a long time have had the experience of seeing a child whom they have patiently but firmly helped over many, many months gradually become able to take care of himself and to participate in ward activities, and finally to behave in accordance with his chronological age and somatically matured capacities.

WORK WITH PARENTS

In work with parents of schizophrenic children, we have come to recognize the schizoid, obsessional part of each parent's personality, which is often not immediately obvious. That is, we have come to recognize the ways in which the parent is frozen and conflicted about the expression of *childlike* feelings, simple and spontaneous feelings of sensuality, sexuality, tenderness, self-considerateness, anger, and the like. The regressive behavior of the parents—consequence of repression of such spontaneity within themselves and with each other—and especially their helplessness with the child, indicates the severity of their own conflicts. Each of the parents of a child —although one sometimes more than the other—unconsciously seeks, and with frozen horror defends himself against, the satisfaction, in relation to the child, of his own regressive and dangerous infantile libidinous needs, which are not satisfied with his mate. Such highly ambivalent parental attitudes are thus funneled into the schizophrenic child's experience. Such satisfactions, repressed and rationalized, cannot be fulfilled for the parent by the child, who himself requires parental equanimity, steadiness, and executive ability in order to learn to acquire skills essential to growth— that is, to satisfying and productive living. The parent cannot help the child learn what he himself has never learned, or what he has lost because thwarting in his current life has led to intensification of his conflict, with consequent regression.

The therapeutic task with parents also centers around helping them to liberate themselves from the tyranny of their own circular, unconscious conflicts about repressed, distorted libidinal impulses. As in therapy with the child, we have learned the importance of attending to every detail of the parents' speech and behavior, and of even accepting silence with unanxious silence. The therapist's nonanxious, noncoercive attentiveness to the expression of all feelings helps the parents to begin to say more of what is in awareness.

Often the parent has a characteristic mode of discharging tension from repressed libidinal impulses in the therapeutic situation—for instance, by smoking, by chewing gum, by facial or bodily movements, or by silent visceral tensions. After the therapeutic relationship has been sufficiently established, the therapist may suggest that the parent attempt voluntarily to control such activities so that the underlying unconscious impulses may come into conscious awareness and be expressed in speech.

We have learned to understand a parent's questions and comments about his sick child as being also statements, in some sense, about the 'sick child' within the parent himself—something which is not at the time clearly perceived by the parent, but which he often confirms later, sometimes years later, in therapy. Such statements often appear in demands for advice and reassurance; in criticism of clinic fees, of the ward setting, and of the nurses' handling of the child; in questions about what is being done to the child in treatment; in demands for more laboratory tests, spinal taps, electroencephalograms, and so on.

On such occasions, the therapist has an opportunity to behave fairly and firmly toward the frightened, hungry, hurt, angry, self-deprecating 'child' within the parent. Again, the therapist begins to help the parent resolve his conflict by his evenly hovering attention and his consistent effort to understand the central motivational conflict of which such doubts, criticisms, and demands are often a symptomatic expression. While the therapist can state his own convictions about the value of continuing the present treatment, his lack of internal coerciveness leaves him free to consider the parents' wishes and suggestions, and, if there is any medical indication for them, to carry them out. When the parents see no progress and get discouraged, he can express his understanding of their feelings and his own professional convictions about the value of the work, and yet freely offer to help them stop work with him and seek help or custodial care elsewhere.

COUNTERTRANSFERENCE PROBLEMS WITH PARENTS

With the parents, as with the child, the therapist's freedom from anxious coerciveness, undue ambitiousness, and competitive need to succeed with the family too soon—that is, his freedom from attempts to satisfy his own otherwise ungratified needs—is important. In addition, his conviction from previous experience of the helpfulness of this method has resulted, in critical moments with some of these parents, in an integrative experience and a more solid continuation of the work. Thus, the parent, too, gradually learns by identifying with the firm and fair behavior of the therapist toward him. He learns that impulses of whatever kind can be nondestructively expressed in speech in the therapeutic situation for the primary and ever-present purpose of clarifying and resolving his own conflicts.

FAMILY HOMEOSTASIS AND THERAPY

Gradually, the regressive attitudes of each family member enter more and more into the therapeutic situation. There are, of course, numerous fluctuations in this development of the transference neurosis in the therapy, and simultaneously, fluctuations in the severity of acting-out within the family. We have often observed that any reduction of conflict in any one member of the family resulting from therapeutic work—or conversely, an increase of anxious tension incident to working-through—is usually promptly reflected in the other two members in therapy, sometimes in paradoxical ways. Eventually and slowly we have experienced, in the relatively few successful instances, a resolution of conflict with more durable reduction of tensions in the family situation. The following cases may serve to illustrate this.

Case 1: The mother of a silent, hostile, destructive, autistic four-and-one-half year-old boy began to verbalize, around the sudden illness and incapacity of her husband, many hostile feelings toward the therapist because he did so little for her. Each time, as she was encouraged to express all her feelings and thoughts, she would go on to recall how her mother, sisters, friends, and husband had previously babied her. She would recall how "nice," and at the same time how stultifying such "babying" was, and how unsure of herself and vulnerable she felt in all situations in which others failed to do for her what she had not learned adequately enough to do for herself. She reported that her husband decorated the home and managed all finances. She also said that he constantly derided her. She felt defensively guilty because she could never get her house cleaned and because she needed a nurse for the children. As the weeks went on, angry attacks on the therapist, because he "expected" her to do all the work at home and in the therapeutic sessions, were followed by floods of early childhood memories of being infantilized and cheated. During this period she drove the family car in city traffic for the first time, was able to care for her husband without help, and was able to have the hospitalized child at home for a while. When the child engaged in aggressive outbursts, she reacted without anxiety and with greater firmness than ever before. At the end of this phase of the work, she redecorated her home, despite her husband's skepticism, and was very pleased with the results. Her husband, however, was quite ambivalent about his wife's successes.

i.e. She was quite right!

Case 2: Both parents of a five-year-old boy were in therapy. The boy was mute and withdrawn, but had marked mechanical skills. In therapy, the father frequently talked of his disappointment that this, his only male child, would not be able to follow in his footsteps through exclusive schools to a successful career in his own profession. For many months the father could talk only of the boy's symptoms and of the impatience he felt with his son when the boy was home on weekend visits from the hospital. In the therapeutic situation, he appeared uncomfortable and sat silent for long periods. After many months during which the therapist alternately gently encouraged him to speak, patiently waited, and offered tentative interpretive comments about his possible thoughts and feelings, the patient gradually began to talk about his own driving and ambitious mother, and the feelings of isolation and worthlessness at not being able to live up to her expectations which he had experienced until he got into professional school and blossomed out. He talked about this with much affect for a number of sessions. At the same time, he began to reduce his leisure-time activities of selling used cars and insurance after his regular work. As he became more content with his own achievements in his professional work, and less fearful of his tender feelings, he relaxed more. He was then able to spend more time with his family and even became able to enjoy playing with his silent son without constantly pushing him and demanding of him that he talk or do things. The boy eventually began to talk. The father reported that for the first time he could enjoy holding and playing with his infant daughter, and being "silly" with all his children.

The mother of this family had two babies during the two and one-half years of therapy with the family. By the time the first of these was born, some ten months after treatment began, the mother had been able to work through much of her conflicts about bodily contact, and about cuddling and mothering a child, as she relived her own childhood experience with her "cold" mother and "perfectionistic" father. The new baby was thought by strangers to be the mother's first child, not her fourth, so tenderly did she handle her and so greatly did she enjoy nursing her. Simultaneously her schizophrenic son became less stiff with her and began to laugh, sing songs, and say a few words.

FAMILY SECRETS

Some of the parents of the most severely disturbed, mute children are found, in the process of therapy, to have open secrets between them—problems which are vital, which both are aware of, but which are rarely or never fully discussed between them. In one family it was the fact that the husband was not the father of the child, our patient, a fact known to both parents for nine years and never talked about. Moreover, the fact had never been mentioned, for fourteen years prior to therapy, that the husband's penis, scarred from surgical efforts at repair of a severe hypospadias, did not permit intromission and sexual satisfaction for either husband or wife. In another family the artificial insemination necessary to conceive a child—our patient—as well as the husband's untreated, chronically draining mastoid, which evoked revulsion in the wife, were never fully discussed during twelve years of marriage. In still another case, the violent feelings of both parents about the father's subservience as his brother-in-law's employee, and his failure to take opportunities for independent business ventures, had not been discussed for eleven years. The subject was brought into the open only after eighteen months of therapy.

ONE THERAPIST FOR A FAMILY

We have found that one therapist *can* work with an entire family. He learns not to cross-communicate information received from one member of the family to another; he learns, in effect, to behave as a separate therapist with each family member. One could say that he behaves as three therapists in one. He begins to understand each patient in terms of his unique past experience expressed in his current relationships with the members of his family. The therapist is thus less likely to overidentify with one patient against the others, and each family member experiences a therapist who has learned to be equally attentive to every impulse. Such experiences have been useful to each parent in resolving old sibling rivalries. In successful instances, such simultaneous work with child and parents by one therapist *may* be more rapid than in those cases where there have been unresolved ambivalences between several therapists. Work with the family by several therapists who are equally skilled and who have no interfering problems with each other can, however, be equally effective and fruitful. Finally, simultaneous treatment of child and parents seems to reduce somewhat the disadvantages of less frequent sessions with each, although the duration of the total work is probably not shortened. We wish we had time to see each family more frequently.

As energy is released from circular conflicts and their destructive compromises in any one of the family trio, it is then freed for more constructive living within the family. As both parents become capable of more consistently genital, sexual mutuality with each other as adults, they can become more actually parental, and their child's living with them as a child then becomes freed of its dangers.

i.e. the less severe the case!

PROGNOSIS

From these experiences our impressions about prognosis are, briefly, that the greater the ego integration of the child prior to therapy, and the earlier therapy is begun, the more successful the outcome is likely to be. The younger the parents and the better their general life adjustment and self-satisfactions, the better the prognosis. Factors in the therapist also affect the prognosis; the greater his skill and experience, and the fewer his unresolved pregenital conflicts, the more successful the work is likely to be.

We cannot report uniform success, or even very many successes, from these therapeutic efforts. Of the more than one hundred psychotic children we have seen—not all in prolonged, systematic therapy—nine are well or very much improved; several are not improved very much and are in state hospitals; and in the remainder, some of the most severe and incapacitating symptoms have been somewhat reduced. We have nevertheless been encouraged by this experience to continue to test our hypotheses and our working methods with even more critical precision.

REFERENCES

1. BETZ, B. Strategic conditions in the psychotherapy of persons with schizophrenia. *Amer. J. Psychiat.*, 1950, 107:203-215.
2. HOLT, E. B. *The Freudian Wish and Its Place in Ethics*. New York: Henry Holt, 1915. Pp. 3-4.
3. KNIGHT, R. P. Psychotherapy of an adolescent catatonic schizophrenia with mutism. *Psychiat.*, 1946, 9:323-339.
4. PIOUS, W. L. The pathogenic process in schizophrenia. *Bull. Menninger Clinic*, 1941, 13:152-159.
5. ROSEN, J. N. *Direct Analysis: Selected Papers*. New York: Grune & Stratton, 1953.
6. SZUREK, S. A. An attitude towards (child) psychiatry, part II. *Quart. J. Child Behavior*, 1949, 1:36-54.
7. SZUREK, S. A. The family and the staff in hospital psychiatric therapy of children. *Amer. J. Orthopsychiat.*, 1951, 21:597-611.
8. SZUREK, S. A. Some lessons from efforts at psychotherapy with parents. *Amer. J. Psychiat.*, 1952, 109:296-302.
9. SZUREK, S. A. Childhood Schizophrenia: Psychotic Episodes and Psychotic Maldevelopment. Read at the meeting of the American Orthopsychiatric Association, February, 1955.
10. WEXLER, M. The structural problem in schizophrenia: the role of the internal object. *Bull. Menninger Clinic*, 1951, 15:221-234.
11. WEXLER, M. The structural problem in schizophrenia: therapeutic implications. *Internat. J. Psycho-Anal.*, 1951, 32:157-166.

10

The Unique Role of the Child Psychiatry Trainee on an Inpatient or Day Care Unit

Irving N. Berlin, M.D.
and
Adolph E. Christ, M.D.

The trainee in child psychiatry who is involved in an inpatient or day care setting is beset by many problems, perhaps the most ubiquitous of which is that of finding a unique role for himself. He discovers that nurses, teachers, occupational therapists, etc., who spend most of their day with the child, have more information and in some instances a more intimate relationship with the patient than he is likely to have. Each worker feels that his interaction with the child is the most vital to his recovery. The child psychiatry trainee, having lived through similar feelings early in his adult inpatient work, is again beset by uncertainties about how much his few therapeutic hours with the child are worth in contrast to the time and effort of his collaborators. When he finds that other child care personnel are also involved on a daily basis in helping parents learn to interact more effectively with their child, he often wonders what he does have to contribute that is his and only his (7, 8, 9). In addition to the psychotherapeutic role, we have come to believe that the synthesizing or integrating role is a potentially unique one for the trainee. We shall describe our efforts at delineating that role somewhat later.

The concepts to be discussed have concerned teachers of child psychiatry and directors of child psychiatric inpatient settings for many years (1, 2, 14, 15, 16, 17, 18, 20, 21). We have tried to analyze our experiences, consider

Reprinted from: Berlin, I. N. and Christ, A. E. The unique role of the child psychiatry trainee on an inpatient or day care unit. *J. Amer. Acad. Child Psychiat.*, 1969, 8(2):247-258.

many of the issues raised by our trainees, and synthesize our formulations for our own learning and to stimulate discussion with others.

The specific tasks which the trainee should master can be roughly classified as follows: (1) assessment of psychopathology in the child and parents; (2) evaluation of emotional level of development of the child, especially in terms of degree of ego development needed to plan a therapeutic milieu program; (3) assessment of cognitive development of the child, in Piaget's terms (11, 22), to help plan the steps in educational experiences to promote mastery and cognitive growth; and (4) psychotherapeutic work with child and parents.

The assessment of parental pathology, defenses, and ego strengths, which help decide how to assist parents to provide a facilitating milieu for their child, is a collaborative task for the trainee and ward staff. In addition to the trainee's role as collaborator and team member, he is expected to provide leadership. One of the recurring miracles is that many trainees do manage to master these tasks and find their unique role in the process. It also reassures the teachers and helps them expect more of the impossible from their students.

PSYCHOTHERAPY WITH THE CHILD

Psychotherapeutic work with the child and family enables the therapist gradually to identify and isolate the areas of nuclear psychopathology and to define those in which the child and family are most ready to engage therapeutically. As the therapist can share the psychotic experience or empathically understand the child's feeling, he may become aware of the child's ambivalent fear of involvement with and investment in another person. Such fears result from serious deprivation of nurturance and may be expressed in psychotic behavior. Similarly, the therapist may understand the child's terror about communicating feelings, especially expression of angry, sexual, sensual, and tender feelings experienced from and toward another person. Guilt, rage, hate, love, fear, strong desires for nurturance, and fear of retaliation from adults for direct or symbolic expression of negative feelings are all present. The resulting admixture makes understanding the meaning of behavior as well as the therapeutic work difficult.

With even the most primitive child, the therapist must learn as his first task to follow the child carefully in play therapy. Later he may need to focus actively and sometimes forcefully on the emerging nuclear conflicts. This may be done by clarifying one aspect of the emotional interaction between them. The therapist tries in various ways to describe both verbally and nonverbally his state of feeling and his perceptions of the interactions so that the child, from repeated experiences, finds a dependable base for his interactions. Diagnostic understanding of nuclear conflicts comes not only from direct observations of child and parents, but also from data gathered in a careful evaluation of the family events which preceded the illness. There is no need to stress the importance of the data which slowly take shape from the past history of each family member and reveal their resultant integrative and conflictful capacities for living. The interactions of family members in response to specific stresses presented by the child's emerging pathology and his response to therapeutic efforts give further clues which help clarify nuclear conflict areas. As the family members are involved in a search for ways to meet each other's needs, clarification and beginning resolution of these core conflicts result in gradually increasing sensitivity to mutual needs and a greater repertoire of satisfying interactions. In the child this results in a greater readiness to move beyond the areas of fixated or regressed emotional and cognitive development.

THE THERAPIST'S ROLE AS A TEAM MEMBER

In his role vis-a-vis the other team members, the trainee has a twofold task. The first is to share his growing insight about child and family with the other team members, thus alerting them to the possible meaning of the child's behavior as it is continually observed in the milieu. It helps them focus on using each experience with the child to contribute to the clarification and refinement of the meaning of the child's behavior. Increased understanding and awareness begin to provide a different, more integrative and responsive milieu experience for the child.

The trainee's second function is to facilitate a collaborative interchange with the ward staff so that their interactive behavior with the child, parents, or child and parents together, leads to a better understanding of the family. It is no easy task to integrate and synthesize data so that the behavior of the child or parents as observed on the ward and in psychotherapeutic work can be understood as an expression of their circular psychopathological conflicts rather than as oppositional or malicious.

Senior child psychiatrists must first provide examples of such integration of data and help the trainee and ward staff experience its usefulness. This is particularly true in the interpretation of anxiety-producing behavior of the parents in their interaction with ward personnel. As such behavior becomes understandable to the staff, therapeutic handling of interactions with child and parents also becomes important in altering the behavior and attitudes of each. The material which results from all such therapeutic interaction is considered available to the psychotherapist in fostering insight and conflict reduction in his patients. As part of the therapeutic contract parents and child are helped from the beginning to understand and agree to the exchange of observations of the ward team with the psychotherapist. The trainee's transition from having a theoretical understanding to providing practical examples of how the staff might use these interactions therapeutically around specific activities is usually not achieved until some time in the second year of child psychiatry fellowship. Hence, the responsibility for development of strategies on the basis of such complex understanding rests with the more experienced psychiatric social workers, psychologists, chief nurse, and senior child psychiatrists, until the trainee can assume this function with his own cases.

FACILITATING EMOTIONAL DEVELOPMENT

The therapist's role in facilitating the emotional development of the child is twofold. First, he needs to enlist the collaboration of all the ward staff in elucidating elements of the child's present stage of development. He then encourages the staff to utilize their knowledge and insight to help the child achieve the very next developmental steps. Thus, when a child being cared for by a new staff member indicates a need to be fed or cuddled, the experienced staff members and trainees can describe from their experiences the sequences that might be expected to occur as the child works through this particular stage and is ready to move on. Nurses can be particularly helpful by describing in case vignettes how their own involvement for a time precluded recognition of the child's readiness to move on because they were enjoying the feeding or cuddling so much themselves. The trainee needs to develop skills which facilitate other staff members' contributions to the learning of all the staff. How a particular child may be helped to take the next step requires close and free collaboration, sharing of information, and freedom to alter the plan as new data are gathered and assessed in the team effort. The capacity of the trainee and other staff members to predict sequences of behavior and direction of growth makes it easier for inexperienced staff to recognize readiness for change and thus to be helpful to the child.

Close collaboration between staff and psychotherapist is essential, as a child may sometimes function on different levels with milieu staff and therapist. Thus, in psychotherapy the more primitive core of his nuclear conflicts may still be worked on after he has progressed through several successive stages of psychosexual development, especially in terms of ego function with the ward staff.

How are these sequences learned by the fellow? We have found that most trainees are deficient in applicable knowledge of the emotional developmental stages of the child. In lectures, seminars, and journal seminars they learn the theoretical framework of emotional maturational stages (3, 4, 5, 6, 10, 11, 12, 13, 19). They are, however, still a long way from using this theoretical framework to understand the observed behavior of the normal, neurotic, or psychotic child.

Furthermore, we find it is very difficult for the trainees to separate out in a behavioral sequence those aspects that represent regressive pathological distortions from those due to fixation. Essential as this differentiation is for the therapist in play therapy, it may become crucial at times for the ward staff. Understanding the conflictful components of behavior which have resulted in the symptoms permits corrective interaction. However, in developmental arrest an environment must be created which is suitable for emotional growth and development at the emotional level of the child and which facilitates the next steps beyond it. For example, destructive behavior may be symptomatic of unconscious conflict and may engage the adults in a characteristic way for that child and family. However, the child's striving for autonomy and independence indicates not only conflict but the need to be helped toward greater self-direction. He needs to be given choices or he gets drawn into severe power struggles (22).

Thus, when Sandy, a four-year-old psychotic boy, initially hit himself and others at every opportunity, this could be understood historically in terms of conflicts from experiences with his harsh, punitive father and helpless, nonnurturant mother. The ward staff was alerted to interrupt his assaultiveness by restraining him until his experiences with the staff and playing out his terror and anger with the therapist made it possible for him to relate to others with verbal demands and abusiveness which slowly merged into permitting physical closeness.

Jenny, at age five, however, began to lash out at everyone as she emerged from autistic isolation and frozen immobility. She slowly reacted to the warmth, nurturance, and cuddling of the nurses and to the patient engagement of her therapist who used her inert hands in his to mold clay. The violent striking out was seen as a developmental phase combining assertiveness and testing of her world as she slowly lost her fear. Jenny was helped to channel her anger into more effective use of large and small muscles. Thus, with each outburst she was given a choice of clay to pound, paint to splash, or wet sand and flour to mash. These were her first vehicles for discharge of feelings and later opportunities to select areas for mastery in clay modeling and building. Each outburst was viewed as an opportunity to provide Jenny with alternative ways of asserting herself and of selecting the vehicles for learning and mastery. With the development of large and small muscle skills and greater independence and initiative, she was then able to take her place in the ward kindergarten group.

When the staff understands the child's behavior in terms of efforts to master developmental tasks, they are quickly able to recognize any new signs of increasing maturation and to foster independence and autonomy with rapid reduction of the destructive behavior. They are also less disturbed by the sometimes necessary brief periods of regressive behavior. The child psychiatry fellow can achieve such learning through repeatedly observing someone else attempting this differentiation. Thus, he slowly acquires competence in classifying levels of the child's emotional development, in translating the theory and applying it to concrete behavioral examples given by the ward staff, and involving them in planning ways to help the child develop.

When sequential development is not specifically fostered, the child's conflicts may be reduced, but he often fails to mature. The milieu may in this way iatrogenically produce a new conflict area. Thus, Frank, a six-year-old autistic boy, very gradually was able to move out of his shell and to communicate in clearly heard words rather than frightened, barely audible whispers. The self-rocking stopped and echolalic singsong TV commercials were more audible as he responded to the nurturance and encouragement of ward staff and engaged in the playroom in alternately feeding the baby doll and then, with gradually increased vigor, smashing it to the ground. For several months the repetitive verbalizations were clear and strong. He moved with confidence and could be persuaded to join in group activities, though on the periphery. Parents reported greater vigor in speech and movement with occasional single word commands for food or a toy. Then he began to fade into his old soft, hardly audible speech, moved about less, appeared awkward, and became isolated. Close analysis of this phenomenon brought into focus staff contentment with the first behavioral changes without any clear plan to assess where he was in terms of ego development and to work toward the next step to help him move toward more age-appropriate behavior. Our second and planned efforts had to overcome the massive withdrawal and then utilize his readiness at each developmental stage to provide opportunities for relationships, learning, and mastery appropriate for the next stage via nurses, nursery school, occupational therapy, dance therapy, etc. This time the milieu facilitated continued progress rather than being content with the prolonged plateau which usually ends in regression.

EFFORTS AT COGNITIVE ASSESSMENT

We now come to the area of cognitive development of the child. Using Piaget's model (11), we observed that most of the severely disturbed psychotic children who require hospitalization operate in the sensorimotor or preoperational stages of development. The task of the therapist is to involve a collaborative team of teacher, occupational therapist, nurse, and psychologist in an attempt to clarify the thinking level of the child. Does he have an inkling of casuality? Does he recognize the permanence of the object? How much and when can he structure his environment? Is he capable of using any make-believe or imagination? Are there any areas where he can distinguish between self and others? Can he find the thread that relates several behavioral sequences? These are but some of the questions to which therapist and staff must address themselves if they are to make teaching of the child possible. The major task of teaching while the child is on an inpatient or day care unit is to help him acquire those precursors to academic skills which will enhance his satisfaction in learning and eventuate in his being able to learn and participate in the school situation after discharge.

The therapist's role in this area is to stimulate the recurrent analysis of the child's cognitive level. Thus, the psychologist's evaluations and the teacher's observations must be correlated with other staff observations and data from the psychotherapeutic work. Often such an assessment takes many weeks of close observation and careful testing and retesting of the parameters of the child's cognitive functioning. Sometimes a child's disruptive behavior will not be an expression of psychopathology as much as an expression of utter frustration because the environment is making intellectual demands on him for which he is not ready.

Another task of the therapist is to serve as a stimulus to the other members to collaborate with him in the exciting discovery of methods and techniques which will teach the child such things as the difference between self and others, what is pretend play, fantasy and reality, and to help him understand that hitting a child and getting hit back by that child are related. They must also find ways to help the child begin to experience object constancy.

Still another task is to encourage and help the teacher and nurse to relay their experiences to the parents. His intimate knowledge of the parents' psychopathology, resistances, and defenses allows the therapist to clarify with the teacher and nurse the best possible methods by which this can be done. Should parents be observers and participate in some activities with other children, or are they ready, with help, to be engaged with their own child in ward activities? How is all this learned? Usually the fellow is totally unprepared for this task.

The greatest problem in the trainee's learning about cognition is in structuring the day care program in such a way that he is not left out of this process. Usually the teacher, occupational therapist, and nurse bring these areas up with the ward director or the psychologist when the trainees are not present. In part it is out of his province, hence it does not require his involvement. Since this material is not taught elsewhere in a general or child psychiatry program, he must learn it in this setting. Since it does not deal with psychopathology or psychotherapy, he may prefer not to be involved in an area for which he is so ill-prepared. Besides, until he learns about cognitive development, he feels anxious and vulnerable and requires support from senior staff members.

This is an area of particular importance to the child psychiatry trainee. It adds a dimension for understanding and discussing the child which enhances his contacts with educators, either as a therapist of the schoolchild or as a school consultant. A major collaborative effort, particularly on the part of teachers, psychologist, chief resident, and ward director, is required to discuss the cognitive aspects of the child's problems in meetings where the trainees participate in order to clarify these concepts and to become familiar with them. The senior child psychiatrists must then repetitively help the fellows carry out observations and engage in discussion until these concepts are useful and familiar to the trainee.

One final unique area in the role of the child psychiatric trainee is responsibility for planning termination of the day care experience for child and family, with transition to outpatient treatment and involvement in other community resources such as school. The intense involvement of the ward staff with a severely disturbed child, so necessary for the child's improvement, demands that the trainee maintain sufficient objectivity to help the ward staff make the termination a therapeutic experience.

THE SYNTHESIZING ROLE

The trainee uses his psychotherapeutic work with the child and parents to provide additional data for understanding the degree of psychopathology and emotional and cognitive levels of the child, as well as to facilitate overall planning for the next steps toward which the team should work. As the trainee learns to assume the synthesizing role, he is faced with examining data from all sources and trying to integrate them for himself and for the team. He must similarly learn to explore gently and uncover the data available in the observations of team members and himself to explain a crisis and to help resolve it. This learning process occurs with some difficulty and discomfort. As has been indicated, it requires the model of a senior child psychiatrist who demonstrates the process to the trainee and whose involvement in this process decreases as the trainee gains experience and competence.

Another aspect of the child psychiatry fellow's work with the child differentiates him from his collaborators. He begins to use his growing understanding of psychopathology and psychotherapeutic methods not only to contribute to the child's general gains, but also to consolidate each step of the growth occurring from all aspects of the therapeutic milieu efforts with the child and parents. Thus, interpretive behavior, comments, and play therapy activities timed in terms of the overall movement may serve to focus sharply and resolve conflicts at a moment when symbolic mastery is possible. With the very sick child he may be the only one who can permit himself to share the child's psychosis as a way of understanding the conflicts and slowly begin to find methods of conflict resolution. This is another aspect of the synthesizing role.

Thus, Phil, a seven-year-old child whose oral-sadistic behaviors were gradually reduced in ward activities and in school, with increased mastery through a variety of living and learning tasks, did not make full use of his energies. He could not move on to the next step in conflict resolution until, in the light of this progress, an old theme in play was reintroduced by his therapist to permit symbolic playing out of a conflict. The therapist brought out alligator and frog puppets which had been abandoned months before. In the ensuing five play therapy sessions, biting, chewing, and swallowing of the frog were increasingly free and voracious as the therapist first made the appropriate sounds and verbalizations for both puppets. Finally, the child joined in and then took over with increasing freedom. This was quite different from the violent, anxious, and desperate play of some months back. In the last of these hours he, as the alligator puppet, restored the frog he had just killed to life with a grand gesture. Subsequently the child's capacity to learn, to pay attention, and to experience pleasure noticeably increased on the ward as his teasing and aggressive behavior decreased at home.

A similar consolidative function occurs in work with parents. The variety of therapeutic efforts by all team members and the parents' experiences, both successes and problems in dealing with the child and their efforts in psychotherapy, are synthesized in terms of their past history and their intra- and interpersonal conflicts. Well-timed interpretive comments often permit the parents to move to the next step in their work.

SUMMARY

The specific tasks of the child psychiatry trainee are to learn to use his growing knowledge and competence to synthesize all the data provided by every team member, to define the psychopathology of the child and parents, the emotional and cognitive levels, and to help evolve a collaborative therapeutic program step by step for his patients. He synthesizes all of the data from the setting and his psychotherapeutic work in order to evaluate and promote the next steps in emotional and cognitive growth for the child and conflict resolution for the child and parents. Most important, his psychotherapeutic engagement with child and parents provides the base for all his learning.

REFERENCES

1. BERLIN, I. N. Some implications of ego psychology for the supervisory process. *American Journal of Psychotherapy*, 1960, 14:536-544.
2. BERLIN, I. N. A history of challenges in child psychiatry training. *Mental Hygiene*, 1964, 48:558-565.
3. BRIDGES, K. M. B. Emotional development in early infancy. *Child Development*, 1932, 3:324-341.
4. BRUNER, J. S. *The Process of Education*. Cambridge: Harvard University Press, 1960.
5. BRUNER, J. S. *Toward a Theory of Instruction*. Cambridge: Harvard University Press, 1966.
6. BRUNER, J. S., OLVER, R. R., GREENFIELD, P. M., ET AL. *Studies in Cognitive Growth*. New York: Wiley, 1966.
7. CHRIST, A. E., CRITCHLEY, D. L., LARSON, M. L. and BROWN, M. L. The role of the nurse in child psychiatry. *Nursing Outlook*, 1965, 13(1):30-32.
8. CHRIST, A. E. and GRIFFITHS, R. Parent-nurse therapeutic contact on a child psychiatry unit. *American Journal of Orthopsychiatry*, 1965, 35: 589-593.
9. CHRIST, A. E. and WAGNER, N. Prevention of iatrogenic factors in child residential treatment. In J. Masserman (Ed.), *Current Psychiatric Therapies*. New York: Grune & Stratton, Vol. 6, 1966. Pp. 46-54.
10. ERIKSON, E. H. *Childhood and Society*. New York: Norton, rev. ed., 1963.
11. FLAVELL, J. H. *The Developmental Psychology of Jean Piaget*. Princeton: Van Nostrand, 1963.
12. FREUD, S. Three essays on the theory of sexuality. *Standard Edition*, Vol. 7, London: Hogarth Press, 1953. Pp. 125-243.
13. GESELL, A. and ILG, F. L. *Studies in Child Development*. New York: Harper, 1959.
14. GREENWOOD, E. D. The role of psychotherapy in residential treatment. *American Journal of Orthopsychiatry*, 1955, 25:692-698.
15. ITTELSON, W. Some Factors Influencing the Design and Function of Psychiatric Facilities. Progress Report of the Department of Psychology, Brooklyn College, 1960.
16. PAVENSTEDT, E. The nursery school, day care centers, and developmental studies. *J. Amer. Acad. Child Psychiat.*, 1966, 5:349-359.
17. REDL, F. The concept of a "therapeutic milieu," *American Journal of Orthopsychiatry*, 1959, 29:721-736.
18. ROBINSON, J. Planning institutional programs for children. *Quarterly Journal of Child Behavior*, 1951, 3:233-239.
19. SPITZ, R. A. *A Genetic Field Theory of Ego Formation: Its Implications for Pathology*. New York: International Universities Press, 1959.
20. SZUREK, S. A. and BERLIN, I. N. Teaching administration in the training of child psychiatrists. *J. Amer. Acad. Child Psychiat.*, 1964, 3:551-560.

21. SZUREK, S. A. and BERLIN, I. N. The question of therapy for the trainee in the psychiatric training program. *J. Amer. Acad. Child Psychiat.*, 1966, 5:155-165.
22. WHITE, R. W. Competence and the psychosexual stages of development. In M. R. Jones (Ed.), *Nebraska Symposium on Motivation.* Lincoln: University of Nebraska Press, 1960. Pp. 97-141.
23. WOLFF, P. H. The developmental psychologies of Jean Piaget and psychoanalysis. In *Psychological Issues*, Monograph 5. New York: International Universities Press, 1960.

11

A Milieu Treatment Program for Psychotic Children

R. W. Brunstetter, M.D.

For a number of years past the inpatient ward of the Children's Service of the Langley Porter Neuropsychiatric Institute has been utilized primarily for the treatment of children whose emotional disorder is so severe and pervasive as to warrant the diagnosis of psychotic reaction. In a series of papers, Szurek, Boatman, and others (Szurek (8), Boatman and Szurek (3), Szurek and Berlin (9), Szurek (6), Sheimo, Paynter and Szurek (5), Szurek (7), Boatman, Paynter and Parsons (2)) have described our ongoing program of clinical research into the psychological aspects of the etiology of childhood psychosis and some of the clinical concepts that have evolved out of the work on the ward. The present paper is concerned with one facet of the operation of the ward—the planning and organization of a therapeutic milieu for severely disturbed children.

Over the years more than two hundred strange and withdrawn children have undergone treatment in our clinic and on our inpatient service. Many of them have been mute, many incontinent and seemingly unable to care for themselves in the simplest kinds of ways. Some are continuingly preoccupied with bizarre rituals and repetitive bits of symbolic behavior. A number have been so viciously self-destructive that they have required almost constant surveillance and restraint to prevent them from inflicting real and lasting damage upon their own bodies. All of them are shut off and inaccessible. They seem desperate for warm and loving contact but they resist any kind of meaningful approach with a practiced skill that often proves discouraging to new and enthusiastic staff members.

The core of the process of treatment on the ward is the psychotherapeutic resolution of conflict in playroom sessions and the construction and reconstruction, particularly through the interventions of the psychiatric nurses,

Reprinted from R. W. Brunstetter, Every Day on an Inpatient Ward for Psychotic Children. *The Psychiatric Quarterly Supplement*, 42:203-217, Part II, 1968.

of a functioning and effective ego. But these activities cannot go on in a vacuum. Even the most skillful psychotherapist and psychiatric nurse would not be able to operate in an environment which was empty save for their own actions. Indeed, anyone who has ever had the opportunity of observing a ward full of withdrawn and apathetic schizophrenic children cannot help but have appreciated the fact that no activity for the psychotic child, when imposed for large parts of the day, is almost always a negative experience which fails to provide stimulation and promotes retreat into a world of inner distortions and angry fantasies. To fill the need for substance in the lives of children in residence, a wide spectrum of activities, referred to usually as "the program," or "the milieu," must be planned and carried out with care and imagination.

Bearing responsibility for the creation out of nothing of a whole pattern of life for a group of children is no small task. It is surprising how much there is to do and how complex the problems are. Redl(4) has contributed a particularly lucid discussion of some of the pitfalls inherent in the planning and operation of a therapeutic milieu of this type.

Normal children receive much of their living experience ready made because of their membership in already existing family units and community groups. Their lives fit into the lives of others in such a way that many activities occur in well-established institutions like school or derive from the pursuit of social or vocational goals by their parents or peers. Parents do need to spend time and thought on the lives of their children, but they can do so at some leisure because so much is provided automatically by the world around them and its existing culture.

On an inpatient ward there is unfortunately no such stable, pre-existing framework of activities into which the children's lives can fit. It must all be built up from the very beginning. So many details of dressing and eating, of coming and going, and of a thousand other things, which seem to take care of themselves in the life of the normal child, must be planned on the ward that the job sometimes is overwhelming.

The preservation of an atmosphere of naturalness is difficult in a situation where everything needs to be planned. When, for instance, we find ourselves going so far as to schedule time for "spontaneous activities," there is good reason to question whether things may not have become too artificial.

There is also something artificial and perhaps not altogether healthy about a situation in which everything is done for the sake of children. It does not happen this way in the real world, and we sometimes wonder if such child-centeredness may not invite overinvestment by the staff and tend to sustain unduly the parasitic dependence of the psychotic child.

However, with all of these disadvantages and difficulties, there is really no choice. The children must exist; and, in the sterile atmosphere of the ward into which their illness has forced them, if something is not planned for them their existences will be barren and the work of therapy will be undone. And, in the long run, the fact that the children's lives have to be planned from the ground up is an opportunity that can be turned to therapeutic advantage. Although difficult, it is a chance to shape the milieu of the ward in accordance with psychodynamic principles and, within limitations imposed by reality, it offers the possibility of fashioning the life of each child to meet his individual clinical needs.

With this end in mind, an attempt is made through the therapeutic milieu to provide the kind of experiences for each psychotic child which will afford him a maximum opportunity to alter within himself all of the disordered emotional perceptions and defenses which have become incorporated into his personality in the process of his development. The environment thus should be one in which interactions similar to those which led to the original disorder occur with minimum frequency so that the child has little real need to defend himself and so that his view of the world as a dangerous place may be replaced by experiences with individuals in a new living situation where fear, frustration and rage are not continually evoked as they had been previously.

To an extent, we probably also hope that the environment will go further than this and actually supply certain kinds of emotional gratifications which are necessary in life but hithertofore have been missing for the child. This is a hope tempered with scepticism. The demands of the schizophrenic child for anaclitic love and attention seem limitless and impossible to fulfill. Nevertheless, it is evident, when we stop to examine our practice, that the concept of some kind of replacement therapy is a part of what is done, even if intellectually we do not really think that it is possible.

THE PROGRAM

The weekly schedule shown in Figure 1 represents schematically the version of the program which was in use on the ward at the time this paper was written. The day contains a number of structured activities like school and crafts, but it also is designed to allow ample time for freer interactions between nurse and child. The program is conceived of as a designed life experience through which the child and nurse move, day after day, experiencing pleasure and some challenge within a framework of security. It is intended to offer, from the standpoint of external reality at least, maximum opportunity for the replacement of fear and frustration with increasing mastery and confidence.

FIGURE 1: WARD SCHEDULE

Time	MONDAY	TUESDAY	WEDNESDAY	THURSDAY	FRIDAY
7:00-8:00	WAKING AND DRESSING				
8:00-8:30	BREAKFAST				
8:30-9:00	SELF CARE				
		SCHOOL: Charley	SCHOOL: Charley and Sid	SCHOOL: Charley	SCHOOL: Charley
9:00-9:15	STAFF MEETS TO DISCUSS AND PREPARE DAILY SCHEDULE				
9:15-9:30	SHARE AND TELL				
9:30-10:15	WEEKLY PLANNING MEETING	COOKING: Primary Group / SCHOOL: K.G. Group / ED. ACT. PROG.: Sid, Steve, Charley, Joey, Ted	OUTING	CRAFTS: Pri-mary Group / SCHOOL: K.G. Group / ED. ACT. PROG.: Sid, Steve, Ted, Joey, Charley	TREATMENT REVIEW
10:15-11:00	SNACKTIME AND STAFF COFFEE BREAKS				
11:00-11:45	SHARE AND TELL	K.G. Group / Pri-mary Group / Paul, Ted, Charley, Joey, Steve	OUTING	K.G. Group / Pri-mary Group / Paul, Ted, Charley, Steve, Joey	COOKING: Paul, Charley
11:45-12:15	PREPARE FOR LUNCH	PREPARE FOR LUNCH		PREPARE FOR LUNCH	
				SCHOOL: Sid, Charley	SCHOOL: Sid, Charley
12:15-1:00	STAFF PLANNING MTG. WITH PSY-CHIATRIST	CRAFTS: Joey		LUNCH	
1:00-2:00		LUNCH / REST HOUR		REST HOUR	
2:00-2:45	COOKING: Joey / SCHOOL: Steve / ED. ACT. PROG.: Others	CRAFTS: Charley, Sid / SCHOOL: Ted / ED. ACT. PROG.: Others		ADMINISTRATION MEETING	CRAFTS: Steve / SCHOOL: Ted / ED. ACT. PROGRAM: Others
2:45-3:30	COOKING: Steve / SCHOOL: Joey / ED. ACT.: Others	Ted / Steve / Others		ED. ACT. PROGRAM	COOKING: Ted / SCHOOL: Joey / ED. ACT. PROGRAM: Others
3:30-4:00	SNACKS, PLAY TIME				
4:00-6:00	EVALUATION MEETING FOR STAFF / PLAY TIME, T.V., CHARTING, SHIFT CHANGES				
6:00-6:30	SUPPER				
6:30-8:30	PLAY TIME, T.V., STORIES, RECORDS, BATHS, PREPARATION FOR BED				
8:30	BEDTIME				

Seen Individually: Steve, Joey, Ted

Kindergarten Group: Paul, Buddy, Lynda

Primary Group: Cheryl, Bobby, Carl

Older Boys: Sid, Charley

1. *Meeting Biological Needs*

One part of the program is built around the rhythms of recurring biological needs. As much as possible, individual nursing attention is provided for the child as he rises, dresses, grooms himself, eats, eliminates and sleeps. If it were possible one nurse would be assigned to each child throughout the day. Such a situation would provide optimal conditions for the resumption of psychological growth. Since the size of the staff precludes one-to-one assignment, we try to encourage at least a constant attitude of awareness of the individual child rather than the group so that, for instance, as four or five nurses help all twelve children to get ready for breakfast in the morning they can shuttle back and forth from child to child, moving in to help when the need is there and moving on to someone else when the child is able again to do for himself.

Even though the ideal of a one-to-one relationship cannot be realized most of the time, we do still formally assign each child to an individual nurse. Throughout the week, although she may often need to divide her attention, the nurse is responsible for knowing what is going on with the child, from the everyday level of clothing needs and bowel habits to the more complex matters of emotions and sequences of interaction on the ward. She maintains liaison with the child's parents and meets regularly with the psychotherapist to give and receive information, which becomes part of the constantly accumulating clinical understanding of the child's behavior and needs. Above all, she is someone to whom the child belongs, for our clinical experience suggests repeatedly the validity of the commonly held belief that belonging to someone is necessary for growth.

The activities associated with recurring biological needs are basic experiences which the child has with the management of his own body and its demands. In the course of the developing emotional disorder they have often become severely distorted and invested with shame and anger so that their daily repetitions are sadomasochistic experiences which only increase the likelihood that the next occurrence will also be pathological. The interruption of this body-centered cycle of cause and ill-effect seems a particularly strategic goal to be pursued in any treatment plan. Our clinical experience seems to bear out the idea that mastery in these areas, more than almost any other, can play a critical role in the foundation of a sense of accruing confidence in the self and the world.

2. *Facilitating Learning and Accomplishment*

The remainder of the program is derived from experiences which are more related to the outer world of ideas and objects and which pursue more directly the goals of learning and accomplishment.

The structured day begins with a twenty minute period called "Share and Tell." It is modeled after the kind of opening exercise which has become customary in the primary grades of public school. All of the children and the majority of the nurses on duty gather in the day room. Their chairs are arranged in a semi-circle, around the teacher. After the Pledge of Allegiance is recited, the date is circled on the calendar and a weather report is given. The day's schedule is presented and discussed, and finally the session ends with a song or story.

This kind of formal beginning to the day's activities has been employed for a number of years now and appears to have considerable value. It allows all of the children to be brought together for one of the few times during the day that this is possible. They quickly become familiar with the brief, pleasurable ritual and look forward to it. Their sense of belonging to a group is enhanced. In such a setting, where controls are maximal and there is little demand being made upon them to learn, they seem able to absorb the formal aspects of the school situation, and some learn quite readily to pay attention and remain seated. These skills, once acquired, carry over, to a degree, to the regular classroom situation.

School itself is conducted off the ward in a room specially outfitted for the purpose. It is probably the most pleasant room on the service, and the children like to go there. Teaching psychotic children is, at best, an unperfected art. Teaching them with only two or three sessions a week to do it in is so difficult that it is very hard to be sure how best to proceed. We have tried many methods over the years, exploring the applicability of both group and individual sessions and experimenting with a spectrum of approaches that has ranged from quite structured academic work to more permissive play-oriented programs. The negativism of the children and their slowness to respond make it hard to discern what course is correct. Currently, we employ a flexible approach which takes into account both the clinical needs of the child and also the way in which the particular teacher assigned to the ward at the time feels most comfortable in working. This appears to be effective and is, by and large, satisfying to everyone concerned.

The experience of the ward staff over the years has led us to believe that the learning process in a schizophrenic child is not qualitatively different than it is in the normal; and that, despite the tantrums and almost unendurable periods of prolonged indifference, the same underlying educational principles are operative. Thus, although often falling short, in the classroom we pursue the goals of motivation and attention and build the teaching process around clear and vivid presentation and many patient repetitions, much as a teacher in a regular school might.

Curriculum is an enormous problem. The children are so abysmally unprepared in some areas, and they mask so well their skills in others, that it is hard to know where the teaching job should begin. Even if this were not so, the extreme variation from child to child and the lack of adequate time would prevent the mounting of a full scale educational program. Instead we are more likely to select some fragment of a program, like reading readiness, and concentrate on it, knowing that the effects will generalize to some extent. We have considered for some time but have not yet attempted a curriculum based on subjects of emotional import to the children. There is both theoretical justification, and also some actual experience, that would suggest that it might be possible to engage them more directly around matters like "The Body and How It Functions," "Food," "Feelings of Love and Hate," "Family Life," and so on than it is in more traditional subjects.

The cooking class in which each child participates is an outgrowth of this kind of thinking. Certainly there is no functional area in which the schizophrenic child is more fundamentally disturbed than that which has to do with eating and oral activity. The earliest and most basic emotional relationships of the infant arise out of the rhythmic cycle of hunger and its satisfaction by the mother. In the fossil symptoms of the psychotic child we can read the record of massive anxiety which interfered at one time so terribly with this fundamental transaction of life. One child is still drinking milk from a bottle at the age of five. Another will not eat anything but spaghetti cooked in a particular pan. Many are afraid of foods; in some this is formalized enough to approach a delusion about poisoning. A group of schizophrenic children at mealtime is a pathetic sight. The aggregate impression of the mouthing and smelling, the fear of chewing, the bolting of food, the use of hands, the spilling, and the compulsive messiness is compelling testimony to the overwhelming tension with which this simple, three times daily, process of gratifying a bodily need has become invested.

For the past three years, one part of the ward's approach to this particular area of conflict has been the cooking class. The children take part in this either individually or in small groups, once a week. A well-outfitted kitchen in a large recreation room with ample table space is available. With the assistance of nurses and guided by the occupational therapist who acts as cooking teacher, the children are given the opportunity to prepare and eat simple, attractive foods. Cookies, cinnamon toast cut-outs, and candy apples are typical examples. On occasion, more ambitious projects like salads, desserts, or even whole meals may be attempted, particularly for cookouts or picnics. The chance to become truly familiar with food in a setting in which few demands are made has had a salutory effect. Along with a simultaneous painstaking, thoughtful effort on the part of the nursing staff to understand and work with the problems of the children at mealtime, it has helped to bring about a real reduction in the amount of oral conflictual behavior on the ward.

The regularly scheduled snacktimes are an allied endeavor. A special cart which is equipped with a toaster and completely stocked with as complete a line of jams, jellies, peanut butter and so on as the budget will allow has been designed and built for snacks. Gadgetry seems somewhat inappropriate in the midst of the subjectivism of the psychiatric world, but this particular innovation and the will to use it to provide gratification for the children has made a pleasant daily ceremony out of what previously was disorganized whining and begging all day long for food.

Along similar lines, although not shown on the schedule, is the fact that each child has money to go off the ward once a day with his nurse for a candy bar or similar treat. We sometimes are subject to nagging doubts about overindulgence, and try to deal with the regressive demand for this when it occurs in the child, but on the whole we have come to believe that successful nourishment both nurtures the child physically and provides for independent striving and so is to be considered an important part of the treatment of the psychotic child.

Craft activities were once held in the occupational therapy workshop which is located on the floor below our ward. Long experience finally taught us that the time required to transport the children to this well-equipped facility and the restlessness induced in them by the move were too high a price to pay for its advantages. The sessions are now held in the ward dining room, which indeed is pressed into service for many different functions between meals. Pursuing the "cart approach" successful in other areas, the staff now uses a mobile workbench fully equipped with all necessary tools as a base for craft activities.

The occupational therapist has employed a number of methods and activities over the years, ranging from rhythmic exercises and finger games to the more traditional work of attractive projects of one kind or another. Her basic purpose is to provide the children with a variety of experiences in sensory and motor gratification and to help them acquire a sense of mastery through making and doing.

Projects and activities are planned primarily for groups of children, but an effort is also made to discover the particular modality which for each individual child has most meaning. One very destructive boy, for instance, has literally "worked" out his conflicts over the years through the medium of a rough sort of carpentry that at first was primarily an outlet for aggressive energies in hammering and sawing but now has progressed to more precise activities and to real sublimation in constructive building.

The craft session is also a useful place to help the children learn component skills like cutting, pasting, and crayoning, which they need for functioning in other areas like school but may not yet have acquired.

The educational activity program is still an experimental effort to provide organized experience for the children during a greater part of the day than had previously been possible. Because of the need to work in small groups, only a part of the children can be involved at one time in a structured activity like school. If enough nurses were available to be assigned individually to the rest, the time when they are not in school might be put to excellent use but unfortunately most of the staff is occupied in the structured activity where a one-to-one relationship is usually required. This year our nursery school level teacher has been assigned to help with the children who remain on the ward. She functions as a resource person, making available materials and ideas to the nurses and helping with activities to provide a supplemental program of games and play. An effort is made to coordinate what is offered in the educational activity program with what is going on in school at any given time. In this way, the child meets with an organized environment in which repeated exposure maximizes the opportunity for learning. Free play and experimentation on the ward seem to be essential for the development of real mastery over skills acquired tentatively in more formal situations.

As a part of the general effort to coordinate the program as much as possible use is made of the device of a central theme, a notion borrowed from the "unit of study" approach in public schools. For each period of four to six weeks, an overall area of interest is chosen. It may be "Transportation" or "People Who Work in the Community" or "Foods We Eat" or something similar. For that period, the content of all of the activities on the ward is more or less closely related to the theme. If it is, for instance, "Transportation," the reading in school may be a story about trains, the outing may be on a ferryboat, and the educational activity program might involve toy cars or magazines from which to cut out pictures of cars for a scrapbook which in turn might be read in the next school session.

The Wednesday Outing is a featured part of the program. It is no easy logistic task to transport a group of psychotic children to a dairy, to a nearby park, or to a deserted beach for a picnic, but the feeling of the staff has been that it is well worth the effort. It is easy to settle into a rut within the private confines of the ward. Reaching out periodically into the outside world counteracts that tendency. It offers new kinds of experiences to children whose scope has been severely limited by emotional illness and maintains their contact with a world and with patterns of behavior to which we hope they will ultimately adjust.

DISCUSSION

The children are divided into small groups for almost all activities, except the outing and Share and Tell. Experience has shown that more than four or five together make for such a concentration of pathology that something is ✓ almost always going wrong and a high level of distraction is hard to avoid. Dividing schizophrenic children into groups is no easy matter. On a ward like ours, the children range in age from nursery school to early adolescence, and their capacities and symptomatic preoccupations are so varied that they are nearly too individual to deal with on anything except a one-to-one basis. Grouping is therefore a difficult but highly important art, which lies at the heart of the planning process. As the children change with new admissions and discharges or as their clinical status is altered by remission or relapse, established groups must be rethought and altered to fit new needs. Yet the altering of groups cannot be indulged in indiscriminately without exposing the children to more change than they can tolerate and without interrupting the slow development of the sense of group identity which we hope will take place.

The need to reevaluate constantly the composition of the childrens' groups highlights another aspect of program planning which has seemed increasingly important. The program now in use has undergone a number of revisions over the years. In the beginning, there was a tendency with each replanning to think that the program in its current form would be permanent; and we were always surprised and a little alarmed to find after some months that what had been created with so much labor and emotional investment not only was not perfect any longer but was seen as a burden and in need of drastic revision. Repeating this cycle many times has led us finally to believe that change is a necessary element in the milieu program of a residential ward. It must be responsible change, carefully thought out and sensitive to the mood and methods of working of the entire staff rather than the demands of individuals; but within these limits the program should be an organic, evolving process rather than a static set of prescriptions. Only in this form is it free to adapt to the shifting needs of deeply disturbed children and to the fluctuating skills of a staff whose membership is constantly changing.

Out of the work of caring for the children and out of growing insight into the genesis of their individual disorders, there should come a flow of thoughts and hypotheses about what is functionally wrong with each child and what can be done concretely to help. One of the responsibilities of the program is to remain free enough of inertia to be able to incorporate, test, and refine the staff's clinical ideas. To the degree to which it is able to maintain this kind of flexibility, the program will not only be a significant part of the ongoing process of study and treatment but also can become an important medium for the professional growth of staff. The hours of evaluation and planning, of questioning and of searching for underlying principles are a vital form of self instruction, more illuminating by far than any formal seminar.

Any discussion of principles needs to be interpreted in the light of the constantly changing nature of the program. What we do is derived from a body of theoretical assumptions, but it should not be misunderstood as rational and wholly deductive. It is more alive than that—something that is added to, altered, quarreled over, compromised about, and shaped in so many meetings and in response to so many pressures that it does not correspond with perfect fidelity to any set of concepts.

With this qualification in mind, there are some observations, however, which do broadly describe both the intent and practice of the planning process.

1. Our primary goal is to offer to the children a structure of normal, age-appropriate experiences and, within the context of these experiences, to identify and reduce the emotional conflicts that prevent participation, and teach whatever skills an individual child may prove ready to acquire.

2. To attain this goal, we believe it important for the program to be cohesive and coordinated, so that each element is related to the rest and so that what is done in the future arises in an orderly way out of the results of what has been tried in the past.

3. The best of what we do is probably, at its core, a sophisticated form of what has always been done instinctively to care for lost and frightened children. Comfort, support, protection from harm, and discriminating reassurance are a part of our interventions at every level. They are just as important a part of program planning as they are of actual nursing care or psychotherapy. For instance, much effort goes into the provision of a schedule that is understandable and simple. As much as possible, activities are planned at the same time and place each day. Mistakes are anticipated, and ample leeway is allowed for confusions or delays in starting or stopping so that the day flows easily from beginning to end without pressure or anxiety. The order of each day's activities is discussed at Share and Tell. The children begin to learn to look forward to what is in store for them. In this and other ways, we try to offer the safety and assurance of a predictable world.

4. Pleasurable experience for the children is an important goal deliberately pursued in the planning process. It is our intention to help them to find gratification with such regularity and freedom that they will come to perceive the world as reliable and good. Thus, for example, birthdays and holidays are celebrated with considerable ceremony, and the opportunity that they offer to pay extra attention to distrustful and unhappy children is

relished by the staff. Similarly, toys are chosen with special care. Interesting movies and cartoons are shown almost every week. Outings are planned to offer a maximum of enjoyable contact with the outside world. All of these are conscious efforts to encourage the children in the experiencing of pleasure of such a kind and degree that the vital element of motivation, so lacking in everything they do, may be rearoused within them. The schizophrenic child who becomes capable of wanting has made an important step toward recovery.

5. We also try hard to promote learning and the acquisition of mastery in whatever form and at whatever level the child is capable of accepting it. In formal school sessions and in the less formal but equally important teaching of the myriad skills of childhood—from shoe tying to bike riding to roller-skating—the staff works, through the program, to give to the children the experience of accomplishment and to help them approach the encounters of everyday life with increased skill and confidence.

6. For each child, the experiences of the program should occur within the context of an ongoing relationship with a mature and unconflicted adult. As Bettelheim and Sylvester (1) pointed out many years ago, without this vital ingredient children suffer from "psychological institutionalism" which is a true deficiency disease, a starvation for interpersonal meaningfulness.

7. Because of this, it is important that the program should be planned with just as much attention to staff and their welfare as to children. The program should be clear and readily understood. It should be consistent with the sense each doctor and nurse has of the nature of the problems of the child for whom they are responsible and ought to adapt itself to permit the best use of each person's particular skills. The staff needs to have a sense of involvement in the planning and should carry a continuing responsibility for contributing to modification of the program in the light of clinical observations.

8. The schedule should not become overdemanding. There is a temptation to crowd in as many activities as possible, but if this leads to pressure, fatigue and anxiety in the staff, the benefits to the child will only be undermined.

9. A balance must always be struck in the planning process between group and individual needs. Planning for groups of children is usually easier and takes less time and effort. More attention can be paid to the activity itself, and the result is likely to be more highly elaborated and directly satisfying. Nevertheless, the important thing in the program is not the activity but the individual child, and this perspective must be maintained. A child who is temporarily bewildered and frightened by a family crisis may derive little from sitting in school no matter how well the lesson has been planned. Far better that such a child should have available to him through the day an individual nurse who can take him out of school if necessary and who can

contain his aggressive and self-hurtful symptoms and offer him comfort and reassurance. But at the same time, another child may require exactly the firm limits of a regular school program to help prepare him for placement in the community. Another may be ready for playground experiences with normal children, still another may need to find sublimative outlets for aggressive energies freshly released. Individual needs vary widely. The program cannot hope to meet all of them with any kind of exactness because of the overwhelming complexity this would entail, but any compromise that is struck should maintain at its heart awareness of the importance of the individual child and his clinical needs.

SUMMARY

We have attempted to present in this paper a description of the supportive functioning of the ward milieu program in a residential treatment center for psychotic children. The current form of the program has been described in detail and the importance of correct grouping of the children and the need for continual replanning of the program have been discussed. The goals of the planning process have been reviewed and the importance of the needs of the individual child has been emphasized.

In focusing on emotional support, gratification, and learning as its primary goals, the program is, in essence, providing what is needed for normal growth and development. When these goals are pursued with care and precision, the ward milieu in its most effective form is a framework of activities and opportunities which supports the psychotherapeutic task of conflict reduction and aids the psychiatric nurse in her work with the daily functioning of the psychotic child.

REFERENCES

1. BETTELHEIM, B. and SYLVESTER, E. A Therapeutic Milieu. *Am. J. Orthopsychiat.*, 1948, 18:191-206.
2. BOATMAN, M. J., PAYNTER, J. and PARSONS, C. Nursing in hospital psychiatric therapy for psychotic children. *Am. J. Orthopsychiat.*, 1962, Vol. 32, No. 5, October. Also in S. A. Szurek, I. N. Berlin and M. J. Boatman (Eds.), *Inpatient Care for the Psychotic Child*. Palo Alto: Science and Behavior Books, 1971. Pp. 168-179.
3. BOATMAN, M. J. and SZUREK, S. A. A clinical study of childhood schizophrenia. In D. D. Jackson (Ed.), *The Etiology of Schizophrenia*. New York: Basic Books, 1960. Pp. 389-448.
4. REDL, F. The concept of a "Therapeutic Milieu." *Am. J. Orthopsychiat.*, 1959, 29:721-736.
5. SHEIMO, S. L., PAYNTER, J. and SZUREK, S. A. Problems of staff interaction with spontaneous group formation on a children's psychiatric ward. *Am. J. Orthopsychiat.*, 1949, 19:599-611. Also in S. A. Szurek, I. N. Ber-

lin and M. J. Boatman (Eds.), *Inpatient Care for the Psychotic Child.* Palo Alto: Science and Behavior Books, 1971. Pp. 122-137.

6. SZUREK, S. A. Dynamics of staff interaction in hospital psychiatric treatment of children. *Am. J. Orthopsychiat.,* 1947, 17:652-664. Also in S. A. Szurek, I. N. Berlin and M. J. Boatman (Eds.), *Inpatient Care for the Psychotic Child.* Palo Alto: Science and Behavior Books, 1971. Pp. 138-154.

7. SZUREK, S. A. The family and the staff in hospital psychiatric therapy of children. *Am. J. Orthopsychiat.,* 1951, 21:597-611. Also in S. A. Szurek, I. N. Berlin and M. J. Boatman (Eds.), *Inpatient Care for the Psychotic Child.* Palo Alto: Science and Behavior Books, 1971. Pp. 138-154.

8. SZUREK, S. A. Childhood schizophrenia: Psychotic episodes and psychotic maldevelopment. *Am. J. Orthopsychiat.,* 1956, 26:519-543. Also in S. A. Szurek, I. N. Berlin and M. J. Boatman (Eds.), *Inpatient Care for the Psychotic Child.* Palo Alto: Science and Behavior Books, 1971. Pp. 264-279.

9. SZUREK, S. A. and BERLIN, I. N. Elements of psychotherapeutics with the schizophrenic child and his parents. *Psychiatry,* 1956, 19:1-9. Also in S. A. Szurek, I. N. Berlin and M. J. Boatman (Eds.), *Inpatient Care for the Psychotic Child.* Palo Alto: Science and Behavior Books, 1971. Pp. 92-119. See also Chapter 9, this volume.

Section IV

CLINICAL RESEARCH

"Attachment and Psychotic Detachment" assesses Bowlby's integration of child development research and his theoretical positions which stem from his own research as well as his review of others' work as they apply to research and psychotherapy with psychotic children. "Clinical Work and Clinical Research . . ." looks at the elements of clinical work required for valid clinical research. The next seven chapters use the data accumulated on the Langley Porter Children's Service for over 25 years to review outcome statistics in the light of a number of variables such as diagnosis on admission, age of onset and severity of illness as assessed by senior staff evaluations, mutism, electroencephalographic findings, duration and intensity of treatment and parental characteristics, etc. The chapter on the Rimland Checklist evaluates the use of a checklist as predictive of outcome and examines the criteria used by Rimland as applied to the Langley Porter population. Other criteria for a more meaningful checklist are suggested.

189

12

Attachment and Psychotic Detachment

S. A. Szurek, M.D.

Clinical research on psychotic disorders of childhood has been a major interest of the author. The hypothesis which with colleagues on the faculty has been tested in a clinical setting for more than two decades is that family psychopathology is a critical variable in the genesis and continuation of psychoses of childhood. The method of testing this hypothesis has been clinical research through the simultaneous treatment of the psychotic child and his parents.

This writer has long held general biological interest with respect to comparative interorganismic behavior in infrahuman phyla and its possible implications for human interactions especially in infancy and early childhood.

It has been his premise that all psychotherapeutic work, but especially with the family, has all the elements of an experiment. These assumptions were early strengthened by the contributions of Harry Stack Sullivan. His clinical and theoretical studies of interpersonal processes in humans appear more germane in many respects than some classical psychoanalytic metapsychological concepts that appeared to leave little room for the importance of the family in clinical work and clinical research in child psychiatry.

The most recent work of John Bowlby on Attachment has been of particular interest in the above context. His review of phylogenetic phenomena of attachment and his emphasis on the experimental approach resonates with the present writer's experience and relates very well to clinical data accumulated over many years. Bowlby's unique synthesis from his own research in mother-infant interaction and his exhaustive review of aspects of child development research in the first year of life is not generally familiar to most physicians. It has been exciting to note the relevance of much of Bowlby's summary of this research for the clarification of the hypotheses generated by some clinicians in their work with children and their families.

These remarkable efforts of Bowlby to relate such research to clinical

191

observations have important implications for the clinical work of all those who are therapeutically engaged with children and their families. The restatement of the findings described by Bowlby as they relate to clinical psychotherapeutic work and research with children, particularly seriously disturbed children, and their families is one purpose of this chapter.

One other objective is to focus on Bowlby's challenging theoretical position derived from these data and to review this new theory in the light of our clinical research findings and observations from psychotherapeutic work with children and their families.

John Bowlby's first of two volumes entitled *Attachment* contains much of interest to clinicians in child psychiatry. Any mental health professional who has found it difficult to keep abreast of recent developments in the behavioral sciences will find this volume a rewarding review and an index for further reading.

Advances in analytical biology and control theory have elucidated basic principles underlying adaptive, goal-directed behavior and, according to Bowlby, constitute a "theoretical breakthrough" in the search for a well-based theory of instinct—the absence of which Freud lamented half a century ago. Three empirically based sciences, ethology, experimental psychology and neurophysiology, have exploited this breakthrough and, complementing one another, are contributing to the emergence of a unified behavioral science. Bowlby describes how analytical biology and control theory have begun to contribute to fundamental principles elucidated in these three basic sciences and have contributed much to modern child development.

This discussion requires a condensation which cannot adequately represent Bowlby's impressive effort to lay a foundation, derived from modern biological science, for the final topic in the remainder of the book, namely, that of the ontogeny of human attachment. This last central notion of human attachment behavior seems also an important contribution not only to the general field of child development but a central contribution as well to clinical science in child psychiatry. Hence, an abbreviated and arbitrary condensation of this kind will permit more space and attention to the last part of the volume and to what strikes one clinician as possible applications to the psychopathology of the psychotic disorders of early childhood.

INSTINCTIVE BEHAVIOR AND ATTACHMENT BEHAVIOR

The first of the two major concepts is Bowlby's redefinition of "instinctive" behavior; the second, his separating out from other instinctive behaviors or behavioral systems that of attachment as one that is primary and autonomous.

In defining the concept of instinctive behavior, Bowlby, a psychoanalyst, points out that the assumption of "psychic energy" in classical psycho-analytic metapsychology (49, 70) must be rejected as well as those meanings commonly attached to such terms as "instinct" or "instinctual." His basic reasons for this rejection are that psychic energy is logically unrelated to central psychoanalytic concepts of unconscious processes of repression, transference and childhood traumas as the origin of neurosis; and also that it was derived and applied to psychology by Freud in an effort to bring it into the sphere of the "proper" science of his day, not from his clinical data (as were the central concepts), but from the applications of the notion of "force" and energy and its conservation which Helmholtz and others were busy applying to physiology in the last half of the nineteenth century. Assumption of a separate "psychical" energy is untestable in direct observations and by experiments in human behavior.

It is, of course, a truism to remind oneself that if a theory in science is tested repeatedly, frequently and rigorously, its status is higher and better for the purposes of science because it is more supported by such accumulated observations and experimental data. Such a theory stands until further data are gathered which are not explicable by the theory, which then requires a new and wider hypothesis which explains both the older as well as the newer data. Although for clinical work the reconstructive or historical approach is useful and necessary, and even though there is nothing unscientific about making assumptions that help to organize and make perhaps more understandable such retrospective data, there are certain and now rather obvious limitations to this method of theory construction.

The ultimate power of an assumption in science is that capacity of an hypothesis for predicting future events and of being capable of confirmation by *prospectively* obtained data from experiment or observation (70). Freud himself pointed out, looking *backward* in analysis at an individual human being's life history, its course appears strictly determined by all events reconstructed. Looking forward, however, prediction, or synthesis, cannot be made since the quantitative assessment of the person's reactions to the particular combination of possible events and influences in their unpredictable chronological order cannot be foreseen. Thus although some of the basic assumptions of psychoanalysis already mentioned have been drawn from direct *clinical*, psychoanalytic experience and are capable of being confirmed by subsequent events in the course of therapeutic work with new patients, that of psychic energy is not. The assumption of psychic energy also does not help to explain for example why some instinctive behaviors are at times activated, then terminated and again activated on the basis of the assumption that psychic energy is discharged upon accumulation and shortly thereafter accumulated to be once more discharged. This is especially true when such activation or termination of behavior can be seen to be repeatedly connected to some change in the organism's relation to events and situations in its environment.

In view of such and other considerations, Bowlby nevertheless retains the name "instinctive" for certain very striking regularities of behavior—despite their complexity, their variations from moment to moment, from day to day, from season to season, from one species to another and even from one individual to another within the same species. He retains the name "instinctive" *provided* it is used *purely descriptively,* particularly without implication of *any* particular theory of causation *and* provided these regularities of behavior play an important part largely in the survival of the individual but particularly in the survival of the species.

Despite such variations, as Bowlby states it, that behavior which in the past has been commonly termed instinctive has four general characteristics: first, it has a recognizably similar and predictable *pattern* (not necessarily stereotyped) in almost all members of a species or all members of one sex; second, it is not a simple response to a single stimulus but is a sequence of behavior that usually runs a predictable course; third, certain of its *usual* consequences are of obvious value in contributing to the preservation of an individual or the continuity of the species; and fourth, many examples of it develop when all the opportunities for learning are exiguous or absent.

He points to the fact that behavior that he calls instinctive can no longer be so considered only on the basis of whether or not it is "innate," or "acquired" by learning. This antithesis is unreal inasmuch as every biological character, morphological, physiological or behavioral, is a product of the interaction of the genetic endowment with environment. In place of this antithesis, of inherited or acquired, biologists, like Hinde, now consider a continuum of characters which extends from one extreme that is termed environmentally stable to that termed environmentally labile. The characters classed in the first extreme are those still commonly termed innate, while those in the second extreme and in the middle ranges are those termed acquired. The latter are learned, that is, made possible in experience as maturation of the innate equipment of the organism proceeds during its ontogenetic development.

He also distinguishes rather sharply between the *function* and the *causation* of instinctive behavior or of a behavioral system. The function of such behavior refers always to the entire *species,* or to that portion that is an interbreeding *population* of the species. The causation of instinctive behavior, on the other hand, refers only to its activation and termination on any occasion in the life of any *individual* of such a population.

The function originates in the processes of phylogenetic evolution such as those mutations that increase the probability of a differentially greater propagation of the mutants. Such increases in probability of propagation are of course those that increase the chances of survival of this portion of the population of the species in their environment. The result and concomitant, naturally, of such processes is that of improving progressively the adaptation of the resulting population of the species to a particular environment which is then its environment of adaptedness.

The return by ethologists to Darwinian principles of evolutionary theory as regards the behavioral equipment of animals makes understanding of behavior more possible in terms of its contribution to species survival in the natural habitat of that species. Bowlby's thesis is that following this same principle will make the instinctive behavior of man more comprehensible.

The *causation* of the given instinctive behavior results from several factors, each with its predictable outcome in nutrition, reproduction, defense of territory, or self-protection. Among these factors are those which are: 1) *internal* to the organism, e.g. characteristic of the phase of its life cycle, the hormone level, the nature of the organization of the central nervous system, the results of experience and learning by the individual and the like; 2) those which are *external* to the organism, such as events in the environment, e.g., the presence or absence of food, a ripe mate, the immature young, a competitor, or dangerous proximity or presence of a predator and the like; and finally, 3) those factors that constitute information from internal and/or external sources about the results of action already taken. This latter factor represents the contribution of control systems theory.

Teleological assumptions are thus avoided. The structure of an instinctive behavioral system, originating in the phylogenic adaptation of a given species, determines its *function* for the population. The activation and termination of such a behavioral system in an individual of that species occurs when internal and external circumstances of the organism are sufficient and adequate as *causes* of the behavior. The goal corrected aspects of such behavior as responses of the organism to the results of action already taken lead to the predictability of its outcome. The flexibility of the instinctive behavioral systems, particularly in the subhuman primates and in man himself especially, stems from their being environmentally labile. That is, the particular form that the behavioral system takes in the adult is left open for learning experience during development and rearing and in subsequent living to determine the particular adaptation of the individual to a particular environment.

This flexibility, however, has a price. A particularly and unusually destructive environment (of course, especially that of the human environment) may make adaptive learning especially difficult in the early phase of the life cycle of an individual. The effect upon the environmentally labile behavioral system's characteristics of such circumstances is a miscarriage in the organization of the behavioral system or systems as far as their adaptive effectiveness for the individual organism is concerned. One result of an effective, or a relatively ineffective, organization of a behavioral system (or of the integration of several behavioral systems) may be that although many or all components of behavior are performed and its predictable outcome is achieved, nevertheless its function is not attained or only partially or poorly attained. Bowlby cites the example of a confirmed homosexual as an illustration of this form of miscarriage of the flexibility of instinctive behavior. In this instance the predictable outcome of orgasm with a partner of the same sex is present, but the functional consequence of reproduction as a means for the survival of the species does not follow. Despite such results in *some individuals* of unadapted or maladaptive forms of behavioral systems for the described reasons, the *species* persists with the potential to develop adaptive forms of the behavioral systems preserved in its genic equipment.

Another aspect important to clinicians is that almost any behavioral system in birds and mammals can be deviated in its development by suitable manipulation of environment so that its final form in an individual is *functionally* ineffective. Thus the systems responsible for locomotion, nest-building, courtship and parental behavior have been observed to develop in a way that functional consequences rarely or never follow their activation.

Of course, if a vital system such as that responsible for food intake is sufficiently seriously maldeveloped, the individual may not survive. But some behavioral systems, such as those responsible for sexual and parental behavior, when even markedly maldeveloped, need not have so fatal a consequence for the individual. Hence, Bowlby suggests, this may be "one reason why so much of psychopathology is concerned with behavioral systems responsible for sexual and parental behavior: whenever it is concerned with a more vital function the individual dies before a psychiatrist sees him." Another and not any less important reason for the frequent involvement of parental and sexual behavior in pathological development or maldevelopment, he suggests, is that both sexual and parental behavior when functionally effective are the integrates "of a very large number of behavioral systems that are organized in very special ways." During the immaturity of the individual an atypical environment then results in more or less severe malintegration of these various behavioral systems.

ATTACHMENT BEHAVIOR

The second main idea which is presented is that of attachment behavior. Bowlby reviews the data of ethologists' study of a number of species of both birds and mammals, as well as their observations especially of the subhuman primates. He collates this animal data with observations on human infants by both clinicians as well as students of child development and concludes that attachment is probably one of the instinctive behaviors in all of these species. He theorizes that it is autonomous and independent of all others. As such it has a function that serves to promote survival of the species: namely that of protection against predators.

There are differences between the various species in the time of the appearance and the intensity of the attachment and in the object toward which it is directed in different early periods of the life cycle. Usually there is a gradual diminution of intensity as puberty and adulthood are approached but evidence of it often continues throughout life. Bowlby considers at some length how application of control theory explains many of the observed phenomena of its occurrence. He discusses in some detail the factors or variables which underlie its appearance, intensification, and particularly its activation and termination—i.e., its causes on those occasions when individuals manifest it.

It is of particular importance, especially for clinicians, to note that it is an *interorganismic* manifestation, that innate biases of *both* the infant and the mother-figure (or other older individuals) predispose to the appearance and development of attachment behavior. The observed data strongly suggest that in all these species it is a primary instinctive behavioral system and *not* a secondary, or conditioned, or learned one as a result of the feeding experience or certain other aspects of mothering care. Thus, at certain times, the behavior is manifested despite punishment from attachment figures, which even strengthens or intensifies it, even though this is not quite the case at the early appearance of this behavior. Thus, appears the attachment of young and immature individuals of a group of animals to the protective strong males, which in circumstances of danger especially punish these immature individuals for their proximity to them at the periphery of their protective barrier to the predator.

There are differences among the species as to the periods after hatching, or after birth, when the attachment occurs to another individual (of the same or another species) or even to inanimate objects. These sensitive periods when such imprinting occurs appear related to the state of maturation upon beginning of the organism's independent existence. The more capable the newborn or the young is of pattern perception, of locomotion, and especially of clinging (among mammals and particularly in the subhuman primates), the earlier after birth is the initiative for attachment seen in the infant. Otherwise, the initiative for maintaining proximity and contact comes from the mother. If, as in the gorilla and the human, the newborn lacks the strength to clasp the mother (or her ventral hair in the case of the gorilla) and support itself, the mother supplies the initiative and the infant receives support from the mother until it can cling.

The initiative for the maintenance of proximity between mother and infant—the goal of the behavior of both—shifts back and forth between them depending upon such variables mentioned as well as the distance between them, the presence of danger, the age and maturational stage of the infant. Thus, in such subhuman primates as the rhesus monkey, the baboon, the chimpanzee and the gorilla, the infant clings to mother soon after birth in a ventro-ventral position with both arms and legs clinging to her hair clasping a nipple in its mouth. The infant is either gathered by mother to her body and supported there by her if necessary, whenever mother or infant is alarmed or whenever mother begins to move for any other reason. In later maturational stages in most or all of these primates, the infant at such times climbs aboard and rides her back.

Although the newborn *human* infant has a moderately strong grasping reflex for a short time, it is generally carried by the mother for several months, as is the gorilla infant. This is especially and more continuously true of the human infant being carried on her back or hip in the simpler societies of hunters and gatherers than of other more advanced cultures. There is thus a discernible continuum in respect to these aspects of the attachment behavior of mother and infant from lowest primates to Western man. In all, proximity between them is very generally maintained whichever, mother or infant, takes the initiative depending upon circumstances with progressive increase of initiative coming from the growing infant.

Although a human infant takes up to three months to begin to discriminate his mother from other people, most infants reared in family settings at four months smile and vocalize more readily when they see their mother's face and hear her voice and follow her with their eyes for longer than they do when they see or hear anyone else. Infants in the tribe of Ganda in Uganda, Africa, have been observed to be generally more rapidly maturing in locomotion than those in Western societies. They were observed occasionally to cry and attempt to follow a mother leaving them by crawling as early as 15 or 17 weeks, though most of them did so by six months of age.

Between the ages of seven and nine months infants, even those of Western cultures, begin to cling to mother when alarmed as in the presence of strangers. Such children also begin to follow and show signs of attachment to other familiar figures such as father and siblings. By 12 months of age, when the child is more mobile, all these signs of attachment to mother, i.e., of attempting to keep proximity to her actively and showing distress on observing any signs of her departure, become much more definite and quite strong in most of them.

Thus, the range of the *appearance* of definite signs of attachment in human infants is from four to twelve months. The aforementioned intensity of this attachment continues until the third birthday after which it is observed very gradually to decrease unless relations with mother are disturbed. Nevertheless, the attachment continues as a dominant trend although in somewhat modified form throughout the period known as latency from the age of four years through adolescence.

Throughout life, internal and external factors temporarily and periodically increase intensity of attachment. Bowlby lists hunger, fatigue, and illness among internal factors, and alarm as the general external factor. He notes also that the attachment of daughter to mother is generally stronger than between mother and son, and the former (that is, the mother-daughter attachment) appears thus more in evidence throughout life. As an additional point, Bowlby objects to designating the increase of the signs of intensity of this attachment in adult life, in effect throughout life from cradle to the grave, during sickness or calamity as "regressive" or as excessive "dependency" as very misleading—as some writers have done. It overlooks the "vital role that attachment plays in the entire life cycle of man."

Briefly, then, six responses are listed as leading to attachment behavior: crying and smiling tend to bring mother to infant and maintain her proximity to the infant; following and clinging bring the infant to mother and retain him close to her; the infant's calling mother by short, sharp calls after four months, and later by her name, is also important. Sucking is not easily categorized and requires further study.

Among the criteria of attachment used then are crying and following when mother leaves, greeting and approach on her return as well as movement towards her and clinging to her when alarmed, and differential smiling at mother. After crawling begins and especially after eight months of age, the child begins to make little excursions from mother, exploring other objects and people and may even go out of her presence returning to her as if to assure himself of her proximity. If, however, the child becomes frightened, or if mother moves away, then the child quickly returns to her with some degree of distress. It has also been observed that in mother's presence such excursions and explorations of the child are markedly more confident; while in the presence of strangers the child is then much more timid and not infrequently collapses in distress. This is particularly true of an infant whose attachment to his mother and hers to him is and has not been secure.

If one discards, as Bowlby does, the learning theory (or secondary drive) as incapable of explaining the facts of attachment behavior, the question arises what hypothesis can replace it. He turns to the question of imprinting (or of sensitive periods very early in life during which attachment may occur) found by ethologists among both many birds and species of mammals. When this question was raised at one conference, the present writer heard a child psychiatrist remark facetiously, "Imprinting is for the birds!"

The reference to birds in this humorous comment is valid to the extent that the original *sense* of the term imprinting stems from the early findings of Lorenz in 1935 from his pioneer observations of attachment of goslings and ducklings to moving objects which these birds followed shortly after hatching. Lorenz also defined his original formulation of the phenomenon of imprinting quite narrowly, saying, "—imprinting (i.e. the attachment behavior which comes quickly to be focused on a particular object or class of objects) has a number of features which distinguish it fundamentally from a learning process—(which) has no equal in the psychology of any other animal least of all a mammal." These features of imprinting Lorenz identified were: 1) that it occurs *only* during a brief critical period in the life-cycle; 2) that it is *irreversible*; 3) that it is *supraindividual* learning (that is, attachment to a class and not to a specific individual); and 4) that it *influences patterns of behavior that have not yet developed* in the organism's repertoire, e.g., the later selection of a sexual partner. Finally Lorenz defined the phenomenon as one occurring in the course of the particular activity: that of following a moving object.

However, in the thirty years since this narrow view of imprinting by Lorenz was stated it has been broadened by other ethologists in the light of later gathered observations. Thus, it has been observed also in a number of mammals: 1) that neither the critical period nor the irreversibility is as clear cut as Lorenz supposed (e.g. selection of sexual mate may not be so determined); 2) that it can occur when the organism is exposed to a stationary object or pattern; and finally 3) some of the features of imprinting (that is, of attachment) apply to other types of learning especially in mammals. For these reasons ethologists currently use the term imprinting in a more generic sense, referring to whatever processes are at work leading a young bird or mammal to become preferentially and stably attached toward one (or more) discriminated figure or figures. Extending this more generic usage it has also been used to refer to processes leading to other forms of behavior directed preferentially toward particular objects such as maternal behavior toward particular young, and sexual behavior toward particular mate or mates.

Hinde emphasizes that, despite the striking similarities in the phenomena of attachment among birds and those among mammals, they need to be considered as the results of convergent evolution to meet a similar survival problem. It does not mean that the mechanisms of attachment evolved in these two phyla are therefore the same.

In the light of such developments in the study of attachment behavior—and particularly in subhuman primates—Bowlby concludes that at present attachment behavior in human infants although much slower "is of a piece with that seen in subhuman mammals." His contention is that "much evidence supports this conclusion and none contradicts it." In support of this he lists the present knowledge of the development of attachment behavior in the human infant and child under the same eight aspects as those summarizing the present knowledge of imprinting in birds as follows:

i. In human infants social responses of every kind are first elicited by a wide array of stimuli and are later elicited by a much narrower array, confined after some months to stimuli arising from one or a few particular individuals.

ii. There is evidence of a marked bias to respond socially to certain kinds of stimuli more than to others.

iii. The more experience of *social interaction* an infant has with a person the stronger his attachment to that person becomes.

iv. The fact that learning to discriminate different faces commonly follows periods of attentive staring and listening suggests that exposure learning may be playing a part, i.e., it is probably not dependent on reinforcement.

v. In most infants attachment behavior to a preferred figure develops during the first year of life. It seems probable that there is a sensitive period in that year during which attachment behavior develops most readily.

vi. It is unlikely that any sensitive phase begins before about six weeks and it may be some weeks later.

vii. After about six months, and markedly so after eight or nine months, babies are more likely to respond to strange figures with fear responses, and more likely also to respond to them with strong fear responses, than they are when they are younger. Because of the growing frequency and strength of such fear responses, the development of attachment to a new figure becomes increasingly difficult toward the end of the first year and subsequently.

viii. Once a child has become strongly attached to a particular figure, he tends to prefer that figure to all others, and such preference tends to persist despite separation.

We may conclude, therefore, that so far as is at present known, the way in which attachment behavior develops in the human infant and becomes focused on a discriminated figure is sufficiently like the way in which it develops in other mammals, and in birds, for it to be included, legitimately, under the heading of imprinting—so long as that term is used in its current generic sense.

Hence, without reviewing here in detail the data of attachment behavior given by Bowlby and obtained by investigators like Harlow with rhesus monkeys and that of others with other primates and with other mammals in the generic sense of the term, one can say that imprinting may not be "for the birds" alone, but also for mammals and among them the human instance. Otherwise one would create "a wholly unwarranted gap between the human case and that of other species."

"ONTOGENY OF HUMAN ATTACHMENT"

Space does not here permit more than a very rough outline of the considerable detail and the wealth of references to specific studies of the four phases of the development of attachment behavior of the human infant during the first twelve months of his life that Bowlby includes in the last section of his book under this title. To those with a scientific interest in early development these last four chapters are an invaluable review and an index to the relevant recent studies of the subject. For the child psychiatrist whose knowledge regarding this period of life is less likely to be as thorough (either from usually insufficient direct clinical experience or from his previous, not very clearly formulated theory), it may be of even greater importance. That is, it is a text which forms a guide for the clinical study of the beginnings of the behavioral development of this phase of life. It is becoming ever more evident that it is essential to include much more than in the past of this phase of human life in the training of future practitioners of this sub-specialty. The various, extant, theoretically speculative formulations about the normal behavior and the psychopathological problems of older children they see clinically could be better evaluated then, from such clinical experience with the first 18 to 24 months of life.

It is a field which is very probably a source of still deeper comprehension of the disorders of later childhood and particularly of those most severe of these disorders, namely the psychoses. Such deeper comprehension may then give still better clues to more effective therapeutic measures for these grave congeries of disorder—as well as for those disorders of milder severity but many of which are still quite difficult to ameliorate. It goes without saying, of course, that the hope of what is still rather wistfully called primary prevention might find firmer ground from such increased information and grasp of the relevant factors in these early phases of human development.

Emphasizing that there are no sharp boundaries between them, Bowlby divides these first twelve months or so of life as far as signs of attachment behavior are concerned of children reared in families roughly into four phases as follows:

1. Orientation and signals without discrimination of figure;
2. Orientation and signals directed towards one (or more) discriminated figures;
3. Maintenance of proximity to a discriminated figure by means of locomotion as well as signals;
4. Formation of a goal-corrected partnership.

They are, obviously, closely related to, as well as expressions of, the maturational phases in growth of the infant's biological, neuromuscular equipment as well as of the kind of experience the infant has, especially with his human environment.

The first phase—lasting from birth to not less than eight weeks of age and more usually to about 12 weeks, but under unfavorable conditions till much later—is characterized by orientation towards *any* person: tracking the person's movements with his eyes, grasping, and reaching, smiling and babbling. The baby ceases to cry on hearing a voice or seeing a face. All these activities, of course, are likely to influence the person to increase the time of his proximity to the baby. All these friendly responses increase in intensity after 12 weeks and thereafter are clearly a fully spontaneous, vivacious and delightful expression of innate bias to respond to the human environment—as well as the bias of the adult to respond to the infant.

In the second phase, the infant behaves in the same generally friendly fashion as in the first phase but begins to do so more markedly toward the mother-figure than toward other persons. This differentiated responsiveness to the mother regarding auditory stimuli may begin as early as about four weeks and at about ten weeks with respect to visual stimuli. Both are generally quite evident in most babies reared in families from twelve weeks of age and this phase lasts till about six months of age or longer.

The third phase includes increasing discrimination between people and an extension of his repertoire of responses. With locomotion progressively available to him the infant follows a departing mother, greets her when she returns and uses her as a base from which to explore other aspects of his environment. During this phase his previously rather undiscriminating friendly responsiveness to other persons tends to wane. Although certain familiar secondary, or subsidiary figures (such as father, siblings or grandparents in home) remain as such secondary attachment figures, *strangers* become objects of increasing cautious regard. Eventually such strangers are likely to arouse alarm and withdrawal.

This phase tends to become evident between the sixth and seventh month although in infants who have had little social contact and responsiveness from a main figure for attachment it may be delayed until after the twelfth month. In infants who are more fortunate in this respect, the systems mediating the attachment to the mothering figure become more clearly organized as goal-corrected, namely, modified by mother's behavior in his effort to gain and maintain proximity to her. In such infants by the first birthday, as Bowlby puts it, "the attachment to his mother-figure is evident for all to see." This phase tends to continue throughout the second year and into the third.

The fourth phase—that which Bowlby names "Formation of a Goal-Corrected Partnership"—more and more evidently by means of a gradually better developed (internal) cognitive map, the infant's proximity to an attachment figure is maintained more and more by means of organized goal-corrected systems. By this is meant that with increasing maturation of the cerebral hemispheres and perhaps especially the frontal areas, the child's internally developed map of his environment, the whereabouts or the movements of the mother figure herself becomes included conceptually as an independent object, persistent in time and space and moving about in a more or less predictable space-time continuum. His mobile activity is then more and more evidently modified by *her* activities in order to maintain his proximity to her.

Although at first the infant's grasp of the mother's own behavior as being organized about her own set goals—at times conflicting with his goal of proximity with her—may be beyond his competence, eventually his observations of her behavior and those factors that influence it may make it progressively possible for him to infer more and more of *her* set-goals and of her plans to achieve them. When this is achieved by the infant the internal picture of his world becomes far more sophisticated and his behavior, more flexible. In other words a child may thus be said to begin to acquire what Bowlby calls "insight" into his mother's motives and feelings. Their relationship to each other now much more complex is one which Bowlby calls a partnership—and clearly a new phase. Although there is still insufficient evidence to guide one, it is difficult not to assume that this phase is very likely to begin before the child's second birthday and for many children, probably, closer to, or after, their third.

As Bowlby puts it, it is entirely arbitrary to assert by which of these four phases the child can be said to be attached: plainly he is not in the first; and plainly he *is* attached in phase three and to what extent in phase two becomes more a matter of definition of attachment.

What can be asserted more generally about all four phases are the following principles of ontogeny.

There is:

a) a tendency for the range of effective stimuli for the infant's responses to become restricted (and focussed—this writer's addition).
b) a tendency for primitive behavioral systems to become superseded by those more sophisticated.
c) a tendency for behavioral systems to start by being nonfunctional and later to become integrated into functional wholes.

It is a fascinating story to follow—one that is impossible even to sketch with any adequacy here—which the students of child development are piecing together from their various researches. These researches form in large part the remainder of this section on ontogeny from such aspects as the behavioral equipment of the neonate, its early responses to people, such as its tendency to orient toward them; the head-turning and sucking ("rooting"), grasping, clinging and reaching (the Moro response of embracing), and especially the development of smiling (through the phases of spontaneous and reflex smiling, that of unselective smiling to the phase of selective social smiling).

However, equally important for the clinician as another important social interchange is to learn that the development of babbling to making a large variety of sounds, like smiling, has a time table which is earlier in family reared infants than those reared in depriving institutions. The response of crying—although not welcomed from the infant by adults as are the previously described friendly responses—is also important for social interaction since human responses are the most effective terminators to such infantile expressions or signals of pain, hunger, anger, or distress and disturbance from unpleasant external stimuli (sudden noises, chilling, nakedness, posture, etc.). Each of these cries according to Wolff's studies have characteristics different from each other according to the sources of their arousal (which will not be detailed here) as well as individual qualities most of which attentive mothers learn to identify.

It is of particular importance to clinicians to know from close study of Bowlby's book, of the references he gives as well from the close clinical study of each child and mother they may see, about the crying which has none of the activating causes already named. This is a type of crying which is terminated most effectively by responses of human origin: sounds of the human voice, tactile and proprioceptive stimuli from *non-nutritive* sucking and particularly by the infant's being rocked. The female voice especially in the third week is more effective than the male one. The mother's voice becomes so effective a few weeks later, that it may not only terminate the crying but if continued may also evoke smiling. Hence not only sucking on pacifiers quiets the child but quiets even those infants born with atresia of the esophagus—hence, it is not only intake of food which is the effective terminating stimulus.

Also of considerable importance is the fact, well known by many mothers, that rocking is also quite effective. This factor has tended to become obscured by "a misplaced insistence on the primacy of feeding." A curiously interesting finding from experimental study of rocking as a terminator of crying, which produces vestibular stimulation from a *vertical* movement, is the fact that it is effective when used at the rate of 60 cycles a minute—and *not* effective at speeds of such rocking slower than this, particularly below 50 cycles per minute. At 60 cycles (and in some infants up to 70 cycles) per minute the infant not only ceases his crying, but his heart rate which may reach up to 200 beats per minute during such crying slows sharply; his breathing becomes regular and the baby becomes relaxed. This speed of rocking is one that continues to be effective—i.e., the infant does not become habituated—and may be related to the fact that it is the rate at which an adult walks slowly. And it has been observed that when the baby is carried by mother on her back or her hip and is thereby rocked at not less than sixty cycles per minute, he does not cry unless hungry or in pain. Bowlby adds, "this happy consequence might be due to chance: more likely, it seems, it is the result of selective pressures that have been operating during the course of man's evolution."

He continues in summary: "It is clear, therefore, that as a terminator of rhythmic crying, rocking is on a par with feeding. When a baby is hungry, feeding is the effective terminator; when he is not hungry, rocking is the most effective one. In the opposite set of conditions, neither is effective for more than a short while."

In another experimental study it was found that rocking a baby is effective not only in terminating such rhythmic crying but also in delaying its onset. The child, selected at random in the nursery with others, after they had all been fed and who was rocked for half an hour in its crib, was less likely to cry during the next half hour of observation, than the other children who were not rocked.

Thus, it may be summarized that if a baby is *not* hungry, or in pain, or is cold, in increasing order of effectiveness as terminators of his crying are first the human female voice, second, non-nutritive sucking, and third, most effective of all, rocking. It is therefore understandable that such rhythmic crying is often said to be from loneliness, however unwarranted scientifically it may be to make such assumptions, there may be a grain of truth in it. The facts are that if infants are not spoken to and are not rocked during waking periods they are apt to cry; they seem content and quiet in the reverse condition, and the most probable person to rock and talk to the baby, of course, is the mother.

Another fact of observation that is of interest to the clinician is that, as Wolff observed, as early as the fifth week many babies. quite content when a person is in their line of vision, begin crying when this person disappears and stop when he returns. There is as yet no discrimination as to the person in this matter until after about five months when the particular person who comes and goes with such responses from the child matters a great deal. By nine months such crying upon departure of mother is likely because the child can then—especially among Ganda babies—follow her. Further, the crying is more likely if mother's departure is sudden, noisy and bustling. By twelve months strangers and strange situations begin to evoke alarm, crying and turning to mother. At this time, too, he may begin to anticipate unpleasant occurrences, such as seeing a doctor preparing an injection which has been experienced a few weeks before, or seeing his mother getting ready to depart, and begin crying. All this evidences a rapidly incrasing grasp of the world which the child of this age is acquiring.

NATURE AND NURTURE; INBORN AND ACQUIRED

Bowlby gives a few examples from the research of others of his previous emphasis of the interaction of both the genetic factors with the environmental influences in the development of attachment behavior as in the development of every biological character in the human organism. Thus, such research workers (33) have found that girls at 24 months of age show a profound preference for looking at faces rather than at non-facial patterns; while boys at the same age show no such preference. This may reinforce studies which show earlier neurophysiologic maturation in female infants than in male infants. Further research (52) evidence has suggested that the first appearance of orientation and smiling is affected by genetic variables in that these appear closer in time in identical twins than in same-sexed, fraternal twins. Since both kinds of twins in this comparison were reared at home in the same family, environmental variation was minimized. Nevertheless, it has been the clinical experience of the present writer that in a few instances tendencies toward opposite personality characteristics *did* appear in identical twins and the mother of such twins reported a definite difference in her feeling reactions to each twin shortly after birth—despite the similarity between the babies.

SOME CLINICAL IMPLICATIONS FROM EXPERIMENTAL STUDIES

Bowlby seems to provide for such different development in his report of the research comparing the generally slower appearance by some weeks of smiling and babbling in children reared in depriving institutions in comparison to those reared in their own family homes. After three months the deviation in such development in the institution children is observed to become progressively greater from the home babies. "Institution infants are later to discriminate between face and mask, and between faces. They also make fewer attempts to initiate social contact, their repertoire of expressive movements is smaller, and as late as twelve months they still show no sign of attachment to any particular person. This absence of attachment is especially noticeable when they are distressed: even then they rarely turn to an adult." Such studies therefore emphasize and support the findings of clinicians, namely, that the greater the variation of the environment of the infant and young child during the early maturational (i.e., genetically determined, but more the environmentally labile) phases the greater is that environmental influence upon the child's behavioral characteristics—or personality development.

Although there is considerable debate about what factors in the institution that are responsible for these "retarding effects"—that is, whether the main factor is a "reduction of stimulus input" or the absence of a mother-figure, Ainsworth (2), an active researcher in this field, replying to this states that the mother-figure is by far the main source of the infant's stimulation, providing opportunity for the infant for actively exploring his world both manually and visually. Piaget and later students regard such opportunities as of considerable importance for the infant's sensori-motor development. Bowlby summarizing this argument points to the multiple deprivations an institution exposes the child to: "lack of stimulus input, lack of exposure learning, lack of opportunity for 'self-induced movement in dependably structured environments,' to name some." One might add that clinicians are aware of such deprivations even in some family reared children.

"FOCUSING ON A FIGURE"—CLINICAL IMPLICATIONS

In a good many respects the present writer regards the fifteenth chapter entitled, "Focusing on a Figure," of more interest than many of the others. The reason for this is its implications and bearing on psychopathology and particularly on the psychopathology of the early psychotic degrees of maldevelopment.

Although Bowlby here reviews in a greater detail the various phenomena of the infant's behavior of phase two which are also of considerable importance (orientation and signals directed toward one or more discriminated figure(s)), it is his sections in this chapter entitled "Figures towards whom attachment behavior is directed," "Processes leading to selection of figures," and "Sensitive phases and the fear of strangers" that excite the greater interest of the clinician who has a particular interest in the psychotic disorders of early childhood. His last section which deals with a critique of Spitz's position in sharply distinguishing fear of strangers (Spitz's "eight month anxiety") from separation anxiety as distinct and separable phenomena is also of considerable theoretical interest.

This detailed review of the thirteen identified, *differentially* directed behaviors toward a particular figure of the second phase, based on studies of infants in Boston by Wolff, and in Ganda—the latter by Ainsworth who is the chief source of this review—emphasizes the restriction of the range of stimuli which activate and terminate each of the aspects of such behavior. Together with these studies, one of some Scottish infants by Shaffer and Emerson, although with observational methods somewhat varying from those of Ainsworth give reasonably comparable data for infants reared under such varying circumstances as rural Africa and urban families in the Western countries make it probable that they will be similar in other settings as well. There were variations found both between infants and probably some fluctuations in the same infant in the discrimination of the mother figure.

The reader is referred to Bowlby's text for the details of the range of ages of the appearance of the various items of these behaviors and the criteria used to define them—already in large measure mentioned previously in the present discussion—which become progressively directed toward the principal attachment figure. Briefly, however, they include such phenomena in which the infants begin to show their preferences as differential stopping of crying on being held, crying on mother's departure, differential approach to mother and following her when she leaves, differential greeting of her on her return, and particularly, differential use of her as a base from which to explore and as a haven of safety, and, of course, others.

In summary, differentially directed responses to the mother are few before sixteen weeks of age and are probably better observable when sensitive methods are used and there are more numerous and more apparent differentially directed responses between sixteen and twenty-six weeks of age. Thus Yarrow reports the results of his study of forty or more infants in each age group (using a preferential, selective attention to mother-figure in the presence of a stranger with a positively excited affect toward her and not toward the stranger as the criteria) as follows: 20 per cent of infants showed such preference toward mother as early as one month of age; 80 per cent of them showed definite signs of recognizing mother at three months, and all of them did so at five months. As Bowlby again states it, "in the great majority of family infants of six months and over" such preference for mother in these differentially directed responses "are plain for all to see."

In his discussion of figures toward whom attachment behavior is directed, Bowlby is careful to emphasize that his use of "mother" or "mother-figure" is one that is unavoidable for the sake of brevity but it does *not* mean that mothering should always be provided by his natural mother and also that mothering "cannot be safely distributed among several figures" as Mead misunderstood him to believe. He also emphasizes that almost from the first many children show attachment to more than one person but do not treat the others, the subsidiary figures, as they do the principal figure (mother). Some of them show some aspects of their attachment to the subsidiary figures (father, siblings, or grandparents in the home, etc.) as soon as they show discrimination, although most infants probably do so later and a majority do so toward more than one figure. There was found by some students a hierarchical order among these additional attachment figures as measured by the amount of protest when the child was left by the different persons. In the African study, Ainsworth using a broader range of criteria found that these Ganda children with more than one attachment figure up to nine months of age tended to confine their following upon such a person's departure to the principal figure. Furthermore, they turned to that figure specifically when they were hungry, tired or ill. In these instances the child turned to the subsidiary figures only when in good spirits, as to another, older child, with whom play was habitual. Thus, these secondary persons from an early age may elicit different types of social behavior. Although the matter requires further research study, Ainsworth (3) concludes that nothing in her observations contradicts "the hypothesis that, given an opportunity to do so, an infant will seek attachment with one figure, even though there are several persons available as caretakers."

Concerning the principal attachment figure Bowlby comments that it is most common, probably in every culture, for the child to select from those present in the household the principal and the subsidiary attachment figures. In both the African and Scottish studies already mentioned only those children who were living with their natural mother were selected for observation, and hence it is not surprising that each child showed that his natural mother was the principal attachment figure. The few exceptions to this are of great interest to the clinician.

These exceptions in the Ganda group were a boy and a girl both of about nine months of age, who although attached to both mother and father, were said to prefer father, and in the boy's case even when he was ill or tired. A third child in this group, a girl, showed at twelve months attachment to father and a half-sister but none to her mother. Among the Scottish infants, there were three out of fifty-eight who showed a similar difference; two of them showed first attachment to father and the third, whose mother worked full-time, chose grandmother who took care of him most of the day. Hence, the role of principal attachment figure can be effectively filled for the child by others than the natural mother, particularly if the substitute treats the child in "a mothering way" which briefly means, according to present available evidence, "engaging in lively social interaction with him, and responding readily to his signals and approaches." From studies of other species, such a substitute may be at some disadvantage compared to the natural mother because of the latter's hormonal levels following parturition and stimuli from the newborn himself may be of great importance. Also, because a substitute mother may not come in contact with the baby until weeks or months after his birth, her responses to the child may be both less strong and less consistently elicited than that of the natural mothers. The clinician, even without the possibly and probably relevant data about the natural mother's hormonal levels, may add to all this his experiences with some natural mother's highly conflictful attitudes and the intrafamilial conflicts (illustrated in the section of studies of individual families in this volume) toward at least one of her infants which to him may have powerfully negative effects on that infant's development of attachment perhaps not only to her but toward other persons as well, as in instances of autism. Unfortunately for this latter point, there is not sufficient data about such matters in the natural mothers' attitudes included in the exceptions in either African or Scottish studies except for the working mother and the caretaking grandmother.

Some distinctions between the terms "principal" and "subsidiary" attachment figures are made by Bowlby and he comments that these problems require further and closer study. This matter is also of considerable interest to the clinician with a major interest in the study and therapy of psychotic disorders of early childhood.

First, there is uncertainty in both the Scotch and the African studies as to sufficiency of the criteria used to distinguish the principal from the subsidiary figures. Second, the Scotch study (in which parents' reports at monthly intervals were used to gather the data and the degree of protest by the child on mother's leaving the infant as the criterion) supports the view that social behavior of the infant begins to be directed toward the subsidiary figure at about the same time as toward the principal attachment figure; while Ainsworth's study (based on direct, fortnightly observations of the infant's behavior) inclines toward the view that attachment behavior toward the subsidiary figures occurred later than that toward the principal figure. Neither study used methods sufficiently refined to settle the issue. Further, it is possible that in some instances the kind of behavior that the infant showed toward the subsidiary figures differed sharply from his behavior toward the principal attachment figure, seeking proximity when ill, tired or alarmed. In other instances both kinds of behavior might be manifested toward the same figure particularly if the natural mother engaged in both kinds of interaction with the child, or if an older sibling, father or other person did likewise. In both instances the distinction might be left unclear as to "principal" and "subsidiary" categorization.

Lastly, the relative strength of attachment toward the principal and subsidiary figures is also of great interest to the clinician as well as to the student of development. Although it might have been supposed that the attachment of an infant with more than one attachment figure might be weak to his principal figure and that an infant with only one principal figure might be particularly strongly attached to this person, just the reverse is the case. And this also conforms in general to clinical experience with young psychotic children. In both the African and the Scotch infants it was found that those infants who begin by an intense attachment to their principal figure were also those who were more likely to direct social behavior toward other discriminated figures as well. On the other hand, the converse has also been found to be true, namely that those whose attachment is weak toward their principal figures are likely to direct little if any social behavior toward other persons.

Ainsworth speaks of all this in terms of security and insecurity of the attachment. In short, "the more insecure the infant's attachment is to his principal figure the more inhibited is he likely to be in developing attachments to other figures." Bowlby expands this explanation, either as an alternative, or as an addition to it: that the more insecure the child the more inhibited is he in developing play relations with other figures. He adds that it is an error to consider that the child "diffuses his attachment over many figures in such a way that he gets along with no strong attachment to anyone, and consequently without missing any particular person when that person is away." This supports an earlier contention of his that there is a strong bias for a child's attachment behavior to be directed toward one particular person in a particularly possessive way. This he referred to in his earlier writings as "monotropy" and now it seems to him to be well established with far-reaching implications for psychopathology.

All these findings of the students of development support the observations of clinicians of many disorders of childhood but particularly their observations of the symptomatology in the most severe and early withdrawal and affective unresponsiveness of the very autistic child. The colleagues of the present writer studying a considerable variety of degrees of the psychotic disorders—during a period of over twenty years at Langley Porter Neuropsychiatric Institute—have observed that those psychotic children with a history of the earliest onset and with the most obviously greatest and most ambivalent relations with their parents and especially with their mothers are also quite generally the most withdrawn from their siblings and other children.

This withdrawn behavior is clearly observed while they are in the hospital. They are also much more likely to be mute, or least verbally communicative, negativistic toward approaches of the adult staff, take much longer to develop intensely possessive attachments to such staff (and toward the particular nurse assigned to their care) and respond less readily and less completely in progressing toward integration (if at all) to their therapeutic efforts. This staff has also had the experience that the parents of these children also show the greatest psychopathology (that is not always very overtly observable outside their family life). Such psychopathology not only involves their relations with this child and their spouse, particularly before or after his birth, but it is also such as to present the greatest difficulty (e.g., clinical evidence of increase of child's symptoms chronologically related to traumatic events in family during therapy) in their psychotherapeutic progress with their individual therapists and the rest of the milieu staff. They are also the most likely to decide to separate themselves from the psychotic child after sometimes years of therapeutic effort. Or if they accept the child back into their homes they appear in their relations with him to remain aloof and highly ambivalent sometimes for years. (See Chapter 15 in this volume.)

In some contrast to this we have had experience also with children whose unresponsiveness and other symptoms have been less severe and less pervasive (sometimes also somewhat later in onset) and been less severely detached from their parents, less apathetic to their departure from the hospital or to their return. These children have been relatively more quickly responsive to the staff (i.e., becoming more quickly attached) than those of the previously mentioned group. This is particularly true if seen at a younger age. Their parents, too, have shown less severe emotional disorder, giving anamnestic information more readily, early in the clinical contact, that is psychologically more easily comprehensible not only toward the "identified" patient but their other children and their spouses. They also have been more readily responsive to the staff's therapeutic efforts. In both categories we have found no diagnosable, organic disease in the children. These latter children seem comparable if not altogether similar to the "symbiotic" group described by Margaret Mahler (37).

All these considerations recall a personal communication from Whitehorn many years ago. He stated to this writer that the schizophrenic person seems not to have lived through nor resolved developmental problems in his "vertical" personal relations (i.e., with parental figures). Therefore, his "horizontal" relations—that is, with persons like his siblings and age-mates— remain intensely uncomfortable or in Bowlby's terms, characterized by less intense or quite insecure attachment toward subsidiary figures. The patients that clinicians classify as less overtly psychotic or "schizoid" show similar but less severe psychopathology. In other words, they tend to be aloof, quite reserved (although perhaps capable of rather isolated self-maintenance outside of hospitals) easily hurt and rebuffed and subject to intensely, revengeful destructive inner turmoil.

To return to the psychotic children and their families, other experienced clinical students have also noted similar characteristics to those at Langley Porter. Thus Kanner and Eisenberg (21, 30) speak of the "refrigeration which has been the common lot of the autistic children" in their homes—even though they postulate a difference in them from the beginning of their extra-uterine existence. Goldfarb (24, 25), too, separates a group of psychotic children whom he calls "nonorganic" whose parents manifest a great "perplexity" about their rearing of their psychotic child. Most uncompromising of all these students about the psychogenic etiology of the autistic disorder, Bruno Bettelheim, appears most convinced of the importance etiologically of the role of parents' attitudes toward the child who develops autistically (10).

INANIMATE OBJECTS

In considering the role of inanimate objects toward which the infant's attachment behavior is also differentially directed, Bowlby calls attention not only to such well known activities as non-nutritive sucking and clasping or clinging to mother's breast (but *not* feeding behavior that he considers outside of attachment behavior). But he also refers to other objects such as a "dummy" (pacifier), the child's thumb in the early weeks of life and later toward the end of the first year, to other soft, cuddly objects as some particular bit of cloth, blanket or toy. He makes the interesting point that in the simplest societies in which the infant spends most of his day and night in contact with his mother's body, such sucking and clinging is directed toward her body as in all species of subhuman primates unlike infants in other societies including our own. In these latter societies, in a high proportion of children, the inanimate objects and such other treasured possessions (Winnicott's "transitional objects" (72), play the role of substitutes not only at night but are also demanded by the child during the day especially when he is tired or upset. Boys and girls, according to the evidence he cites, do not differ in this respect and such attachments to inanimate objects do not bode "ill for a child" and coexist with satisfactory relations with people.

Of interest in regard to this latter point are data from studies by Provence and Lipton (46) of infants reared in a depriving institution during their first year, none of whom became attached to "a favorite cuddly object." Hence the absence of such interest in soft objects "may give grounds for concern." He cites an observation by Stevenson (59) of a child with a strong dislike from early infancy of soft toys who had been rejected from the first by his mother who later deserted him. This could be thought of as possibly expressive of his dislike for his mother. He further considers the point that not only is attachment to inanimate objects quite compatible with satisfactory relations with people, and that prolongation of such attachments into later childhood and even into the school years may be commoner than supposed, but also that this latter fact may *not* be a certain sign that the child is insecure. However, he states, *"the position may be different when* the child *prefers* an inanimate object." (Italics ours.)

Bowlby then quotes several examples from Stevenson (59) of children in whom this was present. One of these, his mother reported, always asked for his duster when he fell down and not for her comfort. Two other mothers told of their sons' first requesting their objects on regaining consciousness after operations. One of the latter, at age six, after a tonsillectomy asked for "squirrel," and having obtained it he went to sleep peacefully.

Bowlby presumes that "it would be possible for the whole of a child's attachment behavior to be directed toward an object and none toward a person" which "were it to last any length of time would almost certainly be inimical to future mental health." He then refers to the findings of Harlow and Harlow (26) in their studies of the rhesus monkeys and to Winnicott's theory of the role of "transitional" objects as occupying a special place in the development of object relations. The rhesus monkeys whose attachment during infancy was directed exclusively to dummy figures were found grossly disturbed later in all their later social relations. He offers a critique of Winnicott's theory suggesting that a more parsimonious view is that inanimate objects may be regarded as "substitute objects" (rather than the widely accepted term "transitional") toward which certain components of attachment behavior come to be directed or redirected "because the 'natural object' is unavailable."

The support of this more parsimonious theory, he feels, is strong in the observations of monkeys and ape infants' attachment behavior raised away from their mothers. These subhuman primate infants, like human infants, readily accept the bottle for food, and comforter and thumb for non-nutritive sucking. These animal infants also direct their non-nutritive sucking to parts of their own body such as toes, and occasionally to her own nipple in the female and to his own penis in the male. They cling to a dummy mother-figure provided it is soft. There are also reports of chimpanzee infants clinging tenaciously to human foster mothers. But one of these was also described as accepting a soft towel as a substitute when such a foster mother sought relief from such unremitting attachment behavior of clinging to her.

From all this, Bowlby concludes that infants, human or monkey, can direct attachment behavior toward inanimate objects as substitutes, as a subsidiary attachment "figure," for the principal attachment figure where the latter is unavailable. This is especially true when such an infant is tired, ill or distressed. Of course, such attachment to inanimate objects as substitutes for the principal figures probably occurs at ages of the infant in the different species which are characteristic for its species. In the human infant the question that may need eventual answers through further research is whether such attachments occur prior to the infant's being able to explore the environmental objects manually and to experience the satisfactions of the sensual stimuli from hands and fingers which some observers place close to the sixth month. A similar question is whether the human infant can and does form definite attachments to such substitute objects prior to his capacity to explore such objects manually before about twelve months of age when maturation makes possible increasing finger-thumb opposition and adequate grasping.

All this data about inanimate objects are of interest to the clinician for a number of reasons. The complaints and anxieties of some parents of relatively undisturbed, or mildly disturbed, children about thumb-sucking, hand-sucking, genital self-stimulation, use of either the corner of their own bed blanket to suck, or to rub nose and mouth, especially on going to bed, are all quite well-known. Clinicians have suspected some disturbance in the mother-child relations in some of the more disturbed of these children, or have made therapeutic efforts especially with mothers to uncover the sources of such anxieties and to reduce them. Thumb-sucking has even been the focus of concern to orthodontists and about its possible role in maldevelopment of dental arches. Attachment to other special cuddly toys or other inanimate objects may generally be less disturbing to parents unless special and excessive concern is aroused for a variety of reasons. There is also some interest on the part of parents to supply cuddly animal toys or dolls to their children. There is also a well-known and popular cartoon strip in the United States' newspapers in which a "security blanket" of one of the child characters figures rather prominently. This may indicate some acceptance of children's attachment to such objects.

The clinical studies of children with psychotic disorder at Langley Porter (and probably by other clinicians elsewhere) have revealed a not infrequent incidence among them of a sometimes long-lasting and strong attachment to a variety of inanimate objects. Such attachments have been observed as preferred to people, often including their own parents and siblings, toward whom they show a marked affective unresponsiveness. Such objects are carried about all day, often quite tenaciously, in the context of other activities toward which they often are negativistic. They are not always soft and cuddly toys but may be such things as a piece of garden hose, balls of string, a purse.

They pick up leaves, sticks, and other such objects which they twiddle and usually gaze at intently for long periods sometimes with their back turned away from the group of other patients and staff. They may show particular interest in touching, smelling, or mouthing bed sheets, blankets, corners of their own clothing, or looking at their own fingers held close to their eyes with intense absorption, and so on. A few have repeatedly stimulated parts of their own bodies, such as genitals, anus, or lips. Such self-stimulation may in some involve squinting at and intensely peering at lamps, the sun, along edges of objects or into openings and holes.

At times such interests have been self-hurtful and in a few, self-mutilating: as biting corners of their mouth or tongue till bleeding and ulceration resulted; punching their heads till cataracts of the ocular lens resulted; banging heads against walls or with their own knees, resulting in bruises, lacerations, or breaking of their teeth, or licking walls, floors, eating garbage picked up from streets, etc. Whether these latter self-hurtful activities belong under rubric of "attachment" or a negative one is perhaps a separate question but it appears to clinicians as also expressive of their attitudes toward themselves as well as toward human persons. In some of such children such preoccupations with inanimate objects has decreased or disappeared when therapeutic work has resulted in the reduction of their unresponsiveness especially to adult persons.

Such clinically observed behavior appears related to the phenomena of attachment behavior to inanimate objects—or its possible opposite in the self-injurious instances. These observations possibly support Bowlby's thesis.

PROCESSES LEADING TO SELECTION OF FIGURES

In discussing the processes which produce the attachment behavior of an infant to particular persons, Bowlby repeats three or four of these processes he has identified earlier and emphasizes the fourth with supporting data from observational studies already referred to previously. The first three are: 1) the infant's "inbuilt bias to orient toward, to look at and listen to" those classes of stimuli that originate from human sources; 2) exposure learning resulting in the infant's becoming familiar perceptually with the person caring for him and discriminating such a person from all others; and 3) "an inbuilt bias to approach whatever is familiar" which leads the infant, as soon as motor maturation permits, to approach and follow the discriminated person.

The fourth process is the result of that learning which augments or reinforces any piece of behavior by the feedback of its consequences. His review of the observational data and experiments of the students of infantile development already referred to previously leads to the conclusion that it is "the way the baby's companions respond to his social advances" that are the most effective processes of augmenting or reinforcing the infant's attachment behavior. He reemphasizes that neither feeding nor satisfying other bodily needs by a person have been found by such research as being effective. In the Scottish study, it was found that such variables as feeding, weaning, toilet-training, the sex of child, birth order or developmental quotient were not related, among 36 children at 18 months of age, to the intensity of their attachment to mother, as measured by the degree of their protests on her departure. Only two variables were found clearly significant: the readiness of the mother to respond to the child's crying and the amount of her initiating social interaction with him. These two varied in direct proportion to the child's intensity of his attachment. Although these two variables overlapped they were not associated with statistical significance. That is, some mothers responded quickly to crying but spontaneously interacted with him rarely, while others who discouraged the baby's crying still interacted a great deal with him.

Similar findings regarding attachment behavior toward subsidiary figures supported the conclusions in regard to mothers. In other words, persons who gave no physical care to the baby but responded to his crying tended to be selected as subsidiary figures, and conversely those who gave physical care at times but did not respond socially were not likely to be selected. Although the persons who responded and initiated social interaction were also those most available, this was not always so. In some families it was found that the child's attachment to father was more intense than that to mother if he, although less available, interacted strongly with the baby when he was present, while mother, although more available, was less responsive and initiated interaction less but gave adequate physical care. Some of these mothers complained of such fathers ruining "their policy of not 'spoiling' the child." They complained also that their children although quite undemanding all day when they were alone with them became much more intensely demanding of father's presence and attention whenever he was about during evenings, weekends and holidays. Similar conclusions were drawn from the African study by Ainsworth although these were more cautiously stated because of her recognition of some deficiencies in her observations.

Of considerable interest regarding this matter are reports on the intensity of the child's attachment toward his own parents from the Kibbutzim in Israel. All observers seem to agree that despite having contact with their infant for only one or two hours a day and all day on the Sabbath (while the rest of the week he is cared for in the nursery by a nurse (metapeleth)) the parents become the principal attachment figure for the kibbutz child. Since the nurse has several children to care for, must prepare their food, change their clothes and so on, she has actually less time with an individual child for social play with him than the parents who have twice as much time with him for this in his first eight months in the kibbutz. Hence, perhaps the finding that in psycho-therapeutic work with individuals reared in kibbutzim, the metapeleth is never a figure of long-lasting, or strong ties, while their parents and siblings are their main object-relations is not surprising and supports the other data. The security and love provided the child by parents in these situations are provided by no one else, according to another observer, who adds, "if anything, the attachment of the young children to their parents is greater than it is in our own society" (58).

All such data supports Bowlby's theory and none of it the traditional theory that food and other bodily care are the crucial reinforcers of the child's attachment to mother. These conclusions are further supported by experimental findings in which the smiling of three month old infants was increased by the experimenter's simply smiling back, cooing, picking him up and cuddling him every time the baby smiled. Other students were able to increase the babbling of babies of the same age by smiling back broadly, making three "tsk" sounds and lightly squeezing the infant's abdomen each time the baby babbled. Both the babbling and smiling of the infant decreased or stopped when the responses of the experimenters decreased or stopped (47).

DELAYED ATTACHMENT

There are some observational data regarding delay of some infants in developing differentially directed attachment from the usual period of about nine months of age to until well into their second year which Bowlby considers consistent with his theory. That is, the evidence in these instances suggests that the delay is due to such infants having experienced much less social stimulation from their mothers than those whose development in this respect has been faster.

He mentions again the study of 75 infants reared in an impersonal institution from the age of five weeks or earlier, none of whom showed any indication of such attachment. Ainsworth's study of Uganda infants tends to support such data. She found four of the 27 infants in her group markedly delayed in manifesting attachment. Two of these four, half-sisters by different mothers, "showed hardly any discrimination or attachment at 11 and 12 months, respectively." The other two, twins (boy and girl), by 37 weeks when the observation ended showed virtually no attachment behavior. The mothers of these four non-attached infants left their babies for long periods, shared mother care with others even when they were themselves available and were rated among all 27 mothers as in the lowest two categories on a seven-point scale as to the amount of care each gave to her baby. The babies were found to have received much less care from mother or anyone else, except one, of the remainder of the infants who became attached. Although the observer in this research pointed out that the dimension of "motherly care" used in this study was too unspecific, the most important component of this care was believed to be social interaction and not routine care.

RECEPTORS IN SOCIAL STIMULATION

The question of which receptors of the infant play an indispensable and most powerful role in the development of attachment behavior, which also was studied in these researches, is also of great interest not only for Bowlby's theory but also for clinicians studying symptoms of their young child patients. These more recent studies do not support the older theory in which feeding was assumed the essential experience and that tactile especially, but also kinaesthetic and olfactory, and particularly oral stimulation were in the earlier months probably the more important in the development of attachment. Students of early child development, like Rheingold (47) and Walters and Parke (71), emphasize in contrast that "from quite early weeks, an infant's eyes and ears are active in mediating social interchange . . ." and they question the special role previously attributed to tactile and kinaesthetic stimulations. Lipsitt (34) has also studied infants in the first days of life reacting to and activating either sounds or a light show. Studies of attention in the human infant made by Kagan and Lewis (28) are relevant in this context as well.

This writer's attention was called by a colleague, Dr. John I. Langdell, to the very interesting work of Bower in 1971 (12) (not referred to by Bowlby because it appeared after the publication of his book) on new born infants and infants in their second week of life as well as infants between 16 and 20 weeks of age which further extends the observations and impressions of Rheingold, and of Walters and Parke just mentioned. Bower found that none of the infants of between 16 and 24 weeks of age, supported in a sitting position, showed surprise or distress when they reached and touched a real object hung in front of them. However, where a virtual object was presented (by means of a shadow caster, in which two oppositely polarized beams of light cast a double shadow of an object on a rear-projection screen and by means of polarizing goggles over the infant's eyes) every infant showed marked surprise when he reached and failed to make contact with the virtual image he perceived in front of the screen. Within a fraction of a second after the infant's hand reached the place where the object seemed to be, "he emitted a coo, a whoop or a cry, accompanied by a change in facial expression so marked as to seem a caricature." The older infants responded even more vigorously, "staring at their hands, rubbing them together or banged their hand on the chair before reaching again for the virtual object."

Encouraged by these observations that by 16 weeks of age the infants already expected a tactile feedback from visual expectation of the solidity of the object, Bower turned to the study of the newborn and of infants under two weeks of age. After learning from Heinz Prechtl's work that infants of this age are probably never fully awake while lying on their backs and after he himself observed no defensive behavior in them in this position to an approaching real or virtual object, he repeated these latter experiments with them after supporting them in a sitting position leaving their hands free to move. He then found that all seven of the infants under two weeks of age showed marked defensive movements of pulling their heads back, putting their hands up between their face and the *approaching* real or virtual objects and by distressed crying so intense the experiment needed to be terminated earlier than planned. There was no such defensive reaction when either the real or the virtual object was moving *away* from the infant. The experiment of allowing *newborn* infants to reach for both a real and a virtual object perceived hanging in front of them led to exactly similar results as with the infants 16 to 20 weeks of age: no surprise or distress when they reached and touched a real object and "a howl as soon as the infant's hand went to the intangible object's location"—even though they did not reach for objects in the same way as the older infants do.

These observations (and others regarding tracking moving objects visually behind a screen for which space here does not permit review) of this student led him to the conclusions that "one aspect of eye-hand interaction is built into the nervous system" at birth and that perhaps some degree of object permanence is also a partially built in property that is further developed with growth and experience. The latter was inferred from the different reactions of infants of various ages to single and multiple images of their mother: to single and multiple images the younger infants reacted with pleasurable coos and arm waving; the older infants, with distress to multiple images of her; all infants, the younger and older, ignored images of strangers. Bower concludes that the discovery of the object concept must simplify the world of the infant more than almost any subsequent intellectual advance—"even though we do not know why the object concept (identity of figure) must be discovered rather than being built into the neural system"—"as so many other kinds of perceptual knowledge are"—nor how the discovery is made.

Robson (48) stresses that not only smiling and babbling but also eye-to-eye contact "seems to play a very special part in developing a bond between infant and mother." That the latter activities are important is the observation that while giving the baby routine care the mother holds him in such a way that only rarely does face to face position contact occur; on the other hand, she regularly faces him when she is being sociable with him. This also happens when anyone to whom the infant becomes attached initiates such social interaction with the infant as against those persons who give him only routine care and to whom he is less likely to become attached.

The latter observations, particularly eye-to-eye contact, are of considerable interest to clinical students of the early psychotic, autistic, disorders of children, inasmuch as absence of eye contact by such children is a symptom quite often observed especially in those assessed as most markedly detached.

To return to the observations of the role of the various receptors in the development of attachment behavior, Bowlby reviews the work and opinions of Schaffer and Emerson (55) who reported their observations of 37 infants in the Scottish study previously mentioned and of Ainsworth's work (74) with a sample of infants in Maryland in regard to the infants' enjoyment of, or resisting, being cuddled. Nine of the Scottish group at 12 months were reported by their mothers to be "actively resistant to being cuddled" from their early weeks ("He won't allow it; he fights to get away," said one mother); 19 enjoyed cuddling and the remaining 9 were in an intermediate position in this respect. The non-cuddlers were rated at this age as different from the rest only in the lessened intensity of their attachment. At 18 months this difference between cuddlers and non-cuddlers, though persistent, was no longer considered significant; and there was no difference between the two groups as to the number of figures to whom they directed their attachment.

Bowlby cautions against interpreting these findings to mean that physical contact is unimportant in the development of attachment. The non-cuddlers still enjoyed being romped with, swung around, were content while feeding to sit on mother's knee, and when alarmed *held* their face against her knee and held mother's skirt. Thus, although they probably received less tactile stimulation than the cuddlers, this was not negligible. In short, the non-cuddlers primarily resented being restrained.

Further, Ainsworth is skeptical of a mother's retrospective report that a baby "was never cuddly" because her work in Maryland suggests that some non-cuddlers are babies who had been held little during their earliest months. Moreover, she and her assistants made a special point of picking up babies reported by their mothers as not cuddly and found them cuddly, concluding from this that these mothers did not like to cuddle a baby. However, later on they found these babies squirming when held having become non-cuddlers. She adds that some brain-damaged babies are hypertonic and may be from the beginning non-cuddlers.

Such latter data is of great interest to clinicians because of their experiences with some young, disturbed children—especially those of autistic degree

—avoiding and very reluctant, even negativistic, about offered bodily contact with their nursing staff personnel in the first period of hospitalization, i.e., some of them later in the therapeutic work came to seek cuddling contact with their assigned nurse or psychotherapist when other signs of attachment to them also became manifest. These children had been similarly reported by their mothers as non-cuddlers from very early life. As thorough anamnesis and neurological examinations as possible revealed no brain damage or hyper-tonicity. In some of these instances when therapy with their parents was successful it often eventuated in the mother's acknowledgement of her con-flictful difficulty in cuddling or otherwise initiating social interaction with the one of their children whose later maldevelopment brought him to clinical attention. Some of these mothers recalled their moderately severe depressions after the birth of such a child; while others expressed a very intense desire to have the child to be the best—as a desperate compromise solution, to a variety of very conflictful attitudes from their past lives, at times exacerbated by current frustrations. Some of the clinical reports in other chapters of this volume illustrate and exemplify the neuroticisms involved in these mothers' difficulties, despite which many of them gave their babies adequate routine care in regard to nutrition, cleanliness, protection against extremes of tem-peratures, injury, and so forth.

Bowlby mentions the "ambiguous results" of some studies of the develop-ment of attachment in blind children in that various reports differ as to whether the blind child's attachment is both weaker in intensity and speci-ficity as to figure; and some reports that a blind infant when alarmed readily exchanges a familiar attachment figure for an unfamiliar person is not unlike the sighted child who tends to cling to whomever is present in the temporary absence of the familiar figure. To these opposing views he offers the possible solution that the development of attachment of blind children to a particular figure is slower than in sighted children, but is more intense and persists so for longer once attachment develops in the blind, than in the sighted children.

He concludes this discussion of the roles of the different receptors in the development of attachment behavior with the statement "that data do not yet exist for answering the questions posed." (This is also true for all the details of the experience of both the child and mother in many instances of autistic maldevelopment.) Although the role that distance receptors play is far more important than previously recognized, this is not to say that tactile and kinaesthetic receptors are unimportant. As a matter of fact when the infant is much distressed, "bodily contact seems vital," as well as rhythmic 60 per minute movements in early months or later. Hence "in all likelihood all modes of social interaction play a major role . . ." The redundancy in the organization of attachment behavior makes it possible that a deficiency in one mode can be made up within wide limits through another mode. Such a "plethora of alternative means" by which survival requirements can be met is quite common in the animal world.

Here, too, in this context of the functioning of the various receptors, clinicians have had experience with the psychotic child's symptoms which are relevant. Some students (e.g., Bergman and Escalona (9)) have postulated particularly great sensitivities, a lowered threshold, in receptors (as in hearing, vision) as determinant factors in the child's withdrawal in self-protection from ordinary stimulations. Others have considered the possibility of heightened thresholds or reduced sensitivity, as in a lessened sense of pain.

In our own experience we have observed several patients produce a variety of several injuries: lacerations, contusions, and cataracts either by banging their heads against walls, against their knees or other objects. Some have punched their heads with their own fists. Others slapped their faces very severely and almost incessantly. A few bit their tongues or lips to the point of lacerations. One, despite efforts at restraint, knocked out or broke several of her teeth. We have seen one child almost sever the terminal phalanx of a finger by putting it in the jamb of a closing door without any apparent overt reaction of pain, or in another, the burning of his own skin against radiators, or in still another, cutting his own prepuce with similar absence of overt evidence of pain. The unresponsiveness to parental voices has led some parents of such children and some clinicians seeing them to consider and examine for hearing loss or decrease of hearing.

Clinicians have also seen blind as well as definitely deaf children with many of the other persistent symptoms of severe disorder of attachment to almost all people. Other children with such disorders are seen repeatedly touching smooth or textured surfaces of bed clothing or other textiles. Still others manifest great interest in record music, or in watching closely and for long periods the turntables of record players, twirling tinkertoys or leaves. Kinaesthetic receptors appear involved in unusual ways in a proportion of such disordered children in their frequent whirling themselves around, walking on tiptoes, and frequent flailing of their arms.

These preferences for such motor activities, as well as persistent tonic reflexes, led to conjectures about maturational lags of the central nervous system and to study of the so-called neurological "soft signs." Other children twiddle pieces of paper, leaves, or sticks for long periods sometimes squatting with their back to groups of other patients and staff. In some instances they observe the twiddling very closely, in others they appear not to look at their hands. One child has been observed frequently to look at lights or the sun, so often and persistently as to arouse concern of nursing personnel about possible damage to the retina.

These and other idiosyncratic self-stimulations appear as problems for clinical understanding as to their determinants—organic disease or dysfunction or some unusual maldevelopmental experiences.

SENSITIVE PHASES AND THE FEAR OF STRANGERS

Bowlby returns to the question about the presence in man of a phase during which the infant most readily develops attachment behavior to a preferred figure and considers the evidence for such a phase which has been now well established in other species. He concludes that the reported observational data by several students leads them to suspect in the first five or six weeks of life the infant is not yet ready to develop such attachment behavior, and this for two reasons: neither perceptual capacities, nor the level of organization of behavior during this period are such that—except in very primitive ways—the infant can interact socially. However, the infant can learn in this time.

The infant becomes progressively able to discriminate after this time what he feels, hears and sees, and his behavior is better organized. A consequence of this is that the differences between infants reared in institutions and those reared in families in their social behavior become more obvious. From such evidence and because the neurological maturation of the infant is rapid, the tentative conclusion is that although the readiness of the infant to develop attachment is low in the first weeks after birth, it increases in the second and third month.

Since by the end of the sixth month many infants manifest elements of attachment, it is possible to consider that in the interval between the ages of three months and six months most infants are in "a high state of sensitivity for developing attachment behavior." There is no evidence that this sensitivity is greater in any one of the latter months than in another, hence beyond this generalization it is not possible to go.

There is some evidence that sensitivity to the development of a discriminated attachment behavior persists in many infants for some months. From some studies it seems possible to conclude that if an infant is given plenty of social interaction in the middle and in the latter half of his first year of life he will do so quickly when given the opportunity. On the other hand he will be much slower to develop attachment behavior toward a discriminated figure without such social stimulation.

Thus Schaffer (53) in 1963 observed one group of eleven infants who were cared for in a hospital with little opportunity there for either social or other stimulation (despite one to four or five visits by some mothers per week) and another group of nine infants placed in a baby home (to avoid infection with tuberculosis at home) where they received much social stimulation from a large staff of nurses. All twenty infants in the middle of their first year spent ten or more weeks in these settings and all returned home when they were somewhere between thirty and fifty-two weeks of age. All but one of these infants developed attachment behavior by the time they were twelve months of age. However, the delay in the development of attachment varied very markedly, from three days to fourteen weeks.

It was found that neither the age of the infant on return home nor the length of time away from home were relevant to the variation in this delay. The factors which were easily identifiable as relevant were the opportunities for social stimulation while the infant was away and the conditions and his experiences on his return home.

All nine infants who had stayed at the baby home developed attachment to mother much sooner than the eleven who had been in the hospital. One of the nine baby home infants after an absence of thirty-seven weeks on returning home at twelve months of age began showing attachment on his third day. Of the remaining eight, all but two were showing attachment within fourteen days. On the other hand, all but one of the hospital infants did not show attachment until from four to seven weeks after returning home. The occasional visits of the mother to these latter infants while they were in the hospital, although better than nothing, were insufficient when the general level of social stimulation during such absences was low.

Additional data on the baby home infants were that seven of the nine showed attachment within two weeks after returning home, while it was considered that "almost certainly" one of the other two showed delay beyond the two weeks because he received little social attention after his return. This boy, thirty-six weeks old on return after a twelve weeks absence, and whose parents who were fond of him, was cared for by an invalid father while mother worked and could therefore see little of the boy, received little attention from either of them. Attachment behavior was not observed in him for two and a half months until mother gave up her work. She devoted herself to her family and within a few days after this, the boy, now nearly twelve months of age, "developed a strong and specific attachment to her."

Such observations suggest that readiness to develop attachment is maintained in at least some infants until the end of the first year, provided some minimum of social conditions for the infant are present. What this minimum is, as yet remains unanswered. Also unanswered are two other questions: (1) whether the later development of attachment affects its strength and stability in comparison to that which has developed earlier; and (2) to what length of time into the second year can the readiness to develop an attachment be thus maintained.

Another aspect of these last three questions—all of which to the present writer have considerable bearing for the clinician in regard to the etiologic factors contributing to the psychotic syndromes of early childhood—that whatever the margin of safety may be, Bowlby is certain that after the age of six months the circumstances for the development of attachment become more complex. The most important of these latter factors is the strength and the greater ease with which the infant responds with fear.

REDUCED SENSITIVITY—FEAR OF STRANGERS

Like the young of other species, the human infant's response of fear to anything strange including individuals of his own kind who are unfamiliar to him increases with his age and this increases his likelihood of withdrawing rather than approaching such persons. Hence he becomes less likely to develop an attachment to new persons. Students of child development distinguish three phases in this response to strangers that are useful to emphasize. The first phase occurs before the infant manifests any visual discrimination between familiars and strangers. The second phase is that in which the infant responds fairly readily and positively to strangers (although not as readily as to persons familiar to him) and lasts about six to ten weeks. The third phase, lasting usually four to six weeks, is one during which he sobers at the sight of strangers and stares. Following this phase he shows orientation and movement away from a stranger, crying or whimpering with a facial expression of dislike; behavior all of which is typical of fear.

Although the appearance of such fear varies much from infant to infant—from a few at twenty-six weeks to a minority in the second year—it is present in the majority by the eighth to ninth month and occurs earlier on being picked up by a stranger than at the sight of him. One observer reports in his sample of infants the following incidence of evidence of fear of strangers: 12% at three months, 40% at six months, and 46% at eight months.

Different observers account for delayed appearance of such fear by different factors. While some point to any delay in the development of attachment to a discriminated principal figure as a reason for the delayed appearance of the fear of strangers, others report that infants who habitually encounter more people also show a later onset of fear of strangers. There may be other variables.

There is also some variation of observations among students as to the peak of intensity of such fear of strangers, although in most or all infants it becomes more evident with increasing age. Some report that this peak intensity occurs at from seven to nine months; others, in the second year; and still others report a marked increase at nine or ten months with a great variation not only from infant to infant but also that in any one infant there tend to be inexplicable variations from month to month.

Some of the differences in the reports of different observers may be due to different criteria used to identify the fear response. Thus, one student observing a sharp reduction in the smiling response to a stranger of infants of fourteen to sixteen weeks of age suggests that fear responses may be present before the overt behavior previously described is seen. Bowlby, however, is not certain that this opinion is justified; and if it is, it seems to him that this "response is at low strength and is quickly habituated."

A variety of circumstances may determine in an important degree the occurrence and the intensity of the fear of strangers in any one infant and constitute a great difficulty in the determination by observers of both the onset of fear and its peak intensity. Thus, the distance the stranger is from the infant, whether the stranger does or does not approach the infant and what else he may do all may affect a great deal the infant's reaction of fear and its intensity. The infant's response to a stranger also may depend upon whether the infant is fresh and rested or fatigued, and whether he is well or ill, and whether he is in familiar or strange surroundings. A particularly important factor, which has been studied, is whether the infant is away from his mother or on her knee. Results of the latter study demonstrate that an infant after eight months shows much more fear when he is only four feet away from her than when he is on her knee which probably relates to the fact that after this age the child begins to use mother "as a secure base from which to explore."

Another study demonstrating that increased age of the child plays an important role in his fear of strangers is one by Yarrow. This student observed seventy-five infants who were shifted from temporary foster homes to adoptive homes at varying ages between six weeks and twelve months. None of the infants between six and twelve weeks was seen to become disturbed; a few of those of three months of age were upset. Beyond this age a larger and larger proportion of the infants showed more and more intensity and pervasiveness of disturbance with increasing age. Thus 86% of those aged six months showed some disturbance, while every one of those aged seven months or more "reacted with marked disturbance." This disturbance was described as both a decrease in the social responses of babbling, smiling and increase in crying, clinging, unusual apathy, disturbance in sleep, feeding as well as loss of previously acquired abilities.

In summary and conclusion regarding the problem of sensitive periods, Bowlby, quoting Caldwell (16) and Hinde (27), states that the problem is complex and that probably there is a different sensitive period for each separate response. It matters much whether students of the problem are concerned with the development of a discriminated attachment or with the effects of a disruption of an already established attachment. He thinks there is no doubt that an existing attachment is particularly vulnerable for several years after the infant reaches the end of his first twelve months.

He considers it "plain" that infants are ready and sensitive to make a discriminated attachment during the second quarter of their first year of life. They can still do so after their sixth month but difficulties increase with subsequent passing months. It also seems clear to him that these difficulties are already great in the second year and that they do not diminish.

The implications of these data on sensitive periods in the first year of life are many and varied for clinicians and particularly for those much concerned with early psychotic disorders of childhood. They will be considered later.

<h2 style="text-align:center">CRITIQUE OF SPITZ'S POSITION</h2>

Bowlby closes this chapter on "Focusing on a Figure" with a critique of Spitz's theories regarding the development of object relations. In reaching his conclusion that these widely accepted theories are untenable in the face of all the observations he has presented, Bowlby first summarizes the essentials of Spitz's (57) position, namely that true object relations are not established before eight months, when almost all infants are held to manifest "eight month's anxiety." This latter phenomenon Bowlby equates with what, as he has already made clear in the foregoing discussion reviewed here, he calls "the fear of strangers."

The four aspects under which Spitz anchors his argument (about the appearance of true object relations) to the eight months anxiety are summarized as follows:

1. Spitz's *observations* that most infants withdraw from strangers at about eight months;
2. An *assumption* that this withdrawal cannot be due to fear since the stranger has caused no pain or unpleasure to the infant;
3. A theory that such withdrawal is not from something frightening, but that it is a form of separation anxiety, i.e., that the infant reacts to the stranger confronting him as not his mother and that his mother has left him; and
4. An *inference*, from this data and theory, that this marks the age at which the child discriminates the mother-figure from all others and thus forms "a true object relation," which Spitz considers a true love as a consequence to his developed ability to distinguish her from all others.

In reply and refutation to this position of Spitz, Bowlby makes three points: 1) Strangeness *per se* is a common cause of fear. Hence Spitz is crucially in error in considering that the child's fear develops only as a result of experience of unpleasure or pain with another person. 2) Since a child can and has been observed to show evidence of fear of a stranger even in the presence of his mother, this fear of strangers is "quite distinct from separation anxiety." Although Spitz replied to this point that it was a rare exception for a child to behave this way, Bowlby maintains that this reply is not sustained by careful experimental studies of Morgan and Ricciuti (39). These observers found that thirteen out of thirty-two infants from ten to twelve months of age (or almost half of them) manifest such fear. Bowlby's third and final reason for his refutation of Spitz's position is the abundant evidence "that an infant can discriminate familiar from unfamiliar long before he shows overt fear of strangers."

Thus the central flaw in Spitz's position, Bowlby holds, is the supposition that an infant cannot experience "realistic fear" at the sight of a stranger which follows from the assumption that "realistic fear" can only arise as a result of a previous experience of unpleasure associated with an object or person.

He also points to the adverse effects of Spitz's theory; first, that by regarding "eight-month's anxiety" as the first indicator of a true object relation, it distracts attention from the observational facts that a majority of infants manifest both discrimination of a familiar person and attachment behavior long before the eighth month; and second, that it has confounded anxiety as a response to missing and longing for a loved person (i.e. separation anxiety) and fear of strangers that Bowlby regards as a realistic fear due to the unfamiliar and strange object, person or situation. Bowlby considers it vital to keep these two responses distinct. Incidentally, the definition of anxiety just given is in accord with Freud's usage in his formulation of 1926 in "Inhibitions, Symptoms and Anxiety" (23). Furthermore, because fear of strangers appears at different ages, and in different infants follows a different course, as well as being influenced by many variables, the term "eight-month anxiety" is also unsatisfactory for these reasons.

Bowlby cites a number of students who also hold his position on the basis of their observations that, although they are related forms of behavior, fear of strangers and separation anxiety are distinct and appear independently of one another. Thus Schaffer (53, 54) found that among twenty-three infants three showed separation anxiety after fear of strangers, in twelve, the two appeared in reverse order, while in eight both appeared simultaneously. Benjamin's (7) report is cited to the effect that in his sample the appearance and peak intensity of the fear of strangers are earlier by some months than the same phenomena for separation anxiety. Although differences of opinion exist as to the relation between the two responses, probably because of the different criteria used by different observers and because of the number of variables involved, there is general agreement that the relationship is not a simple one. There is no evidence that the two run a parallel course or have simultaneous origins. Hence, since Freud and most analysts consider that fear of an alarming object in the surroundings and anxiety are not the same reaction, distinct terms for each are necessary.

Bowlby offers in conclusion to this discussion the following formulation of the distinction between fear of strangers and separation anxiety: In the first, the infant tries to *withdraw* or *escape* from an alarming situation, while in the second, he tries to *remain with,* or *in,* or go *toward* some person or place that evokes a feeling of security. The first comes close to Freud's notion of "realistic fear" generally accompanied by a sense of fright or alarm. The second type of behavior is what Bowlby throughout has termed attachment. In the latter when proximity to the attachment figure cannot be maintained because some barrier intervenes or the person is lost, or when the loss of the person is threatened, there follows a striving and searching for the person which are accompanied by a more or less acute sense of disquiet. It was this disquiet at the threat of, or actual, separation that Freud came to regard as "the key to an understanding of anxiety" in his later work (1926). Conversely, of course, no unpleasant feeling ensues as long as proximity to the attachment figure is maintained.

A CLINICIAN'S REFLECTIONS ABOUT SENSITIVE PHASES, FEAR OF STRANGERS AND SEPARATION ANXIETY

The clinician, with long psychotherapeutic experience with a wide variety of psychotic disorders of preadolescent children, finds the data on the development of attachment summarized by Bowlby very germane to his own clinical work. This may be particularly true of those clinicians who, in their clinical practice and experience with such disorders as well as with other forms and degrees of severity of children's psychiatric problems test psychogenic hypotheses of etiology in their therapeutic work. This includes usually those clinicians who regard the nature of the child's experience with his parents and theirs with him as highly relevant not only to the understanding of the psychopathology of the child, its genesis and maintenance but also as matters which offer data that may be of great importance in choosing and applying maneuvers, procedures, and particular experiences which would enhance the chances of the reduction and resolution of the particular symptomatology in all three of them.

Such clinicians seeing a psychotic child have often been discontent at the time of the first evaluative contact with the family during the first eighteen months of the child's life, and this discontent persists subsequently in longer, more systematic psychotherapeutic work with them. That is, such detailed information was not always available for a number of reasons in the study of enough of these children and their families. Although this was true, some of these clinicians did nevertheless obtain sufficiently clear anamnestic information about the subjective state and behavior of the parents during the first twelve, eighteen or more months of the life of the psychotic child in enough families studied to entertain an etiological hypothesis based upon natal and postnatal, experiential clinical data. This hypothesis was formulated on the basis of such clinical data and guided the search for data to corroborate or negate the hypothesis in subsequently studied families as early as 1946 although it was not first published by the Langley Porter students until 1949 (61), 1956 (63) and 1960 (11). These children were studied anamnestically for evidence of prenatal, paranatal or postnatal trauma or other disease, particularly of the central nervous system. The search was negative in a large proportion of the psychotic children studied in the past twenty-four years at this center. The analysis of the findings in two hundred and sixty-four such children studied clinically between 1946 and 1961 are presented in this volume in another chapter. (See Chapter 14.)

More detailed reports of such psychological and behavioral factors negatively affecting the infant's development in individual instances are also presented in several other chapters as clinical examples of the probably experiential etiology. In other instances of such psychotic maldevelopment of attachment—or of psychotic detachment of an autistic character—there were found a variety of events in the family chronologically related to the appearance or exacerbations of the child's disorder. Such events either precipitated an emotional disturbance in mother and father, or probably more frequently, exacerbated an already existing personality disorder even in the premarital life of one or both parents. For examples of such events the reader is referred to these other chapters in this volume already referred to previously.

One may here summarize such data by the statement that the common factor in such events affected negatively the emotional responsiveness of the mother to the child's maturing social abilities, that is, those of her social responses to the child's signals or her initiative in such transactions with him. This was true in varying degrees in the same mother-child couple from one period to another, or between different couples even though the child who became the patient later generally received adequate nutritional and other physical care.

In some instances it was only one of several of the children of such parents whose development was so severely affected. There were a few families with more than one child affected but there were none with twins in the group of children studied at this center. Although time of this clinical staff was not available to study systematically all the siblings of the psychotic child patients seen, there were some families in which some of the other siblings *were* seen clinically, and in more families there was indirect information from the parents during their therapeutic work about at least some of such siblings who manifested other forms and degrees of personality disorder. In families of a psychotic child in which the siblings were essentially free of disorder, the prenatal and postnatal history of the psychotic child most frequently revealed severe family stresses. In a few instances when therapeutic work with parents, most often with the mother of a psychotic child, was sufficiently successful and an infant was born, during this period often she spontaneously reported to her therapist how much more "motherly" and emotionally responsive she felt and how much more she enjoyed the new child. Such subsequent children developed without the evidence of the disorder present in the psychotic sibling in therapy at the clinic.

This staff has observed both among the psychotic group studied evaluatively and 135 families engaged in prolonged and systematic psychotherapeutic work, variations in the degree of severity of the child's disorder, as well as variation in the age of onset of the disorder or its exacerbation. These clinical differences have been represented in a retrospective subclassification of the sample of the psychotic children seen. As detailed in the chapter on the statistical study, the data from retrospective studies leave much to be desired. The most severely autistically disturbed children appear to have manifested their disorder early in their life. Thus in over 58% of seventy-five of this subgroup the onset was reported as at one year of age or under, and in 21% more, at two years. A large proportion of this group was severely withdrawn, unattached to, or detached from parents, their siblings, other children. Forty-five percent of this sample were also mute, and the remainder showed marked maldevelopment of speech. All of them were negativistically fearful (anxious) about new persons, situations and about learning any new skills. Those of this group who could be engaged in therapy took longer to become attached to the staff persons assigned. They also took longer to show some reduction of their disorder and fewer were rated as improved than in two other subgroups that were less severely affected and with a later onset. The outcomes on a modified followup study (See Chapter 15) were also less satisfactory.

Such clinical data therefore tends to corroborate Bowlby's conclusion regarding the presence of sensitive periods during the last half, or latter three quarters, of the child's first year of life. The fact that a proportion of even those most severely affected did eventually show attachment to the therapeutic personnel of the staff and improvement in their disorder tends in the same way to support his opinion that attachment may still be possible even after the second and third birthdays although with increasing difficulty. Likewise the poorest therapeutic results with such clinical efforts when the work began much later in the first decade of such a severely autistic child's life points in the same direction. The fear of strangers coupled with little or no secure attachment to a primary figure decreases markedly the possibility of development of a sufficiently secure, rehabilitative attachment.

Of course, it needs also to be stressed that it is not alone the maldevelopment, or non-development, of attachment behavior to a principal figure which constitutes the entire syndrome of psychotic disorder of the autistic child. Following the thesis Bowlby presents, the appearance of the fear of the stranger (and perhaps even of the unresponsive mother herself as a "stranger") also leads to the stultification or maldevelopment of the vocal and verbal expressive functions. The poor or absent secure base from which to explore the personal and impersonal environment leads to unavoidable consequences such as cognitive deficiencies as well as conflictful ("negativistic") avoidance of learning various selfcare and other motor and intellectual skills. The deficient, or relatively absent, or mutually satisfying "partnership" phase between mother and child in the second, third and later years has its counterpart in all those psychological maldevelopments of an "internal object" emphasized by Piaget and of a self or autonomy stressed by Bettelheim. These defects are thus understandable aspects of the later psychotic disorder. The fact that even among the most severely autistic there were observed either minor, or transient attachments and associated reductions of disorder, however, is also of interest. It goes almost without saying that in this older group the staff also encountered the greatest difficulty in being therapeutically helpful to the parents, and again particularly with the mother of these children.

Among the deficiencies in the anamnestic data of such clinicians in their study of many of these children and their families is the lack of information about the earliest evidences of the infant's readiness for discriminated attachment: namely, about such phenomena as differential smiling, visual, auditory responses, vocalizations, babbling (especially with children who are later mute), impulses to cuddle, cling or approach the mother, crying when not hungry, ill or fatigued and so forth. There is also insufficient data about later phenomena of social development: namely, the more definite discrimination in focusing on a primary figure as against secondary figures, siblings, appearance of fearful reactions to strangers, as well as the appearance of protests at mother's departure, efforts to bring her back by crying, or attempts to follow her after locomotion is possible, and signs of greeting her upon her return and such other criteria of attachment, or its delay or nonappearance.

Although one quite often in such initial evaluative studies finds statements about the rather gross landmarks of maturation as to when the infant's dentition appeared and he began to be able to sit up, crawl, walk and often when, if any, words were spoken—in short, the vocabulary learned in more traditional pediatric history-taking about "growth and development"—there is frequently a lack of information about what Bowlby calls "social interaction" of parent and child. This writer would prefer—following Dewey and Bentley (20)—to use some such term as interpersonal or social *transactions* for such phenomena since it would encompass the notion of the initiative or its discouragement, occurring from both infant and parent, with responses from each to the other.

There are probably a variety of reasons for such deficiencies in anamnestic data regarding the social transactions. Some teachers of trainees of child psychiatry themselves have not had opportunity to learn of the findings of students of child development here gathered in Bowlby's volume and hence do not emphasize their importance for psychiatric study in the demonstrations to trainees in initial evaluative brief service. In short, these aspects of infant development remain in part a terra incognita for the child psychiatric specialists. Another reason is the frequent lack of time in these evaluative sessions for both the psychiatric interviewers and the parents to permit adequate ventilation and some catharsis about parental anxieties, guilts, fear of being blamed, etc., to free them to consider and recall what they can of these early periods and events in their disturbed child's development. The well-known difficulties of parents to recall accurately such events often discourage the interviewer from closer and more therapeutic efforts (See Chapter 17 by Walker and Szurek in this volume) to help parents through such "fading" of these memories. Further, it is a very common additional factor that the conflictful tensions of parents tend to result in the repression of particularly painful recollections, or to suppression of frank and accurate expression of those of their own behavior and the feelings which they experienced toward the infant and which they *do* remember during these first twelve or eighteen months of the child's life. The first is corroborated by the not infrequent emergence from repression of such recollections during later periods of systematic therapy with them. The second is corroborated in those instances when parents later in periods of successful therapy acknowledge that they did, indeed, remember, even in the beginning of the clinical contact with them, the depressive feelings, or anxieties that they might hurt the child because of their extreme, and enormous intolerance of the child's distressed crying. In other instances parents expressed fear that the child would become as "dependent" upon them as they had felt toward their own mother, that is, they remembered how such feelings interfered with taking initiative in interpersonal transactions with their infant or to respond to his overtures (at times leaving the infant alone in his crib in another room for long periods) but were too ashamed, guilty about them and too anxious that the clinician would blame them for such "inadequate" mothering.

The initial statements of other parents that the child was from the beginning quite "good," i.e., rather unresponsive, or not fussy or crying often, is accepted then as data for some inborn or prenatally determined, perhaps "temperamental" difference (although these in some infants may be factors) (68, 67). Factors such as deficiency or of disease not yet capable of being diagnosed directly are attributed to "minimal brain damage," often without sufficient evidence, as paranatally occurring from anoxia during birth, etc.

Additional factors influencing "organic" interpretation of such gaps in anamnestic information are biases of physicians that such severe disorders as autistic or other psychotic maldevelopments of children are much more likely to have "endogenous" etiology than otherwise. On the other hand, some clinical students of childhood psychoses have expressed a strong aversion to the possibility that human parents could either behave so destructively to their own progeny or that any such interpersonal experiences are capable of resulting in so severe a maldevelopment: that is, as if such behavior had been consciously and willfully hostile rather than an expression of psychopathological disorder, especially when such parents also express what is simultaneously a genuine interest and concern in the welfare of their psychotic child. This possibility of trauma or primary heredo-familial, degenerative disease (38), or of even one of a molecular nature (e.g., Phenylketonuria (31, 32)), of course, needs to be constantly borne in mind and if possible excluded as far as developed diagnostic methodology permits. The negative influence of such search for "organic" factors is evidenced only when it leads to neglect of experiential factors during particularly vulnerable maturational phases of the infant and child. Such phases, i.e., sensitive periods, from the point of view of later personality disturbance, are particularly susceptible to positive or negative influences of human responsiveness.

Another rather insidiously operating environmental factor is the influence of obscuring anxiety on the part of a mother. She in effect obscures and disables her capacity to observe the effect of her own behavior on the child's responses. It is a common experience for mothers to be utterly mystified by the infant's unrelievable and inconsolable crying, general distress, disturbed sleep, poor feeding when they themselves are tense, anxious because of one or a number of a variety of conflicts. Such conflict tensions may stem from overcommitment in their own schedules. They may be worried by financial reverses, deep disagreements or estrangement from their spouses because of various temperamental differences between them. The latter problems may lead them to feel resentful and guilty about their own sexual unresponsiveness at times. Other worries about the health or disability of their own aging or dying parents may be one of such sources of anxiety. They further may feel discouraged by their own inability to measure up to their own or their spouse's expectations and standards of housekeeping and management of finances. Moreover, many of them become extremely uneasy about the absences of the father due to military service and consequent overt or covert destructive criticism from their own mothers, or mothers-in-law, about their rearing methods with the infant if they live with them or near them during such periods. Or finally, quite often there are present some combination of such negative influences, including the opposite influence; the presence of a neurotically disturbed father increasing mother's emotional turmoil with the infant who later develops psychotically, as against other siblings' experience with her when father was away during their first two years or more of their life (e.g., away on sea duty).

They are, as mentioned, unaware of their own tensions in their responsiveness to their infant until relief through therapeutic work or decrease in such destructive pressures upon them comes and the child's behavior changes even moderately for the better. This peculiar "blindness" to the connections between their subjective state and behavior and their child's behavior may persist or recur over and over again despite the therapist's clinical awareness of it and his efforts to help the mother to achieve insight. The mother's responses to such efforts or those of even well-meaning friends, neighbors and relatives is often an increase of her turmoil, defensive resentful denial and further increase in her discouragement about her inadequacy or inferiority as a person, housewife or mother. Only prolonged repetitive working through to a different solution to such problems in their own behavior can then bring more lasting insight.

Also a great number, if not the majority, of mothers of autistically developing children initially manifest no very obvious, gross personality problem to the clinician and tend to emphasize the care that they have expended upon such a child. All this is true; the child is obviously well-nourished and physically generally well-developed as a result of the physical care given him. The mother's story is clearly corroborated. It is obvious that there is no ordinary gross neglect of the child. Whatever psychological turmoil or disturbance such a mother may manifest may even seem then to the clinician as probably arising from the child's organically caused maldevelopment. It is, of course, quite true that undisturbed parents, perhaps especially mothers, do react with anxiety, worry about the child's future, with conflictful tension about any additional burdens upon them in rearing a child who is manifestly organically defective from birth in any diagnosable or obvious way, or who later is found to have a severe disease (e.g., diabetes, intellectual defect, etc.).

However, as Bowlby makes clear in the last two chapters of his volume, it is also true that each member of the dyad of child and mother contributes during the first year to the kind of partnership which is established between them and found in their relationship after this twelve months of experience with each other. Each influences the other's behavior, feelings and expectations of the other in gradual and often minor ways as well as being influenced by the other. This partnership, whatever its variation from that of any other such mother-child dyad, tends not only to be a highly characteristic pattern of transactions for the partnership but has also been found (18) "to persist in recognizable form over at least two or three years." Clinicians with even longer experience of therapeutic work with psychotic children and their parents simultaneously are familiar with such patterns persisting even much longer.

Some clinicians have also had experience with disturbance or attenuation of attachment behavior in a number of children (and their mothers), instances that appeared to be determined by both of two factors: a physical illness of the child and a simultaneous great stress of the mother. In some of these instances the behavior of the child was psychotic-like. The somatic illnesses of the children included asthma, at least one instance of ulcerative colitis and the somatic effects of anorexia nervosa.

In a few instances repeated review of anamnestic data during prolonged therapeutic work with several families whose child was hospitalized made more and more clear that either onset or exacerbation of particular symptoms of the child's psychotic disorder was chronologically related to other diseases of the child and the parents', especially mother's, emotional state. Such conditions as hemolytic purpura in a sibling, inversion of one or both feet requiring application of braces at night, Perthes's disease of the hips, and the occurrence of a severe measles encephalitis. Particularly related were the conflictful efforts of the parents to apply the braces to the inverted feet of the child to which the child reacted with extremely violent opposition. Since these more dramatic events are only those easily recollectable and not the results of systematic review of our records, they do not represent all such correlations of an illness of the child and the emotionally disturbed state of the mother that were found in the group of children reported in another chapter of this volume.

VARIATIONS IN ATTACHMENT BEHAVIOR

In the final two chapters of his volume Bowlby discusses the patterns of and contributing conditions and what little is known of the organization of attachment behavior. In these as in previous chapters and sections of his book he again approaches the interests of all clinicians concerned with childhood. Perhaps it would be more precise to say that his approach is to the interests especially of those clinicians who in their study of the psychopathology of early childhood have been for many years concerned with, and interested in, the psychogenic or experiential factors in the genesis, maintenance, and the reduction of such psychopathology by psychological therapeutic methods, as previously emphasized.

It needs to be immediately added and emphasized that the clinicians referred to are those who are *also* simultaneously careful in their study of any possible contributions to the etiology of such disorders of *disease* factors. By disease factors is meant here such factors as the hereditary, congenital, prenatal, paranatal or postnatal variables stemming from the non-personal, or impersonal, processes of trauma, infections, intoxications, degenerations, dysplasias or aplasias, and the molecular, or the enzymatic defects or deficiencies affecting the physiological *growth* processes of the newborn human organism. All these latter factors—termed here *disease* in contrast to disorder—are often summarized by the terms "organic" or "somatic" etiological variables.

It hardly needs to be said that an essential requirement of a complete diagnostic evaluation of a clinical problem of a child is as thorough an assessment of the presence, absence, or any degree of contribution, of such impersonal disease processes to any behavioral, psychiatric disorder as is possible by established appropriate medical study. It is essential because of the complex relations between disease and disorder as defined above to distinguish one from the other. Thus any primarily disease process may and does in various degrees affect negatively the functioning of an organism and hence also its behavior. On the other hand, it is also known that a primarily psychiatric disorder not only affects behavior but may also affect general organismic, physiologic functioning and even contribute to the development of disease processes (e.g., obesity and consequent metabolic dysfunction, or affect the vigor of the organism by decrease of physical fitness so frequently a part of inactivity or self-neglect, etc.). Further, disease and disorder although they may be more or less independently determined, may coexist and not only potentiate the deleterious effect of each on the child's behavior, and development, but each may also require its separate and appropriate therapeutic attention and intervention. Finally, it is as much an error of clinical study and therapy to overlook an organic disease in psychiatric evaluation as the obverse.

From the standpoint of the emphasis placed both by the clinicians interested in the postnatal experiential influences upon the child's psychological and behavioral development and by Bowlby upon the development of attachment behavior, there is need for an equal attention to similar problems, if any, of the organic health and the emotional integration of the parents and, of course, especially of the mother figure. For, in view of the data Bowlby presents and reviews in this discussion, any deleterious influence from either factor upon the parental responsiveness to the infant's incipient social behavior ("signals" or initiatives of the child are Bowlby's terms) is of equal importance to what ensues in the dyadic partnership of mother figure and infant during the first year of the latter's life and later.

Those clinicians with long experience with the psychotic degrees of disorder in early childhood *and with their parents* are familiar with the variations in the mother-child relationships. They are familiar with not only variations between such children and their families but also with differences in the same child and his family from one period to another. There are also differences in the experiences of the parents with the siblings of the child patient due to differences in the variables already indicated in the sensitive periods of these siblings. These data have led the present writer to express these facts of such observations in the statement to staff and students that "the different children of the same family do not necessarily have 'the same' parents." These clinical differences as mentioned before concern such phenomena as the age of onset of the disorder, the appearance, exacerbation or recession of particular and distinguishable symptoms, the severity or intensity of the disorder and of such discrete symptoms, their duration or persistence, the presence, absence and degree of severity of organic disease or some signs (e.g., abnormalities in the electroencephalographic tracings) which *may* indicate central nervous system dysfunction whether such signs are confirmed and established or not by other evidence from thorough neurological and general medical clinical examination and laboratory study.

The aforementioned clinical experience with the *families* of the psychotic children has revealed a variety of events chronologically related to the changes in development (attachment) of the child in both directions. That is, deleterious influences, psychologic or somatic, affecting parenting behavior has been repeatedly found chronologically related to the appearance or exacerbation of the psychopathology of the child. When the factors negatively affecting especially maternal responsiveness are reduced the obverse, namely, recession of the child's symptoms, has been observed. Such correlated changes are found not only in the anamnestic data obtained in careful, chronological study of the events prior to the beginning of clinical attention, but they are also observed during the course of prolonged and relatively intensive psychotherapy with child and both parents. They occur—as illustrated and documented in other chapters of this volume—both as concomitants of the process of working through and of integrative and dis-integrative events determined by factors external to the therapeutic situations of each member of the family triad.

For all these reasons, such clinicians find the Bowlby discussion in his sixteenth chapter on the contributing conditions to the patterns of attachment germane to their own experience. Some of them may even find the discussion enlightening to their understanding of it in the sense of beginning to think of their own clinical data in a somewhat different way. Others of these clinicians also may consider that such data of their experience as referred to above may contribute partial answers to the questions about this aspect of development that Bowlby raises.

He opens this chapter by presenting four classes of problems to be solved if the urgent need is to be satisfied of distinguishing between the conditions that promote either favorable or unfavorable development of attachment, if attachment is as important for mental health as is claimed. These questions concern:

1) The range of variation in attachment behavior, descriptively, at any age of the child and the dimensions in terms of which the variations are best described;
2) The antecedent conditions that determine the development of each variety of pattern;
3) The stability of each pattern at each age; and
4) The way each pattern is related to later personality development and mental health.

Bowlby acknowledges both that there are no simple answers to such questions and that conclusions are difficult to draw from the numerous research studies aimed to reply to these and related questions. The reasons he gives for this state of affairs are that the issues involved are very complicated, that no single inquiry can be expected to be enlightening to more than a portion of them, and that most of the research thus far reported appears to him as inadequate, either theoretically or empirically, to the tasks for which they have been undertaken.

Once more he calls attention to the theoretical inadequacy of the concept of "dependency" in relation to the phenomena of attachment. In support of this he quotes Sears' conclusion (56), when Sears' own research on various measures of dependency of children had "shown practically no intercorrelation," and therefore that "the notion of a generalized trait of dependency is indefensible." Empirical inquiries, too, he finds have been unsatisfactory to clarify problems of attachment for such reasons as that: studies of such "antecedent variables" as those of child-rearing methods of feeding, weaning, toilet-training or discipline seem now "only indirectly related to attachment";

and that information about these techniques has commonly been gathered by methods subject to inaccuracies and misinterpretations, namely, by parents from whom retrospective accounts have formed the basic data of such studies. Therefore, Bowlby thinks it is "necessary to start afresh."

Parenthetically, inaccuracies and misinterpretations of retrospective information from parents probably are suspect as to their reliability particularly if such statements of parents are obtained by more or less structured questionnaires whether these are written and answered by parents, used by research workers in single interviews in some such systematic effort to gain either simple "yes," "no" answers to questions or graded answers as to severity, frequency or duration by simple checking of printed forms. The same unreliability of data in complex life situations in the past results from similar efforts of clinicians in similar, single anamnestic interviews at the outset of a brief evaluative or diagnostic study.

However, clinicians engaged in prolonged and intensive psychotherapeutic work with parents of disturbed children would probably not wholly agree with such reservations about the reliability of their own data for several reasons. In the first place there is an opportunity in repetitive systematic psychotherapeutic sessions to review the information originally obtained in the initial evaluative study. With such review, the therapist can obtain a wealth of more detailed data about each and many episodes of past events together with accounts of the parents' own responses not only to the child's behavior but also about other factors affecting their lives during those periods of the child's life. That such fuller recall of the actual behavior of all concerned depends upon a number of interrelated factors is of course true and such work is not uniformly successful in this regard depending on the frequency of sessions, the severity of the neurotic conflicts of the parents, the duration of the work and not least upon the experience and skilled judgment of the therapist. When, however, these latter factors are present in favorable combination and have resulted in a more truly collaborative effort of an advanced stage of the psychoanalytic situation between parent and therapist, then the resultant information is much less subject to the earlier distorting factors of repressive and suppressive tendencies of the defensive aspects of the parents' conflicts. There remains naturally the problem of adequate recording of such data by the clinical, therapist-investigator for reports which may be convincing to colleagues in the field. Then not infrequently problems still remain as to the reception of such reports by these colleagues, although these colleagues may be experienced and well trained, but who may still not have had as much, if any, similar clinical experience of concomitant therapeutic work with all three members of the triad, or who may be unreceptive for reasons of differing theoretical preconceptions, or perhaps because of unresolved countertransference obstacles.

Furthermore, the psychotherapeutic clinician with such experience of working thus with all three members of the family triad is not solely dependent upon only the recall of parents or child of past events. These memories which occur early in therapy are subject to various distortions of the actual events by their own conflictful reactions to them and by the negative effect upon their ability to recall them accurately, and of the repetitive occurrence of such events. They also have the opportunity to observe the *current* transactions between the family members and the transference behavior of each of them in the therapeutic situation of each of them with the therapist himself. In such aspects of the therapeutic experience the *present* behavior of each family member may not only be comprehensible as deviant responses to similarly psychopathological behavior of the other two members of the triad. But it becomes also comprehensible in some aspects as continuing repetitions of their transactions in their common experience in their own past when the child was younger as it is more and more clarified by their often spontaneous, detailed recollections, and in other aspects, as understandable also as further maldevelopments in the intervening years.

Moreover, the influence of the grandparents of the child upon the parental attitudes toward each other and toward the child may become evident from two sources. One of these is the progressive recognition of the neurotogenic experience of each parent in *his* own childhood with his parents from the frequently inevitable recollections which occur in their free-associations to current events. The other source is the continuing transactions of younger parents of the child with such grandparents if the latter are still living, and at times nearby, in visits to the family that is engaged in therapy, or even more clearly if one or both grandparents may be living in the same home. Inevitably the psychotherapeutic clinicians obtain informational data about both the integrative or disintegrative factors which have operated in the past or continue to operate in the present so to speak in three generational depth.

Furthermore, as regards the reliability of the data obtained in clinical psychotherapeutic investigation both about past events in the family from the earliest days and weeks of the child patient's life as well as the recurrent episodes after clinical work with the family has begun, for further suggestions and discussions the reader is referred to several chapters in this volume.

In these chapters the reader will find discussion of the problems of psychotherapeutically oriented efforts to obtain earlier historical data, the affective reliving by parents of such past experience, often first in the transference reactions in the therapeutic situation followed by recall of the original experiences. The problems of recording such data perhaps both by audio and audio-visual means is discussed with the need for *prospective* planning of such therapeutic work and results of studies of comparability of the patients' symptomatology to make subgroup classifications. The use of modern methods of data management by methods of Boolean algebra, Venn diagrams to represent the spectra of syndromes are suggested by Alvan Feinstein for more precise studies of therapeutic experiments and prognosis. Both Feinstein and Bettelheim suggest the need of appropriate surveys in the community, rather than of only patients in the clinic and hospital, for valid studies of etiology. The training of students in these investigative methods is essential to the future for such research. Equally essential is the collation of such studies by various research teams in regional, national and even international conferences to obtain agreement of naming and eventual specification (as suggested by Dewey and Bentley (20)) of behavioral and psychological characteristics of patients and families as the appropriate means to approach the goal of transforming such clinical studies into warranted statements meriting the title of clinical science.

To return to Bowlby's discussion of starting afresh, he refers again to the conditions, implicit in his previous summary of data of observers, as probably contributing to whether or not attachment develops towards any one figure under two categories. The first, the reader will recall is "the sensitivity of that figure in responding to the baby's signals"; and the second, "the amount and nature of interaction between the couple." If these conditions are truly important ones, Bowlby thinks that the basic data necessary to answer the questions he poses at the beginning of this chapter are obtainable only from first hand reports of observers "of mothers' and children's interacting." Although few such studies have been performed and reports of them are of preliminary findings largely concerning the first year of life, for Bowlby "they carry promise of great advance." He finds difficulty in drawing upon some of these studies, however, inasmuch as the observations of the child's attachment behavior and those of "the amount and pattern of interaction that a child has with his mother are not always kept distinct." (Bowlby, p. 332.) He reminds his readers, however, that a child's attachment behavior is only a part of a larger system of the transactions of child and mother.

In spite of these arguments against the existing reports of studies, there is considerable value in such "most instructive" reports as those of David and Appell (18, 17), who give first hand accounts of such mother-child pairs interacting. Bowlby summarizes the "lively reading" provided by the accounts of a number of contrasting mother-child couples of these authors by stating that these reports impressively document three characteristics of the patterns of attachment found. These three are: 1) an extraordinary range of variation in the kind and amount of interaction found among a compared series of mother-child couples; 2) that each such couple by the end of one year usually had developed a highly characteristic pattern of interaction; and finally, 3) that each pattern so developed persists for up to three years in a form recognizable for that couple.

Among the elements Appell and David note in their study that compose these variations of pattern from one couple to another, but remain characteristic for each couple, are the quantity, mode, length of their sequences of interactions and which of the two tends to initiate and which terminates them: that is, the percentage of waking time the child is interacting with his mother, whether by touching, holding, or looking at one another and what distance is typically maintained between them. They further note the child's reactions to separations from his mother, his behavior towards strangers when in his mother's presence or absence as well as the mother's responses to the child's explorations or friendly behavior towards others.

Bowlby comments on the striking "degree of fit" that is achieved in these patterns of a given mother and child during their twelve months of coming to know one another, and how each has "shaped the other" in the expectations each has formed of the other's reactions to their own behavior in very many small and large ways. He concludes with a comment that the aforementioned clinicians would completely agree from their own experience, namely, that in considering the different patterns of attachment each child forms to his mother, it is always imperative to know the mother's particular pattern of mothering.

CRITERIA FOR ATTACHMENT BEHAVIOR

After considering the criteria used by students of child development to describe attachment and referring particularly to Ainsworth's (1) reflections on the relation of the problem of the *security* of a child to the apparent strength of his overt attachment behavior, Bowlby concludes that the concept of strength of attachment to one or more discriminated figures is just as much oversimplified to be useful as that of a unitary dependency drive has proved to be. In this review he quotes Ainsworth's ideas to the effect that some of the Ganda infants she observed manifested little protest on mother's departure or separation anxiety, yet they "seemed most solidly attached to their mothers" and "—showed the strength of their attachment—through their readiness to use her as a secure base from which they could both explore the world and expand their horizons to include other attachments." In short, Ainsworth raises the question—with which again clinicians would agree—whether the child who clings fearfully to mother and avoids acquaintance with the world of things and people is not thus manifesting his insecurity rather than the strength of his attachment.

For these reasons Bowlby concludes that new concepts need to be developed which await more systematic collection of the relevant observations and time to formulate them. As a beginning in this direction he points to the need for recording the child's various forms of attachment behavior in terms of his activity in various circumstances, of his responses to such conditions, all of which are clearly specified.

The forms of his activity or behavior, then, would include: a) those that initiate interaction with mother, such as greeting her, approaching, touching, embracing, scrambling over her, burying his face in her lap, calling her, talking and smiling, and the hands up gesture indicating his wish to be picked up; b) those behavioral responses including those just mentioned, in response to mother's initiatives as well as from the child's watching her; c) those behavioral forms, such as crying, following and clinging, that clearly indicate efforts to avoid separation from mother; d) those behavioral activities that are clearly exploratory and particularly how these occur in reference or orientation to the mother; and e) those forms of behavior that are obviously expressive of fear and withdrawal from strange people and situations again in orientation and reference to the mother.

To emphasize clearly the *conditions* under which the various forms of the child's behavior just referred to are to be observed and recorded, Bowlby goes on to list them discretely. In this list, as minimum, he includes: mother's whereabouts (i.e., whether she is present, absent, departing or returning) and her movements; the presence or absence of other persons and whether these are familiar or strangers to the child [and mother?]; the specification of the non-human environment as to whether it is also familiar, a little or very strange to the child [and mother?]; and finally a description of the condition of child himself [and his mother?], namely, whether the child [and mother?] is (or are) healthy, sick or in pain, fresh or fatigued, hungry or sated. The bracketed additions about mother are a clinician's suggestions from his experience which are almost, if not always, equally important concomitant aspects of the conditions to be considered in a total description and specification of the observed situation. Bowlby would probably agree not only to this addition, but also that the sequences of events both prior, during and after the episode observed as equally relevant for a more complete collection of data as basis for the development of the new concepts.

How a child behaves when fatigued or in pain, Bowlby emphasizes—what clinicians have also observed—is often quite revealing about his degree and quality of attachment to a mother figure. Most children in either condition seek out the mother. A child who is detached because of long deprivation of mother responsiveness or an autistic child is not likely to do so. He quotes Robertson's reports of a detached child's behavior (in Ainsworth and Boston (4)) and cites that of an instance of an autistic child described by Bettelheim (10, 65) when both were in severe pain.

The staff of the Children's Service of Langley Porter Neuropsychiatric Institute have had experience with even more distorted behavior from psychotic children with respect to pain whether this resulted from accidental or self-inflicted injury (see Chapter 27, Gianascol's report of a self-mutilating child in this volume). Another child whose relation with her own parents was extremely disturbed inserted the tip of one of her little fingers in a closing door jamb when the attention of a hospital nurse to whom she had begun to show some intense, ambivalently demanding attachment was for a moment unavoidably distracted by the needs of another child. She then without any outcry of pain showed the almost severed tip of the finger to this nurse. Another child, mute and severely autistic for almost ten years, cut the prepuce of his own penis (see Chapter 33 by Berlin in this volume). There were several other children also psychotic who were prone to injure themselves in various ways: e.g., by repeatedly, very severely punching at their own head to the point of inducing a cataract of an eye; or producing severe bruises, burns, lacerations, fractures, cuts, broken teeth and even brain damage, or slapping their own face violently, etc. Such self-injuries occurred often so suddenly that nursing personnel often had great difficulty in preventing such self-mutilations and injuries by appropriate protective restraint. All of such instances occurred without evidence of the usual reactions to pain or of seeking relief or consolation from the adults of the staff. In some of these instances particularly in the accidental minor hurts the child promptly rejected proffered sympathetic attention from an adult by abruptly turning away also without tears, crying or overt evidence of pain. In others the self-inflicted injuries at times alternated with vicious attacks upon the attending nurse or upon another, usually smaller and weaker, child.

The antecedent experience of such children was not always easy or clearly obtainable in the efforts at therapeutic work with their parents, although in some of these instances there was obtained from their parents a guilty account of one of the parents, often the father, of having struck the child in moments of impotent fury and frustration at the child's unresponsiveness to their requests or offered attentiveness. From some mothers of such children their psychotherapist sometimes obtained accounts of the mother's immobilization from intense anxiety and fear about the child's dangerously self-hurtful behavior, or when the child in some enraged disappointment attacked the mother.

These latter instances of self-injurious behavior of some psychotic children, as well as violently hostile aggressive attacks by other children upon others occurred when these children began to emerge from an often prolonged mute intensely isolated state of behavior. They may perhaps not be quite the same sort of psychodynamic condition as those referred to by Bowlby in the aforementioned context. They are clearly instances of much more intense, conflictful developments of the mother-child transactional patterns. Nevertheless, they seem to this writer also disturbances of what Bowlby terms attachment behavior.

However Bowlby and other students would view such phenomena in relation to the further study of attachment behavior and the relevance of such clinical observations to the development of new concepts, one can agree with Bowlby in his thought that "In practice, perhaps a fairly limited selection from such a theoretically complete range of conditions might give an adequate picture of a given child." One might also agree that he may be correct in his expectation that a child's attachment behavior might eventually be describable as a profile of the child's behavior "in each of that number of selected conditions."

It seems certainly true that those clinicians with experience with parents as well as the child would agree with Bowlby that a complete picture could only emerge if "a complementary profile of how the child's mother behaves" both in response to the child's initiations in a comparable series of situations and when and in what manner she takes the initiative toward the child. Only then can the pattern of transactions between them and the child's behavioral contribution to it be more completely grasped.

EXAMPLES OF ATTACHMENT PATTERNS AT TWELVE MONTHS

To illustrate the variations in patterns of attachment among infants reared in their own homes with stable mothers, Bowlby reviews the initial findings of a recent study by Ainsworth and Wittig (5) in some detail. For a more comprehensive description of this research the reader is referred to Bowlby's volume (pp. 335-339) or to the original report. Here only the essential conclusions will be summarized of the results of the short longitudinal observations made upon fourteen of a projected thirty-six middle-class white American couples.

Briefly, the method employed consisted of four hour observational sessions in the homes of the child-mother couples at intervals of four weeks during the first twelve months of the infant's life followed by an interesting set of experimental situations at the end of this first year. The method permitted the study of the behavior of the infant in a variety of typical domestic situations and the behavior of both mother and child in the testing situations. Thus, during the periodic home visits these observers noted the behavior of the child both when mother was present and absent, how she responded to him and how the child behaved with other members of the family and with strangers.

At about the first birthday of the child the experimental conditions under which the behavior of both mother and child were studied consisted of a series of about three minute periods, in a strange room equipped with toys, arranged as follows: first, mother and infant are joined by female stranger; second, mother leaves the child with the stranger going out as unobtrusively as possible; third, mother returns; fourth, mother leaves the child alone for an interval that is relieved by the stranger's return, and finally by mother's return.

Such a testing, or some suitably close variant of it, strikes the present writer as conceivably useful and applicable in clinical study of young children. One could possibly test and measure changes in both the child's and the mother's behavior toward each other in diagnostic evaluations and in relation to a variety of therapeutic procedures. Changes due to age of child and experience of mother and child outside the therapeutic situation need to be considered.

In the Ainsworth study there was much variation in behavioral patterns observed in the fourteen infants and, as Bowlby states it, "the similarities between the majority of them were often as striking as any differences." Thus in all but two instances, the children when first alone with mother were seen, while keeping an eye on mother, "busily exploring the novel situation" and there was practically no crying. "There was still virtually no crying" when the stranger came into the room, but this was followed by reduction of exploration "by almost all the children."

The differences between the children which divided them into two groups became more apparent when mother left the child with the stranger. Six of the fourteen, although showing awareness of mother's leaving and indicating "at minor intensity" a wish to join her by going to the door and perhaps trying to open it, cried little or not at all, continued to explore. All of the remaining eight cried a great deal despite the mother's unobtrusive departure; five of them, in acute distress, rejected the stranger's efforts to comfort them; six of these eight plainly showed their desire to rejoin mother, half of them strongly; while the remaining two appeared helpless and hopeless in their acute distress and made no such efforts to rejoin mother.

On the mother's return all fourteen again showed more behavioral similarity in that all but two immediately approached her; those who were crying tended to stop especially when picked up, and five of them clung tightly to her. The next step in the experimental step began only after mother settled the child into contentment by comforting the infant whereupon mother again left the child, this time alone. This time many more of the infants reacted strongly;

crying, trying to rejoin her by banging on the door or trying to open it and with greater intensity. It was not clear whether this greater intensity of reaction was due to being left alone, or to being sensitized by the first separation, or to the combination of both factors.

All of the mothers except one picked up her child on their second return, and ten of the infants, in place of only five on the first return, upon rejoining their mother, clung tightly to her but all tended to diminish their crying on being picked up.

In summary considering their behavior in the two separations from mother, more than half of the infants observed reacted similarly on both occasions, but more intensely on the second, than on the first. Three of them appeared little distressed on either separation but attempted to rejoin her on each occasion. Four manifested more or less acute distress *and* efforts to rejoin mother; while one child although acutely distressed on both separations, made no effort to rejoin his mother. Of the remaining infants, who showed more change in behavior, two attempted to rejoin mother on each separation but cried only on the second occasion and then strongly. Three others cried and attempted to rejoin mother on the first separation, cried also on the second occasion but made no effort to rejoin her; while one infant was acutely distressed in both occasions and made no attempt to rejoin his mother on her first return but did so on the second.

Such data as the above Bowlby cites with Ainsworth as drawing "attention to the absurdity of trying to arrange these children in simple linear order of strength of attachment—". A number of scales, he thinks, are required to do justice to the facts.

The dimension which Ainsworth finds useful is the one clinicians have been long accustomed to using, namely that of the *security* of the child's attachment to the mother. She points to such phenomena of a twelve-month-old child's behavior as evidence of his security as the following: his ability to use mother's presence as a secure base to explore a strange environment; his not being distressed by the appearance of a stranger in such a situation; his evident awareness of where his mother is in her absence, and he weathers such brief periods of her temporary absence even though he may be distressed by it; and finally his greeting her on her return. At the opposite extreme, that is, as evidence of an infant's insecure attachment to mother, she uses such criteria as: an infant's inability to explore even in his mother's presence; his being much alarmed by the advent of a stranger; his reaction to mother's absence by crumpling into an unoriented and helpless distress; and his *not* greeting her upon her return.

Ainsworth has also communicated to Bowlby her serious consideration of an index which seems to her as possibly a particularly valuable one of security: namely, the manner in which the child responds to mother on her return from a very brief absence. Studying her data suggests that the securely attached child greets her, approaches her, seeks to be picked up, to cling or to remain close to her. This Bowlby interprets as an organized sequence of *goal-corrected* behavior in terms of the control theory he repeatedly advances as a more parsimonious way of looking at behavior. On the other hand, other children (less securely attached) show either disinterest in the mother's reappearance, or distressed tantrums without any such organized efforts to approach her.

All this is reminiscent to the present writer of both similarly organized, or more disorganized, behavior of twelve-month-old infants on tests with pellets and bottle, blocks, putting pegs in a board and persistent search for a block hidden from their view by a screen in children who have been observed by Sylvia Brody as socially responded to, or not responded to, by their mothers during feeding throughout their lives previous to these tests.

Further, clinical observations of psychotic children brought for admission to the hospital for therapy by their parents have shown similar differential reactions to their parents' departure from, or on their return to, the ward at Langley Porter on such occasions. Those children who are observed to be more indifferent to the coming and going of their parents to and from the ward are the more withdrawn and unresponsive (or in Bowlby's terms, detached or unattached) not only to their parents and siblings but also to staff and other child patients on the ward. These children are those who are also often mute, avoiding even eye-contact and manifest other severe symptoms. These symptoms prove to be more durable and more difficult to reduce by therapeutic efforts of the staff often for years. Some of these children although manifesting little or no overt distress on the departure from the ward on first admission did, however, manifest delayed, indirect disturbance in behavior sometimes many hours or even several days later. These manifest delayed disturbances included some degrees of anorexia, sleep disturbances, not easily identifiable as to immediately prior events, temper tantrums, tendency to reject the approach and the offer of comforting efforts of ward staff, or marked tendencies to isolate themselves not only from adults of the staff but also from other child patients on the ward even of their own ages.

Less severely disturbed psychotic children, on the other hand, are seen showing more distress, tantrums, clinging to mother (or father if he is the more primary attachment figure) on the same kinds of occasions.

All this is similar to Ainsworth's findings that the children rated more secure in this index are also those who have been observed in their homes prior to the experimental tests described above as active at home and content while mother is present and crying only when hurt, unwell or in mother's absence. Those children rated on this index as less securely attached in the experimental setting, however, tend to be fussy and inactive at home even in mother's presence and cry readily and frequently.

Furthermore, any clinician with psychotherapeutic experience with pregnant mothers who continue their therapeutic work after the child's birth during their child's first twelve to twenty-four months of life can attest to similar differences in the child's behavior reported by the mother from time to time. Each episode of distress, irritability, sleep or feeding disturbance, negativism and of regressive behavior of the child (such as loss of bladder or bowel habits already somewhat acquired) is clearly chronologically related to the mother's own episode of exacerbation of her neurosis. These latter exacerbations may be the result of one or more events disturbing her, such as: some severe disagreement with, and consequent estrangement from, her husband; with her own parents or her in-laws; with a friend; an overcommitment in her own schedule, and the like. Depending upon the phase in her own therapy and the nature, duration, and severity of the problem initiating the episode, her intercurrent turmoil may be terminated sooner or later. When the causes and effects of such factors are ameliorated, reduced or resolved through the mother's own efforts regarding such situational disturbances, following their clarification and with the insight gained in the therapeutic sessions, the child's disturbed behavior often rather promptly stops, perhaps to recur with another similar episode of the mother's exacerbation of her neurotic conflicts.

While Bowlby suggests that such an index of the security-insecurity dimension of the child's attachment to mother may be of great importance for future research and possibly of predictive value when confirmed, it occurs to the present writer that some such test or experimental situation would be of considerable importance on which to collect data during clinical assessments of degrees of maldevelopments of mother-child relationships as well. Such an index might also prove useful as an approach to the measurement of changes in each, child and mother, and in the relationship between them in the course of therapeutic work.

CONTRIBUTING FACTORS TO VARIATION IN FIRST YEAR

In the second section of this chapter on Patterns of Attachment, Bowlby reviews the conditions in the first year of the child's life which may eventually be proved as contributing to the observed variation of the patterns in mother-child relations. It is both an evident fact and a constant problem to both students of child development as well as clinicians that a particular form a given child's attachment behavior takes depends upon several factors. It depends partly upon "the initial biases that infant and mother each bring to their developing partnership." Also it depends partly on how each affects the other in the course of its development. In short the problem is how much it is determined by their individual biases and how much it results from their influence upon each other. Bowlby thinks that "systematic research is still embryonic" and yet the range of possibilities is almost infinite. For these reasons he gives only a few examples.

Among the biases of the infant and his influence upon the mother's behavior he mentions three examples: (1) the sex-linked differences; (2) those due to neurophysiological damage; and (3) differences in disposition as to activity or passivity of infants of the same sexes and at the same ages.

In support of the first bias of the infant, that is, the sex-linked difference, Moss (40) found that on balance boy babies have a tendency to cry more and sleep less than girl babies do. For this reason he believes that probably on the average boy babies receive, up to three months, from their mothers more holding and rocking contact and social attention than girls. Although it is unknown how this affects future transactions between child and mother, Bowlby would be surprised if it had no effect.

Concerning the second bias of the infant, the influence of neurophysiological damage, Bowlby cites the work of Ucko (69) who studied the differences during their first five years between thirteen boys recorded as having suffered asphyxia at birth and a control group of two boys. The first group were from the first more sensitive to noise, more disturbed in their sleep, more upset at changes in their environment such as those entailed in moving from a house, during a family holiday and by a brief separation from a family member than the controls. They were also more apprehensive and clinging on starting nursery, and regular school. Those who had suffered asphyxia were "far more frequently rated as 'very difficult' or 'difficult much of the time' than were the controls" when available information on their behavior during the entire five years was assessed. There was, too, a significant correlation between the degree of asphyxia recorded originally and their rating on the behavior scale.

Such data from studies of infants with recorded asphyxia during birth, together with other observations of Prechtl (45) and Yarrow (73) lead Bowlby to conclude that the kind of behavioral bias present at birth in infants may not only persist "in its own right, at least in some degree, but apt also to influence the way a mother responds." Bowlby cites the following observations of Prechtl who describes both the hypokinetic apathetic baby who responds weakly and cries little, and the excitable baby who cries readily, over-reacts to slight stimulation and who is difficult to pacify when unpredictably wide awake and equally difficult to arouse when just as unpredictably he shifts to a state of being drowsy. Both the first type as well as the second syndromes are ascribed by Prechtl "as occurring commonly in infants *with minimal brain damage*." Italics, mine, connote this writer's doubt derived from clinical experience about the adequacy of neurological evidence often used to categorize children with this diagnostic title.

Such clinical experience is further supported by Benton's (8) recent overview of clinical neuropsychology of childhood in which appear statements such as the following: "more recently there has been considerable work with children (i.e., those designated as cases of learning disability or minimal brain damage) in whom brain damage is a presumptive or working hypothesis rather than an established fact." And, "Turning to the areas of 'minimal brain damage' and learning disability, we have to concede that at the present time this is truly a mare's nest. Some years ago Gomez (1967) equated 'minimal cerebral dysfunction' with 'maximal neurologic confusion' and he was surely on firm ground in doing so. The confusion is inherent in the term itself. A child is observed to be hyperactive, distractible, motorically awkward, unstable in behavior level or perceptually handicapped. These disabilities are relatively minor as compared to global retardation or frank cerebral palsy. Then by a process of neurological myth making, the relatively minor behavior manifestations are transformed into relatively minor brain abnormality. There is, of course, no justification for doing this. On the one hand, all these behavioral disabilities may have come about because of a faulty nurture (using this term in its broadest sense). On the other hand, they may be the expression of major (not minimal) brain damage."

Such babies, even though infants with either of these syndromes may improve during the first year, present greater problems to their mothers than do normally reactive babies. That is, the over-reactive and unpredictable infant may arouse mother's exasperation, which may lead to her intense anxiety in mothering efforts, or to desperation about her effectiveness and to an inclination on her part to reject him. A clinician could add that both maternal reactions may alternate, and his agreement with Bowlby that in any such situation the pattern of mothering "can be significantly changed from what it might otherwise have been." He could also agree with Sander's findings (1969) that a non-neurotic (Bowlby's term here is "equable") mother's effectiveness need not be affected negatively—at least to a persistently severe degree.

In further support of the effect on mother by the third type of initial bias of the child Bowlby quotes from Yarrow's (73) studies of infants in adoptive and foster homes. Yarrow's observations are that the infants of the same sex and age, in the same home, who are "actively disposed" may receive much more social response from the mothering person than those "passively disposed"; and this for the reason that the active children both demand it and reward it more when they succeed in evoking it. Vivid quoted descriptions of such contrasts from Yarrow confirm not only what experienced clinicians have observed even in twins (6) identical or fraternal, reared in their own homes, but also common observations of many people outside of strictly clinical situations. Bowlby's ending comment to these examples is to the effect that there was much resemblance between the actively and passively disposed infants *only* in respect "to the amounts of physical care each received."

The latter comment evokes again in the present writer the thought already expressed in his published review of Bowlby's book (60). This is the fact that only one child among 264 psychotic children (see Chapters 8, 14) seen at Langley Porter between 1946 and 1961 was in any appreciable degree malnourished and definitely physically underdeveloped. This patient at age three years presented a picture of a severe agitated depression, restless, wringing her hands with an extremely tense facial expression and speaking little and often not at all, and showed little sign of attachment to any staff member. For further details about this patient see Chapter 8 in this volume. (Langdell, J. I. "Depressive Reactions," under subtitle "Marasmic Type.")

Otherwise, most of the remainder of this sample of psychotic children showed none of the signs of failure to thrive, or similarity to the marasmic characteristics this child did. In short the psychotic condition appears to justify the impression that these children do not suffer any *physical* neglect and generally develop well as far as nutrition, motor maturation and development and the like are concerned. They often manifest—but not uniformly— fearfulness in the use of their bodies, such as in going downstairs one step at a time, in the use of play yard equipment, roller skating, bike riding, swimming, etc. Such fearfulness has decreased a great deal even in some quite autistically disordered children when the duration of psychological therapy has been long enough and during which the child has developed even uncertain and still rather insecure attachment to their assigned nurse, teacher and/or psychotherapist.

Bowlby concludes this discussion of the influence of the infant's bias on the later pattern of attachment—which he adds does not need to be supposed as generally present only at birth, but perhaps appearing later—by remarking that the examples he gives emphasize "the degree to which an infant himself plays a part in determining his own environment." He adds the very pertinent note that until methods "for determining the existence of such biases" are developed, discussion of them "tends to degenerate into speculation."

Thomas, Chess, and Birch (68, 67) in their study of temperamental differences in infants note that these appear from birth, that these differences may result in estrangement from mother if not dealt with by an alert pediatrician, and also that these temperamental differences persist throughout the studies that have been done. These authors attribute most of these differences to genetic endowment, rather than to birth trauma.

Bowlby gives somewhat more space to the discussion of the bias of mother and its influence on the baby. He mentions what clinicians, experienced in simultaneous psychotherapeutic work with the parents of such psychotic children, know well; namely, that what the mother brings to the situation is much more complex including not only her "native endowment" but also those influences from relations not only in her own family of origin and perhaps additionally within other families and "from long absorption of the values and practices of her culture." However, he dismisses the examination of such numerous interacting variables and the manner in which they produce the varieties of mothering which he sees as beyond the scope of his volume.

Nonetheless he cites a number of students of child development. Their outlines of longitudinal modes of study of both mother and the child's behavior toward each other and their observations as well as those of two clinicians especially experienced in the work with psychotic maldevelopment in early childhood, namely those of Bettelheim (10) and Mahler (36) are mentioned. He has apparently not had occasion to see the reports from the Ittleson Center in New York by Goldfarb and his coworkers (24, 25) nor those of the clinical students of this problem at Langley Porter Neuropsychiatric Institute in San Francisco (61, 63) whose reports on this factor are in a considerable measure confirmatory in this respect.

All of this data leads him to the conclusion that they suggest that the mother has had a much larger role than the infant by the end of the first birthday of the child in the determination of the quantity as well as the quality of the transactions that occur between them. He finds it—in view of such data regarding "the nature of the variables that now seem of importance in determining patterns of attachment behavior"—not very surprising that studies of certain child rearing techniques have resulted in "so many negative results" (15). The latter group of studies (which he sees of little relevance even if accurate) includes those collecting data on such matters as "breast versus bottle-feeding, self-demand versus schedule, or early weaning versus late."

He refers to Brody's (14) demonstration that breast feeding is no guarantee of a mother's sensitivity to her baby's signals, nor that holding the infant during feeding assures that either intimacy or rapport will develop between the partners. Still, since during the early months particularly the feeding situation is an important opportunity for contact between mother and child, how a mother shows sensitivity to the baby's signals, her responsiveness to his rhythms and social initiatives may become predictive of the way an infant's attachment behavior will develop. Hence, there is little reason to regard their transactions during feeding as wholly irrelevant and to dismiss them.

Space here precludes more detailed review of the research data of a number of students of child development that Bowlby gives in support of the biases brought by mother to the subsequent development of the attachment behavior of the child, or to express the matter in this writer's preferred terms, the transaction between the partners. It is possible here to give only a précis of the chief conclusions of the studies mentioned.

Moss (40) found that among twenty-three women those whom he had rated "as accepting of a nurturant role" two years later were more readily responsive to their own baby's crying in his first three months than those rated lower on his scales regarding these attitudes. Bowlby adds that, although Moss did not give information on the later outcomes in the development of these children, he would expect that the babies with the more responsive mothers would develop "differently" from those with less responsive mothers. Moreover, he also adds that these differences in development in turn influencing the mothers' behavior would exemplify how the circular processes thus begun (63) might have far reaching effects on the nature of their subsequent partnership.

Evidence from recorded longitudinal studies of the transactions of mothers and their babies reported by other students supports not only the effect of her baby's initial bias upon the mother's responsiveness but also the "idiosyncratic" ways different mothers treat their children. Thus, one mother may be encouraged by her baby's social advances, becoming more solicitously responsive to his crying, while another mother may evade the advances, becoming more impatient. In these ways the mother's behavior toward her infant is "a complex product reflecting how her own initial biases have been confirmed, modified or amplified by her experience with him."

Bowlby cites also David and Appel's (18, 17) findings to the effect that the highly characteristic differences in the pattern of transactions between one couple and another at the child's first birthday are immense in range not only in quantity but also in their quality. The quantity of their transactions varied not only in the length of their responsiveness to each other but also in their frequency as to mother's initiative in whatever episodes were observed occurring between them.

Although these studies gave too little information to draw clear inferences as to the reasons for these differences between couples, nevertheless it is evident that the mothers "varied far more than did the infants" in the extent to which a partner responded more to the other's initiatives. In other words, every infant observed almost always responded to his mother's initiatives; while every mother ignored some of her infant's initiatives, and while one mother responded to well over half of them, others hardly ever did so. It is not surprising then that the more responsive mothers enjoyed their infants, while the others appeared to find their child a burden except when they themselves had taken the initiative toward their child.

Observations of mother-child transactions by other students also point strongly in the same direction; by the first birthday of the infant the behavior of the mother determines the amount of such transactions between them much more than does that of the infant. The variation in the pattern of the transactions in the groups and couples observed varied in a continuum from very little to almost constant and the principle variable appeared to be the extent to which the mother ignored or responded to the child's initiatives.

This latter factor, i.e., the way the mother treats her child whatever its causes, plays a leading role in the nature of the resulting pattern of attachment the infant develops and is supported by much research data. One such research is by Yarrow (73) of the development of forty infants while in either foster or adoptive homes during their first six months. At the end of this period there was indirect evidence for the above conclusion from observations of the children's behavior in tests and in situations of social interactions as well as from interviews with the mother figure. These data were then correlated with ratings of the infants' experience in the home made during the previous months by the observer's visits there. Significantly high correlations were found between the child's ability to cope with frustration and stress in the final tests and such characteristics of maternal behavior as: the amount of physical contact mother gave the infant; the degree of her holding the child was adapted to his characteristic rhythms; the extent of effectiveness of her soothing techniques, and in stimulating and encouraging him to respond socially; to express his needs or to make developmental progress; by the provision of materials and experiences provided that were suitable to his individual potentialities; and finally the intensity and frequency of positive expressions of feelings toward him by mother, father and others. All the mentioned indices of maternal behavior were positively correlated (coefficients 0.50 or higher) with the infant's capacity to cope with stress. The highest coefficients of correlation, however, were found to be between the infant's capacity to cope with stress and the degree of the mother's adapting herself effectively to the infant's rhythms and development. These aspects of maternal behavior were also positively correlated with the quantity of social initiative of a given infant, but in all infants the capacity to cope with stress was higher than tolerance of stress.

Yarrow, however, did not give any evidence of how his measured indices of maternal behavior were correlated with the infant's pattern of attachment at twelve months or later. The findings of other students, especially those of Ainsworth, strongly suggested to Bowlby what they probably would be.

Thus in Ainsworth's longitudinal study (5) the list of indices of maternal behavior that in her observations contribute to the development of secure attachment contains items similar to Yarrow's, but contains two additional ones. These are: "an environment so regulated that the baby can derive a sense of the consequences of his own actions"; and "the mutual delight that a mother and infant find in each other's company." The latter Bowlby considers as much a result of the other conditions already listed as a condition in its own right, to which the present writer completely agrees.

Other workers, especially those with clinical experience (Bettelheim (10), Mahler (36), Sander (51, 50), David and Appel (17, 18)) also regard several of the conditions mentioned of great importance in their contribution to the child's development. They stress particularly whether the child's social initiatives lead to his experience of predictable results, especially the degree of success he has in securing reciprocal transactions with his mother. If the conditions are present, happily active transactions ensue and a secure attachment develops; if only partly present, friction and discontent follow in the transactions, and attachment is insecure. If the conditions are practically absent, "grave deficiencies of interchange and attachment may result." Bowlby includes in the latter possibilities great delay in attachment due to quantitatively inadequate transactions and—of greatest interest to the clinicians experienced with the psychotic degrees of childhood maldevelopment— "some forms of autism, owing to the child's finding the social responses of his mother-figure too difficult to predict."

In support of the last statement he quotes Bettelheim and Mahler. The first holds that the child has "given up goal directed action . . . (and) also prediction" as a result of his experience that his social transactions with people have no predictable effects in contrast to his behavior toward impersonal objects which commonly continues goal directed. Mahler, the second experienced clinician (36), is quoted to the effect that unpredictable mothering can result in the child's "retreat into secondary autism." This writer can add that Goldfarb (24, 25) has written of "parental perplexity" toward some of the psychotic children his group has studied. It may also be added that from the reports of the Children's Service of the Langley Porter Neuropsychiatric Institute (61, 63, 11) that this staff has seen in their concomitant therapy with parents as well as with the psychotic child for over twenty-five years severe and such pervasive conflictful rearing by often both parents of the one of their children (and sometimes of more than one of them) that patients' psychotic maldevelopment appeared rather obviously chronologically related to this experience. In these other chapters—especially those studies of therapy with the individual child and his family—the reader will find documentation of the exacerbations of mother's conflicts especially, but also of father's pre-marital neurotic conflicts by intercurrent stresses as well as those primarily deriving from the parents' own conflictful relations to each other.

Bowlby's concluding remarks to this section nevertheless point to the fact that the hypotheses regarding these aforementioned conditions during the first year that are likely to be relevant to the development of attachment behavior are still "little tested and must be treated with caution," and expresses the hope that they will soon be rigorously tested. Some testing of these hypotheses by psychotherapeutic work as illustrated in some of the chapters in this volume reporting the work with such families in this volume seems to have already been done. Similar successful work particularly by Bettelheim, primarily with the child himself, at his center are also supportive of these hypotheses. Even in those children whose attachment is seriously maldeveloped but in whom there is also evidence of organic disease or mental defect there appears to be fairly convincing data of similar psychological variables also operating.

STABILITY AND PERSISTENCE OF PATTERNS

The last section considers the questions of the stability and persistence of the characteristic pattern of transactions between a given mother and child couple that results from their experience with each other in the first year; and particularly "of its two components, the child's attachment behavior and the mother's caretaking behavior." The answers to these questions he considers complex.

It appears plain to him that the more mutual satisfaction is experienced by each member of a couple the more stable it is likely to be. The converse also seems very likely since one or both of a couple experiencing dissatisfaction in the pattern that has evolved will tend constantly or intermittently to change the current pattern. Despite this he finds evidence (17) that whether or not it is satisfying, the pattern evolved by the end of the first year tends to persist for at least the next two or three years. He suggests that a partial reason for this is that each member of the partnership has come to expect certain kinds of behavior from the other and each generally is unsuccessful in changing, or avoids eliciting the customary response of the other. Thus expectations of each tend to be confirmed, "and whether for good or ill" such processes result in a stability of transactional patterns of the couple that is independent of each of the partners separately considered.

Nevertheless, all sorts of events such as chronic illness, an accident of the child, a distraction or depression of the mother, birth of a sibling, a period of separation on the one hand, and more integrative events such as "more perceptive" acceptance of the child's attachment and treatment of the child by the mother on the other hand, may lead to changes in the established pattern for the worse in the first, and for the better, in the second instance. Here again clinicians with long experience in therapeutic work with families would wholly agree (62). Hence there is no invariable prognostic value of the probability of persistence of a pattern present between a couple at the child's first birthday, although this is likely to be true for most couples.

Bowlby also emphasizes that any prognostic statement made about a twelve-month-old child's future degree of autonomous stability, as distinct from the transactional pattern of the couple of which he is a partner, "is even more hazardous than to make about the interactions of a couple." The reason for this is the probability that the organizational stability of a child's behavior at this age is much less than that of the dyad of which he is one part. Bowlby acknowledges how very little is known about the lability or stability of the behavioral organization of *young* children considered as individuals. "All that can safely be said is that as the years pass, lability diminishes; whether it be favorable or unfavorable, whatever organization exists becomes progressively less easily changed."

As for the stability of the transactional pattern of couples Bowlby supposes that this occurs more quickly since whatever pattern becomes established has arisen from mutual adaptation, and hence the pressure to sustain it derives increasingly from both sides. Such stability of the pattern is then both its weakness and its strength. It is strong when the pattern is favorable for the future of both partners. When, however, the pattern is unfavorable for one or both partners, its stability constitutes a weakness because a change in the pattern as a whole can only come about from a change in the organization of behavior of each partner. It was with this purpose that the work at Langley Porter was based on concomitant therapy with all three members of the family triad.

He again concludes with a statement that makes clear he is a clinician of considerable experience—an experience that he shares with other clinicians who have progressively become aware and alert to the ineluctable importance of the entire family in comprehending the nature of a child's psychopathology. Therefore it follows that any therapeusis of such pathology of the child may often, if not usually, require consideration of what changes it may be possible to expect in the transactional pattern of the other members of the family in the context of which the child's maldevelopment arose. In short when Bowlby speaks in this concluding statement about the most significant development in child psychiatry in recent years being the increasing recognition "that the problems its practitioners are called upon to treat are not often problems confined to individuals" but the stable transactional patterns of two or more members of their families, and when he mentions that diagnostic skill consists of "the assessment of these patterns and of the current biases in each family member that help to perpetuate them," and "that therapeutic skill lies in techniques that enable changes to occur more or less concurrently in all members of a family so that a new pattern" can emerge and be stabilized, then he speaks for at least the long-held principles of this writer (61), his colleagues on the staff and for all the child psychiatric clinicians of similar persuasion.

FURTHER DEVELOPMENT IN ORGANIZATION OF ATTACHMENT BEHAVIOR

Bowlby concludes his volume with a brief chapter which he acknowledges as "one inadequate to its theme," (and then appends a relatively succinct review of psychoanalytic literature which he considers pertinent to the "Child's Tie to His Mother," which will not be considered here). The developmental processes reviewed in this final chapter that are, as he puts it, "touched upon [here] are not only of great intrinsic interest but they are the very processes that make man different from other species." He finds that although there is "no doubt" more to say about the developments in the organization of attachment behavior during the second and third years of life than he presents in the chapter, perhaps there is "not much more." There is, he says, "still a continent to conquer" in this least studied early phase of human development during which the child acquires "all that makes him most distinctively human." By this he refers to man's ability to use symbols, language, to plan, to build models, and "his capacities for long-lasting collaboration with others and for interminable strife" which all have their beginnings in these first three years, and they are all utilized from the first few days in the organization of attachment behavior.

He repeats again his earlier statement that attachment behavior persists throughout life to either old or new figures selected and proximity and/or communication is maintained with them. Thus although the outcome of such behavior continues the same as in childhood, the ways and means for achieving this outcome become progressively and increasingly diverse and sophisticated. Both the older child and the adult maintain their attachment to the other persons by not only the basic elements of such behavior evolved by the first birthday but also by adding "an increasingly varied array of more sophisticated elements." As an example of this he compares the school boy's seeking and finding his mother at a neighbor's home, pleading with her to allow him to accompany her on her planned visit to relatives the following week with the same boy's first attempt as an infant to follow his mother as she left the room—which illustrates the greater degree of the school boy's behavioral organization over that he showed in infancy.

These more diverse and more sophisticated aspects of an older child's attachment behavior also exemplify his behavioral organization "as plans with set-goals." Such capacity to plan goal-corrected behavior to bring about the circumstances (the set-goal) that would terminate the attachment behavior by achieving proximity to the attachment person does not begin to appear until after the child's eighth month and as he approaches the end of his first year. Prior to this there is probably no planned effort to achieve the conditions that terminate with his attachment behavior. Either mother is there—as in his own home this is likely to be among the predictable outcomes of whatever attachment behavior he then manifests—and he is content; or she is not, and he is distressed. His behavior in these first three quarters of this first year is not yet goal-corrected.

After this he becomes more skillful, appears to discover "what conditions are that terminate his distress" and bring him security. Thereafter he begins to plan his behavior to achieve these conditions, and thus "during his second year he develops a will of his own." Depending upon the varying intensity of the attachment behavior of a given child at any given time that happens to be elicited by a variety of factors, the terminating conditions vary also as do the child's set-goals from one occasion to another. That is, nothing less than sitting on mother's knee will be his obvious determination at one time, while on the other occasions the sight of her through a doorway will satisfy him. Whatever is necessary at any given time to terminate his attachment behavior becomes the set goal of any plan he adopts for his effort.

Whatever the structure of such attachment plans are as to the simplicity and speed of their executions or as to their degree of elaborate complexity depends on several factors. These factors are partly the set-goal selected the child's estimate of the situation of himself and his attachment figure, and his skill in devising the plan to meet that situation. Also whatever the plan's simplicity or complexity, it is devised only by the child's capacity to construct "working models" of the environment and of himself. Hence, such planning is possible only when he is capable of constructing and elaborating these working models.

Bowlby refers to the experiments of Piaget (43, 41), repeated by Décarie (19) with Canadian children confirming Piaget's results, that it is a very exceptional child who can make a plan before he is seven months old, and that the great majority of children eight, nine months of age, or older show for some months longer only "embryonic" ability to plan and about the simplest of situations. Piaget uses the terms "intention" or "intentionality" in place of Bowlby's "plan" or "goal."

Bowlby agrees that such planning involving first influencing, i.e. changing, the behavior and later grasping the set goals of the attachment figure, is at first primitive: simple pushing, pulling, request or commands, such as "come here" or "go away." He may later, when older, begin to grasp slowly that his mother at times has her own set goals that may possibly be changed. His behavior then begins to be more "sophisticated," although still quite often nevertheless "sadly misconceived"—as in the instance of the boy who attempted to obtain the return of his teddy bear that she had taken from him by offering her his knife. Such efforts illustrate how inadequate still are his working models of his mother.

Hence, it is clear that the requirements of forming a plan, the aim (set goal) of which is to modify the aims (set goals) of another person's behavior are: an ability to attribute to such another a capacity to have her own aims and plans; to infer what these may be from whatever clues are available; and finally, the possession of skill of framing plans that may have some chance of modifying such aims of other persons. All of these requirements presuppose a considerable competence in cognition and model building.

Competence to comprehend the mother's behavior as being directed by her own goals "may perhaps be fairly well established by the second birthday." Competence to grasp what these goals of another are, however, is "still only embryonic." The chief reason for this is something which children have particularly very poor ability to do, namely, to see matters from the other person's point of view. Such ability according to the evidence available grows extremely slowly and "it is not even reasonably well developed until after a child has passed his seventh birthday." Experienced clinicians would add that in a considerable proportion of their "borderline" adolescent and even adult patients with whom they are engaged in intensive psychotherapeutic work such competence is still sadly inadequate and undeveloped by reason of conflictful experiences during these early years with parenting persons who are themselves more or less seriously conflicted about various aspects of their own living. These experiences appear to have had the effect of thwarting their development of: a competence of clearly comprehending their own wishes (aims, set-goals); a capacity to order them as to their priority in importance for their own immediate and ultimate welfare; and an ability to persist in any, even embryonic, plans they may be capable of framing to attain them.

As Bowlby says about the grave limitations upon all children's social relationships and that such inadequacies lead them frequently to be misjudged, so the aforementioned clinicians could echo similar opinions about their older patients. For Bowlby's case with children (as with the patients of clinicians) "a brief digression may be useful."

"THE HANDICAP OF EGOCENTRISM"

The "useful digression" is to "one of Piaget's earliest and best validated findings" (42, 44), namely, "that the child under seven years of age has extreme difficulty in seeing anything from the point of view of someone else." Despite his awareness "in principle" that the other's viewpoint may not be the same as his own, the child is still not able to do so in practice; when this is tested he is able to imagine clearly only his own. Piaget termed this "cognitive limitation" *egocentrism.*

Because the present writer has found essentially similar characteristics in patients in therapy who are much beyond their seventh birthday, he is inclined to quote verbatim the paragraph of Bowlby on these characteristics of egocentrism.

Thus (p. 353): "Egocentrism affects and limits every area of a child's dealing with other people, whether at a verbal or a non-verbal level. In his verbal communications to others, for example, a child of under seven is found to make little attempt to suit what he has to say, or the way he says it, to the needs of his listener. His assumption seems to be that any and every listener is as fully cognizant as he is himself of both the context and the actors in any incident he wishes to relate, and that only the details that are novel and interesting to him need be described. As a result, whenever the listener is not familiar with context and characters, the account is apt to be incomprehensible."

To introduce another brief digression into Bowlby's digression, this just quoted statement appears to be a very good description of the so-called "free-associations" of many analysands in many hours of their analytic sessions. An additional similarity is how extremely slowly some of such analysands learn to express more completely the context and all essential actors in a given event which comes to mind as a result of the analyst's efforts of repeated, patient questioning for such additional details. The fact that these additional facts are not usually difficult for the analysand to supply (although with some very notable and important exceptions that have succumbed to repression) indicates that the "cognitive limitation" is not always a maturational fact as in the child under seven years of age. That such tendencies of the older patient are similar to that of the child (but usually upon therapeutic resolution clearly a compromise solution to psychopathologic conflict) may tempt one to speak of it in terms of "egocentrism" which would be one additional terminological obstacle to scientific meaning, definition and eventual precise specification in the sense of Dewey and Bentley (20).

To illustrate how children have the same difficulty in grasping how the external environment is to others and what their aims may be in the practical sphere, Bowlby quotes the results of some experiments of Flavell (22) with both three year olds and six year olds. These concerned: selecting a gift suitable to give mother on her birthday from a variety of objects (from a toy truck to a lipstick); to show a picture in a way that it would be upside down to a person sitting opposite to the child; and third, to tell whether a stick soft at one end and pointed at the other, would be soft or not to the experimenter if the child said correctly that his end felt soft. Not more than half of the three year olds succeeded in any of these tests and only a quarter of them succeeded on some of them; whereas either all, or the great majority, of the six year olds succeeded on all of the tasks. A typical example of the performance of the three year old was the child who chose a toy truck to give his mother.

From such evidence it is probable that in these years the child is only gradually elaborating a model of his mother which would help him to make plans to modify her behavior towards him. Since there is no evidence at present that this process can be accelerated, that is, the comprehending of another's viewpoint, it appears probable that the rate of growth of the brain may limit this kind of cognition.

Bowlby emphasizes the distinction between this "egocentrism" and egotism. Egocentrism is a capacity that is concerned only with the child's model-building of other people: an ability dependent upon his developed cognitive equipment. It has nothing to do with egotism which is probably no greater in the child than in adults. A child may demonstrate as genuine a concern and willingness to do whatever he can for the welfare of another as did an emotionally integrated older person. His well known difficulty and frequent failure in achieving action that is welcomed by the other does not stem from his lack of willingness to do things beneficial to the recipient, but from his inability to comprehend what actually would be of benefit from the standpoint, or need, of the other person.

Bowlby does not attempt "to broach the large, difficult, and profound questions of how a child gradually builds up his own 'internal world'." Mentioning that it probably begins towards the end of his first year and continues particularly actively during the acquisition of "the powerful and extraordinary gift of language" in the second and third years, the child's working models are constructed not only of how his mother, he himself and significant other persons but also the physical world may be expected to behave. In the resulting framework of these models he makes his evaluations of particular aspects of his situation and plans, especially of his attachment plans.

Just how the models are constructed and thereafter "bias perception and evaluation," how valid or distorted as representations they become and hence how adequate and effective for planning, are all matters of great importance as children grow older for understanding the various ways that attachment behavior becomes organized. He decides that systematic research on these questions "has only just begun and little that is firm is yet known," and therefore it is not sensible for him to attempt to deal with them in this volume. Furthermore these questions raise "too many giant problems (and giant controversies)."

Some of these problems clinicians have struggled with and found necessary to deal with in their work with older patients. A few comments on some aspects of these problems have already been made throughout this discussion and illustrated in other chapters of this volume.

PARTNERSHIP: COLLABORATION AND CONFLICT

A partnership between mother and child becomes a possibility when the child's attachment behavior becomes organized on a goal-corrected basis, Bowlby states, and simultaneously their relationship becomes more complex. This complexity has several distinguishable, possible elements, or possible patterns of development. Although a truly collaborative pattern is one possibility between them, the other is "intractable conflict." In this connection MacKay (35) is quoted to the effect that in terms of control theory, when each of two persons are trying to change the goals of the other, "it may become logically impossible to dissociate the two goal-complexes." Their relationship, in short, has become one in which "their individualities have partly merged."

Bowlby continues with the possibilities in a more or less durable, transactional pattern of the relationship. One of these is that there is a prospect of their sharing a common goal and plan, even though each person is able to make a plan. When a common goal and plan is shared, their transactions acquire new characteristics (as he puts it, "altogether different from those of an interaction based, say on chains of interdigitating fixed action patterns"). These new characteristics of "sharing a common set goal, and participating in a joint plan to achieve it" and thus acquiring "a rewarding sense of common purpose" and likely to identify with each other, all justify to Bowlby the term of partnership.

However, he points out, this partnership style of a transactional pattern can be bought only at the price of each partner's readiness, in case of a necessity to maintain the collaboration or the partnership between them, either to relinquish or to adjust his own personal set goal to that of the other partner. Which of them relinquishes or adjusts his own set goals to suit those of the other on which occasion varies with the many circumstances that may arise. Each of the partners in a mother-child partnership is apt to make many such adjustments to suit the other partner and thus occurs the constant give and take of a happy partnership. Nonetheless, each of such a partnership may at times "dig in heels and demand his own way" even in a happy relationship. Hence even in this case minor frequent conflicts occur during periods when each of their set-goals require time for their alignment. As an example of such conflicts and their adjustments, although a mother may often, or even usually, comply or agree to her child's demands, she may on the other hand, on other occasions not do so; and particularly with a small child "she may use a strong right arm." With an older child the mother makes efforts to attain her purpose by "reasoning" with him to change his set-goals.

During the course of a given day a two-year old's mother's attempts to change the child's attachment demands are likely to be numerous. She may under different circumstances try to get him to keep his distance, or conversely to keep him close to her. Thus, on a street, or during her shopping in a store his remaining close is generally her goal; while during visits of friends, or when parents are still in bed, his staying away from her skirts or their bedroom respectively is very likely to be her aim. Her methods to regulate the child's distance from her may include encouragement, discouragement, bribes and punishment. In these efforts her set-goal is to change the set-goals of the child's attachment behavior.

The child from his side seeks often to change his mother's behavior and her distance from him by various ways which may include methods that are similar to hers.

By the time the child has passed his third birthday the mother experiences in the ordinary relationship some reduction or easing of the child's demands. This is especially true when in his development (when this is "normal") he is less frightened by various, previously alarming, situations and events and when other activities and interests attract him. His progressively developing cognitive competence is a factor not only in the less frequent and less intense activation of his attachment behavior but also its termination is possible in newer ways. His much improved capacity to think in terms of time and space, to understand and thus to know where she is even when she is away, or when he is certain that she is available when he needs her, all these contribute to his feeling content, secure under such circumstances for longer and longer periods of time.

By the fourth birthday such cognitive ability, that is knowledge of mother's easy availability in her absence, is apt to be for most children of great importance—which contrasts with the little significance such information carries for a two-year-old.

"THE REGULATION OF MOTHERING"

Under this subtitle Bowlby closes this final chapter of his book with a section which considers the question very frequently raised by both mothers and professionals. This is the question about the wisdom of a mother's acceding to all of her child's demands for her presence, proximity and attentive responsiveness. The dilemmas behind, or implicit in, this question appear to be numerous and they are well known to clinicians experienced with children and their parents.

Some of these questions are: Is there danger of "spoiling" the child by too much yielding by mother to his demands? If she "overmothers" him, will he not demand and expect that she do everything for him if she does "give in" to too many of his demands? If she does this, how will he ever become "independent?" Just "how much mothering" is best for his best development of his own potential capacity? This writer may add to these questions an hypothesis of some clinicians to the effect that some, not too clearly specified, experience of frustration of the child's wishes (or whims?) is wise, necessary and even essential for the development of the strength of his "ego" and his learning of reality testing ability.

Bowlby's reply is to compare such questions from the "same perspective as the question 'How much food is good for the child'?" As he says, the reply to this is now well known: follow the lead of the child from the earliest day forward. It will probably be nutritious if he is given more when he wants it and it will not be detrimental to him if he refuses to eat. Unless there is some hereditary (such as phenylketonuria, etc. or other metabolic disease), the child's hunger is the best indicator to his biological self-regulatory mechanisms as to the quantity and quality of food. Hence, generally mother's following his initiative is the safest procedure.

With respect to the child's attachment behavior, he affirms, particularly in his earliest years this same principle holds. The child's own rhythm in this regard as expressed by his behavior towards his mother is also the best indicator. If mother follows this indicator she will then also be most safely guided by his inherent self-regulatory mechanisms—as in the case of food—in regard to his "intake" of her presence and attention. In short no harm to him will follow if in her usual mothering activities she gives him as much of her responsiveness as he seems to want. He can from the beginning be permitted to decide how much of it he needs; and only after his sixth or seventh birthday when he is already in school "may there be occasion for gentle discouragement."

Bowlby also points out that, from observations by students of child development of the happiest mother-child couples in their homes quoted earlier, this was true when the mother was not only perceptive of her child's signals but also promptly responsive to them in ways appropriate for the child. In these instances the child thrives and the relationship is mutually satisfying. On the other hand, the converse is true when mother is not perceptive, or not responsive, or responds in ways that do not satisfy the child's wishes.

He further asserts that in the Western World the most frequent reasons for the great variety of disturbances of attachment behavior stem from too little mothering or from mothering from a "succession of different people," rather than from too much mothering which is much less common. Moreover, the latter instances arise because of the mother's compulsion "to shower . . . on him" love and attention rather than from the child's insatiability for them. Close observation of such mothers demonstrates that, instead of taking her cues from the child, she insists on being close to the child, guarding him from danger or occupying his attention. This is just what mothers do who have children who are overfed; in short, they insist on "filling him with food."

He comes finally to those instances of disturbed attachment—of the very greatest interest to the many times aforementioned clinicians in this essay— "of which," Bowlby states, "there are a multitude of kinds" that can be best understood as due "to distortions of patterns of mothering that a child receives or is receiving." These he sharply distinguishes from those who receive either "too little" or "too much" mothering. He pursues the discussion of these named instances no further because it is in the domain of the psychopathology of attachment and because in this volume "it would be easy" in a few paragraphs "to oversimplify."

With the latter statement, that completes his discussion of the developments in organization of attachment behavior, this writer completely agrees —as evidenced by the clinical and theoretical data in other chapters of the present book. The complex and multifariously intertwining factors that compose the distortions of mothering are illustrated particularly in the data reported in those chapters on therapeutic studies of individual children and their parents.

The authors and editors of this volume stress throughout that one begins to glimpse these many factors entering into the distortions of "parenting" (rather than only "mothering") for several reasons discussed and indicated in these reports. Many of the aspects emphasized by Bowlby in discussing the mother-child partnership and its problems can be seen not only in this portion of the intrafamilial life but also in the marital "partnership" considered as another aspect of the total intrafamilial processes that have their impact and effect on the child himself as well as on the mother-child dyad. As these clinical studies of families indicate, the other members of the rest of the family, that is, the other siblings, the members of the extended family, namely the collaterals of the parents, the uncles and aunts (and even cousins) of the psychotic child patient, all exert their influence upon the child's parents and thus upon the child himself. Still more relevant contributions to the distortions of parenting of the one child, or at times two children, who develop psychotically come from the parents of the parents of the child, namely the grandparents of the child patient. As sometimes clearly seen in the reports these grandparents' influence may be distinguished as two-fold. In other words, the first is their influence on the early childhood development and the consequent later degree of mental health and disorder of personality of each of the child's parents; and the second is the not infrequent continuing, complicating influence upon the parents at, during and after the child's birth, i.e., their more current influence during the child patient's early years of life.

What also needs emphasis is that the influence of all these other persons may be, and often is, also conflicted or expressive of their disorder which may vary in degree not only from one to another person but also may vary in degree in any one of them from one time to another. And these variations in the intensity of the disorder of the parents—as well as that of the other significant persons mentioned—gives rise to the differences between various psychotic children in the total spectrum of the disorder observed clinically. Of course, such differences between psychotic children are here assumed to be not only those differences which would arise from the child's *experience* during the first and second years, but probably also those of the third year and possibly later ones. Additional sources of differences in the symptomatology of particular psychotic children that need to be kept in mind are those differences which stem from *genetically* determined differences in such characteristics as intellectual endowment, sex linked differences in activity level (e.g., "temperament," automonic reactivity, etc. . . .) and probably genetically determined differences in sensory modality preferences as in the auditory, visual and motoric spheres of endowment (52, 29). And finally those differences arising from genetically given *disease* factors or those impersonal disease processes of trauma, infection, metabolic disorders, degenerative or neoplastic processes and the like. The contributions of the latter to the emotional disturbance of the mother *and* father and hence to either integrative or malintegrative influence upon the child's development has already been commented upon previously.

DISCUSSION

Some clinical implications of Bowlby's concept of attachment have been described with particular emphasis on childhood psychoses. The somewhat detailed review of research with which Bowlby verifies his own views of attachment behavior has clinical significance for a variety of psychopathology in childhood most clearly the psychophysiological disorders, the severe character disorders and perhaps the neurotic disorders. Most evident is its validity for understanding the most severe and intractable psychopathology of childhood, the psychoses. The fact that so many of these disorders occur during the first year of life and that psychotherapeutic efforts with parents reveal severe maternal and paternal conflicts often with maternal depression and isolation from the infant has long been known. However, the particular form of the impact on the infant has never been so precisely clarified as in Bowlby's investigations and the derivative concept of attachment.

The length of this chapter and its effort to summarize the issues and research around the concept of attachment resulted from this writer's conviction that the clinical implications were important and needed to be related to the concepts and data which underlie the theory.

Psychiatrists, especially child psychiatrists with a strong biological orientation, will find the experimental data to be convincing and the concept of attachment an holistic one without a division of psyche and soma.

My colleagues and I feel much indebted to Bowlby and hope this overview effort at clinical application of the concept of attachment will cause the reader to read the original work and use it for his own thinking in clinical research and teaching.

REFERENCES

1. AINSWORTH, M. D. The development of infant-mother interaction among the Ganda. In B. M. Foss (Ed.), *Determinants of Infant Behavior.* Vol. 2. London: Methuen and New York: Wiley, 1963. Cited by J. Bowlby, *Attachment and Loss. Vol. I: Attachment.* New York Basic Books, 1969.
2. AINSWORTH, M. D. The effects of deprivation: A review of findings and controversy in the context of research strategy. *Deprivation of Maternal Care: A Reassessment of Its Effects,* Public Health Papers No. 14. Geneva: WHO, 1962. Cited by J. Bowlby, *Attachment and Loss. Vol. 1: Attachment.* New York: Basic Books, 1969.
3. AINSWORTH, M. D. Patterns of attachment behavior shown by the infant in interaction with his mother. *Merrill Palmer Quarterly,* 1964, 10:51-58. Cited by J. Bowlby, *Attachment and Loss. Vol. 1: Attachment.* New York: Basic Books, 1969.
4. AINSWORTH, M. D. and BOSTON, M. Psychodiagnostic assessments of a child after prolonged separation in early childhood. *Br. J. Med. Psychol.,* 1952, 25:169-201. Cited by J. Bowlby, *Attachment and Loss. Vol. 1: Attachment.* New York: Basic Books, 1969.

5. AINSWORTH, M. D. SALTER and WITTING, B. A. Attachment and exploratory behavior of one-year olds in a strange situation. In B. M. Foss (Ed.), *Determinants of Infant Behavior, Vol. 4.* London: Methuen and New York: Barnes and Noble, 1969. Cited by J. Bowlby, *Attachment and Loss. Vol. 1: Attachment.* New York: Basic Books, 1969.

6. ALLEN, M. G., POLLIN, W. and HOFFER, A. Parental, birth and infancy factors in infant twin development. *Amer. J. Psychiat.*, 1971, 127(12): 33-40.

7. BENJAMIN, J. D. Further comments on some developmental aspects of anxiety. In H. S. Gaskill (Ed.), *Counterpoint.* New York: Intl. Univ. Press, 1963. Cited by J. Bowlby, *Attachment and Loss. Vol. 1: Attachment.* New York: Basic Books, 1969.

8. BENTON, A. "Clinical Neuropsychology of Childhood." Paper presented at the 78th Annual Convention of the American Psychological Association, Miami Beach, Florida, September, 1970.

9. BERGMAN, P. and ESCALONA, A. Unusual sensitivities in very young children. *Psychoanalytic Study of the Child*, 1949, 3(4):33-352.

10. BETTELHEIM, B. *The Empty Fortress: Infantile Autism and the Birth of Self.* New York: The Free Press, 1967.

11. BOATMAN, M. J. and SZUREK, S. A. A clinical study of childhood schizophrenia. In D. D. Jackson (Ed.), *The Etiology of Schizophrenia.* New York: Basic Books, 1960.

12. BOWER, T. G. R. The object in the world of the infant. *Scientific Amer.*, 1971, 225(4):30-38.

13. BOWLBY, J. *Attachment and Loss. Vol. 1: Attachment.* New York: Basic Books, 1969.

14. BRODY, S. *Patterns of Mothering: Maternal Influence During Infancy.* New York: Intl. Press and London: Bailey and Swinfen, 1956. Cited by J. Bowlby, *Attachment and Loss. Vol. 1: Attachment.* New York: Basic Books, 1969.

15. CALDWELL, B. M. The effects of infant care. In M. L. Hoffman and L. N. W. Hoffman (Eds.), *Review of Child Development Research.* Vol. 1. New York: Russell Sage Foundation, 1964. Cited by J. Bowlby, *Attachment and Loss. Vol. 1: Attachment.* New York: Basic Books, 1969.

16. CALDWELL, B. M. The usefulness of the critical period hypothesis in the study of filiative behavior. *Merrill-Palmer Quarterly*, 1962, 8:229-242. Cited by J. Bowlby, *Attachment and Loss, Vol. 1: Attachment.* New York: Basic Books, 1969.

17. DAVID, M. and APPELL, G. La relation mere-enfant: Etude de cinq pattern d'interaction entre mere et enfant a l'age d'un an. *Psychiat. Enfant.*, 1966, 9:445-531. Cited by J. Bowlby, *Attachment and Loss. Vol. 1: Attachment.* New York: Basic Books, 1969.

18. DAVID, M. and APPELL, G. Mother-child relation. In J. G. Howells (Ed.), *Modern Perspectives in International Child Psychiatry.* Edinburgh: Oliver & Boyd, 1969. Cited by J. Bowlby, *Attachment and Loss. Vol. 1: Attachment.* New York: Basic Books, 1969.

19. DECARIE, T. GOUIN. *Intelligence and Affectivity in Early Childhood.* New York: Intl. Univ. Press, 1965. Cited by J. Bowlby, *Attachment and Loss. Vol. 1: Attachment.* New York: Basic Books, 1969.

20. DEWEY, J. and BENTLEY, A. F. *Knowing and the Known.* Boston: Beacon Press, 1949.

21. EISENBERG, L. and KANNER, L. Early infantile autism, 1943-1955. *Amer. J. Orthopsychiat.*, 1956, 26:556-566. See especially p. 562.

22. FLAVELL, J. H. The ontogenetic development of verbal communication skills. Final Progress Report, NIMH Grant M-2268.
23. FREUD, S. *Inhibitions, Symptoms and Anxiety, Vol. 20.* Standard edition of the complete psychological works of Sigmund Freud. London: Hogarth Press.
24. GOLDFARB, W. *Childhood Schizophrenia.* Cambridge, Mass.: Harvard University Press, 1961.
25. GOLDFARB, W., MINTZ, I. and STROOCK, K. W. *A Time to Heal: Corrective Socialization—A Treatment Approach to Childhood Schizophrenia.* New York: Intl. Univ. Press, 1969.
26. HARLOW, H. F. and HARLOW, M. K. The affectional system. In A. M. Schrier, H. F. Harlow, and F. Stolnitz (Eds.), *Behavior of Nonhuman Primates, Vol. 2.* New York and London: Academic Press, 1965. Cited by J. Bowlby, *Attachment and Loss, Vol. 1: Attachment.* New York: Basic Books, 1969.
27. HINDE, R. A. The nature of imprinting. In B. M. Foss (Ed.), *Determinants of Infant Behavior, Vol. 2.* London: Methuen and New York: Wiley, 1963. Cited by J. Bowlby, *Attachment and Loss, Vol. 1: Attachment.* New York: Basic Books, 1969.
28. KAGAN, J. and LEWIS, M. Studies of attention in the human infant. *Merrill-Palmer Quarterly,* 1965, 11:95-127.
29. KAGAN, J., ET AL. *Change and Continuity in Infancy.* New York: Wiley, 1971.
30. KANNER, L. and EISENBERG, L. Notes on the follow-up studies of autistic children. In P. L. Hock and J. Zubin (Eds.), *Psychopathology of Childhood.* New York and London: Grune and Stratton, 1955.
31. LANGDELL, J. I. Phenylketonuria: A long term multidisciplinary study of the effects of dietary treatment. In S. A. Szurek and I. N. Berlin (Eds.), *Psychosomatic Disorders and Mental Retardation in Children, Vol. 3. The Langley Porter Child Psychiatry Series.* Palo Alto, Calif.: Science and Behavior Books, 1968.
32. LANGDELL, J. I. Phenylketonuria: Some effects of body chemistry on learning. *Ibid.*
33. LEWIS, W. C., KAGAN, J. and KALEFAT, J. Patterns of fixation in the young infant child. *Child Development,* 1966, 37:331-341. Cited by J. Bowlby, *Attachment and Loss, Vol. 1: Attachment.* New York: Basic Books, 1969.
34. LIPSITT, L. P. Learning in the human infant. In H. W. Stevenson (Ed.), *Early Behavior: Comparative and Developmental Approaches.* New York: Wiley, 1967.
35. MACKAY, D. M. Communication and meaning: A functional approach. In F. S. C. Northrop and H. H. Livingston (Eds.), *Cross-cultural Understanding: Epistemology in Anthropology.* New York: Harper, 1964.
36. MAHLER, M. S. On early infantile psychosis. *J. Amer. Acad. Child Psychiat.,* 1965, 4:554-568. Cited by J. Bowlby, *Attachment and Loss, Vol. 1: Attachment.* New York: Basic Books, 969.
37. MAHLER, M. S., ROSS, JR., J. R. and DEFRIES, Z. Clinical studies in benign and malignant cases of childhood psychoses (schizophrenic-like). *Amer. J. Orthopsychiat.,* 1949, 19:295-303.
38. MALAMUD, N. Heller's disease and childhood schizophrenia. *Amer. J. Psychiat.,* 1959, 116:215-218
39. MORGAN, G. A. and RICCIUTI, H. N. Infant's responses to strangers during the first year. In B. M. Foss (Ed.), *Determinants of Infant Behavior, Vol. 4.* London: Methuen and New York: Barnes and Noble, 1969. Cited

by J. Bowlby, *Attachment and Loss, Vol. 1: Attachment*. New York: Basic Books, 1969.

40. MOSS, H. A. Sex, age and state as determinants of mother-infant interaction. *Merrill-Palmer Quarterly*, 1967, 13:19-36. Cited by J. Bowlby, *Attachment and Loss, Vol. 1: Attachment*. New York: Basic Books, 1969.

41. PIAGET, J. *The Construction of Reality in the Child*. New York: Basic Books, 1937, English trans. 1954. Cited by J. Bowlby, *Attachment and Loss, Vol. 1: Attachment*. New York: Basic Books, 1969.

42. PIAGET, J. *The Language and Thought of the Child*. London: Routledge and Kegan Paul and New York: Intl. Univ. Press, 1924, English trans. 1953. Cited by J. Bowlby, *Attachment and Loss, Vol. 1: Attachment*. New York: Basic Books, 1969.

43. PIAGET, J. *The Origins of Intelligence in the Child*. London: Routledge and Kegan Paul and New York: Intl. Univ. Press, 1936, English trans. 1953. Cited by J. Bowlby, *Attachment and Loss, Vol. 1: Attachment*. New York: Basic Books, 1969.

44. PIAGET, J. and INHELDER, B. *The Child's Conception of Space*. London: Routledge and Kegan Paul and New York: Humanities Press, 1948, English trans. 1956. Cited by J. Bowlby, *Attachment and Loss, Vol. 1: Attachment*. New York: Basic Books, 1969.

45. PRECHTL, H. F. R. The mother-child interaction in babies with minimal brain damage. In B. M. Foss (Ed.), *Determinants of Infant Behavior, Vol. 2*. London: Methuen and New York: Wiley, 1963. Cited by J. Bowlby, *Attachment and Loss, Vol. 1: Attachment*. New York: Basic Books, 1969.

46. PROVENCE, S. and LIPTON, R. C. *Infants in Institutions*. London: Bailey and Winfen and New York: Intl. Univ. Press, 1963. Cited by J. Bowlby, *Attachment and Loss, Vol. 1: Attachment*. New York: Basic Books, 1969.

47. RHEINGOLD, H. L. The effect of environmental stimulation upon social and exploratory behavior in the human infant. In B. M. Foss (Ed.), *Determinants of Infant Behavior, Vol. 2*. London: Wiley, 1961. Cited by J. Bowlby, *Attachment and Loss, Vol. 1: Attachment*. New York: Basic Books, 1969.

48. ROBSON, K. S. The role of eye-to-eye contact in maternal-infant attachment. *J. Child Psychol. and Psychiat.*, 1967, 8:13-25. Cited by J. Bowlby, *Attachment and Loss, Vol. 1: Attachment*. New York: Basic Books, 1969.

49. ROSENBLATT, A. D. and THICKSTUN, J. T. A study of the concept of psychic energy. *Int. J. Psychoanal.*, 1970, 51:265-278.

50. SANDER, L. W. Adaptive relationships in early mother-child interaction. *J. Amer. Acad. Child Psychiat.*, 1964, 1:231-264. Cited by J. Bowlby, *Attachment and Loss, Vol. 1: Attachment*. New York: Basic Books, 1969.

51. SANDER, L. W. Issues in early mother-child interaction. *J. Amer. Acad. Child Psychiat.*, 1962, 1:141-166. *Ibid*.

52. SANDER, L. W. and STEELHER, G. Adaptation and perception in early infancy. Terminal Report, National Institute of Mental Health, USPHS# JDO-1766, June 1970.

53. SCHAFFER, H. R. Some issues for research in the study of attachment behavior. In B. M. Foss (Ed.), *Determinants of Infant Behavior, Vol. 2*. London: Methuen and New York: Wiley, 1963. Cited by J. Bowlby,

Attachment and Loss, Vol. 1: Attachment. New York: Basic Books, 1969.

54. SCHAFFER, H. R. The onset of fear of strangers and the incongruity hypothesis. *J. Child Psychol. Psychiat.,* 1966, 7:95-106. Cited by J. Bowlby, *Attachment and Loss, Vol. 1: Attachment.* New York: Basic Books, 1969.

55. SCHAFFER, H. R. and EMERSON, P. E. The development of social attachment in infancy. *Monogram Social Research in Child Development,* 1964a, 29(3):1-13. Cited by J. Bowlby, *Attachment and Loss, Vol. 1: Attachment.* New York: Basic Books, 1969.

56. SEARS, R. R., RAU, L. and ALPERT, R. *Identification and Child Rearing.* Stanford: Stanford Univ. Press and London: Tavistock Publications, 1966.

57. SPITZ, R. A. *The First Year of Life.* New York: Intl. Univ. Press, 1965.

58. SPIRO, M. E. Is the family universal? *Am. Anthrop.,* 1954, 56:839-846. Cited by J. Bowlby, *Attachment and Loss, Vol. 1: Attachment.* New York: Basic Books, 1969.

59. STEVENSON, O. The first treasured possession. *Psychoanal. Study Child,* 1954, 9:199-217. Cited by J. Bowlby, *Attachment and Loss, Vol. 1: Attachment.* New York: Basic Books, 1969.

60. SZUREK, S. A. Review of John Bowlby's *Attachment and Loss, Vol. 1: Attachment. Amer. J. Orthopsychiat.,* 1970, 40:531-534.

61. SZUREK, S. A. An attitude towards (child) psychiatry. *Quart. J. Child Behavior,* 1949, 1:22. Also in S. A. Szurek and I. N. Berlin (Eds.), *Training in Therapeutic Work with Children.* Palo Alto: Science and Behavior Books, 1967. Pp. 1-116.

62. SZUREK, S. A. The child's needs for his emotional health. In J. G. Howells (Ed.), *Modern Perspectives in International Child Psychiatry.* Edinburgh: Oliver & Boyd, 1969.

63. SZUREK, S. A. Childhood schizophrenia: Psychotic episodes and psychotic maldevelopment. *Amer. J. Orthopsychiat.,* 1956, 26:519-543. Also in S. A. Szurek, I. N. Berlin and M. J. Boatman (Eds.), *Inpatient Care for the Psychotic Child.* Palo Alto: Science and Behavior Books, 1971. Pp. 92-119.

64. SZUREK, S. A. Chapters in S. A. Szurek and I. N. Berlin (Eds.), *The Langley Porter Child Psychiatry Series, Vols. 1-5.* Palo Alto, Calif.: Science and Behavior Books, 1967-1971.

65. SZUREK, S. A. Essay review of *The Empty Fortress: Infantile Autism and the Birth of the Self* by Bruno Bettelheim. *Social Service Review,* 1968, 42(2):241-251.

66. SZUREK, S. A. *The Roots of Psychoanalysis and Psychotherapy.* Springfield, Ill.: Charles C Thomas, 1958.

67. THOMAS, A., CHESS, S. and BIRCH, H. G. *Temperament and Behavior Disorders in Children.* New York: New York Univ. Press, 1968.

68. THOMAS, A., CHESS, S., BIRCH, H. G., HERTZIG, M. E. and KARN, S. *Behavioral Individuality in Early Childhood.* New York: New York Univ. Press, 1963.

69. UCKO, L. E. A comparative study of asphyxiated and non-asphyxiated boys from birth to five years. *Dev. Med. Child Neurol.,* 1965, 7:643-657. Cited by J. Bowlby, *Attachment and Loss, Vol. 1: Attachment.* New York: Basic Books, 1969.

70. WALLERSTEIN, R. S. and SAMPSON, H. Issues in research in the psychoanalytic process. *Int. J. Psychoanal.,* 1971, 52:11-50.

71. WALTERS, R. H. and PARKE, R. D. The role of the distance receptors in the development of social responsiveness. In L. P. Lipsitt and C. C. Spiker (Eds.), *Advances in Child Development and Behavior, Vol. 2.* New York and London: Academic Press, 1965. Cited by J. Bowlby, *Attachment and Loss, Vol. 1: Attachment.* New York: Basic Books, 1969.

72. WINNICOTT, D. W. Transitional objects and transitional phenomena. *Int. J. Psychoanal.*, 1953, 1-9. Reprinted in D. W. Winnicott, *Collected Papers.* London: Tavistock Publications, 1958. Cited by J. Bowlby, *Attachment and Loss, Vol. 1: Attachment.* New York: Basic Books, 1969.

73. YARROW, L. J. Research in dimensions of early maternal care. *Merrill-Palmer Quart.*, 1963, 9:101-114. Cited by J. Bowlby, *Attachment and Loss, Vol. 1: Attachment.* New York: Basic Books, 1969.

74. MARY AINSWORTH. Personal communication to Bowlby. See footnote 1, p. 320, in J. Bowlby, *Attachment and Loss, Vol. 1: Attachment.* New York: Basic Books, 1969.

13

Clinical Work and Clinical Research as Scientific Inquiry: Five Conceptual Barriers to Clinical Science

S. A. Szurek, M.D.
and
Irving Philips, M.D.

For too long clinicians seeking to develop their work scientifically have found the path to this goal beset and obscured by a number of obstacles. As a rather sophisticated observer of human psychological processes (hopefully not only those of his patients but also of his own), the psychodynamically trained psychiatrist is not too surprised to have it pointed out to him that these obstacles are primarily internal to himself. In a book appropriately entitled "Clinical Judgment," Alvan Feinstein—to us an elegantly clear thinker and an excellent writer—among many very pointed suggestions and prescriptions for the malady of clinicians, makes a " 'diagnosis' of the intellectual infirmity in our current state of clinical science."

In chapter four of his book he lists five conceptual barriers to clinical science. It is with a review of these barriers that we wish briefly to concern ourselves in this discussion and to consider how his suggestions to reduce or eliminate these barriers might apply to clinical work and clinical research in some problems in child psychiatry. Such a brief discussion cannot do full justice to Feinstein's thought. But perhaps even this brief discussion will arouse enough interest in those readers who have not yet had the opportunity to read him to place his book higher on that list we all have, entitled "Books

Delivered in part at the annual meeting of the American Academy of Child Psychiatry at Des Plaines, Illinois, on October 19, 1969, and in its totality to the Langley Porter Neuropsychiatric Institute staff on January 7 and January 14, 1970.

I Shall Read When I Have Time." The present writers confess to a little hope that this discussion may excite some readers enough to place it at the top of that list.*

Those of us smarting and defensive after long decades of contumely from our fellows in the world of science might find Feinstein's ideas clarifying, relieving and useful as therapeutic management of our "disorder." More of us might then be able to bestir ourselves in ways which could reduce and mayhap even rid ourselves of our self-derogation and the derogation heaped upon the wooly-headed, intuitive clinician. We might even more clear-headedly transform ourselves into clinical scientists or take a few more firm steps in that direction. For, as Feinstein makes clear, there is no invention, apparatus or possible substitute from other fields for the clinician in this venture. No one else than the clinician is in possession of the knowledge of the problems or of the needed skills. No one else than the clinician is in the position to make the necessary observations, the therapeutic experiments, and the consequent studies of prognosis, humanely and precisely, needed for the transformation.

One of the most delightful aspects of Feinstein's "diagnosis" and "prescription" is that in essence it fits so well with that principle and working goal which Freud bequeathed to us and which we think is so good for both ourselves and our patients. It is that fundamental notion that it is supremely useful to make every possible subjective process explicitly conscious and repetitively and progressively clear. From this effort the *order* of all events in nature becomes more defined. The similarities and differences between observations are identified and enumerated. Moreover, the possibilities and probabilities of modifying the processes observed more to our own advantage with greater predictability appear more obvious. Therefore our intuitive clinical judgment is more readily recognized as largely the explicit recall of past experience in assessing a current clinical problem.

Another very satisfying aspect of his analysis is what amounts to putting out to pasture that sacred cow of "basic science." As we all more or less dimly suspected a science does not become "more basic" in respect to others merely because the size of the unit or particle it studies is smaller or larger than those of other sciences. That may help to reassure some of us who have wondered recently whether molecular biology on the one hand and some of the more global implications of community psychiatry on the other might

---

* When a shortened version of the paper was read by two colleagues prior to the Academy meeting, their comments to one of us (SAS) were to the effect that it was hardly anything more than a book review. The co-author of this paper so approached, disagreed. It is a review primarily of only one chapter of a book.

not swiftly revolutionize all medical education and medical practice and perhaps squeeze those of us still interested in the individual child and his family quite quickly into the limbo of obsolescence. To make Feinstein's point about basic science concisely, we would like to quote a few of his concluding phrases about this matter and show you one of his diagrams. He says (page 382):

> Every aspect of human knowledge is constantly, inevitably basic to something and applied from something else. There is no such thing as 'basic science.' The term is a misnomer, and the concept is a malformed mental mirage.

His diagram is in the form of a circle and represents his conception of the actual relations of the various sciences to one another. Thus, it begins near the top right of the diagram with the science of human health, which he considers basic to that of human development, which in turn is basic to that of human speech and so on through the other sciences represented in turn in a similar relation to one another until the science of physiology is represented as basic to clinical medicine. This closes the circle considered basic to human health.

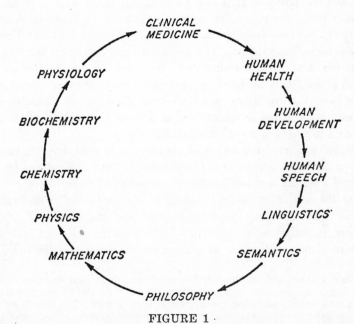

FIGURE 1
The chain of conceptual dependency in "basic" and "applied" science.

Now we return to the point and purpose of this discussion. At least five conceptual barriers to clinical science are identified by Feinstein. He likens them to hallowed beliefs which like axioms are "deeply imbedded in the matrix" of the clinician's thinking. These beliefs are put there by most of the teaching of his medical school years. They are perpetuated by his subsequent training, reading and experience and thus transmitted through the medical generations as intellectual legacies by teacher and student. Each of these axioms, he says, "—is like—an established principle, which, though not a necessary truth, is universally accepted." The five clinical ideas have to do with (1) scientific motivation, (2) reasoning, (3) observation, (4) correlation and (5) classification.

I. SCIENTIFIC MOTIVATION

With respect to the nature of scientific motivation Feinstein makes the point that many clinicians are still not sufficiently clear about which questions the usual clinical research may be able to answer. Too often, he thinks, clinicians have the notion that the only worthwhile question for research to deal with is the question, "Why?". In other words, too many clinicians feel that it is valuable to search only for causes of disease and that phenomena whose causes are unknown cannot be properly managed.

Feinstein acknowledges that the curious person always asks the "Why" about natural phenomena and that he ceases to have useful ideas as soon as he stops asking this question. Nevertheless his discussion including a quotation from Claude Bernard makes abundantly clear that the most successful research students must content themselves with partial answers to the question "How?". How does this or that phenomenon, event or process occur is not only the usual result of investigative work, but also, if answered, generally provides validly useful knowledge. It forms also a firm base for further explorations of other "Hows." Hence, the achievement of relative and partial answers or truths—the result of investigations in all experimental sciences—has increased knowledge and broadened man's power over nature. Even though the more complete understanding of phenomena may escape our grasp, what we do learn may nevertheless permit us to produce or to prevent such phenomena.

Feinstein gives numerous examples of how clinical research has resulted in effective therapy, prophylaxis or prevention of organic disease despite a lack of knowledge of the "cause" or even of the diagnosis of the diseases in question. Thus, Lind's oranges and lemons began to prevent scurvy before anyone knew of vitamins, and Jenner's cowpox vaccinations prevented smallpox a very long time before the virus causing it was discovered. Pasteurization of milk and sanitation of water prevented numerous diseases the identities and causal agents of which were unknown to many.

In the same manner in our own field of child psychiatry, some observations in a ward of psychotic, preadolescent patients began to suggest several possibilities. For example, consider the observation that in time, or following certain kinds and qualities of experiences with nursing personnel, a good number of these children begin to manifest affective responses to the nurse, however conflicted or disordered these responses may be. Such events suggest that perhaps the affective unresponsiveness may not, or not always, be an unmodifiable, inborn characteristic of autism. But whatever the truth is about the etiology of such affective unresponsiveness, observations of this kind can raise doubts about certain aspects of the older theory of narcissistic neuroses. These doubts center on whether all patients with such disorders are indeed incapable of developing a transference relation to a therapist and whether, therefore, any psychological therapy has much likelihood of being in any degree effective. Such empiric observations then lead more and more clinicians to begin, and to continue to experiment with psychotherapeutic programs with autistic or psychotic children.

As another example, when discussions with the mother of such a child are observed to be followed by even transient changes in the child's detachment or indifference to her, the idea is born that psychological therapy with parents may possibly contribute to the amelioration of the disorder in both the parent and the child and some improvement in the relation between them.

We do not need here to extend the list of such clinical observations in our field that begin to form the basis for the hypotheses on which many, many other therapeutic experiments are based and carried out. The data from such clinical therapeutic experiments (which need to continue) may not provide sufficient evidence to prove or to disprove a theory of etiology.* Elucidation of etiology and pathogenesis of this and other disorders of childhood may require other than strictly and purely clinical studies (7, 9). More definitive studies of etiology require comparisons of the frequency of the disorder in groups exposed and not exposed to the suspected causative factor or factors which can be obtained only in epidemiological surveys of younger and younger children in the populations outside the hospital and the clinic. Parenthetically, whether such surveys can be accomplished by students without considerable clinical acumen correctly to identify the pertinent clinical phenomena seems to us somewhat doubtful. However, such work would probably differ somewhat from our usual current clinical practice.

---

* See Bender, L. and Grugett, A. E., "A Study of Certain Epidemiological Factors in a Group of Children with Childhood Schizophrenia," *Am. J. Orthopsychiat.*, 1956, 26, p. 2, which is Reference 4 of Chapter 14, "A Statistical Study of a Group of Psychotic Children," in this volume for further comment on epidemiology of psychotic disorders of childhood.

Nevertheless, as Feinstein is at some pains to point out, purely *empiric* observations and studies by clinicians during their usual practice of caring for patients mentioned previously when made with appropriate and necessary precision and care have extremely important scientific goals. Even though etymologically "empiric" from the Greek means *"in experience"* or founded on experiment," the word "empiric" has in recent times acquired a rather scientifically "dirty" connotation as possibly an ingredient of quackery. Despite this, he points to instances of such empiric, clinical therapeutic experimentation which have withstood the test of time. One such example is the purely empiric work of William Withering in 1785 in defining the appropriate dose through therapeutic trials of preparations of fox glove leaf for the phenomena of "dropsy." Withering knew little or nothing about what we now know about congestive heart failure—which name we now use in place of "dropsy" for the same phenomenon. He did not have our various purified preparations of digitalis in place of his extracts of fox glove. He may even have been wrong in some of his anatomic cardiac diagnoses. But, as Feinstein says, we still treat the same phenomena he did with the same substance he used, with the directions for therapy he gave, with successes not much better than his.

Thus, in the course of his clinical activity the clinician may not be able always to search for etiology and particularly for pathogenesis of disease. But he has many other opportunities for therapeutic experiments which, as Feinstein says, "are fundamentally important and desperately in need of science." These goals are just as intellectually challenging as those of his colleagues in the laboratories studying etiology and pathogenesis. They are often more attainable, and they offer the chance of changing nature instead of just understanding it—if only he asks the right questions. It may be, of course, that in psychotherapeutically oriented child psychiatry that separation of methods to study etiological factors, the processes of pathogenesis on the one hand, and of those directed towards therapeutic experiments on the other may not be as marked as in impersonal organic disease. During therapy of individual members of the family, we often not only see the pathologic and the possibly pathogenic processes operating or unfolding but also obtain strong clues regarding etiology.

II.   REASONING AND MATHEMATICAL ORGANIZATION OF DATA

Concerning the second obstacle, or barrier, to clinical science, Feinstein states that the clinician believes "that his thinking has too many intricate and unquantified elements to be expressed in the mathematical structures used for other types of scientific analysis" and "that his intellectual organization of clinical observations is rationally amorphous."

In his effort to point out a pathway around or through this obstacle, Feinstein briefly reviews three types or systems of mathematical symbolism used to describe the relationship of things, or of properties—called variables—which people think about. The arrangement of the mathematical symbols indicates: 1) the relations between the variables; and 2) the places where numbers are to be inserted to identify magnitudes and for statistical analysis or interpretations.

We shall not do more here than mention two of these three types of organizational arrangements for different variables used in biology.

The first, a common and simple type, is to indicate the relation of equality, of more or less, or of before and after.

The second type provides for equations and graphical representations of the relation between two variables which change continuously through an indefinite range of magnitudes *dependently* related to one another. These equations and the straight lines or curves representing them are either simple or complex. They use the binomial or polynomial structures of algebra, analytic geometry and the calculus. Depending upon our degree of basic exposure to mathematics, and our subsequent use of them, we are as clinicians generally, or more vaguely, familiar with them, or we find them somewhat strange and rather time-consuming to review or to learn.

The third type of mathematics, relatively new since it is only about a century old, is usually unfamiliar to biologists—among whom clinicians may be counted. It has the somewhat strange name of Boolean algebra from the name of its discoverer George Boole (1815-1864) an English mathematician (3), and its Venn* diagrammatic representations (8). Most of us may tend to react with some awe and uneasiness to it as to many things unknown and unfamiliar. Yet it is so simple that it is being taught to our children in their seventh or eighth grade, or earlier, mathematics courses, and it is capable of being mastered by any intelligent adult willing to devote a few hours to its study. Incidentally, mastery of the principles of this "new" mathematics does not require skill and familiarity with the "old" mathematics.

It is a system of describing the relations between the variables, i.e., the attributes or the characteristics of an object or person, or of a group of objects or people, at a specific time. This contrasts with the previous system or second type of mathematics just mentioned which is concerned with changes of one variable in relation to changes in another variable. Thus, it is possible to use it to describe the relation of classes, or of sets of objects or people which have many different characteristics or properties. Since these

---

* John Venn, 1834-1923, a British logician who introduced this form of illustration for sets.

attributes of the individual members of a set or class may be multiple; and since each attribute may be discrete or noncontinuous because it is describable with a finite number of categories; and since each attribute is independent in the sense that its presence or absence is often unrelated to the presence or absence of another attribute; this system of mathematics may be called a type of "classification of multiple, discrete, independent variables."

Let us consider an example. The characteristics of a patient such as his age, hair color, sex, ethnic origin, vocation, education, financial and/or cultural status, his somatic state of health, the degree of emotional integration or disorder are multiple, discrete and independent attributes. Their presence or absence can form the more or less arbitrary basis (but useful for some purpose) to place him in a class or set of other patients with similar characteristics.*

Within the field of our interest the variables may be clinically important characteristics such as his intelligence, various symptoms of psychological or behavioral disorder each of which needs to have clearly defined criteria. These characteristics need reliable confirmation by independently observing, equally trained and experienced clinicians. These clinicians observing the same patients will need to have agreed to clearly specified criteria for each characteristic of the patient. They will need also to have agreed as to the terms or names they will use to denote the clinical observational data as well as the name for the characteristic of the patient—the variable—thus identified. Such clinical procedures can then result in classifying patients into groups on the basis of the presence or absence of the clearly identified characteristics. Such similar groups can then more validly be used for comparisons and evaluations of therapeutic experiments; that is, for studies of outcomes or prognosis. Studies of this sort can then provide a more solid basis for sharpening subsequent clinical reasoning and judgment in application to clinical problems presented by new patients.

Again, as it will be noted later, it is essential to notice that the properties or variables, which are clinically important, need not be numerical dimensions but can be qualitative or anecdotal descriptions. As many different attributes of patients as seem relevant to include and study can be codified in this system of symbolization. Therefore, patients can by these techniques be distinguished as to their characteristics into separate or overlapping groups and subgroups to portray with any degree of precision and accuracy attempted or desired the possibly simple, and more often, the complex spectra of various

---

* For further discussion see Chapter 10, "A Clinical Primer of the 'New' Mathematics," in Feinstein (5).

diseases, or in our field, of disorders in a given population.* The comparability of patients may thus be approached and achieved and permit the only kind of reproducibility of therapeutic experiments which is possible in the clinical field.

For these reasons, Feinstein believes that these new forms of mathematics make profound, and mayhap revolutionary, contributions to clinical reasoning. He states, "with these techniques, a formal mathematical structure can be established for clinical reasoning applied in the deductive logic of diagnosis, in the inductive predictions of prognosis and in the quantitative assessment of therapy."

III. OBSERVATION

The third obstacle, or conceptual barrier, that clinicians often experience in their goal toward clinical science deals with their attitude towards their description of symptoms and signs. Because of the inevitable use of nouns, adjectives, verbs and adverbs—rather than numerical dimensions of measurement—they believe that their descriptions of clinical phenomena cannot be scientifically precise. Clinicians have felt lost in a dilemma. One horn of this dilemma was represented by Kelvin's doctrine that one's knowledge is unsatisfactory and meager when it cannot be expressed in numbers; in short, that measurement was a prerequisite to science. The other horn of the dilemma was "how could a clinician measure headache, angina pectoris, dysuria, or anxiety" and other subjective sensations, qualitative signs and personal reactions—even if he *could* measure such clinical phenomena as "height, blood pressure, urinary volume and cardiac output." Hence, the clinician could never become scientific in his work if science required dimensional measurement.

The clinicians have attempted to escape this dilemma for about fifty years by measuring and developing increasingly precise measurements for everything that could be measured, namely, primarily entities observed in the laboratory; everything, that is, except the phenomena at the bedside or in his office, phenomena for the observation and study of which the clinician alone is competent.

Clinicians working in laboratories—paraclinical activities, Feinstein calls them—believe that number is the "language" of science and that statistical analysis is its "grammar." These beliefs, which lead them often to forsake the bedside for the laboratory as the locus of research, are correct. The concept of measurement, however, is not. Measurement in general biology is

---

* Further elaboration of these applications are found in Feinstein (5), Chapter 11, "Spectrums of Disease and Other 'Mathemedical' Constructions."

often restricted to the use of a scale or yardstick to determine a dimension that represents the amount of a substance. Many clinicians also restrict themselves to this notion that this dimensional mensuration is the only form of measurement.

Feinstein, as already indicated previously, however, emphasizes that another form of measurement, namely enumeration, or counting, also produces numbers. A counted number as the sum of similar units is just as much a number as a dimensional number representing a proportional amount, quantity, or number of units of a substance. The former measurement is *enumeration* answering the question, "How many?". The latter measurement is dimensional mensuration replying to the question, "How much?".

Thus, both dimensional mensuration and enumeration produce a number. However, for scientific reliability of the number, the precision and accuracy of the observation and the comparison of the phenomenon with a standard *or with criteria* which the number represents are all important. We need not here review in detail the care with which identification of a substance by extracting it from a mixture and comparing its quantity with a calibrated scalar standard—all largely chemical in paraclinical laboratory research—needs to be carried out in order that the number expressing the dimensional measurement of the substance in the mixture be reliable.

We *do* need, however, to consider more thoroughly what clinicians need to do to make their observation of clinical phenomena, i.e., the attributes of a whole patient, be accurately identified for comparison with similar attributes of other patients. Since each patient will represent a number to be counted in a group or subgroup of other patients with similar attributes, the scientific reliability of such numbers in enumerational measurement depends upon the accuracy, the precision and the completeness of the *verbal* description of the important attribute or attributes being studied. Their identification and comparison to the attributes of other patients determine the group in which they are to be included. Since most *clinical* observations of pathology and of subjective sensations, or in our own field, of behavioral and psychological characteristics, are primarily describable in words, these descriptions are vital for the reliability of the number.

It is essential for clinicians to digest and to assimilate one of Feinstein's emphases in connection with this matter of establishing enumeration as a reliable and valid method of measurement. This is the fact that precise and complete verbal descriptions by the clinician of all aspects of the patient's subjective complaints *and* of the clinician's observations of the patient's behavior and his incorporation of both in his medical record are the important first steps for the clinician to move towards the scientific goal. We have already done this in some measure. To do this more thoroughly and to treat the results as the basic data by which the patients can be placed in comparable groups is an ineluctable necessity for the kind of reproducibility possible in clinical science. Without this care, studies of the results of the maneuvers of therapeutic experiments cannot be collated for scientifically warranted statements (4) of prognosis.

Other matters are left for closer study of Feinstein's text and its numerous illustrations, such as that concerning the drastic differences in the mathematical methodologies which are appropriate to the statistical analysis of dimensional measurements of paraclinical laboratory research of the old mathematics on the one hand, and those of the new mathematics of Boolean algebra which are appropriate for the enumerational measurements of clinical data on the other. Suffice it here to say with Feinstein, "laboratory workers often measure dimensions and equate" while "clinicians classify cases and count." It may also be mentioned that different computers are necessary. For the laboratory data the analog computers measure dimensions and their circuits use the differential and integral equations of continuous variables. On the other hand the digital computers count units with circuits which use the Boolean algebra of discrete variables.

Let us consider a brief example of the possible application of all this in our own particular field. It is fairly well agreed among the most experienced students of psychotic disorders of preadolescent children that there are differences among the syndromes which are included in the total group whatever name is used to denote the entire category of the disorder. Several subgroupings of the entire category have been proposed with more or less definition of the criteria used to subdivide them. The next steps for the further clinical scientific study of the problem would be as follows:

1) That each clinical research group undertake a painstaking study of its own clinical criteria of primary characteristics of childhood disorder to be included within the spectrum of psychosis. Agreement among the group as to the name to be used and the specific clinical phenomena to which the name refers are essential for interobserver reliability. These agreements need to be thrashed out among the members of the group on the basis of observations of each patient by each or by several members of the group, perhaps aided by audio-visual recordings for repeated detailed review by all participants.

As technology improves equipment, electronic apparatus will be cheaper and more widely utilized. Transistorized television cameras will allow the taking of pictures of the behavior of children in their everyday routine. Clinical investigators may then view, study and discuss the same clinical data and be more likely to arrive at an agreement on what is being described by specific terms and develop valid and reliable naming.

2) That clinical *differences* between patients need similar clear definition, specification of criteria and agreed upon naming of the symptoms. Here one thinks of such matters as the age, sex, the more or less definitely established age of onset of particular symptoms, their exacerbations, remissions, severity, etc., their relation to other events, the presence or absence of particular skills, traits, interests, the nature of relations towards self and others, somatic symptoms of identifiable diseases, and so on.

3) That elaboration from all this be undertaken of criteria of subgroups with similar congeries of characteristics. These subgroups may, and probably would, overlap depending upon the presence of some common attributes and the absence of others.

4) That enumeration of the various subgroups be performed for their frequency and for subsequent comparisons of the numbers of each subgroup responding, and not responding, to therapeutic maneuvers. Such data may be stored in computers for retrieval by various groups of investigators. The computer may be used to analyze such data with efficiency and rapidity to apply tests of statistical significance such as chi square and other procedures as well. And finally,

5) That conferences be held between regional and eventually national, or even international, groups of such clinical research teams for review of the gathered data and for elaboration of agreements as to names, criteria, therapeutic outcomes, estimates of prognoses, and for the delineation of areas requiring further study.

All of the above would also be consistent with Dewey and Bentley's conditions related to naming, as scientific methodology. They state, for example: "(1) the names are to be based on such observations that are accessible to and attainable by everybody; (2) . . . the use of reports upon it are to be tentative, postulational and hypothetical; (3) . . . naming is adopted to promote further observation and naming which in turn will advance and improve. . . ." (4) Consensus in regard to these matters may not be easy to achieve between various groups of research clinicians. However, it may be possible eventually to secure refined comparability of syndromes, that is of symptom and sign clusters, and thereby make assessment of therapeutic results and prognoses more accurate.

We hope we have indicated at least sketchily why Feinstein says that Kelvin's demand for scientific measurement in clinical studies of therapy can be achieved. This can be done if appropriate attention to the ways in which data are acquired and modern mathematical systems of data management are applied. The discrete clinical phenomena may be described verbally, but the data will be in numerical form as the sum of counted patients. Thus symptoms and signs of patients need to be reliably observed, described and re-

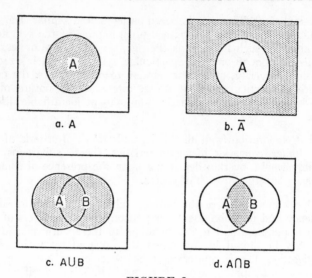

FIGURE 2

The sets produced by Boolean operations of complementation (b); union (c); and intersection (d).

corded by the only instrument capable of doing this—this irreplaceable, human clinician.

To illustrate briefly some of the ideas just discussed concerning Boolean algebra, Venn diagrams and of the possible applications to clinical research, two figures from Feinstein's book are herewith included.

Figure 2 exemplifies some basic operations and relations of sets: namely, (a) set A in a given universe; (b) the complement of set A, symbolized by "$\overline{A}$," and the shaded portion of the diagram, i.e., the universe outside of set A; (c) the union of two sets within a universe, symbolized by the notation A∪B; and finally, (d) the intersection of two sets indicated by the shaded area of overlap of two circles in the diagram and symbolized by the notation A∩B.

Figure 3 is a Venn diagram representing the results of Feinstein's clinical study of a number of patients with rheumatic fever. The clinical differences and similarities of these patients permitted separating and classifying the entire group into A) five main sets, those with: 1) arthritis, 2) chorea, 3) carditis, 4) severe carditis, and 5) those with arthralgia, represented by five circles with different shading; and B) seventeen subsets represented by the portions of each of these five circles which did not, or did, overlap the other four circles.

Thus, there were found patients with: only arthritis, only carditis or severe carditis, only chorea, or only arthralgia, but all of them with rheumatic fever

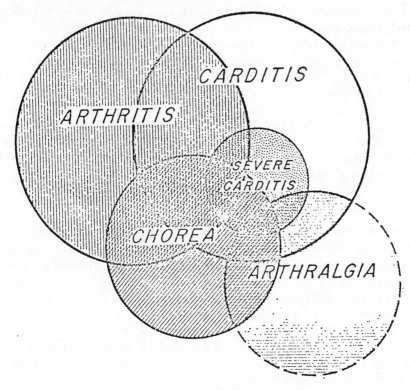

FIGURE 3
The clinical spectrum of acute rheumatic fever.

proved by appropriate diagnostic, serologic and clinical findings. Further, there were found subsets of patients with two, three or four of these major clinical symptoms and signs represented by the overlaps of the four main circles. It is to be noted that there were found no patients with both arthritis *and* arthralgia which is represented by *no overlap* between these two circles. The various other combinations of these clinical characteristics forming the remaining subsets are represented by the other overlaps of the circles.

Thus, the diagram permits one to see at a glance the variety of syndromes based on *clinical* findings found *in each patient studied* among patients with the same disease. The clinical spectrum of a disease is thus as accurately represented as the clinical study and description permits. This, of course, is much more useful to the clinician than a simple "diagnosis" of disease correlated with only paraclinical data in tabular form which ignores the clinical similarities and differences between patients in various aspects of their *illness*.

The reader is referred to Feinstein's text for further illustrations of how such diagrams with the numbers of patients included in the various subsets may be used in the appropriate circles and overlaps in the diagram not only for quantifying the various aspects of the spectrum but also for more accurate assessment and enumerational measurement of effectiveness of therapeutic maneuvers, and most important, for acquiring a more scientific basis for prognosis. For an approach to similar use of Venn diagrams in a statistical study of psychotic children, see Figures Nos. 2, 4, 5, 13, 13a, and 15 in Chapter 14 of this present volume.

IV.   CORRELATION

The fourth of the five obstacles to clinical science is the clinician's mistaken belief that the correlation between abnormal structure and abnormal function is a constant. Because of this belief he frequently obscures clinical differences between patients by anatomic or structural "diagnoses." This, of course, leads to confusing and invalid conclusions from studies of therapeutic experiments and to errors in prognostic reasoning.

There are innumerable examples to substantiate the primary concept in biology that form and function are constantly associated, that there is no difference between structure and function, and that these are, as Szent-Györgi says, the two sides of the same coin. The latter student goes even so far as to say that "if structure does not tell us anything about function, it means that we have not looked at it correctly." Both in general biology and in medicine instances of this direct correlation between the form of the organ or organism and its function are very numerous. Men with legs walk; fish with fins swim; and birds with wings fly. The human brain thinks; the eye sees; the ear hears; the stomach digests and absorbs; the uterus incubates. A yellow skin quite frequently correlates with hyperbilirubinemia; angina pectoris, with coronary arteriosclerosis; cyanosis, with hypoxemia; "lid-lag," with hyperthyroidism and its high, protein-bound iodine; and so on through many, many other such correlations between dysfunction and structural and/or formal physiological abnormality.

The principle of the frequency of the association between form and function and its correlate in medicine is so well established that it is often difficult to see the numerous exceptions to it. As Feinstein says in response to Szent-Györgi's statement, there are still many entities in current biology awaiting correct observation of the correlation of structure and function. Very many uniquely human functions cannot at present be explained by known structural attributes of "people, organs, tissues or cells that perform the functions." It may be that these distinctions of functions, differences in behavioral or psychological traits may some day in the dim, distant future be correlated to differences in their molecular or inframolecular components and configurations. But at present it is still necessary to describe and evaluate in a different language such attributes as the reactions to pain and frustration, the rate of stomach secretion, a given baseball player's skill involved in throwing a curve ball and another's lack of skill despite similar muscular structure, and the qualities of temperament or imagination of a person; in short, in a language different from that necessary for the description of the structure of the body of the organism, its stomach, its muscles or its brain.

It is, as a matter of fact, because of the frequently found discrepancy between function and structure, between the presence of structural changes and the absence of symptoms and complaints, or the obverse, that clinicians have learned to do a complete physical examination, or in psychiatry, a complete mental status and the assessment of psychological abilities in addition to somatic study. It is because there may be a variety of disease processes, and/or stresses to the personality, that may result in similar, or dissimilar symptomatology that a whole variety of diagnostic procedures in both somatic and psychiatric medicine are used in clinical study of patients with apparently similar clinical syndromes. The amount of azotemia may be unrelated to the changes found in a renal biopsy. Therefore, the clinician does both the biopsy *and* the measurement of blood urea nitrogen. Anginal pain may result from pulmonary hypertension and not from coronary arteriosclerosis, and coronary disease may produce no angina. The skin may be yellow because of hypercarotinemia and the serum bilirubin may be high without jaundice. An anemic patient may not become cyanotic for this reason even though he *is* hypoxic. As Feinstein puts it, the term schizophrenia may be used to name a person whose huddled body may be found in the back wards of a large mental hospital, or of a person who walks the streets, functions fairly well at work and even at times holds high public office, and so on through many other examples of such discrepancies between form and function, discrepancies between a structural change and symptom, and those between a "diagnostic" title and behavior.

Thus, the tendency to obliterate the clinical differences between patients and in the same patient from one time to another by a brief anatomic name or a title from an accepted nomenclature occurs probably too frequently. Such clinical differences, often scrupulously obtained from diverse sources of the clinical history, the examination, the laboratory work and other diagnostic procedures in both nonpsychiatric and psychiatric clinical work, when so obliterated or disregarded, serve as an important obstacle to clinical science. Discrepant results of different therapeutic studies then lead to confusion, uncertainty, if not to chaos, with regard to choice of therapy and to judgment of prognosis. The anatomic diagnosis, or the short title, precludes, or leads to disregard of, adequate separation of patients with the same general syndrome into subgroups based upon *clinical* similarities *and differences*. Only if these sources of error are reduced or removed can different results from the same therapeutic experiment be correlated to the possible or probable clinical differences in patients.

Thus, for example, in our field the syndrome of childhood psychosis has been and still is beset with problems of diagnosis, of a variety of theories of etiology, of a variety of therapies and their assessments. Insufficient differentiation of syndromes (e.g. of psychosis from mental defect, or the presence of both), attribution of symptoms to inborn factors, to prenatal or paranatal factors of disease or of deficiency, to ill-defined "organic" factors or "soft-signs" on the one hand, or to similarly insufficiently delineated experiential or psychogenic influences on the other, and so on, abounds in the mushrooming literature. The need to recognize the problems implicit in the present difficulty is great. Similarly, the probable impossibility of correlating all clinically well observed, thoroughly described behavioral and psychological dysfunctional characteristics to presumed structural damage or physiological malfunction is obvious unless these latter, i.e., the structural damage or physiological malfunction, *are independently established by appropriate procedures*. But this does not mean that progressive scientific study is impossible if the suggestions of Feinstein in this regard are followed.

V. CLASSIFICATION OR TAXONOMY

The fifth and last barrier to clinical science identified by Feinstein not only concludes his "diagnosis" of the clinician's "intellectual infirmity" but also leads him into the "therapy" he prescribes for this disorder. This occupies much of the rest of his volume. His discussion of this obstacle with a great wealth of illustrations fills three chapters totalling about fifty-five pages. In this brief review one can hardly hope for a succinct summary of the detailed evidence he presents of the existence of this barrier. One can only offer some indications of his conclusions as to its nature.

He defines this barrier as the clinician's belief "that he adequately identifies human illness by categorizing sick people with diagnostic names that represent the morphologic and laboratory abnormalities of disease." After discussing at some length the resurgence of interest of creative minds in modern problems in taxonomy, after reviewing considerable history of the changing conceptions of disease in medicine over the centuries, and after noting the clinician's general disinterest in, and disregard of, classifying clinical phenomena, he gives as his conclusion that the clinician has no taxonomy of his own. That is, he has no taxonomy for his own unique experience of human illness which could guide him with clear, conscious logic in therapeutic decisions and acts and in his clinical judgment of prognosis.

Morbid anatomy and physiology have especially in modern times along with the technologic revolution of the last half century developed a taxonomy of *disease* with the very useful adjuvants to his (the clinician's) diagnostic acumen. But the clinician has tended to disregard many old and new problems in his practice of *therapy* of the clinical states of the patient. For these the techniques and terminologies of the clinical pathologist or the clinical laboratory scientist are insufficient or inapplicable. Biopsies, roentgenographic silhouettes, instrumental measurements of physiological functions, a host of chemical tests and the like are at best indications of the state of the patient *at one time.* They are not *always* reliable evidence of the disease. They cannot always, or often, be performed or they may be even too dangerous to repeat.

The clinician, however, observes his patient and the changes in his illness over a period of time, sometimes for years, and his observations cannot be always correlated or even described in the terms of his colleagues in the laboratories and in the morgue. He sees phenomena that are not even accessible to these colleagues. In short, while making full use of the contributions of these colleagues with their instruments and procedures of precision especially in diagnosis, he needs to develop a taxonomy, an explicit classification, of the clinical phenomena he alone observes, decides about and experiences. This he requires to reason with for his own unique work.

The clinician has, Feinstein says, a taxonomy of the disease and a taxonomy for the host but not one for the illness of the host. He needs a nomenclature to classify not only the disease of the pathologist, but one that will classify a host *and* an illness *and* a disease. The modern diagnostic and therapeutic techniques have transformed the old passive observation of clinical medicine in which the illness was often undiagnosed till necropsy and which was without the specific, potent therapies of the present into the modern, *experimental* discipline of therapeutic medicine. But this modern discipline is still being stifled by an ancient taxonomy of the morgue, without room for classifying clinical observations under therapy. The clinician's observation of "the strength of his patient's hands, the posture of his body, the noise in his chest, the smell of his breath, the sweat of his brow, the grimace on his face, the quaver of his voice and the anguish of his family" may lead him to the timing, the dosage or the withdrawal, of chemical, or psychologic therapy.

For these phenomena, which he observes and classifies informally or sub-consciously, treating them as nuances rather than thinking of them specifically, clearly distinguishing them, the clinician often has no classificatory vocabulary with which to reason about them explicitly, consistently, and consciously.

Thus, he often cannot "classify symptoms and signs except by losing their distinctions with an inferred translation into the diagnostic vocabulary of pathologic taxonomy. In the midst of the articulate science that surrounds him, the clinician is left scientifically aphasic, cacophonous or mute." Without a taxonomy of his own, his clinical knowledge and practice is not easily expressed in words and concepts. It is squeezed into "irrational" spaces of his mind that are not occupied by the rational concepts and data of "disease." He remains uncertain of how, when, or whence his strictly clinical observations and experiences got there or how he retrieved them. The clinician then cannot clearly identify the process because it had been done without a conscious order and under these circumstances he tends to regard what he calls his clinical judgment as an unscientific hunch, an intuition or mystique. How often this is true in our own field of psychiatry in contrast to that of somatic medicine needs some comment and probably more debate in the field.

There may be some differences in this regard between the situations of the nonpsychiatric and the psychiatric clinicians. The diagnostic nomenclature of psychiatry in general and some proposed symptom classifications in child psychiatry are, we believe, primarily the creations of clinicians themselves rather than of any nonclinical colleagues. Although they include some clinical syndromes associated with disease entities, an important segment of them are brief definitions of clinically observed syndromes. Still, these often imply a nosological entity, which at least resembles the problems of "disease" versus the illness of a specific person. Furthermore, it is probable that many psychiatric clinicians have at least a modicum of difficulty in squeezing a specific patient under a single title which would completely characterize him and his individual symptomatology and traits.

Hence, however useful a step toward a measure of classificatory order in the present knowledge or consensus such nomenclature and such lists may be, to term them as *diagnoses* in any completely comparable sense to those in somatic medicine involves at best some intellectual strain and a sense of a gap in knowledge. They may in a measure be an approach to the clinical taxonomy advocated by Feinstein. At the same time it is clear to many of us, for example, in referrals of a patient from one psychiatric clinician to another, that the use of only such titles seems rarely sufficient. One feels impelled to add much more information to make the characterization more satisfyingly complete. At times it is the latter additions of individual traits which may be used rather than the short title from the standard nomenclature. Furthermore, it is probably often true that the clinician receiving the referral has a definite sense that nothing short of his own direct experience of contact—especially in psychotherapeutic work—will give him the kind of sense of grasp or of understanding the prognostically important aspects of the patient's personality.

It is in this connection that a statement of an early psychiatric teacher, Dr. H. Douglas Singer, often comes to mind. For him the word diagnosis etymologically and literally meant "knowing through and through" (diagnosis). For him many psychiatric syndromes could only be classified—and, one might add, only rather roughly.

Another aspect of the problem for the psychotherapeutic clinician is that some clinicians seem to behave as if the creative endeavor of the psychotherapist is an *art* developed by intuitive skill, humanistic and compassionate concern, and bears little if any relation to science. Sometimes a therapist reports an experience with his patient as if change occurred following an interpretation. This is reported as if by insightful intuition the interpretive comment was uttered at the chosen moment and behavior was modified. What is lacking in such reports is the close attention to all the preceding details of the transactions of the patient and the therapist that led to the gradual evolution of the new behavior of the patient (and probably of the therapist) prior to the interpretation. It is not often that one sees reports of the painstaking steps, of the repetitious interventions of the therapist, and of the patient's responses to these, that preceded the eventual, gradual change, so that such an experience would be more comprehensible. Thus, what may have had all of the elements of a scientific experiment if it had been discretely recorded and later reported, is instead considered an art. Experience in the therapeutic encounter with patients therefore is, or can be, as much an experiment as any other scientific endeavor if adequately performed under an hypothesis. The psychotherapeutic clinician has observed frequently that if repeated observation of characteristic sequences are fully understood, appropriate verbal or behavioral responses by the therapist may have a gradually modifying influence. To repeat, what needs stress is the necessity for careful, regular observation of all details in every sequence, and of any variations in a given pattern of behavior of the patient and oneself. If then observations are fully reported, they are susceptible to comparison to similar data accumulated by other experienced clinicians. Unfortunately, this has not often been the case for such obvious reasons as the difficulty in recalling, recording and reporting all such details. Agreement then is difficult to achieve. Another problem that complicates this is the terminological one, especially in comparing reports of clinicians of different theoretical persuasions.

In any case it appears true that the need for a clinically more useful taxonomy in general psychiatry and in child psychiatry, with the more recent emphasis on developmental assessment, remains great. Advances in psychodynamic understanding of psychopathology and of integrated behavior already achieved and still to be attained from psychoanalytic therapeutic work also press for inclusion into the extant nomenclature or to transform it from a relatively undynamic descriptive system into a more clinically useful taxonomy.

Without such changes in the technical vocabulary, the transmission of knowledge to trainees, and of mutual understanding between trained and experienced clinicians of therapeutic experiments, of their evaluations and hence of prognosis will continue to be difficult if not retarded.

Thus, currently it is still common for us psychiatric clinicians also to strive for a short title from an accepted standardized nomenclature as a "diagnosis." This is in a way similar to, if not altogether the equivalent of, the non-psychiatric clinician's tendency to find a pathologist's term to name the disease of his patient. We need not expatiate on how often our most thorough efforts with somatic study of our patients gives us little or no clue as to any disease of the patient in the pathologist's terminology. Even though this is in some instances to some extent successful, we do not then always find the definable disease as a wholly and satisfactory explanation of the psychological and behavioral disorder of the patient. We are with many other patients even more pressed to compress all that we do and can learn from clinical, psychiatric, especially psychotherapeutic, study and observation about the patient's psychological behavioral characteristics very neatly into any title in the standard nomenclature.

Although the need for revisions, which this nomenclature has undergone, is continuously necessary, it also suggests that perhaps some of these efforts at ordering the thought of psychiatry may have been somewhat premature. If this is true, it may have, as Bronowski suggests, contributed somewhat to its stifling. As he says—"a science cannot develop a system of ordering its observations—until—(it) has passed through a long stage of observation and trial" (5). Otherwise the premature order may hinder for a long time its development as occurred with modern physics and chemistry under the influence of ancient theories of taxonomy in these fields.

If some or all of these considerations hold, our problem then is that we may be in need of more systematic observations and accurate verbal descriptions in the purely clinical sense which would more adequately characterize the disorder in living of each patient. Such descriptions may make possible some approaches to *clinical* quantification of both the degree of psychopathology and of integrated behavior. Scales of severity of disorder might then be developed with painstaking and persistent efforts from observation and description of the frequency, the duration, the degree of maladaptive (i.e., symptomatic), behavior (from the point of view of the patient's own welfare), as well as of his adaptive functioning and behavior in the clinical setting. This latter, the clinical setting, of course also needs clear specification. In other words, an added dimension, or source, of quantifying differences in the severity of qualitatively similar traits or symptoms can be the measurement of their persistence or response to similar therapeutic efforts.

From such studies clearly stated criteria could arise for names of symptoms by progressive agreement among various observers as to the actual data of observation. The association of such symptoms in different patients then could give a foundation for names of syndromes. The differences either in severity, or in the kinds of symptom groups, between patients could then form a much firmer foundation for subgroup classification of the spectrum within a syndrome. All such observations, often otherwise evanescent, and their descriptions might be more adequately preserved for subsequent and repeated study and comparison as mentioned before by audio-visual means.

When such clearly delineated subgroups begin to be formed in clinicians' minds, then similarly observed, described (and perhaps also audio-visually recorded excerpts of) psychotherapeutic maneuvers—which could be clearly thought of as experiments—might give us a more solid base for studies of prognosis in really comparable groups of patients.

Space does not permit any extensive illustration. However, to return to our previously used example of the psychotic disorders of preadolescent children, it may become immediately obvious that, in this field of a motley group, of congeries of clinical phenomena and syndromes, the need is great indeed. Clinical phenomena such as the nature of timing of the onset, the clear establishment of prenatal and paranatal disease, if any, the delineation of the familial circumstances under which a given symptom or sign of maldevelopment occurred, was exacerbated or receded, the multiple, often discretely definable aspects of the child's disorder and of his competences under clinical study are all already the subject of much attention.

In our experience in the treatment of psychotic children and their families, we initially saw young children and older ones and occasionally an adolescent whose disorder was an acute psychotic episode or a chronic one that had begun early in life. Some children used speech, others did not; some were violently self-destructive while others rocked quietly in a corner. After long periods of treatment some responded more readily than others. We have begun to identify and separate for consideration those elements that may have led to some success and others to failure, i.e. such factors as age, family relationships, presence of speech, duration of disorder since onset, presence of organic signs, skill of the therapists, staff-to-children ratio, etc. We are planning to study more thoroughly these factors as well as some elements of therapy that may have significance in future studies for scientific assessment of therapeutic results. (See Chapters 14 and 15.)

It has also come to the attention of some of us in this field of childhood psychoses that in all probability *comparability* of the severity of the syndromes included under the same diagnostic title is at least unclear if not lacking. Results of therapeutic research in different centers are then less likely to refer to the same, or to similar degrees of, disorder. The ensuing prognostic implications therefore lead to doubt and confusion in the field. Thus, for example, some time ago a prominent and creative investigator visited our ward on which are treated primarily psychotic children. He observed our program, talked to our staff, and examined briefly some of the children. Later, in comparing our respective work, he remarked that it was obvious we were working with what he called "the primitive schizophrenic," a group that his center does not admit. After fully assessing such children and from his long experience in working with many subgroups of schizophrenic children he elected with his methods not to treat this group intensively over long periods of time in his facility for various reasons and perhaps because of his estimate of the poor prognosis. We both report our work and results in the literature, but we may be talking about different groups of children.

In the taxonomy of psychiatric disorders, the new American Psychiatric Association's nomenclature (1) lists only "Schizophrenia, childhood type." Yet in the literature there are several other terms referring to several syndromes. We have read about childhood schizophrenia, childhood autism, atypical development, psychotic episodes and maldevelopment, symbiotic psychosis, the borderline child, and perhaps others. As we study the clinical vignettes in such reports, we frequently recognize that we are using similar terms to describe similar children and also the same terms for a variety of subgroups of the same disorder. The clinical descriptions sometimes suggest different degrees of severity of the disorder. Hence, it is not quite clear whether such descriptions are related to disorders of similar severity, which may have different prognoses for as yet not clearly determined reasons. For instance, we see few reports from other centers that describe the severely self-mutilating child that we have encountered in our work. (See Chapter 27.) Although we have noted some similarities in respect to self-injury in reports by other clinicians of very severely disturbed schizophrenic children, it is uncertain whether the children reported do injure themselves as severely and continuously as those we have seen.

We agree, therefore, with those who think that what is needed is less ready theorizing as to etiological factors, which cannot be very rigorously substantiated by only clinical work for given clinical phenomena, and more thorough observation, description and classification of them followed by similar study of effects of defined and precisely specified therapeutic endeavors.

These endeavors include, for example, decisions as to whether, and when, to make interventions or to remain silent, to offer restraint or to allow expression, to verbalize a child's thoughts or to help him express them in play. Such decisions are influenced by past experiences with other patients and by previous, repeated experiences with the patient before the therapist (6).

Such work may require generations of students, among whom nursing, or child-caring, personnel need to be included (2). Such students need to be trained in such methods as previously indicated to advance towards the goal of clinical science.

If the obstacles defined by Feinstein can be lessened as barriers to our clear thinking as clinicians, we may be able to work with even more excitement and enthusiasm. Our work can be as basic as in any science. We can be open to advances in any of these other sciences that can have relevance to our particular segment of the field of human biology. We may then be able to contribute to their advances with data as "hard" as their own. The long-held feelings of some of us that clinical work with each patient thoroughly enough performed and recorded is a piece of research in a larger program of clinical inquiry can then be confirmed as a warranted scientific statement.

All figures included in this Chapter are reproduced by permission of the copyright owners, Williams and Wilkins Company and the author of *Clinical Judgment*, Alvan Feinstein.

REFERENCES

1. American Psychiatric Association. *Diagnostic and Statistical Manual of Mental Disorders*. II. Washington, D. C.: American Psychiatric Association, 1961.
2. BOATMAN, MALETA J. "The Nurse, the Treatment Team and the Patient." In *Inpatient Care for the Psychotic Child*, Volume V of the Langley Porter Child Psychiatry Series. Edited by S. A. Szurek, I. N. Berlin, and M. J. Boatman. Palo Alto: Science and Behavior Books, Inc., 1971.
3. BOOLE, G. *An Investigation of the Laws of Thought. On Which Are Founded the Mathematical Theories of Logic and Probabilities.* 1854. Reprint: New York: Dover Publications, 1951. Cited by Feinstein, 1967.
4. DEWEY, JOHN and BENTLEY, ARTHUR. *Knowing and the Known.* Boston: Beacon Press, 1949. Chapter 2, p. 48.
5. FEINSTEIN, A. R. *Clinical Judgment.* Baltimore: The Williams and Wilkins Company, 1967.

6. SZUREK, S. A. "A Child Psychiatrist's Comments on Therapy of Schizophrenia." In *Inpatient Care for the Psychotic Child*, Volume V of the
   Langley Porter Child Psychiatry Series. Edited by S. A. Szurek, I. N.
   Berlin, and M. J. Boatman. Palo Alto: Science and Behavior Books,
   Inc., 1971.
7. TREFFERT, D. A. "The Epidemiology of Infantile Autism." *Archives of General Psychiatry*, 22(5):431-438. May 1970.
8. VENN, J. *Symbolic Logic*. London: Macmillan Co., 1894. Cited by Feinstein,
   1967.
9. WING, J. K. *Early Childhood Autism: Clinical, Educational and Social
   Aspects*. New York: Pergamon Press, Ltd., 1966. Especially Lotter's Survey of Children in County of Middlesex, England.

14

A Statistical Study of a Group of Psychotic Children

Dorothy Bomberg, M.A.

S. A. Szurek, M.D.

and

Jacqueline G. Etemad, M.D.

This report is a summary of available actuarial data on a sample of 264 children with varying degrees of psychotic disorder, studied on the Children's Service of the Langley Porter Neuropsychiatric Institute in San Francisco, over a span of 16 years, from 1946 to 1961. In 1956 one of the authors (29) characterized a statement of clinical experience with a portion of this same group of children as "preliminary, impressionistic and largely unstatistical." This was so then because time was unavailable to collate the data from clinical records. What follows is an effort to supply some of the deficiencies in that previous statement.

We will present this material in three parts: first, a description of the sample as a whole; next, our categorization of the subjects into seven subgroups; and finally, our data on treatment response.

PART I: SAMPLE

Before beginning a detailed examination of the factors studied, it might be of some interest to review the ratio of children classified as psychotic as compared to the total population offered service at Langley Porter Neuropsychiatric Institute during the 16-year period with which we are concerned.

This work was prepared with the assistance of an NIMH Grant # M-2032, furnished by the National Institute of Mental Health.

TABLE 1

Patient Population Trends*

Year	Total New Patients	New Psychotic Patients	Percent of Psychosis
1946	223	13	5.8
1947	166	13	7.8
1948	131	9	6.8
1949	91	6	6.5
1950	93	25	26.8
1951	100	17	17.0
1952	88	24	27.2
1953	97	23	23.6
1954	98	18	18.3
1955	106	22	20.7
1956	111	19	17.1
1957	103	15	14.5
1958	60	16	16.6
1959	136	24	17.6
1960	114	17	14.0
1961	96	16	16.6
Total	1813	277	15.2

* The discrepancy between the psychotic cases reported in Table 1 (277) and the psychotic population considered in this study (264) is accounted for by the elimination of three cases because of insufficient data and ten cases in 1961 which were reported after the data processing for the study was terminated in mid-1961.

Table 1 shows the changes and trends in the percentages of childhood psychoses in the treatment load over the course of the years. In all patients the diagnosis of psychosis represents the agreement of at least three staff psychiatrists.

As can be seen, after four years of accepting psychotic children for treatment, a substantial and sustained increase is evident in the percentage of such children in the treatment load. Since 1950 a large portion of staff time has been allocated to this effort.

These figures regarding the proportion of patients with psychosis of the total number of children seen in the clinic has, of course, relatively little epidemiological significance about the incidence in the population from which all the patients came. For two recent studies concerning the latter, see Treffert (33). Treffert quotes Lotter's recent survey (in Wing, 1966 (34)) of children in the county of Middlesex, England, of 8, 9 and 10 years of age

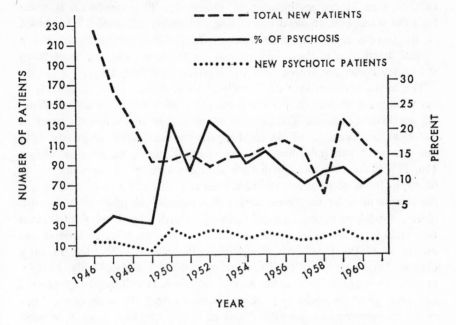

GRAPH OF TABLE 1. PATIENT POPULATION TRENDS

FIGURE 1

among whom he found a rate of 2.1 per 10,000 of a "nuclear syndrome" (infantile autism) and 2.4 per 10,000 with many autistic features but not of the "core" variety. Thus Lotter found a total rate of 4.5 per 10,000 of both infantile autism and childhood schizophrenia.

Treffert's survey of the State of Michigan resulted in a prevalence rate of 3.1 per 10,000. Two hundred and eight children under 12 years of age were identified during a five-year period between 1962 and 1967 by all mental health facilities of the state. This sample was subdivided into: 1) classic infantile autism, 25%; 2) psychosis with later onset, 57%; 3) psychosis complicated by demonstrable organicity, 18%. Whether a census type survey in the community as a case-finding method would result in a very different rate of incidence or not, of course, awaits such an expensive and difficult study.

Reed and Hagen (24) in their 1952 review, sponsored by the Child Welfare League of America, of twelve treatment centers for emotionally disturbed children, made the following descriptive statement about the relative degree of severity of our sample: "As a group the children at Langley Porter Clinic appeared to be the most disturbed of any of the groups of children seen in centers included in this study. This conclusion is made from the standpoint of social functioning and reality adjustment. It is based on the records read and observations of the children on the ward." For a clinical description of these children and the treatment program undertaken at Langley Porter see Szurek (29) and Boatman and Szurek (9).

The increase shown in Table 1 reflects growing community awareness of our willingness to attempt study and treatment of this difficult and challenging psychiatric problem. The increase might also be understood in terms of historical developments within child psychiatry during this period. In 1943 Leo Kanner began publishing his now classical studies on infantile autism (16, 17). Kanner's papers, with their clear descriptions of the autistic syndrome in terms of profound isolation evident before the second year of life, the intense need for the "preservation of sameness," skillful* relations with objects, intelligent appearance and facies along with a low level of intellectual functioning and severe language disturbance, served to heighten interest and awareness of the possibility of incapacitating affective disorders in early childhood. In a review of the literature on childhood schizophrenia, Ekstein, et al. (11) hypothesize that the idea of psychosis in childhood represents a sufficient threat to adults to produce a need to deny the designation. They report an immense increase with almost 10 times as many studies reported in the decade of 1946 to 1956 as in the preceding decade. Fifty-two items appeared in the literature between 1936 and 1946, and 515 between 1946 and 1956. It was this latter decade in which we witnessed the spurt in incidence of psychosis in our own clinic. (For a more recent summary of the literature after 1956, see L. Bender (3).)

Some investigators have suggested that the increased incidence in the diagnosis of childhood schizophrenia is a function of clinical error. Mosse (22) in 1958 writes, "Children in trouble for many different reasons are not likely to be so diagnosed. . . . Children may react in a bizarre way to severe trauma but that does not mean they then have schizophrenia or will develop it later on in life. . . . Childhood schizophrenia is at present in the U. S. a fashionable and much abused diagnosis. Careful clinical study indicates that far more often than not this diagnosis is wrong. This is not only a threat to children living in a difficult milieu, but also hinders the progress of psychiatry as a science."

David Beres, in a thoughtful paper published in 1956 (5), proposes the concept of ego deviation to describe behavioral aberrations which, while extreme, do not justify the gloomy prognostic implications which sometime accompany the psychotic diagnoses.

---

* Bosch, quoted by Bettelheim (7), disputes the characterization of the autistic child's manipulation of objects as being in the full sense "skillful."

Our own direct experience has been such as to make us feel sympathetic with these points of view. Szurek in 1956 (29), addressing this problem, said: "We can agree with those experienced students of this problem who feel that clear-cut criteria for a nosological entity are not easily defined. . . . We are beginning to consider it clinically (that is, prognostically) fruitless, and even unnecessary, to draw any sharp dividing lines between a condition that one could call psychoneurotic and another one could call psychosis, autism, atypical development or schizophrenia. The concept of a *gradient* of severity of disorder, or that of a psychopathological spectrum is for several reasons becoming for us one which fits our experience most closely."

It is only in recent years with a widening sophistication emerging nationally and internationally in the use of the terms childhood psychosis and childhood schizophrenia that we have employed these terms, secure in the knowledge that the connotations of immutability, constitutional defect, and inevitable deterioration are no longer associated with them. We are not unfamiliar with the wide range of violent disruptions of behavior that may appear transiently in children under stress. In our own usage we have employed the diagnostic category of Primary Behavior Problem to deal with those situations where obvious and severe external stress is present and a history of long and severe maldevelopment is absent.

It is our very strong impression that many of the children referred to us for study would have been unquestioningly diagnosed as mentally defective in the years prior to 1950. We have had increasing experience with local pediatricians, schools, and social agencies who now consider the possibility of emotional factors complicating diagnoses that in earlier years would have been unhesitatingly categorized as primary mental defectiveness on the basis of developmental retardation. In our sample we have a group of 27 children who were previously and from our findings, erroneously diagnosed as instances of primary retardation, i.e., mental deficiency. Of this group seven have shown marked clinical improvement. We have seen fourteen children who were previously diagnosed as deaf, when deafness was ruled out during our period of work with them. It is our impression that the increase in sophistication about severe emotional disorders in childhood in our community and at large in the last two decades as reflected in Table 1 represents a widening perceptiveness and understanding of the maldevelopment that can occur in children.

METHOD

For the statistical survey of our sample, we constructed a list of 93 items including variables relating to clinical experience, family history, and the child's development. A summary of the data sought from the records reviewed can be found in the Appendix. A summary of the variables relevant to a description of our population as a whole follows. In later sections we will relate these same variables to our diagnostic subgroups and to our improvement findings.

All items have been stated in discrete (noncontinuous) form and treated by a nonparametric statistical technique.

1. *Clinic Status*

Ninety-two of our subjects (35%) were seen for diagnostic study only. Following application interviews with a member of the social service department, the diagnostic study is conducted by a member of the psychiatric staff and usually consists of four or more sessions (generally weekly) with each family member. This initial investigation includes a review of the history of each parent, of the marriage, of the child's development, of the course of his illness and of his medical history. Physical and neurological examination, including electroencephalography, blood studies, bone age studies, x-rays and special medical procedures as indicated are performed at this time. The child is seen in the playroom or interview situation, and the opportunity for

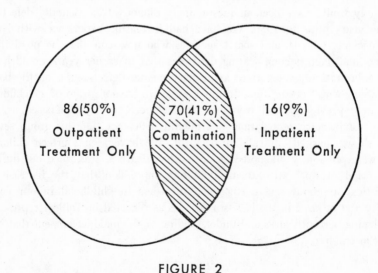

FIGURE 2

DISTRIBUTION OF OUTPATIENT, INPATIENT, PSYCHOTHERAPY
AND COMBINATION OF BOTH IN 172 TREATED
PATIENTS (65% OF TOTAL GROUP)

brief psychotherapy is afforded his parents. A psychodiagnostic evaluation by a member of the psychology staff is also made during this period. In the period since this study was terminated, evaluations by a speech therapist and an educational psychologist have been added to the study procedures. At the conclusion of the study the family is furnished with the findings, a diagnostic formulation is postulated, and plans for follow-up work are made as indicated. These investigations may require upwards of 20 hours of psychiatric service if the study is conducted on an outpatient basis. The study might be conducted on an inpatient basis if required by medical purposes, or if 24-hour observation of the child seems preferable. Nineteen of the 92 studies (20%) included inpatient study.

One hundred and seventy-two or 65% of our subjects were seen for psychotherapy which for purposes of this report is defined in terms of more than 24 sessions beyond the study visits and following the assignment of the family to staff psychotherapists. For a fuller description of both diagnostic and psychotherapeutic methods at Langley Porter during this period, see Boatman and Szurek ((9), pp. 419-426). Of the 172 treatment cases, 16, including one day care patient, or 9% were seen for inpatient therapy only. Eighty-six or 50% were seen as outpatients, and 70 or 41% were seen in some combination of outpatient and inpatient work.

2. Age of Application

Age of the child at the time of first contact with us ranged from 11 months to 17 years. Three of the children were under two years at the time of application, 17 were three years old, and 34 were four years old. Thus, 54 or 20% were under the age of five when first seen. Approximately 30 fell into each chronological age interval between five and nine. Fifty-six or 20% were between nine and 12, and 36 were 12 and older.

3. Sex

Of the total sample, 183 or 69% were male, and 81 or 31% were female. This is an overall ratio of more than two to one predominance of male to female.

4. Ethnic Distribution

More than 90% of our study population were Caucasian. We saw 13 Black children (5%) and seven Orientals (2.77%). The 1960 census report lists the Caucasian population of San Francisco at 81.6%, Black at 10.1%, and Oriental at 6.2%.

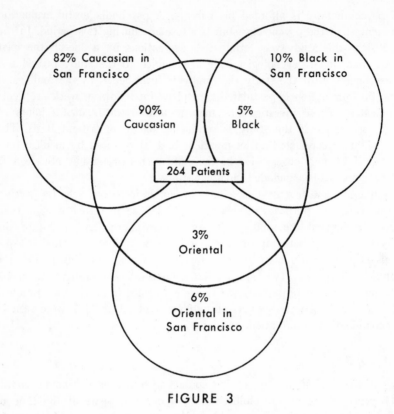

FIGURE 3

ETHNIC DISTRIBUTION OF ENTIRE SAMPLE IN COMPARISON TO ETHNIC DISTRIBUTION IN CITY POPULATION

5. *Duration of Treatment*

Forty-four and three-tenths percent of the total sample or 117 subjects were seen in psychotherapy for one year or less. A little less than five percent or 13 subjects were seen for nine years or longer. About 18.5 percent or 49 subjects were seen for five years or more. In terms of hours of treatment, including hours spent with both parents and the child, the totals are as follows: 77 subjects and their families or 29% were seen for under 50 hours; 52 subjects and their families or 48% were seen between 50 and 200 hours; 57 subjects and their families or 21% were seen for more than 200 hours of therapeutic work; and eight subjects and their families or 2% were seen for more than 800 hours.

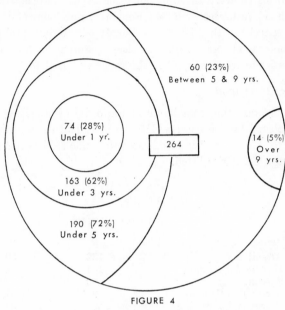

FIGURE 4

DISTRIBUTION OF AGE OF ONSET
AMONG 264 PATIENTS

Ninety-two subjects and their families, or 53% of the 172 treatment cases were seen by a single therapist for one year or more. For a discussion of the continuity afforded by this method of assigning a single therapist treating the family as a whole, see Boatman and Szurek ((9), p. 424).

At the other end of the continuum of treatment, 24 families were seen by more than 11 different therapists. This figure includes the practice of assigning three different therapists to a single family for a given period of work.

6. *Age at Onset of Illness*

Seventy-four of our patients, or 28%, are reported to have suffered the onset of illness at under the age of one year. Onset at year three or under is reported for 62% or 163 children; at age five or under, 190 children or 72%. Onset after age nine is reported for 14 children or 5%.

7. *First Symptoms*

Of first symptoms noted, speech problems rank highest with 44 children or 17% manifesting symptomatology first in this area. Next are mood disturbances and instability with 40 instances or 15%. Third is withdrawal and isolation with 36 instances or 14%. Fourth is developmental disturbances (other than speech) with 26 instances or 10%. Feeding problems, neurological phenomena, hyperactivity, and sleep disturbances are also reported, and in that order of frequency, all in the range of less than 10%.

8. *Presenting Complaints*

Table 2 lists presenting complaints in the order of frequency with which they were reported by the parents. Each subject had usually multiple problems leading to referral, and in some cases the same subject has five or more of the complaint categories listed.

TABLE 2
Presenting Complaints

Disturbance	N	%
Affective	132	50
Hostile Aggression	107	41
Speech	99	38
Social Relationship	97	37
Perceptual-Thinking	91	34
Speech (Mutism)	80	30
Motility	74	28
Toilet Training	65	24
Eating	47	18
Somatic	45	17
Interest-Activity	45	17

The rank order of these complaints perhaps represents to some degree the order with which parents find these various problems disturbing. The high frequency of aggression as a complaint may reflect a greater readiness to report aggressive behavior than for example interest-activity disturbance.

Affective disturbances include:
a.) Absence of affective expression, e.g., flattened facies, no tears, unresponsiveness to pain or gratification.
b.) Rudimentary, massive discharge with excitation, e.g., flailing arms, thrusting torso, incontinence.
c.) Manneristic expression of affect, e.g., grimacing, mirthless laughter.
d.) Extreme fearfulness, phobias, explosive affect, e.g., screaming, violent rages.
e.) Moodiness, irritability, volatility, manifest unhappiness.

Hostile aggression includes:
a.) Violent behavior toward the self or other-directed, ranging in complexity from violent motor discharge in banging, slapping, rubbing.

b.) Persistent voluntary muscle tension to the point of structural change, e.g., teeth grinding, biting.
c.) The assailing of others with body products.
d.) Nondiscriminatory physical attack on objects, animals or people.
e.) Destructive behavior directed toward specific objects or people.
f.) Antisocial behavior such as fire-setting, sexual aggression.
g.) Verbalized threats of violence or of suicide.

Speech disturbances other than mutism include:
a.) Unintelligible vocalizing.
b.) Speech arrest or retrogression.
c.) Absence of parts of speech such as pronouns, particularly personal pronouns, especially that of *I*.
d.) Limited application of speech, e.g., the use of speech infrequently or in only a few specified situations.
e.) Obsessive-compulsive speech.
f.) Pressure of speech.
g.) Marked use of profanity.
h.) Manneristic speech, parroting, or echolalia.

Social relationship disturbances include:
a.) Isolation from adults, siblings, and other children.
b.) Indiscriminate acceptance of affection.
c.) Clinging.
d.) Simultaneous or alternating affection and assault.
e.) Selective avoidance of others.
f.) Indifference about appearance.
g.) Expressions of interpersonal discomfort as in suspiciousness or the anticipation of ridicule.

Perceptual-thinking complaints include:
a.) Unresponsiveness to sensory stimuli.
b.) Confused chaotic behavior.
c.) Learning arrest, pseudo-stupidity.
d.) Thought aberration such as hallucinations or ideas of reference. There were only three or four instances of hallucinations, all of them in adolescent patients.

Motility complaints include:
a.) Total inertness.
b.) Inhibited movement of parts of the body, e.g., hand use, hand to mouth movement, inhibited ambulation.
c.) Poor coordination.
d.) Well-coordinated overactivity.
e.) Motility restricted by ritualistic or symbolic gestures or movement.
f.) Random overactivity.

Toilet training problems range from complete incontinence or retention of feces to obsessive-compulsive or phobic toilet behavior.

Eating complaints include the refusal of solids, voracious or indiscriminate eating, the refusal of foods or liquids, ritualized eating pattern.

Somatic complaints include epileptic seizures, allergic reactions including skin and respiratory disorders, obesity or anorexia, hysterical paralyses.

Interest-activity complaints include:

a.) Massive inhibition of curiosity and exploration.
b.) Exclusive preoccupation with the body.
c.) Limited repetitive activity, e.g., interest confined to circular movement of objects or to a few items like light switches or doors.
d.) Ideational preoccupation, e.g., religious, somatic, sexual.

9. *Birth Order*

Fifty-one children or 19% were only children. Thirty-seven of these 51 were males, 14 were females. Seventy-five children or 28% were youngest children of their families. Ninety-one children or 35% were oldest children.

Summarizing birth order from the point of view of ordinal position, 142 (100 males and 42 females) or 54% were first born, 69 or 26% second born, 38 or 14% were third born, 10 or 4% were fourth, and 5 or 2% were fifth

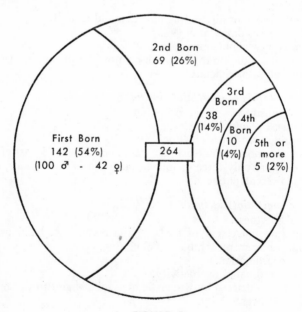

FIGURE 5

ORDINAL POSITION OF 264 PATIENTS
IN SIBSHIP WITHIN OWN FAMILY

or more. Thus it can be seen that there is a tendency for these children to be first born or oldest in the families, with males predominating in a ratio of more than two to one.

In 37 of the families or 14% of the 264 children studied, there were found to be more than one child with evidence of emotional disturbance. Of these, seven or 2.6% were severely enough disturbed to be classified as psychotic.

10. *Socioeconomic Factors*

Kanner (18) reports that of the first 100 cases of infantile autism studied by him there was a preponderance of parents from professional and managerial occupations. Because of this report and because Rimland (26) especially has stressed the preponderance of high intelligence of the parents of the children with this disorder, or of a particular ethnic factor (namely, Jewish), these factors were also analyzed. The following is a summary of the

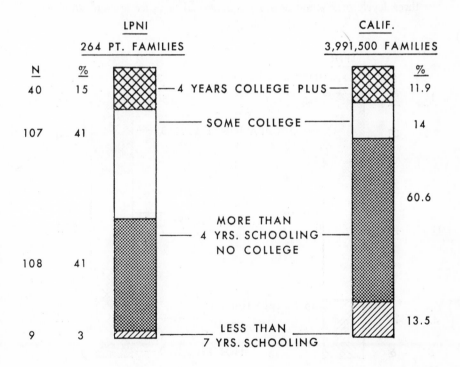

FIGURE 6. COMPARISON OF LEVEL OF FATHER'S EDUCATION IN LPNI PATIENTS' FAMILIES WITH CALIF. FAMILIES (1960).

results of the analysis of data bearing on these questions in our total group of 264 patients.

Educational levels of fathers: A little over 55% of our fathers entered college in comparison with 25.9% of heads of families in California in 1960. If we compare the percentage finishing college, however, we see that the percentages are no longer so discrepant. Fifteen percent of our fathers had four years or more of college, compared with 11.9% of heads of families in California. Our fathers tended to enter but not complete college.

Only nine or three percent of our fathers had less than seven years schooling, compared with 13.5% of heads of families in California.

Occupational levels of fathers: The largest percentage of our fathers, 125 or 47%, were found in skilled labor, clerical and sales, compared with 36.1% of heads of families in California. Although our fathers' educational levels were higher than the heads of families in California, only 31% were in the top three levels of Hollingshead's Occupational Scale compared with 29.9%

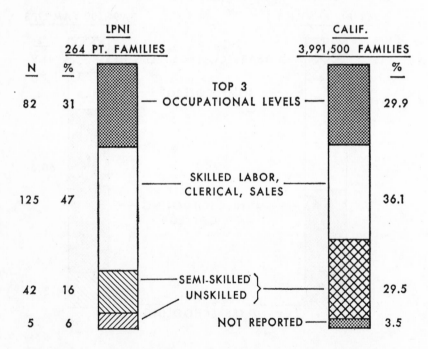

FIGURE 7. COMPARISON OF FATHER'S OCCUPATIONAL LEVEL
IN LPNI PATIENTS' FAMILIES WITH CALIF. FAMILIES (1960).

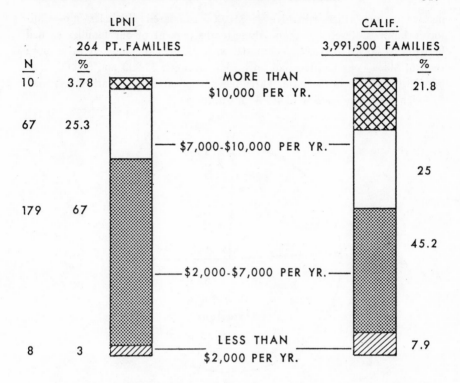

FIGURE 8. COMPARISON OF LEVEL OF INCOME OF LPNI
PATIENTS' FAMILIES WITH CALIF. FAMILIES (1960).

of employed heads of families in California. It raises the question of whether or not our fathers might be viewed as under-achievers.

Twenty-two percent of our fathers were in semiskilled or unskilled levels of occupation compared with 29.5% in the heads of families in California.

Income levels of families: Of all our measures of socioeconomic factors, income is the least reliable. Income of families in the United States has almost doubled from 1947 to 1960. The median income for families in the United States rose from $3,031 in 1947 to $5,630 in 1960, an increase of 85%. Income data on our families was collected throughout this period. It has also been noted that for many reasons, income both in the census and in studies is often inaccurately reported.

When the incomes of our families are compared to the incomes of families in California reported in the 1960 census, our families are earning less. Four percent of our fathers earned over $10,000 compared with 21.8% of California families. Twenty-five and three-tenths percent of our families earned between $7,000 and $10,000 compared with 25% in the state. A little more than 67.8% of our families had an income between $2,000 and $7,000 compared with 45.2% in the state. Three percent of our families earned less than $2,000 a year, compared with 7.9% in California.

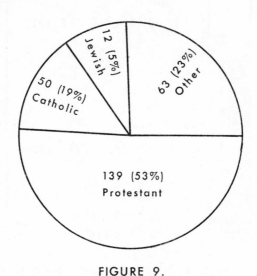

FIGURE 9.

DISTRIBUTION OF RELIGIOUS AFFILIATION
IN TOTAL GROUP OF 264 FAMILIES

These data from the last three figures are not, of course, direct evidence of the intelligence of both parents but only indirect indications of the probable intellectual capacity of only the fathers.

These findings also tend to support Bettelheim's suggestion that psychotic disturbances in children are probably not limited to any one socioeconomic level even though the actual distribution in the population of any community may be different than it is here represented.

Various workers have mentioned a preponderance of Jewish families in their work with schiozphrenic children (1, 18). Our own findings do not confirm this. Only 12 of our children, or 5% are of Jewish background as compared with 3% in the general U.S. population. Fifty-three percent or 139 are Protestant, 19% are Catholic.

11. *Trauma and Other Precipitating Events*

Eighty-one percent, or 214 of our subjects' histories, report no problems of pregnancy and delivery. Only five pregnancy complications, 10 instances of prematurity, four Caesarians, and 16 birth trauma cases are reported in all.

Overt parental disharmony is reported as a precipitating factor to the child's disturbance by 78 families or 29%. A separation in the family is reported as a precipitating factor by 70 families or 26%. Other precipitating factors reported are birth of a sibling, 48 cases or 18%; physical illness of the child, 33 cases or 12%; death in the immediate family, 29 cases or 11%; geographical or financial changes, 27 cases or 10%; miscarriage previous to onset of illness, 5 cases or 2%. Twenty-three of the children or 9% are recalled by their parents to have been unwanted.

TABLE 3

PRECIPITATING EVENTS TO THE CHILD'S DISTURBANCE
AS REPORTED BY THE PARENTS

Factors	N	%
Overt parental disharmony	78	29
Separation in the family	70	26
Birth of sibling	48	18
Physical illness of the child	33	12
Death in the immediate family	29	11
Geographical or financial changes	27	10
Miscarriage previous to onset of illness	5	2
Child unwanted by the parents	23	9

12. *EEG Findings*

Because before 1952 electroencephalographic examination was not routinely performed upon those children considered psychotic, there is a record of such examination in only 204 children or a little more than 77% of the entire sample here studied of 264 patients. The findings as rated by the electroencephalographer are tabulated in Table 4.

TABLE 4

	N	%
Normal EEG	84	41.2
Mildly Abnormal EEG	59	28.9
Moderately Abnormal EEG	48	23.5
Severely Abnormal EEG	13	6.4

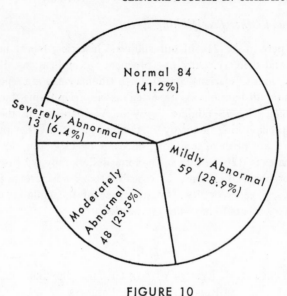

FIGURE 10

DISTRIBUTION OF EEG FINDINGS AMONG
204 PATIENTS EXAMINED

Thus, if those records termed "mild disturbance" are grouped with those called normal, then 143 or 70% of those examined show little or no deviation.

Looking at the type of EEG abnormalities that were observed we find that in 27 or 22.5% or the 120 abnormal tracings, there was some degree of diffuse slowing. Forty-five or 36.7% of the abnormal tracings had recognizable foci. In 16 or 13.3% of the 120 abnormal tracings there was superimposed fast activity. Paroxysmal activity was observed in 78 or 65.0% of the abnormal tracings. These abnormalities were not mutually exclusive, thus there is considerable overlapping of the categories listed above.

EEG findings for these 204 children have been reviewed with regard to relationship of EEG findings and response to treatment as well as with regard to changes in EEG findings for those children who had more than one tracing. This review, along with a more detailed discussion of the EEG abnormalities noted for each of seven diagnostic subgroups can be found in Chapter 18.

13. *Somatic Disease Reported*

Study of the 252 charts in which information concerning somatic factors was recorded revealed the following data as tabulated:

TABLE 5

SOMATIC DISEASE REPORTED

Pathology Reported	Number	%
None	210	83.2
Blindness	6	2.4
Deafness	4	1.6
Convulsive Disorder Alone	10	4.0
Presumed Cerebral Pathology	12	4.8
Primary Mental Defect	10	4.0
Total	252	100

There were another ten patients for whom somatic disease was reported, but a subsequent review of these records led us to exclude them because of the minor nature of the impairment. Among the group with presumed cerebral pathology there were three with degenerative disease of the central nervous system, four who had suffered traumatic injury to brain tissue, two with phenylketonuria, two with pneumoencephalographic evidence of brain abnormalities where the etiology was not known, and two with severe EEG disturbance without convulsive disorder.

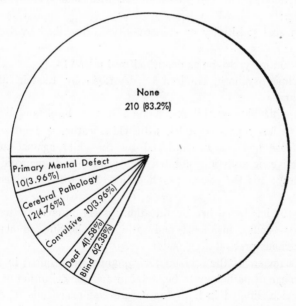

FIGURE II
ORGANIC DISEASE FOUND IN 252 PATIENTS

Thus, of the group where information was available, less than 17% showed evidence of diagnosable organic disease.

Both because of the still controversial status of the meaning of the so-called "soft neurological" signs and because of other problems precluding the systematic inclusion of such examinations in the whole group reported here, we have no data to record on this point.

PART II: CLASSIFICATION OF SAMPLE INTO SUBGROUPS

Various workers have attempted to develop diagnostic categories to encompass the wide variations in the clinical pictures classed as childhood schizophrenia. Hirschberg and Bryant (15) suggest a group of related and overlapping clinical syndromes in which the child displays symptoms arising from regression or arrest in ego development. They outline seven clinical groups:

1. Nuclear schizophrenia as described by Bender (1), an organic dysfunction akin to encephalopathy, involving a maturational lag at the embryonic level characterized by a primitive plasticity;

2. Early infantile autism, as described by Kanner (16, 17, 18);

3. Symbiotic psychosis, as described by Mahler (21), arrest at the most primitive stage of ego development with undeveloped body image differentiation;

4. The unusual sensitivity or vulnerability as described by Bergman and Escalona (6);

5. Organic brain syndrome as described by Fuller (14);

6. Borderline psychotic children as described by Ekstein and Wallerstein (12); and

7. Pseudo-schizophrenic children, as described by Rank and Kaplan (23).

Bender (4) has suggested a tripartite classification system based on the type of defense mechanism employed by the child against anxiety—the pseudo-defective or autistic, inhibited child; the pseudo-neurotic child with evident anxiety; and the pseudo-psychopathic child with prominent tendency to act out.

Despert (10) has based her classification system on onset, describing three major groups—acute, insidious, and insidious following an acute episode with an exogenous precipitating factor.

Our staff's review of the schizophrenic population resulted in an elaboration of the range of pathology to be included and the definition of descriptive categories which differed in both the nature and magnitude of disturbance. It emerged from such discussion that the experience of the staff made possible the formulation of seven separate groups into which our sample fell. We compared our seven groups on the basis of the 92 items of history, development and treatment factors summarized above. What follows is a clinical description of the groups and a review of the item analysis findings which described statistically how they differed one from the other. All the statistical comparisons which follow are at the 5% level of significance or better, using chi square.

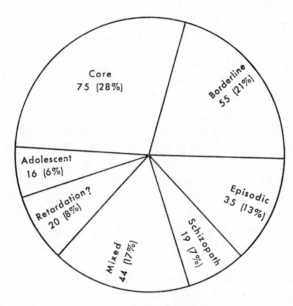

FIGURE 12

DISTRIBUTION OF ENTIRE SAMPLE OF 264 PATIENTS INTO SUBGROUPS

1. Core

What we have called our core group most closely approximates Kanner's syndrome of infantile autism (16, 19). In this group pathology is severe, pervasive, and almost wholly incapacitating. Seventy-five of our sample or 28% are represented in the core group. Part of the definition of core is age at onset. In most of these cases signs of arrested development appear in infancy. In 58.6% of this group onset has been placed at one year or under. The analysis of this group as to age of onset is shown in Table 6.

Thus in over 79% when information was available, the onset was stated as two years of age or earlier.

TABLE 6

	N	%
No information as to age on onset	6	8
At one year or under	44	58.6
At 2 years	16	21+
At 3 years	7	9.3+
At 4 years	1	1.3+
At 5 years	1	1.3+
Totals	75	99.5

Usually, although not always, speech is absent or idiosyncratic. Fifty-five percent are mute. Learning is retarded in most areas, although sometimes there is specialized knowledge or skill in some solitary sphere. They have the least formal schooling of our groups. Application for treatment is associated with family anxiety about developmental factors. There is a medical history of no major illness or physical pathology. Their EEGs tend to be normal. Pregnancy and delivery is reported as normal. The ratio of male to female is three to one. The fathers in this group are highest in occupational level. Both mothers and fathers are highest in academic training. They are youngest in terms of age at application. In their experience with us they have the longest terms of treatment, 24% of the group receiving more than 400 hours. They tend to have more inpatient treatment than any of the other groups. As a group they are well described by Kanner's criterion, including profound isolation, "preservation of sameness," intelligent appearance with poor intellectual performance.

2. *The Borderline*

This group resembles the core group in nature of onset, early and progressive, but the pathology is less severe and less incapacitating. There are 55 children (21%) in this group. The autistic signs of isolation and withdrawal, blocked learning, oblique communication, etc. are present but to a lesser degree. The preponderance of male to female is even greater, four to one. Speech disturbance is reported as a primary complaint in 44% of their records, but mutism is rare. Often these children are able to remain in the community and attend school on some marginal basis, with poor school adjustments (27%) or in special classes (31%). Only 16% are aged five or under, but the discrepancy between age of onset and age of application is greatest. Application tends to be associated with extrafamilial concern, e.g., concern on the part of pediatrician or school. There is an absence of major illness or physical pathology. They are seen most often in outpatient treatment. The term Borderline was chosen to designate that borderline area which lies between the very severe obsessive-compulsive and the psychotic diagnosis. These children manifest less integrated development than the child we would classify as neurotic.

3. Episodic Group

This group displays psychotic phenomena similar to those found in the core group but differ in their history of illness with a later and acute onset. Further experience in therapy almost invariably discloses information about neurotic manifestations in earliest years which was not available from parents' reports at the time of initial exploration. The characteristics which distinguish the group from the core group are in the history, where development is described as asymptomatic to a certain point, e.g., the child was reported to have learned to talk but suddenly stops. The behavior of children in this group when first seen at the clinic is often quite similar to that of the core group children. Sometimes differentiation becomes quite difficult to make, and the line between the two groups grows finer as the clinician becomes more familiar with the family and hears more and more about what might have been amiss in supposedly "premorbid" years, making the designation of acuteness of onset more questionable.

In this group there were 23 males and 12 females, a ratio of almost two to one. The 35 children or 13% of the sample classified as episodic received less treatment than any other group. They were least likely to get into treatment and spent the fewest hours in treatment when they did. Their family histories were overtly the most traumatic, and *manifest* parental anxiety was highest. These families appeared both more volatile and responsive clinically. The frozenness and ambiguity, so often encountered with parents in the group as a whole, were absent here, and it was often possible to make psychological sense of the histories offered in relatively short periods of work with the family. It was interesting to note that the affective disturbance of the child was named as a complaint by 66% of the parents of this group, while in the core group, where affective disorders were at least equally apparent clinically, they were cited as complaints by only 27% of the parents.

4. "Schizopath"

The term was coined in staff discussion of those aggressive children whose actively destructive behavior was unlike that of the withdrawn and self-absorbed core children (see Bender's term pseudo-psychopathic) and whose excitement was less highly organized and focused than the destructive behavior of the nonpsychotic antisocial child. These children combine the symptomatology of both the hostile destructive acting out problem and the autistic. Included would be children without identification with antisocial outgroups, who show destructive behavior that is unusual and idiosyncratic, isolation greater than is seen in the usual delinquent, and contact with others often of compulsively destructive or driven nature. This group is distinguished by a greater activity which might at first view give the impression of outgoingness. The ratio of male to female is highest, 84% to 16% or 5.2 to 1. Onset is both insidious and acute. They are late in ordinal sibling position, only 16% being first born, and 58% being youngest. This is a small group of 19 children, representing only 7% of the sample.

In the years since the collection of the present data so few instances have been seen that could be placed in this category that we have some question about the usefulness of the category.

5. *The Mixed Group*

This group includes children with both severe emotional disturbance of autistic pattern and pathology of a known organic nature. Forty-four children or 17% of the group fall in this category. The sex ratio is almost one to one, 54% male and 45% female. This group has received more psychotherapy than any other group except the core group. Inpatient observation was often indicated to facilitate thorough medical exploration and to further the intensive observation required to differentiate between psychologically and somatically determined symptomatology. By definition they have the most physical pathology, including primary mental retardation, cerebral pathology, and sensory defects.

6. *The Retardation? Group*

Although defined in a negative fashion, this group appears to be one of our most homogeneous groups. It includes those children for whom the differential diagnosis of primary intellectual retardation has not been possible to establish or to rule out. The question of to what, if any, extent does the atypical development result from a primary retardation, has for them remained unresolved. There are 20 children or 8% of the total population in this category. These children closely resemble the descriptions given by Bender of her "pseudo-defective" group with physical lability, inadequate muscle tonus, retention of primitive features of development at an embryonic level. In his recent reviews of the literature, Rimland (26), in an attempt to differentiate schizophrenic children from autistic children who he feels do not fall within the diagnostic category of childhood schizophrenia, describes the schizophrenic child as consistently showing somatic problems as thin, pale with blond hair and blue eyes, receding chin, almost foetus-like appearance, doughy muscle tone, choreoathetotic finger and hand movements, seductive and molding to adults like plastic or dough, hallucinatory, and poorly coordinated with gait problems. With the exception of the observations about coloration and hallucination, this is a fair general description of our retardation group.

They vary markedly from the group as a whole in sex ratio, being the only group in which the ratio is reversed, female being predominant (60%). Forty percent are oldest children. Motility disturbances are common. They tend to have major illnesses in the first year of life, generalized dysrythmia appears in 20% in their EEG findings. Of all the groups they are most inclined to interrupt therapy contrary to staff recommendation. Throughout treatment, they are the most problematical and thwarting clinically, provoking staff divergence about both diagnostic and therapeutic issues, uniformly frustrating therapeutic attention while offering the least stimulation to therapeutic interest.

7. *The Adolescent Group*

This group is composed of 16 children (6% of the sample) who develop psychotic symptoms at or after puberty. There were 11 males and five females, a ratio of about two to one. They are by definition oldest at onset which tends to be acute. They are also the oldest at application, and have the shortest span between onset and application. They are seen almost exclusively as outpatients, have the least evidence of somatic pathology and the greatest number of somatic complaints. Their most frequent presenting complaint is of a perceptual-thought disorder. They differ from the other groups on socioeconomic factors. Both fathers and mothers in this group have less education than those in any of the other six groups.

Sex Ratios

The previously mentioned overall sex ratio of 183 males to 81 females (or somewhat more than two to one) in the total sample of 264 children is also closer to that of Bettelheim's series and that of Shain and Yannet (28) (both less than two to one) than to the sex ratio reported by Eisenberg and Kanner of four to one. There is a notable variation in this sex ratio among the seven groups of our total sample.

For a greater convenience of comparison of the differences in sex ratios, the entire sample of 264 patients is tabulated and presented in graphic form.

TABLE 7

Subgroup	N	%	Sex Ratio: Male to Female
1. Core	75	28	3:1
2. Borderline	55	21	4:1
3. Episodic	35	13	a little less than 2:1
4. "Schizopath"	19	7	5.2:1
5. Mixed	44	17	almost 1:1
6. Retardation?	20	8	1:1.5
7. Adolescent	16	6	about 2:1
Total	264	100	

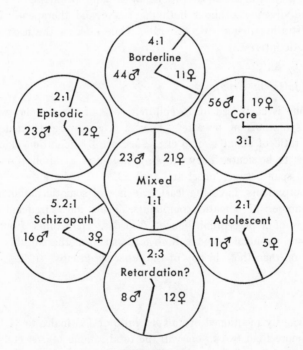

FIGURE 13

SEX RATIO IN VARIOUS SUBGROUPS

PART III: RESPONSE TO THERAPY

Ratings on improvement-unimprovement were obtained for the group of 135 closed patients who had had therapy; the remaining 129 were studies of patients still in therapy. The criteria for improvement employed have been: 1) Recorded evidence of increased social adjustment, e.g., ability to succeed in a school or work situation, increased responsibility for self-care, decreased need for supervision, decreased hostile aggression or self-destructiveness; 2) Evidence of intellectual development, e.g., the appearance of speech in the mute child, increased use of speech for communication, the acquisition of academic skills in the child with a learning arrest, improved performance on psychological testing; 3) Ability to adapt to family and society to an extent obviating institutional placement when placement previously was required.

The ratings represent agreement of the research psychologist and three psychiatrists about 1) the behavior factors suggesting change, and 2) the degree of change or improvement. Where such agreement was not possible, the rating of ambiguous was used. The ambiguous rating represents the failure to achieve the above described unanimity, or the absence of recorded evidence upon which annotated ratings could be secured. Thirteen children or 9.6% were classified as ambiguous.

Fifty-one children or 37.7% of the treatment group were classified as improved. Six of the 51 moved during treatment from essential muteness and extreme isolation to attendance in regular public classes. An example is a three-year-old who at admission did little more than gaze at his own hands and whose mastery of basic executive skills was so limited as to exclude even masticatory functions, and who at discharge two years later had assumed responsibility for his own toileting, fed himself, walked with a steady gait, used words, had stopped his head banging, and was affectively responsive. His mother who continued to suffer repeated severe episodes of anxious depression refused to return to our clinic for further outpatient therapy after her first therapist left the staff. This was despite repeated offers of such work from the staff. Nevertheless, after several periods of therapy elsewhere in which only the boy and father participated and after four years of placement in a foster home, the child at nineteen years of age was expecting to graduate from high school. His father had found a possible job for him after graduation. He continued throughout this period to have relatively few friends.*

Seventy-one children, 52.59% of the treatment group, were classified as

* We are indebted to Dr. Gwen McCullough for the clinical and follow-up data on this extremely interesting patient and his family.

unimproved. Where no demonstration of expanded social freedom or facility was present beyond improved relationship to staff, the rating of unimproved was used. The phrase "relates more to therapist" when found in the record was regarded as a designation more likely to reflect the therapist's sense of familiarity rather than a decrease in estrangement with other people.

The behavioral evidences of change that were employed have been organized into nine categories and are as follows:

1. *Response to psychotherapy*
2. *Physical improvement of child*
   a. Improved EEG
   b. Sensory handicap diminishment
   c. Improved motor coordination
   d. Decreased somatic manifestation of anxiety
3. *Speech improvement*
   a. Use of words following muteness
   b. Ability to speak in sentences
   c. Increased use of speech
   d. More coherent speech
4. *Psychological test performance improvement*
5. *Increased emotional expression*
   a. Expresses feeling more directly
   b. Decreased obsessive-compulsive manifestation
6. *Improved school adjustment*
7. *Social development*
8. *Improved ward behavior*
9. *Parental change*
   a. Less guilt and ambivalence toward child, hence more genuine affection and firmness
   b. Increased understanding of child's behavior
   c. Decrease in somatic problems
   d. Less displacement of anxiety onto child

The improvement findings are more enlightening and meaningful when the findings of the seven groups are considered separately.

Of the 75 total *core* children, 37 or 49.3% were in the group who received therapy. Of these 17 or 45.9% were classified as improved, 14 or 37.8% unimproved, and 6 or 16.2% were ambiguous.

Of the 55 total *borderline* children, 32 or 58.1% were in the group who received therapy. Of these 16 or 50% were classified as improved, 16 or 50% unimproved, and none were ambiguous.

Of the 35 *episodic* children, 12 or 34% were in the group who received therapy. Of these 8 or 66.6% were classified as improved, one was ambiguous (8.3%), and 3 or 25% were unimproved.

Of the 19 *schizopaths*, 9 or 47% were in the group who received therapy.

Of these, 2 or 22.2% were improved, 3 or 33% were ambiguous, and 4 or 44.4% were unimproved.

Of the 44 *mixed* children, 24 or 54.5% were in the group who received therapy. Of these, 6 or 25% were rated improved, 1 or 4.1% were ambiguous, and 17 or 70.8% were unimproved.

Of the 20 *retardation?* children, 12 or 60% were in the group who received therapy. Of these, none were improved.

Of the 16 *adolescents,* 9 or 56% were in the group who received therapy. Of these, 2 or 22.2% were rated improved, 2 or 22.2% were ambiguous, and 5 or 55.5% were unimproved. Table 8 summarizes these findings.

TABLE 8

Treatment Ratings

Group	Received Therapy	Improved	Ambiguous	Unimproved
1. Core	49.3%	45.9%	16.2%	37.8%
2. Borderline	58.1%	50 %	0	50 %
3. Episodic	34 %	66.6%	8.3%	25 %
4. Schizopathic	47 %	22.2%	33.3%	44.4%
5. Mixed	54.5%	25 %	4.1%	70.8%
6. Retardation?	60 %	0	0	100 %
7. Adolescent	56 %	22.2%	22.2%	55.5%

When the first three groups, core, borderline, and episodic, are combined, the improvement rate is 50.6%, ambiguous is 8.6%, and unimproved is 40.7%. Groups four through seven, schizopathic, mixed, retardation?, and adolescent, combined have an improvement rate of 18.5%, 11.1% are ambiguous and 70.37% are unimproved. It thus appears that the isolated typically "atypical" child, free of complicating secondary diagnostic features is more responsive to a psychotherapeutic approach, particularly when onset is acute. As can be seen, the retardation? group was the least responsive as reflected by outcome as well as clinical experience, where confusion about differential diagnosis tends to obscure questions of what is clinically relevant at a given moment and impedes the possibility of therapeutic understanding continuously increasing the accuracy of diagnostic formulation.

These findings largely conform to clinical expectation. The episodic group, although formed of children with severe and incapacitating psychotic reactions, manifested a less frozen and entrenched position than is seen where maldevelopment begins early and is continuous and progressive in its course.

Comparing the above mentioned improvement ratings on the list of 93

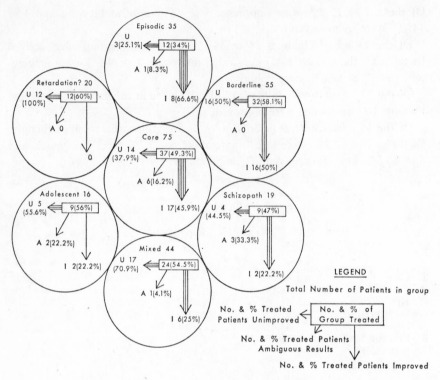

FIGURE 14

RESULTS OF THERAPY IN 135 PATIENTS IN TREATMENT GROUP

history variables produced a single finding. Disturbed EEG records are associated with poor response to therapy.

In a further attempt to refine our data, an effort was made to identify the extremes of the sample by means of a five point rating scale describing a continuum from improved to worse which was submitted for ratings to a group of senior staff psychiatrists, the psychology and social service department staff, and the nurse in charge of nursing training. These weighted ratings provided a group of 30 children representing the extremes of response to therapy, the 15 most improved and the 15 least improved. When these ratings were compared using our 92 items, again only one variable differentiated them. Clinical improvement was associated with shortness of span between age of onset and age of application. For 47% of the improved group the discrepancy between age of onset and age of application was less than

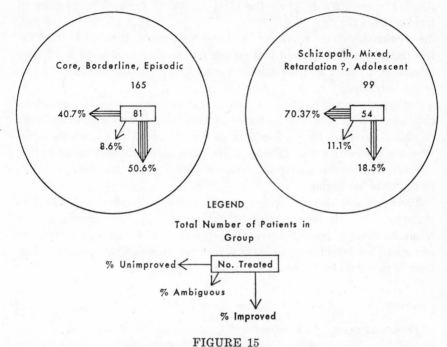

FIGURE 15
GROUPED TREATMENT RESULTS

two years, while the unimproved group revealed a discrepancy of five years or more.

For further treatment of this and additional data with respect to outcome, see Chapter 15.

PART VI: SUGGESTIONS FOR FURTHER RESEARCH

A clinical hypothesis which has not been substantiated by empirical test is that children who at some time in their history prior to application for therapy were placed outside of the home in residential placements had a less hopeful prognosis than children for whom there is no record of such placement. No significant statistical differences were discovered in comparisons between improved-unimproved and placed-nonplaced groups. The clinical experience underlying the hypothesis that out-of-the-home placement is an unfavorable prognostic sign contains the expectation that placement suggests a limited readiness on the part of the family to meet the demands of a psychotherapeutic program. A second hypothesis about the prognostic implications of a readiness to place the child is that it indicates a measure of freedom from the type of strenuous and binding conflict which characterizes the relationship of the psychotic child and his parents. It might be that the two factors are both present and oppose one another to produce a negative finding. A separate and more minute examination of the placement group seems warranted.

An hypothesis which can be tested is that the appearance of a psychotic child in a family results in an increased likelihood of emotional disturbance in siblings who are born subsequent to the patient. This hypothesis stems from the observation that familial stress, particularly as experienced by the mother, gains momentum rapidly once the difficulty with an emotionally disturbed child has begun.

The hypothesis that the acute psychotic syndrome in children is closer to the severe neurotic disorder than to the typical psychotic development in terms of psychogenesis requires further investigation. Projective tests of personality on parents may be a possibility for securing quantitative descriptions of parental characteristics for comparative purposes.

Comment

These findings reflect in some ways the historical development of the staff of Child Psychiatry of the University of California Medical Center at San Francisco and of the ideas of this staff during the years covered by this survey of records. The basic purpose of the Institute and of its Children's Service was and is training, research, and the kind of clinical service that would further these goals.

When a new director came in early 1946 with a psychoanalytic orientation in child psychiatry, there was one child clearly psychotic in a total of 16 children on the unit. The new director had had a very limited experience elsewhere with psychotic disorders in early childhood: Two children seen prior to 1946, one of whom improved markedly in a relatively short time. With an increase in referrals of psychotic children, it was natural then to seek first to broaden and deepen this experience and second to test the psychological hypothesis developed previously in experience with other disorders of childhood.

The increase in referrals of children with very severe disorders soon transformed the inpatient population into an almost entirely psychotic group. It led even to trials of psychotherapy with some of them in the outpatient service. During many of these years children between the ages of two years and ten months and twelve years were accepted for inpatient therapy without regard to the severity, nature or duration of the disorder or the possible presence of organic disease for trials of psychotherapeutic approach. This was, of course, combined with as thorough a study in each instance for organic factors as the resources of the medical center permitted. Acceptance for such work was limited only by the available hospital bed space and staff time. Because of prior experience with other types of childhood disorders in which parental participation was found to be of very great importance in the progress of the work, parents, and even occasional grandparents in the home, were regularly invited and then required to participate in psychotherapy efforts or be involved in the work with the child.

The problems and difficulties implicit in simultaneous efforts to provide an opportunity to a constant stream, and an increasing number, of trainees to learn the skills of psychotherapy while attempting to perform clinical therapeutic research with disorders of major severity and complexity are probably reflected in the therapeutic results. The gradual growth of the staff from these trainees, made possible by funds available from the Federal Government under the National Mental Health Act, reduced somewhat these difficulties but did not eliminate them. The interest and persistence of this staff permitted some children and their families many years of service. It provided this staff with a very broad and deep experience with the variety of these clinical syndromes.

This experience included an increasing sense of the prognoses of the different syndromes as well as of the kind and duration of therapeutic effort necessary to effect any change. Marked improvement in some and gradually lessened severity of disorder in many more kept alive the interest of the more experienced of the staff to continue the clinical experiment under these very trying and often discouraging circumstances. In addition the continuing turnover of staff in all disciplines, often of the most experienced and skillful psychotherapists, nurses, etc., affected the milieu as well as the individual psychotherapy. Other trying circumstances included marked skepticism and even open disapproval of nonsomatic efforts at therapy not only in the staff but also in the community. This was in part because the generally poor prognosis for these children led some staff and parents understandably to grasp at any other shorter possibilities for cure, however unsubstantiated. Such factors tend to influence relatively inexperienced staff negatively.

In an unsystematic way the effort provided this staff with what is a deeper experience with the variety of outcomes than the ordinary follow-up, as a number of the earlier patients grew to middle adolescence on the Children's Service of the Institute or young adulthood either eventually in a state hospital, or in a fewer, more fortunate situations, through high school and even college outside of the hospital.

The present statement makes little or no effort to provide data for or against the psychogenic theory of etiology or of such factors in etiology. The data in the records proved—as in many retrospective studies of records of this sort—too difficult to make even an approach to some quantification in any sense reliable with the time for the study available under the supporting grant. Further, for a substantive contribution to any theory of etiology, the necessity to compare similar data from control groups of families was also impossible for similar reasons.

These facts, however, are not in any sense a retreat from the possibility and the probability of the importance of psychogenic factors in the etiology of most, if not all, of the instances of such disorders. It is only possible to comment here that such data remain recorded in the continuing daily past and present clinical experience of the most experienced members of the staff. To transform such clinical experience into more quantified form, recorded on paper, requires a designed *prospective* study. It awaits for time and opportunity further to develop methods of observation, of measurement of signs and symptoms for more accurate and comparable grouping of patients and families and of more precise recording and the necessary comparisons.

Nevertheless, despite the fact that closer search of all records for evidence of conflictful tensions of parents was not possible, as reported under Trauma and Other Precipitating Events on page 319, very obvious and overt parental disharmony, separations in the family, lack of desire for the child and other such facts and events often productive of emotional tension were recorded in a very appreciable number of the families studied. Moreover, in several families who held most tenaciously to an organic explanation of their child's psychosis, the parents' anger with each other and incapacity to relate to each other kept them on the verge of divorce for many years.

Subject to the same limitations of inference regarding etiology are the data concerning birth order (Fig. 5). The relatively high incidence (54%) of first born or oldest children in the present sample is comparable to the data reported by Bettelheim (7). That is, the degree of predominance of first born among psychotic children is not as great as that reported by others than Bettelheim. This higher incidence of first born by itself as a fact cannot be taken as significant evidence for the psychogenic hypothesis. It is only in the context of evidence of maternal, and especially interparental, intensification of neurotic conflict that the first pregnancy and the first child can gain such significance. Since such data, as mentioned, could not be gathered in a satisfactory way on the entire sample, the etiological inference for this and other reasons is here not drawn.

Although the subgroup, schizopath, has tended to be a "vanishing" group in the later years of our experience in the period here under review, several comments occur to us. The fact that 58% of the schizopath subgroup are the youngest born may indicate the operation of factors more likely to occur around the birth and early years of the youngest child. It might indicate that mothers of such children would be either older or more under stress because of having more children or more likely to be experiencing tensions arising from mounting marital problems which are not infrequent in the later years of a marriage. Further, illness or loss of their own parents with whom they may have had particularly ambivalent relations are more likely to contribute to such tensions. Some of the latter factors were found operative in two instances of one of the writers, Szurek, early experience with very severe disorders of the youngest child. One of these was published (32). In both families there were older children developing in a relatively integrated manner. In addition, the fact that the schizopath subgroup, even in a relatively small number of 19, showed the highest male to female ratio of all our subgroups (five to one) may be an indication that either one or both of two factors may be operative in the genesis and maintenance of this syndrome: namely, the sex of the child presents particular stressful psychological connotations for the mother, or the inborn temperamental characteristics of the child (e.g., of greater vigor of responsiveness to inner and outer events and/or the findings of greater autonomic lability of responsiveness among male newborn babies (25, 27) may pose a greater stress for a mother who may be neurotically too inhibited to respond to such a child adequately for his needs). All these speculations obviously require closer study not undertaken in this survey.

The reversal of the sex ratio in the small retardation? subgroup might be considered in relation to the almost one to one sex ratio found in our mixed subgroup which is more than twice as large. The mixed subgroup is defined as those children with diagnosable organic disease in addition to signs of psychotic disorder. The retardation? subgroup which was so classified because of strong clinical suspicion, although not definitely established, of the presence of primary mental defect also had signs of general immaturity as described. Further, this group tended to have major illness in the first year of life, and 20% of the group were reported to have a generalized dysrhythmia in their EEG tracings or a grossly abnormal record. Although closer comparison of each child in both groups is indicated for more thorough and precise assessment of these factors, nevertheless, one might consider the data given as at least an indication of the possibility that the presence of organic disease may tend to predispose infants and children of both sexes more equally to emotional maldevelopment of a severe degree. We suggest here of course that not only the child's own organic handicap, but also the stress such handicaps may evoke in the parents and perhaps particularly the mother who is neurotically predisposed to such stress contribute to the child's emotional maldevelopment.

For our subgroup of adolescents which was also small we have no additional comment concerning the relatively low male to female ratio of two to one, except to point to the similar sex ratio in the episodic subgroup. The history in both subgroups of a relatively more acute onset of clinically severe symptoms of disorder after a period of more integrated personality development (at their different periods of life) may indicate the operation of similar factors, such as more sudden intensification of intrafamilial stress and tension. Such similarity of factors, of course, would not explain the higher incidence of disorder among male children which is found in all varieties of emotional disorder of children and adolescents. Whatever the factors are which eventuate in this higher male incidence, our conjectured similarity of factors might still operate to decrease the sex ratio seen in our remaining two subgroups.

The sex ratio of three to one in the core subgroup, perhaps most similar to the autistic child as described by Kanner, is less than the ratio of four to one which Kanner reported but it is higher than that reported by Bettelheim and by Schain and Yannet of slightly less than two to one. The higher sex ratio of four to one in our borderline subgroup is still closer to the findings of Kanner than to the latter investigators. Whether such differences in sex ratio between the various studies would be resolved by more epidemiologically oriented surveys of the general population is an open question. Within the context of our sample, limited from the epidemiological standpoint, we can only point to one more or less common factor in the two subgroups, core and borderline, in contrast to our other five subgroups; namely, a tendency to an earlier onset of disorder in the life of the child.

If a general epidemiological survey were to confirm and establish that earlier the onset of disorder, the higher the proportion of male children affected, then the way would be clearer to posit possible explanations and to study them. In the present state of our knowledge any further speculations concerning this datum would be mere additions to the guesswork about this matter already in the literature and that contained elsewhere in the present report.

Bettelheim's (7) data tend to support the findings of Kanner as to the preponderance of somewhat better education and socioeconomic status (but not that of high intelligence) among the parents of autistic children. Bettelheim surmises that such preponderance is an artifact. He argues that it is probably the well-informed parent who would be the most likely to learn of such facilities as that of Kanner or of Bettelheim and only the well-to-do who could travel to such centers with their children from all over the

country and even the world. The findings in our sample concerning education and income of parents (Figs. 6 and 8) tend to be similar to those of
Bettelheim and others, namely, a relatively greater proportion of fathers
with higher education, occupational levels, and higher income than of those
in the lower levels in respect to all three attributes. Still, perhaps because
our clinic has provided service to all residents of the state, even those unable
to pay any fee at all, the lower levels are also represented. The latter fact
may indicate that Bettelheim's surmise is correct; namely, a general survey
of all three-year-old children in one of the metropolitan centers would reveal
that the disorder is more evenly distributed among all groups of the population. Since our studies, like those of other students, did not include direct
measurement of intelligence of the parents, our findings cannot be used
except by inference from educational and socioeconomic data to support the
reports of Kanner and Rimland concerning the predominance of very high
intelligence among parents of autistic children. Bettelheim concludes from a
review of the reports of others and of his own data (7) that very high intelligence among the parents is not frequent. Our experience tends to corroborate
this conclusion. In passing it may be noted that our data do not confirm the
reports of Kanner and Bender about the higher frequency of psychotic
disorder in children of Jewish parents.

The subdivision of the total sample into the seven subgroups is a rather
rough effort to categorize the variety of clinical phenomena we encountered
in our effort to gain as wide an experience with this major disorder of childhood as unsolicited referrals to the clinic permitted. In light of such an analysis and suggestions as contained in the recent volume by Alvan R. Feinstein
(13) on clinical judgment, the criteria for a taxonomy to attain a more
accurate spectrum of any disorder for a prognostic and therapeutic study
require still closer attention to such matters as a more precise identification,
closer observation of symptoms and signs with their specification, designation,
rating, clustering and clinical course, and so on. Perhaps of particular
importance in such a future and prospectively designed study is Feinstein's
suggestion that a complete spectrum of a disease or disorder may comprise
separable *but overlapping* sets of patients. This separation of patients into
sets or subgroups is achieved on the basis of clinically well-observed differences and similarities treated as multiple, discrete, independent variables.
Such overlapping subgroups are then capable of mathematical, statistical
treatment by use of the techniques of Boolean algebra, symbolic logic, Venn
diagrams and the digital computer for a more explicit, scientific study of
prognosis and of the therapeutic experiment. These, in brief, are the elements
of purely clinical judgment and work which transform the less explicit study
of patients by the clinician into clinical science.

From this point of view our subgroups represent a relatively groping attempt to define and describe the "universe" of the disorder presented to us. Although we were struck by some of the differences between patients seen, which the subgrouping represents, we did not account as clearly and sufficiently for the clinically obvious similarities by such a separation into distinct groups, except by the inclusion of all of them in the universe. Without apology for such lack of sophistication as suggested so recently by Feinstein, we submit our findings as we made them for whatever contribution they make toward such improved methods of the future.

Despite such deficiencies as these of our taxonomic efforts, nevertheless some steps toward the clinician's goal of study of prognosis are indicated in the differences in therapeutic outcome between our subgroups. We cannot of course attribute these differences in rates of improvement between the subgroups solely to the differences in clinical attributes of the patients or their families. Psychological therapy as used with the group called "treated" by psychiatrists in training and by the nursing personnel obviously was not a unitary or uniform influence either with all patients or even with the same patients from one year or two to the next phase during the period of work herewith surveyed.

In spite of this, of course, serious attempts to approach consistency and uniformity of therapeutic procedures have been continuous throughout this period. As an indication of this attempt, we wish to quote from a relatively recent formulation (8) of some basic principles underlying the work of especially the nurses by one of the senior psychiatrists of the staff.

Therapy Goals

"The staff's experience from continuous efforts to understand the needs of and to achieve an adequate psychotherapeutic program for psychotic inpatient children led them to place increased emphasis on several of their original assumptions. These include the following concepts.

1. The goals of every staff person need be to behave at all times in that precise manner which may:

    a. Help the child to reduce his disorder (i.e., his internalized conflict), however it manifests itself at a given moment or in a given activity.

    b. Provide opportunities for the child's development of more integrated behavior at whatever level is timely for his own particular maturational and emotional capacities.

2. The degree to which hospitalization of a psychotic child is a positive part of the psychotherapeutic program depends in large measure on the degree to which the nursing staff can achieve the above goals in the moment-

to-moment 24-hour care of the child. This is particularly true in the areas of the necessary daily activities of living such as rising, dressing, toileting, play, eating, going to bed, and sleeping.

3. The skill required by the nursing staff in the attainment of these goals must be based in knowledge and understanding of psychopathology, of childhood, and of the goals themselves and must encompass the ability to apply this knowledge and understanding effectively. It therefore includes the ability to make prompt, independent clinical judgments which are consistent with the psychiatrist's therapeutic aims in addition to the exercise of spontaneous intuitiveness and technical proficiency.

"As a result of continuous observation and reflection with the senior nurses, the senior psychiatrists formulated even more specifically their concepts as to the nature of the skill needed by the staff in this setting as follows:

1. Any destructive activity of the child, although symptomatic, requires firm, nonretaliatory, promptly protective restraint, which is gentle and continuously personal.

Further, this restraint needs to be so applied that it leads the child toward reduction of projected fears about his own sensual wishes for contact; in short, so that it leads to the child's greater relaxation, self-confidence, and trust in the staff.

2. Sensual self-gratifications of the child, which are not destructive and which often appear following restraint of the type described, need to be so understood that they will not be suppressed by any action of the staff.

3. Any of the child's regressive behavior, such as self-absorption and withdrawal, needs to be so understood that the staff will be able to remain attentively, but nonintrusively, available so long as the behavior contributes to the child's reduction of his anxiety, or, to help the child redirect his activity if and when it leads to mounting anxiety in himself.

4. Any of the child's own emerging spontaneity and interest needs to be so promptly recognized and attentively followed that timely but noncoercive encouragement may be offered.

5. Any of the child's efforts to learn and master skills of self-care or other satisfying activity needs such timely offer of help as is necessary to reduce self-frustration and to provide repetitive opportunities for achievement.

6. In addition, in all aspects of the work, each staff member needs to discriminate his own role in the child's experience so clearly that this in no way interferes with the child's relationship to his own parental persons, with the work of the individual psychotherapist of the child or parent, or with any other staff persons' contribution to the therapeutic environment. In other words, all this requires that kind of collaboration with other staff members

which can be described as an integration of the entire staff in the work toward a common therapeutic goal."

These general guiding principles for work with the child and with parents have been repeatedly discussed and repeatedly illustrated by specific daily events between child and nurse in ward rounds and in numerous other staff conferences over the years with nursing personnel, teachers, occupational therapists and such volunteers as may be working on the ward for short periods. More detailed descriptions of such work by nurses and other staff, efforts regarding the milieu and its integration, have been published (30). Similar illustrations of the work of the psychotherapists with the child and parents are the subject of other chapters in this volume. Much more recently some of the senior supervising nurses have undertaken a seminar review of behavioral therapy principles with some psychiatrists and an interested psychologist. The purpose of this seminar is to explore what specific procedures of this approach are, as some of us suspect, quite congruent in principle with those already elaborated in the work and illustrated above (31). The goal is to determine whether the work of nursing personnel might be further delineated and sharpened by these explorations.

Nonetheless, the core staff persisting in the total work throughout this period is well aware of changes, and of differences, in skill and effectiveness with patients not only in themselves, but also in the stream of trainees previously mentioned and perhaps more important in the fairly continuously changing nursing personnel. Nevertheless, the survey of results does express the general impressions of the core staff as to the prognostic differences among patients very probably related to differences between them in clinical attributes such as severity, very early onset, duration of disorder, presence or absence of organic factors, and so on.

It is difficult to compare our results of improvement with those of others such as Eisenberg (as quoted by Bettelheim (7)) and those of Bettelheim because it involves some uncertainty as to whether the criteria applied in each are quite similar. Without therefore assuming strict comparability in this respect to the reports of these others, it may be said that an overall improvement in 36.7% of the treatment group, including all seven subgroups, and an improvement in 48.78% of the combined core, borderline, and episodic subgroups (with the interesting differences of improvement between them), are at least an indication of support for the contentions of those like Bettelheim that 1) children with this disorder do not have a universally hopeless prognosis, and 2) the psychological approach is not ineffective with at least a certain fraction of them.

Time and funds were not available to make another interesting study; namely, later outcomes in all of the patients seen in therapy and those for whom staff time, hospital space, and at times lack of willingness of family, did not permit such an effort. A modified study of a portion of this group has been performed and is included in Chapter 15 of this volume.

SUMMARY

A group of 264 children with varying degrees of psychotic disorder were studied on the Children's Service of the Langley Porter Neuropsychiatric Institute in San Francisco from 1946 to 1961. An inventory of 93 items describing family history, developmental history, and clinical experience was devised and utilized to describe the sample as a whole, to compare the seven subgroups into which the sample was categorized, and to compare treatment response groups.

The increasing appearance of psychotic diagnoses in child psychiatry in the years 1946 to 1961 as seen in our own study and as recorded by other observers is noted and discussed in terms of an increasing clinical awareness, furthered by a growing literature of descriptive studies.

Ages of the children studied ranged from 11 months to 17 years. The overall sex ratio was that of a two to one predominance of male to female. More than 90% of the study population was Caucasian. Socioeconomic findings suggest that parents of our group consistently exceed the average of California population in income, occupation, and educational levels. The sample as a whole showed little evidence of organic pathology of any sort, 78% having no recorded organic problems.

The formulation of seven subgroups of psychotic disorder is presented, and each of these is further described in terms of an item analysis using the inventory of 93 items mentioned above.

1. The *core* group represents the typical "atypical" child where signs of arrested development appear in infancy, and the pathology is severe, pervasive, and almost incapacitating. Usually speech is absent or idiosyncratic. Learning is retarded in most areas, although sometimes there is specialized knowledge or skill in some solitary sphere. Generally the child attempts to isolate himself and avoid contact with others. Twenty-eight percent of the sample are represented in the core group. In about 59% of this group, onset is placed at one year or under. Fifty-five percent are mute. Occupational and academic level of the family is highest. Length of treatment is longest. Sex ratio is three to one, male to female.

2. The *borderline* group resembles the core group in nature of onset, but pathology is less severe. Twenty-one percent are in this group. Mutism is rare. Almost half of the group are able to attend school under special arrangements. Discrepancy between age at onset and age at application is high. Sex ratio is four males to one female.

3. The *episodic* group is distinguished from the core group by a late and acute onset. They represent 13% of the sample. The sex ratio is almost two to one, male to female. They spend the fewest hours in treatment, are the most responsive to it, and have overtly the most traumatic family histories or those most easily recognized as such.

4. The *"schizopath"* or hostile aggressive group represents only 7% of the sample. The ratio of male to female is highest, 84% male to 16% female. Fifty-eight percent are youngest children of their parents.

5. The *mixed* group includes children with both severe emotional disturbance and pathology of known organic nature. Seventeen percent of the sample are in this category. Sex ratio is almost one to one, 54% male to 45% female.

6. The *retardation?* group includes those children for whom a differential diagnosis of intellectual defect has not been possible to establish or to rule out. Although negatively defined, they represent eight percent of the total sample. Their sex ratio is the reverse of the rest of the sample, with a predominance of female, 60%. Forty percent are oldest children. Motility disturbances, major illnesses in the first year of life, and disturbed EEG's are common among them.

7. The *adolescent* group is defined in terms of onset at or after puberty. Six percent of the sample are found in this category. Onset tends to be acute. They reveal the least evidence of somatic pathology and the greatest number of somatic complaints. Their families are lower than the other groups in socioeconomic status. The sex ratio is about two males to one female.

Ratings of response to therapy were made for the group of 135 closed treatment cases, and on a group of 30 cases representing the extremes of response to therapy. Both these groups were studied for factors associated with improvement, using the 93 history, development, and clinical items. Only two items were found to be associated with improvement. Disturbed EEG's were associated with poor treatment response, and improvement was associated with the shortness of span between onset and application.

The seven subgroups varied significantly in response to therapy—of the episodic group, 63.6% were improved; of the borderline, 47%; of the core, 45.9%; of the mixed, 25%; schizopathic, 22.2%; adolescent, 22.2%; and retardation?, none were improved.

Considering the group as a whole, the improvement rate of those treated was 36.7%. Combining the core, borderline, and episodic groups, the treatment response was 48.78%. Combining the schizopathic, mixed, retardation?, and adolescent groups, the improvement rate was 18.5%. It thus appears that the isolated child, free from complicating secondary diagnostic problems, is the more responsive to a psychotherapeutic approach, particularly when onset is acute.

REFERENCES

1. BENDER, L. Childhood Schizophrenia. *Am. J. Orthopsychiat.*, 1947, 27, 68-79.
2. BENDER, L. Schizophrenia in Childhood: Its Recognition, Description and Treatment. *Am. J. Orthopsychiat.*, 1956, 26, 499-506.
3. BENDER, L. The Nature of Childhood Psychosis. In J. G. Howells (Ed.), *Modern Perspectives in International Child Psychiatry*. Edinburgh: Oliver and Boyd, 1956. Chapter XIII, Pp. 649-684.
4. BENDER, L. and GRUGETT, A. E. A Study of Certain Epidemiological Factors in a Group of Children with Childhood Schizophrenia. *Am. J. Orthopsychiat.*, 1956, 26, 131-145.
5. BERES, D. Ego Deviations and the Concept of Schizophrenia. *The Psychoanalytic Study of the Child II*. New York: International Universities Press, Inc., 1956.
6. BERGMAN, P. and ESCALONA, S. Unusual Sensitivities in Very Young Children. *The Psychoanalytic Study of the Child, III & IV*. New York: International Universities Press, Inc., 1949.
7. BETTELHEIM, B. *The Empty Fortress*. New York: The Free Press and London: Collier-MacMillan Ltd., 1967. P. 484.
8. BOATMAN, M. J., PAYNTER, J. and PARSONS, C. Nursing in Hospital Psychiatric Therapy for Psychotic Children. *Am. J. Orthopsychiat.*, 1962, 32(5), 810-811. Also in Langley Porter Child Psychiatry Series, Vol. 5.
9. BOATMAN, M. J. and SZUREK, S. A. A Clinical Study of Childhood Schizophrenia. In Don Jackson (Ed.), *The Etiology of Schizophrenia*. New York: Basic Books, Inc., 1960. Pp. 389-440.
10. DESPERT, J. L. Diagnostic Criteria of Schizophrenia in Children. *Am. J. Psychother.*, 1952, 6, 148-163.
11. EKSTEIN, R., BRYANT, K. and FRIEDMAN, S. W. Childhood Schizophrenia and Allied Conditions. In Leopold Bellak (Ed.), *Schizophrenia: A Review of the Syndrome*. New York: Logan Press, 1958. Pp. 555-693.
12. EKSTEIN, R. and WALLERSTEIN, J. Observations on the Psychotherapy of Borderline and Psychotic Children. *The Psychoanalytic Study of the Child, IX*. New York: International Universities Press, 1956.
13. FEINSTEIN, ALVAN R. *Clinical Judgment*. Baltimore: The Williams and Wilkins Company, 1967. P. 414.
14. FULLER, D. S. A Schizophrenic Pattern of Behavior in a Child with Brain Injury. *Bull. Menninger Clinic*, 1954, 18, 52-58.
15. HIRSCHBERG, J. C. and BRYANT, K. N. Problems in Differential Diagnosis of Children. *Assn. Research in Nervous and Mental Diseases*, 1954, 34, 343-361.
16. KANNER, L. Autistic Disturbances of Affective Contact. *Nerv. Child*, 1943, 2, 217-250.
17. KANNER, L. Early Infantile Autism. *Am. J. Psychiat.*, 1951, 108, 23-26.
18. KANNER, L. Early Infantile Autism. *J. Pediat.*, 1944, 25, 211-217.
19. KANNER, L. Feeblemindedness: Absolute Relative and Apparent. *Nerv. Child*, 1948, 7, 365-397.
20. KANNER, L. Problems of Nosology and Psychodynamics in Early Infantile Autism. *Am. J. Orthopsychiat.*, 1949, 19, 416-476.
21. MAHLER, M. S. On Child Psychosis and Schizophrenia, Autistic and Symbiotic Infantile Psychoses. *The Psychoanalytic Study of the Child, VII*. New York: International Universities Press, Inc., 1952.
22. MOSSE, H. L. The Misuse of the Diagnosis Childhood Schizophrenia. *Am. J. Psychiat.*, 1958, 114, 791-794.

23. RANK, B. and KAPLAN, S. A. Case of Pseudo-Schizophrenia in a Child. *Am. J. Orthopsychiat.*, 1951, 21, 155-181.

24. REED, J. H. and HAGAN, H. R. *Residential Treatment of Emotionally Disturbed Children: A Descriptive Study.* Langley Porter Clinic, Children's Inpatient Service. New York: Child Welfare League of America, Inc., 1952. Pp. 201-221.

25. RICHMOND, J. B., LIPTON, E. L. and STEINSCHNEIDER, A. Observations on Differences in Autonomic Nervous System Function between and within Individuals during Early Infancy. *J. Acad. Child Psychiat.*, 1962, 1, 83-91.

26. RIMLAND, B. *Infantile Autism.* New York: Meredith Publishing Company, 1964.

27. SANDER, L. W. Regulation and Organization in the Early Infant Caretaker System. In R. Robinson (Ed.), *Brain and Early Behavior.* London: Academic Press, 1969. Pp. 311-332.

28. SHAIN, R. J. and YANNET, H. Infantile Autism—An Analysis of 50 Cases. *J. of Pediatrics*, 1960, 57(4), 560-567.

29. SZUREK, S. A. Childhood Schizophrenia: Psychotic Episodes and Psychotic Maldevelopment. *Am. J. Orthopsychiat.*, 1956, 26, 519-534. Also in I. N. Berlin and S. A. Szurek (Eds.), *Learning and Its Disorder.* Vol. I, Langley Porter Child Psychiatry Series.

30. SZUREK, S. A., BERLIN, I. N. and BOATMAN, M. J. (Eds.). *Inpatient Care for the Psychotic Child.* Vol. V, Langley Porter Child Psychiatry Series. Palo Alto: Science and Behavior Books, 1971.

31. SZUREK, S. A. A Child Psychiatrist's Comments on Therapy of Schizophrenia. In S. A. Szurek, I. N. Berlin and M. J. Boatman (Eds.), *Inpatient Care for the Psychotic Child.* Langley Porter Child Psychiatry Series. Palo Alto: Science and Behavior Books, 1971.

32. SZUREK, S. A. Notes on the Genesis of Psychopathic Personality Traits. *Psychiatry*, 1942, 5, 1-6.

33. TREFFERT, D. A. The Epidemiology of Infantile Autism. *Archives of General Psychiatry*, 1970, 22(5), 431-438.

34. WING, J. K. *Early Childhood Autism: Clinical, Educational and Social Aspects.* New York: Pergamon Press Ltd., 1966.

APPENDIX

ADMISSION—DISCHARGE DATA

Name: IP No.:   OP No.:
Age: Birth Date: Sex: Race:
OP Admissions: IP Admissions:
OP Closings: IP Closings:
Total Time: City of Residence:
No. of Hrs.:   Total: No. of Therapists: Total:
     Child: Child:
     Mother: Mother:
     Father: Father:
Diagnosis:
Age at Onset:
First Symptoms:
Chief Complaints:
Nature of Onset:
Previous Diagnoses:
Previous RX:
School History:
Age and Sex of Siblings:
Others in Home:
Family Income Level:
Occupation of Father: Marital Status:
Occupation of Mother:
Year of Parents' Marriage:
Educational Level of Father:
Years Mother Employed: Educational Level of Mother:
Religion: Mother's Age:
Referred by: Father's Age:
Previous Placements: Other Marriages of Mother:
Factors Influencing IP-OP Decision: Other Marriages of Father:
Reason for Application Now:
Physical Illnesses, Accidents:
Accidents or Illnesses During RX:
Self-Destructive Tendencies:
Special Interests and Skills:
Major Family Trauma and Dates:
Events in Family During RX:
Reaction of Each Parent to Ward:
Known Precipitating Events:
Events Associated with Improvement:
Parental Explanation of Child's Difficulty:
EEG Findings:
Medical Investigations (Special):
Positive Medical Findings:
Mixed Diagnoses:
Reasons for Closing:
Condition on Closing:
Group:
Follow-up Data:

15

A Modified Follow-up Study of a Group of Psychotic Children

Jacqueline G. Etemad, M.D.
and
S. A. Szurek, M.D.

I. INTRODUCTION

This is a report of an effort to obtain some follow-up data on a number of the patients discussed in Chapter No. 14 of this volume entitled "A Statistical Study of a Group of Psychotic Children."

II. SELECTION OF SAMPLE

Due to limitations of time and staff, it was not possible to investigate the entire group of patients dealt with in the aforementioned earlier work. Because of an interest in testing the reliability of criteria used in the previous study to assess response to therapy, we chose from the original sample only those patients who had remained in treatment at this clinic; that is, those that were seen for 24 or more therapy sessions beyond the study visits and following the assignment of the family to staff psychotherapists. To follow those patients who were seen for brief evaluation only would be of considerable interest as an additional group for comparison with those who undertook therapeutic work with us, but will have to wait for a later effort.

We further limited our follow-up group to only those patients who had been classified in three of the seven subgroups, namely, the core, the borderline, or the episodic groups in the original study. The full definition of the criteria by which patients were classified into these groups, may be found in "A Statistical Study of a Group of Psychotic Children" (see Chapter 14). Briefly, the core, borderline and episodic patients taken together represented a group of preadolescent children whose illness was uncomplicated by any definable organic factors known to our staff or to consultants of the medical center at the time, or by probable mental deficiency or unusual hyperactivity. The borderline children differed from those in the core group as to severity of the disorder, while the episodic group differed in onset and in having a remitting and relapsing course. As indicated in our earlier report, children from these three subgroups appeared to be more responsive to psychotherapeutic efforts than children whose illness was complicated by organic factors or by mental deficiency. By these criteria, from the 264 patients discussed in the earlier report, we selected 105 for a follow-up effort.

III. METHOD

The follow-up undertaken in this study was a modified one dictated by the availability of time and staff. We began by reviewing our own clinic records, many of which contained requests for information from agencies, schools or therapists with whom our patients or their families had contact subsequent to termination of therapeutic work with us. Some records also contained letters from families or patients directed to members of the clinic staff. Following this review of records we wrote or telephoned agencies, schools and therapists referred to in our records or whenever possible approached families or patients directly in an effort to obtain current information. We also consulted current and former clinic staff members, some of whom had maintained contact with patients or their families. In many instances we did talk directly with patients or their families, but we did not have the time or facilities to establish such contact with all of them. Finally we reviewed State Hospital records of admissions and discharges.

By these means we were able to obtain current information on 22 of our patients. For another group of 68 patients we did not obtain current data, but did have *some* information about them in the period following termination of therapeutic work with us. For 15 patients, we found no data for the period after they left the clinic.

Following the device adopted by Eisenberg (7), we chose to designate a span of five years from a patient's first contact with the clinic to the last time information regarding him was obtainable by our methods as the minimum period for inclusion among the followed cases. There were 84 such patients among the 105 for whom follow-up was attempted, and these 84 formed the group for whom later outcome was determined by the methods outlined below. A graphic representation of our contact with a few patients may help to clarify further the method of sample selection.

TABLE 1
METHOD OF SAMPLE SELECTION

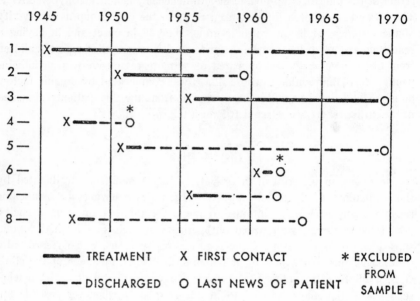

━━━━ TREATMENT   X FIRST CONTACT   * EXCLUDED
                                          FROM
━ ━ ━ DISCHARGED   O LAST NEWS OF PATIENT SAMPLE

IV. DETERMINATION OF OUTCOME

As we began to accumulate follow-up data, we observed a spectrum of outcomes which ranged from apparently successful adaptation as an independent adult at one extreme to what appeared likely to be permanent institutionalization at the other. After examination of the kind of data which were available, we defined criteria for assignment to each of four outcome groups. The criteria fell into two general areas: 1) Amount of time spent in an institution following termination of therapeutic work with us including whether such institutionalization came early or late in the follow-up period; and 2) presence or absence of certain achievements in clearly defined areas of living which seemed indicative of different levels of functioning. We recognize that assignment to categories represents only an *estimate* of functioning, and is less reliable than it might be if direct study of patients had been possible. However, it should be remembered that the range of outcomes is very broad so that even the grossest distinctions can be of some usefulness. Robins (9) has rightly questioned the use of hospitalization per se as a criterion for outcome. In the case of psychotic children, however, based on our experience with children who have come to us from a custodial care program as well as on subsequent contact with patients who move to such settings from our program it is our impression that custodial hospitalization represents a gross failure in adaptation and is associated with a poor prognosis.

V. CRITERIA FOR ASSIGNMENT TO OUTCOME GROUPS

1. Class I
   a.) To the best of our knowledge the patient had *not* been hospitalized since discharge from our treatment program. Hospitalization here refers to a custodial care facility whether for mentally ill or mentally retarded, and not to an intensive treatment program; and
   b.) The patient demonstrated at least *one* criterion of independent functioning. The criteria for this independent functioning were:
      1) Gainfully employed at time of last contact,
      2) Marriage concluded since discharge from our program,
      3) Military service completed or under way,
      4) Performing in regular school setting at a level commensurate with age.
2. Class II
   a.) The patient had been hospitalized *less than half* the time since discharge and was *not* hospitalized at the time of contact for this follow-up; and
   b.) The patient demonstrated one of the criteria under 1. a.) above, or one or more of the following criteria of productive or self-satisfying activity. These criteria were:
      1) Participating in sheltered workshop or other vocational rehabilitation program,
      2) Engaged regularly in hobby such as reading, model building, collecting, etc.,
      3) Involved in structured social or recreational activity program,
      4) Enrolled in special class in school.
3. Class III
   a.) The patient had been hospitalized *less than half* the time since discharge from our program but was hospitalized at the time of contact for this follow-up; and
   b.) The patient demonstrated *none* of the criteria of independent, productive or self-satisfying activity listed above.
4. Class IV
   The patient had been hospitalized *more than half* the time since discharge from our treatment program.

VI. CLINICAL EXAMPLES

The following vignettes describe one patient from each of the four outcome groups.

The selection of patients for description here was made primarily on the basis of the amount of information available to us, particularly for the follow-up period. This information is in each instance less complete than we would like it to be. In particular, we note a paucity of information about early events which might give us a clearer picture of precipitating stresses as well as data regarding the presence or absence of integrative capacities in the parents which may in part account for differences in outcome. It is here we feel most keenly the handicaps of a retrospective study.

As it happens, each of the patients described is from the core group. Thus we regret a comparison among subgroups is not possible. The reader will note also that these four patients illustrate not only a spectrum of later outcomes but also demonstrate a variety in terms of presenting symptoms, nature and timing of environmental stresses, intensity of treatment and degree of success in therapeutic engagement of patient and family. Any comparisons of these four patients with one another should therefore be made only in light of the obvious differences among them.

> *Class I Outcome:* A reserved, defensive and emotionally isolated couple, Arnold's parents described themselves as having no problems. Arnold had seemed "normal" throughout his infancy but according to the parents responded apathetically to any attention. However, his mother's conflict about her own responsiveness was also manifest as she said, "I wanted to breast feed but didn't because in those days you were a 'schmo' if you did." Much later in therapy she recalled Arnold nuzzling at her breast when she still had milk and became tearful as she remembered pushing him away. (This patient exemplifies our recurrent clinical experience that parents may recall very little that is out of the ordinary in their child's early development at the time the initial history is taken. Later, after some period of psychotherapy, the parent may begin to recall emotion laden events which were at first inaccessible to recollection. The reader is referred to Chapter 12 of this volume for further elaboration of this point.) During Arnold's infancy his father was involved in his work and had little to do with his son except to question whether his wife was doing all she could to encourage the boy's development.
>
> Arnold's motor development was normal, but speech was always meager. At the age of one year he muttered an indistinct "mama" and "dada" only with much urging from his parents. Even after he was two and a half years of age, speech was limited to a few isolated words and phrases. From the time Arnold was three his parents made a series of efforts to "find an answer" to their son's difficulties. This included a two-year placement in a school for the deaf. By the age of seven, however, organic impairment and mental deficiency had been ruled out, and Arnold had been given a diagnosis of Childhood Schizophrenia at another Medical Center.
>
> Arnold came to us as a tall, thin, frightened-looking eight year old. He did not appear to look at people or hear what was said to him. He sat in a chair, grinning and rocking back and forth repeatedly touching

his eyelids with the small fingers of each hand. He could communicate his wants through gestures or by pushing or pulling adults, but he spoke only rare isolated words and these were difficult to understand. When we failed to grasp his wishes and carry them out, he stamped, screamed, wept and slapped his head or other parts of his body. He showed interest in toys and puzzles and was rated better than average on performance items of psychological tests.

With considerable reluctance and apprehensiveness, Arnold's parents accepted our offer of an inpatient treatment program for Arnold which included their own participation in psychotherapy. Despite their misgivings the parents made good use of their therapy time. Over three and a half years Arnold's speech developed to a nearly age-appropriate level. His preoccupation with rocking and other isolative behavior nearly vanished, and he began to manifest a voracious interest in learning, particularly about electricity, space and the universe. He remained very restricted in the ability to express his feelings directly to others but was able progressively to confine to his therapy sessions elaborate fantasies about "gas" people who preyed on human beings.

At the age of twelve, by mutual agreement of parents and therapists, Arnold moved from the ward to a public school setting while he and his parents continued in outpatient treatment. The following year, however, he was placed in a class with a teacher who was less permissive of his frequent questions and restless movement about the classroom. When this movement was prohibited, he became disruptive and was excluded from school. With no school placement and tensions high at home, the decision was made to place Arnold in a residential treatment center where he spent the subsequent year. He returned home at fourteen and was able to adjust to a regular school. After he left this setting he had no further psychotherapy at Langley Porter Neuropsychiatric Institute. At eighteen he still had not completed the regular high school curriculum, so he continued part-time until he received his diploma at the age of twenty.

One of our staff described Arnold at 19 as a tall, slender youth with a noticeably tense rigidity to his posture and a tight, strained smile. His movements were a little jerky as though he was forever unsure whether to approach or to move away.

Arnold's mother reports by letter that at 23 Arnold has few social contacts. She considers his ideas on religion somewhat peculiar, such as his interest in finding a means of communing directly with God. However, she says, he continues to do well working full-time as an electronics technician, a position he has held for two and one-half years. He owns his own car and pays room and board to his parents with whom he still lives.

Class II Outcome: Barry was conceived in the early weeks of his parents' somewhat shaky marriage. Tensions mounted as Barry's father failed to find work and mother suspected he was seeing another woman. Frequent disagreements ended in mother's withdrawing temporarily to a locked room ignoring husband and infant. A large placid baby who demanded and received little attention, Barry developed normally except that speech failed to appear on schedule. As a toddler he was exceptionally fearful and protested vigorously any change in routine such as the failure of his favorite TV program to appear on Saturday. When he did begin to speak after the age of four or five, it was an anxious, insistent, repetitive whisper which has persisted over the years of our work with him. Barry rarely showed anger, but at times had tantrums of such severity he kicked holes in the walls. At other times he was slyly destructive, stuffing objects in the furnace or, undetected, breaking the light at the back of the stove.

Barry was diagnosed as mentally retarded until we saw him at the age of eight and were able to document for the first time his age-appropriate skill with puzzles and his phenomenal memory. During his years of therapy he could always recall the names, whereabouts and tenure at this clinic of every therapist he ever had—thirteen in all.

During a brief evaluation period on our inpatient ward, Barry's face was a tense mask—a perpetual, worried frown. He asked endless questions, the answers to which he already knew. He rarely looked anyone in the eye, moving restlessly from place to place and object to object with a facial expression many staff members described as a leer. His lack of involvement with other adults contrasted with his bullying of his mother and sullen submission to his father's dominance.

Barry moved into outpatient therapy, the only program in which staff time was available. This program included individual sessions with each parent with the later addition of regular family meetings. During such meetings Barry fidgeted, fiddled or whispered to himself. Barry's parents demonstrated again and again how consistently they underrated Barry's abilities and acted on these expectations. Over the years our staff, trainees and ultimately to some extent Barry's parents came to realize how frequently his capabilities were hidden by his fearful manner and cryptic, telescoped speech. Gradually a program of activities outside the home was developed. Full academic participation was never achieved, but both recreation and vocational rehabilitation activities were progressively expanded. At 16 Barry became separated from his parents at the clinic one day, and much to their amazement, proceeded home alone on the bus making two transfers along the way. This display of independence paved the way for summers at a camp for the handicapped and gave him the freedom to move about town.

Now at 21, in his thirteenth year of therapy with us, Barry works 20 hours a week packaging small items in a permanent, sheltered employment situation with fifty other handicapped adults. He goes to and from work alone and has never been tardy. Two evenings a week he bowls, dances, or goes to movies with his age-mates at a recreation center for the handicapped. Last year he was president of the center's youth group. He likes popular music and has a record collection paid for out of his own earnings.

Barry still approaches our staff members with insistent whispered questions, "What is your name? What is my name? Is my name Barry?" He still wears his worried frown. However, his current therapist reports that in recent family meetings when his parents are talking calmly and seriously, his face relaxes and he listens.

Class III Outcome: Charles was the product of an unwanted fifth pregnancy, during and after which his mother had for the first time in her life recurrent "hysterical screaming fits" which required sedation. He was a robust infant who was able to suck his thumb even in the early weeks of life. Determined to do her best for him, his mother added her own internal demands to the advice of a well-meaning physician. Using various mechanical devices, she denied Charles the use of his hands from two months until nearly two years of age; she did this to prevent the thumbsucking which she feared would both deform his mouth and entice him into a world of self-gratification from which he would never return.

When we first saw him at three, Charles appeared unable to use his hands and still held them as though they were in restraining cuffs. Though motorically well developed, his only vocalization was repetitive humming of tunes he had heard on the radio. His mother was ashamed of her failure thus far to "break him to the toilet." Following a brief evaluation the family broke contact with us for reasons that were not entirely clear, returning two years later and at that time accepting an offer of inpatient treatment for Charles. Despite persistent efforts on the part of staff then and over the ensuing years, the parents' commitment to their own therapy remained tenuous.

Charles' seven years on our ward are remembered by the staff with a combination of warmth and sadness. He seemed to want physical contact but was afraid of it. He moved slowly and with reluctance towards the accomplishment of some small goal only to destroy what he had achieved as soon as his gain was acknowledged. In early years, he was preoccupied with collecting and destroying magazines or with endless knotting and winding of string, the intricacy and symmetry of which belied any suspicion of subnormal intelligence. In seven years he spoke no more than a few isolated words. The last year, with persistent effort on the part of staff and therapist, Charles showed a somewhat greater interest in human contact; arousing staff hopefulness about him; but by this time Charles was outgrowing our ward program—a program which because of limitations in physical plant and staff time is better suited to smaller, preadolescent children. Thus at 12 Charles moved to an outpatient treatment program. His parents, however, soon elected to discontinue their work with us.

They returned· seven years later with a request for dental services. At 19 Charles was bigger, heavier, perhaps, but otherwise little changed. He sat between his parents rocking and grimacing, looking frequently and fixedly at his hands. As a dental examination was discussed, he grunted and moaned and once reached out to his mother in a beseeching gesture. But he handled the actual examination with ease as his mother held his hand and reassured him it would not hurt.

The parents described Charles as gentle and tractable at home as long as his routine was not disturbed. In most instances when upset he could be calmed by assurances that nothing unusual would be asked of him. They said he feeds and dresses himself, watches TV or roams about the house. He still collects magazines and plays with string. The parents conveyed the impression that if they don't bother Charles, he doesn't bother them. They expressed an interest in exploring the possibility of some outside activities for Charles as well as in making arrangements for regular medical and dental care. However, at this time they did not follow through on efforts to obtain such services even though they were potentially or actually available in their community. Charles' parents expect him to remain at home with them indefinitely.

Class IV Outcome: Donald was described by his parents as a sweet, if somewhat quiet, infant until nine months of age when he witnessed the electrocution of his three year old brother on a heater in their playroom. Thereafter he seemed quieter still, and from 13 months on, following the birth of his sister, he was virtually silent, often sitting for long periods staring at objects or listening to the radio. Seen at our clinic when nearly five, he reacted to separation from his parents by flailing his arms and moving in a circular fashion. He brought toys and other objects to his mouth one by one and then discarded them. Communicative speech was limited to a few single words and phrases. For the most part he ignored people, averting his gaze and staring at the wall. Psychological testing at that time could not rule out deficiency, but subsequent test results were characteristically those of a child with normal intelligence, whose poor performance on standardized tests is a result of severe emotional disturbance.

During the course of outpatient therapy Donald began to respond to any overtures of his therapist or of other adults by spitting and smearing saliva on them. He often laughed hysterically when his therapist spoke of her serious concern about this behavior. Never very deeply involved in their own therapy, Donald's parents elected to discontinue their own therapeutic work with us when Donald was 8½. Their decision to leave coincided with their therapists' departure from the clinic. It was hoped Donald could attend a public school class for the mentally retarded. At the last interview he was quiet—no laughter, no spitting; and he accepted an affectionate hug of farewell, shook hands and said "good-bye."

Ten years later a member of our psychiatric staff happened on Donald during a visit to a state hospital. This staff member wrote: "Now in his eighth year of hospitalization, Donald is a husky and well-developed 19 year old of moderate height. He sits in his chair in a most frightened manner, tense and rigid. He has many squirming, ritualistic movements of his fingers. Often times his eyes flutter. He answers most questions with a brief, curt 'fine.' His voice is high-pitched and squealing. On command of the ward aide, he can sing a song in its entirety. His responses seem to be somewhat mechanical.

"The ward aide stated that Donald is episodically a management problem. He compulsively and openly masturbates, and when this is prevented by having him wear tight coveralls, he beats himself severely or bangs his head against the wall. He also spits at patients and ward personnel. His family visits him every month and takes him out overnight."

TABLE 2

COMPOSITION OF SAMPLE

Age First Seen (in years)

	Mean	Median	Range
Core	6.0	6	2-17
Borderline	8.1	8	3-14
Episodic	6.9	6	3-12
Total	6.7	6	2-17

Duration of Treatment (years)

	Mean	Median	Range
Core	5.6	5.0	2-10
Borderline	3.3	2.0	3-8
Episodic	7.0	2.5	2½-20
Total	4.9	4.0	2-20

Time Span of Contact (years)

	Mean	Median	Range
Core	12.6	12	5-23
Borderline	11.9	12	5-23
Episodic	13.1	13	5-18
Total	12.4	12	5-23

Age at Last Contact (years)

	Mean	Median	Range
Core	18.5	18	10-34
Borderline	20.1	20	11-33
Episodic	20.0	21	11-26
Total	19.2	19	10-34

VII.   COMPOSITION OF THE SAMPLE

Of the 84 patients in the follow-up group, 62 or 74% were males and 22 or 26% were females, a ratio of almost 3 to 1. Seventy-five or 89% were Caucasian; 4 or 4.8% were black; 2 were Oriental; and 3 were not classified as to race. Forty-six or 56% had been designated "core group" in the earlier report. Twenty-six or 31.8% were "borderline" and 10 or 12.2% were "episodic." The average age of these 84 patients when first seen at this clinic was 6.7 years (median 6 years) ranging from two years to 17. They remained in treatment with us for an average of four years (median 3 years), ranging from two years to 20 years. The span of time from first contact until our last report of them averaged 12 years, ranging from 5 years to 23 years. The age of the patients at our last contact averaged 19.2 years, ranging from 10 to 34 years.

VIII.   OUTCOME OF THE GROUP AS A WHOLE AND BY SUBGROUPS

Figure 1 shows outcomes for the groups as a whole. Of the 84 patients in the follow-up group 24 or 28.6% achieved an outcome rating of I., 20 or

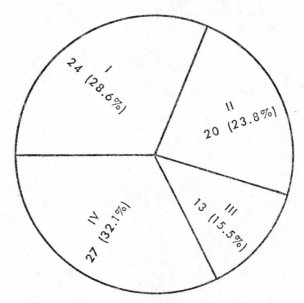

FIGURE 1.

LATER OUTCOME FOR
84 PSYCHOTIC CHILDREN

23.8% were rated II, 13 or 15.5% were rated III, and 27 or 32.1% were rated IV.

We were interested in comparing outcomes for the three diagnostic sub-groups—core, borderline and episodic. Figure 2 shows later outcome for each subgroup.

Of the 47 *core* children in the follow-up group, 9 or 19.1% were assigned to Class I, 8 or 17.1% were rated II, 9 or 19.1% were rated III and 21 or 44.7% were rated IV.

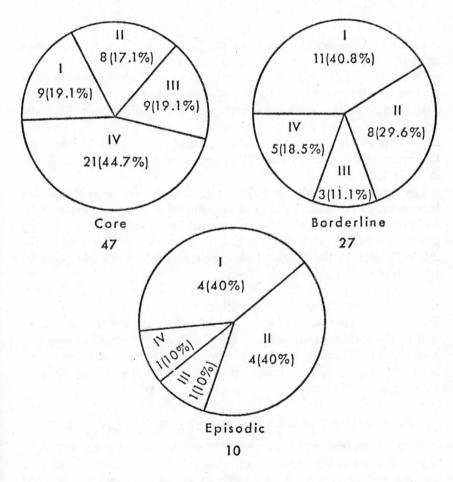

FIGURE 2

LATER OUTCOME BY SUBGROUP

TABLE 3

Diagnostic Subgroup vs. Outcome

	Core		Borderline & Episodic		Total
Class I & II	17	(36.2%)	27	(73%)	44
Class III & IV	30	(63.8%)	10	(27%)	40
Total	47	(100%)	37	(100%)	84

$x^2 = 9.8143$ df $= 1$ p $= .01$

Of the 27 *borderline* children 11 or 40.8% were rated I, 8 or 29.6% were rated III, 3 or 11.1% were rated III and 5 or 18.5% were rated IV.

Of the 10 episodic children 4 or 40% were rated I, 4 or 40% were rated II, 1 or 10% was rated III and 1 or 10% was rated IV.

It is apparent that outcomes were better for the borderline and episodic groups in comparison with the core group. In order to test the statistical significance of this difference, we combined I and II outcomes and contrasted that group with combined III and IV outcomes for the three groups as shown in Table 3.

The outcomes for borderline and episodic children were better than would be expected on the basis of chance when compared with the group as a whole, while outcomes for core children were poorer than would be expected when compared with the group as a whole. The difference was significant at the .01 level; that is, the likelihood that such a distribution would occur on the basis of chance is one in a hundred.

These results parallel the response to treatment as rated at time of discharge which was reported for these three groups in our earlier study and lend support to our clinical impression that within the group of preadolescent psychotic children without evidence of deficiency or organic impairment, a subgroup which we have designated core can be identified and that assignment to this subclassification may have relevance for prognosis, particularly with our modes of therapy.

IX.   COMPARISON OF LATER OUTCOME WITH RESPONSE TO THERAPY

We were also interested in comparing later outcome with response to therapy as assessed in our earlier report. Figure 3 shows a comparison of later outcome with response to therapy. Sixty of our 84 children had been rated previously as to treatment response at time of discharge. The other 24 children were still in therapy at the time of our previous study, and thus were

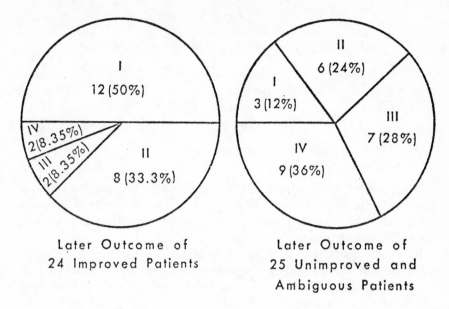

Later Outcome of
24 Improved Patients

Later Outcome of
25 Unimproved and
Ambiguous Patients

FIGURE 3

LATER OUTCOME COMPARED
WITH RESPONSE TO THERAPY

excluded from the ratings. For another eleven patients less than five years had elapsed from time of discharge to time of follow-up, and these we excluded as well. For the remaining 49 patients we compared response to therapy as rated at the time of discharge and later outcome as determined in this follow-up study.

Of these 49 patients 24 or nearly half had been rated improved, twenty or 40.7% were rated unimproved, and 5 or 10.2% were rated as ambiguous. Of the 24 improved children, 12 or 50% had a Class I outcome, 8 or 33.3% had a Class II outcome, and two each or 8.35% had a Class III or Class IV outcome.

Of the 25 children rated other than improved, 3 (or 12%) had a Class I outcome, 6 (or 24%) had a Class II outcome, 7 (or 28%) had a Class III outcome and 9 (or 36%) had a Class IV outcome.

It is clear that the group reported as improved in therapy has fared better in terms of the post-therapeutic follow-up data on outcome. Again for a test of statistical significance we have combined Class I and Class II versus Class III and Class IV outcome groups as shown in Table 4.

TABLE 4

Treatment Response vs. Later Outcome

	Improved		Unimproved & Ambiguous		Total
Class I & II	20	(83.3%)	9	(36%)	29
Class III & IV	4	(16.7%)	16	(64%)	20
Total	24	(100%)	25	(100%)	49

$x^2 = 9.4816$ $df = 1$ $p = .01$

Outcomes for improved children are significantly better than would be expected on the basis of chance for the group as a whole. Similarly, outcomes for the children other than improved were poorer than for the group as a whole. Significance was at the .01 level.

In an additional refinement of improvement ratings, our earlier report made note of the 15 children most improved and the 15 children least improved as rated by a group of senior staff psychiatrists, the psychology and social service department staff and the nurse in charge of nursing training. Figure 4 shows the later outcome of the children so rated.

It happened that all 15 of the "most improved" children were rated as to later outcome in the present study. Nine or 60% had a Class I outcome. Three or 20% had a Class II outcome. One or 6 2/3% 'had a Class III outcome and 2 or 13 1/3% had a Class IV outcome.

It happens that only 9 of the "least improved" children happen to have been rated as to later outcome. Three or one-third attained a Class III outcome. Four or two-thirds attained a Class IV outcome.

Though numbers are too small for a test of significance, when outcome is compared with the extremes of treatment response, the correlation is striking. In fact, none of the "least improved" children attained a Class I or II outcome.

This correlation between response to treatment and later outcome may be cautiously regarded as an indication that there can be lasting benefits from our form of therapy. However, one must also consider the possibility that responsiveness to treatment is in itself indicative of a lesser severity of disorder for which a better outcome might be predicted.

Conclusions that might be drawn from this relationship of treatment response and outcome are further complicated by the lack of uniformity in our treatment program. Some of our patients, the outpatients, were seen only once a week; others, the inpatients, were involved in an intensive program of milieu therapy, psychotherapy, and education for most of their waking hours.

FIGURE 4

LATER OUTCOME COMPARED
WITH FINE IMPROVEMENT RATING

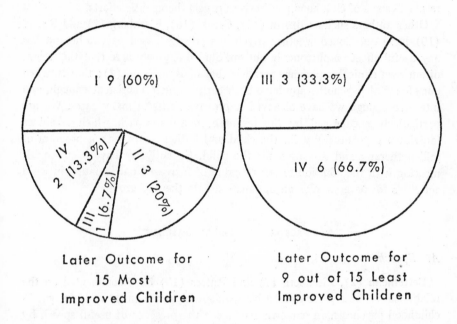

Later Outcome for
15 Most
Improved Children

Later Outcome for
9 out of 15 Least
Improved Children

Some were seen by trainees, others by experienced clinical staff. All were exposed in varying degrees to a lack of continuity of staff including nurses, teachers and psychotherapists.

One may ask why there should be a number of children who responded very well to our treatment efforts and yet attained a Class III or IV outcome later on, while on the other hand, some children rated unimproved ultimately achieved a Class I or II outcome. One possible explanation has to do with the duration of our experience with the patients. Of the 14 patients for whom treatment response and later outcome differed, 8 had been in treatment for a year or less. Perhaps with psychotic children a year is scarcely enough time either to assess accurately responsiveness to treatment or to begin to effect the kind of change which will make for lasting improvement.

In addition, the course of some patients following discontinuance of our therapeutic efforts is not well known to us. We know that at least two who were rated unimproved and later achieved a good outcome continued in psychotherapy elsewhere for many years after they left our program.

We regret it has been impossible for this study to review a group of untreated children with whom to compare those in our treated group. A follow-up of those who were seen for evaluation only would be useful in this connection and may be the subject of a later effort.

It is beyond the scope of this report to go extensively into the question of responsiveness of childhood psychosis to psychotherapeutic efforts.

Other authors such as Brown (14), Creak (16), Eisenberg (7) and Rutter (10) have questioned whether psychoanalytically based psychotherapy has any useful effect on outcome in autism. Suffice it to say here that the weight of our own clinical experience parallels that of Bettelheim (2); that is, when our efforts at psychotherapy have been early enough, consistent enough, and intensive enough we have observed impressive shifts in many cases. We are particularly encouraged by the response to an approach which combines individual psychotherapy for the child and both parents with a program of milieu therapy and education for the child. Recently we have been experimenting with the addition to our program of increased participation in ward activities for parents, plus an optional parents therapy group.

X.   FACTORS RELATED TO OUTCOME

A. *Speech*

Bettelheim (2), Eisenberg (7) and Rutter (10) have commented on the relationship that appears to exist between speech development and outcome in childhood psychosis. In our own experience the presence of useful speech by the age of five does bear a positive relationship to prognosis. Our results are shown in Figure 5 and indicate that for the 64 speaking children, 23 or 35.9% had a Class I outcome, 17 or 26.6% had a Class II outcome, 6 or 9.4% had a Class III outcome and 18 or 28.1% had a Class IV outcome.

Of the 20 mute children in our sample, only 1 or 5% had a Class I outcome, 3 or 15% had a Class II outcome, 7 or 35% had a Class III outcome and 9 or 45% had a Class IV outcome.

Comparing the Class I and II outcomes with Class III and IV outcomes, we find a difference from that expected on the basis of chance which is significant at the .01 level as shown in Table 5.

The numbers of mute children in the borderline and episodic groups are too small for meaningful comparison among the diagnostic subgroups. As reported in Chapter 14 mutism was much more frequent in the core group.

This comparison of "mute" and "speaking" children is only a beginning effort on our part. We are interested in exploring further the abnormalities of language development which are observed in psychotic children and in

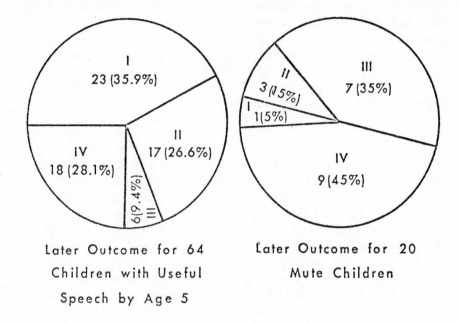

Later Outcome for 64
Children with Useful
Speech by Age 5

Later Outcome for 20
Mute Children

FIGURE 5

SPEECH DEVELOPMENT AND LATER OUTCOME

TABLE 5

SPEECH DEVELOPMENT VS. LATER OUTCOME

	Speaking		Mute		Total
Class I & II	40	(62.7%)	4	(20%)	44
Class III & IV	24	(37.3%)	16	(80%)	40
Total	64	(100%)	20	(100%)	84

$x^2 = 9.3964$ $df = 1$ $p = .01$

pinpointing more precisely the relationship of the various manifestations of mutism to prognosis. In particular we note the fact that there were a *few* mute children who improved during therapy and later achieved a "good" outcome. In closer study of such patients there might be clues as to why the gross symptom of mutism, or some degree of it, was not in these instances a poor prognostic sign. Or one might learn what more, and when, could be done to reduce the usually poor prognosis of mute children. This investigation is discussed in Chapter 16 of this volume.

B.   IQ Scores

Recently Rutter (10) has reviewed the experience with autistic children at Maudsley Hospital and has reported a relationship of measured intelligence both to later educational attainment and later social adjustment. We hope at some point to review our own psychological test results in relation to later outcome. Even without such a review, our general experience would indicate that children who remain essentially untestable in several efforts at psychological evaluation are ones with a poorer eventual outcome. Similarly it seems clear that children who perform at or near an age appropriate level on psychological tests are often though not always ones with a better outcome. It seems to us less likely that IQ scores as currently obtained would be regularly predictive of the finer shadings of later outcomes. We base this notion on our impression of the relative imprecision of IQ scores especially for a group which presents such difficulties to testing as autistic children do.

Rutter does not give us detailed information on how his IQ scores were obtained though he implies that many children had IQ estimates based on performance items alone. It is not clear whether the children had one testing session or more. In our own work it has frequently been more productive for children to have several sessions with the same examiner. However, it is difficult to relate results of such an assessment with a single trial of testing. The more one deviates from a standardized format, the greater the problems of comparing scores from one individual to another.

It is possible that a single trial of a performance test such as a formboard could give a clue to eventual outcome. Such an evaluation might be as much a test of negativism as of intelligence. Our examiners have often commented on the frequency with which autistic children will do consistently and precisely the opposite of that which is asked of them. In such cases the wrong response clearly requires as much if not more intelligence than the right one.

It is our impression that the depth of negativism in autistic children is a fine indicator of severity of the disorder as well as a major problem in therapy. (One of the most important signs of progress in our therapeutic work with a child is the at times imperceptible reduction in the child's use of oppositional behavior.) A method of evaluating negativism would no doubt have relevance for prognosis; however, just how much can be inferred from results of an early and perhaps isolated test result remains to be more conclusively demonstrated.

In general we feel that the relationship of IQ scores and prognosis in childhood psychosis is not clearly understood and is certainly worthy of further exploration with all due attention to the complexities involved.

C. Other Factors

Based on our own earlier work we had anticipated that a better outcome might be associated with shortness of time span between age of onset and age at application to our clinic. (This time period may reflect to some extent the degree of denial used in the family—a factor which appears to have some relevance to ability to engage in therapeutic efforts.) Taking the group who had no psychiatric contact prior to coming to us we compared outcome with time span between onset and application to us (where such information was available). We found that those patients who sought help from us sooner tended to have a better outcome, but that the results were not statistically significant.

Similarly we felt that a prior diagnosis of mental deficiency or organic brain dysfunction might be associated with a poorer outcome. Here again the results were suggestive of a relationship, but for this small group of patients were not statistically significant.

In the same fashion we looked for a relationship between our later outcome results and each of the following variables: Age of Onset, Age of Application, Duration of Treatment (years), Intensity of Treatment (years divided by hours per week), Number of Overt Stresses Reported, Number of "Precipitating Events Reported," Number of Symptom Categories Reported, and Frequency of Treatment Transfer. In no case were statistically significant results obtained. It is our expectation, however, that our clinical hunches may be borne out when we are able to combine variables into symptom patterns which will then have prognostic significance. Such work is beyond the scope of our present effort. However, our division of patients into diagnostic subclassifications represents a first and not a wholly satisfactory step in this direction.

XI. OTHER STUDIES OF OUTCOME IN CHILDHOOD PSYCHOSIS

Eisenberg (7), Bettelheim (2), Bender (1), Creak (6) and Rutter (11) have reported long term follow-ups of psychotic children some or all of whom were given the designation "autistic." The common diagnostic criteria used

new Kanner

by all these authors are those of Kanner's original description as restated by
Eisenberg (7), i.e. 1) extreme *self isolation* present in the first year of life
and 2) *obsessive insistence on the preservation of sameness.* These criteria
are applicable to many of the psychotic children we see, particularly those in
the core and borderline group.

Other authors have stressed the separation of autism from the other psychotic disorders of childhood, whether like Kanner and Eisenberg they view it
as "one of the group of schizophrenias," or like Rimland (8) as an entirely
separate disease entity. Our own view has been, and still is, that there is a
spectrum of psychotic disorders of childhood varying in time of onset, duration, severity of symptomatic expression and in presence or absence of such
complicating features as organic central nervous system pathology, mental
deficiency, physical or neurological handicaps. Some of our initial efforts
to develop a subclassification of the childhood psychoses have been discussed earlier.

In this follow-up of psychotic children we have chosen to exclude those
patients for whom there is a strong presumption of either primary mental
defect or organic brain dysfunction and those with a later onset of the disorder. These same exclusions are implied or stated by all the above authors.
Thus it appears that the children they describe are in many ways similar to
those in our own follow-up group. Whether these children also resemble our
group in regard to severity of the disorder is not possible to answer with the
information available. Comparison among the various studies is complicated
by differences in information provided about outcome by each of the authors.
With the exception of Eisenberg and Bettelheim, no two authors have used
the same criteria for assignment to outcome categories. It had been our
intention to pattern our outcome groups after those of Eisenberg and Bettelheim. However, we soon found it necessary to fashion our own categories in
accordance with the spectrum of outcomes *we* observed and the kinds of data
available to *us.*

Bearing in mind all these qualifications, if we chose the best outcome
group for each study, we observed the following:

1. Eisenberg reports a "good" outcome for three out of 64 patients or 5%.
2. Bender describes 5 or 10% of 50 patients who are functioning as
   independent adults.
3. Creak reports that 17 out of 100 patients had improved to the level
   of age appropriate adults.
4. Rutter indicates that 11 out of 63 or 17% of the Maudsley group did
   not require supervision.
5. Our own Class I group comprises 24 of 84 patients or about 29%.

TABLE 6

COMPARISON OF FOLLOW-UP STUDIES

Study	Total Sample	Best Outcome Group Number	%
Eisenberg	64	3	5%
Bender	50	5	10%
Creak	100	17	17%
Rutter	63	11	17%
Langley Porter	84	24	29%
Bettelheim	40	17	42%

6. And finally, Bettelheim reports that 17 or 42% of a group of 40 children had a "good" outcome which implies as it does for Eisenberg a nearly normal level of functioning.

These results are summaried in Table 6.

It is of interest to note that Bettelheim's group had to the best of our knowledge the most intensive long term psychoanalytically oriented treatment program of any of the groups studied. Our outcomes, which fall between those of Bettelheim and the other authors, are of course for a group of children all of whom were in treatment though of varying duration and intensity. We note that the figures are consistent with the possibility of a relationship between psychotherapy and outcome. *But note p. 367*

XII. SUGGESTIONS FOR FURTHER WORK

Fully recognizing the limitations imposed on this study by its retrospective nature as well as by lack of staff time, we are hopeful that future work from this center can incorporate many of the approaches to clinical inquiry as research which are reviewed by Szurek and Philips (12) in their discussion of Alvan Feinstein's book, *Clinical Judgment.* One approach we are already exploring is an effort to improve interobserver reliability in description and classification of symptom patterns by the use of audio-visual aids for the recording of behavioral sequences. These sequences can then be examined by members of the staff who seek in discussion together to attain agreement regarding clinical findings. From such study of evanescent behavioral events it should be possible to begin to name and classify certain characteristics of behavior by a consensus of the study group. Ratings of the severity of each such named, agreed upon, observed phenomenon can also be achieved by repeated study. The constellations of these phenomena as observed with respect to individual children can then form a clearer basis for assignment to diagnostic subgroups.

Another approach already under way in our setting is the direct study of younger and younger psychotic children—sometimes before the age of three. Our hope is that with closer proximity to the events surrounding the onset of the disorder the reliability with which events, symptoms and other clinical variables are recorded will be enhanced.

A third approach is in the direction of finding ways to recover more fully anamnestic data from parents regarding early development of their psychotic children. It has been our clinical experience that parents are able to recall more early developmental data and more of the affect associated with events after they have had a period of psychotherapy. Thus we have been returning to parents for additional history taking sessions in subsequent years of treatment. We are also endeavoring to acquaint our staff and trainees more fully with the skills of psychotherapeutically oriented history taking. (See Chapter 17.)

When these three approaches can be combined in a prospective study of patients some of whom receive psychotherapy and others of whom do not, and when comparisons before and after therapeutic maneuvers are more precise, it may be possible to approach more accurately the question of treatability and prognosis in the childhood psychoses. But at the very least, the accumulation of such data will add greatly to our knowledge of the spectrum of childhood psychoses and the natural history of the disorder.

XIII. SUMMARY

We have reported here results of a modified follow-up study of 84 psychotic children, designated core, borderline and episodic in our own classification of diagnostic sub-groups of childhood psychosis. These children were seen at the Langley Porter Neuropsychiatric Institute Children's Service between 1946 and 1961 and continued in treatment with us for at least 24 psychotherapy sessions beyond the initial outpatient evaluation. All of them were children about whom we have been able to obtain some data spanning at least five years from the family's first contact with the clinic to the last available information about the patient. We have defined four classes of outcome based on 1) timing and amount of hospitalization subsequent to termination of therapeutic work with us, and 2) presence or absence of certain achievements in clearly defined areas of living which seemed indicative of different levels of functioning. We have presented clinical vignettes to illustrate each of the four outcome groups.

We found that 24 or 28.6% of our 84 patients attained a Class I outcome;

20 or 23.8% obtained a Class II outcome; 13 or 15.5% attained a Class III outcome and 27 or 32.1% a Class IV outcome. The mean time from first contact to time of follow-up was 12.4 years.

We have noted differences in outcome for the three of our seven diagnostic subgroups which lend some support to our clinical impression that these groupings have prognostic significance. We have reported a statistically significant correlation between later outcomes and results of an earlier study of response to treatment in our setting which had included 60 of the patients from our follow-up group.

We have reviewed some earlier follow-up reports of psychotic children and discussed some difficulties in the way of accurate comparisons of our data with those of other authors.

REFERENCES

1. BENDER, L. "The Life Course of Schizophrenic Children." *Biol. Psychiat.*, 2 (1970) : 165
2. BETTELHEIM, B. *The Empty Fortress*. New York: The Free Press, 1967.
3. BOMBERG, D., SZUREK, S. A., and ETEMAD, J. G. "A Statistical Study of a Group of Psychotic Children." Chapter No. 14 of this volume.
4. BROWN, J. L. "Prognosis from Presenting Symptoms of Pre-school Children with Atypical Development." *Amer. J. Orthopsychiat.*, 30 (1960) : 382-390.
5. CREAK, M. "Juvenile Psychosis and Mental Deficiency." Edited by B. W. Richards. *Proceedings London Conference of Scientific Studies of Mental Deficiency*, Vol. II. Dagenham, May & Baker, 1962.
6. CREAK, M. "Childhood Psychosis: A Review of 100 Cases." *Brit. J. Psychiat.*, 109 (1963b) : 84-89.
7. EISENBERG, L. "The Autistic Child in Adolescence." *Am. J. Psychiat.*, 112 (1956) : 607.
8. RIMLAND, BERNARD. *Infantile Autism: The Syndrome and Its Implications for a Neural Theory of Behavior*. New York: Appleton-Century-Crofts, 1964.
9. ROBINS, A. J. "Prognostic Studies in Mental Disorder." *Am. J. Psychiat.*, 111 (1954) : 434.
10. RUTTER, M., GREENFELD, D., and LOCKYER, L. "A Five to Fifteen Year Follow-Up Study of Infantile Psychosis. II. Social and Behavioral Outcome." *Brit. J. Psychiat.*, 113 (1967) : 1183-1199.
11. RUTTER, M. "Autistic Children, Infancy to Adulthood." *Seminars in Psychiat.*, 2 (1970) : 435.
12. SZUREK, S. A. and PHILIPS, I. "Clinical Work and Clinical Research—A Scientific Inquiry: Five Conceptual Barriers to Clinical Science." Chapter No. 13 of this volume.
13. WALKER, J. F. and SZUREK, S. A. "Early Childhood Development of Psychotic Children: A Study of Anamnestic Methods." Chapter No. 17 of this volume.

16

Mutism among Psychotic Children

Jacqueline G. Etemad, M.D.
and
S. A. Szurek, M.D.

Jacqueline G. Etemad, M.D.
and
S. A. Szurek, M.D.

INTRODUCTION

Mutism, or the failure to speak, is one of the abnormalities of vocal behavior frequently characteristic of the symptomatology of childhood psychosis (15, 32). In our review of 264 psychotic children seen on the Langley Porter Neuropsychiatric Institute Children's Service between 1946 and 1961 we noted that 80, or 30%, were totally mute or showed a marked paucity of verbal expression relative to expected age norms when first seen. (See Chapter 14.)

Earlier work by Eisenberg (8) and Bettelheim (2) has indicated that an inverse relationship exists between the symptom of mutism and outcome in childhood psychosis. In our own follow-up study of 84 children (see Chapter 14) we also observed that children who used speech with fluency and with what seemed to be direct communicative intent by the age of five had on the average a better outcome on follow-up.

In this chapter we wish to explore some further questions regarding the symptom of mutism in the childhood psychoses. What does it mean to say that a child is mute? What is the role of age in the question of reversal of mutism? What can be learned from psychological tests administered to the mute child? What is known from the study of others' writings or in part gleaned from our own experience that might be speculatively formulated as one or more hypotheses regarding the genesis of mutism? What can be proposed as to possibly effective therapeutic approaches to the mute child? Is there a possible basis for a subclassification of mute children which

372

might have relevance for prognosis? These are some of the questions to which this chapter is addressed.

In our discussion we refer to a further review of records and other available information regarding 52 of the 84 mute children from the study group of 264 psychotic children referred to in Chapter 14. These 52 patients were ones who continued with us in therapy for one to twelve years beyond the initial evaluation. We also base our discussion on our general experience with more than 350 psychotic children evaluated at Langley Porter Neuropsychiatric Institute since the inception of our program in 1946. Some of the descriptive material refers to children who are currently with us.

Our principal hypothesis at the outset and to date is that mutism among psychotic children who do not show definitive signs of severe genetically determined intellectual defect, prenatal, natal, and postnatal cerebral injury due to malnutrition, viral disease or anoxia during birth, may be an outgrowth of early malintegrative life experiences, particularly with the mothering figure. Our discussion will thus reflect an emphasis on possible psychogenic factors in the genesis of mutism.

Part I. Toward a Definition of Mutism

To say a child is mute is to indicate that he does not speak. This failure to speak, however, might rest on an unwillingness to speak, as is presumed to be the case in elective mutism (5), or on a postulated inability to speak. If we refer to inability, we may further distinguish between those who possess language but lack the capacity for expressive use of language through speech and those whose failure to speak rests on a relative or absolute failure of the development of language itself. To clarify this point, an attempt to draw a distinction between the terms "language" and "speech" is in order.

According to Lenneberg "there is something distinct from speaking which we may call language—and which takes shape very early in life" (16). The presence of language is not detected directly but primarily as it is reflected in actual acts of speaking or hearing—the encoding and decoding of speech—which McNeill, following Chomsky, has termed *performance* (20). Secondarily, language may also be reflected through derivative behaviors of reading and writing as well as through body language, facial expressions or other behaviors which serve to express the individual's cognitive abilities and feeling reactions to events. If these behaviors are understood, communication occurs. In this view speech is but one aspect of linguistic performance. As distinct from this performance, McNeil and Chomsky refer to *competence*, which is the knowledge of syntax, meaning and sound that makes performance possible. This notion of competence seems close to what Lenneberg terms "language."

Current thinking in the field of linguistics suggests that language, as distinct from speech, is not learned as was formerly believed (22), but is rather an innate capacity which develops ontogenetically in the course of neurophysiological maturation (18). Maturation brings cognitive processes to a stage of language readiness which uniformly proceeds to actualization of latent language structure in an environment where spoken language is used. The linguistic input from the environment forms the raw materials which are assimilated and restructured into a form that is unique for each individual in terms of its finest detail but which resonates with the language (or languages) experienced in the environment.

According to Lenneberg (18) the acquisition of language is relatively uninfluenced by environmental factors and proceeds regularly for each individual according to a predictable time schedule. He refers, for example, to the period of rapid increase in vocabulary in the first half of the third year of life. "This 'naming explosion' is only one of the extraordinary activities which mark the coming of language. . . . As far as we know it occurs at about the same age in every healthy child throughout the world" (17).

Speech, on the other hand, is a vocal means for conveying or receiving the verbal messages which constitute the outward expression of language. Normally speech develops in a parallel fashion with language, though language competence at each stage exceeds actual performance by a considerable margin. In the absence of language acquisition, there can be no development of speech. However, language acquisition can occur in some instances in the absence of speech development (11).

In the course of discussing mutism among psychotic children we will want to explore to whatever extent is possible with the information at hand whether (and when) we are dealing with a deficiency in language competence, language performance alone, or some combination of the two.

Part II. Age as a Factor in the Reversal of Mutism

Because of references in the literature to an association between duration of mutism, i.e. up to age five years, and eventual prognosis, we wish to explore our own data about the question of how late reversal of mutism may occur.

First, on theoretical grounds, just how high might we expect the upper age limit for development of language and speech to be? Lenneberg (18) discusses the evidence for what he terms a "critical phase" in language development extending from about age two up to the age of puberty. He notes that after puberty accents appear and persist when a new language is learned. In his review of experience with victims of aphasia due to unilateral cerebral lesions acquired in childhood vs. adulthood, he states that children recovered fully when their aphasia was acquired somewhat before the age of puberty. After puberty there was an increasing residue of language disability, and while aphasic adults showed some recovery of function, there was no evidence of new acquisition of language skills.

Although aphasic children apparently may continue the process of language acquisition until puberty, they must start the process somewhat earlier to allow for the amount of time necessary to complete the process, particularly if at a slower than normal rate. In this connection Lenneberg has described how mongoloid children continue to improve language skills into their teens and then stop, still deficient, presumably because with a slower rate of acquisition the end of what he terms the critical period of "language readiness" has come too soon for full acquisition of language.

Another influential factor appears to be the age at which the language acquisition process is begun. Congenitally deaf children show persistent deficits in language skills if deprived of linguistic input before school age, while the outlook for children with acquired deafness is progressively better the longer they have been previously exposed to linguistic input (14).

Where reversal of mutism refers to acquisition of language as opposed to learning of speech, the concept of "critical phase" may well apply with puberty serving as a theoretical upper limit. However, experience with persistent disabilities among deaf children suggests the possibility of a lower practical limit for the full acquisition of language skills, perhaps as early as school age or even earlier.

Turning to the question of speech development, we know that language may be acquired well in advance of speech (11, 18), but we do not know how late speech alone can be acquired. It is possible that speech development is similar to the establishment of an unused or inhibited motor capacity which is dependent on practice. Such a task may increase in difficulty with age, perhaps in slowly accelerating linear fashion, but there may be as yet no defined theoretical upper limit of age as is suggested for language acquisition.

Table 1 summarizes the improvement in speech noted among our 52 mute children compared with age at application to us for services. Age at application is taken as an indicator of how late the onset of speech was delayed. More pertinent might be the age at which the children began to acquire directly communicative speech, but due to lack of time to locate and fully review old records this information was not always readily available to us. (If it had been possible we would also have liked to report on the number of our child patients where the anamnestic data revealed that varying amounts of speech did appear before the age of five and then ceased suddenly or more gradually during periods of increased stress within the family.)

For def. (very germans) see 381

TABLE 1

IMPROVEMENT IN SPEECH COMPARED WITH AGE AT APPLICATION
FOR 52 MUTE CHILDREN WHO HAD THERAPY

A. FIVE AND UNDER

Age at Application	Became Fully Communicative	Spoke Short Sentences and Phrases	Acquired More Words	No Change	Total
Under 2 years	1	—	—	—	1
Under 4 years	5	—	1	4	10
Under 3 years	1	—	1	1	3
Under 5 years	1	3	1	8	13
Total 5 and under	8	3	3	13	27

B. OVER FIVE

Age at Application	Became Fully Communicative	Spoke Short Sentences and Phrases	Acquired More Words	No Change	Total
Under 6 years	4	—	2	4	10
Under 7 years	1	2	—	4	7
Under 8 years	3	—	1	—	4
Under 9 years	—	—	1	1	2
Under 10 years	—	—	1	1	2
Total over 5	8	2	5	10	25

TABLE 2

ACQUISITION OF SPEECH BY MUTE CHILDREN COMPARING CHILDREN WHO
BEGAN THERAPY BEFORE FIVE WITH THOSE WHO BEGAN AFTER FIVE

Began Therapy	Became Fully Communicative	Did not Become Communicative
Before Five	8	19
After Five	8	17

X^2 .0324   1 d/f   p greater than .98

If we compare the number who showed marked improvement in speech when therapy began before five with those for whom therapy began after five, we find that a chi square test supports the hypothesis that there is no statistically significant difference between these two groups. (See Table 2.)

Prior to collating these figures we had thought it likely that the younger children would have acquired speech with greater frequency. We assumed so first because we had included in our mute group all children who used virtually no speech when first seen regardless of their age at that time. Even though the severity of their disturbance suggested otherwise, we considered the possibility that some of these children might fall on the late side of the normal range of distribution of time for onset of speech. If so, there could be a few in this younger group who might be expected to develop speech spontaneously in the course of further maturational development.

Second, the literature regarding mutism and prognosis suggested a greater difficulty of speech and language acquisition after the age of five. It was not possible for this study to evaluate in detail the depth of disorder in the children of these two groups to see to what degree they were comparable. We do know, however, that our diagnostic subcategories, which in some ways reflect severity, were about equally represented in each age group. (See Chapter 14 for a discussion of diagnostic subcategories.)

The fact remains that in our therapeutic setting 32% of the mute children admitted after five did acquire fully and directly communicative speech as compared to 29% among the younger group. Thus our experience goes along with the theoretical discussions reviewed above suggesting that at least speech and perhaps also some degree of language competence may be acquired past the age of five.

The findings that nearly one-third of mute children admitted past the age of five did develop speech deserves some emphasis, for we have heard other professionals, parents, and even our own less experienced staff, make the assumption that work with a mute child past his fifth birthday is a hopeless and essentially useless undertaking. Our experience indicates such is not always the case. The child described in Chapter 30 is one case in point. This is not to say that the task is not likely to be easier if one begins earlier. But when we are dealing with individuals rather than statistics, it is only in those instances where staff, parents and even the patient himself have put forth their best efforts, given all the limitations imposed by reality, that we are likely to know what progress might possibly be made.

Part III. Psychological Test Findings

We turn now to results of initial psychological testing and what light they may shed on the question of which mute children acquire fully and directly communicative speech.

Rutter has suggested that the I.Q. score of the psychotic child is an important prognostic indicator (26). He found a correlation of .80 between initial and follow-up I.Q. scores and noted that recovery was rare among children who tested below 50. Eisenberg subsequently agreed with Rutter that "the observation of presence or absence of useful speech at age five as a predictor of outcome may have been largely due to the high correlation between absence of speech and low intelligence" (9).

We have discussed previously some problems in interpretation of I.Q.

scores obtained in testing psychotic children. (See Chapter 15.) Since that work was done we have reviewed the test results of our own mute group.* We must state at the outset that our test results do not lend themselves to interpretation in terms of I.Q. scores. It is no doubt a reflection of the severity of disorder in our group as a whole that only five out of the 42 children for whom test results were available could be assigned an I.Q. score based on completion of even the performance items of a standardized test. For the rest the psychologists have given us an estimate of intelligence based on what portions of tests the children did complete or on observations of the children's behavior. A review of the psychologists' reports led to our setting up the following categories for results:

A. *Average Intelligence or Above:* Children who obtained valid I.Q. scores in the average or better range based on performance items.

B. *Probably Average Intelligence:* Children who completed portions of tests at the average level but not a sufficient proportion of the subtests to assign a valid score.

C. *Possibly Average Intelligence:* Children who did not respond to test materials but whose behavior suggested average capacity in puzzle solving, mechanical skills, etc. Among these were included children who did consistently the opposite of what was asked.

D. *Probably Below Average Intelligence:* Children who performed below average level on the portions of the test material they completed.

E. *Definitely Below Average Intelligence:* Children whose performance was rather even at a below average level.

F. *Cannot Estimate:* Children whose response to test items and general behavior gave no clear basis for a guess as to intelligence.

The results of initial psychological examination of 42 mute children are summarized in Table 3 and compared with subsequent speech development.

We note that 12 out of the 14 children who acquired fully and directly communicative speech did give some indication of average or better potential. With regard, however, to the children who did poorly on testing, we note that the two categories of "possibly average" and "cannot estimate," which we are designating the "untestable" groups, account for 17 of the 28 children who did not acquire speech. (See Table 4.)

An absolute probability figure for this distribution is .0096; i.e., the chances are less than one in a hundred that such results would occur by chance.

Even though only two out of 19 "untestable" children acquired speech, many of these children gave an impression of intelligence. Sometimes their

---

* At the time of this review some records had been transferred to a central storage area of the state and either lost or destroyed. Thus test results were recoverable on only 42 children.

TABLE 3

INITIAL I.Q. SCORES COMPARED WITH LATER SPEECH DEVELOPMENT
FOR 42 MUTE PSYCHOTIC CHILDREN

Test Results	Became Fully Communicative	Did Not Become Fully Communicative	Total
A. Average	3	2	5
B. Probably Average	7	2	9
C. Possibly Average	2	10	12
D. Probably Below Average	2	6	8
E. Below Average	—	1	1
F. Cannot Estimate	—	7	7
Totals	14	28	42

TABLE 4

COMPARISON OF "TESTABLE" VS. "UNTESTABLE" CHILDREN

	Became Fully Communicative	Did Not Become Fully Communicative	Total
"Testable" (A,B,D,E)	12	11	23
"Untestable" (C,F)	2	17	19
Totals	14	28	42

performance seemed expressive of the conflict about showing what they knew. For example, a five year old girl doing a form board "paused for a moment with the round block over the round hole . . . it seemed as if she were much tempted to put it in but was overcome by a sudden fear. She finally set several pieces beside the appropriate holes and seemed to lose interest in them."

To be sure these "untestable" children may have a poor outlook as regards acquisition of fully communicative speech, but we wonder if their low scores are properly equated with "low intelligence."

It may be that negativism, or a greater propensity for oppositional behavior, is the prognostically important characteristic which shows up on testing of those psychotic children who are not defective in intelligence. A method which assessed more accurately and comprehensively the depth and fixity of negativism among these children might be a most useful prognostic indicator. It is possible that efforts to correlate psychological test behavior with carefully recorded segments of behavior in other areas of the child's program could be productive in further elucidating and classifying this phenomenon of negativism.

In summary, our findings indicate that results of psychological testing may be a useful prognostic indicator, not just as a measurement of "intelligence," but as a recorded sample of behavior the characteristics of which may bear some relationship to outcome. We should emphasize, however, that in our experience test results among psychotic children are most sensitive to influences known to be factors in outcome of testing. In particular, number of testing sessions (which may reduce anxiety about the relatively strange examiner) and personality and experience of the tester seem strongly to influence results. In our setting where children were given ample and repeated opportunity (some for as many as 10 testing sessions) to show what they would and could do, most of the individuals who later acquired speech gave some clue to this capacity on initial testing. We would be hesitant, however, to place great prognostic weight on the results of testing where the setting, the child's reaction to the efforts of the examiner and other circumstances in the child's life at the time of testing were not well known to us.

Thus, the ability *plus* willingness of a child to demonstrate average or better capacity in the psychological test situation appears to be a useful prognostic sign at least as regards subsequent speech development. The meaning of a poor showing on such an examination is less clear but may be predictive of a poor outlook.

Part IV.   Therapy for the Mute Child

Let us look first at the changes noted in the area of speech for our group of 52 mute children. Of the 52, 16 or 30.8% were described as fully and directly communicative at the time of ending their work with us.* Five or 9.6% had progressed to the point of using phrases or short sentences for purposes of direct communication. Eight or 15.4% used more words for direct communication than at time of admission, while 22 or 44.2% showed no change. These results are summarized in Table 5.

Since we have no control group of untreated mute patients we cannot draw the conclusion as a scientifically warranted statement that our efforts

---

* We use the term "direct communication" here to refer to that use of speech which to the clinical observer is clearly expressive of wishes, observations, memory of past events, reasoning and of subjective affective states. Much of the speech used by our children is not readily understandable except to one who has begun to know the individual child well enough to recognize what is being conveyed. To our minds the speech of psychotic children along with every other aspect of their behavior is expressive even if not apparently intentionally communicative. It is only the clarity, directness of ease of comprehensibility which may be a matter of doubt to the observer.

I.e. a very very generous definition!

TABLE 5

IMPROVEMENT IN SPEECH AMONG MUTE CHILDREN DURING OR AFTER THERAPY

	Number	Percent
Fully Communicative Speech	16	30.8%
Phrases or Short Sentences	5	9.6%
More Words	8	15.4%
No Change	23	44.2%
Total	52	100.0%

brought about the observed improvement in speech. A look, however, at what is known about the possible sources of mutism may lend some support to what we think is probable, namely, that in many instances our approach has been a factor in the improvement noted.

According to Lenneberg all that is required for language acquisition is a state of "language readiness," which is a function of neurophysiological maturation, an environment where vocal language is used and an intact hearing apparatus (18). He does not mention the role of the mother-child relationship as a factor in language development. However, according to Morley, speech habits are responsive to environmental influence presumably including interpersonal relationships (21).

For Piaget the assimilation of auditory experience and its combination with vocal patterns represents one aspect of the maturation and/or development of sensorimotor intelligence (12). He refers to the role of the mother as a model and provider of corrective feedback, but without reference to the nature of the mother-child relationship.

Psychoanalytic writers have tended to focus more on the role of mother-child interaction. Freud and Burlingham stress the importance of the opportunity for emotional interplay with the mother. They postulate an urge of the child toward expression and communication with the loved person—a pleasure based on object relationship (13). Escalona discusses the importance to the child of being responded to by the parent as if he had communicated (10). Spitz has emphasized the role of frustration and defensive maneuvers of identification with the aggressor as factors in development of communication (28, 29).

Experimental evidence regarding the role of social interaction in language development comes from studies of institutionalized infants (23). It has been suggested that retardation of speech and language development in such settings may be due to deprivation of sensory input rather than to a lack of certain psychological experiences (6). However, Rheingold's observation that infant babbling can be increased or decreased by social responsiveness or unresponsiveness of the adult to the child's social initiatives (i.e. of smiling, babbling, crying, following, cuddling the child in response to a hands up gesture as a sign to be picked up) focuses attention on the roles of both quantity, or frequency and quality of interpersonal experience (25). The extent to which the deficits in institutionalized children are reversible has also been the subject of discussion (18). With regard to the role of the infant, Wolff has emphasized the importance of its state (i.e. hungry, sleepy, etc.) as a modifying factor in the outcome of interpersonal transactions beginning as early as the third week of life (34). Recently Ainsworth has observed active avoidance of adults by infants who were not responded to, suggesting the possibility of the infants' participation in a cycle of avoidance (1).

Bowlby has brought together the literature of psychoanalysis, control theory and ethology placing emphasis on the essential role of attachment (4). (See also Chapter 12 in this volume.) He suggests that attachment behavior by mother and infant which has the *goal* for each of maintaining within limits the proximity of the other, has the *consequence* of providing a relationship of sufficient predictability, duration and intensity for the normal sequences of maturation and development to be traversed. A failure of attachment whether due to absence of a figure or unsuitability (i.e. in the sense of an unresponsive or conflicted motherliness) of available figures may be a deficiency factor in both general cognitive and linguistic development (4).

This concept has interesting similarities to that of Bettelheim who suggests that what is crucial for development of "an autonomous self" is the infant's recognition of his capacity to influence his surroundings (2). Such recognition may well have its beginning in the living, developing partnership provided by his relationship to his mother.

Even this cursory review may give some indication why we find support for the notion that the mother-child tie possibly plays an essential part in language acquisition and more surely in the development of speech.

We have discussed elsewhere our views regarding the role of psychotherapy in the childhood psychoses (30, 31), and have noted the sequence of conflict reduction and resolution leading to the possibility of satisfying transactions with adults first and later with playmates. As regards the reversal of mutism, what we see as an essential feature of our work is the opportunity provided for the child to establish a trusting relationship usually with one staff member first, be it therapist, nurse or teacher. In the context of such a relationship speech seems to develop as a byproduct rather than as an end in itself. Growing out of the pleasure of their association, child and adult may collaborate in interesting new endeavors such as the discovery of the pleasures of sound-making or the fascination of finding new ways to communicate. We suspect that this process is similar to the one mother and infant participate in during the normal course of language and speech development.

Our experience with a nine year old girl in her fifth year of work with us is a case in point. This girl spoke rare single words from her first year onward but remained essentially mute until nearly nine. Excerpts from her teacher's description of their work together follow.* This work, of course, represents but one aspect of a total therapeutic program each portion of which has played its part in the progress noted.

"The mouth play that we have been doing began last fall when I would come to the ward both in the afternoon and before 'share and tell' in the mornings. I would sit on her bed with her and begin with teasing her and making her laugh by making weird sounds with my mouth and throat. I let her touch my face. I then put her hands in my mouth, covered my lips with her hand, and placed her hands to feel my throat. This was a means for me to get to know her better outside of the group activities and it was something both of us enjoyed and looked forward to. During this mouth play she would repeat single words after me. Then my humming and singing rhythms were imitated. Often our class time this year consists of my following her leads, her models in mouth play. Now the humming has a definite syllabic rhythmic quality.

"We have a warm, trusting relationship and often engage in conversations. For instance, during one session in March in which she had been saying many words, she was very relaxed and attentive; I asked her when she was going to let the plug out, meaning—when was she going to let the words flow. She looked at me, doubled her fist, sucked in her lips, hit her mouth and then hit my mouth very hard. I told her that hurt. She looked up and then laughed. I asked if she was giving me the plug, but there was no response. In our conversation in class the next day, I asked her again about the plug and she clenched her fist, but this time very gently touched my mouth with her fist, and I asked her if she was giving me the plug and she nodded.

"Last week, after a fifty minute session of intense babbling, humming and mouth play, I asked if I could keep the plug for good because I felt that she didn't need it any more, and she looked at me and said 'keep, keep' and then cuddled."

At nine this child still lacks fully and directly communicative use of speech. In the past year, however, she has begun to try to communicate with words. Before all her efforts seemed directed toward avoidance of such communication. Academically, except for speech and writing skills, she performs at third

---

* We are grateful to Miss Virginia Abts for permission to use this clinical description of her work.

grade level. After years of isolated rocking on her bed, she now participates, for the most part readily, in ward activities, especially the academic program. Her self-care skills, which had been less impaired, are age appropriate.

It seems probable to us that the teacher's patient, dedicated work with this child coupled with similar efforts of many other staff members over the years have begun to show results in the area of speech for this particular child. Further, we know historically and from direct observation something of the demandingness, ambivalence and anxious tension which have characterized the mother of this child in all transactions between them regarding the issue of verbal communication. We find it reasonable to conclude that the relative lack of these elements in the relationship of the child and her teacher is a crucial factor in the beginning appearance of directly communicative speech.

Regarding the parental role Filippi and Rousey have described neurotic children whose delay in speaking seemed connected with the nature of their relationship to their parents (11). In these children of "angry uncommunicative mothers" receptive language seemed to develop normally, while expressive use of language was delayed in onset. Speech seemed to begin its appearance at the point where the intensity of a conflictful interaction with parental figures was diluted by other interpersonal relationships, often around school age. Other case reports in the literature make reference to difficulties within and between the parents of mute psychotic children (2, 33).

When we review our own experience with the varying factors of parental conflicts in the genesis of mutism, we remember two children. One boy's mother took it for granted that he would talk but was fearful regarding her ability to toilet train him. This child talked before one year, but his mother continued to wipe him after bowel movements until he was nineteen. The mother of another boy, who remained mute past the age of five, revealed in her own therapy a persistent fear of talking lest she use a malapropism, while the boy's father remained silent in therapy for fear of sounding foolish. Another example of the role of parental conflicts and their resolution with mutism and recovery may be found in Chapter 30 of this volume.

Our general conclusion regarding the genesis of mutism based on our experience and our review of pertinent literature is that the nature of earliest transactions with significant adults (i.e. the child's experience with mother's response to such early social initiatives as tracking mother's movements with the eyes or responding to her voice with cessation of distressed crying, babbling, etc. (4)) is of the utmost significance for the later development of verbal communicative skills. Further, the delayed development of recovery of such skills probably occurs in the context of a relationship which recapitulates the same conflictful transactions from the child's viewpoint but with a person less conflicted than the parent toward a different conclusion in the child's experience and resulting behavior. In this context the child can experience some reduction of disorder, a part of which is some possibility of development in the area of speech.

Part V. A Possible Subclassification of Mutism

As we have indicated earlier, the presence of verbal communicative skills is evidence for the presence of "language." The absence of such skills, however, does not rule out the possibility that "language" is present. As Lenneberg observes "some children with psychoses . . . give excellent demonstrations of subclinical language development. There are children who fail to communicate with the world around them including their own parents and who give an impression of muteness and incomprehension from their second year of life on. Yet in response to treatment, or even spontaneously, some . . . begin to talk fluently and in accordance with their age level" (19).

In our own experience with psychotic children we have observed many evidences for some degree of language development. If comprehension can be taken as evidence of having acquired language, then most, if not all of our children, do show language development. The fact that the mute psychotic child may comprehend a good deal is often obscured by what seems to the observer to be an unwillingness or perhaps fear of letting it be known that he understands. On longer acquaintance with these children one can begin to comprehend the delayed, distorted or telescoped behavioral responses to linguistic input, much as one eventually begins to understand the unusual verbal productions of the psychotic child who speaks.

Sometimes the messages are not difficult to decipher. One five year old mute child roused from her usual state of almost totally silent self absorption and avoidance of any interpersonal transaction to strike her nurse while exclaiming distinctly, "no!" At that instant the nurse had casually mentioned to a colleague that she was planning to apply for advanced training at a nearby college.

Other evidences for language development among mute children include acquisition of reading and writing skills. One ten year old boy was able to read and write at the sixth grade level without using any speech save an occasional expletive. He later began to speak stutteringly in his early teens. Another girl, now 10, who is inhibited both in vocal expression and in the use of her hands, exhibits third grade mathematics and reading skills through use of a teaching machine.

Like Lenneberg we have also observed children whose occasional efforts at speech suggested prior years of language development. It is difficult to account otherwise for the rapid progress made by the boy described in Chapter 30.

Others seem even to have practiced speech, perhaps subvocally. Recently a ten year old boy, whose prior utterances were so garbled as to defy comprehension, has said complete and clear sentences such as, "I'm a good boy really.", "I don't like it that way." and "I don't want to go out now."

On the other hand, there are children who have given little if any clue to a developing language capacity even while showing marked shifts in general clinical status as indicated by reduced number of temper tantrums, decreased social isolation and increased self care skills. One such girl in her most relaxed and contented moments begins to babble in the fashion of an infant of under a year. In spite of considerable progress, her academic skills remain preverbal.

These various observations plus our review of the literature on speech and language has led us to consider a subclassification of mutism based on a separation of speech vs. language disorder. The following are two examples intended to represent the extremes of a spectrum of clinical presentations:

Let us consider first children like many we have known who do well on performance tests, who show some acquisition of academic skills prior to the onset of speech, who begin to speak late in the first decade, whose development of speech is particularly rapid and who in beginning to speak fail to exhibit the usual stages of language acquisition traversed by the young child as described by McNeill (20). Such children seemed to demonstrate a relatively high degree of linguistic competence. Filippi and Rousey have suggested a neurotic mechanism to account for delay in the onset of speech (11). Perhaps our linguistically competent psychotic child resembles or even represents the extreme in severity of the children they describe. Our experiences of success in reversal of mutism in children over five may come from this group of linguistically competent children. Also the finding of better outcome in regard to speech associated with better performance on psychological tests may be related. That is, the children with better cognitive function, which may show up on testing, may also have acquired a higher degree of linguistic competence (associated perhaps with less severe, negativistic unresponsiveness in their disorder).

Such children may be contrasted with others in our memory whose general improvement was not accompanied by evidence of much increase in language skills and whose verbal productions resembled the vocalizations of infancy, yet whose behavior at times reflected a complexity of reasoning processes seemingly incompatible with simply deficient intelligence. Perhaps these latter children are relatively deficient in the area of language acquisition.

For further evidence in this regard we must turn for a moment to the group of psychotic children who do speak. Here we see a whole spectrum of linguistic distortions such as have been described by Provenost and by Cunningham and Dixon (24, 7). Bosch in his monograph on infantile autism has not only described the spoken language of autistic children but has suggested ways that deviations from normal language patterns may be explained in terms of the way the autistic child experiences the world around him (3). More recently Wolff and Chess as well as Fish and Shapiro have made efforts to quantify the speech abnormalities observed among psychotic children and have related these findings to clinical severity of the disorder (35, 27).

Parenthetically, among the psychotic children who do speak, there are those whose speech seems clearly expressive of the disorder, i.e., of intensely conflicted motivation about responding to questions. A very good example is quoted by Bettelheim from Kanner's original paper of 1943 and the implications of this datum are thoroughly discussed by him. For reasons of space, only the quotation from Kanner will be given here: About his first autistic patient, Kanner wrote, "Many of his replies were metaphorical or otherwise peculiar. When asked to subtract four from ten, he answered: 'I'll draw a hexagon' " (2).

Later Kanner acknowledged that the boy "obviously knew the answer," and although not commented upon by Kanner, Bettelheim points to the fact that the child's reply was an "ingenious solution" to his problem of wishing to assert himself against the questioner and yet show that he understood the question, could have answered it readily, and that his intelligence even permitted him to reply in Greek by offering to draw a six-sided figure. There is no question here of a symptom of organic defect but an expression of the child's experience of the world that is meaningful and quite idiosyncratic to him.

One possible explanation of the linguistic peculiarities observed among the psychotic children who do speak is that they reflect variations in quality of linguistic development. If such is the case among children who speak, a similar variation may also exist among mute children. Perhaps the most linguistically handicapped of these mute children form the largest part of the group who remain resistant to any form of therapeutic intervention unless it comes very early.

In view of the presumed resistance of language development to environmental influence, how could this postulated deficiency come about? Possibly by a process analogous to that in the deaf child, the psychotic child's response to the anxious conflictful tensions of his surroundings is a relative inattention to, or failure in assimilation of, linguistic input. In the absence of input a potentially irreversible language deficit may be sustained. Such a view is in accord with our psychogenic hypothesis and may be seen to complement other notions of interpersonal factors in the genesis of the various language disabilities associated with childhood psychosis such as those discussed by Bettelheim (2).

To postulate a form of constitutional deficiency or central nervous system insult prenatally, at birth, or afterward whether perceptual or intellectual in nature is also conceivable. Definitive evidence is yet lacking to disprove any of these explanations or to rule out some combination of factors.

We are suggesting then the possibility that mutism in psychotic children may be two separate though interrelated disorders which tend to coexist but may to some extent vary independently of one another. A deficit in language acquisition may be rooted in very early and persistent difficulties in the infant-mother relationship; that is, a failure of, or dysfunction of, attachment. On the other hand, absence or distortion of speech development may either rest on a foundation of language deficit or may come about as a result of later, perhaps more specific, conflicts in the relationship with the mother. Perhaps future work in the area of mutism could profitably focus on methods of distinguishing between evidences of language retardation vs. speech retardation in the very young.

It may be that further work will sharpen methods of assessing level of linguistic competence, which may be one factor in prognosis. However, separate consideration will also need to be given to other factors, in particular the propensity toward oppositional behavior and avoidance of potentially satisfying transactions with other persons. Measures which reflect the intensity or fixity of these characteristics would also be of considerable prognostic significance.

REFERENCES

1. AINSWORTH, MARY D. SALTER and BELL, SILVIA M. Attachment: Exploration and Separation. *Child Development,* 1970, 41, 49-67.
2. BETTELHEIM, BRUNO. *The Empty Fortress.* New York: The Free Press, 1967.
3. BOSCH, GERHARD. *Infantile Autism.* New York: Springer-Verlag, 1970.
4. BOWLBY, JOHN. *Attachment and Loss, Vol. I, Attachment.* New York: Basic Books, 1969.
5. BROWNE, E., WILSON, V., and LAYBOURNE, P. Diagnosis and Treatment of Elective Mutism in Children. *J. Amer. Academy of Child Psychiatry,* 1963, 2, 605-617.
6. CASLER, L. Maternal Deprivation: A Critical Review of the Literature. *Monogr. Soc. Res. Child Dev.,* 1961, 26, 1-64.
7. CUNNINGHAM, M. A. and DIXON, C. A. Study of the Language of an Autistic Child. *Journal of Child Psychology and Psychiatry,* 1961, 2, 193-202.
8. EISENBERG, LEON. The Autistic Child in Adolescence. *Amer. J. Orthopsychiat.,* 1956, 112, 607-612.
9. EISENBERG, LEON. Psychotic Disorders of Childhood. In A. M. Freedman and H. I. Kaplan (Eds.), *Comprehensive Textbook of Psychiatry.* Baltimore: Williams and Wilkins, 1967. P. 1437.
10. ESCALONA, S. K. Emotional Development in the First Year of Life. In M. J. E. Senn (Ed.), *Problems of Infancy and Childhood.* New Jersey: Foundation Press, 1953.

11. FILIPPI, RONALD and ROUSEY, CLYDE L. Delay in Onset of Talking—A Symptom of Interpersonal Disturbance. *J. Acad. Child Psychiat.*, 1968, 7:2, 316-328.
12. FLAVELL, JOHN H. *The Developmental Psychology of Jean Piaget.* Princeton: Van Nostrand, 1963.
13. FREUD, A. and BURLINGTON, D. *Infants Without Families.* New York: International University Press, 1944.
14. FRY, D. B. The Development of the Phonological System in the Normal and Deaf Child. In Frank Smith and George A. Miller (Eds.), *The Genesis of Language.* Cambridge: The MIT Press, 1966.
15. KANNER, LEO. *Child Psychiatry.* Springfield: Charles C. Thomas, 1957.
16. LENNEBERG, ERIC. The Biological Foundations of Language. *Hospital Practice*, Dec. 1967, 65. (a)
17. LENNEBERG, ERIC. The Biological Foundations of Language. *Hospital Practice*, Dec. 1967, 59. (b)
18. LENNEBERG, ERIC. *The Biological Foundations of Language.* New York: Wiley, 1967.
19. LENNEBERG, ERIC. *The Biological Foundations of Language.* New York: Wiley, 1967, p. 149.
20. MCNEILL, DAVID. *The Acquisition of Language.* New York: Harper and Row, 1970, p. 145.
21. MORLEY, M. *The Development of Disorders of Speech in Childhood.* London: Livingstone, 1957.
22. MOWRER, O. H. *Learning Theory and the Symbolic Process.* New York: Wiley, 1960.
23. PROVENCE, SALLY A. and LIPTON, ROSE C. *Infants in Institutions.* New York: International Universities Press, 1962.
24. PROVENOST, W. The Speech Behavior and Language Comprehension of Autistic Children. *Journal of Chronic Diseases*, 1961, 13, 228-233.
25. RHEINGOLD, H. L., GEWIRTZ, J. L. and ROSS, H. W. Social Conditioning of Vocalizations in the Infant. *J. of Comp. and Physiol. Psychology*, 1959, 52, 68-73.
26. RUTTER, MICHAEL. Autistic Children: Infancy to Adulthood. *Seminars in Psychiatry*, Nov. 1970, 2, 4.
27. SHAPIRO, T. and FISH, B. A Method to Study Language Deviation as an Aspect of Ego Organization in Young Schizophrenic Children. *J. Amer. Academy of Child Psychiatry*, Jan. 1969, 8, 36-56.
28. SPITZ, R. *No and Yes.* New York: International Universities Press, 1957.
29. SPITZ, R. *The First Year of Life.* New York: International Universities Press, 1965.
30. SZUREK, S. A. Problems around Psychotherapy with Children. *The Journal of Pediatrics*, 1950, 37, 671-678.
31. SZUREK, S. A. and BERLIN, I. N. Elements of Psychotherapeutics with the Schizophrenic Child and His Parents. *Psychiatry*, 1956, 19, 1-9. See also Chapter 9, this volume.
32. VETTER, HAROLD. *Language Behavior and Psychopathology.* Chicago: Rand McNally, 1969, Chapter 6.
33. WARD, T. F. and HODDINOTT, B. A. The Development of Speech in an Autistic Child. *Acta Paedopsychiat.* (Basel) 1968, 35, 199-215.
34. WOLFF, PETER H. The Natural History of Crying and Other Vocalizations in Early Infancy. In Brian Foss (Ed.), *Determinants of Infant Behavior IV.* London: Methuen & Co. Ltd., 1969.
35. WOLFF, S. and CHESS, S. An Analysis of the Language of Fourteen Schizophrenic Children. *Journal of Child Psychology and Psychiatry*, 1965, 6, 29-41.

17

Early Childhood Development of Psychotic Children: A Study of Anamnestic Methods

J. F. Walker, M.D.
and
S. A. Szurek, M.D.

INTRODUCTION

This report summarizes findings and impressions obtained from an exploratory, pilot study which had as its aim the further investigation of the problems and techniques involved in attempting to elicit from parents more retrospective data concerning the early childhood development of their psychotic child than had been possible previously.

Although the usual clinical study prior to systematic therapy often revealed long-standing, conflictful problems of premarital living in each of the parents and events leading to intensification of such psychopathology after the marriage, and although such crises were frequently chronologically related to the onset and/or exacerbations of the reported symptoms of maldevelopment of their child, such correlations were not uniformly obtained in all families. There were in these latter instances impenetrable obscurities about these matters which did not always yield clarifying information even during subsequent, systematic efforts in therapy with the parents.

Quite obvious sources of difficulties in gaining clear anamnestic information about the earliest months and first year or two of the child's life were noted: 1) massive transference projections onto the therapist's and staff's efforts; 2) complicating countertransference difficulties on the part of relatively psychotherapeutically inexperienced trainees and staff, as well as 3) insufficient general knowledge concerning early childhood development and inadequate mastery of such knowledge which existed; and 4) such additions to anamnestic data as did come to light in the course of therapy were not always noted and recorded in progress notes of the contents of therapeutic sessions, or buried in such notes and not explicitly collated in subsequent summary reviews of therapy.

The study was conducted between July 1967 and July 1968 when research time became available on the part of a psychiatrist who had completed a two year, full-time career training in child psychiatry. It concerned itself with five families, each of which had a psychotic child in residence on the Children's Ward at the time of the study. The age of the children varied from four to seven years, and their stay on the ward prior to this study ranged from a few weeks up to three years.

The psychotherapeutic orientation and work of the staff of the Children's Ward with psychotic children is described elsewhere (1, 2, 4).

A well designed *prospective* study potentially offers the best opportunity for accurate detection and description of significant clinical information (2). Otherwise, the clinician is dependent upon *retrospective* data, in combination with current clinical observation. Unless these retrospective studies have been well observed, described and recorded as well as the therapeutic maneuvers assessed, there may be serious drawbacks in such studies as far as drawing warranted scientific statements from them is concerned.

Some doubts have been raised by others about the validity of retrospective studies and histories of child development in general. Thus, Chess, et al. (3) point out that "all retrospective inquiries involve the possibility that the information obtained will have been significantly distorted in recall." She reminds us of Freud's early experiences with patients, in which reported childhood sexual experiences proved to be false recollections and gross distortions of what had actually happened. Freud was later to conclude that these false reports represented fantasies of important dynamic and clinical importance. Nevertheless, as Chess points out, such reporting, if not later corrected, is inadequate for the study of the actual events which had occurred in the course of the child's development, no matter how useful such fantasies might be from a clinical point of view.

Robbins (5) also presented evidence from his prospective study of child development which clearly demonstrated that even parents of normal children significantly distort their memory of developmental facts in their children, when asked to recall them after a lapse of time.

In the later report of 1966, Chess et al. (3) also described the considerable distortions often made by parents of behaviorally disturbed children, when they were asked to recall developmental factors. The types of distortions made were subdivided into four categories. The first was distortion of the timing of events, so as to make the sequence of these events conform to prevalent theories of causation. Second, was denial or "minimization" of problems reported. Third, was flat "inability" to recall pertinent past behavior. Finally, the last category concerned the "placing of onus" on the child for the parents own convenience.

As will later be described, similar distortions are encountered in retrospective reporting by parents of psychotic children, and to a great degree. Also to be herein described are methods which were used to reduce distortions in recollections and in reporting of historical data.

In discussing the reliability of mothers' histories, Chess quotes Wenar (6) as saying "it may well be that mothers' histories mislead more often than they illuminate." She acknowledges the *clinical* necessity for obtaining and utilizing retrospective data from parents, in the sense that even if the data is incorrect, it may still provide important clues to significant concerns and conflicts of the parents.

Further complicating the problem is the experience of many therapists that confirms our finding that parents of psychotic children are among the markedly conflicted individuals seen in therapy on our service. Distortions in history might therefore be expected to be and are often found to be even greater in degree.

Still, clinical experience with parents has suggested that successful psychotherapeutic reduction of conflict of the reporting parent often results in freer, fuller, and more accurate reporting of historical events. One would therefore find that initial distortions in parents' histories are, to varying degrees, subject to later correction by psychotherapeutic means.

To assist in amelioration of the problems in the initial gathering of anamnestic data, D. Bomberg, M.A., drew up a check-list of categories of events deemed pertinent to a psychiatric history. This checklist was conceived of as a guide to the therapist in interviewing, and also as a guide for recording of data.

We shall present first the methods explored as our study progressed with some examples of the results obtained in each method used, and the time utilized in our initial trials of each method. The last was of importance to us because our ultimate aim was to find not only the most effective method but also one which might eventually be adaptable to the training program. Our hope was to incorporate the method chosen into regular, routine procedures of our initial diagnostic assessment of new future children and their families to improve our future collection of clinical research data by all faculty and trainees.

The Bomberg List as an Interview Guide

·In the few years prior to this exploration several therapists on our service had used the Bomberg list (described in the Introduction) with the parents of their inpatient child in treatment, as an effort to further elucidate historical material. One approach that had been briefly attempted was using the list as a kind of interview schedule itself. In other words the therapist began with the first item in the section on family history and followed in sequence the items as they appear on the list. Parental replies were then simply recorded on the mimeographed forms supplied with the list.

These individual efforts on the part of these therapists did result in obtaining additional biographical information, partly because sufficient additional time had been taken to ask those questions for which there had been no time during the course of routine clinical interviews. Also, it was at least recorded that each of these areas in the Bomberg list had been inquired into with the parents. If the parents were unable to report very much, or even any, information on a given topic, the record would show their response to the question. It was by no means clear, however, how useful such an approach was in terms of eliciting clinically relevant material.

With the first family, the Bomberg list was again used, but in the manner described below. The parents were first informed by their therapist of our interest in attempting to elicit further historical data and asked if they would participate. Regular psychotherapy sessions continued as ordinarily scheduled while the parents were concomitantly seen by the historian. The parents were asked about each item on the list in the sequence in which it appears. They were encouraged to report anything that came to mind in response to the items. Their replies were recorded briefly during the course of the interviews, and these notes were used afterwards for writing the summary of the interview.

Selected for the initial effort were the young parents of Bobby, a seven-year-old psychotic boy on our ward. Bobby had been classically autistic when admitted at age four and had greatly improved in the course of over three years' treatment. His parents, especially his mother, were quite verbal people and had made major gains in their own psychotherapeutic work and might be expected to make a fairly comprehensive effort at reporting. Their selection for this first effort was influenced in part by those characteristics.

Beginning the Study

When their therapist informed them of the study, both parents seemed eager to participate. In fact, the father later reported that he had had fantasies of writing a book about Bobby. Each parent was seen individually. Usually the interview was of 45 minutes' duration. At initial contact the historian reviewed with the parents the nature of our effort as being an attempt to reconstruct a sequential and age-dated chronicle of important events and the feelings surrounding them in the lives of the parents and their child. These parents were convinced that their son's disorder was the result of severe and intense intrapersonal and interpersonal conflicts in the early period of their marriage.

As each parent was asked about each item on the list, neither evidenced major difficulty in responding to any item. In fact, both tended to respond at length to each item.

On several occasions, responding in this way would lead the parents spontaneously to information other than that immediately asked for, in which case the historian would not intervene, but instead would follow the parents' train of thought. One example was when the father was asked what he knew about the degree of closeness, or the degree of conflict, between his own parents. He responded instead about his own relationship to his mother, saying immediately that, "She was a thorn in my side," and then went on with a description of his mother's emotional disorder, saying with emphasis that, "She is so severely disturbed that she needs intensive psychiatric care." This one question had stimulated a flow of thoughts and strong feelings which spread into other areas on the list, including areas under his own personal developmental history. As the historian later came in sequence to the section on his personal developmental history, he acknowledged that father had already said a great deal on the subject, but asked if there was more that came to father's mind now.

Other interventions on the historian's part were primarily in terms of asking for clarification of some point reported, e.g., in reference to age, sequence, context, etc. The historian had already acknowledged at the outset that the parents might find themselves reviewing memories which might be difficult or distressing to review, and that he hoped they would feel free to express their distress should they feel it and when they felt it.

The combined interview time for both parents was seventeen hours and twenty minutes. The combined time for both parents required to obtain the developmental history of the child (excluding family history) was six hours and forty minutes (four hours and ten minutes for the mother, and two hours and thirty minutes for the father).

The Data Obtained: New and Old

A large part of this material represented a focused recapitulation of information which had already emerged during the course of three years' therapy, and which could now be recorded in one location for ease of reference in the chart. There were also areas of new information. For example, the father spontaneously commented, when we came to the questions concerning his sexual development, that he had never discussed this in his therapeutic work because, "It had never come up and no one asked." However, as he began to try to respond to the question, he appeared embarrassed and, when the historian inquired about his discomfort, father then acknowledged that he was embarrassed and that he had never before made any effort to discuss this material. He said that he realized he didn't "have to" answer, but then promptly began to answer the question with a minimum of tension. With this statement he had not only indicated his understanding that he was free to not answer, but he also may have been referring to his inner sense of conflict in this area. No inquiry was made about these feelings, and he did, as mentioned, spontaneously proceed to report.

Dynamically relevant information was therefore obtained by this kind of direct, focused inquiry, which had not yet arisen in the course of therapeutic work.

Parents' Reaction to Interviews

Both parents reported to their therapist that the experience with the historian was in many ways "indistinguishable" from their experiences in psychotherapeutic work. The free associations of both parents during history taking had, on several occasions, led them to verbalizing current concerns to the historian. In each case, and without intervention from the historian, both parents interrupted themselves, saying that they would "leave that" for therapy. They then returned to their efforts to report specifically historical material. Experienced in their own therapeutic work, these parents approached and responded at times to these interviews much as if they were therapeutic sessions.

The Effect of Therapy on the Freedom to Recall and to Report History

The mother spontaneously and with emphasis stated that she would have been unable to give much of this information before she began therapy. She described clearly her own naivete before therapy about her parents, their personal emotional difficulties, and her relationship with them. During her therapeutic work she had begun to question her own previous views of her parents, had made a series of visits back home, and confirmed for herself many newly acknowledged facts regarding herself and her parents. Further, there was some information about herself, particularly about sexual matters, which she previously would have been unwilling to report to a historian in

much detail, but now felt less anxious and embarrassed, and gave one striking example of having uncovered apparently repressed memories in the course
of her therapeutic work.

Shortcomings of This Method

Certain shortcomings of this method were apparent. Most obvious was
that the historical data was presented in an excessively categorical fashion,
rather than in a contextual fashion. Thus, feeding history was presented,
sequentially and with age ranges, but this was not contextually related to
other areas of development, and not to the general family situation. It would
be not an impossible, but certainly a more difficult, task to reorganize the
material obtained into a narrative that would be both sequential, as well as
contextual, in nature. Beyond this, it seemed that using the Bomberg list as a
guide to interviewing tended to interfere with contextual recall and reporting,
encouraging instead a kind of "chopped up" reporting. For example, it would
be psychologically more comprehensible to have temporal correlations between Bobby's negativistic self-assertions around feeding, with those occurring around toileting, etc., as well as the temporally concomitant areas of
more healthy functioning.

The Structured Interview Schedule

With the second family studied, a highly structured interview schedule
was used. In this approach clinically known facts about the disorder under
study were, as much as was possible, translated into specific questions to be
incorporated into the interview schedule. These questions were presented, in
the same sequence, to each parent in interview. The historian asked each
of these questions in precisely the same wording and, as much as possible, in
the same manner with one parent as with the other. Such an approach has
as its aim the standardization of the historian's interview behavior. This is
so as to reduce the likelihood of the parents being influenced, in their reporting, by unrecognized bias on the part of the historian.

Two important implications of this approach are: 1) The interview schedule must include enough relevant questions that would tap, to some significant
degree, differences that might exist in the life experiences of psychotic children as opposed to non-psychotic children. One hypothesis is that, even in
the face of parental defensiveness, enough data would be forthcoming to point
up some such differences between groups, as may exist. 2) Such an approach
would probably exclude much of the kind of data usually obtainable with
therapeutic interview techniques. This refers to data blocked from recall or
reporting by parental anxiety, embarrassment, guilt, shame, etc., which

potentially could be reduced by psychotherapeutic intervention, making possible fuller reporting. However, the possible disadvantage of the latter method is that the approach to each parent would be individualized and therefore no longer standardized (in the usual social science sense, although the interviewer's attitude with each parent could be expected to be similar, as an outgrowth of his professional training and experience).

In spite of this dilemma and in order to get a sense of what the structured interview might produce, the Bomberg list for the developmental history of the child alone was used in conjunction with the historian's own clinical experience to elaborate a preliminary structured interview schedule. The Bomberg list was followed in the sense of division of information into her categories of pregnancy, feeding, etc., but with the questions more precisely defined. Possible parental responses were anticipated and incorporated into the schedule itself to promote simplicity in recording.

This schedule was used with the parents of Judy, a four-year-old newly admitted psychotic girl. Neither parent had had any prior experience in psychotherapy. They also differed from the first parents in that they did not find it easy to elaborate spontaneously or to associate freely in response to questions.

The combined interview time for both parents was five hours and sixteen minutes, of which three hours and fourteen minutes were used for family history, and two hours and two minutes for developmental history. This was less than half the time required by Bobby's parents.

The relatively brief amount of time required to obtain the developmental history was partly, at least, the result of strictly following the structured interview schedule. No effort was made to elucidate further with the parents any answers to questions they had given. The parent's responses were characteristically brief and not elaborated. The resulting protocol was one with a small amount of information concerning each of a wide variety of topics. The relative lack of richness in detailed or contextual information is quite striking in contrast to the information obtained from the first family. It was clear to the historian that these less verbal and less psychotherapeutically experienced parents would require much more help and intervention from the interviewer for them to become freer in their reporting, whereas Bobby's parents associated freely, and with affect, even to the simplest queries.

Throughout the history interviews, Judy's parents remained pleasant and cooperative in their demeanor, and generally appeared overtly neither anxious nor distressed. Obvious reluctance in reporting was not observed in response to any item by either parent. However, statements of not remembering recurred frequently throughout the interview. Both parents gave concise answers, often followed by comments of "that's all," or "I can't remember any more." Because the structured interview schedule was used, no effort was made to intervene further at these points of "not remembering." Covert indications of anxiety and embarrassment were evidenced from the mother by a slight hesitancy, vagueness, or embarrassed smiling in replying.

Mother reported that Judy was held during bottle feedings, cradled against the mother's breast. In answer to the question about whether feedings seemed a comfortable experience for both mother and child, mother replied in the affirmative. The historian noted a flatness of affect during this questioning that might have been a cue for further inquiries by the historian, had the interview not been planned to be structured strictly according to the questionnaire.

Mother also reported, still in response to the questions asked in sequence from the questionnaire, that Judy first drank from the cup at age nine months. She first fed herself with the spoon at age one and one-half years and first used a fork at age three years. She still (at the time of interview) "did not know how, or wouldn't" use a knife. There were some problems in teaching Judy self-feeding in that she seemed "awkward" in learning how to hold the spoon. Mother began offering the spoon at age one year, and by age one and one-half years Judy had mastered it.

Father reported in his interview that it was "difficult" to teach Judy to use the spoon, and that she "would not" feed herself until the family moved to their new house at about age two years plus. Father remembers telling Judy then to feed herself "or starve." Father also reported that Judy did not eat many different foods at the time of the interview, but that there "was a time" when Judy would try any food.

Numerous questions occurred to the historian, which were not asked, however, so as to stay strictly within the limits of the questionnaire. Several examples come to mind. Mother could be asked to elaborate on the question of whether Judy "did not know how" to use a knife or whether she "would not" use a knife. Further description as to *what* was "awkward" in Judy's effort to use the spoon, what mother felt and did in responding to this, etc., seemed important. Father's description of the struggle with Judy about feeding herself does not come through in mother's description. Both parents could individually be questioned further about these memories. The shift in Judy, as described by father, from being apparently open to new experiences with foods to later being highly selective about solid foods is of considerable interest and could offer a focus for much further inquiry. The contrast between mother's bland or flat affect and affectless wording about these memories and father's emphatic statements itself offers cues for further study and inquiry with both parents.

Shortcomings of This Method

Use of this method precludes use of known clinical skills which can reduce parental anxiety and facilitate fuller recall and reporting. Judy's parents were not ready or able to engage in reporting that would even approximate in completeness that of Bobby's parents. They were clearly, in the opinion of the historian, in need of psychotherapeutic experience to become freer in their reporting.

Interest in the details of the child's life prior to and leading up to the time that her psychotic disorder became fully evident, often would seem to lead to a focus of attention on especially the first year of life. With children already beyond the age of five when first seen clinically, as has been usual in the past, this first year of life would of course be the period most remote in time from the point when history was elicited. This same period, theoretically, might also be a period of maximum conflictual tension in the lives of the parents in respect to their disordered child. Either factor might contribute to further difficulty in terms of parents' abilities to recall. One would therefore anticipate the need for use of greater clinical and psychotherapeutic effort in focusing on this first year of life, indeed, on the first two or three years of life.

It seemed, then, that the best use of available time for the remainder of this exploratory effort would focus primarily on and around the early developmental history of the child, fully using clinical skills to assist parents in recall and reporting.

An Individualized Approach: Use of Clinical Skills and
Individualized Techniques of Focused Inquiry

After a review of already available historical information, the next three sets of parents were introduced to the project by their therapist, as before. On first meeting with the historian, the parents would hear a recapitulation of the intent, purpose, and method of the study. They were encouraged promptly to report any feeling of discomfort they might have in response to any question. They were further encouraged freely to report any thoughts or feelings that came to mind as they were answering, even if such thoughts might seem to be "off the subject." This much of an introduction might be sufficient for the parent to begin, with little or no further assistance required from the historian. This was strikingly true of Mary's mother, in the third family.

When the parents instead seemed hesitant or unsure as to where to begin, the historian asked something to the effect "When do you recall first becoming concerned?" He then followed the flow of the parent's memories as they came, in whatever sequence. He intervened where needed in order to obtain more detailed clarification of an episode and of the feelings involved. During the course of the interviews, non-verbalized affect and interview behavior suggestive of conflictual tension were observed by the historian. He then often intervened with such statements as, "I noticed that you hesitated just then," or "I noticed that as you were saying that you appeared to be (puzzled, frowning, etc.)." Such comments from the historian often brought into sharper focus for the parent his or her own sense of conflict relative to what was being said. As a result, a fuller and more direct expression of feeling often followed from the parent.

As this process proceeded, a picture began to emerge, very complete and detailed in some areas with all the hues of affective color, but sparse and sketchy in others. It was to these sparse areas that specific questions were later directed, questions that derived from the Bomberg outline or that derived from the historian's own clinical intuition or hunch. Such a "hunch," or guess, was aroused typically by observing some word, phrase, or perhaps nonverbal cue from the parent that was not itself fully expressive, but which suggested the possibility of other aspects of the situation described.

Examples of clinical problems encountered, as well as of interviewing techniques used, are described below, using material drawn from interviews with each of these last three pairs of parents.

The Third Family

The third family was that of Mary, a seven-year-old mute psychotic girl on the Children's Ward. She and her parents had been in therapy for seven months prior to this anamnestic study.

Total interview time was ten hours and thirty minutes divided over fourteen interviews. Seven hours and thirty minutes were spent with the mother. Father's availability for the study was limited.

Anxious Denial, Maternal Guilt, and Fear of Blame

As might be expected, some questions could elicit anxious or overly emphatic denial by a parent. An example follows. To round out the early feeding history, Mary's mother was asked about the ways in which Mary had been fed in infancy, and whether Mary had always been held for feedings, or sometimes propped. Her response was quick and anxiously emphatic. "Oh! I *never* propped Mary." The historian was not aware of any accusatory implication in his own feeling and attitude in asking the question, but was impressed that the mother seemed to be protesting with much anxiety, as if she felt accused.

The historian simply acknowledged her statement with a nod and then asked her to picture in her mind holding Mary during feeding, or how she usually held her. The mother went on to describe this and to demonstrate the positions. Questions were then directed as to how vigorously Mary sucked, the duration of the feeding, and what she was like to hold. What evolved was an increasingly complete description, with distressed affect, of how "squirmy" Mary had become during feedings and of how agonizing the slowness was to mother with which Mary took four ounces of milk in ninety minutes. Perhaps the historian's attentiveness as well as acknowledgment of his empathy with such a situation, helped mother report these feelings more thoroughly in words for the first time. She later acknowledged that this was the first time she had described these events to a physician. She then volunteered the information that by age three months, because of her difficulty in attempting to bottle feed Mary, she began experimenting with propping Mary's bottles with a pillow and with a Teddy Bear nearby, and noticed that Mary seemed more "content."

In sharp contrast to her earlier denial about propping, mother now reported that Mary was thereafter fed in this manner. No effort was made in the context of history taking, however, to clarify with her the dynamics of her earlier denial, since her sense of conflict about it had already been reduced, and her reporting had already become more complete. She was, in fact, shortly thereafter reporting in a very affect-laden way the intensity and scope of her maternal guilt during that period of time when Mary was in her early months of infancy. Although she may have forgotten the "propping" for other reasons, the possibility seemed, by inference, to be a strong one, that her "forgetting" was related to strong guilt feelings.

Distortions of the Timing and Sequence of Events

Time distortion or vagueness about time was a frequently recurring problem with all the parents. Since it is a common and frequent difficulty to reconstruct temporal sequences from the past, an experienced therapist has no problem in feeling empathic with the parents on this score. Often this problem seemed to be experienced consciously by the parents as a trouble in remembering events to which little affective significance was, at the time of occurrence, consciously attached. This seemed to be especially true of events like early feeding patterns when such patterns were subtle and not particularly striking to the parents at the time, but which clinicians might find significant in the light of other facts at the time and of the subsequent course of the child's development. This will be described from work with the last two families. The historian kept in mind that this vagueness about time or temporal relationships could have been an indication of unconscious processes. If this were the case, recalling such sequences would then be blocked by the repressive forces. Hence, any success in recollection by the parent and reconstruction by the historian of the sequences would require perhaps a long period of working through, in a systematic therapeutic effort, the extremely unpleasant associated affects of the conflict involved.

Guessing as an Aid to Recall

With each of these families, questions about temporal sequence in the earliest developmental years often elicited such responses from parents as, "I don't remember" or "I can't be certain." At such moments the historian acceptingly acknowledged the parent's uncertainty, and encouraged the parent to "guess" what the sequence might have even roughly been, or to say what they did uncertainly recall at the moment. Thus encouraged, they sometimes began to modify their first uncertain recollections, for example, by saying, "No, that can't be right, because . . ." They then gave a wealth of other more well remembered facts surrounding the event in question. On occasion this in turn was followed by return of the memory, with the parent feeling much more certain about the chronology of the events in question. The whole detailed context also then elicited a greater sense of conviction in the historian about the final remembered story of events.

Vagueness about Sequence and Interviewer Bias

Temporal vagueness may also increase distortions in the recorded anamnestic data arising from interviewer bias. For example, the original recorded history in Mary's chart stated that the father had taken a new job and moved to another city before Mary's birth. Knowing from other recorded data how easily her mother became anxious about financial security, the historian's first conscious assumption was not only that the move came close in time before Mary's conception, but also that maternal anxiety about the change might have been present and perhaps be a relevant factor affecting Mary's development. Because of this assumption, and when the parent's own associations during this anamnestic review were leading rapidly in another direction, the historian noted in himself an impulse to follow the parent's train of thought, rather than to ask exactly when the move took place. He did ask, however, and then learned that the move occurred four years before Mary's birth, and that soon after the move both parents found themselves to be very comfortable with the new job, the new home, the new neighborhood and new friends. In fact, they stated that they were more pleased with their situation and each other than they had ever been before.

Denial, without Overt Evidence of Defensiveness or Anxiety

The mother appeared to be quite convinced of their "happiness" during that period. However, the historian's interest in this period led to a more detailed exploration of her husband's employment history during that interval. This chronologically led to her reporting, for the first time during the staff's contact with her, that her husband had quit a very good job during her early pregnancy with Mary in order to work for a man that mother did not trust, creating a situation of mother being secretly apprehensive for the duration of the pregnancy. Her husband, she then reported, lost his job just prior to Mary's birth, but she did not know this at the time. He was present for the birth but then did not visit mother for two post-partum days in the hospital. She had no explanation for his absence then and felt hurt and disturbed by it. Later she learned that he had been looking for a job.

As mother proceeded with this narrative she became tearful—especially when recalling the fourth post-partum day, by which time she had returned home. She was on the bed nursing Mary when the bank called to say that the check from father's employer had 'bounced' and that they were without funds. Her tearful description of the panicky two-week period following this call was particularly vivid. In reporting this she wondered aloud about the possible impact on Mary, and then said, "It makes me feel bad to say that." The historian inquired as to her meaning. She replied that it made her "feel bad" to think that she might have had "someting to do with" Mary's disorder. She then said that perhaps she hadn't remembered to report this to doctors before because she "hadn't wanted to remember" it.

Protestations of Normalcy; Rationalization of Reported Data

Her husband also demonstrated a reluctance to report similar data but evidenced it in a different way. He did respond directly to inquiries about the first year of life. Each time he reported difficulty from that period; for example, Mary's lack of appetite, her preference to being propped for feedings, the absence of anticipatory responses to the approaching bottle, the disinterest in the spoon, etc.; he interrupted himself repeatedly to reaffirm that he had always viewed Mary as "a perfectly normal" infant prior to her blood disease at age 11 months.

He did not display overt anxiety during the interviews but, instead, a rather subdued, yet impatient attitude, as if to say, "Yes, I know you may make something of this but, really, Mary was all right." In contrast to this, in another interview he disclaimed intimate knowledge of Mary's first year by pointing out that children prior to age two or three had always seemed to him to be "blobs," objects requiring care but not people who reciprocate affection. Therefore, he described his involvement with Mary as rather distant until she was older. These statements followed the historian's reflecting back to him how much difficulty he was having in attempting to recall events from this age period.

As he began to talk about Mary at age three and four he again evidenced difficulty. For example, when father was describing the onset of Mary's severe night terrors, the historian asked whether there were other problems in the household during that period. He replied that there were none. The historian knew from the mother that both the other children had had fairly serious illnesses during that time (Perthe's disease in a brother and recurrent nephritis in a sister) and brought this up with father. He then described the illness but in a way that suggested these problems had been dealt with at the time without undue concern or upset in the family. He had marked difficulty in trying to recall the sequence, duration, or chronological relationships during these periods of sickness and, in fact, finally ended by saying that he could not remember, perhaps his wife would know. The historian referred back to his earlier descriptions of Mary's panicky fear of doctors and hospitals and asked whether he could recall Mary's reactions to her sister's being hospitalized. Again he could not remember but volunteered that he didn't think Mary was at all interested, nor even aware, and that certainly this would have no bearing on her night terrors.

Again his attitude in this interaction seemed to be, "Yes, these things happened but they have no relevance to Mary or her disorder." This occurred in spite of efforts to define the task as reconstructing events, not a search for causes. Unfortunately, as the historian learned later, father's therapist had inadvertently told him that the historian would be trying to learn more about "causes" of these disorders.

The Fourth Family

The next attempt was made with the parents of Larry, a seven-year-old psychotic boy whose parents had been engaged in psychotherapy for one and one-half years prior to this anamnestic review. Larry was less disturbed at the time of admission than any of the other children studied.

Total interview time was eleven hours and five minutes, divided over fourteen interviews. Six hours and fifty-seven minutes were spent with the mother.

Use of Memory Aids: Home Movies, "Baby Pictures," etc.

Both parents were quite warm and seemed interestedly involved throughout the series of interviews, and displayed serious concern in their efforts to recall. However, the theme of "I don't remember" recurred rather often with both parents, and always with a sense of regret. On their own initiative they looked up old baby pictures and home movies. A review of these by the parents and the historian and therapist did aid in recalling a few details of discrete areas including behavior at bath time, response to stuffed animals, and character of Larry's rocking in late infancy. One film sequence at four-teen months represented the only recording of mother's holding Larry—under her one arm. As she saw herself on film she commented, "Just like a sack of potatoes." She said, "I seem to remember a discussion (then) about Larry's not liking to be held." Her efforts to clarify further became halting. She felt puzzled, she said, by her difficulty in remembering. The same was true in trying to describe her unsuccessful efforts to teach Larry to use a spoon.

"The Perfect Baby"

Mother at first related that Larry, as an infant, had given her "absolutely no trouble." She said, "I know it sounds absurd to say that I had a perfect baby but I simply can't remember any times when I was upset with him." This was said with a frown and a puzzled shake of the head. Friends had also commented that Larry was a "good" or a "perfect" baby, reinforcing the parents' own interpretation of their experience with Larry. Father was the first spontaneously to comment that at the time he had a "passing thought" that Larry was "too damned good—that he had wished he would raise more hell." This provided the focus with both parents for more detailed inquiry by the historian into the infant Larry's demonstration of initiative, as well as his responsiveness to being held and played with, etc. Father recalled that typically Larry would coo for a short time when picked up but then became quickly "distracted—as if he wanted to be left alone." Father's response was to put Larry down, rather than to continue with efforts to reengage Larry. Mother did not recall Larry as preferring to be alone but remembers him as having "a short attention span." The historian inquired further about Larry's feeding behavior while being held, also asking if Larry watched his mother while feeding. After a pause, and with a frown, she said: "Funny thing, I don't think Larry watched me at all. We always had to work to get his attention."

Overcompliance as a Source of Distortion in Reporting

Father remembered that Larry had been "propped" for many of his bottle feedings and wondered if Larry had been held "enough." Mother, in her interviews, thought that he had been. Father's therapist reported that father had a strong tendency toward "overcompliance," especially to staff. Support-ing this was the historian's experience with father, that he often seemed to work hard at anticipating the historian's next question, so as to ask-and-answer-it himself. The retrospective question, "I wonder if he was held enough" could have been in the service of this eager compliance. When asked, father did clarify that he had not had this concern at the time of those feedings, and was not in any sense certain of this impression in retrospect. At any rate, more detailed microscopic inquiries did seem to help him through his own anxious wish to meet the fantasied needs of the historian, so as to be clearer about events he felt he remembered well, as distinct from recollections about which he had doubts.

Recollections of Relatives and Friends

Details of the latter part of the first year and into the second were difficult for mother to recall until the historian inquired about the reactions of relatives to Larry. She then recalled that the family had stayed with the paternal grandparents for a twenty-day visit, beginning when Larry was age 10 months, and that the grandparents thought Larry was a "slow baby." Until this visit, mother had viewed Larry as the "perfect baby" and had not "really begun to worry." She recalled that the grandparents later made efforts to teach Larry to walk but that she had never tried to encourage him before this. She then reported her earliest efforts with Larry about such things as eating with a spoon, and using the "potty," reporting in detail Larry's repeated refusals and persistent negativism.

Use of Nonverbal Cues as a Basis for Further Focused Inquiry

Mother's facial expression and gestures suggested strong feeling. Helplessness, disgust, and anger all came to the historian's mind. When she did not verbalize her feelings, the historian commented on her gestures and asked what her feelings had been when faced with the dilemma of Larry's refusals.

Her first response was to describe her feelings of helplessness and frustration. She did not mention anger, so the historian then asked her about angry feelings at the time. In response, mother said, "I couldn't really get cross with him. It's hard to get angry with someone who doesn't know why you are angry. However, with Terry (her older son), I had definite ideas on discipline, and he always knew right away when I was angry."

When asked to clarify, she referred again to her feelings that Larry had been a "perfect baby," one who neither "bothered" nor "worried" her. At age eleven months, however, during the twenty-day visit with her grandparents, she began to "worry" that Larry's development was not proceeding normally. Before this time, "when he screamed it was because he wanted something," and mother could discover the need and gratify it. "But after he was a year old, he screamed a lot but didn't seem to know what he wanted, perhaps he was only expressing himself," and mother felt helpless and unable to gratify him.

Later, when Larry began to walk, at 14 months, and to explore, she recalls being very attentive to Larry's "deliberate" efforts to touch and handle objects after being told not to do so. She was emphatic in reporting that "I swore Larry would never be a holy terror," and that she routinely slapped his hands. In recalling this same period, father reported that "we were over-aggressive with the limits." By age twenty months, Larry began to slap his own hand and say "no" to it. Later he began to frequently "talk" to this same hand.

It is possible that mother had already experienced the screaming, negativistic Larry as a "holy terror" and that she had been in considerable conflict about feelings of anger, vengefulness, guilt, etc., which might have been repressed. Then when she viewed Larry at a later period behaving in a "deliberate" fashion, she may have overresponded. Her responses to relatively unconflicted exploratory behavior may then have been determined by previously repressed feelings and anxiety.

Further Aids to Recall: Encouragement; Association

The experience of recalling such details as weekends, pets, etc. may help to alleviate anxiety about *not* being able to remember, thus promoting freer reporting which inevitably leads by association to still more new material.

Mother felt especially vague about temporal sequence at an early point in the interviews when attempting to reconstruct the events during much of Larry's second year. This was, she said, a period of "hum-drum routine," with one day seeming, in retrospect, much like the next. The historian encouraged her to picture in her mind as clearly as possible any details that might come to memory from that period, and then to associate freely to these recollections. Questions about weekends, events in father's job, trips, visits, purchase of the family dog, etc., did help to reconstruct a kind of pictorial and sequential context.

For example, when asked about weekends, she at first said, "Funny thing, I can't remember weekends from that year (age one to two years) at all." She then recalled that father worked long hours during the week, and usually went fishing on the weekends. Then, when asked how she spent her time when her husband was away fishing, she recalled going to visit a friend who was also a mother. This led to recall of Larry's consistently avoiding interaction with the friend's children during these visits.

The historian also asked about family pets during that same year. Mother then recalled Larry's earliest experiences with dogs, and his fearfulness about dogs. Apparently in association to the idea of "fears" mother then recalled Larry's apparent fears of new foods during that same year, as well as recalling her sense of conflict in dealing with the feeding problems that developed.

The Fifth Family

The final attempt was made with the parents of six-year-old David, a psychotic boy with some speech, recently admitted for inpatient study. Both parents presented as interested, concerned, and eager to participate.

Total interview time was fourteen hours, eleven of which was spent with the mother.

Careful and Meticulous Reporting: A Defense?

Characteristic of the mother throughout all interviews was a sense of conscientious effort to report all remembered information to the fullest possible extent. Her replies were characteristically clear and precise, even though she often began hesitantly, doubting her ability to recall. Throughout her reporting she always seemed to be struggling, to be somewhat anxious, and often gestured with both hands in a way that suggested a high level of tension. In several interviews she tiredly commented that she felt "exhausted" by the process. Furthermore, after the second interview David's nurse saw the mother in the hall. She was so struck by mother's tired demeanor that she spontaneously asked mother if anything was wrong.

Mother began the interviews apologetically, saying that she had had four children and anticipated much difficulty distinguishing memories of each of the children from one another in terms of developmental events. The first two hours were mostly spent by her reviewing events in the lives of David's siblings, rather than about David. In spite of this, she went on to give the most detailed account of developmental history that was given by any of the other parents. She was meticulous in her efforts to be complete. Yet, her reporting, in spite of its wealth of detail, shed comparatively little light on conflictual tensions which could have contributed to the child's disorder, in contrast to the data reported by the first family.

As she proceeded, little information was forthcoming concerning possible conflictual tensions in the family prior to when David was four years of age. She returned again and again, in a wearied, puzzled way, to the theme that David was her last child and that for two years prior to his birth and until he was four years of age, life for both parents had been relaxed. The year preceding admission, beginning when David was four, was a stressful year for both parents, but in particular for mother. Thus, father was embarking on an ambitious business venture which entailed the investment of almost all their financial resources; mother was receiving frequent anonymous and sexually suggestive phone calls for several months before the caller was arrested; a death occurred in the family with a great deal of tension and efforts at denial of tension by all family members preceding the death; hypochondriacal fears developed in the mother at the same time; chronic anxiety appeared in mother with associated abdominal complaints for which she was treated with Librax, etc. It was during this year that David's more obviously autistic symptomatology emerged. As mother said, until that year she had viewed herself as being able "to handle" most problems but the events during that year were really more than she could "handle."

In contrast to this focus at age four, mother in another interview reported that David's speech began to regress after age *two* years. However, neither parent was able to report any significant increase in conflictual tension during that time, indeed, not at any time prior to David being four. However, other information about these years was obtained in another context.

Observations from Joint Interviews with Both Parents

In collaboration with the parents' therapist the historian learned that the therapist had obtained the impression, not yet fully documented, of a rather subtle but strong power struggle existing between the parents, with the father typically acquiescing because it seemed the easiest thing to do. The struggle rarely reached the level of overt disagreement for very long, and both parents tended to deny the existence of tension between themsleves.

It was learned from the history taking interviews themselves that a power struggle had ensued between mother and David on at least three different occasions. The first was when David was 18 months of age, when the parents were nightly engaged in the struggle with him to keep on his leg braces. These were applied nightly for correction of an inturning foot. The second struggle, which was quite pronounced, was around toilet training (age two years, three or four months, until age three years), and the third occurred around speech which began at about age three years five months and continued to some extent over the next two year period.

With further reflection, mother wondered if David's trouble had really begun around the age of eighteen months, when he was placed in leg braces. Over the course of several more interviews she returned to this theme with increasing conviction. She now recalled this period as the one when David first began to evidence withdrawal and negativism.

Collaboration with the parents' therapist revealed that in the joint therapy interviews, father had spontaneously begun to wonder whether David had been "that normal" prior to the age of eighteen months. Specifically, he recalled David's higher level of motor activity, as compared to other children, and his "testiness." Striking to the therapist was mother's quick interruptions as father spoke, which had the effect of cutting him off and asserting her denial that anything was recognizably wrong with David prior to eighteen months.

Nonetheless, it was quite clear from the detailed developmental information given by mother, that appeared to be complete, that David had achieved many developmental landmarks at or before expected ages prior to age eighteen months, with the possible exceptions being in the areas of attachment behavior to mother and of speech development.

Puzzlement, Hesitancy, and Anxiety in Reporting

Mother evidenced the greatest difficulty in reporting in respect to three subject areas: first, bottle feeding; second, negativistic behavior in David before age four; and third, in respect to David's nursery school experiences. In each case, it was as if she wished to report everything but had great difficulty in remembering.

In response to questions concerning these three areas she seemed to be not only the most hesitant and vague, but also seemed the most prone to changing the subject. She did so in ways that were subtle, without overt evidences of anxiety. At such moments the historian intervened to redirect the mother to the original question. Hesitancy and anxiety would then again be evident, but often she could proceed and recall more details. About other subject matter she typically "stuck to the subject" with great tenacity, reporting in meticulous detail.

Her earliest comments about feeding behavior were that David had not been as "cuddly" as the other children in that he did not like to be held as long. Still, she did not remember these feedings as being uncomfortable for either her or him. In response to further focused inquiry, she reported that after David was placed in leg braces prescribed for his Perthe's disease, he "definitely" had become "squirmy" at feedings, seeming not to want to be held for very long. Efforts to clarify further details of feeding behavior or details of change in feeding behavior led only to a heightened sense of puzzlement and inability to report further on mother's part.

Mother also evidenced greatest difficulty in responding to questions about "negative" behavior in David prior to age four. She initially stated that David was "never" a hostile child. In response to a series of specific questions by the historian, however, she went on to narrate a number of examples of either potentially destructive behavior or of defiant behavior on David's part, which she then tended to explain away as being something else. One example involved David's nearly injuring her seriously by releasing the emergency brake on the car when she was standing in front of it on an incline. After having reported this, she more freely described a multitude of other kinds of events in which David had vigorously defied limits already learned, far beyond the extent exhibited by her other children at that age of two to three years.

The third area of greatest difficulty in reporting concerned David's experiences in nursery school from age three and one-half to four and one-half years. In her initial reporting mother had completely omitted the fact that David had been excluded from nursery school near the end of his first and only year in school. Father, in contrast, had bluntly reported this right away in his individual interview. Several interviews later, without specific intervention by the historian other than maintaining a non-critical attitude, mother did go into detail about the circumstances surrounding David's exclusion. Her therapist reported that in her therapy hours during this same history taking period, mother had been trying, in response to her therapist's encouragement, to more freely express memories and feelings about which she felt anxiety or hesitancy. It may well have been this concomitant therapeutic work which helped mother later to report history in more accurate detail concerning the nursery school period.

Minimal Affect in Reporting of Events

"Power struggles" between mother and David have been referred to in the preceding material. Facts about each of these were reported by mother in a factual way, with little display of affect. Content was, therefore, most available to inquiry, but mother's feelings in each situation proved to be difficult for her to recall and report.

The first struggle with David, as reported, involved the nightly application of David's leg braces. Mother's feelings during this period were difficult to clarify. She stated that she had had an even more difficult time with her daughter who, years earlier, had required full hip braces.

The second reported struggle concerned David's teasing and negative behavior. Mother's feeling at the time about such behavior was difficult to clarify in retrospect, in view of her pronounced tendency to deemphasize the importance of each occurrence as soon as she had reported it.

The third struggle had centered around toilet training. Screaming tantrums had occurred with considerable frequency. Mother reported having eventually "given up" trying to train David, whereupon he promptly "trained himself." Considerable feeling could be inferred to have been present in mother in response to such behavior, but inquiry in this instance led only to acknowledgement, with affectively detached reporting—perhaps itself an evidence of repression of affect.

A fourth struggle had ensued about speech development. A pediatrician had suggested that the family "make" David say the name of the object which he was requesting from them, before they granted his wish. The first such episode was a 45 minute struggle that proved exhausting to the several family members concerned. At the end David "lost" the "battle" by finally saying the word "apple." Mother then recalled that she had felt some "guilt" after the incident, in the sense that she may not have "expected more" of David in terms of speech prior to that point. It was not possible to get clear what her response had been to David's earlier speech behavior, for example, babblings in infancy, or whether she had talked or made any vocal or social gestures to him to any extent.

The following sequences were reported by mother but without any sense of relevance to David's development on mother's part as she reported it.

Neither parent planned for another child after the birth of David's youngest sibling. Both looked forward eagerly to a period when all their children would be of school age, leaving them freer in the use of their time apart from children. Mother's first reaction to learning that she was pregnant was: "My God! I'm pregnant!" followed soon by a sense of pleasurable anticipation. Spotting then began. Since she had had three miscarriages, she had the fantasy that David would either be miscarried or instead might be born deformed. At that time she often hoped for a spontaneous abortion. When the spotting stopped, she felt relieved. At birth, however, David had a large cephalic hematoma, the sight of which activated mother's fears of deformity briefly. Again, mother deemphasized these occurrences as having been of more than transient significance to her at the time. Further, she displayed no definable affective shifts during the reporting of these events.

SUMMARY AND CONCLUSIONS

The three methods of obtaining historical data illustrate that perhaps only prolonged therapeutic work prepares parents for remembering painful events, feelings, and conflict states of possible significance in the evolution of their child's disorder. However, it is also evident that the use of a formalized method of history taking and data collection by a sensitive psychotherapist who uses his sensitivity to gently explore areas of evident conflict, hesitation, or mixed messages and careful attempts to clarify these may also provide more data than a formalized and standardized method of history taking alone.

Not explored was the utility of information gathered impersonally by questionnaires which are carefully worded to avoid blaming adjectives. However, it is clear that in a few instances data so gathered is also retrospectively not accurate despite reduction in interpersonal tensions in questionnaire data collection.

Not only must the data be collected by a psychotherapeutically trained and sensitive historian but utilized with equal awareness of phases in psychotherapy in which the parents are working to consider what new material could be elicited.

A further aspect of sensitive history taking and data collecting is that it provides material for assessing the developmental state of the child and also may give some indication of the kinds of therapeutic involvement required from milieu staff and the child's therapist. Some staff members agree that part of the total therapeutic effort is restitutive. That is, efforts are made to provide those interpersonal experiences not possible in the conflicted home setting.

The parents' therapists not only have the task of engaging the parents in reducing their own conflict states, but at appropriate moments they must help parents to behave toward their child in such a way as to provide previously not possible interpersonal experiences.

REFERENCES

1. BOATMAN, M. J., and SZUREK, S. A. A Clinical Study of Childhood Schizophrenia. In D. Jackson (Ed.), *The Etiology of Schizophrenia*. New York: Basic Books, 1960.
2. BOMBERG, P., SZUREK, S. A., and ETEMAD, J. G. A Statistical Study of a Group of Psychotic Children. This Volume, Chapter 14.
3. CHESS, S., ET AL. Distortions in Developmental Reporting Made by Parents of Behaviorally Disturbed Children. *J. Amer. Acad. Child Psychiat.*, 1966, 5, 226-234.
4. REED, J. H. and HAZEN, H. R. Langley Porter Clinic Children's Inpatient Service. In *Residential Treatment of Emotionally Disturbed Children: A Descriptive Study*, New York: Child Welfare League of America, Inc., pp. 200-221, 1952.
5. ROBBINS, L. The Accuracy of Parental Recall of Aspects of Child Development and of Child Rearing Practices. *J. Abnormal Social Psychology*, 1963, 66, 261.
6. WENAR, C. The Reliability of Developmental Histories. *Psychosomatic Medicine*, 1963, 25, 505.

18

Evaluation of EEG Findings in a Group of Psychotic Children

Jacqueline G. Etemad, M.D.,

S. A. Szurek, M.D.,

C. L. Yeager, M.D.

and

F. R. Schulkin, M.D.

INTRODUCTION

In the process of tabulating statistical data for a group of children at the Langley Porter Neuropsychiatric Institute, EEG results, where available, were examined for all children with a disorder of psychotic proportion who were seen on the Children's Service from 1946-1961. Since, before 1952, EEG's were not routinely performed on all children, of 264 psychotic children seen in this period there were just 204, or 77.3%, who had one or more EEG tracings taken in the course of their contact with us. The tracings of these 204 children are discussed here as to types of EEG abnormalities found, variations in severity of EEG findings, comparisons of EEG findings with clinical course, and, finally, variations of EEG findings among the seven diagnostic subgroups to one of which each of our psychotic patients is assigned. Because of the lack of a standardized approach to evaluations of EEG findings in children, it is necessary to preface our discussion with some general remarks.

VARIATIONS IN NORMAL EEG'S

The type of changes encountered in clinical electroencephalography are seldom found to be exclusively independent, one from another, a fact which must be kept in mind in the appraisal of any EEG, especially that of a child. For example, a normal EEG recorded from a child does not have the well-organized appearance nor the rhythmicity of the normal tracing in the young adult. Frequently in children the record may be mildly asymmetrical and contain diffuse slow and fast background activity as well as some non-specific hypersynchronous bursts of slow waves.

Interpretation then becomes a matter of judgment. Such alterations of a tracing may be considered mildly abnormal by one interpreter and within broad limits of normal by another. Sometimes these mild variations are found in the EEG's of children with chronological ages above those in which such findings are expected to appear normally. When encountered, these seemingly ambiguous findings are referred to as immaturity of EEG pattern which may reflect some retardation in the physiologic integration of the central nervous system or possibly an obscure minimal organic brain dysfunction. As techniques are improved, some clarification of this indecisive diagnostic area is hoped for.

Abnormalities in EEG tracings may be separated into those findings which are relatively constant and stable for the individual as opposed to those which are relatively transient.

The more constant findings are diffuse slowing, fast activity, asymmetry and focal activity. These findings are believed to reflect the presence of varying degrees of diffuse and/or focal types of organic dysfunction or damage.

The more transient changes consist of various forms of paroxysmal dysrhythmias which in their turn reflect transient changes in brain function associated with the convulsive disorders. Clinically, the paroxysms are in many cases associated with classical or atypical seizure patterns, while in other instances they may be found in association with uncontrolled impulsive behavior outbursts.

Since in general none of the above listed EEG abnormalities excludes the presence of the other abnormalities, it is possible for one or several abnormalities to be present in the same tracing. For example, a tracing may be slow, slow plus paroxysmal, slow, fast and paroxysmal, or could contain all of the listed abnormalities.

EEG FINDINGS

Turning now to our group of 204 psychotic children, who ranged in age from 2 to 17, we observe the following:

Looking at only the first EEG tracing for each patient, a recording generally made at the time of initial diagnostic study, we find that 84 or 41.2%

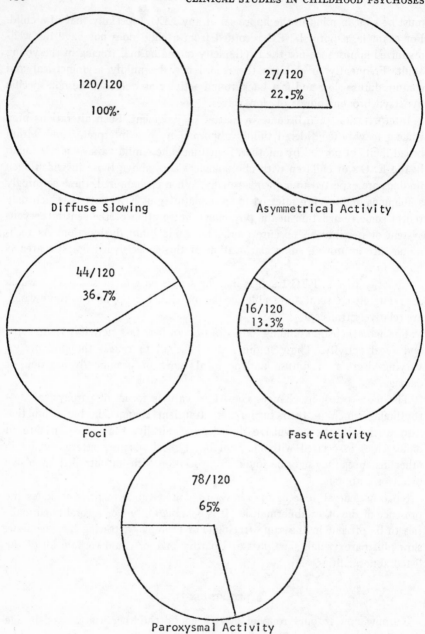

Figure 1.   Distribution of EEG Abnormalities

in 120 Abnormal Tracings

were judged to be normal records. It is interesting to note that when we look at EEG's done on all children for another period (1960-1970) we find that 222 out of 516 records or 43% were judged to be normal. Thus the percentage of normal tracings found among a group of psychotic children does not differ markedly from the percentage of normals in an unselected group of admissions to our clinic. The EEG's in our group of normals were reasonably homogenous and cast no doubt in the mind of the electroencephalographer as to their normality.

The 120 tracings in the abnormal group were considered sufficiently altered from the normal to be reflective of significant brain dysfunction.

As to the various types of abnormalities found within the abnormal group, Figure 1 shows the various incidences. (Note that because the categories are not mutually exclusive, percentages do not total 100.)

a. In all 120 abnormal tracings some degree of diffuse slowing was observed.

b. In 27 or 22.5% of the abnormal tracings asymmetrical activity was present.

c. Forty-four or 36.7% of the abnormal tracings had recognizable foci.

d. In 16 or 13.3% of the abnormal tracings there was superimposed fast activity evident.

e. Paroxysmal activity was observed in 78 or 65% of the abnormal tracings.

DEGREE OF SEVERITY IN ABNORMAL EEG'S

To reflect upon the severity of the disturbance represented by any given EEG tracing is a separate task from that of considering the nature of the abnormalities present. Viewing a number of tracings it is possible to make a judgment as to the degree of abnormality (and the presumed degree of associated organic brain dysfunction) which is present in each tracing. It is then possible to compare clinical findings with degree of EEG abnormality or to compare degrees of EEG abnormality from one tracing to the next in the same individual.

For each of the 204 tracings considered here, a judgment was made as to the degree of abnormality present. The same 84 tracings discussed above formed the normal group, while the 120 abnormal tracings were divided into mildly abnormal, moderately abnormal and severely abnormal tracings. When tracings are rated according to severity, we note the distribution seen in Figure 2.

Eighty-four or 41.2% of the tracings are normal;

Fifty-nine or 28.9% of the tracings show mild abnormalities which are presumed to be reflective of mild organic brain dysfunction;

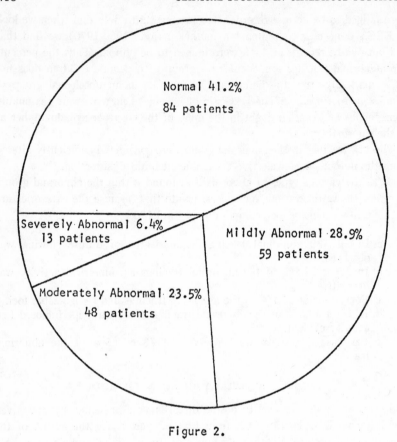

Figure 2.

<u>EEG</u> <u>Findings</u> <u>for</u> <u>204</u> <u>Psychotic</u> <u>Children</u>

Forty-eight or 23.5% of the tracings show moderate abnormalities prob-ably reflective of moderate organic brain dysfunction;

Thirteen or 6.4% of the tracings show severe abnormalities which are associated with presumed or demonstrated severe organic brain dysfunction.

VARIATIONS IN INDIVIDUAL RECORDS WITH REPEATED TRACINGS

Of the 204 patients with EEG recordings, there were 65 who had more than one EEG tracing. Twenty-seven had two EEG's—one at the time of admission and the second usually a year or more later; twenty-seven had from 3 to 5 EEG's; eight had between 6 and 10 EEG's; three had between 11 and 20 EEG's; one had 53 EEG's; and one had 153 EEG's. The large number of tracings for the latter two patients were taken over a period of eight or nine years. As one might expect, two EEG's were most often done when the first tracing was abnormal or equivocally normal. Multiple tracings were most often taken of patients with readily demonstrable EEG abnormalities.

Recognizing the many variables that could not be accounted for, we nonetheless tried to obtain a rough idea of the changes in EEG's by comparing the first and final tracing for each patient with two or more EEG's recordings. We were interested to see whether changes in EEG's would be associated with clinical change or with changes in medication.

There were 24 patients whose final EEG tracing differed by at least one point on our four-point scale of severity from the first tracing. Two of these

TABLE 1

EEG Findings and Clinical Improvement

	Clinically Improved	Clinically Unimproved	Not Rated	Total
EEG Improved n=12	3 (25%)	5 (41.7%)	4 (33.3%)	12 (100%)
EEG Got Worse n=10	2 (20%)	4 (40%)	4 (40%)	10 (100%)
	5	9	8	22

$X^2=0.1619$ not significant

were excluded because the second tracing was taken only a few weeks after the first. Of the remaining 22, 12 or 52.2% showed improvements in EEG tracing, while 10 or 47.8% were worse.

Of the 12 patients where there was improvement in the EEG tracing, 3 or 25% also showed clinical improvement, 5 or 41.7% were ambiguous or unimproved clinically, while 4 or 33.3% had not been rated as to clinical status because they were still in treatment.

Of the 10 patients whose final tracing was rated more severely abnormal, there were two, or 20%, who improved clinically, four, or 40%, did not improve clinically and four were not rated.

For these small numbers there appears to be no clear relationship between clinical change and changes in EEG tracings. However, larger numbers of patients would be required to make a statistically valid statement.

Regarding the question of medication it is of interest to us to note that only two patients from this group of 22 received any anti-convulsant medication. These were also the only two with diagnosed convulsive disorder. These two patients had been studied separately with regard to the relationship of

EEG changes to medication changes (2). For the patient who had 153 tracings note is also made of times that clinical events, such as the death of the patient's grandfather, were immediately followed by a temporary worsening of the EEG tracing.

It seems to us significant that the 20 patients who received no anti-convulsant medication nonetheless showed variations in EEG findings both in the positive and negative direction. There were another 10 patients with multiple EEG's who also received no medication and yet whose tracings varied significantly from one another even though the first and last tracing were similar in severity. Thus 30 or 46.1% of our 65 patients with more than one EEG demonstrated changes in their records not referable to medication. This finding lends support to the notion that while a single abnormal EEG can be

TABLE 2

TREATED GROUP WITH EEG RECORD

	Improved	Unimproved	Ambiguous	Total
Normal	16 (59.3%)	17 (30.9%)	2 (16.7%)	35 (37.2%)
Mild	7 (25.9%)	18 (32.7%)	4 (33.3%)	29 (30.9%)
Moderate	4 (14.8%)	18 (32.7%)	2 (16.7%)	24 (25.5%)
Severe		2 (3.7%)	4 (33.3%)	6 (6.4%)
Total with EEG's	27 (100%)	55 (100%)	12 (100%)	94 (100%)

cautiously regarded as a reflection of possible cerebral dysfunction, to view such a tracing as a fixed or stable indication of cerebral function would be an error. It is also clear that there are many changes in EEG tracings which are not referable to changes in medication or to any obvious or recorded clinical events. What other factors may be involved in such variations remains to be determined. The whole concept of what is normal variation of EEG findings is also, of course, a subject of continuing scrutiny.

EEG FINDINGS AND CLINICAL COURSE

Of the 204 psychotic children who had EEG's there were 94 who stayed with us beyond the diagnostic evaluation for a period of treatment amounting to at least 24 individual psychotherapy sessions and who were rated as to clinical response at time of termination. Table 2 shows a comparison of treatment response and EEG findings.

Observing Table 2 we note the following:

1) Thirty-five or 37.2% of the 94 patients who received therapy and had records of EEG examination were reported to have *normal records*. Sixteen

of these 35 patients, or 45.5%, improved; 17 or 48.5% were unimproved; and 2 or 5.7% were classified as ambiguous.

2) Mild abnormalities in the EEG were recorded for 29 or 30.8% of the treated 94 patients. Of these 29, 7 or 24.1% were rated as improved; 18 or 62.0% were rated unimproved and 4 or 13.7% were rated ambiguous.

3) When the patients in all clinical groups with EEG records read as normal and mild were combined, there was a total of 64 patients or 68% of the 94 treated patients. Of these, 23 or 35.9% were rated as improved; 35 or 54.6% as unimproved; and 6 or 9.3% as ambiguous. Combining the patients rated as unimproved and ambiguous, the number is 41 patients or 64.1%.

In contrast to the above distribution of the 64 patients with EEG tracings classified as normal or mild in the EEG records into roughly 36% improved and 64% unimproved, are the findings on 30 of the 94 treated patients whose EEG tracings were reported with more severe abnormalities. These are as follows:

1) Twenty-four or 25.5% of the 94 treated patients in all the clinical groups had EEG records which were classified as showing moderately severe EEG abnormalities. Four of these patients or 16.6% were rated as clinically improved. Eighteen patients or 75% were regarded as unimproved and two as ambiguous. When the latter two were combined the result was 83.3%.

2) Only 6 of the 94 treated patients in all clinical groups, examined electro-encephalographically, had EEG records rated as *severely abnormal record*. None of these was rated clinically improved. Two or 33-1/3% were rated unimproved and 4 or 66-2/3% were rated ambiguous.

3) Combining the patients with moderately and severely abnormal records, only four of the 30 patients or 13.3% were rated as improved, 20 or 66.6% were rated as unimproved; and 6 or 20% were rated as ambiguous. Again combining the patients rated as unimproved and as ambiguous results in a total of 26 patients or 86.7% (of the total 30 patients in these two groups), with EEG records rated as being the most severely abnormal.

TABLE 3

EEG Findings and Response to Therapy

	Normal and Mildly Abnormal EEG	Moderately and Severely Abnormal EEG	Total
Improved	23 (35.9%)	4 (13.3%)	27 (28.7%)
Unimproved or Ambiguous	41 (64.1%)	26 (86.7%)	67 (71.3%)
N =	64 (100%)	30 (100%)	94 (100%)

$X^2 = 4.053$, 1df, p=.05

When we test for relationships between the variables of normal or milder abnormalities in the EEG tracings and the two categories of moderate and severe abnormalities, we see that patients with normal or milder changes in their EEG examinations show more improvement than those with the more severely abnormal EEG findings (Table 3).

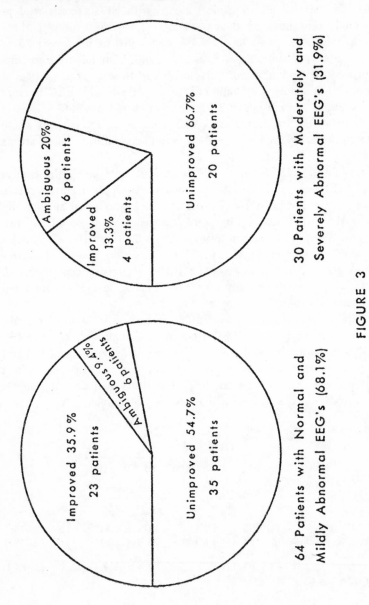

FIGURE 3

COMPARISON OF EEG FINDINGS AND RESPONSE TO TREATMENT

EEG FINDINGS AMONG DIAGNOSTIC SUBGROUPS*

While the findings are not highly significant, it does appear that patients with more severe EEG changes may be on the average less responsive to our therapeutic efforts than those with normal or mildly abnormal EEG's. Figure 3 illustrates graphically the relationship of EEG findings and response to therapy.

In an earlier paper by Bomberg et al. (see Chapter 14) we have described the criteria by which psychotic children are assigned to one of seven diagnostic subgroups; namely, core, borderline, episodic, "schizopath," mixed, retardation? and adolescent. In order to demonstrate the distribution of the various types of EEG findings in each clinical group and to learn what, if any, correlation there was between the type and the degree change from the normal tracing in the EEG record and the results of therapy, the following tabulations were prepared:

Inspection of Table 4 reveals that the number of patients in each clinical group (e.g. Core, Borderline, Episodic, etc.) is quite small for each category of EEG ratings. This is, of course, related to the relatively small number in each clinical group who received therapy and also had electroencephalographic examination. Thus, of the total *Core* group of 75, only 37 were in therapy, but of these only 29 had EEG examinations. Of the total of 55 patients classified as *Borderline*, 32 received therapy but of these only 20 had EEG examinations. Of the 35 patients classified as *Episodic*, 12 were in therapy but of these only 7 had EEG tracings. Only 24 of the 44 patients classed as *Mixed* were included in the group who had had therapy, 3 of whom had no EEG examination performed. In the remaining three clinical groups categorized as *"Schizopath"* (19 patients), *Retardation?* (20 patients), and *Adolescent* (16 patients), the number of patients who both were in the group with therapy and had EEG examinations performed, the numbers were still smaller, namely, 6, 5, and 2, respectively.

We may note in passing that in all groups, except *Mixed* and *Retardation?*, the majority of the patients were found in the first two EEG classes, namely, in the normal and mild categories.

When we compare the *Mixed* and *Retardation?* groups with the remainder of our diagnostic groups, we find that there is a significantly greater number of *Mixed* and *Retardation?* patients with moderately or severely abnormal EEG tracings.

---

* We wish to express our gratitude for the assistance of Mrs. Barbara Levin, M.S.W., in the statistical treatment of the following data. We are also indebted to Mrs. Linda Hinrichs for the preparation of several drafts of this section and of the diagrammatic representations of data.

TABLE 4

EEG Findings and Response to Therapy by Subgroup

Core Group

EEG Findings	Improved	Unimproved	Ambiguous	Totals
Normal	4	8	1	13
Mild	3	4	3	10
Totals	7 (30.4%)	12 (52.1%)	4 (17.5%)	23 (100%)
Moderate	1	3	1	5
Severe	0	0	1	1
Totals	1 (16.7%)	3 (50%)	2 (33.3%)	6 (100%)

Borderline Group

	Improved	Unimproved	Ambiguous	Totals
Normal	5	1	1	7
Mild	2	5	0	7
Totals	7 (50%)	6 (42.8%)	1 (7.2%)	14 (100%)
Moderate	1	4	0	5
Severe	0	1	0	1
Totals	1 (16.7%)	5 (83.3%)	0	6 (100%)

Episodic Group

	Improved	Unimproved	Ambiguous	Totals
Normal	4	0	0	4
Mild	1	0	0	1
Totals	5 (100%)	0	0	5
Moderate	1	1	0	2
Severe	0	0	0	0
Totals	1 (50%)	1 (50%)	0	2 (100%)

"Schizopath" Group

	Improved	Unimproved	Ambiguous	Totals
Normal	2	2	0	4
Mild	0	1	1	2
Totals	2 (33⅓%)	3 (50%)	1 (16⅔%)	6 (100%)

Moderate=0   Severe=0

TABLE 4

EEG FINDINGS AND RESPONSE TO THERAPY BY SUBGROUP (*Continued*)

MIXED GROUP

Normal	1	3	0	4
Mild	1	4	0	5
Totals	2 (22.2%)	7 (77.8%)	0 (0%)	9 (100%)
Moderate	1	7	1	9
Severe	0	0	2	2
Totals	1 (9.1%)	7 (63.6%)	3 (27.3%)	11 (100%)

RETARDATION? GROUP

EEG Findings	Improved	Unimproved	Ambiguous	Totals
Normal	0	3	0	3
Mild	0	2	1	2
Totals	0	5	1	5

ADOLESCENT GROUP

Normal	0	0	0	0
Mild	0	2	0	2
Totals	0	2	0	2

Moderate=0   Severe=0

TABLE 5

EEG FINDINGS FOR MIXED AND RETARDATION? GROUPS COMPARED WITH OTHER SUBGROUPS

	Mixed and Retardation?	Other Groups	Total
Normal & Mildly Abnormal EEG's	27 (47.3%)	116 (78.9%)	143
Moderately & Severely Abnormal EEG's	30 (52.7%)	31 (21.1%)	61
	57 (100%)	147 (100%)	204

$X^2=18.02$ df=1   p=.01

TABLE 6

TREATMENT RESPONSE FOR MIXED AND RETARDATION? GROUPS
COMPARED WITH OTHER GROUPS

	Mixed and Retardation?	Other Groups	Total
Improved	6 (16⅔%)	45 (45.4%)	51
Unimproved and Ambiguous	30 (83⅓%)	54 (54.6%)	84
	36 (100%)	99 (100%)	135

X²=8.1231   df=1   p=.01

When we consider all those who received therapy, with or without EEG examinations, those in the *Mixed* and *Retardation?* groups showed less improvement than the remainder of the groups.

The Mixed clinical group of patients were represented in all categories of EEG ratings with 9 patients in the normal or mild categories and 12 in the moderate or severe.

Of the 10 Retardation? patients, 5 were rated as having milder disturbances and 5 as having moderate to severe abnormalities. These findings may be some indication of a confirmation of our clinical classification.

It may be of some interest that in the Borderline and Episodic groups, despite the small numbers, more patients (71.4% and 100%, respectively) in these groups with normal EEG improved. This was not true of the *Core* group. The difference between the Core Group with normal EEG records and the Borderline and Episodic groups with normal EEG tracings is not, however, statistically significant. The Core group had a larger proportion of patients with improvement than the Mixed, "Schizopath," Retardation? and Adolescent groups, although less than the Borderline and Episodic groups. In the *Core* group with a normal EEG record only 30.8% were rated as clinically improved.

Comparing the clinical improvement-unimprovement ratings with the classification of EEG findings within each clinical group by inspection of Table 4 leads to the following findings.

Core Group

Among normal EEG tracings or relatively mild abnormalities in EEG record 7 (or 30.4%) were rated improved; 12 (or 52.1%) were unimproved and 4 (or 17.5%) were ambiguous.

TABLE 7

RESPONSE TO THERAPY FOR CORE GROUP COMPARED WITH OTHER
GROUPS IN PATIENTS WITH NORMAL OR MILDLY ABNORMAL EEG's

	Core-normal and Mildly Abnormal EEG's	Other Groups Normal and Mildly Abnormal EEG's	Total
Improved	7 (30.3%)	16 (38.9%)	23
Unimproved and Ambiguous	16 (69.7%)	25 (61.1%)	41
	23 (100%)	41 (100%)	64

$X^2 = 0.1728$ not significant

When those in the core group with a normal or mildly abnormal EEG record are compared to all others with normal or mild EEG abnormalities in terms of improvement or lack of improvement, there is no significant difference between the two groups.

It may or may not be of significance that in this group, of the 6 patients whose EEG tracings were rated moderately or severely abnormal, only 1 was rated improved while 3 were unimproved and 2 were ambiguous.

Borderline Group

Here the findings are similar to the Core group. Seven (or 50%) were improved of those 14 whose EEG records were normal or showed mild abnormalities in the EEG tracings. Six (or 42.8%) were unimproved and 1 (or 7.1%) was ambiguous. It may or may not be significant but is possibly of some interest that of the 6 patients showing moderately or severely abnormal records only 1 was improved.

Episodic Group

Again the number of patients (7) in this group militates against any statement of significance although it may be of interest that the single unimproved patient had an EEG tracing rated moderately abnormal.

Mixed Group

The findings in this group have already been mentioned. However, it may be reiterated that the relatively poor improvement rating appears related to the EEG findings.

TABLE 8

EEG FINDINGS AND RESPONSE TO THERAPY FOR CORE,
BORDERLINE AND EPISODIC SUBGROUPS

	Improved	Unimproved	Ambiguous	Total
Normal EEG	13 (59.1%)	9 (33.3%)	2 (28.6%)	24
Mildly Abnormal EEG	6 (27.3%)	9 (33.3%)	3 (42.8%)	18
Moderately Abnormal EEG	3 (13.6%)	8 (29.6%)	1 (14.3%)	12
Severely Abnormal EEG	0 (%)	1 (3.8%)	1 (14.3%)	2
	22 (100%)	27 (100%)	7 (100%)	56

"Schizopath" Group

This is also a small group of 6 patients all of. whom had normal or mildly abnormal EEG tracings but only 2 of whom improved.

Retardation? Group

The findings have already been commented upon. None of this group of 10 patients was rated as improved and the EEG traces were divided evenly between normal and mild versus moderate and severe.

Adolescent Group

Both because this group is very small (2 patients) and because of the clinical features of much later onset of the disorder, this group will not be considered further in the comparisons with the other groups, except to mention the relatively poor clinical outcome regardless of the EEG findings.

Further, to compare the combined first three clinical groups with better results of therapy (i.e., Core, Borderline and Episodic, which were symptomatically more similar to each other except as to onset, duration and severity of disorder) as to outcome and EEG findings, Tables 8 and 9 were prepared. Inspection of the tables shows that a normal EEG is associated with a slightly better outcome.

The diagnostic groups of Core, Borderline and Episodic with normal or milder abnormalities in the EEG tracings showed significantly greater improvement than the remaining groups.

A better chance of improvement seems lessened with increasing abnormality of the EEG, although the decreasing number of patients with the more severe EEG changes also makes statements of significance difficult.

A similar comparison, combining the Mixed, "Schizopath" and Retarda-

TABLE 9

RESPONSE TO THERAPY FOR CORE, BORDERLINE AND EPISODIC PATIENTS
WITH NORMAL AND MILDLY ABNORMAL EEG's COMPARED WITH ALL
OTHER PATIENTS WITH EEG's

	Core, Borderline and Episodic: Normal and Mildly Abnormal EEG's	All Others	
Improved	19 (45.2%)	8 (15.4%)	27
Unimproved and Ambiguous	23 (54.8%)	44 (84.6%)	67
	42 (100%)	52 (100%)	94

$X^2 = 8.7084$ df=1   p=.01

TABLE 10

EEG FINDINGS AND RESPONSE TO THERAPY FOR MIXED,
"SCHIZOPATH," AND RETARDATION? SUBGROUPS

	Improved	Unimproved	Ambiguous	Total
Normal EEG	3 (60%)	8 (30.8%)	0 (0%)	11
Mildly Abnormal EEG	1 (20%)	7 (26.9%)	1 (16⅔%)	9
Moderately Abnormal EEG	1 (20%)	10 (38.4%)	1 (16⅔%)	12
Severely Abnormal EEG	0 (0%)	1 (3.9%)	4 (66⅔%)	5
	5 (100%)	26 (100%)	6 (100%)	37

tion? groups, as to outcome of therapy and degree of abnormality of EEG
records, is made in Table 10.

Although the improvement rate is not good in either the group including
those with normal and mild EEG abnormality [improved 4 (20%), unimproved 15 (75%), ambiguous 1 (5%)] or the group including the patients
with moderately or severely abnormal tracings [improved 1 (5.9%), unimproved 11 (64.8%), ambiguous 5 (29.3%)], it appears to be worse in the
latter group. The difference is not statistically significant.

Because they demonstrate the clinical symptom of hyperactivity, the EEG
findings in the patients of the "schizopath" group are of particular interest.
There are five or 26.3% of the "schizopath" group for whom there is no
record of EEG findings. The findings in terms of severity for the remaining
14 patients are tabulated as follows:

TABLE 11

EEG FINDINGS—"SCHIZOPATH" GROUP

Normal EEG record	9	64.3%
Mildly Abnormal EEG record	3	21.4%
Moderately Abnormal EEG record	2	14.3%
Severely Abnormal EEG record	0	0%
Total	14	100%

In spite of the small number of patients involved, it may still have some significance that 12 or over 80% of this group had normal or only mildly abnormal EEG tracings—this in a group of patients all of whom demonstrated clinically the symptom of hyperactivity which so often in the literature has been linked with the suspicion of organic brain dysfunction.

SUMMARY

We have presented an evaluation of EEG findings in 204 psychotic children at the Langley Porter Neuropsychiatric Institute, Children's Service and have commented on the relationship of these findings to clinical course as well as to variations in findings among diagnostic subgroups.

Based on this study there are some indications that in psychotic children without definite evidence of organic disease, normal or mild abnormalities in the EEG record are not a critical factor in prognosis in psychotherapeutic efforts. There is, on the other hand, a slight indication that severe abnormalities in the EEG record may be a negative factor.

Our findings also suggest that while a single abnormal EEG tracing may reflect some degree of brain dysfunction, to view any such tracing as a fixed or stable indication of cerebral function is unwarranted.

REFERENCES

1. BOMBERG, D., SZUREK, S. A., and ETEMAD, J. "A Statistical Study of a Group of Psychotic Children." Chapter 14 of this volume.
2. SPILKER, B. and YEAGER, C. "Ten Year EEG Studies in Epileptic Children (Two Cases)." Disease of the Nervous System, 30 (March 1969): 194.

19

Comprehension and Negation of Verbal Communication in Autistic Children

Delmont Morrison, Ph.D.

Dale Miller, M.A.

and

Berta Mejia, R.N.

Severely withdrawn children, alternatively called schizophrenic, atypically developed, psychotic, or autistic, have been the subject of increasingly intensive study, treatment, and research efforts by clinical investigators during the past two decades. Clinical and experimental studies have demonstrated that the behavioral repertoire of these children is impoverished (Bettelheim, 1967; Lovass, 1968), with a great deal of the autistic child's activity involving simple non-social activity such as rocking in isolation in a corner, and a small amount of the child's behavior being maintained by age-appropriate social interaction.

The limited range of the autistic child's behavioral repertoire usually is accounted for as the result either of 1) lack of capacity resulting from perceptual and cognitive impairments of an organic nature or 2) motivation on the child's part to avoid interpersonal relationships that would require modification of his behavior as a function of another person. Goldfarb (1956), expressing the organic viewpoint, demonstrated what he believed to be a deviant pattern in the perceptual processes of schizophrenic children. The schizophrenic children he studied tended to prefer contact receptors such as

This research was supported by U.S.P.H.S. Grant MH7127.

A condensed and revised version of the above article appeared in the March 1971 issue of the *American Journal of Mental Deficiency*, Vol. 75, No. 5, pp. 510-18. The article is reprinted with permission of the authors and publisher as it was originally submitted.

touch, taste, and smell and actively avoided use of distance receptors such as vision and hearing. Goldfarb hypothesized that this deviant pattern of receptor activity could result in a fragmentation of the child's perceptual world and could account for some of the behavioral deficiencies observed in such children. He suggested that these unusual perceptual preferences may be caused by constitutional factors or by neurophysiologic processes. Unusual sensitivity to stimulation of several if not all sense modalities in autistic children was noted in a clinical study by Bergman and Escalona (1949). The children in this study were easily hurt and also easily stimulated to joy by colors, bright lights, and smell. The investigators believed that this unusual sensitivity to sensory stimulation existed in their group of children from a very early age, so that they developed defenses against stimulation, culminating in the appearance of autistic or psychotic symptoms.

Working within a psychogenic framework, Boatman and Szurek (1960) closely observed the contradictory, inconsistent, vacillating behavior exhibited by autistic children while engaged in almost any activity, and they considered this behavior to be a characteristic symptom of this group. These authors noted that it is sometimes possible to estimate the basic perceptual and cognitive capacities of the child from his style of dealing with the task at hand rather than from his correct or incorrect answer. For example, many of these children seem always to stop just short of the correct answer or repeatedly demonstrate a negativism so precisely related to the request made of them that their accurate comprehension of the task and its solution may be inferred.

The question of whether the cognitive impairment observed in these children results from basic organic deficiency or from motivational factors is of more than academic interest. Deafness is often the parents' earliest proposed explanation of the inaccessibility of the autistic child. Seven of the 11 patients described by Kanner (1943) when he first introduced this diagnostic category were thought to be deaf or hard of hearing. Certainly psychotherapeutic approaches and remedial education efforts with autistic children would differ if it could be demonstrated that the existing deviant behavior is primarily a function either of organic or of motivational variables. Evidence that motivational factors play an important role in the autistic child's failure to learn and perform is provided in a study by Cowan, Hoddinatt, and Wright (1965) in which autistic children were given a multiple choice task requiring discrimination of color and shape. This study demonstrated that autistic subjects correctly chose the object requested at a significantly less than chance level, indicating that they avoided making the correct response. These experimental findings and the clinical observations made by Boatman and Szurek (1960) suggest that much of the autistic child's failure to learn and to perform results from severe conflict which is manifested in approach-avoidance behavior. One hypothesis derived from these observations is that the autistic child may have various response patterns in his repertoire and is able to perform these response patterns upon request, but that his ability to perform is impaired by his conflictual responses to verbal requests. If this hypothesis is true, the variability in response rate will be a function of the child's conflicts regarding compliance to and negation of verbal communication. The present study investigated the relationship between the receptive use of language and negativistic motivation in two autistic boys.

METHOD
SUBJECT NUMBER 1

The S for this study was an eight-year-old boy, Mike, who had been admitted to the children's inpatient ward at the age of five-and-one-half years. At the time of admission Mike was mute, and his parents stated that he was unable to toilet himself, he would put anything in his mouth, he spent most of his time isolated from people, and he responded negatively to social inter-action. The parents' statements at that time adequately describe Mike's current behavior. His birth was reported to have been normal, and physical examination disclosed no organic defects. Recent psychological testing indicates that he is functioning in the severely retarded range of intelligence (estimated $IQ = 21$), and he has been variously diagnosed as mentally retarded, autistic, or schizophrenic.

Establishment of Imitation

This study was conducted on the ward in a room containing a small table and two chairs. During operant level procedures, the E and Mike sat facing each other by the small table with the various objects to be used placed on the table.

Imitation for Social Reinforcement

Operant Level I. After obtaining Mike's attention, E would say, "OK, Mike, do this," and then perform the response to be imitated. If Mike matched the response within a reasonable amount of time, E said, "OK, Mike," or some other short appropriate encouragement and went on to the next response on the list. If Mike did not imitate, E said nothing and went on to the next response. E recorded on a scoring sheet the occurrence or non-occurrence of Mike's matching response. The scoring sheet contained a list of 120 responses. This response list contained simple responses such as raising a hand and putting a block in a box, and is similar to earlier lists prepared by Metz (1965). Each item on this list was presented to Mike four times and it was established that Mike responded correctly to 14 percent of the total number of opportunities to imitate.

Imitation with Paired Verbal Cues for Social Reinforcement

Operant Level II. The procedures used during Operant Level I were followed, except that after gaining Mike's attention, E now paired an appropriate verbal request with the response to be modeled; e.g., E said, "OK, Mike, do this; put your hand over your head," simultaneously modelling the motor response. Each item on the list was presented five times, and Mike responded correctly to 15 percent of the total number of paired presentations.

Control of Behavior with Verbal Cues and Social Reinforcement

Operant Level III. The procedures followed during the two previous operant level conditions were replicated except that E used only verbal cues to elicit a desired response; e.g., E said, "OK, Mike, do this; put your hand over your head," omitting any physical demonstrations of the item. Each item on the list was presented four times. Mike responded correctly to 3 percent of the total number of presentations. Interscorer reliability was established during Operant Level I by having the E and another observer independently record the occurrence or non-occurrence of the response to be imitated during two complete presentations of the 120 item list. These procedures resulted in 99 percent agreement in recording the behavior. Because of this high agreement and because the behavior under observation was the same during the establishment of the three operant levels, no further studies of interscorer reliability were made. The results of the operant level trials indicated that Mike imitated infrequently for social reinforcement and that verbal cues had little effect in controlling his behavior.

Following the establishment of the operant level performance, Mike was seen for operant training trials at breakfast, lunch, and dinner time, approximately 12 times a week. These sessions lasted approximately one-half hour. All other food intake, such as snacks on the ward, was limited. During these trials, E and Mike sat opposite each other at one end of a table. If an object was needed for the modeling, it was present within reach on the table. A tray of food was on the table next to E. One item at a time was presented for conditioning. E would model the response, pairing it with appropriate verbal cues. If Mike matched E's response, he was reinforced with a bite-sized amount of food. During the early training sessions, it was necessary to shape Mike by physically moving him through the response and reinforcing him at the end of the response. A continuous food reinforcement schedule for correct responses was maintained throughout these trials and the remaining studies. As Mike reached criterion, eight out of ten consecutive correct responses to any given response, a new item was presented. Using these techniques, imitation was established for 25 responses.

Investigation of the Receptive Use of Language

Study 1. The procedures for the establishment of imitation were followed by procedures to establish a shift from the control of imitative behavior by *E's* modeling response and verbal request to control of this behavior by *E's* verbal request alone. Five items were selected for use in the initial training; 1) sweeping the table with a whisk broom, 2) putting a small block in a box, 3) putting a napkin on his lap and then on the table, 4) picking up a milk carton with both hands, and 5) walking around a chair. Mike and *E* were seated facing each other by the table with the necessary items placed in a row on the table within reach. The position of the items was changed after every other response. Mike imitated correctly 100 percent on these five items when *E* employed continued motor and verbal cues.

Two of the responses (1 and 4, above) were selected for verbal cue training, and the other responses were no longer presented. With only the milk carton and the broom present on the table in front of Mike, *E* began fading out the motor cues by making the verbal request and then pointing to the appropriate item. The position of the items was changed randomly, *E* recording the object chosen and its position on every trial. These procedures for position and recording were maintained throughout the studies. Mike quickly made the appropriate discriminations and responded correctly for verbal cues and pointing on both items. Pointing gradually was faded out, until only verbal cues were presented.

Figure 1 shows the shift that occurred in Mike's discriminations when verbal cues alone were presented. During the first experimental session in which only verbal cues were presented, Mike responded correctly to both items approximately 40 percent of the time. His failures (approximately 60 percent) represent responses to the object that was not requested. Between sessions two and five, there is a decided shift in his response pattern, with the emergence of a strong preference for the "broom" item. During these trials, requests for the broom response were given infrequently. In the sixth session, no request for the broom was made at all, yet Mike continued to make that response whenever he was asked to pick up the milk carton.

These data strongly suggest that Mike could discriminate neither the request to pick up the milk carton nor the request to sweep with the broom,

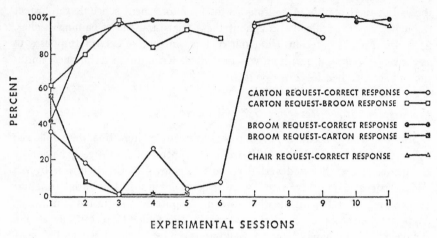

EXPERIMENTAL SESSIONS

FIGURE I

Pattern of Mike's response during initial verbal-cue training trials.

and it could be interpreted as evidence of perseveration. However, his behavior during these sessions suggested that he knew what *E* wanted, but would not comply. For example, he often reached for the milk carton upon request, stopped short of picking it up, and then rocked back and forth before grabbing the broom. When he did respond correctly to the milk carton request, as in the fourth session, he frequently became very angry, biting his hands or refusing the food reward.

As a test of our hypothesis that he understood but would not comply, we added a new item. During the previous training, when verbal cues were presented with concurrent motor modeling, it was noted that Mike frequently responded correctly to the request, "OK, Mike, stand up and walk around the chair." He often performed before *E* could model the response, and seemed to enjoy the activity of going around the chair. This request was added and the request for the broom response was discontinued, the broom being removed from the table. Sessions seven, eight, and nine, in Figure 1, show that Mike now correctly discriminated between the requests to pick up the milk carton and to walk around the chair.

During sessions ten and eleven, the milk carton was removed and the broom made available. On these trials Mike correctly discriminated between the verbal requests to sweep with the broom and to walk around the chair.

Study 2. One possible interpretation of the foregoing data is that Mike will not make correct discriminations unless they involve responses to objects that he shows a preference for. In an effort to establish whether Mike had a

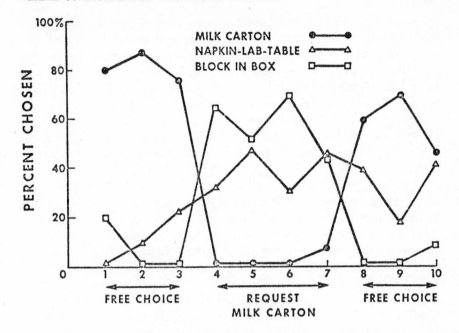

EXPERIMENTAL SESSIONS

FIGURE 2

Pattern of Mike's first choice object as a function of a request for a response to the object.

preference for any of the responses selected for verbal training, we began new procedures. Four objects, milk carton, napkin, and block and box were placed before Mike on the table. Upon being told once by E to "go ahead," Mike responded as he had been trained to all of the objects. After an object was responded to, he was reinforced and the object removed. After all objects had been responded to they were again placed on the table and the procedures were repeated. Figure 2 demonstrates that Mike picked the milk carton as first choice approximately 80 percent of the time during sessions one through three, the remaining two items being chosen much less frequently. Beginning with the fourth session and continuing through the seventh session, before Mike made his first choice E asked that he pick up the milk carton with one of the other objects present. The object that he chose was always removed and he was reinforced if he responded correctly. He was allowed free choice of the remaining two objects and was reinforced after every response. After the last object was responded to, all the objects were presented again, and the procedures were repeated. Figure 2 demonstrates that under these conditions Mike never responded to the milk carton but always responded to one or the other of the objects available. During sessions eight through ten, the procedure maintained during sessions one through three was repeated, with E no longer making a verbal request. Mike responded again to the milk carton as a first choice object, although not at the previous level. Although Mike demonstrated a preference for one response, the presentation of a request for the response in this instance did not result in correct discriminations, but rather in an avoidance of the requested response.

Study 3. It is possible that Mike had made enough correct discriminations and received sufficient reinforcement during our training procedures so that he had acquired verbal discriminations that were not in his repertoire originally and that he now was motivated to avoid performing. However, it is equally possible that our reinforcement procedures had little positive effect on him and that he had these verbal discriminations in his repertoire before he was chosen as a subject for this research. The low response rate occurring at the operant level may have reflected Mike's negativism rather than his inability to discriminate the verbal request. As a test of the latter hypothesis, Mike was trained to imitate three new responses: putting a hat on and taking it off, opening and closing a box, and stacking two blocks. The operant level procedures demonstrated that he would neither imitate these responses nor respond correctly to $E's$ verbal requests that he do them. The acquisition for imitation of these responses followed the procedures described earlier except that verbal requests were never paired with the responses. Once the three imitative responses were definitely established in Mike's repertoire, he was again seated by the table. The objects relating to the three responses were randomly positioned before him, and he was simply told, "go ahead." As before, he responded as he had been trained and the object of his choice was removed. Reinforcement followed each response. When he had completed the final response, all of the objects were presented again and the procedures repeated. A record was kept of Mike's first through third choices. These procedures were repeated 100 times and demonstrated that 95 percent of the time Mike's first response was to open and close the box, while his second and third choice response was random. No position preference was demonstrated. At this point, we altered the procedure by verbally requesting that he open and close the box before he responded to it with the other two objects present. If he responded correctly, he was reinforced. The object of his choice was always removed and he was allowed free choice with reinforcement on the remaining objects. After his final choice, the procedures were repeated. Under these conditions, Mike continued to respond by opening

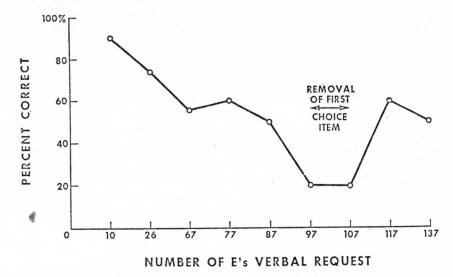

NUMBER OF E's VERBAL REQUEST

FIGURE 3

Pattern of Mike's response during two-choice discrimination trials.

and closing the box 100 percent of the time. E then continued to request the response to the box, and following that response, E also requested that Mike respond to one or the other of the remaining objects. Reinforcement followed each correct discrimination and the object chosen was always removed. No request was made for the remaining object, and after he responded to it and was reinforced the objects were presented again and the procedures repeated. Mike continued to respond correctly when requested to open and close the box; and during the first twenty-six consecutive requests to either put the hat on and take it off or to stack two blocks, he responded correctly 21 times and incorrectly five times. A binomial test of Mike's performance on the two-choice discrimination task comparing the number of correct vs. incorrect responses during trials 1 through 26 indicated that he correctly discriminated $E's$ verbal request at better than chance level (p = .01, 2χ test).

Mike's correct discriminations on the two-choice task indicate that he understood $E's$ request and had acquired this capacity independent of any specific verbal discrimination training known to E. However, between the 26th and 87th verbal requests for the two remaining objects his correct discriminations became no better than chance. This decrement in performance is shown in Figure 3. On the basis of the occurrence of this random performance one could argue that it was an error to reject the null hypothesis that Mike was not making verbal discriminations during the first 26 trials.

Mike continued to respond correctly to the request to open and close the box during the trials in which his performance in the two-choice discrimination became random. One could argue that his response to the box does not indicate discrimination, as he always chose this object first before a verbal request was made for it, and by continuing to respond as before he always received reinforcement whether he listened to *E's* request or not.

Although lack of discrimination learning might be involved, it is also possible that a decrement in motivation was causing the decrement in performance during the two-choice discrimination task. The experimental procedures enabled Mike to receive continuous reinforcement for his response to the box, a response already strongly established in his repertoire prior to the verbal discrimination training. The reinforcing procedure also made it possible for Mike to ignore *E's* verbal request for the two remaining objects and, by responding randomly, to receive 50 percent reinforcement in the two-choice discrimination task and continuous reinforcement for his response to the remaining object.

One test of the hypothesis that motivational factors rather than lack of ability to discriminate was involved in the decrement in performance was to manipulate the experimental procedures in such a way as to increase Mike's motivation to perform correctly responses that were already in his repertoire. One possible method of increasing Mike's motivation was to be more sparing in reinforcement and to introduce punishment contingent upon incorrect responses. To this end, *E* placed only the hat and blocks before Mike between the 87th and 107th verbal requests. *E* asked Mike to respond to one of the objects and if he correctly responded, he was reinforced. The object chosen was removed and the box was then placed next to the remaining object. *E* then requested that Mike respond to one or the other of these objects. If he was correct, he was reinforced and the chosen object was removed. He was then allowed to respond to the remaining object with reinforcement following this response. The objects were presented again and the procedures repeated. If Mike responded incorrectly on the first or second verbal request, *E* removed the objects and delayed procedures for 15 seconds. *E* then presented the same two objects and made the request again.

Figure 3 demonstrates that between the 87th and 107th verbal requests for either the hat or stacking blocks response, Mike's discrimination errors shifted from a random distribution to a decidedly negative one. During this time he was very angry, as was manifested by his biting his finger, stamping his feet, and rocking back and forth in his chair. All of Mike's errors consisted of his choosing the object that *E* had not requested. This shift in errors indicated that the new procedure had resulted in increased motivation not to perform rather than increased motivation to perform the rewarded discrimination. Between the 107th and the 137th verbal requests the box was returned and was presented with the remaining objects, following the procedures used before the 87th verbal request. Figure 3 demonstrates that by return to the original procedures, the discrimination errors for the hat and stacking blocks responses again became random.

SUBJECT NUMBER 2

The S for the second series of experiments was a ten-year-old boy, whom we shall call Ted, who was admitted to the ward when he was six-and-a-half years old. The parents' presenting complaint at the time of admission was that Ted had a speech and hearing problem. However, the results of subsequent complete medical examinations have all been within normal limits. Currently, communicative speech is infrequent, but he is reported to have said sentences such as "sock it to me" and has been noted on occasion to sing. He is erratic in his bowel and bladder control and is generally very timid in participating in social interactions. Attempts at intelligence testing have failed to produce a formal score, although he has never been able to perform on items above a two-year-old level. Ted has been diagnosed at various times as demonstrating mental deficiency, symbiotic psychosis, and childhood autism.

Establishment of the Operant Level for the Receptive Use of Language

Ted was seen in the same room described earlier, during mid-morning and mid-afternoon, approximately ten times a week. During these trials, E and Ted sat facing each other with the various objects to be used placed on the table. Using a shortened list of 50 items taken from the earlier list of 120 items, E would place the appropriate object or objects before Ted and verbally request that he respond in a certain way. The list contained such responses as putting a hat on and taking it off and putting a pencil in a box. If Ted responded correctly to $E's$ request, he was given appropriate praise. If he responded incorrectly, nothing was said. In either case, E continued to the next item on the list, repeating the procedure until the list had been presented six times over a two-week period. Interscorer reliability was established by having E and an observer independently record the occurrence or non-occurrence of the requested response during one complete presentation of the 50-item list. These procedures demonstrated 95 percent agreement between the two scorers. During the establishment of the operant level, Ted responded correctly to 46 percent of the total number of verbal requests. For 15 of the requests Ted responded correctly between 80 and 100 percent of the time; for ten other requests he responded correctly between 50 and 80 percent of the time; and he responded correctly from 0 to 40 percent of the time to the remaining 25 requests. The data from the operant level trials indicated that Ted had a relatively well developed receptive use of language that was controlled to some degree by social reinforcement. Because of the evidence for the control of Ted's behavior by social reinforcement no food deprivation was introduced.

Investigation of Receptive Use of Language

Study 1. During the operant level trials, *E* noted that Ted often would perform correctly the response requested of him on one occasion but would fail to respond correctly on the next. Ted also demonstrated conflictual behavior at those times that was similar to Mike's behavior observed earlier. For example, when asked to sweep the table with the whisk broom he would sometimes do this, but on other occasions he would become agitated, laugh excitedly, and quickly sweep the floor with the whisk broom. This behavior suggested conflict over compliance with *E's* request and avoidance of compliance by sweeping the floor rather than the table as requested. As a test of this hypothesis, Ted was given a series of two-choice verbal discrimination trials. A two-choice situation was selected because it would provide Ted with more alternative ways of avoiding compliance with *E's* request than had existed in the operant levels trials. For example, Ted could avoid compliance by responding to the object that was not requested, as Mike had done. By recording such shifts in Ted's behavior, it would be possible to demonstrate that the impairment in Ted's receptive use of language resulted from avoidance of compliance rather than from lack of ability to comprehend the content of *E's* request.

During the discrimination trials, *E* sat next to Ted, who faced the table. On the table in front of Ted was a four-inch square box with the two objects to be discriminated placed between Ted and the box. *E* verbally requested that Ted respond in a particular way to the objects before him. If Ted responded correctly he was given appropriate verbal encouragement, and if he responded incorrectly nothing was said. In either case, the object responded to was repositioned in front of Ted and another request was made. The left-right position of the objects and the choice of the object to be discriminated on each trial was determined randomly. A record was kept of Ted's response to the request, the position of the object chosen, and whether or not the response was correct. Ted's responses to a series of these requests are summarized in Table 1. During the First Discrimination Trials, Ted was asked to put a small ball of paper or a pencil in the box. During the establishment of the operant level, Ted had correctly discriminated the request to put the

TABLE 1

SUMMARY OF TED'S RESPONSES IN THE TWO-CHOICE DISCRIMINATION TASKS

First Discrimination Trials Paper-Pencil in Box	Second Discrimination Trials Block-Pencil in Box	Third Discrimination Trials Paper-Pencil in Box
Total Trials = 16	Total Trials = 16	Total Trials = 16
Correct = 10	Correct = 13	Correct = 10
Incorrect = 6	Incorrect = 3	Incorrect = 6
P = .45*	P = .02	P = .45

Fourth Discrimination Trials Paper-Open and Close Box	Fifth Discrimination Trials Paper-Open and Close Box	Sixth Discrimination Trials Open and Close Box-Broom
Total Trials = 17	Total Trials = 17	Total Trials = 15
Correct = 14	Correct = 12	Correct = 15
Incorrect = 3	Incorrect = 5	Incorrect = 0
P = .01	P = .14	P = .001

* All probabilities in this table are for two-tailed tests.

paper in the box 100 percent of the time and the request to put the pencil in the box 50 percent of the time. During the First Discrimination Trials his performance was no better than chance. This suggests that he could not make the discriminations involved in this task. However, in the Second Discrimination Trials the paper was replaced by a small block, and during these trials Ted correctly discriminated at better than chance level the request made of him to place the block or pencil in the box. Repetition of the pencil and paper discrimination task in the Third Discrimination Trials again produced chance discrimination performance. Consideration of these three series of discrimination trials alone suggests that it was the request to put the paper in the box that Ted was failing to discriminate, as he was able to discriminate correctly the request to place the pencil in the box when this was paired with another request. However, the strength of the discrimination of the request to put the paper in the box is demonstrated in the Fourth Discrimination Trials, in which Ted correctly discriminated between this request and the request to open and close the lid of a small wooden box that replaced the pencil. He had responded correctly during the operant level trials to 50 percent of the requests to open and close the lid.

During the Fourth Discrimination Trials it was observed that all three of Ted's errors involved his putting the box to be opened into the larger box, when he was requested to put the paper in the box. To see if this was a trend, these requests were continued in the Fifth Discrimination Trials. During these trials Ted's discrimination performance was no better than chance and all his incorrect responses involved putting the smaller box into the larger one when the request was to put the paper in the box. That the incorrect re-

TABLE 2

SUMMARY OF TED'S PERFORMANCE IN THE SIZE DISCRIMINATION TRIALS

First Size Discrimination	*Second Size Discrimination*	*Third Size Discrimination*
Total Trials = 22	Total Trials = 22	Total Trials = 24
Correct = 9	Correct = 17	Correct = 11
Incorrect = 11	Incorrect = 5	Incorrect = 13
$P =$ .52*	$P =$ .01	$P =$ .84

Fourth Size Discrimination	*Size Discrimination in Play*
Total Trials = 24	Total Trials = 16
Correct = 17	Correct = 13
Incorrect = 7	Incorrect = 3
$P =$ .06	$P =$ .02

* All probabilities in this table are for two-tailed tests.

sponses occurring during these trials are not a function of Ted's difficulty in understanding the request to open and close the box is indicated by his correct discrimination of this request during the Sixth Discrimination Trials, when it was presented in a two-choice discrimination task together with a request to sweep the table with a broom. These trials immediately followed the Fifth Discrimination Trials. During the operant level, Ted had correctly discriminated the request to sweep the broom for 40 percent of the requests.

Study 2. The preceding data indicated that Ted had all these discriminations in his repertoire, but because of motivational factors did not perform the necessary responses on certain occasions. However, these responses involved relatively simple discriminations requiring a concrete level of intellectual understanding. A size discrimination task was introduced in order to investigate the hypothesis that Ted was capable of more abstract understanding, but because of motivational factors was erratic in his performance on tasks requiring this ability. Two light brown boxes, identical except for size, were used as the objects to be discriminated. One box measured 4½ x 4½ inches on each side and the other measured 2¾ x 2¾ inches on each side. The tops of both boxes had been removed. During the size discrimination trials these boxes were placed before Ted on the table with a small block between them. E sat on the opposite side of the table facing Ted and asked that he put the block in either the big or little box. The block was replaced by E after Ted's response. Procedures for reinforcement and the recording of responses were the same as described earlier. The left-right position of the boxes and the request of where to put the block were randomly determined.

Table 2 summarizes the results of the size discrimination trials. During the First Size Discrimination Trials, Ted responded correctly at a chance level to the request to place the block in the big or little box. The Second Size Discrimination Trials immediately followed. During these trials E discontinued the request to place the block in the boxes and now asked Ted to hand him either the big or little box. Ted responded correctly to this request at a better than chance level. Ted's correct size discrimination in this condition was followed in the Third Size Discrimination Trials by failure to respond correctly in a replication of the experimental procedures of the First Size Discrimination Trials. The Fourth Size Discrimination Trials replicated the procedures followed in the Second Size Discrimination Trials and resulted in a return to the better than chance level of correct size discriminations.

As a test of the strength of Ted's ability to discriminate size, the preceding discrimination trials were discontinued and Ted was seen for eight half-hour play sessions during a period of a week. A variety of objects suitable for play were available in the room: building blocks, musical instruments, popettes, balls, two cans, identical except for size, and the objects used during the previous discrimination trials. With encouragement from E Ted began to engage in play activity.

During the course of the play sessions, E and Ted played at anything that Ted wished to do. If, during this play, E could request a size discrimination, involving two objects that seemed a natural part of whatever play activity they were engaged in, such a request was made. The frequency of a request for any particular response was limited by E's desire to avoid making the activity task-oriented, with the goals of making size discriminations, rather than spontaneous play activity. Because of these considerations, relatively few requests were made for any one discrimination and the interval between requests was variable, ranging from one minute to a day.

Sixteen requests were made during four different play activities. These were: (1) put a pile of small blocks in a big or little can (six requests); (2) hand a big or little ring made of popettes to E (three requests); (3) put a big or little popette ring on E's head as a hat (three requests); (4) place the big or little box on top of a tower made of blocks (four requests). These were the same brown boxes used in the earlier size discrimination trials. Ted's responses to these requests are summarized in Table 2. During the play activity Ted correctly responded to E's request for size discriminations at better than chance level.

DISCUSSION

The results of these studies are interpreted as indicating that both of these boys understood much of what was requested of them but failed to perform appropriately because of conflictual responses to adult verbal requests. This study supports the results of the study by Cowan et al. (1965) and the clinical observations of Bettelheim (1967) indicating that the autistic child's negativism may be a major cause of his failure to learn and perform at his age level. It would be difficult to argue that Mike's failure to respond correctly was a function of his lack of comprehension, as his response pattern demonstrated a close functional relationship to the request made of him rather than a variability indicating random trial and error that might be expected during the acquisition of new discriminations. When Ted failed to perform, his errors often were random and thus could be interpreted as indicating lack of comprehension. However, as Mike demonstrated in Study 3, random performance does not necessarily indicate lack of comprehension, but can serve as a method of avoiding compliance. Ted's incorrect responses made during the Fourth and Fifth Discrimination Trials were more obvious attempts to avoid compliance. The abrupt shifts in Ted's performance from random errors to better than chance discrimination with the pairing of a new task with one that he had failed to discriminate earlier also suggest impairment of performance resulting mainly from motivational rather than organic variables.

The results of this study indicate that a discrimination should be made between what autistic children have learned and will not perform and what they have not learned and cannot perform. The usual procedures for establishing the existence of an operant level in Behavior Modification Therapy (Leff, 1968) consist of allowing the S an opportunity to perform the responses under consideration prior to the manipulation of the independent variables. The response is recorded as occurring or not occurring with the frequency of occurrence being considered a measure of the strength of the response. These procedures were followed in this study. By primarily focusing on the occurrence or non-occurrence of behavior, this procedure ignores the process whereby S does or does not perform the response E has designated as the dependent variable. As this study demonstrates closer examination of the variability of the S's performance can provide valuable information regarding the S's cognitive and motivational state that is lost when the methods of measurement are dependent on a limited range of behavior. The limited range of behavior typically ascribed to autistic children may be due in part to our limited means of observing and measuring their behavior.

Although it is unlikely that all the autistic child's behavior can be accounted for by conflictual motivation alone, it is possible that this motivation plays a role in much of the deviant behavior observed in these children. The active avoidance of the use of distal receptors such as vision and hearing described by Goldfarb (1956) was shown by both Ted and Mike. Both boys avoided eye contact with E, and both boys often would put their fingers in their ears when a request was made of them. As was noted earlier, suspicion of a hearing loss was one of the main presenting complaints made by Ted's parents. However, in the absence of any evidence of a demonstrable sensory impairment and considering the evidence for comprehension of verbal communication, the most defensible hypothesis is that the instances of failure to respond positively to verbal communication were the result of the boy's active attempts to avoid social communication and compliance with *E's* request, rather than of impairment of distal sensory modalities, as Goldfarb (1956) has suggested.

Our observations of the negativistic, approach-avoidance behavior of Mike and Ted during these studies suggested that both subjects experienced severe conflict in complying with verbal directions or requests to perform simple motor tasks and activities. It is difficult to avoid seriously considering, if not concluding, the probability that this conflict accounted for much of the variation seen in the performance of the two boys. According to Boatman and Szurek (1960), the origin of approach-avoidance behavior in autistic children can be understood as a result of their early conflictual interactions with parents who were themselves in conflict.

Clinical investigation of families with autistic children indicates that the child not only becomes isolated from his parents, but may be either treated as an object or related to with great ambivalence. It is of little consequence whether the child's responses to parental direction are manifested exclusively in either compliant or non-compliant behavior, the result is the same in either case. Because the parents are often extremely withdrawn or introspective, the child's efforts, compliant or non-compliant, may gain little attention in the form of parental approval or disapproval. On the other hand, clinical observation indicates that conflictful, approach-avoidance behavior in the child generally elicits a great deal of parental attention and involvement and, as a result of such reinforcement, may become a dominant feature of the autistic child's repertory.

These clinical observations and the results of this study also have some bearing on the lack of verbal skills typically found in autistic children. There is evidence that receptive language growth precedes expressive language growth in the usual sequence of language development in the normal child. Also, in the normal course of development, the child associates the voice of the parents with a great deal of positive affect, an association which stimulates the development of imitative speech. However, in the case of the autistic child, clinical observations indicate that the parent's voice is associated very early with approach-avoidance conflicts rather than with positive affect. The early development of the autistic child's negative associations with parental verbal communications results in a poorly developed receptive language repertory. These early occurring disruptions in the developmental sequence may account for the lack of imitative speech and expressive language skills typically found in the autistic child.

Undoubtedly, the most controlled and systematic observations of autistic children have been made with recent applications of operant conditioning techniques with these children. No specific mention of conflict is made in these studies (Lovass, 1968; Leff, 1968). Typically, the observation is made that these children fail to respond to social reinforcement, and procedures are initiated to establish social control of the autistic child's behavior. However, some of the behavior noted in the research reported indicates that social stimuli have acquired reinforcing effects on the behavior of the autistic child. For example, Ferster (1961) noted that autistic children have a response repertoire, such as tantrums and self-destructive responses, that generally functions as an aversive stimulus for adults. Since adults usually withdraw when presented with these behaviors, it is plausible that these responses enable the autistic child to avoid social contact that is aversive to him. Although Lovass (1968) stated that autistic children do not perceive or respond to social reinforcement, he also noted that adult demands set the occasion for self-mutilatory behavior in autistic children. These observations indicate that social interaction is not a neutral stimulus for autistic children but rather functions as a negative reinforcing stimulus that these children generally attempt to avoid.

The observations in the present study indicate that this avoidance behavior is one component of what appears to be conflictual behavior. Although systematic observations and discussion of conflictual behavior in autistic children is lacking in the literature on operant conditioning, such behavior could be accounted for within the framework of learning theory (Lundin, 1961). Boatman and Szurek's (1960) clinical observations of the conflictual behavior in autistic children are also compatible with the results of the present study. Further controlled research is needed to determine how this conflict impairs the emotional and cognitive development of the autistic child. The present authors' informal observations of autistic children in a free play situation suggest that many autistic children really spend very little time in isolation but rather spend a good deal of time in conflictual approach-avoidant behavior with any available adult. Systematic investigation of this conflictual behavior is in process.

REFERENCES

1. BERGMAN, P. and ESCALONA, S. "Unusual Sensitivities in Very Young Children." *The Psychoanalytic Study of the Child*, Vol. 3-4. New York: International Universities Press, 1949.

2. BETTELHEIM, B. *The Empty Fortress*. New York: Free Press, 1967.
3. BOATMAN, M. and SZUREK, S. "A Clinical Study of Childhood Schizophrenia." *The Etiology of Schizophrenia*. Edited by Donald Jackson. New York: Basic Books, 1960.
4. COWAN, P., HODDINOTT, B. A., and WRIGHT, B. "Compliance and Resistance in the Conditioning of Autistic Children." *Child Development*, 36 (1965): 914-923.
5. FERSTER, C. B. "Positive Reinforcement and Behavioral Deficits of Autistic Children." *Child Development*, 32 (1961): 437-456.
6. GOLDFARB, W. "Receptor Preferences in Schizophrenic Children." *AMA Arch. Neurol. Psychiat.*, 76 (1956): 643-53.
7. KANNER, L. "Autistic Disturbance of Affective Contact." *Nervous Child*, 2 (1943): 217-250.
8. LEFF, R. "Behavior Modification and the Psychoses of Childhood." *Psychol. Bull.*, 69 (1968): 396-409.
9. LOVASS, I. O. "A Behavior Therapy Approach to the Treatment of Childhood Schizophrenia." *Minnesota Symposia on Child Psychology*, Vol. I. Edited by John P. Hill. Minneapolis: The University of Minnesota Press, 1967.
10. LUNDIN, R. W. *Personality, An Experimental Approach*. New York: The Macmillan Company, 1961.
11. METZ, R. J. "Conditioning Generalized Imitation in Autistic Children." *J. Exp. Child Psychol.*, 2 (1965): 389-399.

20

Attitudinal and Developmental Data from Parents of Disturbed and Normal Children

Virginia Patterson, M.A.

Jeanne Block, Ph.D.

and

Jack Block, Ph.D.

In a prior publication (Block, Patterson, Block and Jackson (2)), the authors reported a study of the personalities of the parents of schizophrenic and neurotic children, based upon Q-sort ratings of projective test protocols. That study revealed no overall group differences between the 20 matched pairs of parents of schizophrenic and neurotic children. However, a typological analysis of the Q-sorts revealed subgroups with statistically significant majorities of parents of schizophrenic or of neurotic children. The Q-sort items characterizing these special subgroups were specified in the article and were considered to represent personality characteristics of "schizophreno-genic" and "neurotogenic" parents.

Since that study relied exclusively upon personality data of an indirect and inferential type, it was concluded that data more directly related to personality maldevelopment in a child were required. Three domains of behavior were assessed: 1) the child-rearing attitudes of the parents of disturbed children, 2) the life situation of the family around the time of the patient's birth, and 3) the early development of the child patient.

A study by Mark (20) suggested that the child-rearing attitudes of mothers of schizophrenic adult males could be statistically differentiated from those of mothers of normal adult males. The Mark scale was designed to build in some *a priori* hypotheses regarding "schizophrenogenic" attitudes. In the present study, a general purpose inventory that included a broad spectrum of parental attitudes was employed, one for which data are available on a variety of clinical groups. The Parental Attitude Research Instrument (PARI), developed by Schaefer and Bell (26) and used in this study, contains 23 scales representing important dimensions of parent attitudes.

The child's early development was assessed by a developmental survey which inquired about circumstances surrounding the birth of the child, important developmental landmarks, and significant events during the first two years of the child's life. All parents of schizophrenic and neurotic children in our original samples were contacted a second time, and both parents were asked to complete the parental attitude scale, while only the mother filled out the developmental survey. To enlarge the original sample, an additional group of parents of neurotic children was obtained from a child guidance clinic. To provide baseline data, a sample of parents of "normal" children from the pediatric service of a medical clinic also completed the two questionnaires. In all, there were 18 families with schizophrenic children (S parents), 48 families with neurotic children (N parents), and 28 families with "normal" children (C parents). The demographic characteristics of the samples are shown in Table 1.

The increase in sample size resulted in less perfect matching on the age variable than had obtained in our original group. The mean age of the parents of the schizophrenic children was significantly higher than the enlarged neurotic sample, which in turn was significantly higher than the mean age of the normal sample. Education and socio-economic variables for the three groups were not significantly different. The questionnaires were returned by mail.

Chi-square, analysis of variance, and t-tests were used, as appropriate to test differences among the groups.

RESULTS

Parental Attitude Research Instrument (PARI)

A two-way analysis of variance of the 23 PARI scales for the three diagnostic groups (S, N, and C) and for the two sexes (Mothers and Fathers) revealed both significant group and sex differences, as shown in Table 2. Significant interaction effects (at the .05 level) were obtained for only two scales (Approval of Activity and Avoidance of Communication) and, because of the well known unreliability of interaction effects, it does not seem worthwhile to attempt their interpretation.

Turning first to the sex differences, it was noted that fathers scored higher than mothers on 17 of the 23 PARI scales including all of those for which

TABLE 1

Demographic Characteristics of Families with "Normal", Neurotic, and Schizophrenic Children

	Normals N=28	Neurotics N=48	Schizophrenics N=18	p
Mean Age of Mothers	33	37	41	*
Mean Age of Fathers	36	41	46	*
Mean Age of Child	7	10	13	*
Average Family Size	2.86	2.73	2.78	NS
Mean Education of Mothers (Hollingshead & Redlich) a.	Partial College 3	Partial College 3.08	Partial College 3.06	NS
Mean Education of Fathers (Hollingshead & Redlich) a.	College Grad. 1.82	Partial College 2.67	Partial College 2.56	NS
Mean Occupation of Fathers (Hollingshead & Redlich) a.	Business Managers 2.46	Administrative Personnel 3.48	Administrative Personnel 3.28	NS

a. Hollingshead and Redlich (1958).
* Kruskal-Wallace sum of ranks significant at .001 level of confidence.

TABLE 2

PARI MEANS FOR MOTHERS OF SCHIZOPHRENIC, NEUROTIC AND
"NORMAL" CHILDREN

PARI Scale	N=18 Schizophrenic	Mothers N=48 Neurotic	N=22 Normal
1. Encouraging Verbalization	18.64	17.58	17.67
2. Fostering Dependency	10.19	9.80	10.63
3. Seclusion of the Mother	10.28	9.74	10.23
4. Breaking the Will	7.94	8.06	8.23
5. Martyrdom	7.25	7.78	7.68
6. Fear of Harming Baby	11.50	12.14	12.61
7. Marital Conflict	15.39	14.94	15.26
8. Strictness	11.89	12.60	13.12
9. Irritability	14.17	14.40	14.42
10. Excluding outside Influences	9.00	8.46	9.50
11. Deification	9.17	9.01	11.45
12. Suppression of Aggression	8.39	8.60	9.68
13. Rejection of Homemaking Role	10.61	11.84	12.27
14. Equalitarianism	17.17	16.06	16.95
15. Approval of Activity	10.78	10.88	11.41
16. Avoidance of Communication	8.17	8.32	9.69
17. Inconsiderateness of Husband	11.79	11.26	11.18
18. Suppression of Sex	7.39	6.74	7.28
19. Ascendancy of Mother	9.50	9.70	10.54
20. Intrusiveness	7.67	8.34	8.00
21. Comradeship and Sharing	18.22	17.81	18.02
22. Acceleration of Development	9.77	8.14	8.91
23. Dependency of the Mother	11.17	10.58	10.89

significant sex differences were found. The following eight scales showed significantly higher mean scores for fathers: Equalitarianism (.05), Excluding Outside Influences (.05), Ascendancy of the Mother (.05), Breaking the Will (.05), Inconsiderateness of the Husband (.01), Acceleration of Development (.01), Dependency of the Mother (.0001), and Martyrdom (.001). The sense of these findings indicates both empathy on the part of the fathers with the problems, anxieties, and restrictions of the maternal role, as well as a definition of the paternal role that includes concern with standards, achievement, and obedience for the child.

The group differences, however, are those of greatest interest for the purposes of this paper. Five scales revealed differences among the three diagnostic groups that were significant beyond the .05 level. The S parents scored highest on Encouraging Verbalization, Equalitarianism, and Acceleration of Development. The N parents scored highest on Intrusiveness, and

TABLE 2 (CONTINUED)

PARI MEANS FOR FATHERS OF SCHIZOPHRENIC, NEUROTIC AND
"NORMAL" CHILDREN

| | | Fathers | |
PARI Scale	N=18 Schizophrenic	N=43 Neurotic	N=22 Normal
1. Encouraging Verbalization	18.11	17.08	17.03
2. Fostering Dependency	10.72	10.86	10.32
3. Seclusion of the Mother	11.00	10.40	10.09
4. Breaking the Will	8.72	9.31	9.25
5. Martyrdom	9.17	9.88	8.52
6. Fear of Harming Baby	11.72	11.47	12.78
7. Marital Conflict	15.28	14.78	14.82
8. Strictness	10.61	11.88	12.08
9. Irritability	14.53	13.80	14.92
10. Excluding Outside Influences	10.11	9.92	9.67
11. Deification	10.61	10.52	11.06
12. Suppression of Aggression	8.67	9.26	8.35
13. Rejection of Homemaking Role	12.22	12.00	12.54
14. Equalitarianism	18.06	17.22	16.24
15. Approval of Activity	12.11	11.72	10.51
16. Avoidance of Communication	9.44	9.29	8.68
17. Inconsiderateness of Husband	13.83	12.45	12.45
18. Suppression of Sex	7.86	8.36	7.20
19. Ascendancy of Mother	10.83	10.82	10.96
20. Intrusiveness	9.11	9.79	9.13
21. Comradeship and Sharing	18.94	17.84	18.58
22. Acceleration of Development	11.14	10.82	8.94
23. Dependency of the Mother	12.94	12.93	12.00

their mean on the Acceleration of Development scale approached that of the S parents. The C parents scored highest on the Deification scale.

Two of the differentiating scales, Encouraging Verbalization and Equalitarianism, have been viewed by Schaefer and Bell as "rapport" scales. The item content suggests that children should be listened to and respected as individuals. The items of the "rapport" scales reverse the direction of the other scales in the inventory by permitting agreement with socially sanctioned attitudes, while the phrasing of items on the remaining scales necessitates a denial in order for the subject to give the socially conforming response.

The findings in the two rapport scales of the PARI suggest an attitude of defensiveness on the part of parents of S children. High positive scores were obtained by all groups on these scales, but the parents of schizophrenic children significantly deviated from the others in placing themselves at the most extreme affirmative position in relation to attitudes reflected in such statements as: "Parents should adjust to the children some rather than

TABLE 2 (CONTINUED)

F-RATIOS FOR PARENTS OF SCHIZOPHRENIC, NEUROTIC AND "NORMAL" CHILDREN

PARI Scale	Sex	F-ratios Group	Interaction
1. Encouraging Verbalization	3.06	3.86*[1]	0.01
2. Fostering Dependency	0.88	0.08	0.78
3. Seclusion of the Mother	0.65	0.58	0.37
4. Breaking the Will	4.90*	0.29	0.09
5. Martyrdom	16.81***	1.31	1.03
6. Fear of Harming Baby	0.004	0.21	0.04
7. Marital Conflict	0.01	0.92	0.30
8. Strictness	0.35	0.27	0.03
9. Irritability	0.30	0.44	0.48
10. Excluding Outside Influences	5.98*	0.46	0.32
11. Deification	2.40	3.01*	1.28
12. Suppression of Aggression	0.12	0.59	2.43
13. Rejection of Homemaking Role	1.57	1.18	0.77
14. Equalitarianism	4.06*	4.50*	1.28
15. Approval of Activity	1.07	0.09	3.00*
16. Avoidance of Communication	0.53	0.40	3.21*
17. Inconsiderateness of Husband	9.85**	1.85	0.32
18. Suppression of Sex	2.88	0.36	1.61
19. Ascendancy of Mother	4.71*	0.64	0.32
20. Intrusiveness	1.50	4.12*	0.05
21. Comradeship and Sharing	1.93	1.93	0.40
22. Acceleration of Development	7.88**	3.41*	2.49
23. Dependency of the Mother	13.22***	0.54	0.56

[1] * Indicates F-ratio significant at or beyond .05 level; ** denotes significance at or beyond .01 level; *** denotes significance at or beyond .001 level.

always expecting the children to adjust to the parents," or "As much as is reasonable a parent should try to treat a child as an equal."

Overall, the responses from all groups to the PARI suggest that parents attributed to themselves the current "right" answers in terms of changing styles of acceptability in child-rearing attitudes. This was true not only of scales reflecting democratic attitudes, but also for other popular positions, e.g., permissive attitudes toward sex and aggression. All three groups scored low on Suppression of Sex and high on the Marital Conflict and Irritability scales, the latter reflecting acceptance that mothers will feel exasperated and annoyed with their children at times. The parents of psychiatrically disturbed children most vehemently rejected the notion of parental deification whereas C parents were more inclined to express agreement with statements about the importance of respect, admiration, and loyalty for parents. The PARI responses from these relatively well-educated families, many of whom were in therapy, many of whom had taken courses in psychology, suggest that the parents were as sophisticated as the test designers in knowing the "right answers" from a contemporary viewpoint. Only the Acceleration of Development scale provides an exception to the tendency to give psychologically esteemed responses to the PARI. All groups denied that they actively encouraged early weaning, toilet training and walking, but the S parents were in least disagreement with items tapping acceleration.

Developmental Survey

The developmental survey completed by each mother in the study covered various aspects of her child's development as well as her own experiences during pregnancy and the first two years of the child's life. The reliability of these retrospective reports cannot be asserted, and published studies (Haggard, Brekstad & Skard, 1960; Wenar, 1961) would lead us to expect both individual and content differences in reporting. It is possible that the parents of schizophrenic children, feeling personally responsible for the plight of their children, might be more defensive, seeking to justify themselves retrospectively on the developmental survey. As we interpret the differences found, this possibility must be considered.

A further restriction on the interpretation of the findings is related to the age differences among the samples that were noted earlier. Because the parents of schizophrenic children were older and, therefore, further in time from developmental events, their reports may be less reliable than those of the younger parents. Again, this limitation must be considered as the results are evaluated.

In order to provide the reader with a perspective for interpreting the differences found on the developmental survey, it should be noted that eighty tests of significance were completed and 21 of these were significant beyond the .05 level. All X^2 were corrected for continuity.

Pregnancy and Delivery. The age of the mother at the time the child-patient was born was comparable among the groups. Although there were no significant differences in symptoms during pregnancy reported by the groups, the mothers of schizophrenic children more often reported complications of birth. However, when the complications were specified and enumerated, e.g., birth injury, blueness, apathy, poor sucking reflex, there were no significant differences among the groups. It would appear, therefore, that the parents of schizophrenic children "felt" that there were birth-associated complications with their disturbed children, but when asked to specify the number and kind, the reported conditions did not differentiate them from those reported by other groups. This may represent a *post facto* rationalization of the anomalies of the schizophrenic child's development.

Early Development. There were no differences among the groups of mothers in frequency or length of breast feeding. However, when asked about the circumstances for stopping breast feeding, mothers of schizophrenic children more often justified the termination by specifying reasons for their stopping ($X^2 = 10.51$ p$<$.01). The reasons did not cluster and could not be compared with those given by other groups, since the latter were less likely to specify reasons for stopping.

The PARI results on toilet training were confirmed by the developmental survey. The mean age for beginning toilet training reported by the group of mothers of schizophrenic children was 7.75 months. The mean age for N children was 12.29 months, and the mean age for "normal" children was 14.95 months. (The chi-square ratio was significant at the .05 level.) There were no differences among the groups in the reported age at which toilet training was completed. The finding regarding age of beginning toilet training might be confounded by the age differences among the samples, since child-rearing styles have been in the process of change. We were able to test this interpretation, however, by comparing the S group with only the neurotic families in the original sample where age was controlled. In this comparison, the S parents still placed greater emphasis on early toilet training than did the matched N families. It is interesting that despite their "advanced" attitudes on other matters, as reflected on the PARI, the parents of schizophrenic children continued at the time of the survey to favor early toilet training as indicated both by their responses to PARI items and by their estimates on the developmental survey of the time at which toilet training was begun. These appear to be reliable differences.

The mothers were asked to rate on a 5-point scale how well their children ate and slept, how active they were, and how cuddly they were. The mothers of neurotic children most often reported sleep disturbances. There were no differences in activity or "cuddlesomeness" among the children in any of the groups as reported by the mothers.

Questions regarding special sensitivities to sounds, colors, touch, and taste revealed a difference significant by chi-square test at the .02 level. Mothers of neurotic and schizophrenic children reported significantly more sensitivities than mothers of "normal" children. Similarly, "habits" developed during the first year, such as thumbsucking, head banging, rocking on knees, etc., were reported least by C mothers and most by S mothers (p. $<$ .05).

An inquiry regarding illnesses during the first year revealed no differences among the groups.

Discipline. The frequency with which punishment was administered revealed significant differences. Parents of "normal" children punished the least, while parents of neurotics reported punishing most frequently, and parents of schizophrenic children were intermediate. The chi-square ratio on frequency of punishment by parents of normals, neurotics, and schizophrenics was significant at the .05 level.

Significant Others. Parents were asked about their use of outside help to assist with care of the infant or the household immediately following the birth. The majority of all parents reported that they had help, mainly from a relative. There was a significant difference ($p. < .001$), however, in how the help was used. "Normals" reported that the assistance had been mainly with household chores, while parents of neurotic and schizophrenic children reported that the help had been mainly devoted to care of the baby. The difference was most striking for the group of mothers of schizophrenic children.

Regarding the use of babysitters, no significant differences were found among the groups. Parents of neurotic children reported that they went out the least number of times (2.62 times per month), parents of schizophrenic children the most (4.86 times per month), and parents of "normals" were intermediate, reporting 3.67 times out of each month. The difference between the number of times out reported by N parents and that by C parents was significant beyond the .05 level.

When asked how the child reacted to the parents' departures (showed little concern, had a temper tantrum, etc.), there were no significant differences among the groups in the types of reactions reported. When asked if they restricted their going out on the basis of the child's reaction, the majority of parents in all groups denied this.

Environmental Stress. To evaluate environmental stresses during the first two years of the child's life, inquiry was made into the following events: serious illness of either parent, death of a relative, number of household moves, major change in husband's job, loss of income, and separations. Questions were asked also about the length and causes of separation, whether due to illness, marital disharmony, or job demands. Chi-square analysis of the distribution of the total number of environmental stresses revealed a difference significant at the .05 level with "normals" experiencing the least stress, neurotics intermediate stress, and schizophrenics reporting the most stress in the first two years of the child's life. Chi-square analysis of the individual items contributing to the total stress score revealed that the schizophrenic families, significantly more often than the other groups, experienced death of a relative during the child-patient's first two years of life. The relative was most often a grandparent on the maternal side. These families also experienced more separations and changes in husband's job. However, the latter finding may have been associated with wartime conditions, reflecting the age differences noted.

DISCUSSION

A comparison of the child-rearing attitudes of parents of "normal," neurotic, and schizophrenic children in this study indicates that parents of schizophrenic children assert more strongly than other parents that they have treated their children well in terms of being egalitarian and allowing them freedom of expression. Whether this reflects an attitude of defensiveness about the fact of having produced a severely emotionally disturbed child, or indicates some personal guilt, cannot be determined. The survey results suggest that parents of schizophrenic children have tried to teach mastery of developmental skills at an earlier age than other parents, and continue to advocate such early training. There are suggestions that the families of schizophrenic children in our study suffered more severe trauma during the early childhood of the disturbed child, particularly the death of a close relative.

Considering the repeated attempts to find attitudinal deviations that characterize the child-rearing attitudes of parents of schizophrenic children our findings are somewhat equivocal. Zuckerman, Oltean, and Monashkin (29) administered the PARI to a sample of 42 mothers of adult schizophrenics hypothesizing that the latter would evidence more controlling and rejecting attitudes than a comparable sample of 42 mothers of normals. The data failed to confirm the hypothesis, since only one out of a possible 20 scales (Strictness) differentiated the groups. They did find significant interactions between the two groups and levels of education.

Klebanoff (16) found that a sample of 15 mothers of schizophrenic children differed significantly from a sample of 26 mothers of normals on a PARI factor of over-possessiveness, but their scores were not significantly different from a sample of 15 mothers of brain-injured children. Horowitz (15) compared PARI results from 30 mothers of adult female schizophrenics, contrasted with responses from 30 normal females, and found significant mean differences on two scales: Fostering Dependency and Seclusion of the Mother. (The "rapport" scales were omitted from the analysis because of their low reliabilities.) The mothers of schizophrenics were also significantly higher ($p. < .05$) on the factor Approval of Maternal Control of the Child.

The outcomes of these studies, and ours, all of which employed the PARI, have yielded negative or, at best, minimal findings. Two factors have been noted as important in the relative lack of discriminability of the PARI: the operation of response sets and its significant relationship with educational level. The interaction between PARI responses and education suggests that the more educated parents are less likely to respond in deviant ways. Although there are occasional consistencies across studies employing the PARI as well as other child-rearing assessment scales (Dworin and Wyant (4); Farina and Holzberg (5); Freeman, Simmons and Bergen (7); Freeman and Grayson (8); Goldstein and Carr (9); Guerton (10); Heilbrun (12, 13); Kohn and Clausen (17)), no regularly identifiable constellation of attitudes has emerged from group studies of parents of schizophrenics. In none of the studies cited has there been cross-validation of the particular differentiating scales.

Our findings on the PARI, in which education level is controlled, suggest that S parents value precocity in the child's development. The S parents tend to reject authoritarianism in their PARI responses, whereas parents of asymptomatic children are more authoritative with their children as well as less demanding with regard to the achievement of developmental landmarks.

We undertook to compare our data on early development with that of other investigators. However, we discovered that published reports seldom cited specific developmental data on schizophrenic children, even when the information had been collected as part of the study. This was surprising to us in view of the fact that developmental deviation was often a part of the diagnosis.

Bender (1), reporting on the epidemiology of childhood schizophrenia, studied case records of 30 schizophrenic children under the age of 6 matched with 30 non-schizophrenic children. She reported that the presenting complaints of the largest proportion (53%) of the sample of children with childhood schizophrenia could be classified as "maturational deviations" compared with 23% of children with this type of complaint in the non-schizophrenic sample. The nature of the deviations was not elaborated. Developmental data were not cited in the article.

Pollack et al. (25) collected developmental histories on 33 schizophrenic and 11 non-schizophrenic hospitalized adult patients and their siblings. Information was obtained from mothers' retrospective reports through questionnaire and interview. Schizophrenics were rated as a group more irritable, shy, dependent and non-affectionate in their childhood than their siblings. Twenty-five developmental variables, subjected to blind analysis by two raters, yielded no significant differences.

A comparison of demographic information on families of children with early childhood schizophrenia and those with other forms of emotional disturbance revealed no differences in sex ratio or ordinal position (Lowe (19)).

In a study of the genetic histories of 60 families with psychotic children, Creak and Ini (3) found that the maternal age of the mother at the birth of the child was 1 to 6 years older than the average for the general population. However, they believe that this finding was probably accounted for by the high proportion of Class I and II families in the sample.

Pollack et al. (24) compared the results of five controlled studies of pre- and perinatal complications in childhood schizophrenia. Four of the five studies reported a significantly higher incidence of complications of pregnancy as compared to control samples. The most frequent complications were toxemia, vaginal bleeding and severe maternal illness. No relation was found between low birth weight alone and the development of psychosis in childhood. Two studies reported that severe illness or prolonged feeding difficulty (up to the age of two) occurred significantly more often among psychotics than controls.

Osterkamp and Sands (22) studied early feeding and birth difficulties in childhood schizophrenia. They found that neither factor taken alone differentiated the groups but that, taken together, they differentiated childhood schizophrenics from those who fell in the neurotic group.

It is difficult to compare the results of these studies with ours since the data were not for the most part comparable. Our findings did not confirm the older age of the mother at the time of the child's birth nor the higher incidence of birth complications and/or feeding difficulties noted above.

The retrospective nature of the data from the Developmental Survey poses limitations since mothers are reporting on events occurring 4-16 years previously. Because of the age differences among our groups, mothers of schizophrenics are reporting on children from the most distant vantage points of any of the groups. Haggard, Brekstad and Skard (11) found in their study of the reliability of anamnestic information that "hard fact" data were recalled more accurately than wishes and attitudes experienced in the past. Consistent with the Haggard et al. findings, the Developmental Survey, which depends more on factual information about the past, was somewhat more discriminating than the PARI, which samples parental attitudes and feelings.

Research efforts in the area of childhood schizophrenia have proceeded in a variety of directions, as indicated by the Annotated Bibliography of Childhood Schizophrenia 1955-1964 (Tilton (27)). Studies of the biochemistry, neurophysiology, genetics, ego vulnerability, and family dynamics are reported. Reviews of the literature have resulted in differing conclusions regarding the role of the family in the etiology of childhood schizophrenia. Lidz (18) has published extensive studies of the intrafamilial environment in which schizophrenic patients grow up, and concludes: "We believe that by now we possess evidence that schizophrenia is related to failures of the family to fill its essential tasks and the outline of a plausible theory of how this transpires is presented." Frank (6), on the other hand, writes in his review article, entitled "The Role of the Family in Development of Psychopathology," "We end this survey by concluding that we have not been able to find any unique factors in the family of the schizophrenic which distinguishes it from the family of the neurotic or from the family of controls, who are ostensibly free from evidence of patterns of gross psychopathology."

Our study points to certain factors that may be of significance in the etiology of childhood schizophrenia. The results are attenuated, however, by our reliance on retrospective reports provided by parents who have a vested interest in the kinds of events remembered and explanations offered. There is a need for assessment of early development, with observation and information collected contemporaneously. Our findings do suggest areas that might be assessed profitably in prospective studies of emotionally disturbed children.

REFERENCES

1. BENDER, L. and GRUGETT, A. A Study of Certain Epidemiological Factors in a Group of Children with Childhood Schizophrenia. *Am. J. of Orthopsychiat.*, 1956, 26, 131-145.
2. BLOCK, JEANNE, PATTERSON, V., BLOCK, JACK, and JACKSON, D. A Study of the Parents of Schizophrenic and Neurotic Children. *Psychiatry*, 1958, 21, 387-397.
3. CREAK, M. and INI, S. Families of Psychotic Children. *J. of Child Psychol. and Psychiat.*, 1960, 61(1), 156-175.
4. DWORIN, J. and WYANT, O. Authoritarian Patterns in Mothers of Schizophrenics. *J. of Clin. Psychol.*, 1957, 13, 332-338.
5. FARINA, A. and HOLZBERG, J. D. Attitudes and Behaviors of Fathers and Mothers of Male Schizophrenic Patients. *J. of Abn. Psychol.*, 1967, 72(5), 381-387.
6. FRANK, GEORGE H. The Role of the Family in the Development of Psychopathology. *Psychol. Bull.*, 1965, 64(3), 191-205.
7. FREEMAN, H. E., SIMMONS, O. G., and BERGEN, B. J. Possessiveness as a Characteristic of Mothers of Schizophrenics. *J. of Abn. and Soc. Psychol.*, 1959, 58, 271-273.
8. FREEMAN, R. V. and GRAYSON, H. M. Maternal Attitudes in Schizophrenia. *J. of Abn. and Soc. Psychol.*, 1955, 50, 45-52.
9. GOLDSTEIN, A. P., and CARR, A. C. Attitudes of the Mothers of Male Catatonic and Paranoid Schizophrenics Toward Child Behavior. *J. of Consult. Psychol.*, 1956, 20, 190.
10. GUERTON, W. H. Are Differences in Schizophrenic Symptoms Related to the Mother's Avowed Attitudes Toward Child Rearing? *J. of Abnorm. and Soc. Psychol.*, 1961, 63, 440-442.
11. HAGGARD, E. A., BREKSTAD, A., and SKARD, A. G. On the Reliability of the Anamnestic Interview. *J. of Abnorm. and Soc. Psychol.*, 1960, 61(3), 311-318.
12. HEILBRUN, A. B., JR. Note on Acquiescence Set in Endorsed Attitudes of Mothers of Schizophrenics and Normals. *J. of Clin. Psychol.*, 1960, 14(1), 104.
13. HEILBRUN, A. B., JR. Maternal Authoritarianism, Social Class, and Filial Schizophrenia. *J. of Gen. Psychol.*, 1961, 65, 235-241.
14. HOLLINGSHEAD, A. B., and REDLICH, F. C. *Social Class and Mental Illness.* New York: John Wiley & Sons, Inc., 1958.

15. HOROWITZ, F. D., and LOVELL, L. L. Attitudes of Mothers of Female Schizophrenics. *Child Develop.*, 1960, 31, 299-305.
16. KLEBANOFF, L. B. 1: Parents of Schizophrenic Children: Workshop, 1958: Parental Attitudes of Mothers of Schizophrenic, Brain-Injured and Retarded, and Normal Children. *Amer. J. of Orthopsychiat.*, 1959, 29, 445-454.
17. KOHN, M. L. and CLAUSEN, J. A. Parental Authority Behavior and Schizophrenia. *Am. J. of Orthopsychiat.*, 1956, 26, 297-313.
18. LIDZ, T., FLECK, S., and CORNELISON, A. R. *Schizophrenia and the Family.* New York: International Universities Press, Inc., 1965.
19. LOWE, L. H. Families of Children with Early Childhood Schizophrenia: Selected Demographic Information. *Arch. of Gen. Psychiat.*, 1966, 14, 26-30.
20. MARK, J. C. The Attitudes of the Mothers of Male Schizophrenics Toward Child Behavior. *J. of Abnorm. and Soc. Psychol.*, 1953, 48(2), 185.
21. MEYERS, D. I. and GOLDFARB, W. Psychiatric Appraisals of Parents and Siblings of Schizophrenic Children. *Amer. J. of Psychiat.*, 1962, 118, 902-908.
22. OSTERKAMP, A. and SAND, D. J. Early Feeding and Birth Difficulties in Childhood Schizophrenia: A Brief Study. *J. Genetic Psychol.*, 1962, 101, 363-366.
23. POLLACK, M. and GITTELMAN, R. K. The Siblings of Childhood Schizophrenics—A Review. *Am. J. of Orthopsychiat.*, 1964, 34, 868-874.
24. POLLACK, M. and WOERNER, M. G. Pre- and Perinatal Complications and Childhood Schizophrenia: A Comparison of Five Controlled Studies. *J. of Child Psychol. and Psychiat.*, 1966, 7, 235-242.
25. POLLACK, M., WOERNER, M. G., GOODMAN, W., and GREENBERG, I. M. Childhood Development Patterns of Hospitalized Adult Schizophrenic and Non-Schizophrenic Patients and Their Siblings. *Amer. J. of Orthopsychiat.*, 1966, 36, 510-517.
26. SCHAEFER, E. S. and BELL, R. Q. Development of a Parental Attitude Research Instrument. *Child Develop.*, 1958, 29, 339-361.
27. TILTON, J. R., DeMYER, M., and LOEW, L. H. *Annotated Bibliography on Childhood Schizophrenia*, 1955-1964. New York: Grune & Stratton, 1966.
28. WENAR, C. The Reliability of Mothers' Histories. *Child Develop.*, 1961, 32, 491-500.
29. ZUCKERMAN, M., OLTEAN, MARY, and MONASHKIN, I. The Parental Attitudes of Mothers of Schizophrenics. *J. of Consult. Psychol.*, 1958, 22, 307-310.

21

An Experience with the Rimland Checklist for Autism

Aubrey W. Metcalf, M.D.

PSYCHOSES, CHILDHOOD SCHIZOPHRENIA, AND AUTISM

The state of diagreement in the diagnosis of psychotic disorders in childhood has been evident in the publications in this field for the past 30 years. With the diversity of theoretical approaches and the difficulty of standardizing behavioral descriptions, such lack of concordance in diagnosis is not hard to understand. Add to this the suspicion of anatomical and/or neurophysiological disease, inherited or acquired, and the issue is compounded. Each investigator then, following his own ideas, has evolved a more or less personal nosology for behavior, symptom and syndrome which has, as often happens in such situations, led to the proliferation of names and prompted an expectable confusion. The difficulty in rendering objective behavioral descriptions of psychotic children without implying etiology has interfered with the scientific quantification that has been so useful in recent years in ethological research with birds and mammals, especially the subhuman primates. Still, in spite of the differing theories and nomenclature, therapists experienced in the attempt to understand children psychologically will most often be able to recognize in the detailed, clinical reports of others some sequences of feelings and behaviors in both patient and therapist which are typical of repeated experiences with their own patients. This being so, one might suppose it to be but a step more to the evolution of a commonly understood, descriptive checklist which would quantify and cluster behaviors in such a manner that characteristic syndromes become more easily recognizable out of the welter of possibilities. In addition to commonly recognized pathological behaviors one might further include in such an assessment the achievements and developmental landmarks in physical, psychological, cognitive and affective areas. Not only would a checklist of this kind be helpful in isolating symptom clusters (and eventually at some point diagnosis with identifiable etiology), but also it would help in more objectively judging progress in treatment, or the lack of it, which would further the evolution of better treatment.

This report is a pilot attempt to find whether a checklist designed by Bernard Rimland, Ph.D. (19), might contribute to the discriminating among patients suffering from the severe disorders of behavior in childhood. The inquiry was made with some inpatient children at Langley Porter Neuropsychiatric Institute during that part of their hospitalization covered from July 1965 to July 1966.

THE HISTORY OF THE DIAGNOSIS OF EARLY INFANTILE AUTISM

In 1943, Leo Kanner first described a syndrome which seemed to him to separate out a group of children from the rest of those seriously disturbed whom we call psychotic. He held that these apparently unique children must have come into the world with an innate inability to form the usual, biologically given affective contact with people: as he said, "an inborn autistic disturbance of affective contact" (11). Since that time opinion has differed on how innate this disturbance of affective contact really is, and what might be done about it. But, there is some agreement that a subgroup of children with behavior as first described by Kanner can be identified, and their isolation in a diagnostic category, "early infantile autism," has had the effect of implying an etiology separate from other severe disorders of children.

Of course these severe disorders had been observed before Kanner singled out from among them the syndrome of "early infantile autism." They have been generally discussed under the name "childhood schizophrenia" and have been reported since 1943 in Kanner's further investigations (11, 12) and the works of such pioneer investigators as Bender (1), Mahler (13), Despert (4), B. Rank (14), Eisenberg (5), Szurek (23), and Goldfarb (10), to name but a few.

Special attention was focused on the nosological differentiation of infantile autism from other severe disorders of behavior in infancy by the publication in 1964 of a monograph on the subject, *Infantile Autism—The Syndrome and its Implications for a Neural Theory of Behavior,* by Bernard Rimland (19). Dr. Rimland, a psychologist, is Director of Personnel Measurement Research Department for the U. S. Navy and has a special interest in the psychoses of childhood. In his book he holds that true cases of Kanner's syndrome can be separated from disorders which simulate it by means of close evaluation of the presence or absence of the classical criteria as laid down by Kanner. To these he added some items described by Bender and

Despert in their studies of childhood schizophrenia and certain other behaviors suggested to him by his experience administering the first draft of the checklist to a number of parents of psychotic children. He believed that if it were possible to separate from the others a group of afflicted children who showed these classic symptoms of autism with little or no admixture of symptoms characteristic of other disorders such as schizophrenia of childhood or mental deficiency, then the cause and cure of this syndrome would be more available to research. Toward this end he proposed a behavioral checklist to quantify the presence of such autistic behaviors, and includes in his monograph a theoretical discussion of the works of students of the problem which supports his ideas on the biological etiology of early infantile autism, and his feeling that the literature on some successes with psychological therapeutic methods should be disregarded. Since 1964 there have been many further contributions to the psychogenic hypothesis most notably those by Ekstein (7), Bettelheim (2), and Szurek (22, 20, 21).*

THE RIMLAND CHECKLIST

On the basis of the current checklist (which appears as an Appendix to *Infantile Autism*) among 80 questions, Rimland lists 54 items which he considers likely to differentiate a child with early infantile autism (EIA) from one who is suffering from some other disorder. He holds this differentiation valid up to the age of 5½ during which time he feels the autistic children follow a pathway of behavior unique to themselves. After this age he reports they lose many of the traits that characterized them previously and begin to adjust to their disability in various highly individual ways which he does not describe further. The checklist questions, then, are to be answered retrospective to age 5½ or before.

For each autistic feature the list provides one positive check point or plus (+) toward a final score which will here, for convenience, be called the autistic quotient (AQ). The diagnosis of early infantile autism according to Rimland's formulation is made when the combination of autistic behaviors (plus points), as noted on the checklist, is sufficient to exceed the numbers of behaviors on the checklist which tend to be absent from classical cases of autism or contravene that diagnosis in the total clinical picture (minus points)

---

* One of the most important issues in the understanding of early development of serious behavior disorders in childhood is the effect of very early insecurity in the mother-child relationship, the failures of attachment, or the detachment of the child. Recently John Bowlby (3) has gathered together his clinical experience with relevant research data from human and infrahuman species to propose a revised dynamic theory of critical periods of attachment in infancy of great interest to students of childhood psychosis. These views are discussed in Chapter 12 by S. A. Szurek.

by the sum of 21. These identifying autistic factors consist of 38 nonverbal and 16 verbal items and are of two types: those which are apparently meaningless to observers, obviously ill-adaptive or bizarre, and those which might seem either normal or even indicate gratifying precocity in the child, but which are highly characteristic of the autistic syndrome when present in sufficient number and in combination with items of the first type. Opposing these autistic items are 43 features that incline away from the classic description of autism. Most of these characteristics are those of normal or subnormal children; some are those of children with conditions frequently diagnosed as psychosis or childhood schizophrenia. An example of this latter type is question number 7: "Appearance of child during first few weeks after birth; 1) Pale, delicate looking, 2) Unusually healthy looking, 3) Average, don't know, or other." Since in Rimland's interpretation of Kanner's work and from other sources he has used, he has singled out the factor that answers number 2) "Unusually healthy looking" (in the first few weeks after birth) is an implicating sign of early infantile autism. Therefore, one positive point is earned if that answer is selected as correct for the child concerned. If either of the other answers are checked, no negative or positive points are scored.

In question number 20, "Before age 3, did the child have an unusually good memory?", any of three broad categories or their combinations were marked with a positive point for autism, e.g., 3) "Remarkable memory for names, places, route, etc." A negative point (that is a sign implying early infantile autism is *not* present) was assigned for answer number 5) "Apparently rather poor memory." Answer number 4) "No evidence for remarkable memory" was not scored either way.

The subjective and difficult nature of the attempt at differentiation for certain behaviors is illustrated by question number 25, "(Age 2-4) Does the child ever 'look through' or 'walk through' people as though they weren't there?" For this, answer number 1) "Yes, often" earns a plus for an autistic trait, while answer number 2) "Yes, I think so," earns a negative point as inclining *away from* the diagnosis of autism.

By subtracting the total negative points from the total positive points Rimland feels he has demonstrated that there is a clustering of true cases of a diagnostic category of early infantile autism from those other disturbed youngsters who have some features of it but not enough to warrant the diagnosis. His initial work indicated there was a bi-modal curve showing a cluster of children above +20 and another cluster below −10, with a few cases scattered in between. He therefore set an arbitrary cut-off point at +20 for the diagnosis of early infantile autism. Those children with scores of +21 and above (after minus points are subtracted) are considered by Rimland as cases of Kanner's syndrome or early infantile autism (EIA). Those in the

+10 to +20 area he considered questionable cases, and those falling below +10 he felt "exceedingly unlikely to be cases of infantile autism" (17). Rimland feels his results have borne out his theory of autism as a unique and specific syndrome free from blends on the basis of more than two thousand checklists submitted to him by mail from parents and physicians all around the world (16).

THE LANGLEY PORTER CHILDREN'S SERVICE'S EXPERIENCE

At the time of the appearance of Rimland's monograph in 1964, the staff at the Langley Porter Neuropsychiatric Institute Children's Service was using diagnostic nomenclature developed at our Institute through work with psychotic children over the years 1946 to 1960 (see Chapter 14 by Bomberg et al. in this volume). It did not include a separate category for children as described by Kanner but considered such youngsters as falling into what we called the "core" group of childhood schizophrenia. Still, it was not hard for our staff to differentiate from among our patients, according to Rimland's characterization of the major symptoms, a group of children more or less obviously disoriented, anxious and confused, given to impulsive, destructive action and rejection of social interaction in any form as opposed to a group more apparently detached, disinterested and aloof, in less apparent conflict with the environment and seeming non-participant rather than reacting. So, without necessarily agreeing with his theoretical notions of etiology, or his methods (questionnaires without clinical study), we attempted, during the period of one year, to accumulate checklists on most of the psychotic children on our ward during that period as well as selected outpatients and former patients, including two brothers diagnosed as having phenylketonuria.

Bearing in mind Rimland's emphasis that the unifying characteristics of EIA may lose their classic configuration after the age of $5\frac{1}{2}$, we were forced, as Rimland is himself in most of his cases, to depend on assessments retrospective to that period between birth and the age of $5\frac{1}{2}$. During the year we worked with the checklist, however, we were able to evaluate four psychotic children under the age $5\frac{1}{2}$ at the time of evaluation, all of whom continued in inpatient therapy with us for more than a year. They were Dan, Martha, Fred, and Willis, who appear in Table 1. Two other youngsters whom we had been working with for some time fell into the same category except that they were six years old at our first use of the checklist to evaluate their characteristics. They were Patrick and Eddy.

We asked both parents to prepare the checklist from their own experience and without consulting each other. At the same time the one staff member (usually the child's therapist and/or assigned nurse) who knew him or her

TABLE 1

Patient	Age when AQ First Assessed	Plus	Minus	Staff Rated AQ
Dan	5	+44	—4	+40
Peter	16	+29	—5	+24
Dick	11	+27	—6	+21
Neil	10	+26	—14	+12
Jim	12	+22	—9	+13
Able G.	15	+21	—14	+7
Bill	8	+20	—21	—1
Patrick	6	+19	—15	+4
John G.	11	+17	—17	0
Bob	11	+16	—18	—2
Martha	5	+16	—24	—8
Eddy	6	+15	—13	+2
Fred	5	+14	—28	—14
Morris	8	+14	—13	+1
Jato	3	+10	—20	—10
Willis	4	+10	—21	—11

best filled in the checklist utilizing the anamnestic data contained in the chart and their own first-hand interview material from the parents and observations of the child. The assessment was retrospective to before the age of $5\frac{1}{2}$ if the child was older than that, or the age of first contact with the staff if the child came to us before that age. The results appear here in Table 1.

Table 1 shows the scores of the 16 children included in this pilot study, as rated by our staff. All, except the two PKU children, Able G. and John G., and Jato, were long-term inpatients. We referred to the total score, plus points minus minus points, as the autistic quotient or AQ. Clearly the first three, Dan, Peter and Dick, are the only ones to qualify in the category of early infantile autism according to Rimland's cut-off point of AQ +20. However, since *all* of the children in our study had ten or more autistic points, and six of them had more than 20 autistic points, they are listed with both the plus and the minus scores so that they may be compared. It became clear that it was the number of non-autistic traits that kept several of them from falling into the autistic group.

The lack of gradations of severity of symptoms on the checklist led to some difficulty with its use. Both Neil and Jim had been thought of by staff as particularly autistic due to the intensity of some of their symptoms, and we felt the same about one other long-term patient, Howard, whom we have not included here because we lack retrospective estimates. We found that they had too many non-autistic points to qualify them for the EIA group. There seemed to be then no clear-cut clinical features that would satisfactorily separate Peter and Dick from Neil and Jim as suffering from differing syndromes except by arbitrary assignment to a cut-off point on the checklist at +20. There also seemed to our staff to be no reason to exclude Neil and Jim from the diagnostic category of the two boys who scored next higher.

There was, however, a striking difference between the score for these four boys and that for Dan. This *does* hint at the possibility of differentiating by checklist. Clinically observed, Dan seemed much less intensely autistic to us than the four boys ranked below him on the list. Part of this might be that all four of these others did not have developed speech and all of them had been in treatment for some time before the checklist was done. Had Peter and Dick developed speech early in life, we are inclined to think they would have scored higher on the autistic side since they had a relative lack of non-autistic features, as did Jim. But that they all were more severely disturbed than Dan was obvious from the first.

This impression is intensified when we look at the checklist on Dan after one year of inpatient treatment. As evaluated by his nurse at age 4 years and 11 months, retrospective to his age at admission of 3 years and 10 months, his AQ was +40 (+44/–4), one of the very highest AQs recorded up to the present date. His mother had assessed him for that period at +44 (+46/–2), the highest AQ recorded by Rimland to date (15). When he was re-evaluated by his nurse for age 5 years and 3 months, after 17 months of inpatient treatment, his score was +25/–19, giving an AQ of +6. His mother's independent scoring for him at that point was +26/–21, giving an AQ of +5. The fall in autistic features was evenly divided between the verbal and non-verbal items, but the total autistic features remaining were not much below those of Peter, Dick and Neil. The shift in diagnosis from the EIA diagnosis made on the Rimland checklist was effected by the steep rise in the presence of non-autistic features, all of this occurring well within the time when autistic children are held by Rimland to still constitute a unique group.

There was clearly little similarity clinically between Dan at age 5, after one year of treatment, and Neil or Jim at the same age and relatively the same AQ as assessed retrospectively. Dan was obviously much less disordered and rapidly improving. Because of this experience we had to conclude the checklist was of more limited use than we had hoped in our attempts to delineate any diagnostic distinction between childhood schizophrenia and early infantile autism or in gauging the severity of either disorder. In addition, as it is now constituted, the checklist yielded no prognostic indications except to emphasize the already documented important factor that regardless of the multiplicity of autistic symptoms, the presence of useful speech is the most hopeful feature (6).

Although in this study the attempt to show clinically how Dan *differed* from Neil or Jim at the same age and relatively the same AQ was not made, that assessment would entail a quantitative estimation of change over time. For example: In which aspects of behavior did one or another of them improve, improve a little, or not improve at all? What was the eventual outcome, in how long a time? What differences were there among them as to age of onset, nature of the symptoms, degree of apparent conflict within the family and within each individual parent, type of therapeutic work, changes in therapists and nurses, degree of the therapeutic alliances with the child, with the parents, and so on?

The number of variables to be taken into account is great, but the clinician's responsibility is to be as scientific as possible so that data can be verified and compared. A method for increasing the reliability of the basic data from such observations has been made by Feinstein in his monograph, *Clinical Judgment* (8). He proposes a way of separating clinical observations into primary and secondary symptoms and thereafter classifying and counting patients with respect to symptoms in common and overlapping groups in the overall picture of the spectrum of a syndrome.*

CHECKLIST RELIABILITY

Because of our experience with the variability of recall of symptoms in retrospective evaluation, we were inclined to doubt the reliability of parents' reports in some cases, and therefore of diagnosis without thorough clinical evaluation and study. Our experience has been that recall of past events, especially those concerning the affected child, often change and expand during the course of effective psychotherapy. The findings of Walker and Szurek in Chapter 17 of this volume on directed and nondirected history-taking points to a variety of factors which enhance the reliability of the data obtained in a history. Among these factors is the beginning resolution of the parents' conflicts so that they feel less self-blaming and thus less blamed and blaming of others, which leads often to recollection of early behaviors of the child previously not mentioned. The trusting relationship with a therapist and other staff genuinely involved in trying to help resolve the problems of the child and family also contributes to the increased ease and "less conflicted" recall of early events. In addition, Walker's study shows that a clinically-attuned interviewer can obtain a much more detailed history than someone who simply goes through a set of questions in a more or less routine manner.

The results for our pilot group of children are listed in Figure 1. Figure 1 shows the checklist scores as filled out by each parent of 13 long-term inpatient children, all but one of which appear in Table 1. As with Table 1,

---

* The relevance of these suggestions to the subject of childhood psychosis is discussed by Szurek and Philips in Chapter 13.

the assessment was retrospective to before the age of 5½ if the child was older than that, or the age of first contact with the staff if the child came to us before that age. The children are listed from left to right in order of decreasing number of positive AQ points as evaluated by staff. The shaded bar is the graphic representation of the degree of discordance between the parents' estimations of their child's AQ. Staff assessment is for comparison. The complete figures for each parent and staff on each child appear below or above the graph in each child's column.

Due to the singular strangeness of some of the behaviors on the checklist one might look for higher agreement between the parents and between them and the staff for those children identifiable as autistic according to Rimland. We do see two of our three AQ +21 and above children high on the list. For the third highest AQ child, Dick, we were unable to get a checklist from his father, but we note a crucial divergence of AQ between staff and his mother in that the staff's assessment of the AQ placed him in the definitely autistic group in AQ while his mother's did not. Neil and Jim, considered quite autistic by staff but who fell in the doubtful category at AQ+12 and +13, had significant divergencies in their scores. Although Neil's parents agreed closely on his AQ at −4, the staff rated him considerably higher. Jim's parents had low agreement, diverging 16 points, with staff agreeing more with mother. With the remainder of the group there was a general lack of agreement in the AQs between many of these mothers and fathers about their own children.

We might further expect that in the case of divergence between parents, the staff evaluation would be closer to the mother's evaluation, as she would be likely to know the child better. Yet a comparison of these shows staff scorings in the direction of agreement with father more than half the time (Fred, Morris, Bob and Eddy) as compared with mother (Jim, Pat and Ian).

Another impressive factor in this comparison is the discrepancy between the evaluations of staff and those of several sets of parents who *agree* with each other relatively. Willis and Neil are striking examples, and in the cases of Fred, Morris, Jim, Ian and Bob the divergence of the parents' evaluations is so great as to draw doubt upon one or the other of the observers and by this seemingly weaken the usefulness of the checklist for statistical purposes.

These divergencies were not as surprising to our staff as one might suppose due to our repeated experience of such amnestic variability (9). The reliability of the instrument as to the basic data of observation using a parental checklist is made more uncertain to us when we see such divergency. Differences in observations between parents and between parents and staff may on the face of it be related to the relative objectivity of each individual who is being influenced by a number of variables. These variables, in our experience,

FIGURE 1

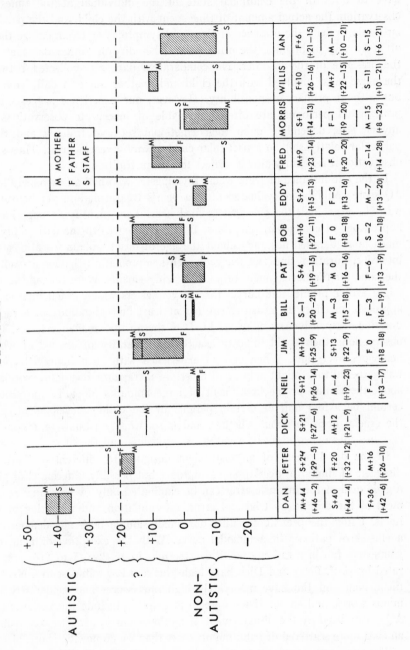

have to do with the emotional state of the individual at the times of observation, the actual amount of time spent with the child, and the particular needs to deny the presence of signs and symptoms or to emphasize them, often by way of blaming the other parent, heredity or "brain damage" for the presence of the disorder. No comparative data was collected between the nurse most involved with the child and another nurse in daily contact, but without primary responsibility. However, our experience suggests that professional personnel are often as capable of inaccurate observations as anyone else, depending upon their emotional set and training and their particular relationship to a particular child at any given moment. Thus staff observational reliability also is subject to human frailties.

In the one instance of Dan, where a youngster who had an extremely high AQ score could be re-evaluated after a year's treatment and yet before he was 5½ years old, the checklist seemed helpful in quantifying our clinical impressions of changes in symptoms. It also pointed us to the desirability of much more detailed accuracy about the age of onset and its variations, the intensity, duration, and frequency of each symptomatic behavior as well as the same for the development of positive achievements. Were this added, one might evolve profiles and curves for our youngsters which would increase or approach an effort at measurement (or at least an estimation) of severity, duration, responsiveness to what kind of therapeutic maneuvers, etc. Our observations then could indicate exactly the quantity of change of which behaviors over time. When enough experience with such improved efforts was gathered they might help us with certain therapeutic decisions, especially about the timing of the investment of large amounts of staff time around certain behaviors and at certain periods in the child's development, e.g., the crucial decision about whether, and if so, when, to allow or encourage certain types of withdrawal, negative assertiveness and the like.

In the development of an instrument designed to differentiate between disorders of similar or overlapping symptoms, but possibly differing etiologies, a good deal of the intrinsic error can be eliminated only by continual refinement of the criteria by trial and error, reformulation and weighting of the items. Using the present checklist our small sample does not demonstrate a cluster of patients in a bimodal curve. With the exception of Dan, our youngsters fall in a rather smooth decrescendo from +29/−5 to +14/−28. As rated by staff, Peter and Dick have high plus and low minus scores. Next to them, Neil and Jim have moderately high plus scores and moderately low minus scores, and so on. If we were to attempt to include the variations in AQs introduced by the disagreement of mothers and fathers, we would have an even more scattered distribution of scores than we do now, in short, blends.

The problems posed by Dan's findings remain. It is hard to imagine a higher autistic score at the beginning, and yet in one year's time between ages of four and five, he lost many of these cardinal symptoms while Peter, Dick, Neil and Jim, with lower AQs and similarly intensive treatment, remained virtually unchanged apropos the checklist items. Disregarding the presence of speech items entirely, Dan would still have been more strikingly high in the plus items than Peter or Dick (nine speech items reverted to non-autistic in that year of treatment), but otherwise the checklist would not have differentiated them in severity or prognosis. Only a course of intensive long-term inpatient treatment determined for us which of these high AQ children could improve with these methods. Those four non-speaking boys with only one-half the number of autistic features as Dan impress us as a diagnostically comparable group, with Dan in a different category altogether. To count Dan to be more autistic than they, would seem to be a paradox as well as contradicting Rimland's statement regarding the uselessness or ineffectiveness of psychological therapy.

This apparent contradiction between autism scores and prognosis, at least in this small sample, needs further attention. In the light of our experience with Dan, and with other youngsters who have come to us before the age of four, the following variables which are not considered in Rimland's checklist seem important in further development of the instrument: 1) The period of the onset of a disorder and when it occurred in the developmental course of the child, especially those factors evident within the first two years of life (age of onset will in part determine how vulnerable the child will be to certain kinds of environmental factors as well as ongoing lack of necessary social stimulations and emotional experiences). 2) The degree of the disturbance when first seen, including the breadth of the symptomatology and the severity of each individual disturbance of physical growth, neurological integration, cognitive, affective and social development, in short all aspects of ego development.

All of these factors, in addition to the items which have been rated by Rimland, must be looked at and weighed to make any checklist meaningful, nosologically in gauging severity and ultimately in estimating prognosis. Even De Sanctis in his paper in 1906 (see Chapter 3 by Jeffress) pointed out that to his surprise *dementia praecocissima* had in many cases been curable. In our present stage of scientific sophistication, and bearing in mind we are dealing with a disorder that has many variables, we must include as many as possible in our assessment and our tabulation to make them meaningful. The step taken by Rimland toward more accurate diagnosis can, we feel, be improved to cover the additional dimensions discussed here, but it seems to us doubtful that it can be done solely through a questionnaire checklist.

REFERENCES

1. BENDER, L. Twenty Years of Clinical Research on Schizophrenic Children with Special Reference to Those Under Six Years of Age. In G. Caplan (Ed.), *Emotional Problems of Early Childhood*. New York: Basic Books, 1955, pp. 503-515.
2. BETTELHEIM, BRUNO. *The Empty Fortress: Infantile Autism and the Birth of the Self*. New York: The Free Press, 1967.
3. BOWLBY, JOHN. *Attachment and Loss: Volume I—Attachment*. New York: Basic Books, 1969.
4. DESPERT, J. LOUISE. Treatment of Childhood Schizophrenia: Presentation of a Case. In Gustav Bychowski and J. Louise Despert (Eds.), *Specialized Techniques in Psychotherapy*. New York: Basic Books, 1952, pp. 135-158.
5. EISENBERG, L. The Course of Childhood Schizophrenia. *Arch. Neurol. Psychiat.*, 1957, 78:69-83.
6. EISENBERG, L. The Autistic Child in Adolescence. *Amer. J. Psychiat.*, 1956, 112:607-612.
7. EKSTEIN, RUDOLF. *Children of Time and Space, of Action and Impulse: Clinical Studies on the Psychoanalytic Treatment of Severely Disturbed Children*. New York: Appelton-Century-Crofts, 1966.
8. FEINSTEIN, A. *Clinical Judgment*. Baltimore: William & Wilkins, 1967.
9. GIANASCOL, A. J. The Psychiatric Evaluation of the Child. In I. N. Berlin, S. A. Szurek, and M. J. Boatman (Eds.), *Inpatient Care for the Psychotic Child. Vol. 5. The Langley Porter Child Psychiatry Series*. Palo Alto, Calif.: Science and Behavior Books, Inc., 1971, pp. 75-79.
10. GOLDFARB, W. An Investigation of Childhood Schizophrenia. *Arch. Gen. Psychiat.*, 1964, 11(6):620-634.
11. KANNER, LEO. Autistic Disturbances of Affective Contact. *Nerv. Child*, 1943, 2:217-250.
12. KANNER, LEO. *Child Psychiatry*. Springfield, Ill.: Charles C Thomas, 1935.
13. MAHLER, M. S., FURER, M., and SETTLAGE, C. F. Severe Emotional Disturbances in Childhood: Psychoses. In S. Arieti (Ed.), *American Handbook of Psychiatry*. New York: Basic Books, 1959, pp. 816-839.
14. RANK, BEATA. Intensive Study and Treatment of Preschool Children Who Show Marked Personality Deviations or "Atypical Development" and Their Parents. In G. Caplan (Ed.), *Emotional Problems of Early Childhood*. New York: Basic Books, 1955, pp. 491-501.
15. RIMLAND, BERNARD. Personal Communication, 1971.
16. RIMLAND, BERNARD. The Differentiation of Childhood Psychoses: An Analysis of Checklists for 2,218 Psychotic Children. *J. Autism and Childhood Schizophrenia*, 1971, 1(2):164.
17. RIMLAND, BERNARD. On the Objective Diagnosis of Infantile Autism. *Acta Paedopsychiatrica*, 1968, 35:150.
18. RIMLAND, BERNARD. Personal Communication, 1965. (Since then this point has been discussed by Rimland, most recently in reference 17 cited above.)
19. RIMLAND, BERNARD. *Infantile Autism: The Syndrome and Its Implications for a Neural Theory of Behavior*. New York: Appelton-Century-Crofts, 1964.
20. SZUREK, S. A. A Child Psychiatrist Comments on Therapy of Schizophrenia. In I. N. Berlin, S. A. Szurek and M. J. Boatman (Eds.), *Inpatient Care for the Psychotic Child. Vol. 5. The Langley Porter Child*

Psychiatry Series. Palo Alto, Calif.: Science and Behavior Books, Inc., 1971, pp. 39-40.

21. SZUREK, S. A. Childhood Schizophrenia: A Psychogenic Hypothesis. In I. N. Berlin, S. A. Szurek and M. J. Boatman (Eds.), *Inpatient Care for the Psychotic Child. Vol. 5. The Langley Porter Child Psychiatry Series.* Palo Alto, Calif.: Science and Behavior Books, Inc., 1971, pp. 92-115.

22. SZUREK, S. A. Review of *The Empty Fortress* by Bruno Bettelheim. University of Chicago: Social Service Review, 1968.

23. SZUREK, S. A. Psychotic Episodes and Psychotic Maldevelopment. *Amer. J. Orthopsychiat.,* 1956, 25:519-543.

Section V

SEXUAL PROBLEMS WITH PSYCHOTIC CHILDREN IN TREATMENT

These two papers analyze the problems of dealing with sexual impulses expressed by psychotic children to aid the therapist to understand and to enhance the therapeutic process.

22

Sexual Countertransference Problems with a Psychotic Child

Adolph E. Christ, M.D.

Although there is no doubt that many countertransference problems arise in the course of psychotherapeutic work with children, the literature is virtually silent on the subject. This is not so hard to understand; countertransference is difficult to discuss perhaps because it deals with such highly personal material. My own interest in the subject was prompted by the difficulties encountered during the treatment of a nearly mute fourteen-year-old inpatient girl who had been considered a childhood schizophrenic since the age of three.

REVIEW OF THE LITERATURE

Countertransference Problems with Children

Although A. Freud (11) and M. Klein (17) have dealt with the technique of play therapy, they have not written specifically of the problems of self-doubt and uncertainty that this work may arouse, especially with severely disturbed children. A few breaks in this silence include the mention of countertransference by S. Levobici et al. (18) who speak 1) of the risk the analyst takes of regressing when he identifies with his patient (child); 2) of the greater difficulty that working with children presents because the analyst must face the child and act; and 3) of the danger of the therapist identifying with one of the parents, particularly when the therapist is a single, childless woman who believes that she can fulfill the figure of the ideal mother for her young patients. Szurek (30) stressed that the therapist, by overidentifying with the child, may increase the parent's conflict or encourage

Reprinted from: Christ, A. E. Sexual Countertransference Problems with a Psychotic Child. *J. Amer. Acad. Child Psychiat.*, 1964, 3(2):298-316.

the child to self-destructive rebelliousness against the parents. Yandell (35) gives six clinical examples of the therapeutic problems related to the expression of sexual drives in psychotic children. He pointed out that the therapist's response may be characterized by actual denial or suppression of awareness of the sexual content of the child's behavior. The therapist's reaction "may be especially angry and retaliatory when a sexual response is aroused in him."

Rather more attention has been paid to the problems of managing hospitalized children. Sheimo et al. (24) showed how unresolved conflicts between and within staff members resulted in greater antisocial activity by hospitalized children. Ekstein et al. (5), describing the schism created between various members of the hospital team during treatment of a "symbiotic" psychotic child, regard it as a manifestation of countertransference. Though not speaking of children, Stanton and Schwartz (25) described the exacerbation of symptoms in hospitalized patients when there is covert staff disagreement. Szurek (28) previously had also pointed out how free staff discussion helps to resolve particular conflicts in hospitalized children.

Proctor (21) discussed various countertransference problems in the treatment of severe character disorders in children. He felt that therapists often "rationalize their counter-resistance by stating they cannot work with a given case in view of the difficult reality circumstances." The therapist may also find it hard to recommend treatment instead of punishment; to "withhold punishment is to condone the patient's impulsivity." He commented that during treatment the child is often sexually seductive and the therapist "must learn to recognize, accept and live with residual and probably irreducible oedipal-castration anxieties" of his own. Also, he stated that "these patients can be maddening, and it is important to sort out the realistic hate they engender" from the therapist's unconscious hate. Szurek (27, 29) emphasized that problems of competitiveness between therapists may emerge in a collaborative effort of psychotherapy when each family member is seen by a different therapist.

Definitions and Concepts of Countertransference

"Definitions of countertransference have varied almost from the first discussions of it, and there remains today wide disagreement as to what the term comprises" (24).

What are some of the trends contributing to the present concept of countertransference? Freud (12) first used the term when he spoke of the patient's influence on the physician's unconscious. Even at that time he warned that the analyst's complexes and resistances limit therapeutic work and in order to be overcome require self-analysis. Five years later, he particularly empha-sized the danger of patients falling in love with the therapist; the therapist must learn this is not due to his charms but is induced by the analytic situation (13). Later authors such as Glover (16) further diversified the concept of countertransference. Stern (26) was one of the earliest to speak of countertransference, defining it as "the transference that the analyst makes to the patient." Ferenczi and Rank (8) have warned of the danger of un-consciously inducing a patient to speak mainly about those things which are pleasing to the analyst's narcissism. English and Pearson (6) broadened the concept to include all that the analyst feels for the patient. Ten years later, Sharpe (23) included the therapist's conscious and unconscious reactions as countertransference, but began to stress that some of these feelings are "healthy." Winnicott (34) emphasized that some reactions of the analyst may be normal, some neurotic, yet both are countertransference. Gitelson (15) added the interesting formulation that if the analyst reacts to the patient as a whole, it is transference; if he reacts to a part of the patient, it is countertransference. That same year, Cohen (2), in a review of the literature, looked for the least common denominator in all the definitions of countertransference and felt it to be the presence of anxiety in the therapist. She then divided the origins of this anxiety into three main groups: (a) reality factors that arouse anxiety in the therapist, (b) unresolved neurotic problems of the therapist, and (c) communication of the patient's anxiety to the therapist. Fliess (9) isolated counteridentification as one part of countertransference and also compared countertransference with *folie à deux*.

A new trend in the present concepts of countertransference has been a shift from viewing it mainly as a factor that interferes with the therapeutic process to regarding it as an inevitable and possibly useful tool. Fenichel (7) felt that the fear of countertransference may lead to the suppression of all humanness in the therapist. Tauber (32) invited an examination of the use-fulness of countertransference data and gave a number of examples where he was able to evoke new material from the patient by exchanging dreams and fantasies with him. Finally, Ackerman (1), in speaking of the dangers of the countertransference, has stated, "The sheer avoidance of emotional engage-ment with the patient may protect a cautious and frightened analyst, but it will not heal anyone."

An interesting re-evaluation of the concept of countertransference was started by Fliess (9) who enumerated four steps in the therapist's instinctive response which Fliess identified as countertransference when, and only when, it takes the form of a repeated infantile response with the patient substituting for the infantile object. Money-Kyrle (19) also linked empathy and counter-transference. He stressed that normal countertransference is "that sense of empathy with the patient on which his insight is based." Such insight comes when the therapist feels the unconscious conflict of the patient as his own, in other words, when he introjects the patient. The therapist then identifies this as arising in the patient when he reprojects him. The analyst must, of course, recognize what elements come from himself and what elements come from the patient.

How are the therapist's unconscious striving and countertransference feelings conveyed to the patient? Freud (14) wrote, "It is very remarkable that the unconscious of the human being can react upon that of another without the conscious being implicated at all." Weiss (33), Ehrenwald (3), and Eisenbud (4) discussed "telepathic feats" where the patient unconsciously perceived the therapist's current situation and core problems. Searles (22) noted that his schizophrenic patients experienced the therapist's unconscious processes as facets of their own personality or as hallucinations; he also found them acting out his own unconscious wishes. He stressed that the therapist can experience feelings "like foreign bodies" which may actually be unconscious processes in the patients.

Though the onus of insufficient analysis still rests on countertransference, I would prefer to define countertransference as those reactions of the therapist to the patient which are motivated by defenses against the therapist's pregenital impulses and which affect the therapist's technique or understanding of the patient. I have purposively left out the usual part of the definition which states that countertransference is a reaction to the patient's transference because there is disagreement as to whether a child whose parents are living is capable of transference. Since the therapist's unconscious defenses against pregenital impulses are stimulated by behavior in a patient, whether the patient is a psychotic child or a neurotic adult, I feel the term countertransference can be validly used when dealing with a child. I have found that if the therapist's genital and pregenital impulses toward the patient are recognized and not unconsciously defended against or acted on, they include some of the therapist's main tools in understanding his patient. These are the foundations on which empathy or insight are built.

There is one other aspect of countertransference that is extremely important in child psychiatry. With the child who may be in the process of destroying the playroom or attacking the therapist, the facial expression of the therapist, his muscle tone, the strength of his grip as he stops the child, or his tone of voice are all registered and reacted to by the child before the therapist may have the time to sort out his therapeutic and nontherapeutic feelings and actions. In the usual less tumultuous therapeutic situation the therapist has leeway in time; thus he can mull over a twinge of anxiety or a primary-process fantasy of his own while the patient is free associating.

The therapist need not respond until he is clear why he feels or fantasies as he does at this particular moment.

Therapeutic work with the mute child demands particularly acute self-awareness on the part of the child psychiatrist at all times since so much of his work requires physical intervention of near-reflex speed and therefore includes somatic nonverbal expression of unconscious affects. That such self-awareness is enhanced by personal analysis was of course stressed by Freud and more recently by Szurek (29, 31). No attempt will be made to give a complete account of the techniques of therapy with the severely disturbed child. What follows rather is a description of psychotherapy with special emphasis on countertransference with a mute schizophrenic child.

CASE PRESENTATION

History of the Patient

Jane is a fourteen-year-old schizophrenic girl who has been an inpatient at the Langley Porter Neuropsychiatric Institute since the age of six. By the age of three, she had already been diagnosed as a case of severe schizophrenic reaction of childhood. Her early history disclosed extreme difficulty with toilet training, which was started at six months, and a refusal of all milk when weaned from the breast at nine months. Throughout the nine months of breast feeding, Jane's mother had painful nipples. In her ten years of weekly and bi-weekly interviews, Jane's mother had been unable to recollect her own emotional reaction to her discomfort during the breast feeding.

Following the birth of her first sibling when she was sixteen months old, Jane's behavior markedly changed. She lost all the speech that she had developed, spent a great deal of time in a crib, and began to paint the bathroom wall with feces. She stood in front of her mother when the latter breast fed the baby sister and deliberately urinated on the floor. Gradually, she became hyperactive and destructive. She did not regain her speech. When examined at three and a half years of age in another psychiatric facility, her therapist described her as "looking through me." After six months of outpatient therapy, "she recognized me by my shoes." Following the birth of her next sibling, Jane became even more destructive and was hospitalized in the Langley Porter Neuropsychiatric Institute at the age of six.

During Jane's eight years on the inpatient children's ward, a major problem was her ambivalence about closeness to people. Over the years she repeated a pattern: when a new student nurse was assigned to her, Jane would act as if the nurse did not exist. After the lapse of a few days or weeks, Jane would then pull her nurse's hair, pick up her skirt, smear saliva on her, and make life miserable for her in a thousand ways. Months later at first, and weeks later during the course of years, Jane would have a few isolated moments when she appeared to enjoy sitting with the nurse, perhaps even cuddling with her. However, even these sessions ended with hair pulling or spitting. Nevertheless, during the periods when she allowed such closeness, she would be more relaxed with the other ward personnel and would make more integrated progress in school and in occupational therapy. When, as periodically occurred, her nurse was transferred to another ward, Jane was inconsolable. She screamed, repulsed everybody by smearing them with saliva or pulling at their clothes, and tried to run away from the hospital. She attempted to hurt herself by trying to get doors closed on her fingers and hugging hot radiators. She would continue this for some weeks or months even after she was assigned a new nurse. Jane reacted in a similar way to a change of therapists or schoolteachers. Since her parents were being seen in therapy, we were able to determine when such a reaction was due to the loss of some important person or to an acute exacerbation of conflict within or between her parents.

Therapeutic Work

A large aspect of my playroom work with Jane has dealt with her fear of closeness, an important determinant of which was her fear of being left or deserted by people important to her. It is perhaps foreseeable how her ambivalence about closeness would bring into play countertransference problems about closeness in me as her therapist, particularly as I realized that her fear of being left would become a reality when I completed my two years of training.

But first, I should explain that in this case the author's therapist and supervisor are identical. The reason is that on the Children's Service, Langley Porter Neuropsychiatric Institute, each full-time child psychiatry resident is assigned to one supervisor who sees the resident three times a week during his two years of training. At the beginning of the training, the resident is given the choice of using his supervisory hours only for supervision or for personal therapy and supervision. I chose the latter.

When I began my two-year Fellowship in Child Psychiatry, I was Jane's fourth therapist. Each therapist saw her for three scheduled playroom interviews per week. She had been an inpatient for seven years. Our first meeting was her 998th therapy hour and my first playroom session. During the first two weeks before regular playroom sessions were scheduled, Jane frequently ran up to me, took my hand in hers, and would lead me to the door of the playroom with a very beseeching, eager look on her face. I felt embarrassed by the intensity of her initial approaches and would disentangle myself as best I could while telling her I would see her as soon as I had my schedule worked out. Her behavior in the playroom in the beginning hours included a great deal of testing. She would begin to cut her hair, touch the floor with chalk or crayons, or start to tear up or break toys. While doing this she would ask, "No, no?" and quizzically look at me. A "No, Jane" or a gesture were all that was needed to have her stop and then continue with the next forbidden activity. One determinant of this continuous questioning might have been her reaction to my initial recoil from her intense approach. Another probably included her trying to define some aspects of our relationship, such as whether I was sufficiently interested in her to stop her destruction, or whether my behavior would be similar to or different from her previous therapists.

As her activities in the playroom became repetitive over the next several months, I began at times to react by daydreaming or feeling bored. I struggled with feelings of incompetence. For weeks she squashed plasticine on a plate, cut it with a knife, then washed the plate. As my attention wandered away from her, she would suddenly stop what she was doing and start scratching the table with the knife, tearing her clothes, etc. During the same time, a twenty-seven-year-old schizophrenic woman I had been seeing in psychotherapy for three years suddenly in near panic described a feeling that she was all alone in the room. I recalled I had been daydreaming for a few seconds. When I told her this, she became furious and then spoke of the fear she felt that I had become too important to her. This helped me understand more clearly that my momentary lapses of attention might provoke Jane to retaliate by destroying something.

As Jane and I became more comfortable with each other, she began more seriously to work out the problems of closeness. She started each session with teasing and provoking which quickly subsided when she saw I was giving her my undivided attention, but the pattern persisted when I failed to do so.

By the second month, I felt more comfortable in expressing pleasure in close physical contact with Jane. Close contact caused uneasiness in me because of my response to her developing physical maturity. During our sixteenth session she spent the first five minutes in her usual teasing, each time coming a little closer, and seemed to enjoy my holding her hand when physical restraint became necessary. I verbalized this, including my pleasure in holding her hands, and suggested she could put her hand directly in mine without first breaking something. She then sat at the toy table and squashed plasticine on the toy plates and called it "ka" (cake). I sat a few inches to her right and she frequently moved her arm back, touching my arm with hers. At the end of the interview, she cleaned up quickly and without protest, then walked quietly to the ward with me. During the next three appointments she seemed intensely and frenziedly occupied with her activities and seemed to exclude me from her awareness. Occasionally, she would start to tear up the playroom but stopped when I said, "No, Jane." I felt rebuffed, disappointed, and hurt. Only by working this through in my personal therapy did I begin to see that this probably was an expression of her fear of closeness, or more specifically, her fear of being seduced.

Eventually, in our 20th interview, Jane's fear of closeness and my resentment at her sudden withdrawal were isolated and brought into sharper focus. She now grabbed the lapel of my coat with hands sticky with plasticine, dashed off, lay down on the floor, and masturbated, shrieking raucously and gleefully all the while. When I lifted her to her feet, she walked over to the toy shelf and broke a few teeth of her comb. She then looked in the lowest shelf with her back to me, stepped on her comb and broke it in half. I suddenly realized I had not stopped her because I was angry. I apologized to her, told her I would try to stop her breaking her own things as I stopped her from breaking the playroom toys. The next twenty minutes were the longest uninterrupted play sequence she had had with me. She had learned to accept that "your things are as important to me as the playroom things." Though this did not become clear until later, she also was starting to learn that though she had acted out a sexual fantasy, one can have human warmth and contact without seducing or being seduced, and without being punished.

During our 24th session, except for a few provocative gestures, Jane played with evident enjoyment for the whole hour, using many more toys than she had before. I sensed a greater warmth and thoroughly enjoyed the hour. As I was closing the door upon returning her to the ward, she made a kissing sound and ran off. She made the same sound again when I left the ward, appeared to blush, then scampered away giggling. Although I immediately sensed that Jane was a little girl who wanted to be held and kissed, I also saw her as a budding young woman and felt immobilized by my sexual taboos and my sense of the inappropriateness of that type of physical response. The same thing happened after the next two sessions except that following a personal therapeutic interview I felt comfortable as I blew her a kiss and grinned. She hung her head and then smiling skipped off to the play area.

Seven sessions later, Jane for the first time tried to put her head on my lap or shoulder. After a few seconds, she viciously grabbed the lapel of my coat, pulled at my tie and hair. During the next several sessions, she repeated this sequence. After a few such occurrences, I began to tense as soon as she got close, even though I knew Jane had taken a long step forward. Before this she would always get me to hold her hand by smearing plasticine on my coat or tearing some object; now she directly initiated closeness and took a chance of being rejected. Nevertheless, I could not prevent my body tensing. I told Jane I tightened up not because she came close to me but because of what she did afterwards. She then put her head on my shoulder for a few seconds longer and seemed to relax, but again grabbed for my tie. I then told her that though she might enjoy being close to me, she might also be afraid. I did not understand fully why she was afraid, but perhaps we could find out together.

By the fifth month Jane started putting her head on my arm or on my lap and after a few seconds would resume her previous activity without spitting and pulling my hair or tie. Over the next five months she relaxed into a routine—she would take some objects such as my keys, my coins, or her own trinkets. She made an imprint of them in plasticine, then took them to the blackboard and made an outline of them with chalk, turned them around and outlined the back, then tried to put in a few lines to represent some features of the object. It was as if she were trying to draw on two dimensions what she saw in three and was puzzling how to do this. Then she took the object to the table and drew an outline of it with a crayon on paper and then washed the object with soap and water. Before starting on the next object, she would put her head on the table for me to stroke her hair. This was a rather calm period in her life. In school she was learning the alphabet and all day long, with her nurse, experimented with new words and sounds.

The next area Jane worked on was how to share an adult with another child. This was a big problem at home. On weekends her mother let Jane sleep longer. She fed the other children and sent them out to play. Only then would Jane get up and breakfast alone with her mother. At night the other children were put to bed early and Jane was allowed to stay up late. Her mother devised this routine because Jane was much easier to handle when they were alone together.

Once a week the full-time child psychiatry residents take care of the ward children for forty-five minutes while the nursing staff has a meeting. On occasions I have been assigned Helen, a self-destructive child whose arms, legs, and face have to be held to keep her from hitting, biting or kicking herself or the person holding her. The staff decided that there would be greater likelihood of understanding Helen's destructiveness and helping her to control it if an adult spent as much time with her as possible rather than fully restraining and isolating her. Helen wore a sweat shirt the arms of which could be pinned to the shirt when this additional restraint became necessary.

The greatest freedom she could usually safely have was when the adult sat next to her, put his leg on her lap, held each of her hands and was in a position to stop her butting her head against a hard object or control her mouth from biting herself or the adult. In past years during unguarded moments, Helen had knocked out a number of her teeth, gashed her face and head, and viciously bitten many of the staff. For months while I held this girl, Jane sat in a far corner, surrounded by magazines and other personal toys, and kept herself frantically busy. She would look at me out of the corner of her eyes when she thought I did not notice. When some of the other residents came to her, she pushed them away with a loud and emphatic "No!" I encouraged Jane to sit by us and slowly she came, first for a few seconds, then for longer and longer periods. During these moments Jane tried to get my attention by grabbing in my pocket, pulling back my shirt collar, putting her head on my lap, and then spitting on me. Yet, there were occasional moments when both Helen and Jane would relax as I talked to them and I began to feel encouraged.

During one of these sessions, Helen had sufficiently relaxed that I had left her head free and unpinned the arms of her sweat shirt to relieve her hands. Jane, who sat next to me, suddenly put her legs over mine as I had them over the legs of Helen and began to rub her legs and rock herself on my lap in an obviously sexual way. At the same instant Helen reacted to Jane's placing her legs on me by trying to kick, pinch, and bite herself and me. I immediately pushed Jane off, got up and concentrated on Helen; Jane got up from the sofa, stood a few feet away, gleefully laughed, undressed, stuck her fingers in her rectum and vagina, then sat on the wastebasket and urinated. At that instant I imagined the disapproving eye of each of my fellow residents on me. I reminded myself of Jane's despair and of her inability to tolerate rivalry and felt guilty when I thought "the hell with that." I felt like hitting her. It took a few seconds to regain control over Helen and of my own feelings. I then spoke to both about their feelings of rivalry for each other and of their rage at me for being unable to stop this sequence. Both relaxed and Jane sat by us as I continued talking to each about the similarity in feelings that both had experienced. I wish I could say that from then on Jane tolerated sharing me with another child. Instead, she continued to struggle openly with her intense jealousy, making life miserable for both of us when I was with another child. Gradually there were more moments when Jane could relax with me and another child. Recently, I was holding Helen; this time her head was free and I had unpinned her hands so they were both out of the sweat shirt. Jane sat by us, then cut out bits of the magazine she had and gave some pieces to Helen and some to me.

Though Jane's course had been a steady slow improvement over the years, as she reached her fourteenth birthday, it was felt that some plan other than ward care should be explored. One of these alternatives was to increase the parents' interviews from once to twice a week. However, they decided to stop their contact with Langley Porter and seek admission for

Jane in a state hospital where their participation in treatments would not be urged.

They had a one-day evaluation at the state hospital. Jane was "as good as gold," sat quietly with her hands in her lap, neither teased nor provoked her examiner. The examiner told the parents, as he later told us, that he felt Jane was mentally deficient and that if she had been schizophrenic, her psychotic symptoms had been "cured." He recommended confinement in a hospital for the mentally deficient. As the parents were relating Jane's history and hospital course to the examiner, however, they became convinced that Jane still needed further psychiatric help. The parents changed their minds and decided to continue working with us and increased the frequency of their interviews.

Jane became very upset with her nurses and with me during these three weeks that we discussed her probable termination of contact with the ward, and her probable transfer to another hospital. During the first part of these weeks, Jane was unmanageable. So long as I was preoccupied with my feelings of loss, she was frantically destructive during the playroom sessions, breaking toys and tearing her clothes. As soon, however, as I had sufficiently resolved my resentment toward her parents, her parents' therapists, and the senior staff for "taking Jane away from me," I was freed to focus on her distress and the destructive behavior stopped. When I finally concentrated on her fully, she looked directly at me. It is difficult to describe that instant. It was as if the veil over her eyes momentarily lifted and with it some I-you boundary took shape. In the months that followed, she experimented more openly with eye contact. At times her face was a few inches from mine; at other times, she studied my eyes almost impersonally. Recently she has looked directly in my eyes when she tried to communicate with me or I with her.

It is of interest to note that Jane's mother mentioned sex only twice in ten years of outpatient therapy, where she was urged to use free association. Once she recalled that the only sexual training she had received was when her brother told her, "Always keep your knees covered with your skirt!" The second time, she began to relate a fantasy of exhibiting herself, blocked, and never again discussed this. The absence of discussion of sex is particularly interesting because of Jane's exhibitionism and open masturbation, and Jane's twelve-year-old sister showing her panties to the boys at the school bus stop.

A few months ago, as Jane's secondary sexual characteristics developed fully and she began to menstruate, she became more sexually aggressive. Instead of putting her head on my lap or shoulder in the playroom sessions and relaxing, Jane would sit tensely on my lap and then straddle my leg and rub her thighs on it in an obviously masturbatory fashion. I pushed her off and tried to stop her, yet my feelings were ambivalent. On the one hand, this made me uncomfortable and aroused sexual and then guilt feelings in me. On the other hand, I was convinced that through these exploratory actions she continued experimenting with closeness. I began to wonder whether we could separate the unpleasant aspects from the potentially quiet, relaxed, mutually pleasant ones.

At first I struggled with the fear that in the process of working this out Jane might find herself caught in a situation where sensual pseudo gratification might occupy all our therapeutic time and preclude all further growth and exploration. I therefore decided to stop her by pushing her away more actively and calling her attention to what she was about to do before she sat on my lap. Still she persisted. I then realized I was misinterpreting the senior staff's guiding remarks as a categorical "Thou shalt not allow sensual contact with a child" without fully thinking this out for myself. There were moments during these sessions when Jane reacted to my lack of clarity by viciously attacking me or lying on the floor, lifting her legs and fondling her genitals while emitting loud, tense laughing shrieks. At those moments I remember wondering if one of the supervisors might be peering reprovingly into the playroom window. Two descriptions of Jane flashed through my mind. Her father used to ride her on his foot when she was four to five years old, and her mother reacted to it as though both were deriving some perverse sexual gratification from it. Her grandfather, who was once apprehended for molesting a minor and was a confirmed alcoholic, had spent time with the family a few weeks before. Her mother described passing by the living room and seeing Jane straddling his lap, rocking herself, giggling. Both seemed to her to be enjoying this sexual type of contact. Though she felt vaguely uneasy, she continued walking past the room and tried to forget the incident. Was I also provoking this persistence?

As I worked through my own doubts and explored my own associations and feelings with my therapist one day, I decided to watch with care and without interruption the full sequence of events from the moment she sat on my lap. Perhaps I could thereby learn what contributed to Jane's struggle. This, however, was not possible until the countertransference aspect became clear. This occurred when I recalled the close similarity of these episodes to a childhood sexual experience of my own. It also explained my fear that the supervisor (my father) might look into the window while Jane was masturbating. I had not fully worked through my uncertainties, but was beginning to identify them and separate them from what I had projected onto Jane. Thus I felt ready to see what Jane was saying in her nonverbal way. On Monday Jane straddled my leg twice, each time for a second, then got up and quietly sat in her chair and continued with her sequence of play. Though I felt tense, I felt more ready to have her continue without interrupting her or stopping her, yet she stopped herself. During the next session she sat on my lap, but this time without squirming, quietly with her head on my shoulder. Without pulling my hair, coat, or tie, she then got up and wrote numbers one through four on a piece of paper. I asked if she would write her name on the other side and she did. She then gave the paper to me and said "Thankee." In this area it was the most integrated piece of behavior I had seen. She wrote correctly, did not scratch out her writing as she usually did, and gave it to me without first tearing it up. By the next hour I learned that her parents were planning a two weeks' vacation and would take Jane out of the hospital for that period of time. I told her so and she again sat on my lap in the same tense rocking fashion. As I spoke to her about her resentment at not having been told before, missing a number of appointments with me, and not seeing her nurse during this period, she relaxed, got off, and then continued playing.

As I continued to observe Jane and myself over the next months, the sequence of events that preceded her sexual assaults began to be clearer. Jane climbed onto my lap and attempted to masturbate either when she was angry or displeased, when she felt particularly close to me, or when I had provoked her without being aware of it. This became particularly clear when during one playroom session I stopped to tie my shoes which she had playfully unlaced and unthinkingly lightly touched her head with mine while we were both sitting at the table. She immediately stopped drawing. Laughing throatily, she straddled my leg. Two hours later, an adult woman patient blocked while recalling an erotic incident. While I watched her struggles, my associations included: identification with her lover, momentary anger at her blocking, awareness of sensuous feelings, then in quick succession flashes of her, my mother, wife, female friend, and Jane. Then I recalled the above incident with Jane two hours before and with sudden clarity saw how my touching her head had precipitated her sexual advance.

It was not for several months, however, that I was able to take one final step in helping Jane to control her seductive, masturbatory behavior. On this occasion she had begun to pull her dress up while sitting at the playroom table. Tensely and throatily she laughed, pushed her chair back and sat on her heels, pulling her panties down and masturbating with the cup she had been holding. She nudged me with her knee, put the cup down, and masturbated with a small baby bottle. Her provocatively enraging laugh suddenly changed and her eyes teared. She put the small baby bottle away and took the large one, put it by her genitals and said, "Pee-pee." I said,

"You must feel very embarrassed—why don't you dress and I'll take you to the bathroom." She quickly got up.

In the whole episode, which lasted about three minutes, I experienced the following sequence of reactions. When Jane first began to pull her dress up and laugh uncomfortably, my immediate impulse was to stop her. I refrained, because I realized that the impulse to stop her was mainly because I was uncomfortable. When she pushed the chair back and pulled her panties down and began to masturbate, I became enraged at her and the instant I felt this, I also suddenly realized that I was displacing this rage. I was enraged at myself for being sexually aroused. By the time she nudged me with her knee and commandingly said, "Huu huu!" I began to sense a shift in both of us. I no longer feared my own sensual experiences and so could focus my attention much more closely on Jane. Since I was not contaminating the situation by converting my own discomfort into action, she more clearly perceived what she was doing. Before this, I believe her self-awareness was lost because my struggle to stop her seemed to channel all her attention to the physical battle with me. Once I had wrestled with my own impulses, I did not need to wrestle with her. At the end when I said, "You must feel very embarrassed," perhaps because I could so clearly sense her desire to stop, she did stop herself without my having to touch her. This marked a rather dramatic turning point in our work together.

In the weeks that followed, there were a number of occasions when Jane gave more and more evidence of an internal struggle before acting on an impulse. She would be drawing or writing and suddenly laugh in the same tense fashion that in the past had accompanied some destructive act, then tightly shut her eyes, clench her fists, and hold her whole body rigid. At times I commented to her on how difficult it is to struggle with oneself; at other times, on how good it must feel to know that one can stop oneself.

At present her behavior has markedly changed in many areas. In school she can copy and print words. With her speech therapist she is experimenting with new sounds. She has made a series of remarkable changes with her nurse, only one of which is evident pleasure in dressing and grooming herself.

There is one final aspect of work with a mute schizophrenic child that needs further mention. The feeling of chaos before clarity ensues is difficult to live with. During these times I often find myself trying to fit the round patient into square theories, only to find later that by doing so I selectively observed the patient and thereby excluded many data from my awareness. This is not to say that theory necessarily hinders therapy, but rather that theorizing can be used as a mechanism of defense to deal with the anxiety generated by feelings of uncertainty and chaos. Fortunately, a patient's verbal comments will in time correct this. With the mute child, however, where play may be repetitive and difficult to understand, the moments of total uncertainty as to what the child is feeling and trying to work through can be very long. Also, feelings and fantasies of the therapist that could either be his projections or an empathic understanding of the child can be confirmed only by following nonverbal cues, which are often highly non-specific and subject to distortion by the therapist.

I am finding that the willingness to work for long periods of time with uncertainty and apparent absence of confirmatory data from a patient is requisite for the therapist working with the nonverbal schizophrenic child. This feeling of chaos may in itself be an empathic understanding of the child's feelings. Perhaps a new phase in treatment comes when as a therapist one can accept this feeling of chaos without anxiety and without attempting to push the child into a theoretical framework in order to decrease the therapist's anxiety and fulfill his need for structure. Perhaps then the child can begin to find the structure in his feelings in the presence of an unanxious, unmolding therapist.

Thus I found it took eighteen months of working with Jane before I more clearly differentiated her discomfort from my own, could more closely look at the source of my own anxiety, and could stand to live with my own anxiety while she worked through her own difficulties in my presence. Only then did I begin to see more clearly the difference between the authoritative position "I'll help you to stop, Jane, because if you go on you will feel embarrassed, hurt and tense" and the authoritarian position "Stop Jane, because I tell you to or because others have told me to stop you" or "because I feel too tense and uncomfortable if you don't." There is a world of difference between, on the one hand, that feeling of clarity and conviction with which one can encourage another to reconsider or stop an act because it is clearly for the other one's benefit and, on the other hand, that anxious, slightly unclear insistence that is perhaps more often based on an inability to identify and face certain feelings and experiences within oneself.

CONCLUSION

I have outlined problems emerging in the course of eighteen months of treatment of a nearly mute fourteen-year-old schizophrenic girl who seemed profoundly influenced by the countertransference. In this period her behavior changed in many areas. I have stressed three major changes that have taken place in the course of our therapeutic work; (1) she now engages in a great deal of direct eye contact with me; (2) she is now very direct in initiating physical contact; and (3) she is now able to let a longer time interval elapse between impulse and act.

In each of these areas I have seen how her progress was delayed as long as I was unaware of my countertransference. Only as I identified my use of such defense mechanisms as repression, denial, displacement, and intellectualization in relation to our work together did her behavior begin to change. Continued identification, clarification, and perhaps even resolution of conflict in the therapist plus longer experience may decrease the countertransference in therapeutic work with psychotic children. The paucity of literature on countertransference with children might seem to indicate that it continues to be a difficult area for all therapists. Unquestionably, here is a fruitful field for further collaboration.

REFERENCES

1. ACKERMAN, N. W. Transference and Countertransference. *Psychoanalysis & Psychoanal. Rev.*, 1959, 46:17-28.
2. COHEN, M. P. Countertransference and Anxiety. *Psychiatry*, 1952, 15: 231-243.
3. EHRENWALD, J. Telepathy in the Psychoanalytic Situation. *Brit. J. Med. Psychol.*, 1944, 20:51-62.
4. EISENBUD, J. Telepathy and Repression. *Psychoanal. Quart.*, 1947, 15: 61-68.
5. EKSTEIN, R., WALLERSTEIN, J., and MANDELBAUM, A. Countertransference in Residential Treatment. *The Psychoanalytic Study of the Child*. New York: International Universities Press, 1959, 14:186-218.
6. ENGLISH, O. S. and PEARSON, G. H. J. *Common Neuroses of Children and Adults*. New York: Norton, 1937.
7. FENICHEL, O. Problems of Psychoanalytic Technique. *Psychoanal. Quart.*, 1941, 10:71-75.
8. FERENCZI, S. and RANK, O. *The Development of Psychoanalysis*. New York: Nervous and Mental Disease Publishing Co., 1925.
9. FLIESS, R. The Metapsychology of the Analyst. *Psychoanal. Quart.*, 1942, 11:211-227.
10. FLIESS, R. Countertransference and Counteridentification. *J. Amer. Psychoanal. Assn.*, 1953, 1:268-284.
11. FREUD, A. *The Psychoanalytical Treatment of Children*. New York: International Universities Press, 1957.
12. FREUD, S. The Future Prospects of Psychoanalytic Therapy. *Collected Papers*, 2:285-296. London: Hogarth Press, 1949.
13. FREUD, S. Observations on Transference Love. *Collected Papers*, 2:377-391. London: Hogarth Press, 1949.
14. FREUD, S. The Unconscious. *Collected Papers*, 4:98-136. London: Hogarth Press, 1949.
15. GITELSON, M. The Emotional Position of the Analyst in the Psychoanalytic Situation. *Int. J. Psycho-Anal.*, 1952, 33:1-10.
16. GLOVER, E. *The Technique of Psychoanalysis*. New York: International Universities Press, 1955.
17. KLEIN, M. *The Psychoanalysis of Children*. New York: Grove Press, 1960.
18. LEVOBICI, S., DIATKINE, R., FAVREAU, J. A., and LUQUET-PARAT, P. The Psychoanalysis of Children. In S. Nacht (Ed.), *Psychoanalysis of Today*. New York: Grune & Stratton, 1959.

19. MONEY-KYRLE, R. E. Normal Countertransference and Some of Its Deviations. *Int. J. Psycho-Anal.*, 1956, 37:360-366.
20. ORR, D. W. Transference and Countertransference. *J. Amer. Psychoanal. Assn.*, 1954, 2:621-668.
21. PROCTOR, J. T. Countertransference Phenomena in the Treatment of Severe Character Disorders in Children and Adolescents. L. Jessner and E. Pavenstedt (Eds.), *Dynamic Psychopathology in Childhood.* New York: Grune & Stratton, 1959, pp. 293-309.
22. SEARLES, H. F. The Schizophrenic's Vulnerability to the Therapist's Unconscious Processes. *J. Nerv. & Ment. Dis.*, 1958, 127:247-262.
23. SHARPE, E. F. The Psychoanalyst. *Int. J. Psycho-Anal.*, 1947, 28:1-6.
24. SHEIMO, S. F., PAYNTER, J., and SZUREK, S. A. Problems of Staff Interaction with Spontaneous Group Formations on a Children's Psychiatric Ward. *Amer. J. Orthopsychiat.*, 1949, 19:599-611.
25. STANTON, A. E. and SCHWARTZ, M. S. *The Mental Hospital.* New York: Basic Books, 1954.
26. STERN, A. On the Countertransference in Psychoanalysis. *Psychoanal. Rev.*, 1924, 11:166-174.
27. SZUREK, S. Some Problems in Collaborative Therapy. *Newsltr. Amer. Assn. Psychiat. Soc. Work.*, 1940, 9:1-7.
28. SZUREK, S. Dynamics of Staff Interaction in Hospital Psychiatric Treatment of Children. *Amer. J. Orthopsychiat.*, 1947, 17:652-664.
29. SZUREK, S. Remarks on Training for Psychotherapy. *Amer. J. Orthopsychiat.*, 1949, 19:36-61.
30. SZUREK, S. Problems around Psychotherapy with Children. *J. Pediat.*, 1950, 37:671-678.
31. SZUREK, S. *Roots of Psychoanalysis and Psychotherapy.* Springfield: Thomas, 1958.
32. TAUBER, E. S. Exploring the Use of Countertransference Data. *Psychiatry*, 1954, 17:331-336.
33. WEISS, E. Regression and Projection in Super-Ego. *Int. J. Psycho-Anal.*, 1932, 13:449-478.
34. WINNICOTT, D. W. Hate in the Countertransference. *Int. J. Psycho-Anal.*, 1949, 30:69-74.
35. YANDELL, W. Therapeutic Problems Related to the Expression of Sexual Drives in Psychotic Children. Read at American Orthopsychiatric Association meeting, Los Angeles, California, 1962.

23

Therapeutic Problems Related to the Expression of Sexual Drives in Psychotic Children

Wilson Yandell, M.D.

INTRODUCTION

Bodily contact between child and staff members is a regular part of work with psychotic children. This may develop either in response to the child's seeking of closeness, or to behavior by the child which requires physical restraint. In either instance the therapist may become the object of or a participant in the child's pursuit of sensual pleasure. The child's intense anxiety about conflict-ridden sexual impulses may be expressed in the massive inhibition of all responsiveness or in the chaotic eruption into behavior of the derivatives of such impulse, whether of oral, anal, or phallic stage of development, or of tactile, kinesthetic, or other sensory-motor modality.

The child's sensual impulses and his frantic effort to stem their expression may influence therapeutic interaction. The ways that therapeutic work may be affected deserve closer scrutiny than has so far been reported. Such scrutiny should lead to the identification of those responses in the therapist most effective in reducing anxiety within the child, who may then gradually feel free to explore less disruptive and more gratifying modes of sensual expression. Of perhaps equal importance for those of us interested in the hypothesis of the psychogenic etiology of psychoses in childhood, we may begin to obtain evidence of the kinds of experience a given child has had with his parents in which the roots of his confusion or disturbance lie. This is particularly true when concomitant psychotherapeutic work with parents pro-

---

This paper was originally presented in somewhat different form at the Annual Meeting of the American Orthopsychiatric Association, Los Angeles, California, March 1962.

vides data to supplement or corroborate that understanding gained in work with the child.

REVIEW OF THE LITERATURE

The literature contains little regarding the effect of the child's expression of sensual impulses upon the therapist-patient relationship. Much has been written particularly in the psychoanalytic literature describing psychosexual development and its relationships to psychopathology. Klein (9) and Anna Freud (7) have each discussed child analysis from her view of the analogues of observed behavior in the psychosexual development of the child. Neither, however, emphasizes problems arising in the analyst or therapist-patient interaction, viewing the events of therapeutic work almost exclusively in terms of the child's conflict-ridden instinctual life.

Some workers feel that psychodynamic considerations do not apply to an understanding of or to work with psychotic children. The content of the psychotic child's behavior may be considered as inexplicable, or as an expression of disturbed brain function (3). Still others view his behavior as an expression of the child's disturbed concepts about self in relation to objects or to orientation in time and space (8). However, hypotheses that the etiology of psychosis is specifically related to disturbed interpersonal experience and its effect upon psychosexual development have been proposed by Mahler (10) and others. Szurek (14) has presented the psychogenic hypothesis for childhood schizophrenia and described the "psychotic maldevelopment" of the child. Boatman and Szurek (5) have described the general experience of the Langley Porter Institute staff in its research investigation of the psychogenic hypothesis and of the efficacy of concomitant psychotherapy with child and parents in the treatment of childhood schizophrenia. Bettelheim in his book *The Empty Fortress* (4) beautifully explicates the psychogenic hypothesis as well as to review conflicting views. In volume 5 of the Langley Porter Child Psychiatry Series, *Inpatient Care for the Psychotic Child* (16), Szurek, Berlin and Boatman have collected much of the work and thought which served as the foundation for the clinical work described in the present paper.

General discussions of play therapy, its techniques and rationale, as in the work of Allen (1) and Axline (2), do not deal with the problems of work with severely disturbed, psychotic children. In their paper "Elements of Psychotherapeutics with the Schizophrenic Child and his Parents," Szurek and Berlin (15) mention as one among many aspects of the therapeutic task with the psychotic child, the problems arising from the expression of the child's sexual impulses, but the scope of the paper does not permit detailed discussion of those problems. Christ, with reference to the original presentation of the present paper has published a case report, "Sexual Countertransference Problems with a Psychotic Child" (6).*

Middlemore (11) has clarified the "uses of sensuality" in the relationships of parents to normal children. He has pointed out not only the child's sources of conflict but also the conflict in the parent aroused by the child's sensuality, with the resultant demands upon them in their interaction. His observations apply equally well to the therapeutic task with the psychotic child, except that here the problems are magnified in intensity and colored by the arousal of anxiety in the child as a result of his past experience and prior failures in resolution of conflicts.

Proctor's observations that countertransference phenomena may contaminate the therapeutic work with children having severe character disorders (12) are equally apropos to work with psychotic children. When the child becomes sexually seductive the therapist "must learn to recognize, accept, and live with residual and probably irreducible Oedipal-castration anxieties—these patients can be maddening, and it is important to sort out the realistic hate they engender" (from the therapist's unconscious hate). . . . "The Therapist . . . can vicariously use the patient to act out for him and then . . . punish the patient for his (the therapist's) instinctual wishes."

Other sources of countertransference problems encountered in coordinated staff work with psychotic children have been delineated by Sheimo, Paynter and Szurek (13). As they point out, unresolved problems of staff interaction may influence a therapist to avoid the expected criticism of staff should he return a wet, soiled, or even angry child to the children's ward. They point also to the competitive struggles within a staff over credit for therapeutic gains which may occur.**

CLINICAL CONSIDERATIONS

In the planning of a ward program for psychotic children, an awareness of the difficulty these children have in experiencing sensual pleasures in an unanxious way leads to efforts beyond those involved in the teaching of self-care, participation in group activities, and the learning of skills, both academic and interpersonal. It also includes provision for the experience of kinesthetic pleasures, tactile and bodily contact experiences, and the achievement of enjoyment or satisfaction in oral, olfactory, and excretory functions. Reduction of the child's disabling conflict will be fostered as he learns that others can be calmly accepting of both his impulses and of his anxiety about

---

* See Chapter 22 of present volume.
** It should be noted that detailed review of the literature since the original presentation of this paper has not been attempted.

them. Should the ideal treatment milieu be achieved, the child's own distortion or inhibition of impulse would remain the primary interference with his satisfactions. Additional interference would stem from the usual frustrations of postponement of gratification and modification of behavior attendant upon developmental expectations and life as a social being.

Much of the moment to moment work with these children, both on the ward and in playroom therapy at the Langley Porter Neuropsychiatric Institute, as it must be in most teaching institutions, is undertaken by trainee personnel. Young workers characteristically feel ignorant and unequal to the intense demands of the task. The manifest behavior of the child may often for long periods remain unintelligible. Mute and autistic withdrawal may accompany negativism to the requests of others. The child's behavior may be characterized by ritualistic and repetitive, seemingly meaningless acts; impulsive, apparently unprovoked attacks upon self or others; or destruction of the physical environment. The child may provoke in the therapist or attending ward personnel such fury, disgust, or anxiety that responses to the child based solely upon relatively clear perception of the child's need become the exception rather than the rule.

Particularly anxiety-provoking for workers, few of whom have completed personal analysis, are derivatives of sexual impulses which color the child's behavior toward all external objects. In the clinical examples to follow we have focused upon these elements in the child's behavior, the therapist's response, and their effect upon the subsequent behavior of child and therapist together. In these examples there has been no effort to convey the sequential development of positive therapeutic engagement leading to resolution of conflict in the child. Instead there is an effort to present those tension-fraught instances of engagement in which the therapeutic problems related to the expression of sexual drives in the child have been pivotal in the outcome of the immediate therapeutic work and the work to follow.

Case 1

Nicholas, an 11 year-old boy, the eldest of three children of a Lutheran minister, had a calcified left choroid plexus, atrophy of the left cerebral hemisphere, and clinical epilepsy. Nonetheless, additional evidence suggested that psychological factors contributed significantly to his speech retardation, generally autistic symptomatology, and behavior disturbances. His parents were markedly inhibited, passively hostile persons, in conflict internally and with each other. They delegated much of Nicholas' management to his maternal grandmother, a dominant and controlling woman, with whom Nicholas resided intermittently near his parents home. In the therapy hours

Nicholas was provocative, often requiring physical restraint. His greatest un-conflicted pleasure in these hours was in physical contact with the therapist. He regularly asked for tickling, kissing, or lapholding. On one such occasion he stood between the seated therapist's thighs, pressing and rubbing against the therapist in what proved a sexually stimulating manner to the therapist. The therapist felt increasing uneasiness and general bodily tension, which was not acknowledged to the child. Instead the therapist suggested brusquely that Nicholas sit on the chair beside him. Suddenly Nicholas spit in the therapist's face. Many hours followed during which the entire focus of both patient and therapist centered around provocative spitting attacks and their control, when bodily contact occurred only as a part of the ensuing struggle.

Much later in discussing this period of work with the staff, the therapist remembered and considered for the first time his own sexual arousal as specifically related to the sequence that followed. He recalled then that Nicholas' mother, with whom he also worked, had, during the same period in time as the above incident, reported with considerable anxiety and hesitation Nicholas' habit of cuddling with her in her bed. She wondered whether it was "right" for Nicholas to fondle her breasts at his age. She immediately interpreted the therapist's silence as an accusation that she was "perverted." Somewhat later she revealed that she had prohibited Nicholas' behavior, feeling that the therapist had told her it was wrong. But guilt about her own erotic response, so implicit in these statements, was not acknowledged.*

Case 2

The therapist found it extremely difficult to restrain large, strong 13 year-old Dan, who, while spitting at the therapist, was attempting to bang his own head against one chair and trying to slam another chair against a cabinet. Only after many such struggles, and increasing acceptance of his own fury with Dan, could the therapist begin to recognize the relationship of Dan's behavior to his anguished wish to be held and cuddled about which Dan was both intensely frightened and contemptuous. His accompanying genital excitement evoked shame, fear, and confusion in Dan. To communicate to the child the therapist's acceptance of all these feelings, as well as to provide an opportunity for the experience of physical closeness without sexual overtones and outside that of combative struggle, became a difficult and elusive therapeutic goal.

---

* For a fuller account of the therapeutic work with this family see Chapter 32.

Case 3

The relationship of Tommy, a 10 year-old Negro boy, with people generally as well as with his therapist and our staff was subject to chaotic and abrupt interruptions and separations. On one occasion, the therapist was delayed by Tommy's father when the child expected to be taken to the playroom. Tommy's request to be held and carried by his therapist enroute to the playroom was denied without attentive efforts to understand Tommy's request. In the playroom Tommy became provocatively aggressive, spitting at the therapist and testing other previously set limits on behavior. Such behavior alternated with feigned helplessness, tensely urgent sucking of the baby bottle, and brief moments when Tommy climbed into the cradle. The child's excitement mounted. He dashed back and forth to the toilet, dribbling urine upon himself and on the floor. He slipped a nursing nipple into his trousers, rubbing it against his anus. Finally after defecating into the toilet, Tommy carried about the tissue with which he had wiped himself. His soiled person disgusted the therapist, and Tommy's speedy movements and gleeful manner provoked in the therapist a mounting fury and sense of impotence. The hour ended as Tommy became ever more boisterous, calling out obscenities and spitting at the therapist.

Retrospectively, Tommy's initial request seemed clearly a response to his anxiety and perhaps anger about events involving Tommy, his father, and the therapist which delayed the playroom hour. This was followed by the therapist's denial of Tommy's request to be carried. As Tommy progressively lost control of himself and received no understanding restraint from the therapist, his actions became ever more frantic.

Neither the possibility that Tommy felt anxious or angry about the events prior to arrival in the playroom, nor the therapist's increasing sense of helplessness, were acknowledged directly by the therapist. Instead the child was returned to the ward in a state of agitation as his exhausted therapist retreated from the scene. As the therapist subsequently learned to be more promptly attentive to the child's requests, as well as more promptly restraining, instances in which there was reduction of tension became more common.

Case 4

Donald, an 8 year-old outpatient, whose elder sister was also psychotic and in treatment by our staff, was mute, spending much of his unsupervised time in rocking, thumbsucking, and genital masturbation. His pleasure and persistent interest in water play filled many playroom hours. He could pour, toss, catch and spew from his mouth streams of water very skillfully. However, it often happened that what began in an unanxious way became replaced by tensely driven excitement. Donald's body became tense, excited flapping motions of his arms accompanied the water play; the spewing became wild, and he quickly soaked his clothing. The sequence could progress so rapidly that the therapist repeatedly defined the first spatter of clothing as the limit to such play, with the understood reason that Donald would otherwise have to make an hour's trip home in wet clothes.

Regularly after such play was interrupted by the therapist, Donald became fretful, angry and began to rock in the cradle. He seldom remained angry long, however, and often moved closer toward communication and contact with the therapist. Donald might approach the therapist to gaze intently in the latter's eyes, or put his cheek against the therapist's. At other times he sat upon the therapist's lap, to rock and snuggle. On one such occasion, Donald quickly moved from his position to play again at the sink. It was several minutes before the therapist became aware that Donald had exceeded the previously set limits. The therapist realized that he had become lulled into a state of reverie, thinking of his pleasure in the cuddling physical contact enjoyed with his own 2 year-old son. It then became clear that similar episodes had occurred previously. The water play might now be seen as a frequent response to the child's anxiety when interpersonal contact was disrupted by the therapist's withdrawal. Conversely, by thus stimulating his therapist, Donald was free to pursue play which may have served as a compromise solution to anxiety.

Case 5

Jane, a nearly mute, 13 year-old pubescent girl, regularly sought with her therapist physical closeness to which he responded with a paternal pleasure marred by ill-defined uneasiness. As work progressed, Jane's behavior shifted from an ambivalent wish for simple closeness to a more frankly sexual advance. She began attempting to masturbate while straddling the therapist's leg. For many weeks the therapist repeatedly reacted with confusion and anxiety, pushing her away. In response, Jane became increasingly silly and would shriek wildly or attack the therapist. In his own analysis the therapist became more and more sharply aware of his guilt about his associations to Jane's behavior. He then became able for the first time to view Jane's behavior as a form of communication rather than as a sexual act per se. He could accept in a more relaxed way her tentative rubbing of her pelvis against his leg and wait for what might follow. Twice in one hour Jane began but quickly discarded her self-stimulating behavior each time neither attacking the therapist nor disrupting her own play. In fact what followed was the most integrated behavior by the patient in their work together. She wrote her name correctly and accepted the therapist's praise. Previously all such efforts had been uncompleted or destroyed. The therapist subsequently observed that Jane attempted such masturbatory behavior when she was angry or was seemingly accidentally stimulated by physical contact with the therapist (6).*

Case 6

Sally, a moderately obese, prepubescent 12 year-old girl, had been an inpatient for five years on the Children's Ward. She communicated with others, including her therapist, primarily by means of fluttering gestures and disconnected, perseverative demands for food. A major focus of the ward staff's effort with Sally was that of helping her to choose alternatives other than eating as a regular means of attempting to relieve anxiety. Sally's response to verbal requests from others was often a blank and helpless expression; when physically urged to respond, she often resisted with active combat or by becoming limp. Much of the playroom work involved jointly executed crayon drawings prompted by the patient's one-word requests for "milk-shake," "crib," "diaper," "bottle." During their close physical proximity at the desk, Sally would often look intently and appealingly into the therapist's face and occasionally her hair would brush his forehead. On one such occasion, she giggled, slid to the floor, and tried to pull the therapist down with her. When she did not succeed in this attempt, as she fluttered her hands she made vigorous pelvic thrusts and put her legs in the therapist's lap. The initial shock at her behavior and his associations to coitus immobilized the therapist. Thereafter in the same situation his behavior ranged from efforts at physical restraint to angry insistence that she could not kick him, and to vain attempts to distract her.

Only when the therapist understood more fully the basis for his own anxiety could he talk directly with Sally about his confusion and his difficulty in being helpful at such moments. He then speculated with her about the confusion she might feel. He suggested that Sally might not know how to express feelings of excitement and warmth, and that she might wonder what people do together with their bodies. Sally became quiet and looked directly and thoughtfully at the therapist. On subsequent occasions of physical closeness (i.e. leaning against the therapist's shoulder) the therapist learned at the first sign of excitement on Sally's part (usually expressed by a widening of the eyes, her pressing hard against his shoulder, or a fluttering of her hands) to speak promptly. He talked to her about the location and intensity of sensations she might feel at being physically close to someone she liked

---

* For fuller description of this work see Chapter 22.

and trusted. In such instances Sally did not slide to the floor, but smiled and returned to her drawing.

THERAPEUTIC PROBLEMS ENCOUNTERED

These clinical examples are presented not as therapeutic successes but as illustrations of therapeutic problems and process. Episodes or sequences of behavior occurring in the work with various children and therapists have been selected to focus upon the impulse, action, and reaction in the therapeutic relationship. Only when there was resolution of the countertransference problems by the therapist could there begin in the interpersonal transaction between therapist and child the reduction of tension. Otherwise anxiety mounted for both until some disruptive behavior occurred.

In some situations the therapist's tension alone may communicate itself to the child, provoking simple disruption of the child's behavior, or expressions of anxiety or hostility. Self-attack, or attack upon the therapist, as in Nicholas' case, may follow. That same sequence illustrates the manner in which the therapist's response to his own tension may be to abruptly reject the child, himself withdrawing from a position of equidistance in the relationship which might promote a setting for resolution of conflict on the part of the patient.

The therapist may be so pressed to deal with the child's manifest behavior, as with Dan, that he fails to consider the affective force behind the behavior, at least during the immediate sequence. The admixture of positive seeking of closeness with hostile, aggressive behavior may be more subtle, as when a kiss becomes a bite; a pat, a slap. Provocative behavior may be endlessly repetitive. One must be prepared to offer the child discriminating and judicious setting of limits in the face of constant physical struggle or of the child's persistent efforts to find compromise solutions to his conflicts. The task is particularly difficult when the child becomes physically repulsive to the therapist as in the case of Tommy. The smearing of feces, or, more commonly, of saliva and nasal secretions, may accompany a child's demand for unambivalent concern and readiness to help, including close physical contact.

Finally, the sensuality of these children is not only direct and openly provocative as in the case of Jane, but may appear so genital in quality as to provoke in the therapist particularly harsh countertransference reactions manifest by surprise, disbelief, and anxiety, as with Sally.

DISCUSSION

I have attempted to convey the sense of complexity and the tremendous distortions of each sensual or possibly sexual impulse which may occur. I have stressed here the interplay of affect, impulse, and response of the psychotic child in the context of his relationship with his therapist, and of the therapist's response. It may be helpful to direct the attention of other workers to ways in which the behavior of these children may be not only explicable, but characterized by great sensitivity to tensions disruptive in all human relationships.

Those problems in the work generated by expression of the child's inhibited, distorted, conflict-ridden sensual and sexual impulses may provoke particularly intense anxiety as a countertransference response in the therapists of these children. The therapist's defensive reaction may be characterized by actual denial or suppression of awareness of the sexual and sensual content of the child's behavior. Intense anxiety aroused by the child's behavior may result in the therapist's disruption of the sequence. His reaction may be especially angry and retaliatory when anxiety about his own sexual response is aroused in him. Even when the sensual expression of the child and the therapist's response are accepted by the therapist, limits of bodily contact or antisocial behavior of the child require some definition in each relationship, by no means an easy task for a beginning therapist. If the therapist tolerates silently but uneasily the child's behavior, it may be perpetuated with mounting tension for the child and therapist. In this way what began as exploratory freedom of expression becomes, as in the child's previous life experience with significant adults, tension-fraught, obsessive and ungratifying, or a distorted derivative of the original impulse. Thus a therapist may behave in a manner which serves to convince the child further of his own essential badness, and may rebuke him when the child most poignantly seeks interpersonal experiences which provide relief of inner conflict, so necessary for self-acceptance.

SUMMARY

Massive inhibition of, or chaotic eruption of, conflict-ridden sensual impulses may be observed in most psychotic children. Such impulses include all expressions of sensuality, whether stage-related, oral, anal, or phallic, or sensory-motor modalities such as the tactile and kinesthetic. These children try often and persistently to experience with pleasure one or another such bodily feelings. Just as often they may not realize enjoyment, but may resort to ritualistic autoerotic behavior in an effort to relieve tension. Quite regularly, too, we see symptomatic evidence of unsuccessfully repressed, distorted impulses in self-destructive behavior and provocative ambivalent moves for contact of the child with significant adults.

The long-term and expensive nature of the treatment of psychotic children, as well as uncertain prognosis, will continue to discourage many from the undertaking. Probably for some time to come, the major number of these children in treatment will be seen by trainee-therapists. As demonstrated by the clinical examples here, considerable anxiety is mobilized for the learning therapist by the distorted expressions of sensuality in these children.

That the clinical examples included reflect no greater measure of success is a factor not only of the symptomatic disturbance in the child. They point equally to the requirements of skill, patience, sensitivity, and freedom from anxiety in the therapist. While such statements might be made about all therapeutic undertakings, their relevance to the outcome of work with psychotic children deserves emphasis.

REFERENCES

1. ALLEN, FREDERICK H. *Psychotherapy with Children.* New York: Norton, 1942.
2. AXLINE, VIRGINIA MAE. *Play Therapy: The Inner Dynamics of Childhood.* Boston: Houghton Mifflin, 1947.
3. BENDER, LAURETTA. Childhood Schizophrenia: Clinical Study of One Hundred Schizophrenic Children. *Am. J. Orthopsychiat.,* 1947, 17, 40-56.
4. BETTELHEIM, BRUNO. *The Empty Fortress.* New York: The Free Press, 1967.
5. BOATMAN, MALETA J. and SZUREK, S. A. A Clinical Study of Childhood Schizophrenia. In D. D. Jackson (Ed.), *Etiology of Schizophrenia,* New York: Basic Books, 1960, pp. 389-440.
6. CHRIST, ADOLPH E. Sexual Countertransference Problems with a Psychotic Child. *Journal American Academy Child Psychiatry,* 1964, 3(2), 298-316.
7. FREUD, ANNA. *The Psychoanalytic Treatment of Children.* London: Image, 1946.
8. GOLDFARB, WILLIAM and MINTZ, IRVING. Schizophrenic Child's Reaction to Time and Space. *Archives of General Psychiatry,* 1961, 5, 535-543.
9. KLEIN, MELANIE. *The Psychoanalysis of Children.* London: Hogarth Press, 1946.
10. MAHLER, MARGARET S. On Childhood Psychosis and Schizophrenia: Autism and Symbiotic Infantile Psychosis. *Psychoanalytic Study of the Child,* 1949, 3, 286-305.
11. MIDDLEMORE, MERREL P. The Uses of Sensuality. In John Richman (Ed.), *On the Bringing up of Children.* London: Kegan, Paul, Trench, Trubner & Co., 1938, pp. 57-85.
12. PROCTOR, JAMES T. Countertransference Phenomena in the Treatment of Severe Character Disorders in Children and Adolescents. In *Dynamic Psychopathology in Childhood.* New York & London: Grune & Stratton, 1959, pp. 293-309.
13. SHEIMO, S. L., PAYNTER, J., and SZUREK, S. A. Problems of Staff Interaction with Spontaneous Group Formations on a Children's Psychiatric Ward. *Am. J. Orthopsychiat.,* 1949, 19, 599-611.
14. SZUREK, S. A. Childhood Schizophrenia: Psychotic Episodes and Psychotic Maldevelopment. *Am. J. Orthopsychiat.,* 1956, 26, 519-543.
15. SZUREK, S. A. and BERLIN, I. N. Elements of Psychotherapeutics with the Schizophrenic Child and His Parents. *Psychiatry,* 1956, 19, 1-9. Also see Chapter 9 in this volume.
16. SZUREK, S. A., BERLIN, I. N., and BOATMAN, MALETA J. (Eds.). *Inpatient Care for the Psychotic Child,* Vol. 5. Langley Porter Child Psychiatry Series. Palo Alto, California: Science and Behavior Books, 1971.

Section VI

THERAPEUTIC EXPERIENCES WITH PSYCHOTIC CHILDREN AND THEIR FAMILIES

We present here case histories and clinical experiences which illustrate the psychotherapeutic work of members of the Children's Service and how the faculty and staff have learned from such work. The evaluation of the methodology and its implications for further clinical psychotherapeutic work and research is detailed in these clinical examples. The use of physical restraint as a therapeutic tool in work with violent, aggressive, psychotic children is described. Work with self-destructive children, with very young autistic children and with the gamut of symptom complexes found in psychotic children is discussed. The role of the collaborative team is closely examined and our experiences in work with parents in both short term and long term psychotherapeutic work with psychotic children are carefully reviewed.

24

Regression as a Phase in Psychotherapeutic Work with Young Schizophrenic Children

Irving N. Berlin, M.D.

Classically, regression is regarded as a retreat from a previously achieved stage of integration or psychosexual development. Such regression is attendant on either severe intrapsychic trauma or conflict, or as a phase in the process of psychotherapy. In the latter the transference relationship with the psychotherapist permits the patient to return to a previous stage of development and to experience with the therapist new and hitherto, not worked through phases of that developmental period.

Freud (1) described fixation and regression as ego phenomena. He gave a very graphic description of ego development as an army marching along and leaving garrisons of soldiers at those points of greatest opposition in the developmental march. Where the conflicts and lack of gratification were the most intense, the largest garrisons were left behind. Thus, the greater the conflict, the larger the garrison left behind, i.e., the greater the fixation and the weaker the army that marches on. Regression then occurs most frequently to areas of greatest fixation.

Such regression in psychoanalytic and dynamic psychotherapeutic work is an essential part of the working through of unresolved conflicts and of a restitution of previously unexperienced parent-child relationships necessary for an orderly and healthy progression through developmental stages to maturity.

In psychoses of childhood and especially those in which the psychosis is

For a symposium of "Regression" in Treatment of Young Children. American Psychiatric Association, 1962.

clearly evident in the first year of life, some interesting questions are raised: (1) In the face of massive fixation, does regression itself occur? (2) Does it occur in the transference relationship with the therapist or other maternal figures in a therapeutic milieu? (3) If it does occur, is it an essential aspect of the treatment and recovery of the psychotic child as it is in the neurotic adult, where regression and subsequent progression march hand in hand?

Answering these questions is difficult. Most of us who have worked with young severely psychotic children have encountered several problems. For instance, when a child who has had little, if any, oral gratification up to age four with his mother, and who bites, tears, and destroys objects within reach, begins to suck on a baby bottle, coo, and rock in the cradle or in the therapist's arms, is this regression? If so, from what, since it is clear this youngster has not passed through the other stages of psychosexual development with any degree of success and remains fixated at the oral stage?

In other instances of early childhood psychoses with marked oral deprivation, a child may have achieved some autonomy, some bowel and bladder control, and show evidence of rudimentary oedipal conflicts. When such a child is helped in the therapeutic experience to attempt, with increasing lack of tension and increasing pleasure, to play with water, sand, and clay, and then finally to embark on a variety of orally gratifying activities, are these evidences of regression in therapy or signs of reduced conflict permitting progressive learning? Is it learning that certain sensual and sexual feelings and impulses in these fixated areas of development, areas of conflict for his parents, can be experienced without hurt, fear, and resulting trauma? In these instances, clear evidence exists of learning about the less forbidden impulses first, with gradual return to re-experiencing and re-learning about the most conflicted areas.

Perhaps one of the most tantalizing bits of therapeutic evidence, concerning regression as a necessary part of psychotherapeutic work with psychotic children, comes from those moments of intense and intensive, sometimes combative, interchange, where the therapist actively prevents a psychotic child from a self-mutilating or assaultive act. When such prevention has been accomplished by a non-retaliatory, non-hostile although sometimes angry and bruised therapist, the child may suddenly relax, smile and begin to suckle contentedly on a baby bottle, permit physical closeness and cuddling. Usually after such an experience the child evidences more integrative and age-appropriate behavior.

Here, in one or several dramatic moments, "regressive" behavior occurs, i.e., experiencing previously forbidden and little-experienced sensual impulses, with very rapid progression to more integrative functioning.

Frankie

Frank, a 5½-year old, non-speaking, destructive, assaultive and occasionally self-destructive child, repeatedly tried to tear the doll house apart in our play therapy sessions just as he had successfully torn apart all the furniture in his own room as well as much of the furnishings when he lived at home. When Frankie first glanced or moved toward a play house, I would warn him that I was going to stop any such behavior. He would glance at me out of the corner of his eye and suddenly make a dash for the play house trying to rip one of the walls or the roof. I soon learned to station myself in front of the play house so that when he ran toward it, I was able to grab his outstretched arms, turn him around, cross his arms in front of him and place him partly on my lap with my legs over his so that he could not kick, elbow or turn his head and bite me. At first he struggled unremittingly, trying to get away from me and to hurt me as much as possible in the process. I would work strenuously to keep him restrained so that he was unable to actually hurt me.

Sometimes this struggle occurred for most of an hour. If I attempted to avoid the struggle by seeing him in my office which had no doll house, Frankie would dart toward my desk attempting to rip the desk pad and papers. Therefore, we concentrated our efforts in the playroom. After several weeks of such restraint, Frank would relax in my arms after being restrained long enough so it was clear he would not be able to get away. When I tentatively let loose so he could pursue other activities, he would dash again toward the doll house and require further restraint.

After several weeks, we were in the playroom one morning when I was momentarily distracted by a knock on the playroom door. Frankie immediately seized the opportunity to stomp on one of the floors of the doll house and partly rip off one side of the roof. Angry because my own distraction prevented my prompt restraint, I grabbed him and in angry tones told him that I knew that I had not restrained him as promptly as before but that I was very angry that he had again tried to destroy the doll house. With unabated fury he tried to kick, elbow, pinch and bite me and succeeded in pinching me as I was trying to restrain his arms. Again, with anger augmented by pain, I described my fury that I had been hurt and my hope that I would be able to contain myself and only restrain him so that he would not be hurt in the process, although part of me wanted him to feel what it was like to be hurt.

As my anger subsided, Frank began to relax, my tension subsided and I also began to relax. I noticed for the first time that Frank was resting his head on my chest and was cuddling up against me rather than simply sitting quietly erect on my lap. As his head burrowed into my shoulder and seemed to nuzzle me, I let go with one arm and reached out for the partially filled baby bottle that the previous therapist had left on the sink. I offered it to Frankie who clenched his lips as I put the baby bottle to them. Then, as I began to tickle his lips with the baby bottle, he began to smile, opened his mouth, eagerly grabbed the nipple and began to suck voraciously. This sucking continued for nearly 15 minutes with increased bodily relaxation.

At the end of this play therapy session Frankie weakly said "Hi" as we left the playroom. As has happened in work with other psychotic children, the experience marked a turning point in my work with Frankie. It also marked a turning point in his relationships with ward staff and teachers and his capacity to relate to them, become involved in learning, and finally to become involved in peer activities.

Jimmy

Jimmy, a 4½-year-old, mute, withdrawn, combative, and destructive boy sat for some hours immobile. As I talked to him about what I guessed his feelings might be, he watched me mold clay objects such as animals, airplanes and trucks. Each time I finished, I held out the object to him, and he dashed it to the floor or threw it at me. I would comment about his mixed anger and desire to enjoy the play with the clay, and slowly offer him some clay to join me in the activity. He would sit motionless, and I would then make another object. My running comments of the pleasure I had in molding the clay were apparently not heard.

At one session, as I tore off a piece of clay, as usual I offered him a piece before I took my own, and to my surprise he took it and held it in his tightly-clenched fist. He watched me as I shaped a long, snake-like object on which I put legs and ears like a dachshund. I gave it to him, and he held it in one hand, his clay in the other. After a few moments, he put my clay figure down and sat staring at his lump in his hand. I took both of his hands and very slowly opened them and began to rub them together to make a ball, then a snake, and finally feet, etc., like my figure. With this, he tentatively settled back into my arms and gingerly stuck his thumb in his mouth for a few seconds. This was the start of the improvement.

Now, how can one describe such behavior? Is it regression to the fixated state, or is it rather progression from the fixated state which makes all sensual pleasure dangerous, especially oral gratification? Were the snakes phallic or anal symbols, or primarily pleasurable, sensual experiences which occurred in the context of the therapeutic relationship as part of learning what was permitted in that relationship? Was the snake a combination of regression with its symbolic components and learning about non-threatening sensual experience?

The general question, then, for discussion is to what extent regression is a necessary part of the therapeutic experience in early childhood psychosis, where massive fixation at the oral stage occurs. Our own experiences cast some doubt about regression being a necessary part of psychotherapy with severely psychotic young children.

Our experience shows that many of the most severely psychotic children are so fixated at early stages of development that regression in psychotherapeutic work does not occur until they have begun to make progress. Then there may be brief regressive periods as they work through conflict areas. One often sees progressive learning fostered by the realities of the therapy and the therapeutic milieu and permitted at home by less conflicted parents now in treatment. For example, a frequent phenomenon after effective therapeutic work with extremely withdrawn, mute, frightened, and isolated children is that they may become angry and aggressive. It is as if they are now able to be self assertive and feel free for the first time to express feelings of anger, and to behave aggressively to assert independence and risk not being meek and submissive. While difficult to deal with, such behavior is progression. When dealt with therapeutically it leads to beginning speech and playing out of conflicts. Return to isolation and withdrawal or hostile, destructive behavior may recur at nodal points in the therapeutic work as signals of what is painfully and fearfully being worked through. Here, as in psychotherapeutic work with less disturbed children, regression portends progress in working through conflicts.

Sammy

Sammy, age 4, came to us because his pediatrician finally forced the mother and father to look at the fact that Sammy had not yet learned to talk. Sammy was extremely withdrawn and frightened of both children and adults. He spent most of his day listening to records and spinning in front of him a tinker toy which contained several spokes. The pediatrician had not been overly concerned with his lack of speech at age 2 because the motor development was adequate. He considered Sammy's withdrawal and noninvolvement with both parents and siblings as something that would pass and that the child would grow out of. He became increasingly concerned as no changes occurred.

We heard a familiar history from mother of the death of her own mother when she was carrying Sammy so that when he was born, mother continued to be profoundly depressed. Father, an extraordinarily busy business executive, paid little attention to the child or to the mother, and mother characteristically withdrew and made no effort to seek outside help. Her own gynecologist and internist did not see anything particularly wrong with her because she masked her own problems whenever she talked with them during her regular examination periods.

Sammy was cared for by the housekeeper who, in addition, took care of the two older children, did household chores, and prepared meals. Realistically, it meant that Sammy spent most of his time during his first year alone in his crib. Since he did very little complaining, he was only picked up for his bottles, some of which were propped, and for regular diaper changes. When placed in the playpen by the housekeeper at age one, he began to crawl and to become involved in walking and became interested in many toys. He seemed especially stimulated by his brother who was two years older. There was a great deal of physical contact and play. Since his brother also had only sufficient speech to make his needs known, their mutual play did not stimulate either of them verbally. We subsequently saw the brother who is in psychotherapy with a colleague and doing fairly well.

When Sammy came to our ward, he reacted to a great deal of attention on the ward, and from the nursery school teacher and to my efforts in the playroom, at first, with mute and frightened withdrawal and some crying, until he became convinced that no one was going to force anything on him. He reacted to the frequent attention of one of the ward nurses by allowing himself to be cuddled, becoming less stiff in his gait and less isolated. Occasionally, lying in her lap, he drank a nursing bottle filled with water or milk. With the nursery school teacher he engaged in a great deal of smearing of finger paint with obvious enjoyment. He was pleased that the nursery school teacher praised each of his efforts. He seemed to become more spontaneous in the use of his entire hand and all five fingers in smearing the paint after tentatively using only one finger at a time.

With me in the playroom he at first either sat mutely or wandered around indifferently as if oblivious to the toys on the shelves that I named as he passed. After several weeks, he was sitting on the floor and I rolled a toy train in his direction making the appropriate chu-chu sounds. With a bored expression, he pushed the engine back toward me and I returned it to him with the same sounds somewhat louder and with much more enthusiasm in my voice. Thus began a game that went on for a number of weeks until Sammy would begin to follow my chu-chu sounds with very weak ch-ch when he pushed the train toward me. Over a period of time, however, these sounds increased in volume and accuracy until chu-chu was very clear. With some pleasure when the train would fall over and I would shout "Bang, it's turned over," he would echo with real feeling and volume "bang, bang."

Very slowly he learned to use a few words including my name, the names of his nurse and teacher and, with them, a few words like "come," "go," and "out." On his visits home he began to correctly identify his mother, father and brothers, saying Momma, Dadda, Ma for Mark and Ha for Harold.

After three months of therapy, Sammy began to use the railroad engine in quite another way. He would pick out the momma doll of the five Flagg dolls and begin tentatively to roll the engine over her. At first he was apprehensive, glancing fearfully at me. However, when I simply calmly reflected that he was rolling the engine over the momma doll, he slowly became less apprehensive and a gleeful note could be heard in his voice as he said, "Maaa Bang."

During this period Sammy showed increased verbalization, contact with adults and freedom in play on the ward. There was also beginning interaction with his age mates on the ward and with normal children of his own age in the park. Sammy was returned from home one weekend with his left arm in a cast. While playing on the stairs with his brothers, he had accidentally tripped over one of the toy cars on the stairs, fallen and sustained a colles fracture of the wrist. Despite his mother's efforts at reassurance, he screamed unceasingly as he was being anesthetized. Her presence after he woke up and during the entire next day in no way allayed his fears and he again became withdrawn, would not talk or let himself be comforted by his mother. On return to the ward he was also isolated, looked very frightened and would not be comforted by any of the staff. However, since the nurses, the nursery school teacher and I insisted upon holding him and talking to him about how scared he must have been when this happened to him, he finally began to relax, to enjoy being held and to relate again to the staff on the ward. He continued somewhat cautious with his mother, father and siblings.

During the two month period during which he had his cast and a sling, Sammy made a great deal of progress in verbalization. He began to repeat parts of stories that were read to him, to recognize parts of the alphabet and say them back to the nursery school teacher, to indicate the various stories he wanted to have read to him and to repeat the favorite portions of them back to his nurse. In the playroom during the first week, I held him a good deal of the time and talked to him. After that he began again to utilize the train engine and cars to run over his mother and finally to bump into and smash his father. He also played through a repetitive episode in which the two Flagg dolls named after his brothers were placed in a freight car which had a collision with one of the other cars in which his brothers always fell down and were hurt. During these occasions, his voice was very gleeful and he would say, "Ma bang" or "Pa hurt."

Sammy began to use a variety of verbs very much more frequently and thus made himself more thoroughly understood to various people on the ward so that his needs could be better met. He also began to jabber and vocalize when certain nursery school rhymes were played on the phonograph as if it were safe then to imitate the sounds. Many of these sounds I heard as a part of the action when he was playing out his game with the toy engine and the various railroad cars.

Subsequently, after five months of therapy, a rather surprising series of events occurred. One day when the nurse came to get him for their usual walk in the park, he kicked her sharply in the shins. When she leaned over to remonstrate, he hit her very hard in the face and turned and ran away. The nurse pursued him, grabbed him by both arms and shook him with a good deal of anger saying that she would not permit this. In the nursery school for the first time he began to spill his paints. On one occasion he actually dropped a bottle but usually he spilled the paints haphazardly over the paper and on the floor and tore up his papers after he had smeared them. Most of his physical aggression came out at his nurse.

In the playroom Sammy continued his very dramatic play in which he destroyed his mother, father and siblings over and over again but with greater use of words. Our only physical interaction occurred on two occasions. Once I stopped his pulling the wheels off the railroad cars. He lashed out at me in a furious temper tantrum so that I had to hold him until he quieted. On the second occasion I prevented him from smashing the car he held threateningly above his head. He then had a milder tantrum which subsided quickly as I held him. He seemed to enjoy both the restraint and the closeness. However, the aggressive behavior on the ward continued for several weeks. He needed to be very quickly restrained by both the nurse and the nursery school teacher whenever he gave any signs of attacking them or breaking the paint bottles.

At home Sammy was increasingly hostile and destructive, pounding away at his mother and his brothers, destroying many of his brothers' toys, and, on one occasion, tearing his father's shirt rather badly when father was trying to restrain him. Some help to the parents in the therapeutic sessions enabled the parents to restrain him more quickly by attending to the signs they could describe but usually delayed acting on. They were progressively able to do it in as non-punitive a manner as possible so that there was a fairly unified approach to his hostile assaults.

Over a month this behavior slowly began to subside. In its place Sammy became much freer in his bodily movements. He began for the first time to utilize a trike and scooter and to swing on swings without evidence of fear. In the playroom he began to play out fairly complex family scenes of eating and sleeping in the doll house. He would eventually kill off each of the family members, usually by having them jump or drop from the doll house and get run over by his favorite toy engine. Sammy's progress continued as he began to learn more and to interact more freely with both adults and peers. He became much more spontaneous in his behavior and much freer about expressing his anger or disappointment, either in words or by crying or stamping his feet, so that the adult could interact with him in a helpful and supportive way.

In less severely psychotic children, regression may occur in various phases of the therapeutic work. Frequently this is only very fleeting and transient. Occasionally the child gets stuck at a regressed stage because resolution in psychotherapy of particular conflicts awaits the therapist's working through his own conflict.

At times problems in the ward milieu setting or unresolved conflicts manifested by the parents at home contribute to the regression. Thus, loss of therapist or nurse or new overt or covert manifestations of parental hostility toward the child which is not understood and dealt with therapeutically, results in periods of regression or exacerbation of symptoms not observed for some time.

One sometimes observes a period of regression without apparent cause to a former state of behavior, symptoms or overt manifestations of severe conflict. If the brief regression is not reacted to with undue anxiety by the therapist or other adults, it serves to test or verify the capacities of the adults in the child's world to deal with such behavior effectively and nonpunitively. Sometimes such a brief regression is followed by a sense of great freedom with the therapist and a spirit of intensive working to resolve a more current conflict. With adults one often hears psychotherapists of psychotic patients comment that if a therapist can allow regressive, helpless, hopeless, child-like, dependent behavior for a bit, the patient is able to again move forward in therapeutic work. These processes may be fairly similar.

Mary

Mary, age 5½, after a year of inpatient therapy, was an attractive little girl who related very well to both adults and children. She learned in a kindergarten setting and was tested as very bright and considerably above her age level. She was clearly the leader of her age group in the kindergarten and one of the favorites of the nurses; there was discussion about termination of her hospitalization and transfer to outpatient treatment.

Before her admission to the ward, Mary had been completely nonspeaking for 2½ years. She was extraordinarily hostile, aggressive and destructive of all furniture, toys, and clothing that came within her reach both at home and in the hospital. She hit at herself, blacked her eyes and had knocked out one of her teeth. She was constantly tearing her dress and underthings.

Mary's mother died at her birth, and Mary had been cared for by a housekeeper. She had been severely maltreated by the housekeeper and malnourished. It was not until 1½ years of age that the father recognized that something was wrong, fired the housekeeper and got someone else the pediatrician recommended. But the mute, angry, assaultive and destructive behavior which had begun was in no way mitigated by the new housekeeper's very tranquil appearance and effort at mothering. Mary rejected all contact.

On the ward Mary responded very quickly to the kind of nonpunitive restraint we have previously described. She began to relate to one of the evening nurses who was the most attuned to her and would restrain her the most quickly when she even looked as if she were going to have some kind of temper outburst or destroy something or hurt herself.

She began very rapidly thereafter to get better. She began to learn to say words, to become involved in learning in nursery school and to be very active in developing fantasy play in the playroom. Soon she responded well to the interpretive behavior and comments of the therapist. She was a delight to her father and a new housekeeper who were pleased to have her at home and to find her an enjoyable and a delightful child.

At the end of that year, Mary suffered a double loss. The evening nurse to whom she was most attached married and moved out of the state. Her tharapist who was a senior fellow in child psychiatry left the service. Very quickly Mary again began to look haunted and isolated. She rejected all approaches and efforts at comforting by hitting out, tearing uniforms on nurses, clothes of the new therapist, spitting, kicking and biting all adults, especially her father when he came to get her. She made weekends at home a living hell.

After such great progress the nursing staff and the kindergarten teacher were furious at Mary for her reversals. It took them some time to reinstitute the measures that had originally helped her begin her therapeutic gains. As nonpunitive restraint was again instituted, Mary very quickly settled down except at home. Her father, in the throes of a love affair and engagement, wanted nothing of Mary and became more distant and punitive when she attacked him. Only after a number of therapeutic hours, he was helped to work through not only the feelings of loss of his first wife but his anxiety about remarrying and investing in someone else who might also be lost to him. After that he began to recognize that he would again have to attend to Mary and be supportive and nonpunitive in restraining her when necessary. Thus, within a brief time father was also able to restrain Mary and to establish their previous relationship. He was even able to help his fiancee to establish a fairly good relationship with Mary although that took a number of months.

The greatest pleasure to both of them was when she began to call this woman "momma," a word she had not previously used for any human being.

From our review of the work with Mary it is clear that only the relaxed vigilance of the ward staff and their willingness to resume nonpunitive restraint for however long was necessary got through to Mary. Previous hostile anger towards Mary only accelerated her problems and father's angry and removed, actual unconcern for Mary escalated his problems with her. She was able to integrate self restraint when she was no longer so hopeless about attaining satisfactions and had proven to herself that other people could and would work with her toward self mastery and independence. When Mary left the ward after a year and a half she was able to enter school at her proper grade. Father and the new mother as well as Mary continued in outpatient therapy for two years. When last seen, Mary was doing very well.

CONCLUSION

Strangely enough, the most obvious so-called "regressive behavior" in psychotic children, i.e., the most clearly defined oral or anal activities, have occurred in my experience when the child is no longer psychotic and is working through primarily neurotic problems and problems of the oedipal stage of development. Then for short periods oral and anal activities reappear as part of working through conflicts in other stages of psychosexual development.

The rapid alternation of explosive, hostile, assaultive or self-destructive behavior with withdrawn or repetitive sensually stimulating activities like compulsive masturbation, so often noted in psychotic youngsters, is not considered by some of us to be regression. Since these activities are at the most primitive levels of development and the child gives little evidence of progression through other psychosexual stages, we tend to look at psychotic children developmentally as fixated at oral levels of development. Those affective, cognitive and motor skills which indicate more advanced development are so fragmented that they appear not to represent any working through and consolidation of ego development or resolution of conflicts in any of the psychosexual stages of development requisite for libidinal maturation. In short, with severely psychotic children regression may not occur as a regular phenomenon in the psychotherapeutic work.

25

The Use of Physical Restraint: Its Relation to Other Forms of Psychotherapeutic Intervention

Samuel Susselman, M.D.

The use of physical restraint, the most active of all therapeutic measures, contributes to an understanding of other forms of intervention in psychotherapy, ranging from limit setting to the most passive technique. My purpose is to discuss physical restraint, to point out how it resembles verbal intervention and how nonintervention seems like intervention to the patient through projection.

Psychotherapeutic work with those individuals who are diagnosed in the categories of schizophrenia and character disorder has necessitated "variations from standard analytic techniques" (6). Increasingly over the past 15 years, alterations in technique and the theoretical implications for these changes have been described in the literature. Noteworthy in recent years is the work of Szurek and Berlin (11), who discuss the use of physical restraint in the early phase of treatment of destructive autistic children; and Hoedemaker (6), who dealt with the role of limit setting. These writers agree concerning the indication for active measures, instead of the classical passive approach, in the preliminary work with severely disturbed persons. They also agree that these more active measures differ in degree rather than in kind from the standard technique, which relies on "interpretation in conjunction with 'the kind of setting of limits' described by Freud" (6).

Active measures were discussed in the literature as far back as 1920, when Ferenczi (3) elaborated Freud's ideas on active interference. Five years later, by contrast, the efficacy of permissive techniques with delinquent children was described in *Wayward Youth* (1). That same year, 1925, Ferenczi (4) in reply to both the criticism and the extravagant praise his earlier paper had aroused, considered the contraindications to the use of active therapy. The debate about active and passive techniques has thus been an issue for 35 years.

Today only a rare clinic would tolerate the destruction wrought by Aichhorn's youths, for something has been learned about the use of physical restraint as a therapeutic tool since Aichhorn did his pioneer work.

I have found relatively few references to physical restraint. Wexler (12) in the course of his work with Nedda, a 38-year-old schizophrenic woman, did what he could to immobilize her when she became assaultive, and at times found it necessary to meet force with force. After almost every struggle, all of which with one exception ended in peace making, some clinical improvement was noted. Axeline (2) and Hamilton (5) briefly discussed physical restraint and some of its indications. Wilkins (13) cited vivid examples and explained "the meaning of external control" to Laura, a 14-year-old schizophrenic girl. Especially interesting is the incident when Laura during the restraint period gave the therapist broad hints about how to hold her more effectively. Redl and Wineman's (7) clinical accounts contain rich examples of the effectiveness of physical restraint with impulsive youngsters.

Szurek and Berlin (11) in their paper, "Elements of Psychotherapeutics with the Schizophrenic Child and His Parents," have incisively discussed physical restraint. They regard it as essential to prevent the damaging effects of serious destructive and self-destructive behavior to person and property. They are careful to stress that it is only a first step in psychotherapy. Destructive behavior that is not stopped results in guilt, fear of retaliation, massive anxiety about the consequences of the behavior and further defiance. When it is halted, not only is the absence of these feelings relieving in itself, but the possibility for progressive work in therapy is enhanced.

They add that other first steps in the therapeutic work are the therapist's attitude and manner in exercising physical restraint, what he says, and what he offers to the child as alternative ways of expressing feelings which lead to destructive behavior. The therapist's actions begin to help the child discriminate between the internal conflict and the external reality of the therapeutic situation. After he has repeatedly lived through the turmoil of conflicted emotions that now cannot be expressed in destructive behavior, evidence begins to appear of previously inhibited impulses toward sensual gratification and of engagement in constructive and satisfying activities. Progressively the child begins to exercise his own restraint against impulses toward destructive behavior. The more he learns to control his impulsive behavior consistently, the more he is able to work through the details of conflict solution. The dynamic problem in therapy then approaches the situation of those individuals with the milder transference neuroses.

Let us start at a moment when the therapist seizes the wrist of a child who is about to slap himself viciously in the face. The child struggles to escape, becomes furiously angry when he cannot, twists in all directions and hits at the therapist with his free hand. In self-defense the therapist seizes this hand, too. Even more furious, the child kicks, and the therapist to protect himself envelopes the child with arms and legs. The child, now impotent to act, strains in fury. If he is not mute, he will shout, curse, and accuse.

Through actual physical contact, the therapist will learn to distinguish when the muscle tone is relaxed and firm, a sign that conflict has receded, and when it is flaccid, melting, deadweight, an indication that resolution has not yet been achieved. These shifts in tone will teach him when to loosen his grip and when to resume restraint. Through these and other perceptions of voice quality, skin color, respiratory rate, etc. he is ever ready to prevent destructive behavior and equally ready not to interfere with the fullest non-destructive expression of emotion possible. He will, as it were, flow flexibly with his patient. Being involved so intimately in the transaction, the therapist must be the "participant observer" to be effective, demonstrating perhaps the ultimate in "evenly hovering attention."

In this way the child experiences the nonauthoritarian (i.e., non-punitive) use of superior strength. He, too, learns through his muscles and in visual and auditory perceptions to discriminate the behavior of the therapist from that of other persons.

The therapist speaks to the child at moments when it seems useful to do so while restraining him. For example, he may reaffirm his determination to prevent injury or hurt, or he may voice his idea or impression about what motivated the sudden eruption of violent behavior. On occasion he may express such things as his concern about not being more helpful, or even his anger at the patient's having injured him.

A sort of confirmatory test for the precision of the therapist's work are those occasions when the child becomes calm and engages in productive and satisfying play. On the other hand, if the child intensifies and prolongs the destructive activity, a search for causal factors in the countertransference and in the environment is indicated.

What the use of physical restraint so dramatically demonstrates is the start of a process by which a welter of libidinous feelings, anxiety and rage are converted from their discharge in destructive behavior to their expression in an alternative and less destructive way (9). When this alternative way is experienced in a relatively relaxed interpersonal climate, there is greater opportunity for resolving conflict and for learning how to gratify libidinous impulses now freed from previous distortions caused by inner, anxious prohibitions and revengeful rebelliousness against these prohibitions. As a result, the intense impulse toward destructive behavior is weakened.

During psychotherapy other forms of intervention that are short of physical restraint do not in themselves alter behavior. It is the patient who ultimately brings about the change, often in response to the intervention. Whether destructive behavior is directly aborted by the therapist, as with physical restraint, or by the patient in response to other forms of intervention, or by the patient himself without outside assistance, the result is the same; namely, the facilitation of an alternative avenue of expression of conflict that is more readily resolvable than is the destructive behavior it replaces.

It would be instructive to discuss all gradations of intervention from the most active, already considered, to the more passive techniques employed in the milder transference neuroses. For example, there is the elective rather than the urgent and necessary use of physical measures, as in restraining a child who is intent on breaking all the new crayons or wasting all the paper towels or cups in the playroom. Next would come the effect of a firm verbal prohibition, succinctly illustrated by Wilkins' (13) statement that when a "firm 'no' checked the motor expression of anxiety, Laura's words poured out in a torrent as if literally a new channel for her impulses had been forced open by the pressure of her thoughts." Or again, the events that occur when the therapist intervenes by reminding the patient that he is not carrying out the conditions of the therapy such as following the method of work, paying his fees, being on time for appointments; that is, acting out in relation to the therapeutic work. Finally, one can consider the more subtle examples of acting out, and equate them with the destructive behavior of hostilely aggressive children. This equation may seem like a giant step, but is not, if the definition of acting out is limited to that behavior in the interview, "inimical to, and the very antithesis of analysis—that is, the progressive reduction or resolution of the conflict evidenced in the transference neurosis" (10).

I wish now to discuss the effect of verbal intervention in work with an adult patient who had had considerable experience in psychotherapy. A phobic individual, he was concerned about his health and was subject to recurrent headaches once diagnosed as migraine. For these headaches and for other complaints, his mother, in his youth, and his wife for the past 30 years, had been over solicitous. He himself recognized how he had been "babied" and how he had invited it. The following is an example of verbal intervention. The patient, appearing preoccupied, opened the interview by stating in a petulant tone, "The back of my neck hurts." He was asked, "Did you hear how your voice sounded?" He paused, repeated his initial statement several times in the same tone as though studying the sound and said, "It sounds like I'm begging." He continued with a new quality in his voice. "It makes

me angry to be corrected by you—to be criticized and ridiculed"—pause—
"but I realize that you didn't correct me—all you did was to ask, did I hear
the sound of my voice." He went on to express his shame and guilt because
of titillating remarks he had exchanged at work with a woman thirty years
his junior. As he continued, his voice became stronger and more assertive.
Soon he remembered a pleasant event in his life and was able to identify a
sense of relaxation and confidence in himself.

The intervention called the patient's attention to a manner of expression
which characteristically appeared under certain stress, often of his own making, and which usually elicited from his mother and wife the kind of response
that fostered both its continuance and the sadomasochistic transaction at
these times of his relationship with them. Because he attended differently to
how he was speaking after the intervention by the therapist (closer attention
was his own intervention) he became aware of the quality in his voice, labeled
it begging and immediately modified it.

This shift when compared to the shift that occurs after the use of physical
restraint seems microscopic only because the forces involved are much less
intense. Nevertheless, it demonstrates a similar phenomenon, namely, the
appearance of an alternative and more constructive way of expression, quite
profound in its contribution to the progress of the therapeutic work. For only
after the intervention did the patient supply the kinds of details which are
recognizable as components of conflict, i.e., anger, criticism and ridicule from
past experiences together with evidence of projection of some of these components onto the therapist. No longer reacting to the therapist as on similar
occasions toward his mother and wife, he proceeded to work through feelings
of guilt and shame about his behavior with the woman at work and gave
evidence of having become more at ease with himself.

Another form of intervention is brought about by the patient in his anxious
efforts to elicit a particular response from the therapist rather than attend to
the work of the hour. For example, he may attempt to evoke a smile from the
therapist to alleviate some sense of uneasiness. He may ask a question such
as "Am I late?" to cover up his confusion when he knows very well he is.
For some reason known only to himself he may say "Hello" on entering the
consultation room even though greetings have already been exchanged in the
waiting room. If the therapist does not match smile with smile or supply
answers to questions motivated by anxiety, if he does not engage in "collu-
sion with delusion" (8), in short, if he does not feed back the response
invited by the patient, an intervention occurs. The patient's gambit, his acting out behavior as herein defined, has failed for such moments in its purpose and must be abandoned for something else. Like the child stopped by
physical restraint, the patient experiences feelings of anxiety and resentment.

He may lash out with comments such as "You make me mad—can't you answer a simple question?" and by these very words return again to the work of the hour.

Many examples can be cited about what occurs after the therapist has intervened and called the patient's attention to such acting out behavior as a breach of conditions of the work.

In one instance a 35-year-old man himself intervened by mastering an impulse to skip an appointment. The patient had a history of delinquency as an adolescent, of truancy and of learning difficulties at school. He had this to say about keeping an appointment: "I felt irritated—despondent—because I'm forced to come here—it's a demand to talk about what's uncomfortable." With some embarrassment he continued: "I went to bed with my wife just before my appointment today. It almost deterred me from coming here because I'd have to talk about it. I resent having to dig all this up. If I didn't come here I could let it pass—but when I do say these things, I feel better. Nevertheless, I don't want to say these things. You are the hour, the time, the one snapping the whip—but I know it's not you."

In this clinical example, a patient whose past history of delinquent and truant behavior made him a good candidate for missing an appointment intervened himself. Having previously solved similar dilemmas in the course of psychotherapy, he could not permit himself to forgo an appointment nor "let pass" the feelings and thoughts he verbalized. The process of self-analysis had become well enough integrated that he was now the one who interrupted an impulse to act out and chose, instead, the more productive alternative. Such interventions by the patient make possible the so-called "passive" role of the therapist, a role now to be briefly considered.

When the work of psychotherapy, as in the second case, has progressed to where the therapist can intervene less often and can sit quietly by, statements have been known to erupt with the suddenness of an impulsive act. "Why are you sitting there so quiet like a bump on a log—you must be laughing at me!" or, "You think I'm stupid!" or, "You don't care!" These statements are obviously projections. They often appear after some pause denoting such things as reluctance to speak or self-preoccupation, and mark an intervention by the patient into his own behavior. Even though he uses the second person, the patient returns to the work of therapy by verbalizing some aspect of what he is feeling or thinking, instead of acting out by remaining silent. The therapist's presence and his demonstrated capacity to intervene with a word, comment or sound even when he remains silent reminds the patient of work to be done; for the patient by himself might well revert to old patterns of avoidance at moments of anxiety.

SUMMARY

When acting out behavior during the interview is therapeutically interrupted, the conflicted emotions represented by this behavior are expressed differently as a consequence, and in a way which lends itself more to conflict resolution than before. It is a reflection of the degree of psychopathology and ego integration whether the therapist does the interrupting with physical restraint, the most active measure, or whether the patient does it while the therapist vocalizes or "participantly" observes. The conversion of acting out behavior into something less pernicious through prompt and precise intervention is an important step toward reduction and eventual resolution of conflict. As the patient learns to assume a more active role in intervention, the role of the therapist becomes more inactive.

REFERENCES

1. AICHHORN, AUGUST. *Wayward Youth*. New York: Viking Press, 1943.
2. AXLINE, V. M. *Play Therapy: The Inner Dynamics of Childhood*. Boston: Houghton-Mifflin, 1947.
3. FERENCZI, S. The Further Development of an Active Therapy in Psychoanalysis. In *Further Contributions to the Theory and Technique of Psychoanalysis*. London: Hogarth Press, 1950, transl. J. I. Suttie.
4. FERENCZI, S. Contraindications to the Active Psychoanalytic Technique. In *Further Contributions to the Theory and Technique of Psychoanalysis*. London: Hogarth Press, 1950, transl. J. I. Suttie.
5. HAMILTON, D. *Psychotherapy in Child Guidance*. New York: Columbia Univ. Press, 1950.
6. HOEDEMAKER, E. D. Psychoanalytic Technique and Ego Modifications. *Internat. J. Psychoanalysis*, 1960, 41:1-3.
7. REDL, F. and WINEMAN, O. *Controls from Within*. Glencoe, Illinois: The Free Press, 1952.
8. REIDER, N. Remark attributed to.
9. SZUREK, S. Playfulness, Creativity and Schisis. *Am. J. Orthopsychiat.*, 1959, 29:667-683.
10. SZUREK, S. *The Roots of Psychoanalysis and Psychotherapy*. Springfield, Illinois: Charles C Thomas, 1958.
11. SZUREK, S. A. and BERLIN, I. N. Elements of Psychotherapeutics with the Schizophrenic Child and His Parents. *Psychiatry*, 1956, 19:1-9. Also see Chapter 9 in this volume.
12. WEXLER, M. The Structural Problem in Schizophrenia: Therapeutic Implications. *Internat. J. Psycho-Anal.*, 1951, 32:157-166.
13. WILKINS, A. The Meaning of External Control to a Schizophrenic Adolescent Girl. *Bull. Menn. Clin.*, 1957, 21:140-152.

26

A Clinical Note on the Reversibility of Autistic Behavior in a 20-Month-Old Child

Irving N. Berlin, M.D.

Billy first came to medical attention when he was hospitalized at 18 months of age because of a severe anemia and ear infection. The pediatrician immediately noted that this child was withdrawn. He spent most of his time in bed lying on his back with his fingers fanning in front of his eyes, apparently totally preoccupied with this behavior to the exclusion of all else about him. Billy also did not make any eye contact or relate with any nursing or ward personnel. During the two weeks of hospitalization, his fanning activity of the fingers increased, with some crying whenever Billy was approached by staff members in the hospital or whenever other children nearby cried. Only during his last two days of hospitalization did he relate at all to a nurse who had been in constant attendance. At that time Billy began to smile at her when she came to his bedside. However, something about the character of his smiling during these last two days was disturbing to the pediatrician and the staff. They described the smile as a kind of grimace without much feeling, almost as if the child actually did not know how to smile.

During hospitalization Billy submitted to all necessary procedures, no matter how painful, such as venipunctures, with no struggle and no real vocal protest, although he did look unhappy. His expression was rather sad and unhappily resigned. Billy's withdrawn behavior and odd mannerisms convinced the pediatrician that the child was severely emotionally disturbed. He therefore spent some time with the mother in an effort to understand the child's developmental and emotional history.

Billy was the second of two children, with a brother two years older. Mother said Billy was different from any other children she had ever seen, especially different from her older son. She described Billy as being unusually good. He never cried. He seemed afraid of people and was withdrawn most of the time.

529

Billy's father was overseas until the child was 14 months old. He only saw Billy once, for a few days, when Billy was eight months old. During the four months preceding hospitalization, Father was in the home. However, Billy was still extremely shy with him. Mother described Billy's activities during the day as sitting in one place, either looking at a magazine picture for hours at a time or listening to the radio, apparently absorbed. He would also sit for hours looking at his fingers as he waved them, fanlike, in front of his eyes. Billy actively resisted being held on his mother's lap. Mother felt Billy resented her affection and cuddling and actually did not want it. Mother described the fanning activity as beginning at two months of age when Billy first began to use his hands. Mother remarked that while Billy seemed to show little pleasure in anything during his daily routine, he listened to and moved his body in rhythm to fast music with some evidence of pleasure. The pediatrician found that the medical history and developmental history were essentially normal. There was no history of injuries or illnesses. Developmentally, Billy sat alone at six months of age and took single steps at 11 months of age. He never ventured more than a few steps at a time, apparently fearful of walking without some kind of support. At seven to eight months of age Billy learned to pat-a-cake in response to Mother's insistence and playfulness. At 14 months of age he began to say a few words, mostly "mama" and "daddy." He was bowel trained at 13 months of age, but was still enuretic at night and insisted upon sitting down to urinate. The pediatrician talked with Billy's mother about her own worries of recent years. She spontaneously talked about her recurrent ulcerative colitis of many years' duration. She felt the colitis was considerably aggravated by Billy's birth and by caring for him during the past 18 months. She expressed concern to the pediatrician that Billy was different from the other children in the neighborhood. The pediatrician described the father as reserved, ill at ease, and difficult to talk with. At the insistence of the pediatrician in the Army hospital, the parents applied to our psychiatric clinic.

FIRST CONTACT WITH CHILD PSYCHIATRY CLINIC

After application six weeks elapsed before the parents actually kept an appointment and appeared at the clinic for their intake interview. During the intake interview, Mother appeared anxious, and Father was sullen and hostile. Mother fearfully asked if her child would have to stay in the hospital. She reiterated that she didn't want to leave Billy there. Their missed appointments appeared to be related to Mother's anxiety that she might have to leave Billy in our hospital.

At intake Billy was 20 months of age, the parents were each 24 years of age, and Billy's brother was four years old. Mother's complaints about Billy during the intake were centered primarily on his failure to talk and his fanning and twiddling of his fingers in front of his face for prolonged periods, especially when anxious or tired. Billy also avoided looking at people. Mother was concerned that Billy had not learned to feed himself. He was fed by his mother although she stated he had no eating problem and ate all foods. Billy's talking had, until he came from the hospital, consisted only of the words, "mama" and "daddy." Since his hospitalization, he had begun a few more words like "choo choo train," "bye bye," and "outside." He had also begun to make efforts to walk. His efforts toward talking and walking were at their height immediately after his return from the hospital. Since then, Billy's efforts had lessened. Both parents, especially Father, were very tense in the interview and reiterated that everything seemed to be getting better, and that, since Billy's anemia and ear infection had been taken care of, he would probably now progress normally. They stated they really didn't think there was anything to be gained by coming here for an evaluation. A good deal of tension between the parents was evident. Finally Mother said she had great difficulty in handling Billy because of his frequent temper tantrums and she was concerned that his recent spurt in walking and talking had ended. Mother also said she herself had been ill, that her ulcerative colitis was flaring up again. Father emphatically insisted his child was all right and there was no point in coming here. Father finally stated that coming to this clinic was an admission that there was something wrong with his boy and he didn't think there was anything wrong.

The parents were told that we were available to them to investigate the problems of the child, and that we did feel there were problems. The intake worker suggested they talk over what they wanted to do and told them they could avail themselves of our services, and we would await their calling us.

About a week later, Mother called the intake worker to state that Billy had almost completely stopped his walking, she was becoming increasingly concerned, and she wanted an early appointment. Billy and his parents were seen about a week later. The psychiatrist and intake worker were immediately impressed by the rather odd look on Billy's face. He looked unusually solemn, quiet, and withdrawn. Billy appeared quite unaware of his surroundings and sat stiffly in the lap of whichever parent happened to be holding him. We were also struck with the odd shape of his head. The occiput was almost completely flat and gave his head a rather towering look. He appeared quite dull and during the initial examination smiled little or not at all. He sat through the history taking from the parents with little change of expression. He occasionally played with his mother's beads. He showed animation only when he became annoyed or frustrated when Mother moved out of reach and he began to cry.

During the physical examination Billy was quite resistive and uncoopera-
tive in sharp contrast to the description given by the pediatrician during his
hospitalization. He struggled to prevent the psychiatrist from looking at his
throat and in those moments appeared quite determined and vigorous. Following the physical examination he relaxed and seemed in better contact with
the adults in his environment. Holding onto the examining table bars, he
actually walked around the examining room and looked at the objects around
him. On returning to the interview room Billy again appeared indifferent and
apathetic. He complained occasionally when Mother may have been unresponsive to his signals toward her. The relationship between Mother and Billy
seemed to be a rather easy one with a good deal of natural tenderness toward
Billy. She made repeated efforts to cuddle the child and to hold him close.
He resisted by sitting stiffly erect. When Father held the boy, they seemed to
be separated by an invisible wall. Father was constantly impatient with Billy,
and tension was apparent between Mother and Father.

The initial psychiatric examination revealed additional details of Billy's
developmental history. Mother said that throughout the pregnancy she had
severe colitis which greatly restricted her movements. She was uncomfortable
and in pain throughout the pregnancy. The birth was normal, with no difficulties during delivery. She suspected that she was again anemic as she had
been about three or four years ago. Mother's high fever forced her to remain
in the hospital for eight days after Billy's birth, so she was unable to nurse
Billy. During the last 20 months she was recurrently ill, felt tired, and her
colitis flared up frequently.

Billy was a very hungry baby; in fact, he was described as a voracious
eater. He was put on solid food and whole milk a few weeks after his birth
because his appetite did not seem to be satisfied by the previous diet. Despite
his lusty eating, he was physically listless, lay on his back most of the time,
and became upset if turned on his stomach. Billy was a "good" baby. He slept
most of the time, cried almost not at all, and offered Mother little trouble in
caring for him.

At about 2½ months he found his fingers and began to fan them in front
of his eyes. He was preoccupied with them and spent hours moving them in
front of his eyes. At 20 months this was still one of his favorite preoccupations
—although he seemed to do this more when he was unhappy or tired. Billy
made no effort to sit and no effort to handle things with his hands. Mother
felt his hands and arms were weak and that he could not grasp things. He did
begin to sit at six months of age, stood at 11 months, and later took a few
steps, always with firm support.

At about 13 or 14 months of age he began to say "Mama" and "Daddy"
and a few other words not clearly recognizable. He said no more until after

his hospitalization at 18 months. Mother described Billy's eating habits as excellent, he ate everything although he refused to feed himself. He would not hold a cup or any utensil. Mother ascribed some of this to her feeding him and not encouraging self feeding because she felt his hands were weak. Besides, she got through the feeding more quickly this way. His toilet training began at about a year of age, and at 13 months of age he stopped soiling himself. At 20 months he stayed dry most nights, but during the day Mother must anticipate his need or else he wets himself. Billy had no serious illnesses until a severe attack of measles at 11 months. After that illness, he awakened two or three times at night and was irritable after each wakening. For two or three weeks he was not hungry which was quite unlike Billy.

Mother described Billy's indifference to children around him and some fear of other adults. He would not look in the direction of older children or adults but seemed fond of babies and happily looked at them. In the past two or three months he had shown some interest in his brother's toy cars and made an effort at pushing them on the floor. However, he spent most of his time sitting and listening to music or looking at a single page in a magazine. If left by Mother, he acted fearful and screamed constantly until her return. Mother said that, in the weeks since his hospitalization, Billy seemed more relaxed with other people, and less frightened if she left him for a few moments. Billy also during the past year had many severe temper tantrums during which he screamed and banged his head on the wall or the arm of Mother's chair. He did this with such great force that Mother was frightened and anxious. The temper tantrums were continuing and occurred several times a day. Mother felt they were brought on by frustration when he wanted something and Mother either failed to understand or refused what he wanted.

During this interview Father participated very little, saying that he had not been home long enough to know much about the boy. He also mentioned that he was about to leave to spend about three months at an Air Force school.

The physical examination performed at this time was like the previous ones, within normal limits except for the odd appearing occiput, previously described. The musculature was of normal tone and strength. However, Billy walked unsteadily and was noticeably insecure and wobbly on his feet and needed to hold onto something for support. There was no indication, however, of weak leg muscles since he was able to hold himself erect with great ease. The picture was more one of fearfulness than muscular weakness in walking.

With the clinical psychologist, Billy was quite irritable, refused to be separated from his mother, and cried lustily when this was attempted. Mother explained his fretful behavior on the basis of his being rather disturbed by the number of people about and also that he was tired because he had had no nap. He played with his mother's beads and at other times engaged himself intently in looking at his fingers as he fanned them. This activity had the quality of a ritual and seemed to exclude everything else and by his intent appearance, to provide internal satisfaction. Billy gave some fleeting and guarded glances at other adults in the room, but never was there a smile or a curious gaze. When he walked holding on, he was stiff legged, toddling with extremely small steps. His score on the Vineland Social Maturity Scale was 13 months. From what little could be observed during the interview, there seemed to be no indication of development in advance of this level. The parents, however, repeated their belief that there had been some progress since his hospitalization.

INTERVIEW WITH MOTHER

Later in the interview with Billy's mother, she began to talk about her colitis, her anemia, her feeling of being tired all of the time, and her sense of weariness of the responsibility of having to care for her two children all alone since Father was overseas most of the time, and now again was about to be away for three months. As she talked, she appeared wan and tired, and obviously was appealing to the psychiatrist for some kind of understanding and support. When asked to describe her colitis she reported that actually she had only few diarrhetic movements daily, but a good deal of lower abdominal discomfort and she felt quite tired most of the time. She said that Billy's temper tantrums were extremely disturbing to her and she felt very tired after each one.

We discussed possible causes of Billy's behavior. I felt it was difficult at this time to distinguish between retardation and autism. At that time some evidence for each appeared to exist. From the pediatric hematology consultant at the university hospital we learned what the effects of prolonged anemia might be on a young child. At the time of his hospitalization he had a hemoglobin of only 2 gm. The hematologist indicated that usually severe anemia in small children did not affect their mental ability and usually the only noticeable effect was some retardation in motor development.

We decided to reinforce Mother's capacity to interact with Billy. The social worker and I discussed with her how vital her efforts were to Billy's development. We illustrated how, when, and where such interactions could be fostered. We suggested times of day, like during the bath, after naps and morning awakening that Mother sing and talk to Billy. We suggested that peek-a-boo, hide and seek, and playing house would help. We also described how the older brother's interactions could be used to facilitate Billy's learning through his participating with Billy and Mother in the games. Because the family lived almost 210 miles from the clinic, we asked them to return in three months. At that time we hoped to be able to determine whether or not

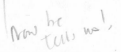

the underlying process was primarily an emotional-autistic one or whether there was some basic retardation.

When Billy and his mother returned to the clinic, Father was still away at Air Force school. Mother reported that Billy had improved enormously. Since our interview with her and the child, Billy had begun to talk more, he had begun to walk fairly well by himself, although stiffly and with difficulty up and down stairs, and that for the first time in his life he had begun to join the children in the neighborhood at play. He was also exploring toys— handling them with evident interest. Billy was less fearful of adults and completely accepted the older children in the neighborhood after whom he now tagged. Mother was extremely pleased at the rapidity of Billy's development during this period. She recounted how her efforts to work with Billy were rewarded by his greater interaction with her, more smiling and eager looks when she came toward him, and rewarding, exciting "Momma's" when he saw her; in Bowlby's terms, increasing development of attachment to Mother in response to her initiative toward the child.

During this visit Billy appeared much less tense and preoccupied. He said a few words to the interviewer and began to explore the room in which he was seen. He played a game with the psychiatrist and returned the trains when they were pushed in his direction. He laughed quite spontaneously and smiled. There was only occasional fanning of his fingers at moments when he appeared tense, or when asked to do something that interrupted his play.

On the next visit, three months later when Billy was 26 months old, Mother said Father had just returned from school and Billy was getting to know him again. She complained that despite his rapid strides developmentally, his temper tantrums had not yet abated. She felt she had to pacify him at all costs, and she indicated that she had been in relatively good health during the past three months.

In the playroom with the psychiatrist, Billy seemed somewhat sad. He vocally objected to his mother's leaving the room but in her presence he began to play games with the psychiatrist and to look directly at him. When Mother and child were left alone in the playroom for a few minutes, the warmth between them noticeably increased. They played spontaneously, both laughing. Billy kept pushing trains and toy cars out of his mother's reach and seemed to enjoy the special efforts required of her to return them to him. He walked about easily, although there was still some stiffness in his gait as if he were not sure about bending his knees freely. Much of the dullness previously noted in his facial expression was gone. However, it was clear the child was still withdrawn in many ways, and also speech was not age appropriate. The psychological examination at this time revealed a Vineland Social Maturity Scale of 21 months and an I.Q. of 89, as against 63 three months ago.

During the psychological examinations Billy was extremely irritable and evidenced a good deal of withdrawal. He played with the materials of the Intelligence Scale, but he responded to any pressure or demands with severe temper tantrums. When pushed to finish a test, Billy screamed and hit his mother. He earned a score of 18-months-level performance on a few Bailey subtests where he enjoyed the use of the test materials.

Mother's description gave some evidence that he was beginning to use two-word sentences. Mother related that much of his play was still solitary, although he did follow the other children and play more with them. Despite the fact that he no longer seemed afraid of others, he would not permit anyone but Mother to touch him or pick him up. He spent as much as two hours in repetitive play such as putting shoes in and out of a shoe box. Mother reported he was still fearful of many things, especially the faces of stuffed animals and dolls belonging to him and his brother.

On the basis of the examinations done over the several months, it was clearly felt that what we were seeing was a severe emotional disturbance with no evidence of mental retardation. The emotional disturbance seemed to be of an autistic character and seemed to be in the process of being reversed.

We again discussed in detail plans for Mother to begin to read to Billy and to encourage play with balls, hopping and running games, and interaction with other children by inviting a few children into the house to play with the two boys. Our aim was to increase Billy's language and sensorimotor skills.

About four months later when Billy was 30 months old, in response to several letters from us, Mother wrote from another state saying she and Father had separated. Father had been interested in someone else, and she therefore returned to her own mother in another state. Mother probably received a positive response from her mother and her depressive reaction lessened. She described Billy as much more social and talkative. He was now reciting rhymes and counting. People in the neighborhood felt he was quite smart for his age. He was completely toilet trained during the day and night, and his finger waving activities were extremely rare and occurred only when he was tired or tense. His walking and running were quite normal. There was still a little difficulty in walking up and down stairs. During the last month or so, Mother said he had ceased pounding his head on the furniture and no longer hit at Mother. He was also not fearful of people, but was still not very friendly with adults. Billy was, however, playing with children of his age and older and spent much less time in solitary activities.

Mother wrote that during the two months before her separation from her husband she had been very nervous and tense but she made no mention of her colitis. She was very pleased with Billy's progress but feared the effect of separation from Father. She briefly described that she had carried out most of the agreed on program with mutual pleasure as Billy evidenced increased speech and motor skills. Also, she could now play with greater ease with both children and enjoyed it. Previously she had been at a loss about what to do with her children at home or in a park.

After this report, our letters at regular three-month intervals were returned marked, "No forwarding address," and we had no further contact with Billy or his mother.

SUMMARY AND CONCLUSIONS

This case presents several interesting questions of etiology. First, here is a child born to a mother who had severe colitis during the pregnancy and continued disability and difficulty during the child's first two years of life. Also, during this time Father, from whom the mother was later estranged, was absent overseas, leaving the entire burden of two children to Mother. This child is described early as being a "good" baby who slept most of the time and otherwise laid quietly in his crib. One wonders about the genetic and interpersonal factors that went into such a reaction on the part of the child. We have some data on the interpersonal factors.

A question also exists about the effect of the anemia upon the child's development, although his solitary play, fear of people, and self-absorbed fanning of his fingers can hardly be accounted for on the basis of anemia.

The factors in the reversal of the autistic behavior are also not fully clear. One can certainly guess at the alteration of Mother's feelings when she got some help and attention from both the pediatrician and the psychiatrist during her several clinic visits. Suggested plans for helping Billy clearly implied Mother's capacity to help her child and indicated that the child was probably not so sick as to require hospital care. The continued improvement of the child, first evidenced in the home with Mother, enhanced Mother's self esteem and sense of effectiveness. The fact that the improvement continued in the grandmother's home might indicate Mother's continued expectation of change in Billy. The return of the mother to the maternal grandmother might also be an important factor in Mother's greater comfort and feeling of support and thus her increased capacity to work with Billy, resulting in decreased autistic symptomatology.

Ask the parents!

This case is of great interest to us since we rarely see such autistic behavior in a child at 18 months of age. The problem of differential diagnosis is a recurrent one.

The author and a colleague in clinical psychology did treat a child with mild autistic symptoms at about 14 months of age, who recovered quickly. This child was largely phobic, fearful of bugs and flies, as well as withdrawn and autistic. After four or five months of work with the child and both parents, the child recovered and acted age appropriately in all developmental areas.

Dr. S. A. Szurek told me of a one-year-old child, a foundling who looked catatonic during the adoptability examination. The foster mother also looked withdrawn. After a transfer to another home Dr. Szurek saw the child six months later. The child in a similar examination setting was alive, responsive, babbled and smiled at adults.

In a personal communication to Dr. Szurek, Dr. Eric Erickson said that he saw an autistic child at 18 months of age, the youngest he'd seen. This had occurred at a social visit and there had been no follow up.

When Billy was first seen, the psychiatrist's impression was that he was primarily retarded with possibly some autistic component to the disturbance. It was the opinion of the psychologist that the primary process was an autistic one. Only subsequent to seeing the child after an interval of three months did it become clear to both that this was primarily an autistic process.

One wonders how many children at this age are seen and thought to be retarded and treated as such. One also wonders what the effect might have been had this child and parent been treated more intensively in the clinic. In this instance it was prohibited by the distance of the clinic from Mother's residence and the difficulty of transportation. I think it is also fair to speculate that had this child and parent been treated in the clinic, the change in behavior to a less autistic and withdrawn child might have been felt to be the result of the treatment activities rather than some change in the relationship between parent and child as Mother involved herself actively with Billy.

These changes probably occurred because Mother was helped to feel more hopeful and competent about helping her child. The specific details of the helping process were probably important to a mother who had few resources available since her illness, the care of an older child, and her husband's being overseas all probably contributed to her inability to nurture Billy as she had the older son. Once the process of withdrawal, mutism, and isolated self-absorbed playing became a pattern, Mother had few resources and little help in altering her interaction with Billy. Feeling tired, alone, and overwhelmed, it was easier to leave Billy to his own devices. The specific suggestions gave her a means of re-engaging her son with the help of "powerful" and friendly allies which seemed to help Mother reassert her latent capacities for nurturance and engagement of the child. The fact that she also commented that she had "learned to play" may indicate some lack of being played with in her own childhood.

Thus, the changes that occurred were the result of Mother's work with the child and the strong reinforcement that encouraged continued work as changes in Billy's behavior and speech became manifest.

not merely her changed feelings!

always feel, never learn to act, even when they did teach her!

27

Experiences in the Psychotherapy of a Non-Verbal, Self-Destructive, Psychotic Child

A. J. Gianascol, M.D.

This report summarizes very briefly my experience with one of the most self-hurtful children treated on the children's ward at The Langley Porter Neuropsychiatric Institute. It is not a success story since the child is now in a state hospital.

The organization of the Children's Service described elsewhere (1, 2, 4, 5, 6) will not be elaborated. Numerous conferences held at various staff levels allow all to share experiences and examine the progress of therapy. These included the therapist's meeting one hour weekly with the child's nurse, as well as frequent collaboration between therapist, technicians, nurses, the teacher, psychiatric social worker, occupational and recreational therapists and other staff involved in ward milieu. These reflect our recognition of the importance of the staff's collaboration and communication concerning a patient's total experience during the 120 hours of each hospital week.

Psychopathology may be considered as stemming from a conflict between opposing motivational forces with ensuing anxiety leading to repression, the formation of defenses, and the return of distorted derivatives of the conflictual impulses as symptoms.

Conflict-reductive psychotherapy as distinguished from other types, such as symptomatic or supportive, may be defined as the patient's agreement with a therapist to try to express all feelings and thoughts as they occur during the hour with the goal being the resolution or reduction of intrapsychic conflict. With a child, play therapy is utilized rather than free

Presented in part at the American Orthopsychiatric Association Annual Meeting, San Francisco, California, March 30, 1959.

association and the agreement for the child's participation in therapy rests with the parents—hopefully the child concurs.

The therapist's role is multifold. He serves to facilitate the patient's expression of feelings, sensation, and thoughts, both by his silence and/or his comments and queries. This may involve his observing aloud any non-verbal modes of communication during a session, such as the movement of a limb, finger, or a facial twitch which may not be verbalized by the patient. In my experience an observation or statement is preferable to a question since the latter may inhibit a patient's verbalization. The therapist also serves as a non-derogatory and non-retaliatory "sounding board" for the patient's feelings providing the patient with a different kind of relationship than hithertofore experienced.

A few pertinent details of the psychotherapeutic work with the patient and her parents will be mentioned, although the primary intent of this report is to summarize those aspects of therapy concerned with the importance of consistent, prompt, personal restraint of self-punitive or assaultive impulses in a non-retaliatory way and in a manner physically and psychologically comfortable for the therapist. Along with this, the therapist remains ready to facilitate the ensuing emergence of relaxed sensual satisfactions in all modalities whenever cued by changes such as in muscle tonus, a quick glance of the child's eyes, a turning of the head, or the slight movement of a foot or even finger. Concurrent with restraint and his non-verbal behavior, the therapist might make non-intrusive, tentative expressions of what the child might be experiencing, along with the demonstration during such sequences that the therapist's feelings can be adequately discharged verbally.

Repetitive, consistent, prompt restraint of self-hurtful behavior in the child to be described led to an internalization of the restraint, so that eventually verbal restraint from the therapist sufficed. With this, the non-destructive and less conflictful expression of her impulses became evident and she demonstrated more spontaneity and integration. As this occurred, her interest was encouraged by all staff members at her pace. Her rate of improvement, however, often proceeded at a snail's pace.

CASE PRESENTATION

The patient, whom I shall call Jane, and her parents were first referred to our hospital when she was 5 years old, from another clinic where the parents had sought aid because of head banging since age 1 year, biting her arms and hands and slapping her face since age 4 years, and never having achieved bowel or bladder training.

Without detailing the parents' background prior to marriage, the development of their individual psychological difficulties and their summation after marriage, was apparent. The ensuing intrafamilial disturbances reached an exacerbation around the birth and infancy of the patient. It was during a peak of parental tensions, shortly after the patient had begun to say single words at age 1 year, that her symptom of head banging began. Her development then became arrested and toilet training and learning did not progress significantly.

During the next three years her symptoms increased, as did the familial tensions until age 5 when her parents sought an evaluation of Jane at our clinic. After out-patient therapy for one year, which included Jane, they discontinued, only to reapply about a year later and Jane was admitted as an in-patient at age 7 years, 4 months and remained until discharge at age 10½ years, three years and two months after admission. Throughout her hospitalization she was seen three hours weekly in play therapy and her parents were each seen in individual psychotherapy for weekly interviews, as well as in conjoint meetings. The psychotherapeutic program is detailed elsewhere (1, 2).

Physical and neurological examinations, repeated blood counts, blood serology, sedimentation rate, and urinalyses including phenylpyruvic acid testing were negative. Repeated chest x-rays were normal, as were x-rays of the skull. Skeletal maturation as measured by x-ray was normal. Repeated electroencephalograms revealed no abnormalities.

Psychological testing on admission and repeated twice during her hospitalization indicated that she was grossly retarded and seriously disturbed emotionally with marked self-punitive tendencies. Her lack of cooperation precluded any data that would allow conclusions about intellectual capacity.

SUMMARY OF THERAPY AND COURSE IN THE HOSPITAL

Following Jane's admission and prior to my work with the family, she and her parents were seen by one therapist for a period of seventeen months.

Initially, Jane improved to a point where she began to explore the playroom, hum, mouth blocks and vocalize monosyllabic sounds, but after six months she regressed until it became necessary to hold her intermittently throughout the entire play therapy hour. No pharmacotherapy was utilized during the patient's hospitalization other than that for intercurrent medical illnesses.

Since this report is not meant to detail the family's course in psychotherapy, it will be limited to correlations between Jane's behavior, the course of therapy with her and her parents, and the staff's experiences in working with her.

At admission, the parents described Jane as non-verbal, but vocal, not toilet trained, unable to adequately care for herself, and having difficulties around sleeping and eating. They reported her persistence in hurting herself by intense, self-inflicted blows and they pointed out many marks and bruises over her body as evidence of long standing, self-destructive behavior.

The nursing staff experienced concern over her symptom of self-destruction and about how to most effectively prevent it, and physical restraint by staff personnel was necessary during the greater part of Jane's hospitalization. Numerous techniques and attitudes were introduced to try to resolve the management problem she posed and it was strongly felt by the staff that had worked long and close with Jane that these played a role in the dramatic shifts seen in her behavior.

During her first eighteen months, the nursing staff reported little significant change, and her attempts to hurt herself were unending. She not only hit herself with her fists, knees and feet, but bit her arms, hands, lips and tongue, and ground her teeth together. At times it was necessary for two staff members to restrain her self-hurtful behavior, but this proved so exhausting that it became necessary for the staff to rotate their time with her.

Other factors which added to the discomfort of being close to Jane were her habits of regurgitating food, picking at the sores on her skin, urinary and intermittent fecal incontinence, and her monotonous groaning and wailing.

Meal times were also difficult and messy as Jane shoved food in her mouth with her hands, smearing herself and the surrounding area thoroughly.

Bedtime was another area of stress. From admission on, Jane had been wrapped in a sheet and tucked in bed in order to prevent her self-hurtful attempts. Occasionally she spent the night in a side room because of her loud screeching.

The structured activities of school, occupational therapy, picnics and outings also were often just one struggle after another.

Fluctuations in her weekly weight (see Figure 1) grossly correlated with periods of regression and improvement, since during her more disturbed periods her refusal to eat required hand feeding by the staff. Losses or gains of as much as eight pounds within a week were evident and we found striking correlations between her weight, symptomatology, and factors such as intra-staff tensions, vacations of staff members or her parents, and changes in the assignment of staff working with her.

When I began therapy with Jane and her parents during her second year

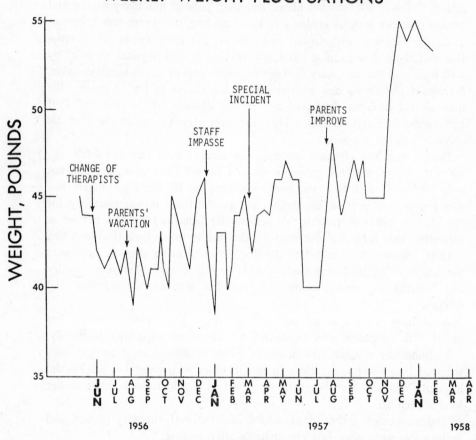

WEEKLY WEIGHT FLUCTUATIONS

FIGURE 1

of in-patient treatment, she was in the midst of a regression with an exacerbation of self-punitive behavior and weight loss which seemed related to the change of therapists. She required extraction of several teeth because she had ground them down to the pulp.

Throughout the initial months I reiterated to her both verbally and by my actions that I would not allow her to hurt herself or me, or any of the playroom materials. Interspersed with intervals of restraint, there were many moments of relaxation, during which she fingered small objects in the playroom. During one session in my fourth month with her, while restraining a flurry of her self-destructive behavior and also trying to express her feelings about my missing several interviews due to illness, she suddenly whacked me painfully on the forehead with her elbow. Initially disappointed and then angry at not having been more alert, I tightly restrained her arms, telling her that I was fed up with her hurtful way of expressing herself. After verbalizing my thoughts, I expressed regret at feeling so angry; and, as I spoke I relaxed, as did she. She then cuddled in my lap and as I became sleepy, she disengaged herself from nominal restraint, stood warmly peering into my face and then hugged me cheek to cheek.

Throughout these initial months, however, I was tardy in getting to know all the ward staff and in appreciating fully the difficulties involved from their point of view in working with Jane. As we began to share experiences, some differences in our attitude emerged and during the twenty-fourth month of hospitalization Jane seemed to become the focus of our conflicts. One weekend when Jane's parents, who usually took her home, left her while they vacationed, a rather marked regression and exacerbation of her self-destructive behavior occurred with a self-inflicted scalp laceration and a broken tooth.

Following this, the nursing staff more directly discussed individual and group problems concerning their care of Jane, and the ensuing ventilation entailed a more organized plan for Jane's care. Their attitude became one of "Let Jane set the pace." She was allowed to stay in bed longer in the mornings and was dressed when she gave some indication of being ready. Her meals were offered away from the group whenever possible and she was offered long tub baths and water play.

However, the stormy periods did not abate suddenly. Occasional expressions of discouragement from those most involved with working with Jane would take the form of, "It's impossible to prevent every self-destructive act," or "What can we expect to accomplish with her?" Discouragement also was expressed in their feeling that they could expect little from her, and they increasingly did things *for her*—such as dressing or bathing her.

During my eighth month with Jane (her twenty-sixth hospital month), a nurse who had not worked with her appreciably described an experience that modified staff attitudes and heightened their expectation of what Jane might accomplish. She had taken Jane to her locker to get a change of clothes. As Jane struggled and pulled away in attempts to beat herself, the nurse stopped for a moment and expressed to Jane for the first time her feelings about caring for her, with some exasperation. She then relaxed her restraint but maintained her vigilance. Jane, appearing very angry, howled, stomped her feet and vocalized, "Na na," but did not attempt to hurt herself. In the midst of this, she then calmly picked up her clothes and handed them to the nurse who told Jane she "could go to hell" before she would dress her when she could demonstrate her ability to do something for herself, such as pick up her clothes. The nurse then turned and left the locker room and Jane, carrying her clothes, followed. When they joined the other patients and staff members in the day room, *Jane slowly dressed herself for the first time,* to the amazement of all present.

In individual therapy with Jane at that time, I had been verbalizing to her how efforts continued on all our parts to examine some of the tensions around her. Verbal restraint of self-destructive behavior would at times suffice, and she frequently expressed her frustrations and negative feelings more openly by slapping her palms on her thighs and stamping her feet rather than by sustained efforts to beat herself.

During this period of improvement, her parents were discussing their difficulties more frankly and they had begun to handle their financial affairs with circumspection. Father explored his self-derogatory attitudes and their projection in therapy, and as his relationship with his supervisor at work improved, he received a salary increase.

During my tenth month with Jane, her behavior entailed an increasing amount of self-injury with numerous secondary infections and I again became more alert to the tensions amongst all of us working with Jane. These reached a climax following an incident in which Jane had cut her lip while with a staff member. In discussing it with the staff member, I became aware of the feeling among some ward personnel that they might be criticized for holding her too tightly if they really tried to prevent all of the patient's self-hurtful behavior. Implicit in their concern I recognized their awareness and my own of how disappointment, anger, retaliatory feelings, and then guilt arose in working with Jane. In conferences, I verbalized my own struggles to express these feelings verbally rather than through other modes of behavior, i.e., allowing passive expression of these feelings by laxity of restraint which allowed her to hit herself even once or more actively allowing these feelings to be communicated to her by restraining her so tightly it caused her discomfort. I shared the travail of having to navigate through the straits between this Scylla and Charybdis of Jane's therapy. I also reiterated the futility of expecting Jane to learn how to express her negative feelings in a non-destructive way if she experienced with us that we did not practice what we preached. I also recalled in conferences how the nurse managed this in the previously described dressing episode. I shared the dilemma of preventing Jane's self-injury through adequate personal restraint without inhibiting any non-destructive expression of her feelings with the staff. I also decided that it might be helpful to demonstrate effective modes of restraint for a prolonged period, so I stayed with Jane in various ward and hospital activities throughout one morning to demonstrate how I achieved restraint.

Our discussions and the demonstration of methods of personal restraint seemed to relieve staff uneasiness about similar methods they might employ. A dramatic change followed in Jane's behavior manifest by several weeks of freedom from attempts to hurt herself. She sought contact with the staff in a laughing, cuddling manner and for the first time, ward personnel vied with each other to be with her. The parents reported the best weekend they had ever experienced with her at home, and they described how she played with a toy without restraint.

After several weeks of improvement, a rapid regression occurred early in my thirteenth month of therapy with her, a time when it was necessary for me to cancel all but one play therapy session in two weeks; a time, too, when staff tensions were mounting. With their resolution and the resumption of regular appointments, her improvement resumed.

During my fourteenth month with Jane, her parents left on a two week vacation without her. An acute regression in the patient occurred and then a period of improvement began, interrupted during my sixteenth month of treatment by an acute staff shortage occasioned by influenza, so that finally we requested that the parents keep Jane at home for several days. Following her return, improvement continued until her discharge, except for a slight regression when termination was discussed with her and her parents.

Throughout the latter months of her third year of hospitalization, Jane's mother was expressing her feelings more directly in therapy. After exploring her own role in perpetuating Jane's seeming inability to do things for herself, she began to report how they were able to do things at home together on weekends, such as picking up toys or bits of paper Jane had torn. Throughout this time, father had continued to do well in his job as he was able to work through his feelings in therapy. This culminated in his submitting some proposals to his employer which resulted in his being recommended for promotion to a position with a more promising future, but which entailed the family's moving out of state.

Concurrent with these events in her parents' therapy, Jane was again initiating more activity for herself on the ward, exploring both herself and objects close by with her eyes, ears, mouth, nose, and fingers. One indication of improvement was her ability to give up being wrapped in a sheet at night. As previously mentioned, she had been wrapped nightly in a sheet which seemed to serve as a token restraint because she readily could free herself at any time (she was nicknamed "Houdini" by the night nursing staff because of this). Jane was given the sheet at night and was told she would no longer be wrapped; and, although she vocalized loudly and stomped about, she went to sleep without being wrapped and without hurting herself. There were many nights when she relinquished the wrap completely. At this time, too, the parents reported that she dressed herself in pajamas at home for the first time.

During the seventeenth month of therapy with me (thirty-fourth month of hospitalization), following Jane's being taken home by her parents at our request, she continued to improve on her return. She more readily accepted from staff verbal control of her self-destructive behavior and group situations seemed less distressful to her. Her vocal activity increased and her repertoire of songs, which she hummed, grew. Although inattentive during school, she would later hum songs heard there, such as "Lover, Come Back to Me" and "Never Let Me Go."

The family, after much deliberation and exploration of other facilities for Jane, decided to move because of the opportunities for promotion presented father and because they felt they could care for Jane at home since she had improved, and they terminated therapy.

Follow-up information after discharge, however, revealed that Jane's behavior worsened when the family moved into their new home and she required further hospitalization. Her regression continued despite several courses of phenothiazines followed by a course of electroconvulsive therapy.

DISCUSSION

Several observations of psychodynamic and psychotherapeutic import emerge from this experience.

First, it was evident that the child served as a sensitive barometer to any pressures within the staff or parents, and as Stanton and Schwartz (3) (see also Chapter 2, this volume) have shown, a hospitalized patient may become increasingly disturbed, serving as the symptomatic expression of unspoken and/or unrecognized staff tensions just as an emotionally disturbed child in the family expresses the symptomatic resultant of the parental conflicts. Although not elaborated in this case discussion, the interaction between hospital staff and a child's parents around visits or their picking up and returning the child for weekend leaves, may contribute significantly to staff tensions which come to focus on the child through displacement and other mechanisms. Staff awareness of these interactions and their effects on the child are enhanced, although not always assured, through close collaboration at all levels of staff functioning.

Although a therapist and other staff involved in the treatment program of a child may frequently reiterate that he and they will not allow the child to do anything that is hurtful to herself or others or property, this does not suffice. It is important for the child to experience through its experience with the staff that they mean what they say. Through their behavior and prompt personal restraint of self-hurtful behavior, the staff can reinforce the child's trust in others. When our non-verbal behavior coincided with our verbal behavior, the child seemed to appreciate that we meant what we said. If, on the other hand, the words do not go with the tune, this serves to further confound and increase the child's distrust and distress. In this child's experience when we demonstrated that we could experience angry feelings and discharge them verbally rather than through hurtful behavior, the child's own self-destructive behavior disappeared.

Psychotherapeutic work with a non-verbal child increases the therapist's awareness of the importance of all modalities of non-verbal communication which in turn enhances the opportunity for his interpretive behavior in play therapy, with an empathy for what the child may be experiencing. The readiness on the therapist's part to verbalize an emerging impulse in a child, even though it may be complicated by conflict and ambivalence, allows him to try to help the child express the impulse be it negative, such as an angry feeling, or positive, such as a move toward closeness and some sensual satisfaction. In the therapy of Jane, for example, the verbalization of her furtive glance at a toy often led to her reaching out and playing with the toy.

The importance of letting the child set the pace in therapy, as well as in all of the milieu therapeutic activities, was recognized, and when the staff's expectations were adjusted to the tempos of Jane's readiness, dramatic behavioral shifts occurred, such as her dressing and feeding herself, as well as participation in other milieu activities. Although easy to verbalize and discuss, the application of this principle entails a constant vigilance on the part of all staff members to prevent their expectations, impatience, and disappointments around intercurrent regressive periods from becoming de-

which guaranteed minimal progress in 3 yrs + final permanent hosp!. What might behav. mod. have accmplx?

mands on the child. With Jane, the staff's readiness to provide opportunities for her expression of increasing ego function without impatience or making demands seemed an important factor in the clinical improvement.

In summary then, although not an ultimate success story, our experience in the in-patient treatment of this psychotic child heightened our awareness of the above factors and facilitated our therapeutic efforts with less severely disturbed children.

REFERENCES

1. BOATMAN, M. J. and SZUREK, S. A. A Clinical Study of Childhood Schizo-phrenia. In D. D. Jackson (Ed.), *The Etiology of Schizophrenia.* New York: Basic Books, 1960, pp. 389-440.
2. GIANASCOL, A. J. Psychodynamic Approaches to Childhood Schizophrenia: A Review. *J. Nervous and Mental Disease,* 1963, 137:336-348. See Chap-ter 5, this volume.
3. STANTON, A. H. and SCHWARTZ, M. S. Observations on Dissociation as Social Participation. *Psychiatry,* 1949, 12:339-354.
4. SZUREK, S. A. A Descriptive Study of the Program of the Langley Porter Clinic, Children's In-Patient Service. In J. H. Reid & H. R. Hagan (Eds.), *Residential Treatment of Emotionally Disturbed Children.* New York: Child Welfare League of America, 1951, pp. 200-221.
5. SZUREK, S. A. The Family and the Staff in Hospital Psychiatric Therapy of Children. *Amer. J. Orthopsychiat.,* 1951, 21:597-611. Also in S. A. Szurek, I. N. Berlin and M. J. Boatman (Eds.), *Inpatient Care for the Psychotic Child.* Palo Alto: Science and Behavior Books, 1971, pp. 264-279.
6. SZUREK, S. A. and BERLIN, I. N. Elements of Psychotherapeutics with a Schizophrenic Child and His Parents. *Psychiatry,* 1956, 19:1-9. See Chap-ter 9, this volume.

28

Intrapersonal, Interpersonal, and Impersonal Factors in the Genesis of Childhood Schizophrenia

Irving N. Berlin, M.D.

On the waiting room couch a handsome, blond, four-year-old boy stood silently and half-heartedly poking at the eyes of a pretty, tired woman in her thirties. She sat half turned away from the boy, pushing feebly at his hands and wearily ducking her head to avoid his jabs. On the other side of the boy sat a dapper man in his forties. He smiled toothily at passersbys and "tsk-tsked" at the boy after each jab at the woman. Every few moments the man would straighten the boy's jacket, smooth his hair, and adjust his shirt and tie. The boy suffered these attentions without interrupting his apathetic poking at the woman's face.

This was our introduction to Danny and his parents, the beginning of almost three years of psychotherapeutic work with this family. This case illustrates three important points in treating childhood psychosis:

1. When working with a disturbed child, psychotherapy may achieve its most pronounced effects through work with another member of the family. In this case the psychotherapeutic work with the father seemed to have the greatest effect on the child, as it influenced the mother's feelings about herself and thus her behavior with the child. These changes *did* influence the child and his degree of integration.
2. The working through of certain conflicts with the child often waits upon the parents', in this case usually the mother's, having made progress in these particular areas.
3. Often before the parents can help care for a disturbed child, they need to have worked out their own conflicts about infantile needs for nurturance to permit reciprocal taking care of each other and more mutual gratification on a mature level. Their conflicts must

551

be sufficiently reduced to let them keep the child at home and to permit improvement to continue.

Danny's case permits the reader to assess the many variables which may, in conjunction, produce childhood psychosis. The long-term work with Danny on the ward and in individual play therapy make it possible to evaluate factors that appear to permit improvement and gradual reversal of psychopathology. These changes allow us to focus on some of the early pathogenic experiences, elicited in the history, which subsequent therapeutic work tended to validate. As Danny improved, and as the parents also changed as a result of psychotherapeutic work with them, each shift in Danny appeared to produce reverberations in parental attitudes and behavior. These shifts sometimes brought into vivid relief earlier parental attitudes and their possible contribution to Danny's illness.

The prolonged therapy also made it possible to obtain a clearer picture of the parents' personalities than was apparent in their histories. The work showed not only how their personalities were affected by their early relationships, but also how alteration in attitudes and behavior toward self, spouse, children, and relatives was influenced by continual reassessment during therapy.

The work also made material available to help weight the degree to which the impact of impersonal factors affected the parents and through them the child.

How much had he spoken before? (before 2)

DANNY'S PRESENTING ILLNESS AND BACKGROUND

A diagnosis of childhood schizophrenia and an urgent recommendation for inpatient treatment made by a child psychiatrist led the family to bring Danny to the clinic. Since the birth of his sister, two years earlier, Danny had rarely spoken. He assaulted his mother and baby sister and for the past 22 months had been so destructive to household articles that he had spent most of each day locked in his room with his furniture bolted down. Danny isolated himself from the children and adults in his environment, and when not engaged in destructive behavior, sat frozen-faced, piling blocks one atop the other.

The following historical material was gleaned from the three years' work with the parents. Many initially vague descriptions became more specific during therapy and many relevant and emotion-laden details were recalled only in the last few months of the work.

Danny, the second child, was accidentally conceived when his brother was five-years-old. The mother dreaded the necessity for a second Caesarean, although her great desires for a daughter tempered these fears. The pregnancy proved uneventful except for fatigue and headaches in the last trimester, which were ascribed to difficult situations at home. The father, a district manager for a state-wide wholesale firm, was in the throes of planning and building a new office in the face of the post-war building materials shortage. He was thus constantly harried, rarely at home, and only mildly concerned with his wife's pregnancy. At this time mother's oldest sister and her disturbed two-year-old son visited for two and a half months. This boy, later diagnosed an untreatable schizophrenic, upset the household by his frequent tantrums and constant rocking and crying. Mother found herself retreating to bed early in the day with fatigue and a severe generalized headache.

Danny was delivered at term by Caesarean section. He weighed seven pounds and was a healthy, strong, but not very vigorous infant. Mother described her acute disappointment that he was not her hoped-for daughter. She attempted to breast feed him, as she had her first son, but was forced to put him on formula after three days, due to insufficient milk. Danny was an exceptionally handsome child, and mother recalled that her only pleasure in Danny came from exhibiting him to friends and family who were loud in their praise over his beauty. He gained well and would sleep, eat, lie quietly, and then sleep again. He was called a "good," that is, undemanding, child. Shortly after Danny was two months old, mother's own mother who had been ill died. In therapy mother dwelt on her close ties to her mother and her hope for a daughter with whom she could re-experience these close feelings. With the death of her mother, she suffered a severe depression. She often cried hysterically, and both parents recalled that the "melancholia" lasted more than six months. After her mother's death, with her husband increasingly preoccupied with building problems, she said she felt alone, helpless, and child-like.

Danny sat up, stood, walked, and talked at the appropriate times, but was considered to be an extremely sober child who rarely smiled and was unresponsive to people. He said "Mamma," "Daddy," "doggy," and "bye-bye" at about 12 months and babbled a great deal, especially with his brother, then almost six. Babbling stopped once he began to walk at 12 to 15 months. During the next year he learned many new words and spoke a few sentences. Unlike the first child, he made little effort to use speech with family members, except for one-word statements of need such as "milk" or "toilet." There semed to be little spontaneity in any of his activities. He was not very curious and did little exploring of his surroundings. In therapy mother related this to her depression and her consequent isolation and withdrawal from Danny.

Danny was just 16 months old when mother became accidentally pregnant again. At first she talked frantically of abortion, but the hope that a daughter might be born as a memorial to her deceased mother prompted her to go through with the pregnancy. Toward the end of the first trimester, mother's fatigue and severe headaches required complete bed rest and the hiring of a housekeeper. This woman doted on Danny and she carried him around like an infant. Danny enjoyed this greatly and subsequently refused to walk, to feed himself, or to talk to make his wants known. He reacted to any demands that he do things for himself and to any thwarting of his desires by breaking china, lamps, or any household article within reach. The housekeeper reacted to these rages as if they were cute and gave Danny what he wanted. By the time she left the home, Danny was 23 months old.

During this five-month period the parents had had little contact with Danny. In the month's interim between housekeepers, mother dealt with the tantrums by locking Danny in his room where he systematically destroyed all his toys and furniture, and tore his clothes and bedding. The next housekeeper, hired when Danny was 24 months old, was a harsh, punitive person who several times beat Danny severely for his tantrums but who mostly kept him locked in his room except for meals. Mother was afraid of the woman, but help was hard to get and she was nearing term, so this housekeeper was retained. Danny became increasingly destructive, self-absorbed, vacant-looking, and unresponsive to the attentions of his father or brother.

A sister was born when Danny was 26 months old. Mother had a complicating pneumonitis after the Caesarean and was ill for six weeks. The new infant was left to the housekeeper's care. Danny spent the whole day alone, pounding on walls and furniture in his room. By now all his furniture had been bolted to the floor and his window shuttered on the inside to prevent his shattering the glass. His reaction to the new baby was one of great interest and he said his first spontaneous words, "Baby, nice baby." However, a few weeks later he attempted to hit the child, to overturn her crib and then to knock down her highchair. When his mother came near he tried to poke at her eyes and strike her. With the whole family, or in company, Danny sat immobile and frozen-faced, unresponsive to any overtures.

Mother was delighted with her daughter who was also a strikingly beautiful infant. As soon as she felt able, mother took over the full care of her cherished baby girl and for the first time enjoyed an infant. She felt close, warm and loving. From his twenty-seventh month on, one month after the birth of his sister, Danny stopped saying "Mamma" and from then on made all his wants known by pointing.

Both parents commented on Danny's stiffness when his father held him and tried to cuddle him. They reported that he would not respond at all to any of the adults or children who visited the home. By age three Danny was still not toilet trained. His destructive and assaultive behavior toward mother and sister continued, and his parents consulted a local psychologist. On his advice Danny was taken out of the locked room and entered in a nursery school. There he quickly learned to signal his toilet needs, began to say "Hi" on demand, and was seen to move his mouth as if forming words when the children sang. His behavior at home did not change. After 10 months at school, when he continued to be frozen-faced, destructive, and assaultive at home, and when friends made frequent comments about how strange Danny appeared, the family decided to take him to a neighboring city to see a child psychiatrist. At his urging the family came to the clinic.

MOTHER'S HISTORY

The mother was an attractive, petite, well-groomed woman in her late thirties who appeared about five years younger. She looked at everyone with an air of appealing, child-like helplessness. She was the youngest in a family of four girls and a boy. The parents were middle-class Greek, one of a few Greek families in a small New England town. They lived in lonely isolation for much of mother's early childhood. She was permitted to play only with the children of the other well-to-do Greek family in town. Although father was a rather successful junk peddler, he was looked down upon by his wife and children for his occupation. Danny's mother described him as a nonentity. He was withdrawn and isolated and had no say in the running of the home, the expenditure of the money, or the discipline of the children. Mother remembered him as unhappy looking. At home he seemed to be in constant awe and terror of his wife and appeared purposely to stay away for long periods of time. Mother remembered her sisters' taunts that she was her father's favorite, in fact, the only child with whom he really made any effort to play. She, however, had no memory of this. Mother said that she learned early that demonstrations of affection toward her father or her mother's male friends evoked her mother's anger. She learned to be affectionate mostly with her mother and her older sisters.

Mother's mother was a controlling woman who kept her four daughters very close to her and paid little attention to her son. This brother was described as extremely passive and dependent, both as a child and as an adult. The mother shared most of her feelings, observations, and convictions with her daughters. She directed their lives, but allowed them sufficient freedom and initiative so that none seemed to want to escape. Danny's mother felt that she was the favorite daughter and that she was showered with a great deal of attention and affection from her mother. She recalled the hostile comments of her sisters that she was "too cute for words," the darling of her mother and visitors, and complaints that she alone was exempt from household tasks. With keen insight she also described her sisters' psychological problems which had made it necessary for each of them to undergo psychiatric treatment.

In school mother found it difficult to measure up to her sisters' high grades. She worked hard and got good marks, but relied on her sisters for constant help with her studies, even in college, when the subjects were foreign to them. She came to feel that she was less intelligent than they and that she could not get along without them.

It was not until the family moved to New York City and became part of a larger Greek community that mother began to feel socially at ease. Thus in high school, and later in teachers' college, mother began to date boys, being careful to conform to her mother's restrictions. At 18 she fell in love with a Greek boy who could not free himself from his mother. At 21 she quarreled with him and broke off their relationship. After graduation her first job was in home teaching. She was disturbed by some of the male children who, ill in bed, would frequently masturbate in her presence. She felt sick and nauseated each time this occurred. It reminded her of experiences with her brother which made her feel that boys were nasty. When she was 11 or 12 her brother, six years her senior, repeatedly exposed himself in her presence and attempted some sex play with her.

Shortly after breaking off with her boyfriend, she met her husband and after a brief courtship decided to marry him, although she was not at the time sure that she really cared for him. The early years of marriage were very disconcerting as mother knew nothing about housekeeping, cooking, or furnishing a home and found herself completely dominated by the tastes of her artistic and competent husband. When they bought a new home it was furnished entirely to his taste. Mother felt that it was not really hers. Only their sexual relations were satisfying to her; other aspects of marriage were upsetting. Housework was extremely distasteful and it took her "forever" to do it. Her prodigious efforts at cooking and maintaining the house were not appreciated by her husband, and she resented having to defer to his opinions on all household matters. She also felt that her husband expected too much of her in the running of the home. Very early in the marriage her husband took over the paying of all household bills since mother's inexperience made it difficult for her to assert herself. Father refused to discuss any of his business problems or successes. Mother resented the expense of his hobbies at a time when he was critical of her for spending so much money on the house or for occasional household help.

With the birth of her first child, a son whom she had hoped would be a girl, she found that household chores became even more onerous. Being a mother was not pleasurable, although she enjoyed comments about her son's attractiveness from others. She felt anxious when he played with his penis, and uneasy when bathing him because of her distaste for cleansing his genitalia.

Mother also developed an active social life, mostly with a number of older women. There were frequent visits with both her mother and her oldest sister. On visits to any of her sisters, mother re-experienced the old feelings of inferiority. She often talked with envy of her oldest sister's marriage to a very wealthy man who later employed her husband. This sister lived in luxury, could care financially for their mother, and thus became their mother's favorite child.

FATHER'S HISTORY

The father, a spruce, distinguished-looking man, looked 39, although he was 10 years older. The youthful enthusiasm in his voice and his pervasive boyishness appeared rather forced at times. He was born in Greece and was an only child. When he was five, his family emigrated to South America and lived there until he was eighteen years old. Life there was difficult as his father earned only a marginal living as a laborer. The family was usually in financial distress. His parents' quarrels were mostly about money, and his mother constantly derided his father for his poor earning capacity. Danny's father guiltily recalled that he frequently had stolen grocery money from his mother and used it to buy candy and toys. He remembered terrible jealousy of his father and a desire for exclusive possession of his mother.

Shortly after the family's move to this country his father, then only in his mid-forties, died. The son, then 18, went to work. He usually took jobs away from home despite his mother's efforts to keep him near her. He prevented his mother's remarriage to a very nice man, although his mother was then only 40. Much later, when his mother was hospitalized for an inoperable brain tumor, he had many mixed shameful feelings of wanting to control her small estate although he had taken great pride in providing well for her.

In business he became an effective office and sales manager for a number of wholesale food chains and finally joined a large wholesale food company owned and run by his prospective brother-in-law. In this firm he was a successful and respected divisional manager. He felt insecure about this position, however, as he was convinced that despite his abilities, only his family ties kept him employed. He lived in constant fear that he might fall victim to his brother-in-law's whims which had led to the firing of other competent executives during business slumps when the boss needed a fall guy.

Father was especially delighted with the freedom of sexual expression in the United States as contrasted to South American countries. From his comments he evidently had led a fairly active sex life, not wanting any permanent ties, until about the time he met his prospective wife. Then in his mid-thirties, he felt that he had had enough of the life of a gay young blade and wanted to settle down and raise a family. Father was also plagued by doubts about his own masculinity. He talked of his feelings about his smooth skin and dapper appearance, describing how homosexual advances had been made to him and of his anger and anxiety at such moments and the doubts they raised. His wife's femininity as a good sexual partner and his masculinity in their sexual relationship was satisfying to him and never a matter of concern. Several times he said that he was particularly attracted to his wife because of her naive and helpless attitude and his feeling that it would be fun to care for her.

By the time there were children in the family he had become angry with his wife for her general helplessness and especially her need for help with the children. He relied on his wife, however, to obtain his yearly bonus for him via her sister, a bonus amounting to one-half his total salary.

At home, when he did find leisure time, he usually locked himself in his study or shop to work on various hobby projects. He pursued each project until he had won national recognition and then would abandon one hobby to take up another.

INITIAL PHASE OF THERAPY WITH DANNY

During the outpatient evaluation Danny appeared fearful and isolated himself from me by turning his back and monotonously pushing a toy car back and forth for most of the playroom session. Any question, tentative comment, or statement about how he might be feeling resulted in body stiffening and momentary cessation of activity. When I continued to sit quietly there was a gradual relaxation of his body and a resumed pushing of the car to and fro. Danny spoke only twice, to utter a harsh "yes" when, at the end of each session, I asked whether he wanted to rejoin his parents.

Throughout the evaluation the parents appeared detached from the child. Interaction occurred only when Danny poked at his mother or when father straightened Danny's clothes. The evaluation results concurred with the diagnosis of childhood schizophrenia and the recommendation for inpatient psychotherapeutic work with the child and weekly psychotherapeutic interviews with each parents.

Both parents appeared uncomfortable during the introductory tour of the children's ward and remarked on the lack of aseptic, scrubbed cleanliness. They noted that the children who had just come in from the playground were disheveled and dusty. The fact that our nursing staff wore street clothes rather than white uniforms also troubled them. Their questions mainly concerned whether Danny would be kept clean and neat and how often he would be bathed.

Danny, on being brought to the ward to stay, immediately detached himself from his parents and joined a warm, firm, authoritative nurse. He paid little heed to his parents' protracted goodbyes and to their departure. Both parents showed visible distress that Danny did not appear to be concerned with their leaving.

Danny was seen three times a week, usually in the playroom. On weekends he returned home. During the first two months of psychotherapeutic work, he isolated himself by turning away from me, running toy vehicles back and forth on the floor, and standing in a corner where he scribbled on the blackboard and hid his chalk marks with his body. I sat nearby and said little.

Danny's first response to me occurred when I correctly interpreted his need to urinate, offered my hand to take him to the toilet, and helped him with his trousers. These attentions were passively accepted but later in the same hour Danny began to finger the doll furniture and other toys on the shelves. As he touched an object I quietly named it. Danny's lips began to move and after several therapeutic hours he started to whisper the names of toys after me. By the end of the first month he would bring a toy and brush against me as he repeated my naming it. During the second month he occasionally leaned against me as we named toys together. On the occasions when we used my office because the playrooms were all in use, Danny would swivel in my swivel chair, at first tentatively and then with increased freedom. There was little evidence of pleasure in his face as he did this, however. He twirled rapidly around, frozen-faced, his eyes catching mine on each rotation.

Toward the end of the second month an incident occurred in which Danny's destructiveness was countered with a non-retaliatory firmness. He had entered the playroom, made a dash for the dollhouse, and tried to overturn it. When I held on to the dollhouse, Danny began to hurl the doll furniture at me. I quickly restrained him, stating: "Okay, you're mad.

I don't know why, but you can be mad by hitting the pegs on the pegboard like this." I hit the pegs forcefully, keeping one arm around Danny, and then gave him the mallet. He hit a few tentative whacks, then, after a glance at me, smashed the pegs with great vehemence, looking at me from time to time. I shouted "slam," "bang" as Danny struck the pegs to encourage more vigorous pounding. For the first time I noted a thawing of this expression. At the end of this session and at the beginning of several succeeding hours, he also banged the cupboard door with great force, watching me as I sat quietly or as I vocally accompanied the noises with loud bangs and booms.

During the third and fourth months emphasis was placed on accepting Danny's fears of animals and strangers and taking the time to permit a trustworthy relationship with an adult to develop. Danny spent three weeks of the third month with his mother and siblings at the beach. On his return to the ward he again isolated himself from his nurse and from me. He refused to go to the playroom and when led by the hand he had screaming, kicking tantrums. I would sit with him on the ward during these rages. Several days after his return he gashed his hand on a broken bicycle pedal and required general anesthesia for the suturing of the cut. This occurred in the evening when none of the staff he knew well were on duty. The next day he appeared frightened of me and would not go near his favorite nurse with whom he had previously enjoyed physical contact.

For the next month I sat in the ward dayroom and talked to Danny without any effort to take him to the playroom. Several times a day I stopped briefly to sit and talk to him. When Danny seemed only minimally fearful I took him by the hand to the playroom. He struggled for a short time in the elevator, crying: "Don't choke me!" In the playroom he relaxed, was friendly, and included me in his play by bringing the toys for us to name together. The next several interviews began with an initial reluctance to go to the playroom. Once there, he pounded on the pegboard and brought toys for us to name. His face appeared less set each time.

At the beginning of the fourth month Danny had a severe otitis media and was confined to bed. He reacted to each of my visits, several times daily, with a warm smile. As he felt better his smile broadened and toward the end of the week he sat up in bed and leaned against me, smiling happily as I read to him from a storybook.

In the first playroom session after his illness, Danny eagerly inspected every toy, named it himself, and for the first time picked up an airplane and zoomed it. When I made the proper motor noises Danny laughed aloud, another first, and zoomed the plane more freely. There was a brief struggle when he wanted to take the plane with him and was told it had to stay in the room where he could play with it the next time. The play with the plane and Danny's delight at my accompanying noises continued for the next several sessions.

DANNY AND HIS NURSE

On the ward Danny slowly made friends with one of the nurses who spent several hours daily helping him to ride on the tricycle. At first he poked at her face whenever she had to leave to attend to another child. However, her prompt restraint and her unambivalent statements, once again a countering of destructiveness with firmness, brought a quick end to this behavior. She told him that when she did have to leave him she would return as soon as she could. He might be angry with her for leaving to help another child, but she would not permit him to hurt her.

The nurse's quick hugs and attuned response to his body stiffening by a relaxing of her embrace slowly increased his tolerance for physical contact until he would seek her out to sit in her lap for a few moments several times a day.

On daily trips to the playground with other children, or to the park alone with a nurse, Danny would impassively permit her to push him on the swings or to rock with him on the teeter-totter. He would not take her proffered hand on these walks. Following surgery on his cut hand he pushed her away whenever she came near. She continued simply to remain with him in his activities and in a few days he put his hand in hers as they walked to the park, as if he had forgiven her for her desertion when his hand was injured.

During Danny's episode of otitis his nurse had to administer penicillin injections. Her discussions with him prior to each shot failed to avert the ensuing struggle. One day she became very angry with him. She forcibly turned him over while telling him how mad she felt that they had to have such a fight when she must give him the medicine to help him get well. She said that she knew he didn't like being hurt and that she did not like to hurt him. This verbal expression of anger seemed to cut through some barrier and after the shot his usually impassive face was wracked with silent sobs and tears as he cuddled in her arms. From that time on there was only token protest with each shot and frequent cuddling, often unrelated to the injection. After his illness he cuddled often, his body relaxing as he cuddled.

INITIAL WORK WITH FATHER

Father began his first several interviews by loudly protesting his inclusion in the treatment plan. He complained of the time it took from his work and of the distance the family had to travel. Father questioned whether we really knew what was wrong with Danny and what would help him; whether it really was necessary to come once a week to the clinic; and how we knew Danny was not simply mentally retarded. He angrily proclaimed that he did not believe in our hypothesis that it was an emotional disturbance which might have its origin in the parents' troubles.

These objections were listened to with respect and then followed by firm statements about our tentative hypothesis and our plans to validate it by concomitant work with the child and both parents. We indicated that there were other alternatives, such as custodial hospital care elsewhere, psychotherapy with Danny alone, or work at other clinics which did not work as we did with the entire family. Father agreed to try working with us.

During the first month of work father was preoccupied with Danny's cleanliness, a subject of concern when he had first toured the ward. He complained often of how dirty and mussed up Danny was when he saw him and of how noisy the ward was. Father was also troubled by an aggressive little girl who spit on him, accepted his bribes of candy, but then continued to spit.

At this time an error in the setting of a fee was discovered and he was told he would have to pay full rather than half fee. Father was very angry and complained that all his savings would be eaten up. However, he did not talk of stopping the work. It was several months later that we learned that his sister-in-law had offered to pay for the hospitalization. When father did mention this he appeared uncomfortable and reiterated: "She's rich and won't miss it."

Father then began to discuss his feelings of insecurity about his position in his brother-in-law's firm. He knew that only his relationship to the boss kept him employed. Father, during this period, began to complain of preprandial and nocturnal epigastric pain and severe backache. This became a pattern as it later became clear that he developed psychosomatic disturbances only in therapy when there was some chance his need for care could be compensated. He took a holiday from work to investigate his complaints but also to permit the new assistant manager, sent in by his brother-in-law to help with the business slump in father's division, to have full control. He hoped thus to demonstrate to the boss that the temporary business decline was not of his making.

In the fourth month of our work, father was hospitalized for a week to begin treatment of his X-ray-confirmed peptic ulcer. In the hospital he felt fine, was placed on a diet, and given a supportive belt for his backache which X-ray proved to be due to a congenital malformation of several lumbosacral vertebrae. His anxieties about how much business his assistant was doing in his absence led him to check the books secretly. Father alternated between relief and concern as business continued to fluctuate.

MOTHER'S INTRODUCTION TO PSYCHOTHERAPY

When we first saw her at the clinic we were struck by mother's prevailing attitude of innocent helplessness and her repeated assertion that she just could not understand how Danny had become the way he was. She reiterated her great love for the child and her bewilderment that he rejected her affection and attacked her. She wondered whether there was any hereditary taint involved since her sister's child had been diagnosed as a hopeless schizophrenic.

Initially mother felt that our insistence on her participation in treatment meant that we blamed her because she had "neglected" Danny. She, too, seemed preoccupied with Danny's cleanliness and talked angrily about the nurses, who did not keep Danny spotless. Mother declared that at least she had done this. She would then be angry at me and the staff.

We tried to restate each time, as clearly as possible, our feelings about the difference between blame and responsibility and explained that we did not blame parents who under a variety of trying circumstances had done the best they knew how to help their child. However, as parents they were responsible for some of their child's troubles, despite the unconscious manner in which their problems affected the child and despite the effect of events over which they had no control.

As she ventilated her anger at me and discussed some of her own guilty feelings about what had been missing in her relations with Danny, she began to understand my comments that our efforts to understand all the circumstances around Danny's illness included the general family problems, the impersonal stresses due to events in the family's life, and her own unconscious conflicts which she now had an opportunity to understand and work through with me. She slowly began to feel that an exploratory question from me did not imply an accusation of malice aforethought in the handling of her child or in her reaction to certain family situations or life events. Mother thus began to talk more readily about herself, but whenever she felt overwhelmed by problems at home or found it difficult to talk in the therapeutic hours, she would again burst out with tearful tirades that we "blamed" her for everything.

In the next several months mother seemed determined to be a model patient. During these hours her many competitive feelings with her three sisters emerged. She frequently asked how she was doing. She reported conversations with her sisters about what they found most useful in discussing in their analyses, so that she could do the same with me. She reacted to any encouragement not to be a copy of her sisters, but to be herself and find herself in her own thoughts and feelings, with hurt, pouting, and appealing looks and with occasional statements of how being tiny and cute didn't seem to count for much in this relationship. She began to discuss her conviction that her "appealing helplessness" and "sincere sweetness," rather than her ability, had won her grades in college and jobs after graduation. She expressed pleasure that what was expected of her in therapy was not different from the expectations reported by her sisters in their sessions. Mother also recalled her sisters' anger because the despised father preferred and played with her when she was a baby.

Mother was distressed, as was her husband, at the resetting of the fee, lest their savings be depleted, but felt that her sister would take care of them. She was alternately critical of her husband for staying with the firm where only his marriage to her kept him secure, and fearful of what would happen if her husband decided to strike out on his own. Mother talked angrily about her husband's costly hobbies, his restrictions on money for household help, and about her feelings of helplessness in managing the home. Around these feelings came very vivid memories of being told what to wear and how to act, of having homework done for her, and of being coached before exams by her mother and sisters.

Mother also talked of her feelings of disgust about boys' genitals. She recalled vividly her brother's attempting sexual relations with her when she was 11; her nausea when male students she worked with masturbated in her presence; and her disgust and revulsion with Danny's frequent manipulation of his penis.

When Danny's cut hand needed surgical repair during the third month of therapy, mother was furious and blamed the staff for the accident. Finally it became clear how guilty she felt that she should resent having to have cut her vacation short and come to see Danny following the accident. When the resentment was accepted as human and understandable, mother relaxed and was able to talk of her anger with her husband for his accusations that her inadequacies as a mother and wife had caused Danny's illness and made their participation in the treatment program necessary. Thus, when father's ulcer symptoms became severe and he was hospitalized, mother expressed anxious glee that father could no longer deny his emotional disturbance.

Father's subsequent dependence on mother both delighted and annoyed her. She voiced for the first time her feelings that one therapist could not be fair to both marital partners. He would have to side with one against the other—more specifically, a man would side with a man. When I invited her to reject anything taken on faith but instead to evaluate this critically for herself, she relaxed but returned again and again to this subject as she anxiously began to feel more her husband's equal and was able to do more for herself.

DEVELOPMENT OF A RELATIONSHIP WITH DANNY

The next phase of work encompassed a period of 10 months. In the fifth month after the start of therapy Danny went home for a week. He was obviously pleased at his return to the ward and upon seeing me, he held my hand warmly going to and from the playroom and began to name objects more freely.

In the next month Danny began to zoom planes and crash them to the ground. At first he looked anxiously at me after each crash. Tension diminished and he crashed the plane in quick succession to my accompanying "crash-bangs." Finally he began to giggle. At the end of the hour he said: "That was nice." On the ward he used my name for the first time and said: "Good-bye Dr. Berlin. See you later." In subsequent hours he began to make his own crude planes. He also asked me to make them and looked tense as he smashed them. At my nod indicating it was O.K., he would go on to make more.

Danny appeared freer in each succeeding hour. As we made planes together he began to lean against me and smile at me. He also returned to the pounding board and after some encouragement began to pound on it with vigor and evident pleasure.

My week's vacation at the end of this period produced a temporary estrangement, evident upon my return. It was as if Danny had not believed what I had told him in preparation for my leaving. However, after two stormy hours of our both making planes, which he violently smashed, Danny began to laugh and turned to investigating the dolls.

He would peek uneasily under the girl dolls' dresses, glance at me, and when reassured, would examine the genital areas more carefully, finally saying that he needed to urinate. Returning to the playroom, he would spend the rest of the session sucking water out of a nippled baby bottle with great seriousness, filling the bottles over and over again with hardly a glance at me. This pattern ended after several weeks when one day he looked only briefly under the skirts of the dolls, drank several bottles of water, and went on to fill the sink with water and to sail the toy boats, which he happily proceeded to sink.

Danny then turned to the trains. Mastering the process of coupling individual cars together occupied him for several hours. Once he succeeded he began to snake the train across the floor, at first simply repeating my train noises and finally making them alone, loudly and with much laughter. At this time he began parroting whatever I said to him. He had several ear infections and when I came to sit with him at his bedside he would hug me and hold my hand, saying my name over and over again. He repeated fairly long sentences after me and appeared to enjoy this.

BEGINNING SCHOOL ACTIVITIES

During this phase Danny's nurse began to involve him in games with her and he became much more spontaneous. He gradually responded to being chased and discovered in hide-and-seek and initiated such games with her on the ward, especially if she were busy with someone else. As he became more interactive his nurse would bring him into the morning rhythm exercises where the children marched and danced to music. With her help he gradually joined in. He responded to her joyful participation and her warm encouragement with fuller body movements and he began to romp with abandon and shouts to his favorite record, a very fast march. He also began to call the nurse by name, but said very little otherwise.

Toward the end of this period he was introduced to the nursery school group. Although he had participated well in a nursery school prior to hospital admission, he joined very cautiously in the fingerpainting and block-building. He listened carefully to the stories and to the songs, looking to his nurse to sing the words. With her encouragement he began to sing the words of "The Farmer in the Dell." After a few weeks Danny's "ee-ii-oh" could be heard all over the children's ward. The story time and singing seemed especially important in helping him to talk again.

In the last few weeks of this 10-month period, Danny's nurse took him to the occupational therapy sessions for the nursery group. When faced with the tools he once again seemed frozen. As his nurse began to hammer and asked his help in holding materials, he slowly joined in, but would not hammer himself.

FATHER'S EXPLORATIONS IN THERAPY

Father began this same period with some tentative explorations of the general theme of homosexuality. When he detected neither aversion nor special interest in response to his general comments and inquiries, he began to talk of his feelings about his dapper appearance, describing advances made to him and the anger and concern they elicited about his own masculinity. When I indicated my understanding of his feelings he seemed relieved, and later said he felt this was a great hurdle and test of my acceptance of him and his feelings.

Subsequent hours centered around the themes of father's anger with his wife for her helplessness as a homemaker and mother. He also expressed his fury, anxiety, and related feeling of helplessness about his job, which was dependent upon his brother-in-law's inclinations. He revealed that he depended upon his wife to obtain his yearly bonuses and that he had not mentioned this bonus when the fee was discussed. He often talked of his need to give his children everything to feel he was a success. At this time his ulcer symptoms were minimal and he had no backache unless he seemingly deliberately did something he was told not to do. Also his business flourished during this period and he was cited the best branch manager in the organization.

When, at father's insistence, Danny was taken home before the Christmas holiday and was hostile and silent for most of the week, father became discouraged about treatment. In the eighth month following the beginning of therapy, father began to talk of his feelings that the therapist, as a man, would like women better and thus that I would be partial to his wife. He felt she was a better patient because she liked to come, while he came reluctantly. Father was invited to evaluate my partiality and to verbalize his suspicions, disagreements and distrust. When the confidentiality of his communications was again discussed, father said he had been watching for slips and at least these had not occurred.

During the 10th to the 14th months, business took a turn for the worse. At this time father was increasingly critical of the nurses' failure to keep Danny immaculate. Whenever father criticized the ward personnel he would look anxiously at me. His epigastric discomfort reappeared and father was agitated as he complained of the ineffectiveness of therapy. When I acknowledged that I could understand these feelings and that perhaps no great gains had been made, father relaxed.

Insomnia, ulcer pain, and business difficulties continued to be the subject of therapeutic sessions for several months. When father was discouraged he complained that his ulcer pain became more severe as he approached the treatment hour. At these times he was encouraged to express all of his feelings. As he talked of wanting to stop his therapeutic work and of how little help I was, his mild voice began to sound angry and his tension appeared less. On one occasion, when he said he wanted to quit, I told him he could do so without any ill feeling on my part, but that I nevertheless felt strongly that it was important for him to resolve the conflicts which made him feel so miserable and were related to his ulcer pain. Again he felt his wife was better liked and understood by me since she said she liked to come.

Finally he was able to say he could not understand how anyone could want to work with a complaining, reluctant, ungratifying patient. His apprehension about being fired by his boss also seemed a reflection of his fear of being fired by me if all his angry, hateful, and demanding feelings came out. Father then repeatedly expressed his admiration of gangsters who took what they wanted by force and related his occasional fantasies of being a gangster. When I suggested he was beginning to know what to do in our hours, to feel less helpless and at my mercy, and to take what he wanted from this experience, father laughed with relief. His ulcer symptoms began to abate during the last few weeks of the 14th month.

MOTHER'S ENGAGEMENT IN THERAPEUTIC WORK

During the fifth to the 14th months mother worked quite diligently. She became increasingly free with her criticism of her husband, her capacity to discuss their "perfect" marriage, and her evaluation of her own difficulties. She was pleased with her greater ease in handling household matters. Then she became apprehensive about what might be uncovered in therapy. She also became aware of how much she and her husband depended on her sister for their financial security, how insecure they felt about their own resources, and how little self-esteem they had. Later she reported with pleasure that they had decided to pay their life insurance premiums themselves rather than accept her sister's annual offer to pay for them. In a subsequent interview mother expressed feelings of depression at the thought of being penniless if father died.

Mother reported greater ease in handling Danny at home, at the same time making accusations that I, like her husband, wasn't really concerned with her. During the eighth month, when she was encouraged to return Danny early from Christmas vacation if he proved too difficult, mother, fearing father's contempt and ridicule, suffered through the entire week. She was blazingly angry because I was not sympathetic and instead inquired about the feelings that had kept her tense, unhappy, and full of self-pity rather than encouraging her to return Danny to the ward as had been suggested.

Several weeks later mother reported her surprise at her ease in expressing warm and sympathetic feelings as she consoled a bereaved friend. This was a task she had always feared and avoided.

During an explosive hour mother again accused me of not being able to understand her feelings as a woman. She was encouraged to try to express all these feelings and she ventilated her anger toward men and their lack of perception of women's feelings. The next week she returned to report with pleasure a clear awareness of the various feeling components within her—the baby, the child, the adolescent, and the woman.

The last several weeks of the 14th month were spent in exploration of her feelings about men. She recalled that her boyfriend's domination by his mother not only aroused contempt for him but also made him attractive to her. She also recalled how secure she felt with her husband because he seemed so sure of himself and took such good care of her. She later talked of how unhappy she felt when she began to realize how limited she was as a person and how insecure her husband seemed to be in his relationship with his brother-in-law. Mother's need to depend on father's strength, and his need to use her to ensure that her sister would take care of them, depressed and frightened her. In a later session she mentioned that her ex-boyfriend was still unmarried—another piece of insurance in the event father died. She began to wonder if she might not really be able to take care of her family herself in the event of an emergency.

THE WORKING THROUGH WITH DANNY

The third phase of the work encompassed a period of about a year, from the 15th to the 27th month, and saw a slow working through of some conflicts with many ups and downs for Danny and both parents. It was also a year in which there were many changes in their ways of living and the means by which father earned his livelihood. There were some clear shifts within each family member and in their relationships to each other.

Danny began his 15th month of therapy preoccupied with the planes in the playroom. He would make the worried reiteration that "propellor cut off Daddy's hand." In reply to this statement, the toy plane and the clay were pointed out as materials he could use to show me what he was feeling. At the same time he was intensely interested in the sex of the dolls and protested to me that he was not a boy but a girl, that his sister had a penis, not Danny. In response I made two dolls of clay and a clay penis and encouraged him to use them to show me what he meant. He began to use the clay girl and boy figures and the clay penis in his play, employing the planes and a clay figure for father. At first these activities were accompanied by anxious, fearful glances at me and by tense, stiff, jerky body movements which gradually relaxed.

The sequence enacted was usually one in which father lost one or both hands in the whirling propellor. This occurred over and over again until, after some decrease of intensity, he turned to making penises out of clay. For the boy dolls he usually made very tiny ones. The larger penises he gave to the girl doll, and said with conviction: "That's Sally." He then pointed to the boy doll without a penis, stating: "That's Danny." He never used the penises which I made out of clay at his request. After this sequence he frequently needed to urinate. My comment each time at the urinal that he still had a fine penis was met with a slight smile. During this period he began to protest at coming back to the clinic and wanted to remain at home.

Several weeks later he ended many of his sessions by picking up the toy pistol and banging away loudly at me. He also proclaimed he wasn't going to clean up, but laughed and jumped up to help when I, with a smile, would start with the task. He was openly affectionate, frequently hugging me and his favorite nurse. As this phase of play therapy came to an end, he began to hold brief telephone conversations with me, using whole sentences. Usually he talked about school activities or about going home. This alternated with furious pounding on the pegboard and great vocal "bang-boom's."

These hours often ended with Danny and the therapist making clay model planes. Danny's increasing skill was mirrored by his pleasure. He would measure his workmanship against mine, since I was able to produce fairly good replicas of model planes. When Danny's models were as good and finally even better than mine, he beamed and boasted to everyone on the ward that "Danny made good, excellent planes." In each such session I helped him analyze how the details could be improved and encouraged him to practice on individual parts until he succeeded. There were times when, in exasperation and angry frustration, he would smash his and my planes and then look anxiously at me. I would tell him that we could try to make them again in the next session. As Danny's planes looked more real, he would fly them about the room, designating various areas on the floor as cities to fly over in a cross-country flight. It seemed likely that these were cities his father mentioned after business trips. This involved us with some geography which Danny mastered quickly and with pleasure. There were numerous crashes at first, which decreased in frequency until most flights encountered many thrilling storms and had to fly around high and dangerous mountains.

INVOLVEMENT IN LEARNING

The nurse took my hint about Danny's preference for airplanes and in occupational therapy encouraged him to nail together parts she had cut out for him. Later she helped him saw pieces of wood to make a plane. He began to talk more volubly, at first in short sentences, but after they had worked together for a while, he would tell her about wanting to fly a plane to various places using longer sentences.

He was able to narrate many of the stories from the nursery rhyme books. The primary school teacher began to spend a few minutes with Danny and his nurse around their story time. Then she began to read new stories to Danny. Three weeks later he was seeking her out in the classroom to read to him. In this way he was introduced to the teacher and the primary class. He made rapid progress there in learning sounds, letters, and numbers, and began to read and to write.

Danny proudly showed off his work and practiced his new words on his nurse. He had an uncanny knowledge of geography and she discovered that he and father often looked at maps, especially the routes and cities where his father flew on his many trips. He rarely mentioned school to me.

Danny responded to his nurse's vacation with greater attachment to the teacher and to another nurse. Although he was noticeably cool towards his own nurse on her return, he quickly returned to their former warm relationship. He was especially pleased when she expressed her appreciation of a valentine card or a drawing he had made especially for her. Most of all he liked to have his drawings taped on the nurses' station window for all to see.

VICISSITUDES OF THE WORKING THROUGH WITH THE FATHER

Father began the fifteenth month of therapy with another series of severe backaches, insomnia, and tension. After weeks of exploration, when the backaches proved clearly related to unnecessary exertion and self-destructive activities, I expressed grave concern and anger that he would seemingly deliberately injure himself. There followed some decrease in these symptoms. Father also expressed concern that Danny had tried to injure his sister, and that he repeatedly insisted that she had a penis while he himself did not—that he was really a little girl. At this point discussion again arose of father's feelings about his own virility along with stories of his sexual prowess, and finally many weeks of discussion dealt with his mixed feelings about the femininity of his domineering mother.

These discussions came to a head when father had to place his mother in a state hospital because her inoperable brain tumor no longer responded to X-ray and her irrational behavior made custodial care necessary. He recalled his jealousy of his father, his possessiveness toward his mother, and having prevented his mother's remarriage. He was troubled by shameful feelings of wanting to control her small estate, then began to see how much he still wanted from his mother. After working these feelings through, he reported how easy he felt with his mother when he visited her at the state hospital. He also reported greater ease with his son and found he could now talk of his son's illness and his own psychiatric treatment with his friends.

Following this, father wanted to reduce the frequency of his sessions as "things were going so well." As this statement was examined, it became clear to father that his close and dependent feelings with me made him feel tense and anxious. After these feelings were explored I voiced my conviction about the importance of continued regular interviews. Father then relaxed, seemed much relieved, and later reported feeling more effective at work.

Increased conflict between his teenage son and his wife some weeks later seemed related to renewed helpless, rageful feelings and to a brief exacerbation of ulcer symptoms. He seemed torn about the consequences of taking sides and of bearing the anger and the loss of love from the family member whom he might oppose. As he explored his roles as husband and father, he began to clarify many of his ambivalent feelings of wanting to be taken care of and to have decisions made for him. At the same time he talked about how he was beginning to understand psychotherapy and why it was a slow process. In subsequent sessions father wondered very tentatively how I might react if he could handle matters well at home, be more effective in his work, and therefore have less need of me. My response that I was pleased with his progress did not fully relieve his tension. At about this time both mother and son were becoming more independent of father.

MOTHER'S TURMOIL IN THE WORKING THROUGH

During this same period mother was very tense as she recounted Danny's insistence that he had no penis and that he was a girl. Danny had said that his sister, Sally, had a penis, and had also insisted that she be the one to return to the clinic and that he stay home with mother. This again brought to the fore the mother's feelings about boys and their dirty penises. She began to discuss her adoration of her daughter and the tension she felt when her daughter now chose to be with father and play house with him. Mother expressed feelings of fear and hurt that she and her daughter would no longer be as close.

During my two-week vacation, mother suffered two severe burns when she overturned a boiling pot and "accidentally" ignited a whole package of matches. However, she was able to be very firm with Danny on visits home and was delighted that he responded by appearing relaxed and that he made only rare efforts to hurt her. After one critical weekend, when she repeatedly stopped his poking her by holding his hands each time he started, he never tried it again. He now cooperated in cleaning his room, would come to mother for a hug, and began to talk in sentences at home.

Mother's conflicts with her teenage son occupied many sessions. His rebelliousness and her stubborn retaliatory behavior came into sharp focus.

Memories emerged of her own hatred, anger, and rebellion as a child. Mother was surprised and frightened to discover these violent feelings, of which she had not been at all aware. As she began to explore these feelings she demanded more frequent interviews. This was evaluated in terms of her situation and mine, and the frequency of visits remained the same.

Mother, in subsequent hours, disclosed that for a month now she and father, not her sister, had paid the hospital bills. The sister had stopped paying without any explanation. Father had not mentioned this at all, although it had coincided with the period when he was talking about his mother and how much he had wanted from her. Mother expressed initial anger with her sister, who could *afford* to foot these bills, but finally expressed relief that they were now on their own. In the following session mother reported that she had never before felt so alive, so competent and efficient, as she had that previous week.

In subsequent weeks trouble with her oldest son, father's special ulcer diet, his lack of appreciation of her efforts, and his deriding of her abilities to be an effective mother and housekeeper, aroused memories of her derogated father. She identified her own helpless and despondent feelings with the way her own father appeared to her and described how she had joined with her sisters and mother in their contempt for him. Now she began to see her father in a more sympathetic light and to understand her own dependent helplessness upon her mother and sisters. Rage at her son, who refused to learn with her help, led to explorations of her own helpless feelings, limited self-expectations, and her great designs for him. He had picked her most vulnerable area, achievement, as a battleground. In trying to help her defiant son with his school work, she re-experienced many of her old feelings about learning. She explored her sense of stupidity and futility with each new subject she had encountered. She also recalled her relief in having been able to turn to her sisters, who were always at hand for help. As she began to understand how unhappy and disturbed her son was, she and father arranged for psychotherapy for him in their community.

Mother began to express fear of her intense dependent feelings on me. She vividly recalled her childhood helplessness and dependence and their continuation in marriage. As she began to express rivalrous feelings toward her husband, who must be my most-loved and best patient, she also began to do more things for herself. This was climaxed by the redecorating of her home without the advice and help of her artistic husband. Mother was very pleased with the result and with her husband's grudging admission that it was "pretty good." For the first time mother also began to drive the car out of the neighborhood for shopping and into downtown city traffic. She now found she could comfortably drive alone in the heart of the city. She had overcome a fear of some 10 year's duration, that in traffic she would lose control of the car and it would kill someone; or that she would be helpless in the maze and press of traffic, would freeze in terror, and not be able to move or find her way to her destination.

During exacerbations of his ulcer symptoms or back trouble, mother was openly furious with her troublesome husband. She expressed anger at me because I still expected her to work in her therapeutic hours notwithstanding her burdens at home. Simultaneously, mother became more able to handle Danny on his visits home and during their short vacations together. She now indicated that she felt free to return him promptly to the ward with only slight qualms of fear at derogation by the staff or her husband were she unable to care for him at home. Return to the ward never proved to be necessary.

During this period, as mother explored more freely and fully her relations with her own mother, she became aware that her fury with her oldest son occurred most frequently when she had suppressed an awareness of her own increasing needs, was beginning to feel helpless, and wanted someone to take care of her. This became clear when her daughter began to stutter and mother demanded that I instruct her on procedures for stopping the stuttering. At my insistence that she explore her own thoughts and feelings, she became furious, wept, and finally began to describe the intrafamilial pressures and the changes in the equilibrium at home. As mother felt more adequate, father appeared more tense and cross.

Mother, in a later session, described how, with some anxiety, she had encouraged father, in Sally's presence, to play house with his daughter and to spend time with her. Sally's stuttering decreased and finally disappeared. Over a period of several months mother discussed more openly her desire to be babied and to be taken care of by the therapist. Subsequently she described her greater ease in babying her husband when he was ill, in understanding her children's demands, and in dealing with these in a helpful way. She reported a marked decrease in her resentful, helpless feelings in the face of the needs or demands from others.

Mother reported that father, for the first time in their married life, began to discuss his business problems with her. They wept together after father described his anxious fears that a new business slump might mean more trouble with the brother-in-law. They shared their uncertainties about the future and the possibility that father might be fired. Mother reported that they both felt better, somewhat reassured, and closer to each other after this episode.

FINAL PHASE OF INPATIENT THERAPY WITH DANNY

The final phase of inpatient therapy with Danny seemed to center around his leaving the hospital and lasted about two months. Since summer vacation, he had been increasingly resistant to returning to the ward after weekends at home. He often asked his parents not to return him. On the ward he would appear lost and troubled for several hours before responding to the staff. He greeted me warmly and eagerly, clinging to my hand to and from the playroom. He often used these moments to say: "I don't want to come back to the hospital. When can I stay home?"

In the playroom during this two-month period, Danny was increasingly free with the toys and explored most of the play potentials of the various vehicles. One playroom hour he picked up a wetting doll which he had only looked at before. He spent several hours soberly feeding her from a nursing bottle and then, with amusement, watching her wet. When I noted his swallowing as he fed the doll, I suggested that Danny had fed the doll well, that it was full and satisfied, and that he now might like to feed himself from the nursing bottle. After several tentative glances at me, Danny tried to suck on the nipple, which proved to be difficult for him. I enlarged the hole and showed him what he could do to suck more effectively. After first dutifully feeding the doll, Danny contentedly sucked on the nursing bottle for portions of several sessions.

Danny then began to play with water and boats. He would fill the sink with water, place several boats in it, and then sink them. After doing this several times and cautiously glancing at me, he picked up a large coat, placed a man, woman, boy, and girl doll in it, and sank them over and over again with increasing spontaneity, laughing and chortling. Finally he said, "There, down you go—they're all bad, very bad," afterwards laughing tensely. Later Danny's utterances during the drowning of the dolls became less strained. He would place these figures in the boat, turn on the faucet, and watch with fascination as the boat was drawn under the running faucet and capsized. He would then come to the aid of the dolls, quickly rescue them, and repeat this process 'til the end of the hour. When we talked of his going to live at home and coming with his parents to see me once a week, Danny's eyes would shine and he would whisper, "Good, good." Later he would shout gleefully, "I'll be at home and visit you. That's right, come to visit you." Not until he actually did go home, taking all of his belongings with him, did he seem to believe it would happen.

THE WARD FAVORITE

Danny became a delightful student. He learned quickly and seemed pleased when his teacher singled him out for praise. He brought each good spelling or arithmetic paper to his nurse for her enthusiastic approval. He also became a vigorous participant in occupational therapy and a leader in the rhythm sessions. After one occasion, when invited to help his nurse make beds, he insisted on sharing this activity with her.

His play with other children was much more cooperative. His nurse had not recognized how ready he was for group play until an afternoon at the park playground when Danny not only had fun taking turns, but also became involved in building sand castles with other children his age. To his nurse's surprise he did not stand out as a sick child among these youngsters in any way.

During these weeks Danny's nurse and mother were able to talk about Danny with greater ease. Previously mother had been quick to report some overwhelming problem with Danny at home, implying that the nurses had not been doing their job or else Danny would not have continued to be so destructive. Or she would immediately begin with a proud recital of some achievement of Danny's, as if she wanted the staff to know how well she handled things at home. Now mutual pleasure in his activities at home and on the ward was evident. Danny held onto his mother's hand when they first came on the ward and would often walk between mother and nurse, holding onto both. Several times the nurse or teacher would demonstrate to mother how they helped Danny learn in school, or how to use tools or new materials with him. Mother would now sit still long enough to watch and would ask questions. Often she would report back on her efforts in the same direction. After she had watched the nurse read a story with dramatic emphasis and noted Danny's pleasure, mother was elated when for the first time she was able to let herself go with him in reading a fairy tale, and he hugged and kissed her with delight.

The nurse and teacher began to plan activities in the ward, park playground, and school which were similar to the kinds of activities Danny would be engaged in at home. He responded with wholehearted involvement, increasing competence, and self-assurance in each of these areas.

BEGINNING OF FINAL PHASE OF WORK WITH FATHER

Father, during these two months, was preoccupied with his poor business and his awareness that he would have to face his boss's wrath and derision. He explored his anxious feelings about facing the boss, and his increased awareness that he had missed some good bets in merchandising which could realistically be assessed to his own misjudgment. He was more aware that Danny wanted to stay home after his visits. He felt his wife could handle Danny, but was apprehensive that maybe things would fall apart again. As we began to explore these feelings, father became aware of his concern that the attention Danny needed from his wife might result in less attention for him at a time when he himself was so in need. Finally, as it looked fairly certain that Danny would go home, father again raised the question about the need for continued work with the family. When I expressed my conviction that continued outpatient work was necessary, he relaxed, smiled, and spoke of his fears that people really had an aversion to him and wanted to be rid of him, just as his boss did. He explored his feelings of needing to ingratiate himself with others through gifts and favors to insure their friendliness toward him.

THERAPY IN THE FINAL PHASE WITH MOTHER

Mother, during these two months, expressed her concern about being able to handle Danny at home with the additional strain of her husband's ill health and their worries about the business. At the same time, Danny's increased freedom in talking and his relaxed behavior at home delighted her. She began to describe her own growing trust in her hunches, her ideas, and her sense of how others might feel. She began to discuss her need to succeed with Danny, to prove to her husband and friends how effective a mother she could be. The feelings of needing to demonstrate that she was no longer helpless were followed by exploration of old feelings of anxiety that there would be no help or support from others if one showed oneself to be grown-up and effective. She began to describe her pleasure in herself when she was able to do things well, i.e., to her own satisfaction. She was experiencing these feelings more frequently and hoped to continue experiencing them once Danny was home. Mother was able, quite realistically, to assess the problems that would be created by his return to the household. While she was aware that she faced some difficult times, she seemed ready to try it.

OUTPATIENT TREATMENT

The outpatient period of the last phase of our work with this family lasted 10 months. Danny and both parents came in for weekly interviews. This period was one of marked change in the living circumstances of the entire family and of turmoil for the parents.

Outpatient Treatment with Danny

Danny expressed some anxiety during our first outpatient session that he might be returned to the ward. Although he appeared to be reassured by my statements that he now lived at home and only visited me, it was two and

one-half months before he expressed a desire to visit the ward itself. Even
so, he mentioned the name of his favorite nurse many times as he walked
from the waiting room to the playroom.

Danny greeted me joyfully each time. His first several outpatient sessions
consisted of his former water play with the doll family in the boat, their
being drawn under the running faucet, drowning, and being quickly rescued.
Once again he looked at me anxiously as the drowning occurred, but seemed
reassured by an answering nod and smile, and continued his play.

In the third outpatient session Danny turned to the dollhouse. Although
he had previously searched the dollhouse at each session for the members
of the doll family, he had never touched the furniture. This time he began
to place the boy and girl and infant dolls in the high chair, on the toilet,
and in the crib. He was silently but intensely involved in this play. Finally,
toward the end of three such hours, he walked over to the baby buggy, lay
down in it, and began to rock very gently. I walked over to it and rocked
it for him. Danny relaxed in the buggy and asked to be rocked more
vigorously. To my low-voiced comment about how nice it felt to be rocked,
he nodded and smiled. I suggested he might also like the idea of being
rocked like this in my arms, although he was a pretty big boy and it would
be hard to do. But he might just let himself think of how nice it would
feel. Danny smiled and replied, "Oh, yes," very happily. He allowed himself
to be rocked for a bit more, then climbed out of the buggy and began to
move dollhouse furniture from one destination to another in a large toy
truck. Since this occurred at a time when his parents were talking about
a move, I commented that he might be moving from his home and he might
be worried about going to a new place to live. Danny did not respond
overtly to my comments and continued his moving activities in an even more
careful and precise fashion. He progressed from a haphazard dumping of
furniture in and out of trucks to a careful arrangement of furniture to fit the
space in the vehicle.

After the eighth outpatient therapy session Danny returned to making
planes and asking me to do likewise. He was pleased when his plane was so
well made that I praised him for his skill. Towards the end of that month
he would make a plane and ask me to fly it with accompanying motor
noises, while he bombarded it with a toy machine gun. He took intense
delight in following all the movements of the plane with his gun and finally
acclaimed that he had hit and shot it down.

The work was interrupted for two weeks by my illness. On my return,
Danny said several times, with much delight in his voice, "I'm so glad to
see you Dr. Berlin." There followed several weeks of continued play with

moving doll furniture and building airplanes to be shot down. These hours were followed by a joyous greeting of his parents in the waiting room.

On one occasion Danny refused to help clean up. He said he did not want to, but if I wanted to, I could. I did so after invitations to Danny were answered by the calm, assertive order: "You clean up yourself."

Danny next began building with blocks in the interviews. He made large forts and castles, playing intently and working with great care. This activity continued for about a month. In the sixth month of outpatient therapy he began to draw on the board. This occurred at the time mother reported that he was enjoying his school work, although his teacher seemed afraid to insist that he do it. At first Danny repeatedly drew crude airplanes. He often turned to me for suggestions, but never asked me to draw a plane. As he became more proficient, Danny began to print his name under his drawings, and was pleased with these results. When his drawings, as had the clay models, drew my comments about how good some pieces of work actually were, he responded with smiles and the reply: "Yes, it's good."

The End Phase of Work with Danny

During the seventh to tenth month of outpatient therapy, Danny alternated between the dollhouse and the airplanes. His dollhouse play consisted of dressing and undressing the girl and infant dolls and bathing or toileting them. He often talked as he did this, describing his activities. "I'm taking baby's clothes off for a bath," he would observe. "Now she's bathing and splashing. It's time to dry her." When playing with the dolls and dollhouse he usually wanted to clean up early and see his Daddy and Mommy. In his airplane games he bombed objects and frequently concluded the hour with laughing threats to bomb me.

Other hours were spent in making clay planes, bombing cars and trucks with clay pellets, standing on a chair and fiercely pretending to bomb me, and squealing with pleasure when I pretended fright. Several times he turned on the tap, wet some paper towels, crumpled them, and threw them with great force into the sink. On each occasion his mocking threats to throw the wet paper balls at me were met with a pleading, "Oh, please don't soak me," and Danny would grandly reply, "Oh, don't worry, I won't," and laugh and bomb the sink. The termination of such hours seemed difficult for him and he sought to prolong them by resuming his play after cleaning-up activities. His teasing was full of sparkling laughter and he seemed to strut about as he threatened to bomb me.

Although recurrent mention of the coming separation had been made during previous months, the subject was discussed in greater detail in the hours before the final session. Danny said little in response to comments on my regret that our work would stop, my hope that I would see him from time to time, and my desire to hear from him. I suggested that he too might feel sad. When I drew two sad faces on the board and labeled them "Danny" and "Dr. Berlin," he smiled. He responded to the emotion in my voice by leaning against me. When, after some abortive bombing of cars and trucks, he wanted to leave and I replied that I would like the full hour with him, Danny hugged me and I responded with a warm embrace. He played with some toy planes, flying them around but staying near me. I continued to talk about the kinds of feelings Danny seemed to be expressing in his play, his reluctance to leave, and my sadness too. At the end of the hour he seemed to want something to take with him and was pleased when I handed him a large box of clay as a parting gift. He grasped this in his hands as he left the playroom. After a quick good-bye hug he went happily with his parents.

Final Phase of Work with Father

In relation to Danny's returning home, father expressed both fear that the family's equilibrium would be upset and also confidence that he and his wife had learned enough about themselves to deal with things.

Father became increasingly concerned with his business and his relationship to his brother-in-law. He reported a sharp increase in gastric pain and insomnia. As business declined and he was accused of mishandling things, father offered to resign, but the boss refused, saying father's leaving would cause too much trouble in the family. Father then began to write a letter of resignation that might leave his brother-in-law greater freedom to act in the face of family ties. As he was writing several drafts, his insomnia and other symptoms vanished. However, instead of sending the resignation, father decided to accept the new assistant manager sent from the central office. His symptoms then returned, but only in mild form. In the next several months father was able to meet with his brother-in-law, discuss with greater ease and objectivity the operation he ran, and admit certain errors of judgment without feeling so depreciated and worthless.

As father discussed his helpless feelings in dealing with the quarrels between his wife and older son and his problems in handling his assistant manager and employees, I inquired about the feeling he was experiencing right then as he talked. This elicited his momentary discomfort. He described feelings of uneasiness, a dread of being disliked, fear of incurring wrath, and his desire to placate everyone involved in any controversy to prevent hurt and anger. At the same time he began to be aware of the devious ways through which his own anger and hostility were expressed if he failed to deal directly with a situation. Father began to discuss anger with his brother-in-law's lack of confidence in him. He described how he would run the branch office were he not forced to go along with the firm's dictates.

Finally, four months before termination of outpatient therapy, father decided to resign from the organization. He felt pleased with himself, although anxious about the future and believed his wife also shared these anxieties. As he began to explore his feelings about facing brother-in-law to get his last year's bonus, which had not been paid, he again became tense and anxious. Father finally marshalled his arguments and listed the pros and cons of his position. He was able to talk to his brother-in-law in a straightforward manner and obtain the bonus. Father was proud that he had not been his usual servile, propitiating self and pleased with his new-found directness.

In the next several months father alternated between elation over his resignation and the pleasurable aspects of his efforts to found a business, and anxiety that he would not succeed in his own venture. During this trying period he had little insomnia, ulcer or back pain. He then suggested that the weekly trips to the clinic were expensive. In the light of no income and limited savings, he felt that the family should discontinue psychotherapy. I said that continued work was important. Then I helped him evaluate the actual costs of the trip and the income available from social security payments, savings, and various investments. It became clear after careful review that there was no realistic basis for discontinuing therapy. Father was much relieved. Later he said he had been helped by this analysis to assess other situations carefully, thus determining the reality of each situation when he felt desperate or panicked.

Paradoxically, as bankers and businessmen in the community offered loans to start his own enterprise, he became depressed and felt that such confidence was not merited. At the same time he talked with admiration of his wife, who was increasingly cheerful and who handled household affairs with a new competence. She held a sale of much of their unnecessary furniture. Father was amazed at her ability and her intuitive feel for what customers wanted to hear.

This period of alternating depression and well-being made father aware that he was able to express his need for help and accept help from me and his wife only if he were ill, depressed, or otherwise helpless. During these last few months of work father was progressively more open in expressing warm feelings toward me. He described his dependency needs and his feeling easier about the desire to be cared for. In conjunction with this increased freedom to talk about all of his feelings, father found it easier to maintain a close relationship with his family and felt less constrained with them. His former fears of being helpless and at their mercy if these feelings came out, disappeared.

His increased closeness with and respect for his wife led to their discussing various business possibilities together. Father was amazed when such discussions revealed that his wife had excellent judgment in business matters and that having these exchanges and listening to his wife's opinions did not make him feel any less capable or belittled, as had been true previously. He found that these increasingly free discussions even enhanced his own business acumen.

Father described the sequence of events around the purchase of a business. He used his wife's ideas and hunches to help him more clearly evaluate for himself how wise such a venture would be. Then he meticulously and exhaustively investigated every aspect of the prospect. Father contrasted this to his former tendency to depend on the owner's word. Father's desire to be liked, to be thought astute and clever, and his fear that any close scrutiny would make people feel he distrusted them would previously have precluded a detailed examination of the elements of a business.

In the final interview father wept without restraint and readily accepted the idea of an occasional interview if he felt it would be helpful. He expressed his confidence in being able to do things both on his own and with his wife, so that he looked forward to the vicissitudes of their moving to another city, of a new business, and of new associates and friends, both with awareness of the difficulties he would face and with eagerness at the challenge for himself and his family.

Final Phase of Work with Mother

During the last period of our work, mother also became increasingly free in describing her feelings. To her surprise she found that while Danny occasionally behaved in the old ways with her, increased awareness of her own feelings made it easier to understand him and her reactions to him. Thus she could begin to behave differently with Danny. She found it easier to be clear about what she expected of him and to be both more firm and more patient with him. Mother was also able to help the public school teacher to be firm and to demand work from Danny.

When her sister gave her $500 as a birthday present, mother found herself glad to have the money, but did not feel as joyous, overly grateful, and indebted as in the past.

Mother then brought up her concerns with her adolescent son, their conflicts, and his insubordination and defiance. She re-experienced many of her old anxieties about boys. Once again she demanded advice and expressed anger that I insisted she work this through as she had worked through other problems, by putting into words everything she was aware of. In this context it became clear that to deal effectively with her son meant to give up a last vestige of helpless dependence in her relationship with me. She recalled her old struggles with her brother, with male students, and with men in general, where to be assertive and authoritative meant to lose something in relation to her mother and sisters. To join them in their contempt for nasty boys and men and to run to them with complaints about her brother's sexual advances had meant increased closeness and protection. To be cute and helpless had always been a way of handling demands or pressures from men.

Mother also began to see that her demands that her son excel in school and his rebelliousness were related to her wish that he do this for her sake rather than for his own. She began to consider in detail the emotional implications of her demands for scholastic excellence, obedience, and fastidious cleanliness of his person and room. She became aware of her own meticulous grooming prior to interviews, so that I would like her appearance, approve of her, and perhaps not expect so much from her. Mother remarked that she seemed to need to have her son be a male replica of herself. She recalled how her good looks had obtained relationships, jobs, and favors which she felt she could not have gained in any other way. When I commented, after a prolonged recital of troubles, that it seemed she felt that the work with me might be discontinued were she to function effectively, mother blushed and acknowledged that this was indeed a fear. She spoke with pleasure of her increasing feeling of competence, laughing as she quoted Danny's perceptive observation to his parents one evening: "Daddy likes to be with Mommy all the time now."

When father resigned from his job, mother was concerned about their future and about father's adequacy as "the boss." She felt that she could be of help in whatever they did. Mother met father's desire to save money (by cutting out the weekly trips to the clinic) by insisting on the importance of continued work for the family. She later was able to get father to discuss with her their exact financial situation, which had previously not been "any of her business." Father's suggestion that they discontinue therapy made mother more clearly aware of her competitive feelings toward father over me, of her old competitive feelings with her sisters to be mother's best loved, and later to be her wealthy sister's most loved sister. She finally became aware of her feelings of needing to be her husband's only child after the birth of their first son. She also became aware of the need to be reassured that I would not give more to father because of his very urgent business problems.

Mother brought up many dreams about me. She demanded interpretations, becoming infuriated when again she was encouraged to make associations about them. These angry attacks continued through several interviews until she perceived how relieved she felt that I had not given in to the alternating anger, helplessness, and demands that I do for her what she could do for herself. Thus, the hateful fury that she always suspected lay underneath her helplessness evoked neither the feared retreat or placation which she had experienced as a child, nor the retaliation which she had always felt would be forthcoming from her mother.

With father out of work and at home, mother alternately felt competent, effective, or angry. She had many backaches and a severe vaginal discharge as she assumed her new burdens and duties. Her relationship to Danny was now warm, yet firm when necessary. She expressed a recurrent delight, as if she had found a new child. At the same time she resented the child in her husband that needed reassurance when she herself felt unsure of the future.

Mother now was able to express more fully her angry feelings toward her husband, sister, and me without the old fear that the relationship would be disrupted. She reported feeling like an adult, and the equal of her sister, for the first time when they visited together. Mother also talked of how pleased she was to find her judgment being seriously considered by her husband and of her delight in discovering that she was a good saleswoman when her enterprise in selling the surplus household furnishings brought in welcome revenue. She found her judgment more mature in many areas. She seemed to be able to consider many aspects of a problem and to talk with people without feeling shy, self-conscious, and withdrawn.

During these last weeks, as mother appeared more mature in her demeanor and dress and reported her increased competence in all areas, she found it easier to express fond and dependent feelings toward me and to experience infant-like feelings without fear when with her husband in therapy. She was thus able to fully express her sadness and regret at discontinuing the work, to assess the strides she had made, and to look forward to her new life with some trepidation about the problems it might bring, but without overwhelming anxiety. In the last hour mother wept freely about the separation and her feelings of warmth, closeness, and gratitude toward me. She, as did her husband, felt she could come back occasionally when and if necessary.

DISCUSSION

The three major factors usually involved in the etiology of mental illness are the impersonal, the interpersonal, and the intrapersonal aspects. Frequently they are difficult to tease apart.

In this case these factors are more readily separable, although the usual amalgam of at least two etiologic factors often makes it difficult to separate certain aspects from one another. It is sometimes difficult to give accurate weight to the categories in which certain events belong, since their effects on the child are usually mediated through the adults. That is, the child's reactions usually result from the conflicted amalgam of the parents' feelings and behavior toward him. Nevertheless, the evidence from prolonged psychotherapeutic work with this child and his parents makes it possible to make certain choices about the category of these etiologic factors, which permit the reader to assess for himself, at least on the evidence presented, where they belong.

The author's biases, the result of long clinical experience, are that a prime etiologic element is the interpersonal one. The intrapersonal aspects of a child's psychotic illness can be viewed from the experiences which shaped him early in life.

The impersonal factor can be divided into the genetic-constitutional givens of the child, the pre-, para-, and postnatal physiological environment which includes the nutritional state of mother during pregnancy and of the infant and child, as well as the toxic, infectious, and endocrine insults to the organism, both gross and subtle. The impersonal factor also includes those life events which affect the child and parents directly. For example, the child's or parent's severe illness, accidents, deaths in the family, etc. may profoundly affect the child. The kind and degree of impact depends on his developmental stage and his general integrative capacities resulting from his previous relationships with other important people in his life. Those aspects of crises in the child's life, mediated through the child's parents and others in his life, become interpersonal experiences, and their effect is determined by the degree of conflict in and between parents which is represented in their behavior. Thus the crisis of a sibling's death or severe illness may result in open discussion and grief with beginning resolution of crisis or in silence and unresolved withdrawal of adults from the child and each other with adverse effects, developmentally and in reinforcing previous anxieties and conflicts.

Such crises may, of course, provide parents with an opportunity to use their energies to effect a new and fuller integration. Their efforts in this respect might also serve an integrative purpose for the child and probably would not harm his psychological development.

Danny's birth by Caesarean section involved no prolonged labor or anoxia. He was a good-sized, strong, quiet, and not very vigorous infant, who demanded little stimulation or attention. At an early age he seemed to cope with his environment and the lack of maternal stimulation by the physiologically established mechanisms of continual sleeping, eating, and lying quietly in his crib. Significantly, his developmental landmarks were within normal limits until he walked at 12 to 15 months, at which time his babbling ceased and his behavior appeared to be lacking in curiosity, exploration, and spontaneity. Danny's constitutional tendencies to be quiet and "undemanding," with little motor vigor, may have resulted in a self-protective mechanism as well as an unusual susceptibility to both impersonal and interpersonal events which affected mother and reduced her interest in him and her capacity to be nurturant and stimulating. Thus while Danny's passivity may have averted acute conflict with mother, it also permitted little interaction and socialization or attachment as described by Bowlby (2).

The death of mother's mother, when Danny was two months old, had seriously aggravated her depression and sense of isolation and helplessness, resulting from her husband's continued preoccupation with construction problems. The fact that Danny was not the hoped-for daughter with whom mother could feel close, compounded these feelings. Similarly, mother's accidental pregnancy with her third child and her reactive depression further interfered with the contacts between mother and Danny.

The first housekeeper, who relieved mother of her burdens during the next five months, indulged and infantilized Danny without much age-appropriate stimulation. His rages, his first vigorous behavior, occurred at this period whenever his desires were thwarted or demands were made upon him. Mother's helplessness in the face of his tantrums, her increased depression, and the advent of a second housekeeper, a harsh and punitive person, were all complicating life events mediated through important persons in Danny's life which possibly aggravated the illness. The birth of the long-awaited sister and mother's preoccupation with her further affected Danny.

Other interpersonal factors in the genesis of Danny's psychosis need to be evaluated in terms of the quality of relationships he had with each of the significant individuals in his life. In each instance the known intrapersonal or intrapsychic conflicts of each of these persons and how each relationship impinged on Danny need to be examined.

For several years father was only minimally involved with Danny. However, father's relationship with mother and his personal expectations of his son in terms of behavior and cleanliness did influence both Danny's illness and his degree of integration. The psychotherapeutic work with father also seemed to have its greatest effect on Danny since it influenced mother's feelings about herself and thus her behavior with Danny.

Father's need to assert his competence, masculinity, and capacity for nurturant care of mother may have been exaggerated, conflictful residues of conflict experiences with his own mother that led to self-doubts. Such doubts about himself may have been revealed in his need to take over mother's functions. This permitted him to demonstrate his superior capabilities and at the same time to derogate his wife for her inadequacies as a housewife and mother. It is interesting that mother's femininity as a good sexual partner and the enjoyment of sexual relations and father's masculinity in the same area were never derogated or questioned by mother or father. It is very likely that this area of relative integration for each and thus of mutual satisfaction with its implications for achievement of genital, psychosexual development is a very important and favorable prognostic sign. Similarly, father's capacity to work effectively in many situations and his superior executive abilities spoke well for his ego development, despite the many lacunae.

Father's own imperative needs to be taken care of appeared to keep him in an untenable and precariously dependent relationship with his employer-brother-in-law. He needed his wife as an intermediary to assure his employment and the payment of annual bonuses. This dependence on his wife in a vital area of self-esteem may have required him to compensate as an effective caretaker of mother and to infantilize her. At the same time this dependence may have elicited his disguised anger that she could not care for him except in his most vulnerable area—that of making certain that his brother-in-law paid him. It is also interesting that father's psychosomatic disturbances did not manifest themselves in acute form until both he and his wife were engaged in therapy. One might speculate that the care and nurturance which these disorders necessitated could only surface when there was some chance of fulfillment. One could speculate further that these particular psychophysiological disturbances might not have occurred had father not been engaged in psychotherapy, his previous adaptation to stress having been severe and incapacitating headaches. It should be noted, however, that his business troubles were increasingly stressful during this period, although he had had similar problems of lesser degree in previous years.

Father's intense preoccupation with his business drastically reduced mother's contact with him. It also reduced the attention he had formerly given to her as an attractive woman, as indicated by the way in which he often playfully babied her. Mother, involved in her own hurts, needs, and problems, was unable to support and encourage father during this period of constant trouble and harrassment. Thus, she found him withdrawing from her, leaving her alone, depressed, and helpless during much of her third, unwanted pregnancy.

Mother had been infantilized and cared for by her mother, her older sisters, and her husband. She viewed herself as an ineffectual and helpless person who could only affect others by being cute, feminine, and helpless. This made it difficult for her to find any areas of competence in which she could gain either self-respect or the respect of others. Her early feelings about males, who were exemplified by her father and brother, were feelings constantly reinforced by her mother and sisters. She viewed men as weak, ineffective, and nasty—only women could be trusted and would take care of you. In her husband she found a man who could care for and baby her as her mother and her "good" father used to cherish her. This may have made it easier for her to accept her husband's sexuality in contrast to the revulsion she felt toward the males who depended on her and looked to her for care, such as her brother, her male students, and her sons.

Mother's depression during her second pregnancy and her dread of having yet another child dependent upon her, were aggravated when the hoped-for girl turned out to be Danny. The fact that he was a good, i.e., non-demanding, baby who required little care was a relief. With the death of mother's mother came a profound depression. There was no one to turn to and no one with whom to grieve. Her uncontrolled weeping and melancholia brought only transient comfort from her harassed husband. Mother withdrew from her baby son even more, carrying out only the bare essentials of bottle feeding and diaper changing. She left him alone in his crib or playpen most of the time while she wept or brooded alone in her room. Thus, mother could not give her baby son the "social" stimulation that Bowlby (2) describes as essential to normal development.

Danny's brother, five years older, was his greatest source of stimulation. It was brother who talked to him and encouraged him as Danny made sounds and began to turn over and sit up. The comments about Danny's sober, unsmiling appearance and his lack of curiosity and playfulness throughout his first three years of life testified to his lack of other nurturant and pleasurable social stimulation. His normal physical development, making of sounds, and saying of words at about 12 months of age indicated his genetic endowment and capacity to withstand lack of nurturance through self-amusement and sleep. Such evidence also spoke for his capacity to utilize stimulation offered by brother or, occasionally, by father.

The first housekeeper was hired when Danny was 19 months old because of mother's pregnancy and ensuing fatigue, headaches, and need for bed rest. For the next four months Danny was totally indulged, so that he did not need to walk, talk, or feed himself. He regressed in these areas temporarily but also began for the first time to show rage when thwarted. In retrospect the rage reactions seem healthier than the previous inertness. The punitive harshness of the second housekeeper and Danny's daily isolation in his room for the next 10 months seemed to solidify the rages and destructiveness. He directed his assaults primarily at his mother and baby sister, not toward his father and brother. It is interesting that a brief nursery school experience at 30 months of age revealed a capacity to relate to adults and a marked reduction of hostile destructive behavior in that setting.

The interpersonal factors in the relationship thus appear to be deprivation of a nurturant relationship with mother during infancy and early childhood and some stimulation from a brother five years older and occasionally from father. These factors had resulted in a withdrawn, largely silent, unsmiling child without spontaneity. Little coherent and communicative speech developed. Prior to hospitalization Danny had little opportunity for investigation, exploration, and rewarded learning. The indulgent housekeeper made it possible, through overindulgence, for Danny to express rage and be destructive in response to frustration and later in response to punishment and being locked up and isolated in his room.

The intrapersonal aspects of Danny's illness can be viewed from the experiences which early in life shaped this physically strong, healthy, and handsome child who, despite stimulus deprivation, initially achieved developmental landmarks in the motor and speech sphere without retardation. His somberness and the vacant stare, described by some friends and seen early on the ward, appeared to be similar to, but less severe than, reactions described by Spitz (4) and others (1, 5) to stimulus and nurturance deprivation. The early development of object relations and the delineation of self from the world were grossly interfered with by mother's incapacity to care for and nurture this child.

Even with its negative aspects, the first housekeeper's affectionate overindulgence of Danny provided the first close physical contact Danny had experienced. This seemed to make possible a beginning object relationship in which rages were elicited when desires and needs were not fulfilled. Thus, Danny, having experienced some warmth, nurturant care, and predictable responses to his needs and signals, could demand that things be done for him. One might say that this relationship began to help him differentiate self from non-self and to depend on an adult to meet his needs and desires. His subsequent rages, destructiveness, and assaultiveness could be described as ego-integrative, that is, assertive and signs of autonomy, despite the low frustration tolerance which resulted in maladaptive behavior.

To assign a stage of psychosexual fixation to a child with these experiences presupposes sufficient ego differentiation to warrant such a delineation. Danny's maturational sequences and age-appropriate physical and speech milestones indicate that there was indeed such primitive differentiation, maturation, and ego development. However, his other behaviors and his progression during psychotherapy suggest that the most massive fixation occurred at the very early oral stage. It is perhaps most meaningful to translate this in terms of Erickson's (3) concept of basic trust as the first adaptive stage of infantile experience. In this sense the long period of therapeutic work required to establish a predictable trustworthy, and honest relationship with adults, along with the ensuing inevitable vicissitudes, were followed by Danny's capacity to suck on a baby bottle with increasing pleasure, to permit being rocked in the cradle, i.e., to accept and later to enjoy the sensual pleasures of body contact and support, which had previously been inaccessible to him.

Although not illustrated in this case, it should be noted that in a number of other instances psychotic youngsters have been able to suckle on a bottle for the first time, permit close physical contact, or obtain pleasure in rocking or being rocked only after a violent physical struggle because the therapist or nurse would not permit some self-destructive or assaultive behavior which previously had not been countered with such firm protective restraints. In the course of the struggle the therapist's efforts would be to restrain the child and prevent such destructiveness. He would try to express in words his own feelings of anger and pain and would strive as well to make evident his valiant efforts not to become retaliatory in the face of the child's violence. These efforts have seemed to provide the child an experience with a more predictable, supportive adult whom he might begin to trust. He could then begin to incorporate and integrate such self-consideration and then could therefore safely explore the sensual pleasures of sucking, caressing, and bodily contact.

With Danny, the therapeutic work, both in individual play therapy and on the ward, revealed a progression during the recovery process which illustrated the resolution of some nuclear conflicts at various developmental stages. The work also graphically demonstrated that the working through of certain of Danny's conflicts waited upon the parents', usually upon his mother's, having made some progress in these particular areas, which then seemed to permit the tentative efforts of early sessions to be more solidly worked through prior to moving on to the next stage.

An illustration of this process was Danny's acceptance of physical cuddling and warmth. His conflict in this regard revealed an inner ambivalence, an inner sense of danger about relaxed acceptance of adult attention. Externally, he demonstrated his inability to rely upon an adult. It is interesting that this basic kind of nurturance, which usually occurs in the first weeks of life, preceded any oral explorations on his part. A patient acceptance of Danny's fears, the willingness to take the time necessary to permit a relationship to develop in which these fears could be repeatedly reduced, together with non-retaliatory firmness which prevented him from being destructive or assaultive were factors which led to his eventual acceptance of cuddling. Both my firmness in countering his efforts to destroy the dollhouse, and the nurse's firmness in administering the penicillin injections, resulted in the reduction of isolation and beginning physical contact. In each instance it was as if a non-retaliatory, unambiguous firmness about protecting him from the injurious consequences of his panicky attacks and revengeful disappointments reassured him. Such "parental" certainty and unambivalence about what was "good" for the child permitted relaxation and trust in the adult.

Later, when the therapeutic work had helped mother to know in an un-conflicted way what was good for herself and hence for her child, Danny was able to express trust in her and to enjoy physical closeness for the first time. For mother also, the first physical closeness with Danny followed a prevention of destructive behavior. His efforts to poke his mother many times a day over one weekend were met with the repeated verbal injunction to "stop it," followed immediately by holding his hands until he relaxed. Her capacity to deal with such behavior firmly and repeatedly came after mother's working through her violent repressed anger at infantilization by her own mother, sister, and husband.

A second illustration of how the solutions of the child's nuclear conflicts awaited parents' progress centers around Danny's concern with his penis. This conflict came up only to be dropped, and then arose again to be worked through. The resolution seemed closely related to mother's being able to work through first some of her pregenital problems about being taken care of and being able to trust someone not to have egocentric, narcissistic and exploitative investment in nurturing her. She then was able to work through some of her own oedipal struggles, which led her to permit her daughter to be close to the father and to play house with him. Dealing with her oedipal conflicts also resulted in reduced anger and contempt of men, with increased tolerance of Danny. At about the same time father began to allow himself to be taken care of by mother and to be more assertive with his boss. Thus, Danny did not need to be a girl to be loved by either mother or father.

The recurring theme of airplane propellors cutting off Daddy's hands in the playroom and Danny's greater freedom to express hostility and anger symbolically via play may have represented not only real anger at father for abandoning him and fear of father in the oedipal situation, but also displaced anger at mother who might be seen as father without his hands (penis).

The early preoccupation of both parents with Danny's cleanliness, to the exclusion of all else, may have represented the only areas where there was some mutual agreement. This concern may also have demonstrated a condensation of both parents' conflicts about hate, hostility, and infantile sexuality, represented by dirt, into cleanliness and neatness, though possibly nurturance, love, and concern also were represented by cleanliness. Danny was permitted to be messy in his activity and dress while playing, only as his mother became less fearful of her angry and hateful feelings, and as father could begin to accept his desires for infant-like nurturance.

Each of these phases of the working through with the parents was previewed in their work with me in the transference. Perhaps most dramatic were those sequences in which each of the parents was able to resolve some aspects of conflict in the transference, followed by a more evident capacity to use the insights so gained. Each would then behave with the spouse in a new way, with next a spurt of increasingly integrative behavior in their mutual living. After a time this would be succeeded by a new freedom and intensity in individual therapeutic work. This pattern was most apparent in mother's working through her rage toward her own mother and sisters, her helpless dependence on them, and her fear of dependence on me, as well as her repeated fury that I expected so much of her. Simultaneously, father was working on his fear of desires to be cared for and his need to be seen as a virile male. His anxieties about homosexual feelings came to the fore along with fears that if he let me "take care" of him in his sessions, he would never be able to be independent of me. As these conflicts about fears of self-assertion on the one hand, and accepting the consequences of his errors on the other hand, were being worked through, mother became more self-confident and effective and father more able both to let mother baby him and to be more unanxiously assertive at work.

A frequent experience in inpatient work with psychotic children is that the child may be ready to live at home before the parents' conflicts have been sufficiently reduced to allow them to keep him at home and to permit improvement to continue. In this instance Danny too seemed ready to live with the family and asked to do so some time before the parents were ready. Parents need to have sufficiently resolved their own conflicts about infantile needs for nurturance to permit reciprocal taking care of each other and mutual gratification on a more mature level, before they can help care for their disturbed child.

I have seen Danny and his parents intermittently during the past 12 years. Danny was able to go on in school and do well scholastically. It was clear after the first follow-up visit, a year after therapy ended, that continued outpatient work with Danny and his parents would be helpful, although impossible because of the distance. Danny still tended to be passive and to isolate himself from other children if permitted. Both parents were so busy making their new business venture a success that they had little time to concern themselves with Danny's problems, now that these were not so pressing.

Father is now very successful in his business and mother acts only in an advisory capacity. When last seen at age 19, Danny had successfully managed a year's service in the Army as a National Guard trainee. He was in college and doing B work in social sciences. Still quite shy, he had a few friends who shared his intellectual interests. Although he dated occasionally, he had no steady girl friends and thought girls were too frivolous. Danny, at this writing, is not psychotic, nor is he normal. He evidences a good many obsessive-compulsive defenses, but seems able to take care of himself and to be fairly effective in his own circumscribed world.

REFERENCES

1. BETTELHEIM, BRUNO. *The Empty Fortress.* New York: Free Press, 1967.
2. BOWLBY, JOHN. *Attachment and Loss. Vol. 1, Attachment.* New York: Basic Books, Inc., 1969.
3. ERICKSON, ERIK. *Childhood and Society.* New York: Norton, 1963.
4. SPITZ, R. A. Anaclitic Depression. In *The Psychoanalytic Study of the Child.* New York: International University Press, Vol. 2, 1946, pp. 313-342.
5. SZUREK, S. A. *The Roots of Psychoanalysis and Psychotherapy.* Springfield, Illinois: Charles C Thomas, 1958.

29

Work with a Psychotic Boy: An Illustration of Concepts of Authority and Physical Intervention

Samuel Susselman, M.D.

Many lessons can be learned from psychotherapeutic work with a schizophrenic child. Examples are the role of physical intervention (2) and concepts of authority (1) that, in turn, contribute to generalizations about punishment and discipline.

Authority that enables one to deal helpfully with others is the competence to persuade, in the sense of the meaning given the word *persuasion* by Whitehead when he wrote, "The worth of men consists in their liability to persuasion. They can persuade and can be persuaded by the disclosure of alternatives, the better and the worse" (4). Aside from ignorance, nothing more obscures one's capacity to discern alternatives than does emotional conflict. When encumbered by conflict, an individual in authority, such as a psychiatrist at work, must exercise his influence ambivalently and often without psychodynamic relevance. Therefore, if he seeks to enlist the patient's collaboration in a "working alliance" and is to help his patients choose better alternatives (more satisfying and wiser) (3), he would do well to recognize those occasions when he, too, is in conflict. This is a first step in freeing himself from conflict and in extending his competence for the therapeutic work.

Often a therapist is forced to take this first step when he must use physical restraint to deter a child's destructive, or self-punitive, behavior. Although a psychotic child is capable of such behavior for reasons internal to himself alone, his keen perceptiveness of even the slightest evidence of conflict in the therapist causes him to react either with further withdrawal or with more persistent, destructive behavior requiring intervention. In the

Presented in part at the University of Utah, Child Psychiatry Workshop, 1965.

act of restraining such a child the therapist may first discover his own previously unsuspected countertransference involvements. He also obtains knowledge about: how physical restraint can assist in the therapeutic work, how this most extreme intervening measure often regarded by many professionals as "authoritarian," can be truly authoritative (2), and how, when behavioral expression of hostile aggressive impulses are thwarted by restraint, a step may be taken in the direction of encouraging verbal expression of such emotions instead. A child can then be persuaded to select more satisfying alternatives either of his own devising or from those offered by the therapist.

CASE HISTORY

Mark Reisner, at age 15, is withdrawn and seldom can be motivated to do any of the simple tasks he has learned, such as mowing the lawn or washing the dishes. The little reading ability he once demonstrated is not now evident. Only with difficulty can he be induced to speak, and he usually gives monosyllabic answers to questions. When he makes spontaneous statements, their meanings are difficult or impossible to understand. He appears compelled to touch the edge of floors or furniture with his feet as he walks through corridors of the institute. Bringing himself to pass through a doorway has become a major undertaking. He stands poised to move forward, but seems held back by some force. Finally, he makes a lunge through the doorway only to return quickly to his original position and repeat the same agonizing struggle over and over. At times he becomes preoccupied with taking off his shoes and socks and putting them on again. Following an acute disturbed episode last year, which required several weeks of hospitalization, he is living at home and takes Thorazine in doses of 600 mg. per day. After 10 years of out-patient treatment, his can hardly be called a success story, yet I have learned much from him and from his parents.

Mark is the third of five children and lives with his parents, two older sisters, and two younger brothers. He was 3½ years old when his parents applied for inpatient services at Langley Porter Neuropsychiatric Institute in the early 1950's. At that time, the chief complaints were that he did not talk, did not dress himself, and was not toilet-trained. He was difficult to manage at home. When he could not be supervised directly, the parents kept him in a bare room with a locked door because of the mess he made (sometimes smearing feces) and because they feared he might wander away. He often disturbed the family with his screaming. In addition, he displayed stereotyped, bizarre movements involving his entire body.

Professional help was first sought for Mark at the recommendation of his pediatrician when he was a year and nine months old. From that time until he was first seen by us, he had been studied at three psychiatric clinics, by four psychiatrists in private practice, and by a neurosurgeon. Several of their reports were made available to us.

FAMILY HISTORY

Mr. Otto Reisner, age 44 years, is the oldest of four children. He was born in Central Europe of Jewish parents. His adjustment at school was uneven; mostly, he performed below his considerable capacity, in part because of his anxious response to anti-Semitic attitudes and behavior of his teachers and classmates. Hitler was already in power when he was 13 years old. At age 15 years, a few weeks before graduation from the gymnasium, he requested and was granted his parents' permission to terminate formal education because he found school so uncomfortable. For a short time thereafter he worked in his father's advertising business. At age 17, because of increasing danger of Nazi persecution, he was sent to England. In 1939, his family escaped from their country by way of Switzerland to London, where his father died of carcinoma. The family, now consisting of his mother, two sisters, a brother, and himself, soon emigrated to the United States. One year later, when he was 21 years old, he met his wife.

Mrs. Ann Reisner, also age 44 years, is the daughter and granddaughter of Methodist ministers. She is the youngest in a family of four girls and was born nine years after her next older sister. When she was four years old, her eldest sister left home for college, precipitating difficulty between Ann and her mother. Some indication of the state of affairs came from my interview with this older sister who said, "My mother was not too well when Ann was born. She never fully recovered (inquiry yielded no further information about the nature of her mother's illness). Therefore, I took care of Ann who used to say, 'I'm my sister's daughter.' My mother resented this. . . . On my first visit home from college (Thanksgiving) my mother deliberately turned Ann against me." By this time Ann had developed "many night terrors," was difficult to calm, and had begun to oppose her mother. When Ann was six, according to this same sister, their "mother had a period of time when she lay in bed . . . a matter of seven days and nights . . . you couldn't wake her up . . . we thought she might have sleeping sickness, but it wasn't. She wasn't really well until Ann was seven or eight years old." At age 15, Ann was sent to boarding school to "separate them." She met Mr. Reisner before the start of her senior year at college after having become acquainted with his mother at a resort where she worked as a waitress during the summer vacation. There was a mutual attachment between the two women which was maintained over the years out of respect for each other's intelligence and sensitivity despite widely different values. She left college a semester before graduation to live in Boston with a sister in order to be near Mr. Reisner.

Six months after Mr. Reisner entered the armed forces in World War II, they were married. A year later, six months pregnant with their first child, Mary, she went to live with her parents in expectation of the birth. After Mary's arrival, she delayed joining her husband until the child was three months old. "I kept postponing—not a devoted wife." Three months later Mr. Reisner was sent overseas and Mrs. Reisner returned to her parents' home for about one and a half years. History repeated itself when Mrs. Reisner yielded most of the care of the infant, Mary, to others (her mother and a sister living in the home); nor was the subsequent relation between Mrs. Reisner and Mary much better than that enjoyed by Mrs. Reisner and her own mother, probably for related reasons.

At the conclusion of the war, for some unstated reason, Mr. Reisner went to Switzerland even though his outfit had been returned to the United States. "He managed to have a lovely time. I resented it. I called him up. We sounded and talked like strangers. When he came home he wanted to go to California. I wasn't too happy with the idea. I didn't want to leave his mother." Nevertheless, he persuaded her to move to California proposing an auto trip cross-country as a second honeymoon. Mary, then almost two years old, was to be flown out by friends. The journey turned into a nightmare of violent quarrels. Sometimes, when Mrs. Reisner's anxiety erupted into fury, she would get out of the car, refusing to ride further; or she would impulsively drive off for miles without her husband until she calmed down enough to return for him.

Sally, the only child planned and the first infant actually reared by Mrs. Reisner, was born a year later when, because of postwar housing shortages, they were living in a crowded basement apartment. By that time, Mrs. Reisner was becoming increasingly disillusioned, discouraged, and anxious about her husband's capacity to earn a living, and no doubt he, too, had become apprehensive about his abilities.

Perhaps some measure of her turmoil and consequent inability to cope with her situation is the fact that it was friends who taught Sally to sit up and to walk, rather than she, herself. This is one reason why Mark's own retarded attainment of developmental landmarks was attributed more to the quality of his rearing than to his endowment. Perhaps another measure of the turmoil shared by both parents was their decision to limit their family to two children rather than the five they had originally planned. She stated,

"We wanted a boy very badly but for economic reasons decided not to have one. No sooner had we made this decision than I became pregnant with Mark."

Mrs. Reisner regarded this pregnancy as her "nastiest" for a number of reasons, including, "terrific" nausea, vaginal bleeding, a severe cold, lack of finances, and violent quarrels with her husband. Mark was a breech presentation at birth, as were her first two children. Delivery and neonatal course were otherwise uneventful. The mother breastfed Mark in the hospital; when he was brought home, a bottle was substituted. He was weaned when he was 20 months and started feeding himself at 28 months.

Most of Mark's early history gives evidence of retarded development and disturbed behavior. He did not sit until he was 11 months old nor walk, even with help, until 17 months old. Not until he was 23 months old did he walk alone. At 22 months, he could say "daw" for dog, and "cookie," but he stopped saying these and the few other words he had learned. Rhythmic movements and head-banging on the mattress were said to have started when he was three months old. His mother reported, "He spent hours rocking himself with apparent enjoyment. I felt guilty when I made no effort to do anything with him. He didn't appear to respond—didn't look us in the eye—was lugubrious—didn't make demands—didn't cry much." Mrs. Reisner stated he was two years old before he looked directly at people. At that time he cried in response to smiles and praise.

He was 16 months old when Mrs. Reisner became pregnant with Johnny, the next child. Because of Mark's "lack of responsiveness about everything," toilet training was started late and was abandoned. His hospitalization on our ward for a herniorrhaphy and circumcision at about age five contributed significantly to his toilet training. He has not wet the bed since age 6½. Earlier, as mentioned, he had smeared his room with feces, but "not until he had awareness and not until he knew he was annoying."

During psychological testing at age 3½, he gave no sign of hearing or of recognizing even his own name. When the psychologist sat him on her lap, he neither resisted nor moved toward her. Such behavioral plasticity caused her to remark that more responsiveness would have been expected from an infant or even a pet. He did the Binet form board at the three-year level without relying on trial and error. Instead of stringing beads as was requested of him, he neatly sorted them into three piles according to shape. Both of these performances were done in a far corner of the room with his back to the examiner. More formal testing was not possible.

He had had chickenpox and measles. Physical and neurological examinations showed normal findings except for his gait, which was somewhat waddling. He is left handed but is unusually dexterous with his right hand. Laboratory findings during the study and his hospital stay were normal except for successfully treated pinworm while he was an inpatient for surgery. An electroencephalogram, reported from a previous evaluation, was normal.

DIAGNOSTIC EVALUATION

His history of inappropriate affective responses from infancy, of withdrawal from others and preoccupation with his own activities, of rhythmic movements and headbanging, loss of what little speech he did acquire and of oppositional behavior such as deliberate smearing of feces according to the mother plus his marked behavioral plasticity pointed to the contribution of emotional factors to his maldevelopment. There were no signs to correlate his gait with a neurological deficit. Mental deficiency was considered in the differential in view of his retarded development but his near-age-appropriate performance on at least two test items, despite the adverse effect on testing of his affective disorder, and a similar though not an abnormal history of slow development in an older sister as well, tended to implicate experiential interferences rather than structural factors in his retardation. At the conclusion of the initial study the diagnosis of childhood schizophrenia was primary, with mental deficiency to be ruled out.

EARLY INTERVIEWS

Outpatient therapy with student psychiatric social workers started when Mark was four years old. My work with the family began when their first therapists, who saw them for six months, left the clinic. Attendance by the family has been regular except for vacations, holidays, illnesses, and the father's occasional absence on necessary business trips.

My first meeting with Mark occurred in the waiting room. While I exchanged greetings with his mother, he seemed not to notice me as he stood close-by indifferently sucking his thumb, which, may have contributed to the prominence of his upper front teeth. When I said "Hello" and asked him to accompany me to the playroom, he drew back. When I proferred my hand, he advanced toward the playroom, obviously knowing what was expected, from his previous visits. He pointedly avoided physical contact; not until the 16th hour did he spontaneously take hold of my hand. There was no verbal response, and I expected none, since I knew he was mute. He descended the stairs, a step at a time, instead of alternating his feet.

In the playroom Mark immediately went to the blackboard, picked up a piece of chalk and vigorously scribbled, using left and right hand in turn. He was truly ambidextrous at this time. Although he eventually favored his left hand, his right hand remained proficient in performing skilled maneuvers. The fact that he so quickly seized on an activity, that he kept his back turned toward me, and that he wrote so forcibly, conveyed the impression that he was frightened. I verbalized that he might be surprised to see me, that he might have expected to see a "lady" (since his former therapist was female) and that he might be frightened. Shortly afterwards, the chalk fell from his hand. He scribbled with a second piece of chalk and that, too, soon dropped to the floor. When several more pieces slipped through his fingers and when he, with seeming inadvertence, stepped on them, grinding them into the floor, I concluded that I was observing a purposeful rather than an accidental behavioral sequence.

Perhaps because of the insistent way I told him that such behavior was not necessary, he soon turned the clay can upside down, dumping its contents onto the bench. Mixed in the clay were shreds of paper and pieces of crayon. Fastidiously, I sorted out the crayons, placing them in their appropriate can, and threw the bits of paper into the wastebasket. He assisted me by picking out some of the bits of paper, but instead of putting them in the wastebasket as I had done, threw them to the floor. I commended him for helping me but said that he, too, might use the wastebasket. He did not seem to hear and played with pieces of clay with his back turned toward me. I moved closer, saying that I wanted to watch what he was doing. As he played, he occasionally looked directly into my eyes and sometimes past me. After a while, he smiled gently. Pleased, I commented that I noticed he had smiled. Immediately the smile was replaced by a look of anger. I said that he was probably angry and that perhaps I should not have said anything. His response was to throw a handful of clay into the sink. I tried to stop his next throw but I was not quick enough. However, when he picked up another piece of clay, evidently with the same purpose in mind, I put my hand over his and he promptly gave up the attempt. This was my first physical intervention. He then collected knives, forks, and automobiles and mixed them among the pieces of clay. When I said he was making a mishmash, he smiled. At the end of the hour he helped me put the toys in their appropriate places.

At times during the hour he engaged in ritualistic, shaking movements. This activity ranged from slight, irregular, almost tremor-like movements of his hands to an apparently ecstatic involvement of his entire body. Most often he would plant his right foot forward and vigorously lunge his body back and forth, at the waist. Simultaneously his arms would extend far behind him, his fingers opening and closing spasmodically, his wrists twisting. He seemed oblivious to everything except for some object on which his gaze would be fixed, his eyes wide open and unblinking. In almost reckless abandon his head would come to within inches of the object. I witnessed these bizarre movements many times subsequently. On rare occasions his flaying hands would strike the cabinets or walls, but never in my presence did he misjudge and hit his head. Most often the mood was less intense and the movements correspondingly gentler. Much of the time he sat on the floor, his knees jack-knifed, his feet splayed at right angles with his buttocks resting between his heels. In the first few years he wore out the inner sides of his shoes brought in contact with the floor by this habitual posture. He stayed meticulously clean, except for rare occasions, even when using finger paints. If his forearms inadvertently became wet during water play he would immediately dry them.

Mark's greeting for the second hour was a fleeting, shy smile. Again, he held back when I asked him to come with me, and when I extended my hand, he disregarded it. Immediately after entering the playroom, he picked up several balls of clay and threw them into the sink. When I said, as I had in the previous hour, that I did not like him to throw clay, he eyed me directly and fixedly for several minutes. His head and body wobbled as though he were making an effort to control stronger and more generalized muscular movements. I was aware of waves of uneasiness in myself and of feelings of helplessness, sensing a more formidable struggle. He turned his gaze from me to scramble pieces of clay aimlessly and then resumed looking at me. I made further attempts to verbalize my reasons for stopping the clay throwing, but there was no detectible response. I sat quietly, silently dealing with my own uneasiness and sense of helplessness. There seemed to be no other choice. After about fifteen minutes he smiled slightly. Again too eagerly, I asked him if he was feeling better. The smile disappeared instantly. Again I sat back. Several moments later the smile returned, much broader this time. More at ease, I told him I knew he was feeling better. He responded by becoming more active, reached into the cabinet for a toy percolator and took it apart appropriately. He then used a knife and fork on the lumps of clay in a fairly conventional fashion. When he reached for the crayons, I offered him a piece of paper and made a few marks to encourage him to draw. He complied briefly, but then, apparently in rebellion, deliberately, but surreptitiously, bore down on the crayon so that it broke. I was aware of feeling disappointed but was at a loss to respond.

His smile was more noticeable when I greeted him for our third hour. He seemed less tense, but occasionally he looked at me in the scrutinizing way already described. I thought I was ready to intervene should he start throwing clay again, but I was unable to stop two quick throws. Each time I voiced my objections, feeling helpless, and each time he smiled. He then looked teasingly at me and tried to throw a large piece of clay. Forewarned by the teasing look, I was able to grasp his hand firmly until I felt his muscles relax and then released him. He smiled and went to the blackboard. His scribbling was less randomly vigorous and, for the first time, parallel lines appeared, drawn with a kind of purposefulness I had not seen previously.

He turned his attention to the doll house, took a toilet and a chair and placed them on the eraser ledge of the blackboard. He picked up the toilet which soon slipped through his fingers much as did the chalk in the first hour. I handed it to him and again it dropped to the floor. To all outward appearances, it seemed accidental but quite evidently could not have been. This time I said that he could get it himself. Instead he picked up the toy chair and threw it to the floor in anger. There was no hint of an accident this time. More certain about what he was feeling I said, with some emphasis, "You're teasing—you're angry," trying to supply words for his feelings. Play became more active, consisting of banging and throwing toys. When he was in danger of breaking the telephone I said that he could make all the noise he wanted but he was not to break any toys. He threw the telephone to the floor, but I caught it before it landed. Again I said that he was not to break the toys regardless of how angry he felt. He picked up two cars, took them to the bench as though to play with them and then unexpectedly threw them into the sink. I verbalized a prohibition sharply now, quite angry, and he seemed pleased. Was my more open anger, somehow, relieving? The rest of the hour was uneventful as he played with the clay, cars, and knives in a fairly relaxed way, helping to put away the toys at the end.

By the fourth hour, I was able to observe more clearly when he was about to throw clay. For example, he would interrupt his activity and stand quietly as though trying to decide whether to throw or not. There was also a look on his face that betrayed his intent. Thus warned, I was prepared. I was about to say "I know you are trying to decide whether or not to throw the clay." Before I reached a decision to speak, he reached for a piece of clay with the intent to throw quite evidently in mind. I put my hand over his, feeling that physical intervention was again indicated. That hour the playroom had been left untidy by the previous therapist, and I began to clean it up. Mark heaped toys on the floor, littering the playroom even more. I verbalized his displeasure at finding the playroom so untidy. In retrospect, I recognized that this was an expression of my own resentment at those thoughtless therapists, whoever they were, charged with the responsibility of leaving the playroom in good order. Mark proceeded to mix clay, knives, forks, and automobiles on the bench, apparently at random. I felt his actions and attitudes were expressions of angry futility. Consequently, I interrupted what he was doing and took over mixing the conglomeration, but in a more vigorous fashion, exaggerating his way of doing it. At the same time I made angry, roaring noises. He responded with a pleased smile. I moved away from the bench and he took over mixing the toys in a way that I interpreted as teasing. I therefore imitated him again, emitting different sounds on what I intended to be a note of exultation, for some reason not clear to me now. I also verbalized my feeling that he was teasing. He looked more pleased and, as though by accident, rested the elbow of his left arm on my elbow. Because this was the first spontaneous physical contact initiated by him, I sat quietly until he moved away.

In the sixth hour he looked at me eagerly and happily when I greeted him. Perhaps embarrassed by a display of open emotion, he quickly became sad and almost tearful as he slowly followed me to the playroom. He continued to throw toys and to mix them. I watched him closely, verbalizing his anger and disappointment as seemed indicated. Finally, I had to limit his behavior when he tore the clothes off a doll, encountering more vigorous resistance than I had learned to expect from him. At one time as he was about to drop a doll to the floor I quickly caught it. My quick movement must have surprised and alarmed him for he raised his arms defensively over his head as though to ward off a blow.

Parenthetically, at about this time his mother reported she had "resumed being firm" with Mark, no doubt because of her own psychotherapy, and that he had responded by saying a "dozen" words, the first in over six months. He could almost say my name.

When he picked up the toy telephone in the seventh hour, I recalled how he had banged it on the floor during a previous meeting. I asked him to be careful, saying that it might break. He gently lowered the telephone to the floor, the first evidence in overt behavior that he understood words and could comply with verbal instructions. In this hour, he started doll play that was continued in several subsequent hours. He placed a rubber doll on the bench, struck it hard, and laughed with glee each time it emitted a squeak. Using the bean bag as a pillow, he placed the doll on it and hit it again. At the end of the hour I asked him to help me clean up. He responded with an exaggerated nod. I tentatively assumed this to be an agreement, exaggerated because such a gesture was new to him. He participated in the cleaning up for a short while. He insisted on taking home the flat, rubber sink stopper, but I refused to let him have it. Its significance did not become apparent until later despite earlier clues of its importance to him.

In the tenth hour he selected a toilet and placed it on the bench. Next he picked up a baby doll, took the doll's panties off, placed the doll with its buttocks on the rubber stopper, whacked the doll until it squealed, picked up the rubber stopper and folded it in quarters as one might fold a dirtied diaper. Only then did I realize how his previous play gave broad hints that he was working out something possibly related to toilet training. As early as the third hour he had included the toy toilet in his play. In retrospect, I realized there had been other hints such as tearing the clothes off the doll, trying to break the toy toilet and placing the doll on the bean bag and striking it. Subsequently he had substituted the flat rubber sink stopper for the bean bag. But I had missed the meaning of these fragments until he put the whole sequence together so unmistakeably in this hour. Even then I couldn't quite decide whether he was saying something about toilet training. It seemed too pat an interpretation! I did, however, venture to ask him if the rubber stopper was a diaper. This comment made him anxious for he immediately and frenetically began to mix together all the toys he could gather on the bench.

Intermittently in subsequent hours he returned to toilet play, adding chunks of brown clay to the rubber stopper, making the sequences more graphic. Once he cleaned brown clay off a toy toilet messed up by some other child who had used the same playroom. Somewhere along the way, assisted by efforts to toilet train him during his brief stay on the children's psychiatric ward for surgery, he became toilet trained. It was impossible to establish the exact time of this achievement since his mother casually mentioned it several months after it had been accomplished.

This then, is some of the flavor of our early interviews. I had never before worked systematically with an autistic child. Much of my activity was unpremeditated, springing more or less intuitively from experience with other patients, staff discussion, presentations, and my own concomitant personal analysis. In retrospect, I recognize several lasting lessons, even in these first ten hours. These lessons were: (1) the essential role of attentive observation in learning about the child and in detecting early steps in a sequence of behavior, especially those leading to symptomatic acts; (2) how much went into discriminating for myself what was acceptable to me in a child's behavior before I could begin to grasp the nature of the opposing impulses expressed in this manner in order to respond in a way most likely to help him reduce and resolve conflict; (3) the importance of making verbal efforts even with a relatively mute psychotic child, for not only may words have more meaning for him than he leads one to expect but the attentiveness and the interest inherent in the effort may not be lost on him; (4) how a contented affect can be dampened by calling untimely and no doubt, anxious attention to it; (5) the shift from random to more structured activity after a child has worked something through in his own feelings; (6) the possibility of dramatizing a feeling, probably dimly perceived by the patient, by making both appropriate sounds and movements to increase his awareness of it; and (7) the efficacy of physical intervention when it is therapeutically employed. Of special importance was the experience of working with a mute child who could provide no spoken clues to his thoughts or feelings, forcing me to rely on nonverbal signals. This experience enhanced my work with other patients whose movements and facial expressions conveyed messages often contradicting their words or who sat in frozen silence.

Despite these instructive experiences, most of Mark's play was stereotyped and repetitive, conveying little meaning to me. Even the variations in behavior produced by the gross shaking movements already described did not relieve the feelings of monotony often induced in me by the sameness of his actions.

Perhaps the main factor engendering feelings of boredom in me was his so-called "lack of affect." This concerned not only his placid, passive facial expression but his bodily responsiveness as well. They combined to hide from me any clues about his feelings or thoughts, especially when I made efforts to introduce an activity or to amplify anything he had initiated. With no discernible signs of response to my interventions, I felt futile and impotent. Only in retrospect did I recognize how great was my disappointment and how persistent my implicit demand for a response in order to prove my own effectiveness. So well did Mark hide his feelings that on those rare occasions when I gave him a present, such as a favorite key, the only indication that he was touched might be an audible exhalation after a long pause. Until I heard the sound of expiration I had no idea he was holding his breath, let alone feeling pleasure.

EMERGENCE OF SPEECH

The interactions described and similar ones that followed, together with the parents' therapeutic efforts, were conflict-reducing, and Mark soon began to speak. Without going into great detail, I should like to mention some of the steps that led to speech and some of the highlights of subsequent interviews.

By the 23rd hour I was urging Mark to say what he wanted instead of pantomiming a request. Three hours later, with my encouragement, he made an effort to talk over the toy telephones, uttering an unintelligible sound after a struggle to speak.

In the 27th hour, when I asked him not to tear off the feather that decorated the toy drum, he gave me a baleful, hostile look, quite different from his usual affectlessness. In the next hour he inserted his hand into my trouser pocket and took out its contents, keys and coins. He again gave me the impression that he was trying to speak. Instead, he made motions for me to take the keys off the ring. While complying, I said, "You can say, 'Take them apart!' " Later, when he again motioned for me to separate the keys from the ring, I asked, "Do you want me to take them apart?" He nodded his head affirmatively and looked into my eyes. This response was so direct, simple, and clear, compared to the few previous awkward, hardly detectible but probably affirmative nods, and was so unexpected, that it had a thrillingly dramatic effect on me.

In the next hour he uttered a sound that seemed to be "ouch" while struggling to clasp a key chain together. This was followed by clicking sounds with his tongue, also new, as he turned to me for help. When I urged him to say "Fix it," he only smiled. On our way to the playroom for the next hour, one of the psychology fellows, as he passed by said "Hi." Mark whispered "Hi" in return. That same hour, he whispered "key" when asking for the contents of my pockets. In several following interviews, he made sounds and his play became more structured. Once I thought he said "boa" for "boat."

In the 35th hour, he said the word "key" quite distinctly. He struggled to say something more. When I heard the consonant "p-p-p," I asked him if he were trying to say "Take them apart." After further struggle he sputtered out something that sounded like "part." I responded by taking the keys off the ring. The next hour, I imitated some of his bizarre movements. He looked startled, then amused. As I persisted, his look of amusement changed to one of puzzlement, and I stopped. When I imitated him again the next hour, he responded with even more amusement. Suddenly a pained expression crossed his face, and although I told him that I was not making fun of him, his play became agitated. In the next hour, when I imitated him again, he made a gesture as though to pick up a sponge. The gesture said, "if you keep this up, I'll throw the sponge at you." However, he seemed more playful than hostile, communicating without speaking.

In the 42nd hour, when I prevented him from tearing a sponge, he hit my arm. The motion started out with vigor but landed gently, as though restrained in mid-air. Parenthetically, his mother told me, much later, that he had made threatening gestures toward her that ended as light "pats." At the same time, she reported, he kept saying, "no hit Mama," yet his eyes were smoldering. She added that he had more control over his actions than she did when angry.

The first evidence that he understood the concept of an adjective occurred in the 51st hour when he pointed to a spaceman and said something that I heard as "B-A-W." When I asked him what he meant, he ignored me. Much later in the hour he again pointed to the spaceman and said "B-R-A-W-K." I then noticed that the spaceman's arm was broken, and when I said "broken," showing him I understood, he smiled with pleasure. In the next hour, he handed me a jar of finger paint saying "Open" distinctly. This was his first use of a verb. By the 53rd hour, he was uttering commands such as "Make a dog." He discovered a new ball and said, "Ball, new."

Much of his verbalization was preceded by a struggle in which he gulped, evidently tensing his vocal muscles, held his breath, and made sounds in his throat. Sometimes a word emerged. A few times it seemed that he was struggling to remember a word. For example, in clay play he asked me to "make a vacuum." As I molded the clay he directed me further by saying "bag," followed by "handle" and then "electric light" without apparent difficulty. Then came a long pause as he seemed locked in a struggle with himself until he remembered or could say the word "wire." After I had made the wire, he said, again without difficulty, "plug."

Once when he was about to throw a handful of tongue blades across the room, he said, "Mark, you are a bad boy," and then answered this self-accusation with mocking and defiant sounds, a beautiful expression of both sides of an internalized authority problem. Other evidence of a similar internalized problem occurred one day as he was about to throw. Laughing with a silly, uneasy giggle he said, "Don't you throw that," but he threw, nevertheless. After thus expressing rebellion in deed, he proceeded to urge himself on in words with "Do it, do it again." He then gathered up the tongue blades, saying, "Pick it up." In so doing he may have modified the impulse to throw, for he commended himself by saying, "Very good," probably savoring the satisfaction of a restitutive act. While I could not be certain that he learned these commending words from me or from his parents, it was plain that words were beginning to identify elements in sequences that formerly had found expression in behavior. It was as though one could see in slow motion what had once been condensed before, during, and after a single, unexplainable impulsive act. There was no doubt, too, in the 215th hour, that communicative speech was occurring when, upon coming into the playroom, he excitedly exclaimed, "I broke the thermos bottle." In answer to my question about how had he broken it, he said appropriately, "On the sidewalk." I do not intend to imply that such meaningful verbal exchanges were common. Actually, they were rare. When they did occur, they reinforced the notion, sometimes shaken and weakened by discouragements in the work, that it was possible for him to achieve meaningful verbal communication.

As to the discernment of alternative choices aided by the use of speech, a most illustrative instance occurred after Mark had misbehaved in the waiting room, taxing the attention of personnel who had duties other than "baby sitting." I asked him if he would behave himself or if it would be necessary to ask his father to sit with him. His instant reply was "No father sit with me." His behavior in the waiting room immediately improved so that supervision there was no longer needed. When Mr. Reisner learned of the alternatives posed for his son, he responded tearfully to the thought that Mark's wishes were respected. Mr. Reisner's own father had "never" shown him such consideration, nor had it occurred to him that Mark could understand alternatives posed in such a way.

THERAPIST-PATIENT INTERACTIONS

Implicit in the description of Mark's behavior is the interplay of my attitude and reactions with his. The following, more detailed account of the transaction between Mark and myself concerns one playroom hour in which he engaged in finger painting. I hoped he would limit himself to one or two of the six colors. He dipped the wooden tongue blade into the jar of red paint and transferred a huge glob of expendable paint to a clean sheet of expendable paper. Things seemed to be going smoothly as I helped him tap all the paint off the stick. He then turned eagerly to the jar of yellow paint but, to avoid contamination with the red, I asked him to wait until I could wash off the tongue blade. Only the day before I had observed one of my colleagues in the playroom. All six jars were open and a tongue blade was in place in each. I liked this method but I hesitated to adopt it because I might thus encourage my patient to follow his usual custom of taking paint from all the jars. Consequently, I persisted with the one tongue blade, pausing to clean it each time and hoping he would not run the gamut of colors.

In a dim way I was aware that when he made a move toward the finger paints something unpleasant happened to me. I personally did not like a mess in the first place. Besides, my protruding French cuffs, smudged with paint once before, were again in danger. In addition, I wore no protective covering, since the preceding therapist had left the solitary smock soaking wet. This was not the first time this had happened and I was angry with him. I was also angry with myself because I had intended to take up this matter with him but had forgotten to do so. Furthermore, I had meant to provide myself with a smock and forgotten to do that, too. I had once inquired about securing clean gowns and was told that they were not part of playroom equipment. Finger paints stained them beyond washability. Only because the housekeeper was kind enough to exceed her authority did we have any gowns at all. I was advised not to mention the problem to her, for I might spoil a good thing. I had considered buying my own smock but could not find the time to shop for it. The truth was that I was reluctant to pay for it myself. Even if I owned one, there was no place to hang it in the office I shared with several others in that crowded clinic, safe from someone else in search of a clean smock. How would I get it laundered, and what would I wear while it was in the laundry? Should I buy two smocks? After all this speculation, I had deferred the whole matter, and there I was in the playroom again with no protection for my clothes.

But this was not all. On opening the jar of yellow paint, I found that it had already been contaminated with the blue. How could I insist that my patient be so meticulously careful? Suddenly I felt how picayune I must have seemed to him. Very apologetically I explained why I had voiced restrictions. Neither he nor I seemed convinced.

Encouraging a child to play as a means of expressing himself and as a way of helping to work out his problems was not a simple matter for me that day. Almost predictably, his play became more and more hectic. Finger paint splattered the counter, the walls, the floor, and myself. The child himself was a mess. When all this was happening I was not clearly aware of all I have just recounted. I was too busy with my own preoccupations and with the child to be attentive to my subjective state. Only in retrospect was I able to piece things together.

This experience taught me to be dressed appropriately for the playroom. On days when it was inconvenient to wear old clothes or when a gown was not available, I could tell him quite easily that he would have to be especially careful because I did not want to be smeared with paint. His response was gratifying. He used the finger paints enjoyably and within bounds. Constant alertness was still necessary to detect early signs of impulsivity. However, now a restraining word was usually sufficient where formerly even a restraining hand was of no avail. It was a mutual learning experience.

Vacillation on my part has at times contributed to destructive play. For instance, on arriving at the playroom one day, we discovered a new set of metal tea dishes. Their shapes were modern and quite beautiful. I expressed my admiration and I thought he, too, seemed pleased. After playing with them for a short time, he deliberately made a light scratch on one of the saucers with a spoon. I debated with myself about stopping him. What was a little scratch, after all? He hesitated for a moment and made another scratch. I hesitated, still undecided. I verbalized unconvincingly that I supposed he was not really hurting the dish. His response was to scratch away so vigorously at the dish that I angrily stopped him. What I had not fully enough appreciated was my potentially deep annoyance at the desecration of a beautiful object. Telling myself that it was only a toy dish was not convincing to me. I did not clearly see at the time how much of my anger was at myself for not taking a stand, knowing from previous experiences what could happen yet half hoping it wouldn't occur this time, and thus the contribution of my own vacillation and indecision to his destructive behavior. Nor did I, until later, recognize in my feelings an element of guilt for not having stopped him before I became so angry.

Such experiences impressed me with the contribution of my own reactions and attitudes to his behavior. Despite his apparent nonreactiveness to me, when I anticipated a reaction he sometimes gave me a clue about what I was doing, either because he was more aware of it than I or because he was reacting as unwittingly in his way as I was in mine. For example, I would note a sudden cessation in what he was doing and only then would I recall that my shoes had just creaked as I had restlessly raised myself on tip toe. It also became clear that he was aware of my activities through peripheral vision on those occasions when I sat almost directly behind him as he played at the counter. For when I crossed or uncrossed my legs, he sometimes, without turning his head, signaled to me what I was unwittingly doing through some change in his activity. Once, I "came to" and found him gazing intently into my eyes. I realized that I had moved my arm into position just a moment before to look at my wrist watch. As he learned to talk, he would turn to me at such times, inquiring, "Clean up?" even though the hour was still young.

FURTHER DISCUSSION OF PHYSICAL INTERVENTION

In order to permit Mark fuller expression, I sometimes decided to risk damage to a toy rather than take it from him. My intention was to intervene only when absolutely necessary and, I hoped, in time to prevent a destructive act. This tactic is, obviously, quite different from the vacillation I have just described. Often crayons were broken because either my verbal efforts failed or my attention wandered at the precise moment before he suddenly snapped a crayon between his fingers, a difficult maneuver to prevent at best, or, when I could not discriminate destructive deliberate pressure on a crayon while he seemed to be scribbling vigorously.

One hour, after he had tested my patience in various ways, he picked up a plastic horse and made teasing, moderately strong motions to tear off its tail. I told him that if he continued to bend the tail I would be forced to take the horse from him, but that I was reluctant to do so. He abandoned his efforts, but soon began again to manipulate the tail. In time, we might have worked things out without damage to the horse, but the tail, partially weakened from previous attempts, came off unexpectedly. I think he, too, was surprised at the ease with which it separated, not having fully intended to tear it off. Evidence of his anxiety was a gleeful, mischievous laugh, which I associated with a destructive impulse and which usually alerted me to intervene should it be necessary. However, it was too late, in this instance, to do anything except to call attention to his anxiety and to acknowledge that he, too, must have been surprised. Parenthetically, parents who misinterpret such a laugh as solely one of pleasure unwittingly miss its connection to a destructive impulse or act. They do not recognize that such a laugh is a conflictual expression of glee arising from revengefulness and from guilty anxiety for the destruction committed and from attempts at reducing these feelings to a "joking" or self-ridiculing attempt to make "light" of the situation and to pretend that one is not anxious. Perhaps other combinations of reactions are fused with these. Lulled by this oversight, parents may not only miss an opportunity to offer their child a corrective experience but, should he carry out in action the hostile impulse inherent in the gleeful moment, they are implicated in several ways. First, they are guilty because they disregarded the warning signaled by a laugh of this quality and thus did not anticipate and prevent damaging behavior. Second, they are angry at their entrapment and impotency. Third, and perhaps more serious for the child, is his own guilt plus whatever self-reprisal he has already internalized, as well as fear of his parents' reprisal, whether or not this actually occurs. Should they react with uneasy helplessness, he is left even more anxious.

In order to help Mark become aware of his anxiety, and at the same time to convey the fact that I was not retaliatory, I said, in terms that he might understand, "You feel bad." He retorted, "No feel bad." I said with conviction, "Yes, you do." He looked quiet and reflective for a few moments and then tried to fit the torn edges together. I then said, "See, you do feel bad—that's why you're trying to fix it. You can stop yourself next time and you won't feel so bad." As though hearing something that had some meaning to him, he repeated softly, "you stop yourself." From then on when he started an activity that seemed deliberately mischievous he would often stop when I said gently, but firmly, "You can stop yourself." By my tone, attitude, behavior, and attention to what he was feeling it was my hope to soften whatever harsh commands toward hostile impulses were already internalized and to reinforce his capacity to intervene appropriately for himself.

As work progressed it was less and less necessary to intervene physically.

In the 279th hour he shut the cabinet doors, banging them with unnecessary force, gleefully looked at me, and repeated the performance. When there was no rise out of me he stopped. I knew with a kind of certainty that we had reached some kind of understanding. This realization came first to me and, a moment later, to him. I knew he would stop and he seemed to know it too. The same kind of understanding came about in his use of the pounding board, upon which he had often purposely and unnecessarily made dents. This hour, after he had pounded the pegs so that their tops were level with the board, he continued to hammer on the vertical ends of the pounding board. His blows, though relatively light, were still causing slight hammer marks on the wood. I felt the testing nature of what he was doing and observed him quietly as he seemed to make studied efforts to attend to the hammering rather than to me. Apparently my silence and lack of intervention was unexpected, for he suddenly looked up and said "Lookee!" as though saying, "See what I'm doing, aren't you going to stop me or say something?" I replied, "You know about stopping" and he stopped. Testing was less necessary when he had experienced my unambivalent readiness to prevent real damage rather than anxious and retaliatory inhibition of his play. He realized and integrated my clear expectations that he could finally stop himself.

Although physical intervention was usually reserved for preventing destructive behavior, I also exercised it to help him do something constructive. One hour, instead of helping to clean up, Mark threw toy soldiers to the floor. I took him by the hands, closed them over the tops and steered him, bodily, toward the cabinet. His body became pliant and almost plastic. He squealed with what I took to be a mixture of chagrin, anger, embarrassment, silliness, and even amusement. He dropped several soldiers on the way. However, one or two remained in his grasp. We deposited the toys in the cabinet and returned, in the same fashion, for those he had dropped. As his body took on more tone, I released him. He continued to put away the toys without further prompting from me, but he expressed his defiance by throwing some of them into the cabinet instead of simply placing them there. However, there was discrimination even in his defiant behavior. For example, he threw a rubber object in with considerable force and the metallic toys more gently.

An incident that is important because Mark's persistence caused me to analyze a self-involvement in his presence, instead of learning by retrospective reflection, also is a dramatic demonstration of his exquisite sensitivity to my reactions.

When I first started to use a ball-point pen, I offered no objection when Mark wanted to play with my cheap, expendable model. Actually, I felt encouraged when he learned to take it apart and put it together properly. Even his drumming on the counter with the filler point caused me little concern, especially after I learned that the writing qualities were not noticeably affected. He took special delight in rubbing out with an eraser the easily removable lettering stamped on each filler.

After experimenting with several ball-point pens, I found one that I liked. The filler was marked "Med. Black." Before seeing Mark I had decided that he could play with the filler, for this had become one of his usual activities on each visit, but there would be no erasing. Without the legend, Med. Black, I might forget which filler to buy when I needed a new one.

No doubt there was something different in my behavior right away, for when he asked for my pen I said, "It's got a new filler." He paused, gave no other recognizable sign, unscrewed the pen and took out the filler. He said, "Rub off the letter, make it shiny brass." I said, "No, I don't want you to." When he persisted, I realized that the only reminder I needed was the letters that spelled out "Med. Black." Consequently, I said, "You can erase everything up to this black line," and I pointed to line A.

FIGURE 1

He looked pleased and immediately went to work, erasing everything from the tip to line A, using longitudinal strokes and taking care not to encroach on line A. He then paused, but soon began to make persistent and teasing passes at the area A to B with the eraser until I said, "You're teasing." He stopped but then made sly and surreptitious attempts to rub out the forbidden area with his thumb. Observing this, I asked him to stop. It then occurred to me that the two black lines, A and B, could go without disturbing the words I wanted to save. So I said, "You can erase the black lines but not the letters," pointing to them to make sure he understood. He eagerly set about doing this, now plying the eraser at right angles so as not to endanger the letters. The task finished, he stopped and made no further effort to erase the letters. It was as though we both knew the end point. His persistence called my attention to something uncertain in the way I voiced my prohibitions, compelling me to recognize that I was not firm and causing me to modify my stand until the essence of my concern was apparent to me, namely, the preservation of the two words. At that point it was unnecessary to do anything to maintain my prohibition because it was no longer necessary to enforce it.

A decision on what constitutes a child's destructive behavior warranting intervention often may reflect the personality and experience of the therapist rather than the actual behavior of the child. A dramatic illustration of these differences occurred many years ago. A graduating resident introduced his autistic, boy patient to a newly arrived trainee, to whom the patient was to be transferred. The child promptly popped a piece of clay into his mouth and chewed it, as he often did when anxious. When he did not spit it out, the first therapist put his finger in the child's mouth and retrieved it. Evidently he had done it before and knew he was not risking injury. It seemed a good demonstration of physical intervention that should have been instructive to a resident unfamiliar with such procedures. But apparently it was not, because when the new therapist subsequently reported his first play session alone with this child, he mentioned that clay chewing had recurred; however, he said nothing about his response to it. I therefore asked, "What did you do?" He answered, "Nothing." I then asked, "What happened?" and he replied, "He spit it out!"

There is no question that sudden, explosive, and violent behavior, injurious or potentially injurious to the patient and the therapist or to property, requires unhesitating use of physical restraint. This is true whether it springs from the patient's psychopathology without being triggered by countertransference involvements or whether it is the end point of the interaction already occurring between therapist and patient. Even if restraint serves the purpose of protection alone, it is therapeutic. Similarly, a therapist will not stand idly by when a child slaps himself in the face and will intervene out of consideration both for his own feelings of not wanting to be a party to a self-destructive act and for his patient's pain and suffering. Physical intervention, when other measures are ineffective, is unquestionably indicated.

However, because a withdrawn child's first efforts to assert himself may take the form of an aggressive act, a dilemma is often posed for the therapist who wants to preserve the potentially positive, assertive, and satisfying components in an act while discouraging those that are self-destructive and self-defeating arising from hostile impulses. A less grossly disturbing act may offer him a greater opportunity to solve this dilemma. It may give him time to consider whether the act was accidental or not; to note the context from which it sprang, helping him draw inferences about its motivation; and to observe how it was done—for example, was it deliberate, sly, teasing? These data may form a basis for pertinent verbal interpretations rather than physical intervention. Thus, he may allow the child to splash water or to use excessive amounts of paper towels or drawing paper until he is clearer about the meaning of the child's behavior or until some useful alternative occurs to him. He may permit the child to pick one or two straws off a broom, for example, making efforts to understand and to deal verbally with him. However, if these efforts do not effect an appropriate response and the child plucks straw number three, and then four, five, etc., somewhere along the way physical intervention would be indicated. The principal issue is not the preserving of the material object in these instances. It is the understanding and resolution, in front of one's self, of a conflict state in the patient and ambivalence or conflict regarding intervention by the therapist.

Acting out, with its subsequent guilt and rebellion against the guilty self-prohibition inherent in another destructive act, must be applied with great precision otherwise a climate largely composed of prohibitions and "don't's" may pervade the playroom. Encouraging assertive expression requires equal precision. The therapist calls upon himself to suggest new avenues of expression, i.e., "this way rather than that way"; to become aware of motivation that he can address; to persist with genuine tolerance in his efforts despite the child's provoking behavior, or to recognize when the limits of his own tolerance have been exceeded, a difficult thing for a zealous therapist to admit to himself; and to recall what he knows from past experience is possible to achieve, despite the discouragements that this work so often generates. In the final analysis, each therapist must judge for himself when physical intervention is indicated. Perhaps nothing will teach a therapist how to behave integratively with a patient short of the self-scrutiny that comes with many playroom sessions, his growing knowledge of a particular child, including details of past and current history, and the review of his work with similarly interested colleagues as well as increased self-knowledge and self-analysis or his therapeutic work with a mentor who can help him understand present ambivalence about restraint in terms of his genetic understanding of these experiences in his own past.

PARENTAL CONFLICTS

The psychogenic hypothesis of the etiology of childhood schizophrenia imposes the task and obligation of searching for the roots of the child's behavior in his experiences from birth on with the manifestations of those parental conflicts that affect him. Therefore, although this presentation is primarily concerned with Mark, a few words about his parents seem indicated.

The Reisners are both intelligent and responsible individuals who are, by societal standards, well adjusted. Mr. Reisner has successfully built up a business that provides for his family of five children. Mrs. Reisner manages the household carefully and well. They own their own home and desire to and are able to educate their children through college.

Mr. Reisner is a handsome, graying man who, though foreign-born, speaks English with only a trace of accent. He is especially sensitive to nuances of language and his speech sometimes takes on a poetic quality. He has a phenomenal memory and is able to recall telephone numbers even from childhood and to describe places he has visited, accurately remembering the contours of hills and the appearance of vegetation. Yet, he has made three mistakes in writing down a four-line order, has misplaced lists of customers he has taken special pains to prepare, and has mislaid important business notes. On several occasions he forgot to close the door behind him before starting his interview and twice seated himself on the hard-backed chair that serves as a foot stool, placing his feet on the soft arm chair on which he usually sat, without detecting his error. Hating detail, he obsessively overloads himself with paper work at the expense of time he might otherwise use for selling or for spontaneously participating in family life.

Mrs. Reisner is a slim, attractive woman usually dressed casually and tastefully. She is intelligent, observant, and highly intuitive. Despite these superior capacities she is extremely self-belittling, perhaps because she often fails, quite consciously, to implement her awareness of what is in her best interest. "I know, but I ignore what I know." Thus, despite her capacity to discern better alternatives she disregards them, reducing her own "liability to persuasion." She speaks with her jaws almost immobile and forms her words mostly through lip movements. She is capable of speaking distinctly, but when she is uneasy, her sentences tend to trail off inaudibly. If asked to repeat a word indistinctly expressed, she becomes embarrassed and seldom complies for fear she has or might commit a "malaprop." Her face readily indicates the play of affect. It is relatively easy to know when she is anxious, depressed, or happy. Anger is revealed by a slight narrowing of her eyelids. Crying occurs infrequently, causing her to bang her fist angrily against the chair arm at a display of such childishness. She presents a curious paradox of order and disorder. Her clothes are usually clean and neat, as are her children's. Yet shirts and blouses may have been ironed just in time to come to the clinic. The bedroom she shares with her husband is called the jungle by him, having become a catchall for papers, books, and clothes.

It is tidied on rare occasions, usually when company is expected. As the family and business bookkeeper, she falls three to six months behind in her entries. Yet they are neat and thorough when they are eventually done. She relies on her husband's prodigious memory, at the expense of his time and patience, to supply details she has forgotten or never knew, and on his ability to find the lost or misfiled documents she needs. Her chronic lateness for appointments manages to be exactly seven minutes, quite a precise inaccuracy in view of the fact that she must drive about an hour to the clinic for each visit. To make amends for the day's procrastination, she stays up until the early morning hours to do her chores. Consequently, she sleeps late, is again guiltily behind in her duties, and, often by default, delegates the job of getting Mark fed and off to school to her husband who is usually up early to undertake his never ending business details. Resentful because of the interruptions to his schedule, but afraid to rebel openly, he responds with outward compliance. As a result, he has been too impatient to foster Mark's ability to do for himself in many ways. It is probable that Mark's inability to comb his hair, a simpler performance than tieing his shoes, which he learned at age eight, and his recent regressive preoccupation with putting on his clothes and taking them off is related to his father's impatient efforts to dress him on so many mornings when his mother is making up for lost sleep. Perhaps such preoccupation with herself in this circular manner, maybe intensified for external reasons when Mark was an infant, accounts for the fact that there is little data about how his early learning and curiosity were facilitated or discouraged.

First attempts of Mrs. Reisner to teach Mark academic skills at about age eight met with gratifying success. He learned colors and words with surprising rapidity for his level of functioning. However, when he subsequently showed resistance to learning, she alternated between pressuring him and giving up trying to teach him for weeks and months at a time. Mr. Reisner, who had resisted his own parents' supervision of his school work ("I used to study the carvings on the desk as my mother tried to help me with my school work"), could not tolerate most efforts made with Mark, whether pressured or not. His repeated statement was, "He'll learn when he's ready." Rarely did he advance concrete notions of how Mark might be helped to learn, other than recommending, when an issue became pressing, that he be left alone. It was not always certain whether "he" was Mark or himself. Nevertheless, Mark was enrolled in a special class at school where he formed an important and productive relationship with a school teacher which lasted for four years.

Significant details of critical events in the parents' interaction are hard to determine. The parents, especially Mr. Reisner, had difficulty in noting those moments when each hurt the other, provoking angry, hostile feelings. The anxious climate generated by a series of such occasions often escaped their notice, but had a negative effect on Mark. Sometimes when it became too intense he called what they were doing to their attention by becoming visibly agitated or by leaving their presence to go to his room. Mrs. Reisner's almost ever present tendency to procrastinate was a recurrent theme that contributed to building up tense situations.

One such situation started when Mrs. Reisner tried to include Mark in the purchase of a Christmas present for one of the family. She drove halfway to the store before she realized that she had forgotten her money. She could have charged the present but felt that if Mark did not actually pay for it in cash himself or see it paid for he might not acquire the real sense of participating in this purchase. She stopped at a gasoline station where she was known, to cash a check, but the station was already closed for the night. She then drove to a store where she often shopped, induced Mark to accompany her into the store lest he wander away if left alone in the car, and managed to make out the check without any misbehavior from Mark. As she was cashing the check, perhaps in sensitive reaction to anxious clues from her of which she was not aware, he walked behind the counter and began some of his bizarre, ritualistic movements, to the awed puzzlement of onlooking customers and to her consternation and embarrassment. In desperation, she said, "I'll give you anything, just come outside with me." Fortunately for her, he complied with her urgent plea. They drove home together (mother stated they were too unnerved to buy the present) both of them silent and dejected.

The next day she picked him up at school and ran out of gas on a busy thoroughfare. She was again fearful that Mark would prove difficult and she had many anxious moments deciding how she would manage with him, e.g., should she leave him in the car while she went for gasoline?; if she took him with her, would he bolt?, etc. Luckily, a passing motorist arranged to have gasoline sent from a nearby filling station. They arrived home in time to go to the clinic with Mr. Reisner. He was interviewed first, then left on a business errand while Mrs. Reisner and Mark were being seen, planning to call for them after their interviews. However, he telephoned to say he was unavoidably detained and Mrs. Reisner agreed to take Mark home by train.

On the way home Mark behaved "beautifully," but his mother remained apprehensive that he might draw attention to himself by his rituals or that he might balk when it was time to get off the train. Therefore, she got him out of his seat early and waited with him in the open end of the car for about the last five miles of their journey. It was raining hard and both were drenched when they arrived at the station. She called home from a public telephone for Sally to fetch them in their second car. For some reason she dialed the wrong number. As she dropped her last dime into the slot Mark bolted towards the tracks. She chased him, fearful that he might be run down by the commuter trains. Again, fortunately, he responded to her pleas and returned to the station with her. She was able to make change, reached Sally, and returned home without further incident.

Only two days later there was another family incident following Mrs. Reisner's and Mark's return from the dentist. They had been forced that day, by Mark's increasingly active opposition, to abandon orthodontic correction of his protuberant front teeth. This decision must have been an important defeat for both of them. Mark found it difficult to dress himself for the trip to the clinic. When he was finally ready Mrs. Reisner pressed the buzzer to her husband's office, signalling that they were ready to go. Busy on the telephone, he did not respond. He told me, "Sometimes when she buzzes me I drop my work immediately. When I get there, I have to wait." By the time he answered Mark had taken off his coat, which Mrs. Reisner felt was his way of saying that he did not want to go—at least she was not prepared to struggle to make him put it on again. Mr. Reisner reported to me, "I asked Mark if he wanted to go to the clinic and he said 'Yes'—so I told him to put on his coat, which he promptly did. My wife still didn't believe it, so she, too, asked him if he wanted to go and, again, he said 'Yes.'" Because of the delay all this entailed Mrs. Reisner went to the telephone to inform me that they would be late for the appointment. Mr. Reisner, in a hurry to get started and probably feeling guilty that he had not responded to the buzzer sooner, said that if she took time to call he would have to drive fast. While he rationalized to me that his urging immediate departure was to prevent Mark's obstructing tactics, which are precipitated by any hesitation or delay, he must have known how terrified his wife is of his fast driving. When rushed, he makes it a point to tailgate cars in front of him, forcing them to move over. Her reaction was to say that she did not want to risk danger and announced that she and Mark would not accompany him. Capitulating, Mr. Reisner said he would drive slowly, but to no avail for she now adamantly refused to go with him. Perhaps to save face with me, he came to the clinic alone, feeling much the culprit and, no doubt, feeling blamed by me for causing his wife's non-appearance, something that his discouraged wife may well have revengefully wished.

EXTERNAL EVENTS

As Mark was approaching pubescence the anxious climate that pervaded the family, rooted in the internal conflicts of each of them, was made more stormy by external events. Mary, the oldest child, who adroitly circumvented her mother's injunctions during adolescence was now, at age 18, openly rebellious and defiant. The father, who stood helplessly by when his wife and his own mother differed, felt equally inept when his wife and daughter were at odds. He rationalized his dilemmas and uncertainties to me at these times by saying that his wife was inordinately restrictive, but he seldom ventured constructive suggestions. When relations between Mary and her mother approached open crisis, and guiltily stirred by his wife's importuning that he do something, he would sometimes arrange an out-of-home dinner with Mary for a father-daughter talk. Rather than speaking to her of pertinent issues, let alone resolving them, he most often settled for a "friendly understanding with her." The impasses at home grew more frequent and more intense.

By the time Mark started back to school in the fall when he was thirteen, tension in the home was high. It was augmented when the parents heard rumors that the school personnel's job assignments were threatened. Perhaps the increased anxiety both at home and at school plus the endocrine effect inherent in Mark's emerging adolescence might have been enough to account for the appearance of new behavior, alarming in its implications for Mark's continuing in school, namely, "exposing himself" by taking off his trousers. Further anxiety was engendered by the fact Mr. Reisner was being pressured by his principal supplier, pushing for increased volume, to add a salesman. Mr. Reisner had always felt that too good a salesman was a potential business rival while too poor a one would cost too much in money and in the time it would take to teach him. Nevertheless, he yielded and hired a salesman in January, coinciding with Mark's transfer from his long-term, very productive teacher to a different class and teacher. We never clearly understood why he was transferred. No doubt his continuing disruptive behavior played some part. His new teacher, challenged to succeed with him for her own personal reasons, persuaded him to resume the preprimer work he had abandoned. However, he soon began to demand all her time. When she turned to work with other children he found ways to plague and to annoy her. Eventually he reacted to her irritation and desperation by more often exposing himself, inviting complaints from the mothers of several girl pupils. While the principal felt he could deal with this problem, Mrs. Reisner was embarrassed enough to investigate Mark's eligibility for the public school self-help program. Soon more embarrassed by further reports of Mark's provocative behavior, she kept him out of school altogether and then placed him in a newly opened private day-care school for the emotionally disturbed. Incidentally, while school matters were discussed with the father at home, he seldom raised such issues with me. In all probability he yielded to his wife's anxieties. In effect, many of the decisions affecting Mark were hers with his tacit, though ambivalent, consent.

In June, Mark was accepted by the self-help class for the fall session. His teacher was to be the former principal of the school Mark had attended for many years, who had been demoted to classroom teaching for reasons not known to us. That same month, the paternal grandmother came for a visit. As her visit became extended, tension increased in all family members.

In September, several things occurred. It became unmistakenly evident that the salesman Mr. Reisner had hired and paid for with money the paternal grandmother had given them, was and had been costing more time and money than he was worth. Mr. Reisner's efforts to assuage a litiginous customer was threatening to lose him an important supplier. The Reisner's learned from Mark that two youthful, male paternal relatives had coerced him into sexual play. Lastly, on the very day Mrs. Reisner heard that her mother was seriously ill with possible cancer, Mark developed a new symptom, namely, not chewing his food.

Shortly afterwards, while Mrs. Reisner was debating whether to visit her mother on the East Coast, considering whether they could afford the money for the trip, and how to get rid of the salesman (who resigned the following January at the Reisners' request), Mark developed another new symptom labelled "tracing" by his father. This was an elaborate ritual with many variations. For example, he would scrape his toe along the whole length of a room where the floor met the wall or, with his foot, would repeatedly touch the bases of door frames before going through them. He would also touch the legs of chairs, over and over again with his feet, sometimes crossing his legs to complete a pattern known only to him. Other rituals occurred.

Soon Mrs. Reisner reported she was becoming afraid of Mark's violent rages, especially that he might open the car door and jump out during the ride to and from the clinic. She reported recurrences of aura-like feelings that she had not experienced for years. Mr. Reisner complained that Mark was spitting inordinately, was picking at his cuticles until they bled, was less tidy about his toilet habits, and was taking an interminable time to dress.

While some of the rituals were seen in the waiting room, Mark exhibited very little of this new form of disturbed behavior in the playroom. However, a new indecisiveness appeared. For example, he would not or could not finish assembling a key chain and key, a procedure he had formerly concluded rapidly and deftly. He would put the chain through the hole in the key, remove it, turn the key around, insert the chain again, remove

This th. has been going on 9 yrs!

it, and so forth for long periods of time. Sometimes the task was not completed until it was interrupted by the hour's end.

I became sick just before Christmas and was away from work for about two weeks. I saw Mrs. Reisner only once in a joint interview with her husband before she went East to visit her mother who, incidentally, recovered from her illness. I would have preferred an individual meeting with her but the pressure of time precluded this. My next individual interview with her occurred after about seven weeks.

While Mrs. Reisner was away, Mr. Reisner looked after all the children. When interviews with Mark were resumed, approximately 25 days after my last meeting with him, he seemed quite upset. By the time Mrs. Reisner returned he was in a frantic state. He was restless, paced up and down in the waiting room, was occupied with rituals, or stood in one spot flipping the pages of a magazine without looking at its contents. He came reluctantly to the playroom and seemed inconsolable.

His attendance at school was cut to half-time because of his disturbed and disturbing behavior. In a conference held with our staff in early February, school personnel felt that school was becoming antitherapeutic for Mark and alerted us to the probability that he might soon be excluded. His teacher (former principal) was present at this conference and, while he professed hope for Mark's improvement and argued for his continuance at school, it seemed clear to me that he was approaching his own limits of tolerance with Mark.

On Mrs. Reisner's return there was visible reduction of Mark's frenetic behavior for a while. I felt that, had she not been away, Mark might not have regressed as much as he had or in the way he did. However, Mr. Reisner soon again reported an increase in Mark's disturbance at home. He found he could not attend to work because of the attention Mark required, and was falling far behind soliciting and processing holiday business, with the time limit for seasonal selling rapidly approaching.

In mid-February the parents phoned me early one morning upset by Mark, who, the previous night, had gotten out of bed, naked, and had rushed angrily at Mrs. Reisner. He was returned to bed but in the early morning hours he took his bed apart in a frenzy. The next day, after a good night, Mrs. Reisner reported that Mark was much better after our telephone conversation and that she had been able to deal with him during the day. However, he became more upset over the weekend and continued to be so disturbed that admission to the acute treatment service was requested by the parents. After seven weeks of hospitalization he was discharged and continued to receive large doses of Thorazine, which has reduced his agitation and made him more compliant. However, his behavior has otherwise not improved. The parents' former assurance about their ability to understand his behavior in order to correct it or to be firm with him when indicated, or to examine their own counter feelings that interplayed with his emotions was now replaced by the fear that he would become too oppositional to take the mollifying medication and they would again be faced with an unsolvable crisis. Mark developed a large rectal prolapse during his hospitalization requiring manual reduction with the associated problem of toilet hygiene. Mark's difficulty in responding to his parents' instructions in toileting increased parental tension.

ANGER AND AUTHORITY

Some of the lessons Mark learned in the playroom and from the beneficial results of his parents' therapy were evidenced by his unique bids for help when struggling with hostile impulses. For example, he would approach his mother with a statement such as "Don't you hit Johnny," a signal that he was fighting against an impulse to act, possibly in retaliation to something Johnny had done, said, or implied. Thus alerted, the parents often were able to inquire about and to settle problems before they got out of hand.

Once, however, after Johnny had "told on him," Mark, long before he grew too big and strong to manage physically, became so enraged that he threw a hammer, barely missing his brother's head. Mr. Reisner was away on a long business trip and Mrs. Reisner, frightened and furious, called me on the telephone insisting that I do something immediately to place Mark either on our ward or elsewhere. She demanded prompt action to get him out of the home and became even more enraged when I asked if she could wait until our next appointment two days hence. Recognizing her panic, I inquired whether there was any continuing danger to Johnny if she and the two older daughters provided the necessary supervision, and she eventually quieted and agreed she could wait.

When Mrs. Reisner came for her appointment, she refused our offer to admit Mark to our ward, feeling hospitalization was no longer indicated. She had arranged separate bedrooms for the boys who until then had shared the same room. Although still shaken by the experience, she spontaneously commented that, in some way, the freer display of emotions by herself and other family members had had beneficial effects despite the recent crisis. Now that she was more frequently recognizing her anger before it became suppressed (resulting in either a state of helplessness or precipitating a hostile tirade) she had learned to express it more directly and simply. In turn, Mark, more and more, glared unmistakably when annoyed or angry instead of looking blank or acting submissive and withdrawn. In general, he had

become more assertive and alert. The other children had by themselves come
to the realization that their own displays of uncontrolled violence were
setting a "poor example for him."

The work with Mark and his parents clearly indicated it is potentially
more productive to identify angry feelings and, if need be, to express them
even vehemently in words rather than to permit their conversion, by default,
into behavior that is impulsively destructive, tensely inhibited, slyly manifested, ineptly disclosed, etc. Inability to express such angry feelings simply
and directly in words rather than through their symptomatic derivatives,
of which a hostile verbal attack is one example and physical punishment
another, maintains conflict and negatively affects the individual's capacity
to exercise concise authority and self-discipline.

A variety of fused, conflicted feelings are implicated in the parent's difficulty in exercising meaningful authority toward his child and in the child's
malintegrated behavior (see Chapter 2 of this volume). Those feeling components that emerge into awareness through psychotherapy and thus find
affectual expression, rather than behavioral, contribute to the reduction of
conflict and to improved behavior. Among these many feelings are those of
helplessness. When identified and even sometimes verbally expressed, helplessness may be relieved enough for a parent to be effctive with his rebellious
child. Anger emerging from conflict is more readily recognized than helplessness, perhaps because anger is a more intense feeling and maybe a less
complicated one. The changes subsequent to the appearance of anger rather
than hostile aggression (which can appear when anger is suppressed) are
sometimes dramatic such as the individual's renewed unambivalent capacity
to exercise authority which was absent a few moments before. Other "describable and essential elements contribute to the quality of firmness on the part
of an authority" (2).

CONCLUSION

I have attempted to show how individual psychotherapy with a psychotic
child can teach the therapist something about the precise conflict state in
the psychopathology of the child and aspects of it in himself. Concomitant
therapeutic work with the parent may effect enough reduction in conflict so
that he may exercise his authority in a way which is more integrative for
his child and, therefore, more satisfying to himself than it had been before.
Aside from contributing to meaningful psychotherapeutic work in all its
forms, this knowledge can improve understanding of what motivates distortions in human behavior and can suggest therapeutic means (persuasion in
its finest sense) to effect favorable changes in behavior.

REFERENCES

1. HOLT, E. B. *The Freudian Wish and Its Place in Ethics.* Chapter IV. Henry Holt and Co., 1915.
2. SZUREK, S. A. Emotional Factors in the Use of Authority. In *Public Health Is People.* New York: Commonwealth Fund, 1950. Reprinted in S. A. Szurek and I. N. Berlin (Eds.), *The Antisocial Child, His Family and His Community.* Vol. 4. *The Langley Porter Child Psychiatry Series.* Palo Alto, Calif.: Science and Behavior Books, 1969.
3. SZUREK, S. A. and BERLIN, I. N. Elements of Psychotherapeutics with the Schizophrenic Child and His Parents. *Psychiatry,* 1956, 19:1-9. Reprinted in S. A. Szurek and I. N. Berlin (Eds.), *Training in Therapeutic Work with Children.* Vol. 2. *The Langley Porter Child Psychiatry Series.* Palo Alto, Calif.: Science and Behavior Books, 1967. See Chapter 9, this volume.
4. WHITEHEAD, A. N. *Adventure of Ideas.* A Mentor Book published by the New American Library, May, 1958, p. 90.

30

Simultaneous Psychotherapy with a Psychotic Child and Both Parents: The Reversal of Mutism

Irving N. Berlin, M.D.

Irving N. Berlin, M.D.

EARLY THERAPEUTIC WORK WITH THIS FAMILY

We saw Teddy from ages 5½ to almost 12 on our inpatient service. He had been mute since birth, having said only a few words like "momma" and "da da" for a very short period of time around age three. We report this case primarily because it indicates that a child who has been mute for a good many years can learn to talk and that the simultaneous psychotherapeutic work with the child and his parents which relieves the conflicts in and between them may be of sufficient help, even at the age of 10 to bring about speech. We also describe this family and our work with them because this is one of the instances in which the parents had another child during the course of psychotherapy and can report differences in their attitudes toward the new infant and toward each other during that period as compared to the period around the birth and infancy of the psychotic child and the other children in the family. This case also illustrates one of the other issues which has been alluded to in several other papers, that is, our sense that in some instances the psychosis of childhood seems to be the obverse of an acting out, hostile, delinquent kind of behavior which may be seen in other members of the same family. This was also true in this instance. One further outstanding feature in this case was the fact that the mutism was with a marked self-destructiveness, hitting and slapping of himself on the face, with such ferocity that at times we feared he would inflict serious self-injury. His self-destructiveness created a difficult bind for both the therapist and

---

I am indebted to Dr. Edward Liska for sharing his clinical material with me.

the ward staff. He was able to utilize the destructive, self-slapping behavior as a way, not only of obtaining attention, but also as a way of enforcing certain kinds of behaviors from both his parents and the therapeutic staff. He appeared anxious around any progress that indicated his own capacity to deal with aspects of learning or environment in a more effective way. Momentary relaxation on the part of the staff with the feeling that Teddy was then beginning to come out of it and could do more for himself resulted in the vigorous slapping at his face until it was bright red which again brought staff or parents to his side to restrain him and which seemed to negate the movement toward independence which he had just seemed to attain.

It is impossible in this paper to give many of the details of psychotherapy for a period of over six years which would very precisely delineate the intra-familial problems as well as the exact sequence of the difficulties that beset our patient early in his life. Teddy was seen for 878 playtherapy sessions, Mother was seen 615 times, Father was seen 530 times. It is certainly impossible to detail the 6½ years of psychotherapeutic work with four changes of therapists. However, for the purposes of our discussion we will simply highlight some of the critical issues both from the history of the child and both parents as well as from the psychotherapeutic work, focusing primarily on the kinds of therapeutic processes which seemed to help both the child and parents to make continuous progress. This resulted in this youngster, at more than 10 years of age, beginning to use speech, after a time fluently, and being able to leave the inpatient ward, enter special education classes in a regular school, and finally to enter a regular school and to matriculate at his age level. When last we heard, our patient, Teddy, at age 20, was still a rather retiring young man but had done reasonably well in business college and was employed and able to earn his own living as a secretary-bookkeeper. Subsequent follow up has been difficult due to the parents' moving.

The therapy of each family member will be divided into the introductory phase with the first therapist, work with the second and third therapists, and finally the last phase of therapeutic work with the fourth therapist.

PAST HISTORY AND PRESENT ILLNESS OF TEDDY

Teddy is the second of three boys, one two years older and one three years younger than Teddy. Mother's pregnancy was essentially normal; although labor was some 36 hours in length, no instruments were used. He weighed over seven pounds, cried spontaneously, and there was no evidence of neonatal distress.

The period prior to Teddy's birth was an extremely difficult one for both parents. Father, a member of the armed services, had just been informed that he would not be promoted and would be retired in a few years, upon attaining 30 years of service. For the first time in their 10 years of married life they had been living continuously together for over a year. Previously, Father had been on overseas duty most of the time with very short periods of family reunion. During each of these periods, because of their many problems and increasing estrangement and difficulty in verbalization, both parents felt constrained not to speak of their problems with each other and in the family. There was no open discussion of the family and personal problems resulting from military life. Father was particularly bitter because Mother had been unwilling to do the kind of entertaining which was important in an officer's life, and Mother was especially bitter that Father dealt with her and the children as he would with a military command, by simply giving orders and expecting instant obedience.

Thus Teddy was born at a time when Father was a post commander on a very small and isolated post, extremely unhappy and uneasy with his wife because he was involved in an extramarital affair about which his wife had some suspicion and massive, silent anger. The oldest child had a severe flare up of rheumatic fever and was hospitalized for several months during the pregnancy which was also of great concern to both parents, but especially Mother. Within two weeks after Teddy's birth, Father was detached from his post and given a foreign assignment. Mother was left with a newborn infant and her young son who was recuperating from rheumatic fever and required a great deal of care.

Teddy was described as a very quiet and contented infant who took his bottle well. If necessary, it could be propped, and he made no fuss when Mother was otherwise busy with household tasks and her older, convalescing son.

Upon Father's return, three months later, Teddy did not seem to know him at all, and Father said he felt hurt and resentful. At six months of age, Teddy fell from his parents' bed and subsequently developed a fear of their bedroom and the overhead light in it. He also began to exhibit a fear of the sound of airplanes that were flying overhead and began to scream and could not be comforted whenever squadrons of planes came over their base. He was also fearful of the objects in the bathroom, especially rushing water in the toilet which made toilet training extremely difficult. This was accomplished at 18 months of age.

He had the usual childhood diseases without complications. His motor development was normal except that walking occurred late, when he was about 15 months of age. However, he became very dexterous and very fleet of foot and was extremely nimble and agile by the age of two. Father relates an incident of having taken his eyes off Teddy for a moment at three years of age and suddenly finding him at the top of a flag pole in front of their cottage. He had shinnied to the top and was screaming with fright because he didn't know how to get down. Father had to get the fire department and its ladder to rescue Teddy.

Father and Mother also described the apparent indifference that Teddy had to danger around him. They described a variety of instances in which he had almost walked off a cliff, almost walked off the street corner into a passing car, and had several bad falls, one when he had simply walked off the edge of the garden wall and dropped about ten feet. Another time while swinging, he simply let go when he was up in the air. He dropped about eight feet without any apparent injury but was terribly frightened. When he was two years of age, the family was moved to a new post and at that time Father again was sent on a variety of overseas assignments. At this time Teddy began to soil himself whereas he had been completely toilet trained.

When Teddy was three years of age his younger brother, George, was born. At this time, Teddy had said no words although he was thought by his grandmother to have said "ma ma" on one occasion. However, he made his needs known by vocalization and gesturing, pushing people in the direction he wanted them to go so that there seemed little need for him to actually talk. From six months on, Teddy's most frequent and welcome companion was his older brother, Sandy. He played with Teddy, talked to him, and when Teddy could walk and run, they roamed the base together for hours on end. Mother said she was concerned but relieved to have them out of sight. Both parents describe this period from birth to about three years of age as an extremely tense and difficult one for them. Mother was very depressed, feeling that she had failed again as a mother. The older son, Sandy, then 5½ and in kindergarten, was having considerable trouble because of his aggressiveness and his stealing from other children, despite the fact that he was a very bright, verbal and alert youngster who was physically very athletic and personable. The school's complaints, her husband's constant anger with her, and Teddy's failure to develop speech and social skills all seemed to indicate to Mother that she was a failure as a mother and a wife.

When Teddy was 3½ years old there was a series of events which increased family tensions. His maternal grandmother died of a stroke and within a month, Father was returned from his overseas duty with severe hepatitis and he was hospitalized. During this period Teddy was hyperactive, in constant motion during the day, and kept the family awake at night with his bedrocking and crying. He wet himself very frequently and had become destructive to some of the furnishings. Especially annoying to Mother was his jumping and bouncing on the couches and beds which seemed to be one of the few diversions that he enjoyed. At the same time he began to slap his thigh and somewhat later he began to slap his face. Although Father doesn't recall the details of the onset of the slapping, Mother believes it followed a spanking by Father when Teddy began to bite his Father in the midst of a demanded kiss. Father hit him very hard. When he was nearly four years old Teddy was first examined in the local hospital, and an EEG was done which they thought was abnormal. He was seen by a well-known child psychiatrist in a nearby metropolis who then made the diagnosis of childhood psychosis. This examination when Teddy was four years of age provides data that his behavior was hyperactive. He ran around the playroom touching the toys, had a very short attention span, and would not involve himself with the psychiatrist or with any of the materials in the playroom. Whenever he was frustrated in his efforts to break something, he would begin to scream and hit himself in the face. He made no attempt to speak, although he seemed to understand instructions well. His responses to some of the subtests of the Merrill-Palmer suggested that in certain areas he functioned at his age level. He did a picture puzzle at his age level and was able to do some items from the performance scale of the WISC at or above his age level. The psychiatrist suggested that Teddy was an appropriate patient for our inpatient setting, and the family brought Teddy to see us. After inpatient admission, Father applied for a transfer to the Bay Area which was granted.

INPATIENT ADMISSION EVALUATION

Teddy was admitted as an inpatient at five years of age. Examinations were all within normal limits, including the EEG which in no way resembled the report we had received from the previous hospital. Repeated electroencephalograms continued to be normal throughout his hospitalization. Psychological examinations could not be carried out due to his hyperactivity and negativism. Teddy was a handsome, brown-haired, sturdy five year old. He screeched to gain attention and was in constant motion. When this motion was stopped in order to engage him in a structured activity or to take him to meals, he slapped his face very hard and often had to be restrained. He needed to be held and fed, although he would feed himself with utensils on occasions. He ignored both adults and children, and when a staff member sought eye contact, he would turn his head, slap himself, and dart away. At night he slept little and often wandered the ward. Bouncing on beds was his favorite activity. At the end of the five-day evaluation all the staff members' observations pointed to a diagnosis of childhood psychosis, core type, that is, with onset prior to two years of age, characterized by isolation, mutism, and massive anxiety in interpersonal relations with family or staff.

MOTHER'S PAST HISTORY

Mother, at the time of Teddy's admission, was 34 years of age and extremely attractive. She was constantly deprecating her accomplishments, her appearance, and her capacities for being an effective mother and wife. She was the youngest of three sisters. The older two were five and seven years her senior, and thus she had little to do with them because they left home for further finishing school while she was still young. Her father was a prominent politician who died when she was 15 years of age. Her mother died during the period of general stress when Teddy was 3½ years of age. She was an attractive child and young woman. She at first described herself as very close to her mother and father, but later she described her estrangement from her mother whose social life involved her in a variety of politically-important activities which kept her away from home. Mother read a good deal and spent most of her time with housekeepers as companions. Her recollections of her father are very vivid. He was a very colorful and positive man who was effective in everything he did. She recalls her relationships with him very tenderly. She often contrasted him with her husband who tended to be much more withdrawn and much less spontaneous than her father who was the ebulient type. Her father always joked and interacted with people easily. Mother contrasted her sense of inadequacy in her social life as an officer's wife with her mother who was never at a loss socially and who entertained a great deal. She also felt her mother had a tremendous amount of support from her zestful father to whom people were constantly attracted. Mother believed her mother and father had complimented each other and were able to work together toward common interests. She felt that she and her husband had never attained that kind of intimacy nor capacity to evolve common goals. Mother described that although her father was very busy with political campaigns, he was nevertheless frequently home so that there was a good deal of home life. She felt her mother and father had the opportunity to know each other both early, prior to her own birth, and until her father's death when she was 15 years old. She expressed a great deal of bitterness that her own mother remarried, scarcely a year after her father's death, to a younger man who promptly squandered their inheritance. The loss of her father resulted in a year-long depression with little recall of that year. She wondered how she passed in high school, and after only a year of college, she had to go to work. She worked for several attorneys as a secretary and office manager and then later was the office manager for a number of physicians. Oddly, Mother has no recall about when she learned to type, take dictation, etc. She felt she had always performed these jobs for her father. It was while working in the doctors' office that she met her husband. She described herself as a lonely, isolated young woman with very few friends. One of the physicians in the office was a friend of her husband's and introduced them. They both seemed to be searching for someone to be with and began to go out together. After a period of two months they were engaged.

FATHER'S PAST HISTORY

At the time of Teddy's admission, Father was 43 years of age, was a senior officer in the military and a graduate of one of the academies. He has memories of violent quarrels between his parents who were separated and divorced when he was five years of age. He and a younger brother were then placed in a foster home for several years until his mother married an Army officer, and the boys joined their mother. Father greatly admired his new stepfather, but after four years his mother divorced him and married two more times prior to the time Teddy's father left to enter one of the academies. He felt estranged from his mother as well as from his younger brother. While he was an outstanding athlete in high school and an excellent student, Father did not come into his own until he entered the service academy and there he became an outstanding cadet, academically and athletically, as well as an outstanding officer who seemed to find the routine and ritual of the service comforting and fitting to his own needs. He recalls the anger of the enlisted men who worked under him at his obsessive concern with very small details during inspections. Father described his intense preoccupation with all detail, both important and unimportant alike, throughout his various commands in the service. He recalls that he felt his marriage to Mother was an opportunity to experience the closeness for which he had been searching. However, only shortly after he was married, he was called overseas on a special assignment. From then on Father and Mother were constantly separated for military reasons. Father had an outstanding military record during the war and he had earned many decorations. During his first extended tour of duty in the United States, he and his wife were able to live together for a period of more than a year, right after Teddy was conceived. This was the period of extreme difficulty and strain for both of them. They found they were unable to communicate. Father found much of the closeness for which he had been looking and hoped would be there was absent. Their brief period of honeymoon after each of his stints of overseas duty never gave him the opportunity to test out how they might live together and what kind of closeness and intimacy they might be able to acquire. Thus he regarded his wife as quite withdrawn and non-communicative, his children as strangers, and his very small post command as very irksome. He turned to find other ways of getting personal satisfaction and understanding and became involved in a love affair with a woman in a nearby town. His wife's awareness of this affair prior to the birth of Teddy led Father to request another overseas assignment which he was granted shortly after Teddy's birth.

THERAPEUTIC WORK WITH TEDDY: OVERVIEW

When he was first seen Teddy was a sturdy five year old, very attractive, brown hair, and with a ruddy complexion which we soon learned was the result of his constant slapping of himself when he was frustrated in any of the activities in which he liked to engage, like jumping on beds, playing with tinkertoys in a solitary fashion, or listening to the radio. He would slap himself if somebody intervened and wanted to bring him into the classroom with other children, involve him in group activities, or involve him in any interactions with the nurses. When his therapist came to take him to the playroom, he slapped himself until held.

Therapeutic work with Teddy can be divided into three phases. The first two had to do with the introduction to a new therapist. Teddy had four of them. The first therapist was only there for a few months. There were recurrent problems in helping Teddy to trust and interact with the therapist and to become involved in playtherapy. The second phase centered around Teddy's beginning to become very much more assertive in his behavior with his therapist, the nursing staff, and other children as he began to work with each therapist. He became much more assertive in his play activities in the playroom as well as on the ward and began to look pleased and to smile while playing and doing non-verbal tasks in the school room. At the end of the tenure of each of his therapists there was a period of very marked regression with a great deal of self-slapping. However, each period of therapeutic involvement was characterized by a much longer period of integrative play, and the period of regression and self-hurting was less intense and of shorter duration.

The constant people in his life on the ward such as the nurses, the school teacher, and the occupational therapist seemed better able, as the years went by, to help Teddy with each of these very difficult periods.

It is not possible to prove that the coming and going of therapists evoked similar anxieties that both Teddy and his mother experienced around the frequent coming and going of his Father with resultant stresses. However, it should be noted that Mother reacted to the departure of each of her therapists with great difficulty and was unable to feel at all convinced that the next therapist could be helpful to her until they had had a period of working together in which there was intense testing of the new therapist. Most hostility was expressed toward the previous therapist for leaving and toward the present therapist for not understanding her and making her "go through the same thing all over again."

Father, on the contrary, seemed to have very little difficulty in making the transition from one therapist to another, although it is quite clear that he was most able to relate to the female therapist who saw him for the longest period of time.

Therapeutic work with Teddy was also enhanced by a growing relationship with one of the women psychiatric aides on the ward. She was able to engage him in a very non-defensive way, to play with him, take him on walks, and especially to be quite playful with this somber, rigid-appearing, and anxiety-provoking child. She was the only one who could tickle Teddy and get him to smile and later to laugh.

The fact that Teddy would at the slightest provocation begin to slap himself audibly so that others could hear impelled the adults who were with him to hold him, try to control and minimize his self-hurting. Rather than expressing their own feelings when they felt helpless to understand his problems and to try to get him to verbalize them or at least to indicate what the difficulty was, they had to quickly immobilize him and hope he would settle down. They experienced that their comments increased the slapping and their bind. Thus, rather than to deal with the anxiety in Teddy and their feelings in a much more forthright way and to engage him in activity which might be more helpful to him and help him feel more effective as a child, they felt stuck and under constant scrutiny when the audible slapping occurred.

It was first noted in the school room, some six to eight months after admission, that the school teacher who was an extremely competent, experienced, matter-of-fact person, was able to contain Teddy's slapping with a very firm, "no, you're not going to start that again, I want you to get back to your work."

It became clear with his third therapist, toward the end of four years (three years with two other therapists) of work, that Teddy was asking to have his hands held, not just because he wanted to hurt himself and test the therapist, but also because he was now enjoying the contact. That therapist was trying to help him recognize that he could have contact without the same kind of teasing which would end up in his hurting himself by asking for it or simply putting his hand out. The fact that physical contact became possible without self-hurt led Teddy to go around and hold his hands out to a number of people who worked with him on the ward. There was very much less of a teasing or angry look in his eyes as he playfully held his hands out to establish contact with the therapist or staff members.

Again, it was the nurse's aide who was able to do more than simply hold his hands. She was able to put her arms around him and to cuddle him a bit which was impossible for anyone else to do and from Mother's report, very difficult for her. She reported, however, that during this period when there was more actual pleasurable physical contact and a seeking out of such contact, Teddy was much easier to handle at home and would simply hold her own hand occasionaly rather than jumping on the couch or striking out at one of the younger children which she knew was a prelude to his slapping.

PLEASURABLE HOLDING VERSUS SELF-HURT

In the playroom during the fourth year of therapeutic work, Teddy began his usual roaming around, touching toys on the shelves, and flipping some of them on the floor. After about ten minutes the floor was covered with toy vehicles, blocks, dolls, etc., and the therapist attempted his usual engagement of Teddy in helping pick up the toys and put them back on the shelf; or alternatively, the therapist replaced some toys while Teddy began to play with the others on the floor, glancing at the therapist. Usually, the effort to obtain Teddy's cooperation resulted in his slapping his face and his hands having to be held. When the therapist replaced toys alone and let Teddy explore other toys on the floor, Teddy sometimes would begin to push cars around or build with the blocks. However, often under these circumstances it appeared as if Teddy was going to step on a toy, and when this was stopped by the therapist, the self-slapping would also occur. Thus much of the hour was spent with the therapist holding Teddy's hands to prevent slapping.

During one session in their second year of work the therapist noted that when he relaxed his grip on Teddy's wrist, Teddy made no effort to hit himself. Teddy instead sat relaxed, leaning on the therapist's shoulder. In retrospect the therapist recalled that the leaning occurred frequently even when he was holding the wrists firmly to prevent the slapping and long before he let Teddy's hands loose.

On the next occasion when the therapist had to control the slapping, he quickly relaxed his grip but maintained contact with the wrists as Teddy was leaning against him and he used one of Teddy's hands to rake a block over. Then as if using the hand as a crane claw, he placed the hand over another block and to appropriate machine noises by the therapist, Teddy obligingly put one block on the next. Thus they built their first big tower. This kind of activity continued for several weeks.

Subsequently, one one playroom hour the therapist sensed it was appropriate to stop Teddy's self-slapping with a comment, "come here and give me your hands if you want to be held so we can play together." Teddy quickly placed his wrists in the therapist's hands and relaxed comfortably for the ensuing building and play with toy trucks. Slowly the self-slapping could be halted by a "Hey, you know where I am."

As the play continued Teddy would take his hands out of the therapist's encircling fingers to alter the pattern of play or change the shape of the tower and then he would put his wrists back. This activity evolved into playing together and holding hands for brief periods during and at the end of the hour.

In the therapeutic work with the fourth therapist during the fifth and sixth years of work, Teddy began to utilize many of the toys much more appropriately. He played with them at first by himself and then finally involved the therapist in a variety of silent dramas. There was a great deal of leave taking in the doll play. The mother and father dolls were frequently leaving the children and each other. Often the children were left alone by both parents who went their separate ways. The therapist would try to verbalize the kinds of feelings the children might have with Teddy looking on very impassively and giving no signs that he understood. There was also a great deal of play in which one or another member of the family was run over by a car, usually a parent but sometimes one of the children. In these instances there was some very vigorous and gleeful chortling as the car would run over the doll repeatedly with great banging, thumping, and sometimes evident fury. The therapist gradually learned in each instance to talk about what he saw rather than what he thought Teddy was feeling since such interpretations usually halted the play. Thus, rather than, "you're very angry and you're trying to kill the daddy or the mommy doll," he would say, "the mommy and daddy doll are being run over by the car and they are really being hit hard by the car," with a great deal of dramatic emphasis that, "they are being squashed, stomped on, torn apart as the car is driving over and over and over again." This kind of descriptive comment would result in the particular drama being played out to the end. Sometimes the particular doll who was being run over would finally be rescued or put to bed. With this last therapist, in their second year together, Teddy began to talk.

TEDDY TALKS

His beginning speech coincided with a number of events in Teddy's life, most notably the mother's change in her attitude toward Teddy and her increased capacity to be attentive to him, to understand his particular feelings and moods, to verbalize them, and to express some physical tenderness. Mother and Father had begun to resolve some of their differences which enhanced not only their own relationship but their mutual capacity to relate to their children. In addition, the birth of a "planned" baby found Mother able to re-experience some feelings she had had with her oldest boy, but with marked enhancement of tender, loving, nurturing feelings and with greater freedom to play and talk to the new baby. These events will be discussed more fully later. However, the amount of tenderness that she felt toward this infant seemed to free her to feel and behave much more tenderly toward Teddy.

In the playroom some three months after the baby's birth, Teddy appeared relaxed and intent on the doll play. As usual, Teddy was running the large truck over the adult male doll. Over and over again with great energy he slammed the figure around with the truck wheels, a tight grin flickering on his face as he pursued the doll with the truck, knocking it about the room. In the last few weeks he had begun to grunt "ugh" as he banged into the doll and sometimes he laughed as he scurried after the doll he had sent sprawling across the room. The therapist moved with him on the floor and continued, as he had learned would enhance Teddy's play, to vocalize and verbalize Teddy's actions. The exclamations were usually, "crunch, slam, that doll sure got knocked way over there." When these accompanying exclamations and descriptions were especially dramatically intoned, Teddy might glance at the therapist. The therapist in turn attended to Teddy's facial expression and his body tones as cues about the intensity of tone he should use. During the course of this hour, as he exclaimed "crunch, slam," Teddy's face turned toward the therapist, and his lips seemed to be forming "s-l-a-m." The therapist continued his dramatic commentary, watching Teddy very closely and thought he heard a whispered "bam." Throughout the rest of the session, whispered "bam" and "slam" could just be heard. Often the therapist was not sure he had really heard the whisper, only to have it repeated a moment or two later. One "slam" was very distinct: The therapist smiled and continued his commentary as the play continued and ended with the doll being carefully patted and put to bed.

When the therapist mentioned with great delight his observations to the staff, with a caution that they should not press Teddy to talk, the staff members agreed they had felt Teddy was about ready to talk because of the increased vocalization and animation in his face in response to the staff and children talking to him.

DEVELOPMENT OF SPEECH

Shortly thereafter the teacher noted that Teddy was also whispering after her as she would go over a lesson with him. He put into words the fragments of their lessons, saying after her the colors or numbers in assignments where they matched colors or added numbers and so on. As she was able to hear him whispering these words, she would go on for longer periods of time, describing what was being done and without noticing very much what he was saying. Later she would simply say to him very matter of factly, "a little louder," and with only slight encouragement he would begin to increase the volume in which he repeated her comments.

In a short time he also began to reply to her questions with a very short and terse "yes" or "no" and finally used a few short phrases. He also began to respond with "yes" or "no" to his favorite nurse's aide when she would ask him a question, especially around food. It was clear from the way in which he spoke that he understood most of the words that were said to him and that he needed very little practice to say words clearly.

In the playroom it was evident that the more animated and active the play and the more verbalization and vocalization there was by the therapist, the greater the range of Teddy's verbal expressions until he was able to say, "that daddy doll, I bump him." He was especially proud when he greeted his therapist by name and said, "shake hand."

At the beginning of his 11th year of life, Teddy began to speak with ever greater freedom. Father was heard to say as Teddy began to speak volubly that he didn't know what was worse, to have a silent, completely mute child or to have one who was constantly chattering.

SUMMARY OF PLAY THERAPY

When one examines the work of the four therapists for almost two years each, it becomes clear there was a constant progression and that each therapist was able to build upon the work of the other, despite the regressive behavior that occurred at each termination. The rapidity with which the last therapist was able to establish a relationship with Teddy was based upon the fact that he was able to quickly cue into some of his behaviors as a result of having heard about Teddy from previous therapists and to utilize this understanding of Teddy's behavior by verbalizing his own feelings about what Teddy was doing and how he felt about it. When he had to hold Teddy's hands to prevent him from slapping, he was not only able to say he felt annoyed or was hurt in the tussle to control Teddy, but he also expressed how sad he felt that Teddy had to hurt himself in order to say something or get somebody to understand him and to be with him. The therapist was also able to follow Teddy's play in a way which did not interfere with his playing out various themes. He seemed to provide support and less interferences with the boy's play. Teddy appeared to be able to hear the therapist's comments that were made which were affectively tuned to his behavior. Thus the self-directed anger and the self-hurting seemed to diminish and turn into playing out his feelings.

Teddy appeared most involved in play when he heard the therapist's verbal accompaniment to the play and in many such sessions, he would hold his hands out to the therapist so that they would sit together holding hands for a few moments during pauses in the hour and before they cleaned up. It became clearer that in all of the self-directed anger and slapping, as well as in the violent play, there were some elements of anxiety about the expression and the feeling of both angry and tender, close feelings. On several occasions when he slapped himself the therapist would hold him and with a good deal of affect talk about his sadness and annoyance that this was the only way Teddy could get to hold hands with the therapist or express his feelings. With increasing frequency after such affective comments by the therapist, Teddy would snuggle up against him. The sequences made clear also that when he played out a particularly violent scene to the accompaniment of the therapist's verbal and vocal comments as the "crunch, slam, they're being run over and smashed," he began, at the end of such periods of play, to want to hold hands and snuggle.

OTHER AREAS OF PROGRESS

Concomitantly, Teddy looked very alert and became responsive to his environment. He began to notice and to comment with single words as he pointed at street lights, stoplights, gas station signs, billboards, trees and birds. Teddy began using each word with an expression of pleasure and "look at me" in his voice. Simultaneously he became interested in games and began to get involved with other children in a whole variety of age-appropriate play, especially basketball. It was noted that he was no longer quite as accident prone and seemed to be alert to potential danger. On one occasion he actually pulled another child out of the way of a closing elevator door.

During the last year of therapeutic work, Teddy not only began to speak freely with more complex sentences and to play out a variety of scenes, but he also began to integrate in every sphere of his living. He made extraordinarily rapid progress in school and he began to read very quickly, according to his teacher, as if he already knew how to read. He had little difficulty in pronouncing any word he had heard. We wondered if there had been constant sub-vocal practicing of words. Thus, during the last six months of his stay in the hospital, Teddy was talking more and more, until he was chattering away most of the time, as if to make up for the lost time. Teddy began to make comments about what was going on around him, gently teasing both the staff and other children, especially when he felt some of their feelings which were not being expressed. Thus, on one occasion when the nurse was very angry with a child for dumping her food on the floor and was saying in a very firm but sweet voice, "I want you to clean it up," Teddy jumped up and said very gleefully, "You're very mad, you're very mad, but you pretend to be nice." Also, he was able to comment about how his parents were feeling, and especially commented with great accuracy on the underlying feelings in Father's usual flat, non-committal remarks. He would say to Father, "you really are mad" or "you really like it" or "enjoy it." On a number of occasions, Father was able to laugh and agree that these were indeed the feelings he had.

EVENTS PRIOR TO DISCHARGE—SEPARATION FEELINGS

Playtherapy during the last few months turned from the aggressive, hostile running over of dolls to repetitive scenes of family life in which the children and parents were able to live together with only minor squabbles. It was during this period that his oldest brother, who had been having some difficulties with the law, was visited by the police as a possible suspect in vandalism in which he had had no part. Teddy expressed concern about the fact that policemen had come to see his brother and inquired how his brother was bad. When the parents were asked to talk with Teddy quite frankly about the problems with his brother which were by then diminishing, Teddy appeared relieved after discussing the situation and said that his brother was not in trouble now.

There was a short period of outpatient treatment before the parents moved to another part of the country. Father, having retired from the service, was preparing to take an executive job with an industry back East. During the period prior to leaving, Teddy was able to work through his separation, this time without much in the way of regression. There was no slapping but a good deal of open crying. He repeatedly cried, "I'll miss you, I'll miss you, no one will say thank you" to both his therapist and his nurse. This last statement referred to both of us thanking him for being helpful in cleaning up in the playroom and helping out on the ward. He learned to say thank you when he appreciated something done for him. His "thank you" when said was always heart-felt, and his eyes "lit up" when he was thanked. During this same period, he was going to a special education program in a nearby school and doing very well.

THERAPEUTIC WORK WITH FATHER

Therapeutic work with Father was interrupted frequently by his periods of service abroad or his being taken away from his area post to carry on inspections throughout the country and in some foreign posts. Thus the therapy with him after his final station prior to and after his retirement, during the last two years of our work together, was the only sustained period of work. Father was a tall, slender man who appeared much younger than his age, looked usually rather tense and stiff, almost an exaggerated military posture as he sat. He was frequently depressed during his interviews and was self-derrogating and bitter about his military career and the fact that he was not to be promoted because of his interpersonal difficulties. He often blamed his wife for her lack of social skills, but mostly he blamed himself. He had an excellent record and extremely high achievement during the war as an outstanding field commander and was widely used by his service as a consultant and special inspector. He was seen, he heard, by superiors as a good tactical person but not as a potential strategist and diplomat. During the first two years of therapy with two therapists he described his "black" moods and his constant feeling of being neglected by both his peers and those who served under him. He compared himself with his son, saying that they were both terribly depressed and felt helpless. He also described the tremendous rage that Teddy evoked in him when he began to slap himself or became very obstinate. When Teddy looked angry and depressed, Father felt he mirrored Father's own feelings and he would often feel murderous and described the restraint he had to place upon himself not to really hurt Teddy when he spanked him for hitting himself.

Father, who during the first year also expressed concern about the younger boy who was now four and also not talking, wondered what it was about their family that led to mute children. Subsequently, this youngster did begin to talk, although only after a good deal of speech therapy and help in a special class. Only during the latter part of his work with the first therapist was Father able to express a sense of needing the therapist and feeling the loss of the therapist after Father had been away. He was later able to begin discussing his relationships with his wife.

Father described his initial pleasure in dating such a lovely young woman and his high expectations that they would be close and that he would experience the longed for feelings of intimacy and being loved and able to love someone else. He was initially very disappointed that they were not able to stay together very long after their marriage because he was immediately called to an overseas assignment, leaving his new wife at the post. He came home to find his wife embittered at the loneliness and the lack of social activity. They started off on the wrong foot and they were thereafter never able to establish any real intimacy. There was always a pretend flavor to their reunions and he felt that even their sexual life which had been initially satisfying to both of them carried an aura of pretense about it, as if they had to show each other that they really cared through their sexual activity. He found himself not enjoying it a great deal and was sure that his wife didn't enjoy it at all. With the first pregnancy, nearly five years after they were married, his wife became very preoccupied with the child, and he felt excluded and once again alone. Father described this feeling of aloneness over and over again during the years of treatment, the sense of being excluded from the family, of having no one of his own to turn to, of his wife's preference for the children. He related that on several occasions when they had moved from one post to another, and he gave the last move as an example, he found no room had been made for his belongings and no work space had been allocated for the work he had to do at home. He usually found all his belongings stored in the basement. He felt no one cared about him and he was not part of the family. Then he would bitterly comment that in some sense, realistically, this was true.

In his work with his second therapist, Father began to recognize more clearly the kinds of problems that he was having with Teddy, especially the way in which he identified with many of Teddy's moods and his sense that somehow Teddy knew how he was feeling and in some way took advantage of it. Father did not talk about their troubles with Sandy's stealing and aggressive behavior in school until near the end of therapy. Father also began to describe his resignation about the impending retirement and lack of promotion. He began to plan with his wife for their future, and this slowly brought them together. They discussed the variety of jobs Father was fitted for and would enjoy and the kind of training that he might need to undertake. Finally, Father decided to take training in business administration and management in a nearby university's evening classes. As he got into his training and found it not at all difficult for him, he could express his pleasure in discovering he was the best student in the class. He slowly felt very much better about himself and could even begin to brag to his wife about what a good businessman he was going to be. He was pleased that Mother could accept his bragging and tease him gently that she expected him to become a tycoon. While Father continued to complain and to examine his feelings about Mother's preference for the children, he was also able to speak with greater tenderness about her capacity to understand his feelings and to encourage him to talk about how he felt. They were able to talk together more frankly about Teddy and they were even able to explore together the possibility that Teddy might have to go to a state hospital. Mother seemed more at ease with the idea than Father who was extremely angry when it was discussed. Each time he would feel tension and he was able to more openly vent hostility toward the therapist and the clinic for not having cured his son. During those moments he looked at the therapist with anxiety, expecting retaliation. When this did not occur he seemed to be more relaxed and finally would even be able to comment on the phenomenon of lashing out at the therapist and expecting to be hurt and feeling tremendously relieved when this did not occur. Instead he was asked simply to understand what the feelings were and to try to express them more fully.

Toward the end of the work with the second therapist Father was again sent on an overseas assignment for several months. On his return he was both able to express his gratitude that he was back and able to talk to someone about his feelings. He also described the great relief he found in being able to work within a new setting without the previously experienced sense of friction and isolation. He felt that he got along better with his subordinates as well as with his superiors. Father even conjectured that feeling as easy as he had on his last assignment, he would probably have been able to work much more effectively on all of his previous assignments so that he would have gotten the promotion. Later, half smiling, he said that since he was young enough after his thirty years of service, he would probably become very productive in another field. During his work with his third therapist he had numerous interruptions as he was called away many times for special assignments and in that period of work did not seem nearly as intensely involved and productive as in the work with the previous two therapists. He talked primarily about his recognition of changes in himself as he worked in various assignments and his capacity to be much more flexible and to tune into the needs of others and also be aware of those moments of depression and anger which previously would lead either to alienation or lashing back and being very harsh with subordinates and sullen with superiors. He also was able to describe in therapy his sense of alienation because the therapist and he did not get to know each other well.

With his fourth therapist there was the longest period of continuity. Father received his last command and was at home most of the time. He also was retired during the last year of therapeutic work. During this period, their last child was born. This was the first time Father was home during the birth of a child. Father felt this was a planned pregnancy, although there was some difference between Mother and Father about this. Father described with a great deal of pleasure the kind of intimacy Mother and he had together and the warm and tender feelings he had toward the new baby. Father was able to carry out his last command with a great deal of ease and continued his night work at the college. He not only finished his course work in business administration but was also able to finish a course in accounting with very high honors and was very pleased with himself. During the last year, just after his retirement, he was able, with the therapist's help, not to plunge immediately into a permanent job but to look very carefully at the opportunities about him before making any commitments. He thus worked temporarily in several local industries to gain some experience and found himself functioning at a very high level. Since he was retired in his late forties, he found himself feeling he could work out a new and satisfying career.

When Teddy began to talk during this last year in treatment, Father was able to talk with Teddy honestly about many of his own feelings. Father learned to respond with affect when Teddy recognized his anger or withdrawal or sullenness and to verify Teddy's observation and say how he did feel. Father's laughing irritation at Teddy's constant chattering brought forth memories of Teddy's infancy and the muteness of both parents with each other and with Teddy and his younger brother. Father played with Teddy and his oldest youngster who were both good athletes. They played baseball and basketball together with mutual pleasure. It was during this period also that Father found himself able to talk about a new found intimacy with his wife. Their sexual satisfaction was increased. Father described a new sense of being able to feel the kinds of tensions his wife experienced when she was tired or harassed with the demands of the house. He was now able to sensitively step in and help her rather than irritably inquiring why she was so silent and removed as he had done in the past. Toward the end of his treatment, Father described that he and Mother had had a number of "honeymoons," the longest which had occurred before the birth of their last child and prior to his retirement when they took an official leave and visited some of their old friends for two weeks. During this last period of therapy Father examined some of his transference feelings toward the therapist and began to speak honestly of the closeness and warmth he felt toward her as well as the anger that he felt when he was not understood and had to put feelings into words at a time when he wanted somebody to understand his feelings and put them into words for him.

Father finally was able to talk about Sandy's stealing from stores and at home and his frequent fights and disruption of the classroom which brought both the school and juvenile authorities to their home. At first Father punished Sandy severely, or in futile desperation left the problem to Mother. He could not comprehend the behavior. Later when stationed near home he began to spend time with Sandy and got to know him. They worked together on his school work and his basketball practice. Father was very pleased at his son's brilliance in math and science and his athletic abilities. He attended his basketball games, and he and Mother included Sandy in their discussions about Father's future work. Although Father recalled his hostile, almost brutal treatment of Sandy, frequent spanking, etc., only now could he talk about these as taking out his anger at Mother and himself or his son.

The therapist and other members of the staff noted that during the last year of therapy, Father, who had been rather strained and stiff in posture, now appeared more relaxed, and the sternness in his countenance had decreased. The parents made several trips back East to look at a company which wanted to hire him as a comptroller. He was able to accept the idea that he would have to serve a period of apprenticeship with the comptroller who was about to retire. He found it not very difficult in the two visits he made to the firm to understand the operations which he would eventually be in charge of and he returned with a sense of his real competency as a business manager.

THERAPY WITH MOTHER

Mother in her therapeutic work was at first provocative and coy with the first therapist, feeling that no one understood her and that no man could be trusted. She felt men could only relate to her because she was an attractive woman and that she would be accused of being a failure both as a mother and a wife by any man who got to know her. It was thus with some real relief that she began to recognize that as she would associate to her early childhood experiences, some of the experiences during her marriage were clarified. Especially, she understood the kind of anger she felt at each separation from her husband, and her rather helpless feelings with Teddy became meaningful as well as the full extent of her helplessness and rage. It was with her second therapist during the second and third years of therapy that she was able to clearly look at her difficulties during Teddy's birth and first few years of life. Her explorations made clear the severity of her depression around the illness of her first son and the death of her mother, the amount of isolation she felt when her husband left her and her need to retreat and not be involved which left Teddy alone and unstimulated. She compared the amount of time she spent with the first born and was able to see that she really had spent very little time with Teddy. She also began to recognize how impotent and helpless she felt when Teddy did not develop normally and would not speak. The slapping and other kinds of destructive behavior which commenced when he was around the age of three made her feel more helpless. Mother was slowly able to recognize the amount of underlying rage, some of murderous proportions, when she felt totally without resources in dealing with her son and felt that her husband did not understand her desperation. During this period Mother had a number of minor illnesses which forced cancellation of some appointments. She was able then to clarify the way in which she utilized going to bed with a severe cold or headache and getting in some help to care for the children as the only way she could feel justified in giving some time to herself and getting some rest. She looked to her therapist for an angry denunciation of her failures in mothering and taking care of her husband when he came home. It was also during this period of treatment that she was able to begin to describe fully the anger and bitterness she felt toward her husband. She remembered very little of the happy first few months of her marriage. She could recall vividly her intense anger and estrangement from him which started with the first separation and grew with every subsequent separation. She described very vividly his abrupt, cold military manner at home and the way in which he would conduct what seemed like court martials whenever one of the youngsters disobeyed him. Mother felt that he considered her a junior officer who must obey his every command. Her fury at Father was often expressed through neglect of Father's explicit need for her. Thus she forgot to get his clothes ready for a trip or could not entertain senior officers or go with him to a variety of functions because she felt ill. Thus, her husband was forced often to go alone to required social events.

Not only Teddy made her feel helpless. Sandy now in elementary school continued to fight in school and disrupt classes by teasing and hitting other students. Several times he stole toys and candy from stores. Each time he was caught Mother had to deal with the authorities and with Sandy. Mother tried to keep Father out of it fearing his potentially violent beating of Sandy. At first she and Sandy could not talk together at all. Mother felt that Sandy, who was "court martialed" by Father at any breach of good behavior, was the fall guy because Father had no one else with whom to get physically angry.

We discussed the possibility of hospitalization of Teddy at this point when they were still unable to keep him at home for weekends after two and one half years of hospitalization because of his self-destructive behavior, his slapping, and sometimes tearing at himself when nobody would attend to him. Mother frequently was tired and could not hold onto Teddy for long to stop his slapping. Thus if she were alone she would turn to her older son to help her and found that despite his other troubles, to her surprise, he was very willing and effective in containing Teddy.

With the third therapist who was a woman, Mother began to work through some of her feelings that all men wanted to use her as a sexual object and that her husband had no regard for her at all. She began then to describe her own more frequent desires to be closer to her husband and to achieve some kind of intimacy. Usually she felt turned off when Father came home and was stern with the children and with her as if they were part of his command. She and Father began to talk more together about the needs of the family, and she was able to understand Father's anxiety and loss of self-esteem about his being retired and not promoted. She was gradually able to express a good deal of sympathy toward Father. Mother understood her failure to be helpful in the kinds of activities which might have been meaningful to Father, although she recognized that when they were together at social events Father seemed to be reserved and withdrawn and not able to interact with other officers and wives with the same kind of spontaneity and freedom she noticed in other officers of his rank.

During this period of work Mother began to lose weight. She looked much more attractive and younger and toward the end of this period she became pregnant. She said she wanted to have another baby but that they had planned not to have another child for some time until things were more clear about Teddy. The parents were able to talk about perhaps needing to have Teddy hospitalized in a state hospital if he were not better after another period of work. Mother could understand Father's panic during these discussions. However, she said she felt sad though less guilty during such talks. Mother was able to be more attentive to the other children. She could relate better to her older son who was still quite hostile in school and often delinquent. As a result of her attention to him and her capacity to understand his feelings and to talk with him quite honestly about her own perception of him and let him talk about his perceptions of her, their relationship changed and slowly much of the delinquent activity ceased. Mother described with pride that she was able to help her son so that he became eventually an outstanding student and athlete. When her younger child had failed to talk by age four, she again had felt she was a terrible mother, but paying close attention to him also and working closely with a speech therapist, they were slowly able to overcome the mutism so that when he entered kindergarten, he was able to talk fairly well although he was not as verbal as the other children.

During her work with her last therapist, Mother was able to consolidate many of her gains. In the transference relationship, she worked out many feelings toward her father and mother, as well as about her use of sexuality.

In one of the early months of work with her last therapist around the 450th interview, Mother came into the office obviously quite annoyed. She sat stiffly in the chair and apparently continued from the last interview a discussion of her anger at the transfer again to a new therapist. She commented again with bitterness that she had to repeat material, but most of all, remarked that getting to know and trust a new therapist was difficult and she was tired of it. The therapist reminded her that he had known Mother for over four years as a staff member. He had been present at the intake, had chatted with Mother from time to time over milieu problems when her therapist was not there, and had followed the work closely so that he was familiar with much of the historical data. Mother angrily snorted and said it didn't make it any easier, "I really don't know you." The therapist responded that he realized how comfortable and close Mother had felt with her previous therapist and he could well understand how much she missed the therapist and how sad she was. It was tough to give up such a warm relationship. Mother began to tear, but looked stubborn at the same time. The therapist inquired about what this kind of feeling, missing someone badly and having to relate to someone else, brought to mind. Mother looked sober at being reminded that she would get more mileage from working than simply complaining. She sighed and said, "Oh, she always thought first of her husband as the recurrent stranger in her life," and then with a flood of words said, "no, it was my mother who appeared to be there but was usually too busy for me so I felt close to the housekeepers who changed every few years." Half to herself, she continued to talk about her father's importance to her, he was always around. After recounting a number of childhood memories about good times with her father, she began to weep. "It was not true, he wasn't really there when I needed him when I was upset or lonely." She then recalled for the first time her feelings of anger and hate toward her father when he would not stay with her in the hospital when she had her tonsils out at age four and was frightened. Her father had to be out of town for a meeting, and her mother told her she was a big girl and shouldn't fuss. She also remembered several illnesses as a child of seven or eight, one a severe otitis media, where again her father would not stay at her side during the painful opening of the ear and only visited the day she was to come home. While her mother came every day briefly, she wasn't very friendly or warm and was always preoccupied with the many other responsibilities she had.

Mother then described how good her genial father could make her feel with his warmth and attentiveness. She recalled that as an adolescent and perhaps earlier, she had felt hurt and rageful toward her father when he displayed the same warmth and attentiveness to many others of their friends and his political co-workers. Passionately she exclaimed, "I really never had either Mom or Dad especially all to myself." At the end of the hour, she smiled and said, "Well, where did that come from?"

In several subsequent hours, angry or hurt feelings expressed toward the therapist for not knowing or understanding her feelings, led to further recall of events in childhood, especially the overwhelming feeling that she had no right to complain because she was given so many nice clothes and "had everything a girl could want."

Later Mother related these feelings to her feelings early in her marriage that she had no right to complain.

A cold which caused the therapist to cancel an hour led to Mother's expression of hurt feelings at being deserted and a clear sense of how dangerous it was to feel close to someone and to express feelings that would make them want to shove you away. Several times she said, "I'll bet that's how Teddy must feel toward me."

It was around the birth of her child that she was able to describe the feelings that she had of wanting to be awake during the delivery and to experience the birth. She described how much she looked forward to having the new baby. For the first time she felt she really was a woman and felt that her husband treated her like a woman. She described their various trips together and the new sense of intimacy which they had. When a baby boy was born she was delighted to find he was an "adorable" child. She found the birth process not terribly painful or difficult and was very proud of herself. She was also pleased that her husband was there with her and was able to be with her during the process of the baby's birth so that they could share it together. Mother expressed her pleasure that Father was there to support her when the baby came home. There was a brief period of colic so that Father more than took his turn staying up with the infant. Her pleasure in nursing the infant was obvious. She had not been able to nurse Teddy or the other youngsters, having nursed the older child for a period of about three months before her milk dried up. Mother described with surprise and delight the sensual enjoyment in nursing which she had never expected to experience. On numerous occasions she remarked that when she took the baby for a walk or into the store when she went shopping, people would stop her to look at this lovely child and to exclaim about the baby and ask her if this was her first child because she looked so happy. This infant's rapid development and Mother's capacity to involve herself with the infant was a pleasure to both parents. Mother described very vividly Father's light-hearted playing with the baby.

During this period of treatment Mother was able to recall the sexual pleasure she and Father had during their honeymoon and the few months before he had to go overseas and leave her with their subsequent estrangement. She talked about the self-deception she felt Father played into so they would never talk about how they felt toward each other and how unsatisfactory their sexual relationship actually was. She and Father were not able to experience a great deal of pleasure and tenderness in their sexual relationship, and Mother described the fact that she was now having orgasms for the first time frequently.

During the last year of her therapeutic work Mother discussed her anxiety about Father's retirement. She had doubts about his ability to find a job where his personality would not stand in the way. She was also concerned that the job be remunerative and give him the sense of status and importance which he needed. At first Mother wanted Father to take any job that was offered to him and only slowly was able to recognize that her own anxiety about their security might lead him to take a job which he really didn't want. She was able to discuss this with her husband quite frankly and to arrive at a decision that he would take several temporary jobs to get a sense of his own competency and then begin to look for the job where he felt he might be able to make another career.

It was during these last two years that Mother was able to analyze her feelings toward Teddy. She talked about her guilt that she had cheated him and that she could in no way make up for the lack of mothering. However, she found that as she was more tuned into his feelings and as he began to talk, they were able to be together and to feel closer than she had ever thought possible. On a number of occasions, when she felt as of old, frozen, tired, and overworked, Teddy was able to say something like, "Mommy, you look mad." Mother was able to laugh and say, "You're so right," and feel that he understood her the best of all the children. She was also able to be physically close to him for the first time, to put her arms around him and to cuddle him without feeling frightened that he would begin to hurt himself or that she would need to contain him and feel again the urge to actually hurt him. All the ward personnel as well as the therapist noted that Mother was much more attentive and warm with Teddy on the ward. She was able to bring him back and forth to the hospital without any anxiety, and they could walk hand in hand and chat together in a free and warm way. Teddy became increasingly concerned when Mother left, asking her each time when he would see her again. Previously he had been indifferent to her leaving. With her last therapist Mother was able to describe some of her sexual feelings toward him and to accept the fact that such sexual feelings from one person toward another were normal ones and did not necessarily mean they had to be exploitative. She then began to recognize the ways in which she had used her own cuteness and coquettishness to get her way, not only with her employers, but with most men and with some disappointment she could relate the fact that only during the first few months of their marriage was she able to utilize this as a way of relating to her husband. Mother related her current life with her husband as increasingly happy and contented. Using her husband's terminology with a laugh, she described them as a "good team." She found she could raise an issue with her husband about a child's misdeeds without the anxiety and fear that her husband would become furious and "court martial" the child and then mete out suitable punishment.

Toward the end of our work, Mother talked freely of her sense of growth and her pleasure in the growth of her husband and Teddy's marked and continuing improvement. The separation was difficult for Mother who felt she would need to continue her therapeutic work to consolidate her gains. The parents and Teddy were referred to colleagues on the East Coast.

We heard each year of Teddy's steady improvement, Father's raises in salary, and Mother's pleasure in her children. Our last contact occurred when Teddy was 20 and had just taken a job after successfully completing business college.

DISCUSSION

This case report reviews the highlights of simultaneous psycho-therapeutic work with child and both parents. In a period of 6½ years with four different therapists working with the family, many changes occurred in each member which could not be predicted in the admission evaluation. Teddy, mute, self-hurting, and frozen at age five had a poor prognosis. Only his exact negativism, his precise use of slapping himself to control adults and his great physical coordination spoke to aspects of ego integration. Possibly, his close relationship with his older brother, his constant companion for five years, explains his capacity to relate and to express acute hurt at separations from meaningful people by self-slapping. It is clear from Mother's capacity to use therapy to reduce her conflicts and her need to denigrate her own capacity as a mother that she may have given more to Teddy than was visible in a mute, frozen, self-destructive child.

Similarly, both Mother's and Father's behavior when first seen and their discussion of their own childhood indicated little capacity for self-examination, understanding, and altered interpersonal relationships. Although Mother was most dependent and helpless and Father most overtly caustic and angry, it was Father who utilized the therapeutic relationship first to begin to resolve some basic conflicts about accepting help and the vulnerability this led to in each relationship. He began to see his sternness, preoccupation with minute and non-relevant details and his isolation from others as problems to be understood and worked through. As he saw himself with less need to defend himself in his relationship with each therapist, he was able to also see his wife and then his children, especially Teddy, in a different light.

Mother, fearful of investing in any relationship, was able to begin to openly express her doubts that anyone would really want to help her, and her fears of being abandoned. Each therapist held firm to their expectations of her in therapy and handling, usually alone, the real life problems with her delinquent older son, her mute younger child, as well as Teddy. Mother slowly found she was indeed more capable of being effective than she had been and certainly more effective than she ever thought she could be. Each change of therapist led to new testing with reassuring results. She could express her feelings no matter how dependent, furious, or sulky she behaved toward each therapist, without recrimination or being turned off by the therapist.

This is one of the few times in my experience that the parents and child seemed to move at about the same pace in therapy. In this instance the parents were a bit ahead of the child, enhancing his potential for improvement.

The phenomenon of two children in the same family at opposite ends of the psychopathologic spectrum was familiar to us from previous work of staff in our setting. In several instances both a psychotic child and a seriously delinquent child were seen from the same family. In two other instances in my own experience, the delinquent child appeared after an "uneventful" first and second year of life to have been neglected, not nurtured sufficiently, and without reliable models for identification in his parents but with sufficient ego function to learn, adapt in his home and school, and to act out his hurt, neglect and anger. In this instance the delinquent child, the oldest boy, also was the victim of Father's anger, stern reprimands, and physical chastisement because, as both parents pointed out in retrospect, he was the only one at hand that Father could pick on. Nevertheless, he identified with Father in many ways as he became a bright student and a brilliant athlete. Athletics was the only evident means of interaction and closeness between Father and son. His delinquency was reduced in mid-adolescence as both parents could relate to him more honestly. They could provide more attention of an appropriate kind and also offer relationships which could withstand testing behavior without the previous withdrawal or hostile retaliation.

Teddy's beginning speech with continued talking was probably the result of the confluences of a number of factors, not all of them obvious. The maturational elements which usually affect the psychotic young child adversely, his increase in size and strength coupled with mutism and unpredictable, often aggressive, behavior usually lead to more anxiety and restraints from staff. Staff tensions interfere with relationships and efforts to encourage and utilize ego strength to resolve conflict. Although Teddy was a large boy, his relationships when seven and eight had already improved so that the increase in size and strength did not result in hostile behavior or alienate adults to impede progress. He was able to use his development to become more age appropriate and competent and relate better to children and staff.

The genetic factors, if any, cannot be assessed; neither parent had much information about mental illness in their families.

The relationships developed on the ward and in the playroom slowly began to help Teddy trust adults and rely more on his own increased effectiveness. The amount of affective interchange in all therapeutic settings also seemed to enhance Teddy's increased capacity to feel, express feelings tentatively, and to try to talk when no one challenged his achievements by claiming credit for themselves. Thus his first speech in barely audible whispers resulted in more of the affectively laden responses from adults which seemed to lead to speech. Only later was he casually asked to speak up, and no one interpreted the speech except to encourage it by their behavior.

The fact that many changes in personality and behavior in the parents and even in the older brother had occurred because of the parents' conflict reduction, we would see this as a major contributing factor to Teddy's onset of speech and the more integrated behavior leading to discharge.

We have repeatedly noted times when a child is ready to move in the direction of less psychotic behavior only to find that one or both parents are still locked in conflict. The child seems unable to sustain his progress and regresses again to a much more psychotic state. In several instances we have noted repeated shifts on the child's part toward integration and in one instance mentioned in this volume the child and parents finally were ready to live together with much less conflict, and the child improved rapidly. In other instances the parents had not been helped sufficiently or their conflicts were so severe that more time was needed to reduce them. Then the child falls back into severe psychotic behavior, sometimes not to approach resolution again.

In this instance the simultaneous working through of conflicts in child and parents we feel was critical to his gaining speech and bing able to live at home and finally go to school and work at a job.

This is an example of simultaneous psychotherapy in its most ideal circumstances with the expected, but not so often attained, results.

Postscript: We recently had a request for information about Teddy from a psychiatric hospital. We received no replies to our inquiries to clarify Teddy's present psychiatric condition and the reasons for his request for help.

31

Can Conflicts in Collaborative Therapy Exacerbate Psychosis?

Maleta J. Boatman, M.D., Mary B. Davis, M.S.W.,
Winifred Donohue, R.N., S. L. Sheimo, M.D.
and S. A. Szurek, M.D.

INTRODUCTION

It is possible to learn a great deal by reviewing the history and therapy of a case which has recovered or improved. Perhaps it is possible to learn as much or more by reviewing the clinical material and therapeutic efforts around a case which has not recovered or has even become worse. In the former instance it is easy and pleasurable to assume that what one thought was done in therapy was responsible for the desired result. In the latter instance it is necessary to examine closely what has occurred in the patient's life and in the therapy with constant questions such as, "Was our evaluation of this situation an accurate one? Was our response to this situation therapeutically rational? If so, what stood in the way of clinical progress at this point?" In such an inquiry it may not be possible to find answers to all our questions, but we may gain a new perspective of the situation which may help us in our future therapeutic efforts. It may also help us and others to evaluate similar problems in other cases with more rapidity.

We feel that some such results have been obtained from our inquiry into twenty-four months of our experience with a particularly puzzling patient and family. Six months before the time of writing this paper the collabora-

---

This paper is written in the present tense despite the fact that it was presented over 25 years ago because it makes for a greater sense of dynamics. The principles learned from this paper were used in the development of the Children's Service.

tive therapists felt that therapy was at an impasse and held a conference with the director and staff of the department to review and discuss the clinical history, the diagnosis and what had occurred in treatment up to that point in more detail than had been possible in the small informal collaborative conferences that had been held previously. It became apparent in the conference that there was available much pertinent information about the complex emotional interaction between the patient and various staff members which for a number of reasons had not previously reached the attention of the director nor been fully recognized by the therapists. The increased feeling of hopefulness which followed this clearer definition of the total situation and the subsequent greater movement in the therapy impressed the collaborative team with the probable value of even more intensive review over a longer period of time. What has occurred in the months which have followed the initiation of this review has been helpful and stimulating to the authors of this paper. We feel a report of the inquiry may be of general interest.

CLINICAL HISTORY

The limitations of space make it possible for us to present only briefly the clinical material on which this paper is based.

Mary, as we shall call our patient, is a white, single, 19½ year old girl, fifth of six children of tenant farmers. Her illness apparently had an acute onset when she was 15½ with a severe anxiety attack. This was followed by seven months of varying somatic symptoms, including headache, fatigue, abdominal pain and weakness. Several physicians were consulted and treatment varied from liver and vitamin injections to an appendectomy. Those symptoms that were alleviated were immediately replaced by more disabling ones. Psychiatric consultation was sought at this point but was abandoned by Mary's parents when the sodium amytal injection she received resulted in a week of near stupor from which she aroused with a crossed paralysis of her right leg and left arm. Her weakness progressed so rapidly in the next two months that she was hospitalized. Complete neurological examination, including several spinal taps, revealed no organic pathology and she was referred to our psychiatric clinic, although it was 150 miles from home. Mary was then 16½ and had been ill for nine months.

ADMISSION TO INPATIENT ADULT WARD

As our clinic has no facilities for adolescents, she was placed on the women's open ward. Because of the nature of our clinic as a training center, there was frequent rotation of staff. Within the first five months three different psychiatric residents were assigned to Mary in turn. Each of them attempted to establish free verbal communication with her using sodium amytal as an aid at times because she was tense and blocked frequently in her interviews. Little was accomplished except the development of feelings of frustration in the therapists. On the ward she proved to be immature and demanding, and showed some affective withdrawal from those around her as well as periods of depression. She ate poorly and showed no interest in her family except as a source of material supplies. Because of her apparent helplessness it was difficult for some of the staff not to cajole and baby her. At the same time the insatiability of her demands for constant attention aroused feelings of impatience. Any expression of impatience produced periods of withdrawal and depression in Mary and feelings of guilt in the staff.

After five months the director of the children's division was consulted. He stressed the necessity to try to understand the patient's communications whether verbal or non-verbal and to respond to them with constant therapeutic behavior as well as verbal expression. He recognized that the ever present therapeutic potentialities of the relationship betwen patient and nurses (5) was particularly great with such a patient. Although Mary was nearly 17 she was moved to the children's ward, the population of which was for the most part 12 or younger. The closer supervision and collaboration available to nurses and residents on this service proved to be an aid to the staff members in reducing their anxiety, making it possible for them to deal somewhat less ambivalently with Mary's excessive childish demands and disguised hostilities. The probable close relation between Mary's illness and her parents' attitudes was recognized, and the parents were encouraged to come in as often as possible for interviews during which we expressed our attitudes of understanding acceptance of their anxieties and gave them recognition of any positive participation they showed in Mary's treatment.

ADMISSION TO CHILDREN'S WARD

During Mary's first weeks on the children's ward, discussion at staff conferences (5) frequently turned to the different ways in which the nurses might work with the patient and particularly to the variety of meanings and results which each approach might have. It was recognized that considerable care of Mary, if given with spontaneity, might give her the valuable experience of kindly, uncritical acceptance of her feelings. The possibility was accepted, however, that the nurses might soon find such care difficult and a source of resentment. It was also recognized that Mary might misinterpret this care as an expression of deprecation of her capabilities and might respond with even lessened attempts to help herself. On the other hand, it was felt that reduction in the amount of physical care given her might be interpreted by Mary as an expression of confidence in her and might therefore result in a lessening of her demands. The possibility that such reduction in care might occur as a result of resentment on the part of the nurses rather than of true greater expectation was examined. It was recognized that if the latter occurred or if Mary interpreted it so, her response might be greater regression, perhaps even psychotic in degree.

By the end of her sixth week on the ward, various changes were noted in Mary which seemed to indicate that the care she was receiving had established considerable rapport between her and some of the staff members. Among other things she was showing renewed interest in her family and home. At this point, also, the nurses felt clear enough in their attitudes toward Mary and among themselves that they felt they could refuse kindly but firmly and without feelings of hostility or guilt, to do for her the things which they knew she could do for herself. This new approach was undertaken and at the end of the first day she slid across the floor to the toilet. On the second day she dressed herself. By the end of a week she was much more alert, trying new things each day with pride and pleasure, and planning with her family a trip home for her birthday. By the end of two weeks she walked unaided to her parents' car to make her first visit home.

In the month which followed she made rapid progress, but the staff noted the close relation between any sign of ambivalence in the parents and transient hours of regression in Mary. Three months after her admission to the children's ward the parents acquiesced in Mary's demands to remain home and, although they were advised against it, the whole family withdrew from therapy, stating that they could complete the treatment which had been started and that trips to the clinic were too arduous and expensive to be continued.

DISCHARGE FROM HOSPITAL AGAINST OUR ADVICE

At home she remained well for about two months and then symptoms began to recur. After five months the parents requested readmission for her. They were seen and our lack of a vacant bed explained to them. Their expressed feelings of guilt over having removed her from therapy were relieved by our attitude of acceptance of their necessity and right to try what they felt was best. At the time the next bed was available they felt things were going better at home and decided against rehospitalizing Mary. They attributed her improvement at this time to chiropractic care. Thirteen months after her discharge, the parents urgently requested and were granted emergency admission for Mary because of long continued refusal to eat solid food and an explosion of rage in which she kicked the father with her "paralyzed" leg. She was then 18.

READMISSION TO CHILDREN'S WARD

It was with considerable feeling of confidence that we undertook to go on from where we left off in therapy. The charge nurse was familiar with Mary from her previous stay on the children's ward. She undertook to carry out the same firm consistent refusal to do things for Mary as before, but the girl's regressive, negativistic attitudes seemed only to become entrenched. She refused all food, anxiously stating it was poison. By the third day she was incontinent. On the fourth day it was recognized that she was in acidosis and I.V.'s were started. On the eleventh day tube feeding was augmented by I.V.'s and although following this she took some small sips of fluid, tube feeding has continued with two exceptions for the sixteen months which have followed her admission. At the end of 1½ months she ceased saying even such things as "Leave me alone. Everyone hates me." She wailed and wrung her hands at any attempt to care for her.

At the end of 2½ months and again at the end of five months signs of alertness led us to allow Mary to do some things for herself. Each attempt lasted only several days, after which anxiety about the condition of the skin on her back and the developing acidosis made it impossible for us to continue because of our great concern about the patient's physical welfare. It was during the second of these periods, however, that the only major change occurred in Mary during this hospitalization. She ceased her anguished wailing and hand wringing and became completely silent and limp. Some of the staff felt this was even greater regression to a near corpse-like state while others felt it was a sign of some relaxation of tension.

There has been no rapid change in Mary in the ten months since this, but those who know her well have come to recognize increasingly frequent response to them in the form of physiologic and behavior changes. Mary frequently hyperventilates when someone expresses warmth toward her. She sometimes holds her breath until she becomes cyanotic. Expression of anger on the part of the nurse will be answered with a flooding of the bed with urine or soiling of the sheets. Grudging or insistent attempts to care for her will be met with board-like muscular rigidity which makes it almost impossible to move her. Wailing occurs only on attempts to move her bed to include her in a ward group activity.

Although at the time of Mary's admission there was no therapist with time available to see her regularly, the child psychiatry resident who came on the service two months later undertook therapy with her. Attempts were made early to verbalize all the feelings which Mary might be having. This therapist's experience of frustration and anxiety at getting no response was similar to that experienced by others previously. She soon realized that only by expressing her own feelings both to her supervisor and to Mary could she tolerate the experience of sitting in the same room with the patient for any length of time. Fortunately, this resident psychiatrist has been on the children's service throughout Mary's stay and has had time to work through some of the initial feelings this patient tends to arouse in those around her with the result that she has gradually had somewhat less ambivalent personal contact to offer the girl.

WORK WITH PARENTS

Mary's parents have been included in therapy since her readmission, and the therapists of both have had significantly similar experiences to that of Mary's psychiatrist. Both father and mother are rather stolid, apparently timid people, with backgrounds of isolated farm life and marginal economic status. Early they presented the appearance of being unable to understand what was expected of them in the interviews and both therapists became frustrated in their attempts to gain any clearer understanding of what had occurred in Mary's life or what the parents were feeling. It was only when each therapist reached the point of giving up and was able to express his feelings frankly that some sense of rapport developed in the interviews. Although the distance the parents must travel and the expense involved have been realistic barriers to frequent visits, they have recently started coming more often, i.e. every other week. They have begun to recognize Mary's illness as a reaction to the intra-familial attitudes rather than as something apart from them, and are beginning to show more freedom of expression of their feelings toward each other, Mary, and the clinic staff.

DIAGNOSIS

Consideration of the range of symptoms that have been observed in this patient has repeatedly raised many questions as to the diagnosis. It would seem that it might have been possible to classify this illness, at some particular stage, in almost every one of our diagnostic categories of functional disorders, ranging from the mildest of neuroses to the severest of psychoses. Indeed, at times the question has been raised whether this might not be an obscure organic condition and not functional at all. It is unlikely that anyone would question the psychotic nature of Mary's present state, yet all who saw her during the first fifteen months of her illness felt the problem was a neurotic one. Early we would undoubtedly have called it an anxiety state. At one point neurasthenia appeared predominant. It seemed obvious when we first saw her that conversion hysteria was the proper diagnosis and yet such terms as "schizoid trends" and "depressive features" would have been applicable. Were these early symptoms in reality the prodrome of psychosis or has a neurosis turned into a psychosis? Is the patient at present a stuperous manic depressive or is she a catatonic schizophrenic? If she is the latter, where is the waxy flexibility of catatonia and how do we explain the intense affect which accompanied her crying? This veritable kaleidoscope of psychiatric symptoms seems to raise questions which are beyond the scope of the paper—questions as to the relationship between neuroses and psychoses and about the validity of our diagnostic categories. It has seemed to point out to us, however, the relative uselessness to the patient and to the therapist of finding a name by which to call the illness and to accentuate the necessity of approaching the problem by attempting to understand the dynamics behind the symptoms and to find the therapeutic responses to them.

PATIENT'S PAST HISTORY

Having decided that nosological diagnosis would not help in treating Mary, our inquiry turned to what had been learned from the anamnesis which might help. Mary is next to the youngest of six siblings ranging from 9 to 27 years of age, all of whom were born in the southern middle west. The father is a farm laborer whose income has always been marginal. Mary's developmental history is relatively uneventful except that she was breast fed until the age of 2½. She is said to have been a cheerful, pretty, active child who was always the favorite of the family. Both parents were ill sporadically throughout her early years and with the birth of the baby brother when she was 11, responsibility for Mary was turned over even more completely than previously to her eldest sister of whom she was very fond. Puberty at 12 is reported to have been uneventful except that Mary became less active. When she was 14, the family moved from the dust bowl to California seeking better employment because of the war-time boom. Although this move involved major changes in Mary's life—in her friends, her home, her church, and the type of community in which she lived—her initial adjustment was an adequate one. The parents, particularly the father, were hesitant about allowing the girls in the family much social freedom, especially with regard to dancing and dating. Yet they did not forbid these things completely and during her fourteenth year Mary had several boy friends but did not appear very serious about any of them. When she was

14½ her one older brother was suddenly called into the Army. Father began to work sporadically because farm jobs for older men were hard to find, and because he was ailing. He felt he had not bettered himself by leaving the south and he missed his own parents who were quite elderly. Mother and the children objected to prospects of returning, however, as they felt California had more to offer the younger generation. About the time Mary was 15, she seemed discontented with school and objected bitterly to several minor moves the family made. Four days before the end of school and after she had passed her final exams Mary collapsed in gym class with a severe attack of hyperventilation. She was then 15½. She later described the great anxiety she felt leading to the hyperventilation.

The parents have reported several major occurrences within the family since Mary became ill. In the period of time she was home between her first and present hospitalizations she accompanied her parents on a trip to their old home in Oklahoma. It was on the way back to California that she began to have increased complaints. During this period, also, her favorite sister became engaged and married, although Mary begged her not to. Since Mary's second hospital admission this same sister has given birth to a still-born son. The other three older siblings have also married and one of them now has a daughter.

It is not just the limitation of space which is responsible for the brevity of this historical review. One of the major obstacles in the work with the patient and her parents has been the reluctance of Mary and her parents to talk freely with us about past family events. Mary has told us little about her feelings toward her family and the parents have repeatedly said there were no more details to give, at least none they could remember. All of the therapists have been impressed by the fact that this very lack of information told them a good deal about the similarity between Mary's way and the parents' ways of expressing their feelings of deep mistrust and anxiety by a withdrawal from any real verbal communication. In spite of the therapeutic handicap, it has seemed to reemphasize for us the value of trying to understand and respond to whatever they may be trying to tell us of their feelings at each moment whether or not we have anamnestic material with which to correlate it (5).

THERAPEUTIC CONSIDERATIONS

In this inquiry our first consideration with regard to therapy has been whether we have approached the problem from the most rational point of view available to us from our knowledge of therapeutic principles and our past experience.* Throughout the past sixteen months one recurrent question

---

* These efforts occurred prior to the availability of psychotropic drugs.

has been whether or not Mary should have shock therapy rather than, or in conjunction with, psychotherapy. The fact that she has not been given electroshock has occasionally brought frank criticism from some members of the child psychiatry service who felt it might be beneficial. Particularly, the child psychiatry residents and nurses have found support for their critical attitude in the bantering remarks by their friends in other services of the hospital where electroshock and insulin were frequently used. Comments like, "Haven't you started shock *yet*? When are you going to give up?" were frequent. During the first six months this repeated opposition resulted in some vacillation on the part of the director as to whether he was justified in continuing a plan of treatment which he felt was basically sound as well as of research significance, despite the possibility that unknown variables might reduce the plan's effectiveness. As will be discussed more fully later, it has since been recognized that this vacillation in itself was one of the factors which was affecting his plan of treatment adversely. It increased the opposition of the staff who sensed the director's uneasiness and interpreted his decision as being arbitrary rather than based on conviction.

Review of the occasions on which the question of shock was raised among the ward staff has seemed to clarify the steps by which the decision was reached that it was not a rational form of treatment in this case. It now seems likely that it was sometimes suggested, not only as a disguised form of resentment toward the director, but as a way in which to express anger toward Mary as well. It is obvious also that it was sought as an escape from the frustrating job the staff was facing and as a means by which they could feel they were "doing something" (1). Confirmation of these probabilities may lie in the fact that when after five months the director consented to a pre-shock workup, the staff found that on completion of the blood tests, EEG, ECG, etc. they no longer felt under any pressure to urge the use of shock treatment itself (3).*

With our increasing conviction that shock therapy in this case would have been more beneficial in the resolution of the therapist's anxieties than the patient's psychogenic conflicts, we decided definitely not to abandon our efforts at psychotherapy. It was suggested, however, that shock therapy might make Mary more accessible to psychotherapy. On closer consideration of this possibility, we have felt this, too, was not a sound basis for treatment. No one has ever had any question but that Mary, without shock, was aware of what was said to and done for her. It might possibly establish some verbal

---

* The relief that shock treatment can afford a therapist's feelings of failure or hesitation to put his therapeutic skills to the test has been discussed by Gottschalk (3) and others.

response in the patient, but it seems unlikely that that would be helpful. We recall the early period of her first admission when she was speaking to her doctor and remember the lack of real communication between them. Even at that time improvement occurred only when increasing emphasis was placed on the communication possible through the total attitude toward her rather than speech alone. Perhaps we can argue that in that event shock would serve most forcibly as a form of non-verbal communication. But we recall the ominous progression of symptoms that followed each semi-assaultive type of therapy: amytal injections, surgery, spinal tap, etc.

THE USE OF COLLABORATIVE PSYCHOTHERAPY

What, then, can we say about the available forms of psychotherapy? Surely we have seen with sufficient clarity that emphasis on catharsis, verbal suggestion, or insight therapy have repeatedly failed with Mary at all stages in her illness. There is no reason to believe that increased emphasis on the verbal aspects of psychotherapy would be more helpful now that she is even more entrenched in her withdrawal than ever before. We continue to believe that establishment and therapeutic use of rapport with Mary through recognition of, and response to, her total person offers the most rational form of therapy. If this is the desired form of treatment, why was her previous improvement with it not maintained? There are two possibilities that occur to us. Perhaps the improvement within Mary was not yet stabilized when treatment was disrupted or perhaps she again encountered within the environment, those conflict-inducing experiences originally responsible for her illness. We recall the brevity of our first period of therapy with her. We remember the observed close relation between symptom recurrence and parental ambivalence, as well as the parents' participation in premature disruption of therapy. It would seem that both of our proposed possibilities are probabilities. Is there any therapeutic approach which might provide greater surety of reduction of the pathological forces which operate to produce or prolong her illness? Our past experiences have confirmed our belief that there is a close relationship between parental problems and emotional disturbances in children, even those who have already reached adolescence. Therapeutic effectiveness still seems to lie in the type of collaborative therapy of parents and child which places emphasis on the pathology within the family constellation as well as within the individual child.

Questions have also been raised about the nature of the therapeutic environment or milieu. Some objections have been voiced about the desirability of placing a patient with regressive tendencies into the regressive milieu, characteristic of a ward of much younger children. Our response has been that an adolescent ward might be more desirable but that in our experience in a situation where the choice has always been between an adult or children's ward, the availability of close collaboration among the staff has proved repeatedly to be more important than the age of the patient population.

The question as to whether in-patient or out-patient therapy would have been better for Mary is perhaps unanswerable. Our experience with previous cases where the problem seemed so clearly an intrafamilial one has emphasized for us the seriousness of such a step as hospitalization which alters as well as diminishes the opportunity for interaction between child and parents during the period of therapy. In Mary's case, however, the distance of her home from the clinic as well as the economic status of the family has made out-patient treatment unavailable at those times when the severity of her illness had lessened enough to make it feasible.

DIFFERENCES IN PARENT INVOLVEMENT

Since our inquiry into the therapeutic possibilities has only renewed our belief that collaborative psychotherapy of Mary and her parents by the nursing and psychiatric staff is the most rational approach to treatment, the question arises as to what have been the difficulties that have blocked Mary's improvement during our second in contrast to our first contact with her. Perhaps we should see first whether there was some essential difference in the two situations from the very moment of planning admission to the ward. On the first occasion the children's ward staff undertook Mary's therapy at a point where the critical anxiety initiating the change was that of previous therapists rather than of the parents. Admission of the girl to the children's ward at that time resulted in greater participation by the parents in Mary's treatment than previously. At the time of the second admission we undertook therapy at a point where it was the parents who were anxious about what they had not been able to do for her. Although they were included in the treatment plan even more than previously, the change represented an actual decrease in their participation in Mary's care. Have we any information which would support the probability that this difference was of significance? At the time of the parents' first reapplication only six months after withdrawal from therapy, their anxiety around the crisis at home was met by us with a calm acceptance of the reality situation of our lack of bed space, reassurance to them about their feeling of guilt over having taken her home against advice, and a frank acknowledgement with them that whatever decision was made at this point would have to be entirely theirs within the possibilities of reality—keep her home, commitment to a state hospital, or wait for our next available bed. This one brief contact with them seemed to have decreased their anxieties enough that Mary showed some improvement and they felt able to care for her for another half year. At the time of the second reapplication they phoned us pressing admission when the director was available for brief consultation only. The resident psychiatrist on whom the responsibility devolved for handling this crisis was relatively unfamiliar with this case and became understandably anxious at the story of near starvation. His feeling was that admission was probably desirable and the director agreed to this plan although feeling dissatisfied about the necessity for making the decision when he had no time to discuss the situation more fully. Hospitalization for Mary was agreed upon, therefore, without anyone having the opportunity of first attempting to alleviate the parental anxiety and guilt and also to help them again make their choice and consider the possibility that they might prefer state hospital commitment which would keep her nearer home and relieve them more fully of the burden of Mary's care than would treatment at the clinic. It would seem probable that the emergency nature of this admission left them with some feeling that their participation in therapy was expected of them as due atonement for their failure rather than that it was part of a plan they had voluntarily chosen to make because they did not feel they were ready to give up as yet. The greater freedom of movement which occurred in their interviews when their therapists finally expressed the feeling that we, too, had failed just as much as they, and that we were all "in the same boat" together would tend to confirm the fact that one obstacle to therapy had been set up at the very moment of hospital intake.

THERAPISTS' PROBLEMS: STATUS, COMPETENCE AND COMPETITION

A second area which would seem to require clarification is why, in the absence of the frequent rotation of the psychiatric staff which had repeatedly broken the continuity of therapy during the first hospitalization, did the present ongoing therapists find it so difficult to establish rapport with Mary and her parents. On review it seems that one source of the difficulty lay in the individual problems of each of the therapists. It is perhaps significant that the child psychiatry resident who has seen Mary during the past fourteen months had come to the clinic from a hospital where she had been in charge of a psychiatric program for a large number of primarily impulsive, aggressive children. Although she had previously worked under the supervision of the director of the Children's Service, it soon became apparent that she had ambivalent feelings about returning to training status, as well as about the necessary shift in her interests to the problems of withdrawn children such as Mary. Although frequent supervisory hours with the director resulted in diminution of the conflict, it was further complicated by the fact that shortly after she began to see Mary, a new position of assistant director was created on the ward. The new assistant director took over officially some of the minor administrative responsibilities which had previously devolved upon this child psychiatry resident. During the first few weeks the resident's tendency to perceive the situation as a threat to her own status was increased by the new assistant director's marked interest in Mary's case, his repeated visits to the patient's room and his frequent suggestions about how one might reach the emotions behind the girl's puzzling symptoms. Resolution occurred when at one particularly discouraging point the resident offered to resign from the case and allow the assistant director to take over, upon which she became aware that his interest in Mary was not derogatory, but a genuine wish to be of help.

The therapist of the mother, at that time a junior psychiatric social worker, likewise had mixed feelings about her position on the Children's Service. Although a relatively mature person, she had only recently finished her training period and was both pleased and somewhat fearful about having been asked to fill a staff position which more experienced predecessors had found difficult. These doubts about her own adequacy, which are common to relatively inexperienced therapists, were accentuated by the fact that she interpreted some differences of opinion between the director of the children's division and the director of the social service department of the hospital as putting her in a position of being caught between them. The director had frankly stated his opinion that there was no basic difference in the psychotherapeutic interviews by psychiatric residents and the casework interviews of social workers since both had as their purpose the reduction of anxieties in the patient and the effectiveness of both depended largely on the level of therapeutic skill and personal maturity of the interviewer. The director of the social service department had stated equally frankly that she felt social casework was in certain aspects basically different from psychotherapy. As the worker became aware that she had a greater degree of maturity than many other beginning therapists, she gradually perceived more clearly that these differences in opinion need not be a threat to her own work with patients if she could work out her own individual feelings about any particular patient and her feelings about her status in each of the departments through conferences with her social work supervisor and the director of the children's service.

EFFECT OF SOME RESOLUTION OF THERAPISTS' CONFLICTS

The resident psychiatrist who has been treating Mary's father for the past eight months has recently become aware that his early work was influenced by feelings of competition with his predecessor on the case. Frequent supervisory hours with the director have aided in gradual diminution of his problem as well as those of the other two therapists. The result has been subsequent greater movement in the therapy with Mary. For the sake of brevity we shall report only one example of the confirmation we have had of this process. When the father's therapist accepted the fact that he might fail as thoroughly as his predecessor, he was able to discuss quite frankly with the father his deep discouragement. Within a week after this interview the father's seemingly serious complaints of dyspnea and cardiac pain disappeared and he has since expressed his feeling that could he choose, he would find it less painful to give up as Mary has than to struggle on with the worry she has caused him.

WARD-STAFF PROBLEMS

A third source of difficulty was the even more complex problems the nurses had to deal with. During the weeks which preceded Mary's readmission, the ward population had shifted to a younger age group with the admission of four pre-school children. A number of the new patients were severely disturbed. In spite of this, there was an unusually small staff during Mary's first weeks in the hospital because of illness and an approaching holiday.

There have been in addition to these problems on the ward some essential difficulties within the nursing staff itself. In the past sixteen months there have been three different nurses in charge of the ward in succession. The first of these had been very interested in Mary during her first hospitalization and voluntarily assumed her care upon readmission. Although she reported that the same kind, firm attitudes were being shown Mary as previously, the rapid regression in the patient made it seem obvious that there were disruptive tensions present which were not being understood. Later it became clear that the other nurses had sensed and resented in this nurse both decreased spontaneity and interest in the total ward program. She was actually planning to leave the profession but hesitated to confide in the other nurses. Although it continued to be her responsibility to make ward plans, the carrying out of many of them devolved upon other nurses who, resenting their unexplained extra duties, found it difficult to express their feeling to her at points of disagreement. Some of the other senior nurses felt that she was wrong in assuming that, because of her own previous experience with Mary, the staff as a whole should be able to feel toward the patient as she did. Because of their other resentments they reacted with a withdrawal of interest in Mary rather than open expression of their feelings. The resultant lack of support of the other senior nurses made the charge nurse's

care of Mary, coupled with her ward administrative duties, an almost impossible responsibility. After one and a half months she expressed in ward
rounds her feelings of frustration and discouragement to the point of raising
the question, "Why has Mary not been given shock?" The possibility that
Mary's care on our ward might be too much for the nurses was accepted by
the director. With this more open discussion of the difficulties involved,
others of the senior nurses expressed willingness to share in her care. One in
particular among them felt it would not be fair to Mary to give up and
sensed a challenge in the situation. She has continued throughout the months
which have followed to assume a major proportion of the responsibility for
the girl's care.

With the resignation of the first charge nurse three months after Mary's
admission, the assistant charge nurse, a woman who was better able to
discuss frankly her awareness and concern about the feelings of the children
and staff, assumed the position. Some of the tensions which had long been
present on the ward (4) because of the relationship between these two disappeared. It seemed that a more direct and less ambivalent attitude was
gradually developing toward Mary and at one point a new attempt was
made to express confidence in her ability to do things for herself. Mary did
respond with increased relaxation, but the senior nurses soon recognized the
signs of increasing anxiety in a portion of the staff, and the attempt was
abandoned until such time as more of them could feel easy about it.

THE PROBLEM OF EXAGGERATED SELF-EXPECTATIONS

Shortly after this, this second charge nurse left the ward for a supervisory
position, and a third nurse who had had relatively little previous experience
with children came to the ward. The staff recognizes that it takes a considerable period of time for a new nurse to adjust to the demands of a ward such
as ours, where the degree of disturbance of the children is a considerable
emotional drain. In addition, the director feels it is possible for the nurses to
participate in the long-term therapeutic program (5), rather than limiting
their sphere of responsibility to the patient's immediate welfare. This expectation that the nurses shall be, not only "eyes and ears" for the doctors,
but also frequently the most effective members of the therapeutic team,
tends to make the nurses feel that their abilities are given more recognition
than on most psychiatric wards. It is frequently perceived by a new nurse,
however, as an added and somewhat threatening demand on her resources.
With this present charge nurse's increasing feeling of security in her position, the tension in the staff and in the children which followed her arrival
on the ward has gradually decreased. It is probable that the increasing emo-

tional interaction that Mary shows with the nurses is in part a reflection of this as well as of the now relatively long continuity of her relationship with one nurse.

GUILT AS A STAFF PROBLEM

We have already indicated that a fourth and very serious problem in therapy consisted of the feelings of inadequacy, frustration, anger and guilt which Mary and her family tend to evoke in all those who work with them. It has been extremely hard for the staff to gain some real understanding that this family had not only the apparent wish but also the ability and right to "defeat" their therapeutic efforts. Their intense desire to succeed with this case sometimes made them set as their therapeutic goal Mary's recovery. The more realistic goal would have been the reduction of anxiety within the family to the best of their ability at any given moment. The resultant frustration at their inability to achieve their goal tended to produce feelings of resentment in them toward the patient and her family, each of whom reacted by increased resistance.

It has been even harder for the staff to recognize the possibility that they might be able to help this family even though their therapeutic skill and personal emotional maturity might not yet be as great as they wished. It was difficult for them to realize that frank acceptance of their limitations without feelings of guilt could be more helpful than attempts to assume attitudes of inexhaustible warmth because they felt a more experienced person might feel this way.

INTRASTAFF PROBLEMS: NEED FOR AND ANXIETY ABOUT ACHIEVEMENT

All of these difficulties might have been more readily recognized and their reduction sought and gained in staff conferences and supervisory hours with the director had not a fifth problem existed in the form of ambivalent feelings toward the director on the part of the staff as a whole in relation to this case. The staff knew that collaborative psychotherapeutic work with families whose children showed serious psychotic withdrawal was of particular interest to him. They were pleased to be asked to participate in this undertaking but were fearful of possible failure. As a result, they resentfully felt that perhaps he was expecting too much of them. Frequent criticism of his program from other departments within the hospital supported their ambivalence and made free discussion with him even harder. The director's repeated attempts to discover the sources of the staff's tension and to impress on them the probable consequences to Mary if it were not reduced, were interpreted, particularly by the nurses, as anxiety about the seriousness of the girl's illness. They entered into a kind of competition to be the one to bring him word that she had improved. Mary responded to their pressure appropriately with more negativism, but their desire to succeed made it difficult for them to recognize this. On review it becomes clear that many things failed to be reported in conferences or were only partially reported. For instance, when Mary drank half a glass of water, it was not reported because it was not positive enough, and when she soiled the bed immediately upon removal of the bedpan, it was not reported because it was too negative. It was recognized that she relaxed during the hours the intravenous fluids were given but it was not reported that the nurse who sat in the room felt calm and useful while watching a Murphy drip and felt angry and impotent while watching only Mary.

THE DIRECTOR'S PROBLEM OF ATTAINING OPENNESS WITH A NEW STAFF

The continued inability of the staff to share their problems fully with the director led to a sixth difficulty in the work with this case. Lacking the minute but significant evidences of interpersonal reaction between Mary and the adults around her, he failed to achieve that grasp of the total situation which in other more long-standing and equally difficult cases had given him a deep sense of conviction that even with the present training level of his staff they might, with help, find this plan of treatment possible. Doubts assailed him as to whether he was not, indeed, expecting too much of them.

In recent months since this review was begun he has gained some greater clarity about the total situation, including the awareness that his previous doubts had in part supported some of the ambivalent attitudes within the staff. He has since been able to express with a more reassuringly authoritative attitude his strong impression that it was unnecessary for them to subtly sabotage their own and one another's efforts through lack of direct discussion of their feelings. As a result they have sensed more clearly that his concern was not about hopelessness regarding the patient's illness but about the intrastaff tensions.

In the last few months we have observed signs of greater movement in therapy of the whole family. On a few occasions Mary has spoken brief sentences to the nurses. Her expression of affect through "body language" is even more frequent and direct. For example, unavoidable failure of the nurse to enter her room for relatively long periods has resulted in finding Mary lying unhurt on the floor beside her bed although she seemingly is unable to move when anyone is present. She has recently vomited after some of her tube feedings and recognition that this might be her expression that she was ready to try something else has resulted in her taking small amounts of fluid offered her from a cup.

In spite of the realistic handicap of the time and money involved in their 150 mile trips to the clinic, the parents have been coming in more frequently than formerly and appear more relaxed. Mother has been able to express her feeling that Mary is fighting them, as well as her feeling that father has always babied this daughter too much. Father says, "Mary will talk one of these days when she gets ready. I think we've been a bit too keen on pushing her."

SUMMARY

For us, at least in this one instance, we have to answer the question raised by the title of this paper in the affirmative. Confusion in one person can be worse confounded by uncertainty in others—a neurosis can be transmuted to a psychosis (1, 2).* We feel that this review of the complex inter-relationships of Mary, her family and our staff has emphasized for us, however, the great potentialities of unambivalent collaborative therapy as well as the multiple difficulties involved in achieving it. Although we have found some effective methods for reducing these difficulties, we recognize that it is too early to predict the degree of probability of therapeutic success. It is also obvious that in spite of our greater optimism about the possibility of achieving it, we cannot at this point venture an estimate as to how long it might take. In other words, one could say that although one knows from experience it can happen, one can never be quite sure that it will. Perhaps all we have been saying in this report is that one reason why more has not happened is that too many, if not all of us, for at least part of the time, did not *know* out of our previous experience that it *could*.

CONCLUSION

These experiences have led to more clearly defined policies of close collaboration and development of greater freedom by all staff members to disagree openly with each other and the director. Our work in this case is frequently referred to by staff members as a reminder that failure to communicate openly may lead to increased problems in working with the very disturbed children in our ward setting.

---

* Betz (1, 2) and others have discussed the possibilities as well as the difficulties of resolving the barrier which the presence of a "schizophrenic pattern" of reacting to others presents, whether or not it is of psychotic degree.

ADDENDUM

We feel that this follow-up information about Mary, fragmentary as it is, will be of interest to the readers.*

DISCHARGE FROM CHILDREN'S SERVICE

In the seven months after the paper was written, there were several cycles of improvement in capacity to interact with others and to feed and care for herself, after which Mary would relapse. This usually had to do with feeling neglected by her mother or therapist and staff because of their illness or other patient commitments. The parents' disagreement about Mary's care came out into the open. Mother was more reluctant to sacrifice time and money. Finally, they decided they could not afford the trips and arranged to hospitalize her in a state hospital near home. They took her from the hospital against medical advice. Mary was again doing well and promptly relapsed when told of the transfer. The diagnosis was Dementia Praecox, Catatonic Type, unimproved.

STATE HOSPITAL COURSE

During Mary's state hospitalization of almost three years, she was given many courses of Electro Shock Therapy. She was slowly able to develop relationships with a male hospital aid and began to verbalize a bit and sit in a wheel chair, attend patient entertainment and then would have exacerbations of immobile catatonia. It is of interest that after admission, as she began to emerge from catatonic stupor in the state hospital, she repeatedly asked for Dr. Szurek, who saw her frequently for a few moments at a time on our ward. He never worked directly with her. She did regard him as did the staff as a vital figure in her treatment. When she talked to her psychiatrist, she angrily remarked that her mother could kill her for being sick. Later she said the family was very upset by the death of her sister's child. Mary felt the family cared more about the baby than Mary and that they rejected her totally. With physical therapy, she learned to walk. She said she was in love with a former male patient who visited her. She then became concerned with her appearance, attended dances and ate in the diningroom. She continued her regressions if attention was diverted from her. After many visits home in a wheel chair, she was on extended leave to her sister and then

---

* We are very grateful to Freeman Adams, M.D., and to our colleague on our staff, Gwen McCullough, M.D., for the follow-up information on the later life experiences of our patient. We thank Dr. Adams for making the records of the Stockton State Hospital available, and Dr. McCullough for the many hours of labor spent in reviewing the voluminous records and compiling an excellent summary for which space here did not permit inclusion in its complete form.

discharged and was able to go home to her parents as essentially minimally verbal, not able to walk or to interact much, but able to eat by herself and not requiring hospital care. The diagnosis was Dementia Praecox, Catatonic Type, Moderately Improved.

MIRACLE CURE

About one year later, at a Revival Church meeting, she was "saved" and walked away from the wheel chair and began to communiciate freely. She had already begun to relate to a divinity student. She was subsequently married twice to a revivalist minister and an Air Force man. She had two children and one further state hospitalization in another state for psychosis and some out-patient care over the next eight years. Our last contact was with a social agency that filed a "neglect of children petition." We have no idea about her mental state at this time, some 12 years after discharge from our care.

These follow-up notes give us some sense of the psychotic, hysterical and borderline psychotic alternations that this young woman continued to experience. There was some hint that her troubles increased after separation from a husband.

REFERENCES

1. BETZ, BARBARA J. Experiences in the Psychotherapy of Obsessive-Schizophrenic Personalities. *Southern Med. Journal*, 1946, 39:249-256.
2. BETZ, BARBARA J. A Study of Tactics for Resolving the Autistic Barrier in the Psychotherapy of the Schizophrenic Personality. *American J. Psychiatry*, 1947, 104:267-273.
3. GOTTSCHALK, LOUIS A. Systematic Psychotherapy of the Psychoses. *Psychiat. Quarterly*, 1947, 21:554-574.
4. SHEIMO, S. L., PAYNTER, J., and SZUREK, S. A. Problems of Staff Interaction with Spontaneous Group Formations on a Children's Psychiatric Ward. *Amer. J. Ortho.*, 1949, 19:699-611. Also in S. A. Szurek, I. N. Berlin and Maleta J. Boatman (Eds.), *Inpatient Care for the Psychotic Child*. Palo Alto, California: Science and Behavior Books, 1971. Pp. 122-137.
5. SZUREK, S. A. Dynamics of Staff Interaction in Hospital Psychiatric Treatment of Children. *Amer. J. Ortho.*, 1947, 17:652-664. Also in S. A. Szurek, I. N. Berlin and Maleta J. Boatman (Eds.), *Inpatient Care for the Psychotic Child*. Palo Alto, California: Science and Behavior Books, 1971. Pp. 138-154.

32

Some Observations from the Treatment of Parents and Their Psychotic Son

Robert D. Wald, M.D.

> "When Nicholas leaves for school, I think to myself, 'Now I am a normal person with two normal children and I can work everything out for myself.' When he comes home, I don't feel normal anymore. It's like I'm afflicted with an emotional illness."

This statement was made by the mother during a treatment session six months after therapy began with Nicholas and his parents. Its few words express data tending to validate the hypothesis this paper would examine. In general, this hypothesis states that the intrapersonal and interpersonal conflicts of the parents are generative of unsatisfying compromise solutions (3) which are anxiety laden. The anxious parent, usually the anxious mother, transmits the anxiety as well as the methods of compromise solution to the child which leads to, to quote from Szurek, "early, continuous distortion of biological tendencies of the human organism after birth by anxieties induced from anxious parents" (11). This general hypothesis is continuing to be examined at this Institute and elsewhere. This case report examines a special aspect of the general hypothesis.

The life histories of Nicholas' parents reveal startling similarities in their backgrounds. Both of them are children of Lutheran ministers, born and raised in church parsonages. From earliest childhood they learned that it was unacceptable to their parents to express "negative" feelings. Disappointment or discouragement was considered a sign of weakness. Fear was dealt with by invocations to prayer, and anger was so unacceptable it led to threats of the loss of heavenly Grace.

The special focus of this paper deals with the nature of the interactions between these parents that occur as a result of their own special early training, and the ways in which their isolation from their aggressive and hostile feelings play a part in the problems of their child. Selected clinical material is used to support this illustration of that specific aspect of the general hypothesis. To be demonstrated is the manner in which the character of the child becomes the resultant of unexpressed conflictual forces that exist in and between the parents.

Stated another way, maladaptive modes of thinking and behaving that we call mental illness of whatever sort are products of the learning of the child in his postnatal experiences, principally with his parents and his world. In a conflict-ridden home, such aberrant modes that do develop, may be not only not "bizarre" or "just plain crazy," but understandable, and describable as resultants. An understanding of the specific conflicts shows such modes to be also purposive and functional. Although Haley was discussing "schizophrenics" in their family settings, his point is well taken here; that the thesis of family origin refines a demonstration of the function of schizophrenic behavior in the family.

Of secondary interest to this paper is Nicholas' somatic illness. At age 22 months he had the onset of convulsions which were investigated at a children's hospital. Aside from a "very abnormal" EEG, physical examination and other laboratory studies were negative. Six years later, roentgenograms of the skull showed calcification which upon detailed study was diagnosed as a calcified right chorioid plexus. He has been on anticonvulsant medication, Dilantin and phenobarbital, for two years. At age 2½ years a diagnosis of "severe mental retardation" was given the family. Subsequent examiners were impressed with the evidences of negativistic and autistic behavior. An a priori association of the convulsive disorder with the psychological disturbance, leading to an assumption of a causal relationship on an organic basis for his psychotic behavior, is untestable and, we feel, open to question (7). The question that *is testable*, and remains so regardless of the presence of the organic findings, is whether conflict reductive psychotherapy of the parents and the child offers the possibility of alteration of the behavior, including the nonlearningness that is involved in the educational and intellectual retardation. The central thesis of this paper is not involved in the "organic vs. functional" argument; for purposes of our discussion, Nicholas' organic illness could be in another organ system. Strauss and Kephart (9) have pointed out that behavior disturbances not related to brain injury are frequently co-existent with evidence of brain injury. Further, Strauss and Lehtinen (10), using Bradley's (4) early criteria of the behavior of children with schizophrenic illness, contrast on eight criteria the differentiation of these children from brain injured children. Only one criterion is shared, "daydreaming."

Nicholas' parents, Charles and Anne, are both "P.K.'s" (preachers' kids). They both were born in and grew up in Lutheran parsonages. And for both of them, in the public eye as "P.K.'s" so often are, the learning of appropriate external characteristics of behavior was preeminent in their parents' view. Equally so, each of them had the weekly occasion to see their father reverently considered on the pulpit, and realistically considered at home. In neither of their homes was the comparison conjunctive.

Charles' father, orphaned when young, could never consistently bring to his home the peacefulness he apparently brought his parishioners. He was highly thought of in the rural and town areas he served in Southern California throughout Charles' youth. But at home, he was something of a martinet, given to spells of dark depression and self-pitying despair. Charles' older brother avoided contact with father at these times, and his mother fled once to a short-termed marital separation when Charles was six and later to chronic alcoholism. The disruption in his home was of grave concern to the young Charles. He learned that if he "babied" his father by rubbing his feet, speaking softly the many blandishments he had learned from his father's own lips, that his father would soften and sometimes appear to be relieved from his own distress. "Smile and the world smiles with you," "Every cloud has a silver lining," and such expressions were apparently effective when offered by the boy in the repair of his father's feelings. For his efforts, Charles felt he was the favorite of his father, although he also knew that for this position he had alienated his siblings. Later in life, when Charles left home to prepare for the seminary training he chose, his father had a severe depression that required a year's retirement from church work. Perhaps because of his responsiveness to his father in earlier years, Charles remembers his home as quiet and peaceful except when father was upset.

Anne's father was the minister of a larger church in a wealthy community, and though not exceedingly well paid for his services, the social situation into which the minister and his family were projected well suited Anne's mother. She was the child of a wealthy family, who had "given up so much" to marry a man of the cloth. Anne's mother was a driving woman who felt the parsonage to be an extension of the church. In her view, all the furnishings and the people in the parsonage were vestments of that church. She was the minister of the home, as her husband was the minister of the church. He was highly regarded by his parishioners as a strong and able person, ready to be of help to them in their personal or marital problems as well as their spiritual problems. But at home, Anne remembers him as a meek person who would "never stand up to" his wife, nor support either of his two children in disputes with their mother. Anne's father had a number of disabling depressions in years gone by, and recently had one of almost psychotic proportions.

Both Charles and Anne learned early that their behavior had to be exemplary; members of their fathers' churches were watching them. Each was taught the importance of appearing happy and cheerful and of denying unhappy and restless feelings.

In Charles' home, the prescription for recapturing outward appearance of smiling tranquility was to recall how much one had to be grateful for, and to remember the aphorisms and proverbs that emphasized the positive.

For Anne, any lapse into despondence or rejection was seen by her mother as evidence that she was getting sick, and any expression of annoyance or anger was willful sinfulness, proving the child's wavering Faith. For Anne to be seen as sick, meant further restriction of her childish freedoms and intensification of her mother's overwhelming control of her. When she would be put to bed, her uneasiness would increase, and she would look at the picture of Jesus above her bed, whose gentle face seemed to speak to her in her mother's words, "Are you doing enough for me?"

Charles and Anne share further common features in their histories through their teens. Neither was interested in athletics nor was either in the center of the social swim in their own settings. Both were, as might be expected, extremely well behaved. Anne had frequent minor illnesses throughout adolescence. Charles experienced a year of chronic depression when he was in his last year in the seminary. His description of his symptoms, months apart in the telling from the description of his father's difficulties of many years earlier, was remarkably similar.

Anne's brother and Charles were classmates in preseminary training. In this way, Nicholas' parents met and ultimately became betrothed and married. They were married by her father, and Charles' first Call was as assistant minister to his father-in-law.

The Call was arranged by Anne's mother, without objection by her father. Mother wanted her child, now newlywed, to be close to her as she felt Anne needed maternal attention because of her "poor heart," "delicate condition," and because "she wasn't well." By this time, although she had no evidence of ill health, the early lessons of "not wanting to cross mother," were so thoroughly learned that she had no objection. It was only with great effort that Charles and Anne were able to rent a place of their own rather than to live in the parsonage with the bride's parents as her mother wished. Charles saw the attention his wife received from her mother as "natural" and thought that his wife would "grow up with marriage" and be able to be independent of her mother. Anne's mother turned to Charles as an ally whenever she felt her daughter was showing signs of "sickness"—the severe anxiety and guilt she felt when she moved toward independence. Charles, from his own background, as a master "peacemaker," enjoined his wife to be reasonable as he agreed with his mother-in-law that they should take care of Anne. Some of his willingness to accept the authority of the elders he saw as an investment in the future; the social station of that church was substantially above his father's, and he saw a bright future for himself there.

Anne's first pregnancy, leading to Nicholas' birth, occurred with planning three years after the couple was married. Except for morning sickness in the first trimester, and the recurrence of the colicky pains that had previously been diagnosed as "gall bladder trouble," she enjoyed the pregnancy. The obstetrician selected was a member of the congregation. At first this was explained that it would be "unthinkable" to go outside the church. Later it was said that "naturally" a member of the church would reduce or cancel his fee to the minister.

Anne had polyhydramnios. When she went into labor, the selected physician was not present. The attending doctor, concerned that an abnormal presentation had caused the prolonged first stage, stopped labor with a narcotic. The appointed doctor arrived and after the 24-hour first stage of labor, did a midforceps rotation and delivered Nicholas after a 70-minute second stage. Although he cried immediately, he aspirated some amniotic fluid and was apneic for an unspecified time. The pediatrician who assumed his care that same day, and who followed Nicholas' progress for the next 15 months, stated that he was normal in appearance and development throughout that time.

Almost from birth Nicholas was noted to be very active and inclined to irritability. He was breast fed for three weeks. He was described by his mother as "always a colicky and nervous baby." An abnormal sleep pattern developed with "night-day reversals." He slept fitfully and awakened the parents from their sleep and distracted them from periods of rest. He was not a "feeding problem."

He sat at 6 months, walked at 9½ months and said his first words by 12 months.

During the first year of Nicholas' life his mother felt he constituted a severe restriction on her freedom. She stated, "I don't want to blame Nicholas" but she felt his birth limited her social life. His continuing and increasing demands to be held, a pattern established in the first few weeks of his life when he cried, disturbed her daytime activities as well as her sleep at night. At the same time her growing discontent with her husband's evening absences from home on church business, as well as her discontent with the physical plant that was the home, added to the stresses she felt. Furthermore, she was increasingly troubled with chronic right upper quadrant pain and tenderness. Her husband quietly, but continually, made known his displeasure with her failure to participate in church affairs, "as ministers' wives are supposed to do." She became agitated and depressed. She couldn't find a moment to herself.

At church services the child would become restless and cry and she would have to leave. She remembers having fears that she would act upon the impulse she felt to stand up in church and shout out "Go to Hell." She felt guilty about this and became more depressed. She thought of killing herself. She stopped attending church and couldn't "make" her husband understand. When she would speak of her fearful impulses to him, he would laugh at her and tell her she was a good Christian woman, and assure her if she had enough faith, all would turn out well. She developed sudden fears that she might strangle Nicholas or smash his head. The more disturbed she became, the more restless and difficult to manage Nicholas became.

Flatulence and bloating, symptoms she had before marriage, increased in intensity during Nicholas' infancy, and when he was 9 months old, Anne had a cholecystectomy. Almost total care of Charles and the baby was then assumed by her mother. When Anne returned from an uneventful hospital course, she didn't regain her vitality as she expected to, and her mother continued to cook and clean for them. But even as Anne did regain some stamina, she found her mother disapproving of her resumption of household duties. Her mother urged her to protect herself, recalling her frail condition, her undefined heart trouble, and so on.

Charles told his wife he was interested in striking out for himself and having his own church. He was growing increasingly restless and anxious about the control his mother-in-law was exerting over his family. Nominally supporting her husband, Anne wavered but did not give in to her mother's threats and demands that the two families stay close together.

The parents moved to another community 400 miles away when Nicholas was 14 months old. Complaints she tentatively offered her husband about their new situation, he hushed up with calls to her need for more faith. His own discontents with the new station never came to awareness as he tackled the flood of work, and his absences from the home increased. Anne felt isolated. She was afraid to stay alone with Nicholas in the house at night. Three months after arrival, she sent for her mother. Mother came and relieved her of many chores. Anne experienced an increase in her obsessive thoughts of suicide and her phobic avoidance of church. Charles dealt with Anne's anxious concerns for her safety and sanity with invocations to greater faith and better Christian living. She said, "He wasn't my husband, he was my minister—and the more I needed a husband, the more he sounded like a minister."

Eight months after they arrived at their new home, five months after grandmother joined them, Nicholas had his first seizure. He was 22 months old. The quality of family interactions didn't change following this; but they became more intense.

Anne's mother and Charles' parents, soon after a diagnosis of petit mal epilepsy, became convinced that the child "should be put away." The parents vacillated in their wishes for the child, but not equally. Anne, becoming more frightened about the baby, noted growing reluctance to touch Nicholas. "I was afraid I might break it . . . I might drop it." Charles, charged with the nocturnal walking of the baby, found that he could walk and sleep at the same time, "I'd forget I was even holding the baby." He began to look forward to their next child, wishing to prove he could sire a normal child.

Anne never cried and rarely openly complained to Charles. For when she did, his response was of such darkening discomfort that her original distress was intensified. They therefore both attempted to remain calm and reasonable in the context of their separately mounting tension and despair. Anne's mother "understood" how upset her daughter was and responded by taking over more and more of the family's decisions.

The part of his wife's complaints Charles could hear had to do with her discontents about their home and the town they lived in; absent from his own awareness was his again growing discontent with his in-laws' interference in their lives. He asked for another church in a small remote area—then he realized he had found a place to the complete dislike of his in-laws. When they arrived at their third home, Nicholas improved measurably. By this time he was three years old.

Nicholas did not speak sentences. A few scattered words, apparently appropriate, were accepted by the parents as all they might expect from a "severely mentally retarded" child. Anne recalls how they used to discuss Nicholas' problems in front of him, "as though he wasn't there," "just like he was a statue." He was no longer having convulsions, but seemed "always on the verge of mischief."

In their new home, six months went by before Anne began to feel oppressed by the weight of responsibility. She didn't like being a minister's wife, with the frequent and unavoidable intrusions on her personal affairs. But each time she felt this keenly she tried harder, encouraged by her husband's wish for her to be his helpmate.

Frequent visits from her mother undermined her adjustment there. In a few months, Anne's mother convinced her to return to the Bay Area where she could get proper medical care for Nicholas. Anne was encouraged by her mother to leave Charles, who, she was assured, would soon follow. As Anne pondered this decision, Nicholas began to have temper tantrums, became more hyperactive, and showed some directly aggressive behavior. Intermittent urinary incontinence were noted for the first time.

Anne returned to the area of her mother's home—Charles followed soon after, feeling very defeated as a husband and a minister. He resigned that church position. He felt he had failed in breaking his wife away from her mother. When Charles returned to the Bay Area, as his mother-in-law had predicted he would, he worked with his father and brother-in-law in a small business they had established earlier. This business failed and Charles moved to various selling jobs until he located his present employment as an organ and piano salesman. The parents and Nicholas lived in a small house which belonged to and was near Anne's parents.

The second child was born when Nicholas was 5 years 3 months old. When his mother returned from her confinement, Nicholas had a single grand mal convulsion. He had been free of seizures and without medication for three years. Phenobarbital was restarted for a few weeks and was discontinued. No convulsions recurred.

Anne accepted her mother's advice to lighten her own burdens by letting Nicholas spend time at his grandparents' home. It soon became the pattern for Nicholas to run over to grandmother's house after breakfast and return in time to be bedded down for the night. At this time Nicholas developed persistent urinary frequency which was thought to be "quite a nuisance" by his parents. Urologic examinations, including urethroscopy, was negative.

Nicholas was enrolled in a nursery school for retarded children when he was 5½. His sibling, brother James, was 3 months old. The medical consultants at that school first thought of Nicholas as severely retarded, but in their later experience with him, were increasingly struck with his withdrawal, autistic behavior, hyperactivity, and his impulsive aggressiveness.

Nicholas' grandmother taught him table manners, neatness of dress and appearance, and nursery rhymes in German, a language not otherwise used in either home. Her attitude was that he would deteriorate and die soon, and her care was directed to make him comfortable and to keep him from being troublesome to her daughter. He continued in nursery school, under the general care of his grandmother, until he was 7¼, when the family was referred to this Institute.

The parents wanted to know how severely retarded he was. Their complaints were varied. "He has intelligence he doesn't use. When you cross him, he has a temper tantrum . . . he is jealous of James and he pushes children at school. He plays with adults but refuses to play with children." They wanted to learn better ways to handle Nicholas and to learn how to help him use whatever ability he had more completely and effectively. They did not feel Nicholas was emotionally disturbed. Clearly, they denied tension or strife which might recommend they participate in therapy.

An outpatient study was started when Nicholas was 7 years 7 months.

A month later, he was admitted to the ward, in part to facilitate further laboratory examinations that could not be conducted on an outpatient basis. The study continued for four months.

Although not formally stated, such a study fulfills the criteria of the World Health Organization's recommendations (5) for the formulation of a "dynamic diagnosis." The criteria are:

1. The study in depth of the child's behavior disorders.
2. The study of the child's personality in its present state, including his somatic state.
3. The study of the child's family (biographical and familial).
4. The study of the various types of milieu of the child's family in all their respects, social, economic, cultural and emotional.

Observed here, Nicholas was described as a child who kissed and hugged without affect, as though taught these techniques without understanding their purpose. He kept to himself. He tapped one palm with a rubber hatchet held in the other. He hummed parts of songs and occasionally clearly shouted single or paired words to the observer. He had a short attention span and was only with effort able to restrain himself when presented with frustration. The emergence of destructive behavior was prominent when outwardly directed aggression was blocked. The hand tapping was easily converted to fierce pounding of self—this also extended to hitting his teeth, lips and cheeks. He responded to control of this self-destructive behavior by others and showed an effort to accept the limits and the control. He tended to be "unpredictably" explosive in response both to expectations of others, to prohibitions and to requests for constructive play activities.

During the first three weeks, he had to be shown the lavatory each time he indicated a need to use it. He seemed unable to remember his way about the ward for two months. He ate poorly. He appeared disinterested in the events about the ward. He didn't make a firm relationship with the special nurse assigned his care. Masturbatory play was common. Mother was observed scolding him for this, which was seen as a prelude to another episode of self-destructive behavior. He remained continent throughout his hospitalization.

Psychological testing was not possible. The Vineland Social Maturity Scale suggested a 2½ year retardation. His failures were in items of cooperative interaction with others and in school achievement.

Physical and laboratory examinations were all normal except for the EEG and the discovery of an intracranial calcification, just under the temporal horn of the right lateral ventricle. Some dilatation of the horn was thought to exist. The EEG showed right hemispheric slowing with a right midtemporal spike wave focus, suggesting the possibility of brain damage. A right carotid arteriogram was negative, ruling out arterial or venous fistulae. Toxoplasmosis, a possible cause of calcification, was also ruled out. Neurosurgical consultants supported our impression that the intracranial lesion was a hypertrophied and calcified chorioid plexus. There was no evidence of increased intracranial pressure. Interval re-examination and re-evaluation was planned to determine any future need for further diagnostic tests or surgical exploration.

During the course of the study, the parents were attentive and polite to inquiries about Nicholas' and their own histories. They offered only the softest questions as evidences of their concerns about the various tests and procedures that were recommended. The observant permissiveness the ward situation encourages allowed some increase in openness from Nicholas, and Mother speculated that perhaps the hospital was making Nicholas "worse." She quickly denied her ability to judge this and explained that we had, after all, told her to say everything that came to her mind. The father, politely interested and attentive to the course of the investigation of Nicholas' organic pathology, never gave any direct evidence of the dread in which he held each test. From his wife we learned of his disapproval and apprehension. Generally, revelation of his anxiety came through his questioning the general value of the hospitalization.

Although it was clear to us that treatment was indicated for the parents and Nicholas upon his discharge from the hospital upon completion of the study and although that was our recommendation, the parents apparently "did not hear" our advice. It was felt that their state of conflict within themselves and with each other was being manifested as "fears and reservations (which) constitute a relevant part of the negative motivation (resistance)" (8).

The third child, a daughter, was born six weeks after the study was concluded.

Nine months later, when the parents communicated with us to have Nicholas' records sent to a local physician, they again heard our recommendation that they enter into regular, systematic treatment together with their son, and this time they were able to indicate their wish for this care. Treatment time finally became available seven months later. Nicholas was then 9 years, 5 months old.

At this writing, the family has been in individual therapy with the writer, each patient seen once weekly, for the past 19 months.

A detailed, or indeed even a sketchy recounting of the therapeutic work with this family is not the intent of the following account. Rather, this protocol is intended to select from the material examples of the kinds of interactions that tend to illuminate the hypothesis described earlier, i.e., that the parents, in their own conflicts unable to deal with hostile and aggressive impulses and feelings, in large part not in their awareness, have nevertheless "transferred," or "induced," the quality of their conflicts to their son in the form of his hyperactive and aggressive behavior. It is to be considered evidence in support of this concept that when therapeutic effort relieves, even if only temporarily, an aspect of their conflict, that the results will be visible in the representations of the conflicts of the child as seen in his performance and behavior. This is a very narrowed view of the whole treatment process, and it would be well to remember that the therapist does not consider this more than a sidelight, albeit of considerable interest, of the total process.

Nicholas' parents are a most attractive couple. Anne is a pretty woman who presents herself as a somewhat self-effacing, mild, mannered, "nice little girl" who seeks answers and reassurances from ostensibly more forceful and certain people than she could ever hope to be. She dresses in moderately priced but stylish dresses and wears sporty shoes. Her makeup is minimal. Her prematurely greying hair is always arranged in the same youngish style. Initially she viewed the therapist as the person with the answers, and if she was obliging and sweet, perhaps she too might learn what the doctor knew.

Charles might also be described as "a nice person." A rather strained smile usually marks his face. When his discomfort becomes more evident, the smile takes on the conformation of a mask. In his early interviews, he felt there was no question about it; he simply did not need therapy. He said he participated only because it was necessary in order to have his wife and son treated. In time he was sure we would see it his way and prescribe the appropriate medication or specific therapy for the other members of his family. From his training as a religious counselor, he knew a counselor or therapist had nothing to offer him. His early hours of therapy were marked by these considerations and his desire to be of help to the therapist in helping his wife. He took the position of co-therapist at the start.

At the time treatment started, Nicholas had been living full time with his maternal grandparents and visiting only briefly each day with his parents and two siblings. He appeared oblivious to the younger children, followed his mother closely about her household tasks, and continually tapped one hand with a rubber hatchet held in the other. Neither he nor his parents gave any open signs that his living away from home was anything other than satisfactory. Anne had withdrawn all objections to her mother's ways of dealing with Nicholas. When she had objected to her mother about some detail of his care, her mother had scolded her and told her she was ungrateful, and if she, the grandmother, was to care for the boy, it would have to be altogether her way. Otherwise, she wouldn't help out at all. Nicholas was always treated politely by his parents and was "given his way . . . because when you cross him, he has a temper tantrum."

Within a few weeks after they began their current therapy and without consulting their therapist, the parents precipitously brought Nicholas home to live. Anne's mother threatened her with court action, suicide and revocation of her right to enter the Kingdom of Heaven for the action against her. The parents had acted without first discussing their plans with the grandparents. This action represented the first parental agreement relating to Nicholas in over three years since the family returned to living near Anne's parents. Despite second thoughts about bringing Nicholas home, Anne and Charles were both surprised they could "manage" him themselves. When the rosy glow of their independent act faded, they talked of putting him into a church run home for defective children. It soon became clear that when either of their hours began with thoughts of putting Nicholas into that institution, it was a signal that there was some disruptive exchange with the grandparents, or that Nicholas had done some specific thing that they didn't *well, why not?* know how to deal with.

Three months after treatment began, Nicholas was admitted to a "Point 2" class. This was viewed unrealistically by the parents as the beginning of his formal education. When he entered school, the character of the parents' interviews changed and they began to talk more of themselves.

Nicholas, in playroom therapy, began his experience by mechanically requesting closeness. When lapsitting was permitted, Nicholas quickly turned it into seductive movements that aroused him sexually. Discontinuation of the activity by the therapist led to disruptive spitting and struggling over control. Though almost without speech and bizarre in his behavior, there was from the start little question about the accuracy of his perceptions of the limits offered.

Although the hours started sometimes disruptively, Nicholas was exposed to a person, the therapist, who was trying to establish communicant order from the apparent chaos of his mixed cuteness and aggressiveness. Frequent statements to the child were made about the confusion the therapist felt, as well as when he felt something had become more clear and certain. For example, early in the work, Nicholas began to sing a song, indicating with smiles, the therapist thought, his wish to be joined in the activity. When the therapist started to follow along in the song, Nicholas stopped. The therapist stopped and the child turned to another activity. When the therapist realized that he had interfered, he said to Nicholas, "I thought you wanted me to sing. If you don't, I won't. If you want to sing again, I won't interrupt you." And Nicholas smiled and began to sing again.

The first clear improvement in Nicholas' playroom behavior came at the time when his mother began to be increasingly confident in her hours that she could with hostile aggressiveness, aggressively and hostilely, criticize her husband. She most especially disliked his Pollyannish attitudes. She felt he never took her seriously. He disallowed any expression in conflict with his benign attitude, "You can do anything if you *really* try." Two modes of speech emerged in her hours. There is a more present childlike speech common in the chronicling of the week's events. It is also heard during episodes of denial, sometimes promoted by premature interpretations by the therapist. The other voice, heard after some months of therapy, is a rather throaty, almost growling, declarative tone that is used to express direct anger with the therapist or in recounting some recent time when she spoke directly to her husband. When she attempted to associate freely, she quickly ran into areas of pronounced affect. She focussed her attention there. Wary and cautious, she allowed herself first childlike, then womanly expressions of discontent, unhappiness, disgust or even hatred of her husband. In thinking of her husband as a minister, she became more free to disclose long held resentments and animosities toward the ministry and the Church. Before each hour was over, she redressed herself with sanctimony and clearly stated she is still a Christian, still believes in God, and "that is one thing therapy will never change."

Charles moved from the initial position that he was the cotherapist in the care of his wife to talking about the pain of his lonely life away from home in seminary training and his feelings that a minister is a beggar subject to the whims of the members. Whenever he was distraught about some problem at work, and there have been many, he asked the same questions about Nicholas' illness, seeking assurances that we considered the possible organic basis for his symptoms. In the first 20 hours or so, the parents were able to talk about some of the areas of their mutual concerns, particularly cementing the solidarity of their family position vis-a-vis Anne's parents. When they began to become critical of each other, they regressed to their more less open ways. At this same time, there was no change noted in Nicholas in the playroom. Testing of limits was still primary.

There were eruptions into arguments and squabbles that were louder interactions than their home had seen before. When one of these is reported, Anne recounts at first tentatively and then with increasing self-assurance that she managed herself well. Charles, less likely directly to report such an event, may at such a time talk about how much better Nicholas is and how well his wife seems to be doing. On one occasion, following a minor melee at home, he reported, "My wife and I have been arguing a lot more lately—ever since we have been getting along better!"

One morning at breakfast, Anne asked Charles a question about some family problem "and he responded like a minister instead of a husband." She threw a cup of hot coffee at him. Nicholas jumped up and laughed, clapping his hands. Well-behaved and tense younger brother, James, asked seriously, "Mummy, does Jesus say it's all right to throw hot coffee?" Nicholas' glee seemed to mirror her happiness with her directness—James' concern made her ponder the consequences of her act. James' sense of rightness and wrongness and her and Nicholas' impulse and their expression were being examined by her. Nicholas went to school joyfully for the next week. One day he came running back to her for a kiss—new behavior.

Nicholas' continuation in school was in jeopardy because the staff at the school felt he was too withdrawn from the other children and wasn't participant enough in the activities to indicate any profit coming to him from the work.

At the time the family was talking about this, Anne became ill for two days and wondered out loud to her husband that perhaps she wasn't strong enough to care for Nicholas. "And then you know what he said? He said it was plain I just didn't love the child. I got so darned mad at him I just picked up the magazine from the table and threw it at him." She laughed. "That's the first time in my life I ever threw anything at anyone. So I threw another magazine at him. He was running for the door and I didn't have any more magazines. All that was left on the bedside table was the Bible—and I picked the Bible up and threw it at him, and it hit him just as he was going out the door." Later she talked it over with him and he said he thought it was too bad she had to throw *that* book. She said she first thought that too, but that then she knew it had more meaning and told him that she felt she was saying to him with that throw, "And you can take your damned Bible with you too!" She was surprised that he somehow understood. Shortly thereafter, Nicholas stopped allowing children in school to take toys away from him. The teacher was tentatively encouraged. But she only became convinced that Nicholas should be recommended to continue in the program when he threw a book at her when she frustrated him in some activity! Previously he had only withdrawn. At this same time in the therapy playroom, he began to indicate some interest in forming the clay that he had previously only chewed up.

Charles discussed the difficulty of shopping for Nicholas or of taking him for a haircut. He always arranged in their small home community for the shopkeeper to stay open longer, or come in on Sunday, "because Nicholas acts up so bad." This became clear when he uncovered his own feelings of embarrassment followed by anger with Nicholas when he made strange noises or "looked stupid" in public. Mother talked about what a mess Nicholas makes of family dinners out and how he cannot be taken into supermarkets. When both parents had the opportunity to confront themselves with the awarenesses that they were ashamed of how Nicholas appeared to others for their own sakes, and that they retaliated for their hurt feelings against Nicholas, they began to be able to take him to more places and although he initially caused some further disruptions, these soon disappeared.

Only because Nicholas embarrassed Anne by charging into a cubicle in the ladies' room just before the beginning of her own therapy hour, was the fact made known that Nicholas, by this time 10 years old, was still taken to the lavatory by his mother because—she wasn't sure just why—but because she didn't know what he would do in a men's room by himself. She talked about this and decided that she would take the chance and try him. He went to the latrine alone and returned promptly, with his pants properly fastened. In the latrine adjoining the playroom following this, his pattern of tense and sporadic urinary flow, repeated perhaps ten times during previous hours, was replaced with a relaxed full stream and apparently adequate voiding for the first time.

An interesting piece of behavior of the child is his hand hitting. The rubber hatchet is almost always with him, and although it didn't make any sense when first seen, the therapist learned after a few months that the patting of one palm with the hatchet held in the other was a barometer of Nicholas' own inner sense of scolding. That is, when he had to be limited from some activity, he would assault his hand fiercely and jump up and down as if being spanked. When the therapist told him, "You don't have to hit yourself here," the action stopped. Mother had already heard and denied an interpretation that her way of turning on awareness of forceful feeling against herself with a repetition of some superego interdiction was similar to Nicholas hitting himself with the hatchet. Then one day she reported that Nicholas had "really gone all out in the hammer department," and described Nicholas walking about their children's play area at home with a carpenter's hammer. She thought it was "cute," and when the safety of this was questioned she laughed and said she did not mind if he used it on one especially disagreeable little boy in the neighborhood. The therapist indicated his concern and she said she didn't think Nicholas was strong enough to do anything dangerous with the hammer. She was clearly told, and heard, "Nicholas is as strong as you!" The next week, Nicholas appeared for his session carrying a potato masher and Anne described his fury when the hammer was taken from him.

Much of the improvement in Nicholas' speech is perhaps attributable to the parents' realizations that they had been talking "differently" to Nicholas than to the other two children. Mother reported that for years, and even today sometimes, problems about Nicholas have been discussed with him present as though he were not present. "We talk about him like he isn't even there, like he can't understand what we are saying." Charles became aware of his special way of talking to Nicholas when James, five years Nicholas' junior, asked his father why he talked "babytalk" to Nicholas. With these have come some changes for them and for Nicholas. He has become more "cooperative" and "responsive" to parental expectations, as their expectations for him have increased.

There has been a continuing and marked improvement in Nicholas' speech in the months he has been seen. He no longer speaks in that parrot-like voice that referred to himself in the third person. "Nicholas' hurt" or "You be good, Nicholas!" that appropriately accompanied, respectively, small injuries and limit settings in therapy. His most common word has always been an expression of an affirmative, either, "O.K.!" or "Yes!" the intensity of these words usually being inversely proportional to his obvious more real feeling. This persists, but he now also says "No!" when he means no, and he has begun to use the first person pronoun most appropriately. "I want to go to the bathroom," has replaced the "Nicholas want pee-pee" of 18 months ago. Formerly, when limit setting required firm physical restraint, even as he fought to be freed, furtively pinching or trying to spit all the while, he would say in a sing-song voice, "Nicholas be a good boy. Nicholas no do dat no more." He is now able to be held the more rarely occurring times he requires restraint, and when relaxed he says something like, "O.K., let me go. I won't do it no more." The diction and pronunciation reflects not only learning but also increased relaxation.

Even though some of the hours have been filled with struggle and turmoil, he never hesitates to come to the next. When Anne had to inform him that his therapist was sick shortly before their weekly trip to the Institute, he cried and said, "I want to see Dr. W." She was softly sympathetic to his tearfulness and when he stopped crying he said, "Can I go to school?", an activity unscheduled the day of his appointment.

Nicholas' most integrated behavior emerged at a time of a great crisis in the family. Charles' employer, the owner of several retail piano and organ stores, who had formerly acknowledged Charles to be his best salesman and had placed him in increasingly responsible jobs, in part responding to worsening business conditions, accused Charles of dishonesty and spoke to him darkly of the possibility that their relationship would be terminated. Charles' response was electric. He immediately called the authorities of the church, requesting a Call to be again a minister. To his wife, he first tearfully told her of his anger with the boss and his disappointment to hear from the boss that fellow employees didn't like him. And although Anne was very upset at the prospect of the change in vocations and the worsening economics of the situation, she felt some glee that her husband was able to respond with such affect. She said, "At least it proves he has feelings!" Perhaps because the parents are inattentive to Nicholas' presence when he is quiet, there was no effort to conceal their feelings from him. In the contemporaneous playroom sessions, Nicholas took an interest in the doll family, and although the play wasn't extensive, it included two adults and a boy child. He began to build towers with wood building blocks and indicated his interest in having the therapist observe and participate in the fun of building up and smashing down the towers. He also cheerily cleaned up the equipment without the attentive hovering that had theretofore been necessary.

It was at this time that the parents agreed to a reduction in his Dilantin-phenobarbital anticonvulsant medication recommended by the therapist. Nicholas appeared improved each of the next three weeks in terms of spontaneity, alertness and cooperativeness about the home. The parents spent their therapeutic time considering the possible move back to the ministry.

In the early period of the discussions between the parents about the plan to return to the ministry, Anne felt her husband was expressing feelings of insecurity and uncertainty. She felt Charles' position (vis-a-vis the change in occupation) was temporary. She was, in her own mind, helping him as she had been helped in therapy. As it became clear to her, however, that he was planning in fact these major changes in their lives and not just expressing his feelings, she became anxious and depressed. At precisely this time, the much agreed upon improvement in Nicholas' behavior, thought by the parents secondary to the reduction in medication, stopped. Docile compliance replaced Nicholas' enthusiastic departures for school. He grew less spontaneous and less responsive to his parents. In the therapy playroom, he withdrew from pleasurable block-building and spent more time looking "aimlessly" out the window.

Charles completely disavowed his former reluctances and hesitations about the ministry. He felt it was his professional calling. He denied his move was prompted by economic peril. He asked the therapist to join him in convincing his wife that this was "for the good of the family." Anne was resolute at first in her refusal to go along with his insistent demands that they return to the ministry and then began to give in on one point after another. From her first position of absolute refusal, she acceded to their reentry if she didn't have to live in a parsonage. Then she abandoned that but insisted that she would not participate in any church work. She lost that point and held out for James and Betty to be kept out of parochial schools. One by one, week by week, her husband argued her into compliance. She began to experience the same sense of guilt she remembered from childhood as each of his arguments turned on her "Christian Duty," her "obligation to God and husband." Although her Adult (2) knew his arguments were illogical and inconclusive, her Child (2) responded to his Parent(2). At this time, six weeks after the reduction of the anticonvulsants, Nicholas became more aggressive, striking out at his brother, trying to choke his sister, and finally, assaulting the woman who drove the school bus. Mother described a group of "seizures," which appeared to be sudden tonic and clonic jerks of the upper extremities made together with piercing shrieks. These had been seen in the playroom throughout his course and had always been considered expressions of heightened frustration. As the time for decision about the future of the family became imminent, Charles and Anne more closely had reestablished the pretherapy condition of dominance-subordination in their home that each of them had experienced in their youth—Charles representing her mother to Anne, and his own father to himself. In therapy, her complaints turned to whines. His review of his status became a parade of rationalizations. In this regressing situation, Nicholas had a grand mal convulsion.

Electroencephalographic study confirmed a "worsening brain wave," and the medication was returned to its earlier level.

The next day, the principal of Nicholas' school told Anne that Nicholas was "a problem" to the school. He was pushing other children, pinching and choking them and was in general "too aggressive." Anne smiled and remembered that just about a year earlier, the school complained that Nicholas was too retiring and wasn't aggressive enough. She told the principal that, "No, there wasn't anything happening at home that would explain the difficulty at school." She rather resented the question. But in the therapeutic interview, she looked at this more closely and corrected it to say, "Well, nothing that is leading to yelling or violence—yet." She laughed, "It's funny the way he (Nicholas) is able to pick up what isn't being said."

The following week, Charles' mercuric boss offered him a subdealership on terms that sounded most generous. The plan to reenter the ministry was dropped as quickly as it had been grasped. Nicholas had no more convulsions and Anne began to return to her temporarily abandoned role.

The reduction of medication, coincident as it was with the period of disruption in the family's life, sharply focuses the difficulty in evaluating effectiveness of anticonvulsant medication in this child's care. We have the feeling that we would again wish to reduce this medication if we could stabilize the field of variables that interact upon him.

Since the medication was increased, Nicholas is less energetic, tends to play in solitude, but responds to inquiries about whether he would like to do something familiar as though they are commands and mechanically sets to it. When this is pointed out to him, he dully stops. At times he seems almost a robot. Most recently he has returned to requests for the seductive body contacts reminiscent of the earliest hours, 19 months ago.

Nicholas' parents are "nice" people. Attitudes and characteristics they highly esteem are reasonableness, pleasantness, ability to get along with each other without friction, and unquestioning equal love for each of their three children.

In the home of Charles' youth, he learned that submission of his own wishes and desires was necessary to arrest his father's wrath. Self-subordination to the point of servility roused father from the despondence that led to wrath. Obsequiousness worked.

In her home, Anne learned that guilt, uncertainty and unrest were the consequences of her thwarted strivings toward independence and self-assertion. Efforts toward "freedom," when expressed, led to violent accusations of ingratitude, nonlovingness, and sinfulness by Anne's mother. The threats of rejection by mother and God caused Anne to lose each day's battle in her struggle for herself.

For each of them, then, modes of adaptation were developed to assure continued relationship with the more hostile, aggressive and disordered parent. Adaptation occurred to prevent emergence of a sense of unlove, or rejection, although the protagonist, child, saw it as an expression of love on his part. The recipient, parent, validated the interchange by accepting this equivalent expression in the form of decreasing the pressure or intensity of his anxiety-provoking behavior. Love thus becomes equated with the avoidance of unlove.

Each of them, Charles and Anne, found it was to their parent of the same sex that surrender had to be made. Each felt and feels that the contrasexual parent was and is weak, ineffective and somehow unresponsive to their plight. Their models of adults of the opposite sex, perhaps a determinant of their marriage choices, appeared to them impotent but nonthreatening.

By selecting each other in marriage, each in a sense seems to have said, "I wish to continue to avoid that threat of unlove I painfully recall receiving from my parent so I select a surrendering person like you who reminds me of my surrendering, contrasexual, parent." By selecting a spouse like the subordinated parent, they were thereby probably identifying with their aggressive parent.

The introjects of the aggressor parent as often occurs remain out of awareness until a stressful disagreement in the marriage provokes anamnestic anxiety. The submissive route to anxiety-reduction—surrendering—a mode that had its genesis in the presence of the aggressor, no longer is the only available course. First timidly, then with more force, the aggressive, anxious, partner enjoins the other to accede, employing the threat of withdrawal of love (of non-unlove), the pattern learned in childhood.

When Charles was becoming successful in his saleswork and beginning to voice to his wife his doubts about the value of church work— in reality startlingly similar attitudes to her own—she raised the question whether he had lost his faith in God. His instantaneous anxiety caused her to withdraw to silence the aggressive feint, but not to forget it. Later, when Anne did not want to reenter church life, Charles invoked her, first pleadingly, then with increasing fervor, to remember her obligation to God. Finally, he threatened to leave her and she capitulated.

When treatment began for this family, neither parent had readily available the experiences with others to use nor the awareness of his potential strength to work in a method of dealing with negative feeling that might lead toward resolution of their stress and difficulty, that is, candor and openness (12). Both felt the perception of negative affect toward the other was in itself threatening. Subjectively, it seemed wrong, bad and sinful. In the years of their marriage, there had not been an intensely angry exchange, a violent word or act. To think a "bad thought" was the equivalent of saying it, which was the equivalent of acting upon it.

Denial has been their principal defense. The conscious and unconscious aggressiveness that so clearly shows in them is generally not in their awareness. What becomes of it?

It is hypothesized that Nicholas, because of his particular problems and troubles, became the expressive instrument of his parents' conflicts. As a radio set detects, amplifies and makes audible certain electromagnetic waves, so Nicholas detects and makes visible and audible his parents' conflicts.

The first descriptions of him by competent observers say, "He kisses and hugs without affect . . . as though taught these . . . without understanding their purpose."

As Nicholas smiles without mirth, so too do the parents carry, through their day-to-day lives, expressions that belie their feelings. A measure of the successfulness of therapeutic work is the uncovering of conflicts and working toward their resolution to the end that new and more self-serving ways of problem solving will evolve.

The hypothesis that Nicholas is the repository and expressive instrument of the parents' conflicts has been examined in terms of specific references to the therapeutic work. At best, this is just suggestive of the leads that might be followed in further investigation of the work with the family. But as they are all three in therapy and not simply "under observation," the field is in constant change. Future re-evaluation of the hypothesis must take into account the dynamic changes in the child as the vulnerable object of the conflicts, as well as in the parents whose intra- and inter-personal conflicts could be seen in this child's behavior.

When Nicholas was first brought home from his Grandmother's home, Anne was for the first time unsuccessfully threatened by her mother. That is, Anne resisted the urgings of her mother that Nicholas be returned, and he began to sleep well. When he entered school, his withdrawal for a long time jeopardized his continuing in that program; the teachers felt he was getting nothing from it. But when the parents at this time began to argue with each other at home, culminating in Anne throwing coffee at her husband, Nicholas began to interact with the children at school after first throwing a jar of paint at another child which, although in itself a regrettably destructive act, was the beginning of a change for him. From then on, he moved toward the other children.

As the parents increased the openness of their interactions with one another and formed a more united front in dealing with the in-laws, Nicholas began to request his mother to kiss him good-bye each morning when he left for school. When Anne acknowledged finally in therapy that sometimes she hates this son and wishes he were "croaked," she also became aware of feelings for him that were less pitying and more loving. When Charles talked about his own embarrassment about taking Nicholas for a haircut or to the store to buy shoes, he clarified his own feelings enough to be able to take Nicholas to the store on regular shopping days and was able to abandon his earlier practice of making special arrangements with storekeepers for after-hours shopping.

Nicholas responded with the appropriate behavior Charles had not dared expect from him. Nicholas' speech began to improve when the parents quite suddenly became aware that they were talking "baby-talk" to him, and that the 5-year-younger sibling, they were addressing as an adult.

Anne "moves" more in therapy and her progress is something of a threat to her husband who sometimes is not ready to talk with her or with the therapist about immediate concerns. This has been noted by her reporting that he would like to drop out of treatment, and in his hours, by return to speculations about the organic aspects of Nicholas' illness. Nicholas' behavior during the last period of this specific activity was generally unchanged except that he developed the habit of lightly touching his mother's arm and saying, "Gentle! Gentle!" It was neither the kinetic energy nor the expression on his placid face that gave her the notion she had—that this was a well-controlled beating she was receiving. Such a speculation has a variety of possible unconscious and pre-conscious meanings but certainly fits both parents' usual symbolic expression of rage.

The issue of the accusation of father's theft led to a change in Nicholas' behavior. His behavior became diffusely disorganized, with an increase in distractibility and perseveration. As the discussions about whether or not to enter the clergy occurred and mother was holding her ground on the issues she insisted upon, Nicholas was playing easily at school, his medication was reduced, and for the first time in the playroom he played a game of his own creation and allowed the inclusion of the therapist in the game. As Anne began to yield to the pressure Charles was applying for his return to the cloth, Nicholas became hyperactive and assaultive to children at school— then later to his siblings—and there was a recurrence of his convulsive disorder. We may have here a replay of the parents' childhood and adult sado-masochistic behaviors and their resulting conflicts reflected in Nicholas' behavior.

Most recently, the parents have been talking of joining their separate talents in mutual efforts in the music store Charles will manage. Together, goes their thinking, they can provide music lessons on three instruments— the organ, piano and harp. Also they will be working together for the first time. They will be able to relieve each other from the sometimes tedium of tending the store. Charles thinks it would do Anne good to get out among people, to think about something other than the children. At first Anne looked forward to being "out in the world" and participating in developing what might become a family business. Nicholas, in the playroom, began to initiate and speak sentences for the first time. In a matter of two weeks, after Anne had accepted the idea of going to work in music, she decided she would prefer to work independently of her husband, and Nicholas' behavior again showed regression. Thus the mother's more integrative self-assertion there was probably increased intra- and inter-personal conflict not yet worked through which may have been symptomatically evident in the child.

With the background of this opportunity concomitantly to see all members of the family in treatment, a sense emerges in the therapist that after seeing Nicholas first on each treatment visit, the degree of covert conflict can be anticipated in the parents by tense and anxious play. Conversely, the degree of overt conflict and/or harmony can be inferred from his more relaxed playing toward integration. Such heralding of conflict states in the parent has been described by others who have first looked at the child's behavior as giving clues to parental tension, anxiety or conflict.

REFERENCES

1. BERLIN, I. N. and YEAGER, C. L. Correlation of Epileptic Seizures, Electro-encephalograms and Emotional State. *Am. J. Dis. Children*, 1951, 81: 664-670.

2. BERNE, E. *Transactional Analysis in Psychotherapy*. New York: Grove Press, 1961.
3. BOATMAN, M. and SZUREK, S. A. In D. Jackson (Ed.), *Etiology of Schizophrenia*. New York: Basic Books, 1960, p. 390.
4. BRADLEY, C. *Schizophrenia in Childhood*. New York: Macmillan, 1941.
5. BUCKLE, D. and LEBOVICI, S. *Child Guidance Centres*. Geneva: WHO, 1960, p. 50.
6. HALEY, J. The Family of the Schizophrenic. *Am. J. Orthopsych.*, 1960, 30:3.
7. LAWRENCE, M. Minimal Brain Injury in Child Psychiatry. *Comprehensive Psychiatry*, 1960, 1:360.
8. LICHTENBERG, P. et al. *Motivation for Child Psychiatry Treatment*. New York: Russell and Russell, 1960.
9. STRAUSS, A. and KEPHART, N. *The Brain Injured Child, Vol. II*. New York: Grune & Stratton, 1955, p. 142.
10. STRAUSS, A. and LEHTINEN, L. *The Brain Injured Child. Vol. I.* New York: Grune & Stratton, 1947, p. 86.
11. SZUREK, S. Childhood Schizophrenia. *Am. J. Orthopsych.*, 1956, 26:519.
12. TILLICH, P. *The Courage to Be*. New Haven, Conn.: Yale University Press, 1952.

33

Lessons from Failure in Ten Years of Psychotherapeutic Work with a Schizophrenic Boy and His Parents

Irving N. Berlin, M.D.

INTRODUCTION

Terrance is now 26. Since 18 years of age he has been in a state hospital back ward and has been treated with electroshock, phenothiazines, and every new major tranquilizer. He remains mute, destructive, and occasionally assaultive, spending most of his days in restraints or heavily sedated, just sitting. His parents are still very devoted, visit him almost every week, and keep the state hospital staff alert to their continued hope that he still may be helped. When his parents are with him they report that Terrance looks alert, and appears to be delighted and interested in his surroundings.

We saw Terry and his parents for almost ten years—eight as an inpatient and two as an outpatient. Terry was eight years old, Mother was thirty-four and Father was thirty-six years old when first seen. Terry was seen three times a week in individual psychotherapy for eight years (approximately 1,100 sessions) and once a week for two years (about 85 sessions). Mother was seen in individual psychotherapy two times a week for almost eight years, once a week for two years, and then on a monthly basis for a part of a year during Terry's admission to a nearby state hospital. Father, whose consultant activities as a nuclear physicist kept him away from home much of the time, was seen every other week for the first two to three years. During the last five years of Terry's inpatient stay a flexible schedule on the therapist's part resulted in nearly once-a-week psychotherapeutic sessions with Father. Because of his heavy increased consultation burden as senior consultant, resulting from his many honors and world-wide recognition for his experimental work, Father was seen again less frequently—approximately on an every-other-week basis—when Terry was an outpatient.

A series of nurses, attendants, and several generations of teachers and occupational therapists worked with Terry during his eight years on the inpatient service. After the first year I was the primary person involved in psychotherapy with this family.

WHERE DID WE FAIL?

Since I saw Terry and his family when he was between ages 9 and 18, a close examination of therapeutic work both in individual psychotherapy and in the milieu is important to an analysis of factors resulting in our failure to help him. In reviewing these 10 years of effort in the light of our present knowledge, many factors which affect prognosis require re-evaluation. Some of the shifts in emphasis on milieu therapy in the last few years need also to be examined in terms of their potential effect on Terry. The very strong and stormy transference and countertransference problems which are part of the learning experiences of a therapist working with severely disturbed human beings also require assessment. Efforts at resolution of transference and countertransference problems, once they have taken hold and are not dealt with adequately, become part of the interacting neurotic conflicts and have a life of their own. To understand these factors calls for careful examination of the therapeutic process. From such an examination I have learned a good deal about the psychotherapeutic work with psychotic children and their parents, about myself as a human being and as a psychotherapist, and about the general vicissitudes of learning to work psychotherapeutically with such families. In addition, the material from such work, brought to supervision, has clarified not only idiosyncratic problems, but general issues about supervision of psychotherapy with seriously disturbed children published elsewhere in this volume.*

The impact of a mute, destructive, assaultive, agile, and generally nonresponsive psychotic boy on all who attempted to engage him has general implications for all workers in inpatient settings. Circular and continuous impact of such a severely psychotic child on his parents, the effect of their troubles on him, and how intrafamilial conflicts are continued and reinforced are also made more explicit in this retrospective analysis.

Finally, what alterations in therapeutic attitudes and efforts might have affected the outcome hopefully can be assessed from the data which emerges. Although such post hoc findings and their implications for the treatment results with this child and his family are speculative, they do represent one pertinent scientific effort which permits the readers to evaluate the relevance

---

* I and many of the authors of this volume are indebted to S. A. Szurek, our supervisor, mentor and teacher.

and cogency of the data for the conclusions which to me stem from the retrospective analysis of these data.

Terry came to us at age eight having already experienced a great many traumata at the hands of previous workers in several institutions, but primarily maltreatment at the hands of his own uncle who had great difficulty in dealing with him. In addition, by age eight he spoke not at all. Since speech as communication is a means of engaging the environment around one, this meant Terry was greatly handicapped in any setting.

Our ward staff, having heard that he was extremely dexterous and that he had been rather severely punished for some of his destructive behavior in removing locks and dismantling toilets and refrigerators, felt that a boy with this kind of capacity surely would be able to work out in our setting. Thus the staff eagerly anticipated his coming, despite his age and our increasing experience that by age eight there was unlikely to be any dramatic improvement in childhood psychosis. Many of the circular problems and developmental issues which may have been related to critical periods during which timely interventions might have been possible had already passed—the circular problems were already well established. Despite all of the obvious predictive signs that we might not be very successful with Terry, our staff elected to have him come into the hospital for a preliminary evaluation. After the evaluation a conference would decide whether or not it was possible for him to stay in the inpatient service as it was then constituted and whether or not we felt we could be of some help to Terry.

During the inpatient phase of this evaluation, Terry was reluctant to leave his mother and was very reluctant to go to bed at night which provided some major difficulties for our staff. It was only after several months of treatment that Terry was able to establish a relationship with one of the day nurses and one of the evening nurse's aides that it became possible to separate him from Mother long enough so we could assess our original evaluation. Previous attempts at evaluation had been seriously hampered by Terry's cowering at his mother's side and refusing to go with anyone else for fear that he again might be permanently separated.

Even during this brief period of over a week, Terry managed to jam several of the locks in the ward which took the locksmith several hours to unjam. He also managed to plug one of the toilets, an action much later understood as a means of indicating his anger at some member of the staff who worked with him and should be with him.

During the seven or eight days that Terry and his mother remained together on the ward, several rather critical issues in the relationship became evident. At first it became clear that Mother's great hunger for meaningful, mutually pleasurable relations with adults led her to hunt up the occupational therapist and some of the teachers. Mother engaged them in discussions and actively pursued some of the kinds of things that she was expert in doing and began to help some of the other children on the ward who needed help in their projects. It was obvious that although Terry remained at her side during this period, he did not receive her full attention and it was impossible for any other person to involve him in similar activities. When Mother tried to get him involved in any of these activities which took considerable manual dexterity, he refused and became very angry with Mother, making whining, "no, no" noises and on one occasion kicking out toward her. These incidents were confirming illustrations of Mother's reports that when she was at home with Terry and began to work on something she enjoyed, the moment she was absorbed in it, Terry would disappear and shortly thereafter some serious malfunctioning in one of the various appliances would occur.

Mother's great hunger for friendships and work-related closeness, especially where she could help someone in an artistic pursuit in which she was proficient and talented, were denied her in almost all settings except when she occasionally attended night school when Father was home to take care of Terry. Thus, Terry controlled most of Mother's behavior when he was with her because she feared he might do something destructive. When it came to eating, his hands, usually so effective with a screwdriver or other small tool used to jimmy appliances, suddenly became totally ineffectual; he would not pick up a spoon or fork, forcing Mother to feed him to prevent severe weight loss, which had actually happened twice with weight losses of 20 and 33 pounds. The latter occurred in the previous inpatient setting.

When other children, most of them very much younger (i.e., three or four years of age) approached him to play, Terry would cower behind his mother and screech as if in great fear. Mother recounted numerous episodes in which other children had hurt him, explaining his great fear of being hurt by those children whose toys he had previously dismantled. For some time it was impossible to get Terry involved with any other children in our setting. After about seven or eight days, Terry realized that no one on the ward was punitive toward him for being mischievous in jimmying a lock or toilet. Through experience in the next several months he learned that although several of the adults tried to get him involved in the variety of activities, they respected his refusal and did not push him overly hard. He also realized that nobody would forcibly remove him from his mother. Thus when he went home over the weekend after forming several warm relationships with staff, there seemed to be very little anxiety about his returning to the ward. Mother commented on this as being greatly different from those occasions when she and her husband had gone down to the residential school where he had been previously treated. When they would take him out of that school for the weekend, each return to the institution would cause an uproar, and he would have to be forcibly taken from them by several of the counselors before they could effect a separation.

One of the day care personnel, a very warm and outgoing aide, took a special liking to Terry primarily because he presented a particular challenge to the ward staff who seemed afraid of so large a boy. This aide seemed to understand the kinds of anxieties Terry evidenced when she tried to separate him from his Mother. She spent her time with him next to Mother engaging him in a variety of activities such as playing with tinker toys and mechanical toys which he enjoyed. Very slowly he was able to trust her to take him to other parts of the ward and finally from the ward to the playground and back to the ward. Finally, when it became clear to him that Mother would visit at frequent intervals, he was able to let Mother leave and was always surprised and pleased when she returned for her therapeutic sessions with me or when she volunteered to help the occupational therapist on the ward. Mother's increased amount of time spent in animated talk with the ward staff and the occupational therapist was usually brought to a halt by Terry's angry behavior when she attended to others and not to him.

Some of the ward staff evidenced anger toward Mother because they had to care for her son, a child who was difficult to manage on the ward and destructive with equipment. Because Mother was very sensitive to these feelings of others, she found herself less and less involved in those activities in which she could have made a major contribution to the total ward milieu.

At this time Terry was the next to the oldest child on the ward. The evening aide paired him with the older child and under her tutelage they helped make beds and followed her around as she made her usual ward rounds seeing that other children were sleeping. They also sat with her while she did some charting, drinking fruit juice while she drank coffee.

It was at this time that Terry's love, delight, and repetitive play with jigsaw puzzles came to the fore; as each staff member began to recognize this talent of his, they would carefully investigate how he was performing. As we all pooled our notes, it became clear that Terry did not look at the picture as a whole but saw each of the individual forms as fitting together with other forms, having no concept of the total picture after it was completed. Several of the teachers and the occupational therapist tried to involve him in learning through the jigsaw puzzles, but their methods were unsuccessful.

In some day care and inpatient units for young psychotic children, the experiences which I am about to very briefly mention may have been described. While we have no way of knowing that these experiences are consonant with those of therapists of psychotic youngsters in other clinics, they have been fairly universal in our own clinic and therefore may be of some value to others.

With Terry as with a good many other very sick youngsters who are brought into the inpatient setting, the intake and evaluation process as they unfold give one the sense of a rather grim picture and a very poor prognosis. Despite the kind of optimism that is found among those who work with very sick children in all of the mental health professions, a child like Terry at age eight who is mute, destructive, completely negativistic and unable to relate to anyone—even his parents—with any degree of attachment, makes the task seem indeed an insurmountable one.

One of the questions to be raised in a paper of this nature is why we undertake such therapeutic work. As in all such undertakings, we noticed that various members of the faculty and staff who have contact with seriously disturbed patients whose prognoses are poor also have a variety of therapeutic experiences with these patients making them more hopeful about their own capacity to help effect change through mutual interaction with the patient.

In Terry's case as in so many others, there was an additional factor: the parents' urgent desire for someone to help them with their child. This was especially true of Mother who repeatedly described experiences in which she was frequently blamed by others as being a "bad or schizophrenogenic mother" or by her relatives, as being a "no good" mother. Reinforcing her own sense of guilt was a very recent experience in which a school and famous institution for the care of disturbed children indicated that she was to blame for Terry's difficulties. They later stated that they were unable to help him and considered him hopeless. This created a sense of urgent need on the part of the nursing staff both to succor the mother and to help her feel more adequate. The staff also felt a competitive sense of being able to help this very appealing boy who, despite his frequently destructive and difficult behavior, always had a kind of winsomeness which made each staff member —whether a nurse, occupational therapist, teacher, or psychotherapist—feel that he might be the one to unlock the terrified, psychotic combination lock and bring about some miraculous change.

We have seen this phenomenon frequently; despite the poor prognosis from the onset, the duration and present severity of the illness, other signs of lack of speech and capacity for interaction, and hostile, destructive, revengeful behavior or total withdrawal, the staff will nevertheless undertake the treatment of the youngster. This is perhaps more true at Langley Porter than at some other clinics because the Langley Porter Children's Service works with both child and parents so there is a sense of greater optimism and hope in the effectiveness of the therapeutic process. Thus the work done in the setting of the hospital or day care unit may also be communicated through the frequent contact with parents. In this way, a similar kind of intervention and helpful or effective attitudes and rewards might be conveyed to the parents. It has also been our belief that the nexus of the problem lies not only in the child's genetic and congenital makeup as well as possible early traumatic experiences but also lies in the early and continuous conflicts within and between the mother and father which may be found expressed in the illness of the child. Thus, the many conflictful states found in each parent make it difficult for them to relate to each other as well as to the child. This is also reflected in their increased difficulty in their work with the child. This conflictful state appears in both parents, but especially in Mother since she acts as the funnel for the conflicts between herself and Father or other family members. It affects her interaction with the child throughout the especially important developmental periods which have been described in several chapters in this volume. Intensive work with both the child and parents has at least in a good many instances been rewarding; therefore, it tends to make the staff feel more effective than they otherwise would despite the many discouraging instances where the staff has not been able to help the very seriously disturbed child. Thus after an extended intake of several months it was decided to embark upon an unspecified trial period of therapeutic work with both parents and intensive work with Terry by milieu staff—the child psychiatrist as psychotherapist to Terry, Mother and Father.

HISTORICAL INFORMATION

Father's History as Related by Father

Father was the only son in a family of three children, having a sister two years older and one two years younger than himself. He was his mother's favorite. A congenital abdominal tumor required numerous surgical repairs and radiation and prolonged hospitalization and nursing by his mother and older sister. His father, a prosperous merchant, spent little time with him. Father's x-ray treatments left him sterile. Throughout school he was very shy, had few friends, but excelled scholastically. His scientific prowess led to scholarships in college where he dated very infrequently and was described by his associates as a recluse. His brilliance in mathematics and physics resulted in fellowships at eastern colleges and he obtained his Ph.D. at a prominent institution.

Throughout these years of study he remained close to his mother, especially following his father's death shortly before he received his degree. Torn between remaining on to do research and an offer to conduct research in nuclear physics for a large private firm often employed by the government, he chose the latter because one of his few childhood friends was employed there in an allied field. It was through this friend that he met his wife-to-be. He'd had no experience with women and, like his mother, she appeared very warm, competent, protective, and made few demands on him. Following her refusal of his first proposal he became very depressed and preoccupied with suicidal thoughts. In this desperate frame of mind he sought her out again and in response to his desperation she agreed to the marriage. He told her they would have to adopt children because of his sterility.

Father felt the first few years of their marriage were idyllic, despite the fact that his wife's ailing mother came to live with them and that the war meant frequent separations as he was asked to supervise the work of a number of physicists at various installations. When his wife became pregnant, father was surprised and wondered if the doctors had been wrong about his sterility, if his wife had gotten artificially inseminated, and only fleetingly whether she'd had an affair. There was never any discussion about the pregnancy. He was concerned that a child might mean less attention from his wife, but he was so rarely home that this seemed not a very serious worry. Throughout this time he remained close to both his mother and older sister who was now married and had children of her own. Father's mother called on him frequently for advice about running the business she'd taken over after her husband's death. Thus, when he was home he spent a good deal of his time with his mother. He recalled very little of Terry's first few years of life except that his crying and sleeplessness interfered with Father's sleep so that he dreaded returning home from his consultation trips.

Mother's History as Related by Mother

Mother was an only daughter, having a brother four years older and a brother two years younger. The younger brother was the apple of her mother's eye. When her father died shortly before the younger brother was born, her mother used the money from his estate to buy a large house in an eastern seacoast resort town. This house was both a summer resort and a boarding house for boys in a nearby college.

Her older brother showed early signs of instability. He had a quick temper and frequently beat Mother as a girl who could get no help from her own mother. He also began to make sexual advances when she became pubescent and she was in constant fear of him. Her mother suffered from hereditary deafness so was not aware of Mother's cries of protest or anger and when confronted by the sexual advances made by the older brother, made light of these.

The younger brother could do no wrong and was a very precocious and bright boy who was adored by all. Mother took care of him and did many household chores to help with the boarding house. She had many friends of both sexes, was very outgoing, bright in school, and took part in many drama and art activities. Her many boyfriends made her older brother very jealous; he opened all her letters and often accused her of sexual misbehavior. While he continued severe verbal tantrums and rages at her, he discontinued any physical advances as she became physically able to defend herself. Mother took advantage of a scholarship to a teachers college in another state to get out of the home. There she did very well scholastically and made many friends. Her brother would occasionally appear, make threats about sexual misbehaviors, embarrass her, and then leave.

During her first job as a teacher, Mother noticed a decrease in her own hearing acuity. It was also during this year that she fell in love with a young lawyer to whom she became engaged. A few days before the wedding she received a telephone call from a woman who said she was the man's wife. When she confronted her fiance he told her he had gotten married while drunk a year before, was having the marriage annulled, and would be free in time for their wedding. Mother was so hurt by his lack of honesty she called off the wedding. It was in this frame of mind that she was introduced to Father, to whom she was attracted because it was clear he was not interested in other women and was pleasant to date. She turned down his proposal; however, upon learning of his suicidal preoccupations she felt he needed her and reluctantly agreed to the marriage.

Mother soon discovered they had little in common and that Father was totally unaware of her feelings or needs. He seemed not aware at all that his abdominal scarring made intercourse unpleasant and his ignorance made it totally unsatisfying for mother. During the first year of marriage Mother's mother had a slight stroke and came to live with them since her sons refused to care for her.

Mother spent her days painting and working in a Red Cross unit with the wives of other scientists in the same company whose husbands were also away much of the time. During this year she met a friend and colleague of her husband's who managed the company's home laboratories. In a short time they fell in love and because this man was not married she felt free to have an affair with him. She was determined to divorce Father after her mother recovered and to marry her friend. When she became pregnant she was determined to have the child, feeling it would not alter the course of events and that she wanted to bear this man's child. Her pregnancy was a period of great satisfaction to her and she never felt better; however, her hearing loss suddenly increased.

When Mother went for her first obstetrical examination a large uterine fibroid was discovered. Mother was not told about this because the obstetrician did not want to worry her. However, she was told she would have to have a Caesarean section because of a small pelvic outlet. Mother accepted this explanation despite the fact that she was a large-boned, broad-hipped woman. During the Caesarean the fibroid could not be separated from the uterine wall and the obstetrician asked Father's permission to remove the uterus; this Father gave. Terry was almost eight pounds, a very strong and vigorous child. A severe post partum infection kept mother in the hospital, semicomatose for several weeks with a high fever. Thus, it was three weeks after Terry's birth that she learned the uterus had been removed and she could have no more children. Mother felt certain this was a revengeful act on Father's part, since he knew he could not be the child's father. Neither parent had ever discussed this open secret. Mother was unable to nurse Terry due to her infection and her only comforts during this time were the visits from her best friend and their plans for Mother's divorce and remarriage.

Shortly after Mother's return from the hospital her older brother came to live with them, ostensibly to help take care of Mother who was doing very well, but actually because he had again become depressed, lost his job, and needed care himself.

During Terry's first six months of life Mother suffered two tragic losses. Her own mother, who was recovering from a stroke, had another stroke and died. Just as Mother was recovering from her older brother's recriminations that it was her attention to her baby son and failure to attend to their mother that caused the death, her lover was killed in an auto accident, leaving Mother and Terry tied to Father.

During this period Terry's crying and sleeplessness and Mother's fatigue and depression resulted in further decrease in her ability to hear. She was therefore even more isolated from her female companions. Her acute depression which lasted during the entire next year, coupled with Terry's increased activity and constant crying and wakefulness, left her in a state of nearly constant shock, feeling like a zombie and trying to exist from day to day. Father never recognized Mother's depression, acute weight loss and withdrawn state though Mother repeatedly and angrily talked about her physical exhaustion and need for household help which Father said they could not afford.

Terry's Past History and Present Illness

Terry was born at full term by Caesarean section and was almost eight pounds in weight. Because of Mother's postpartum infection he was bottle fed and despite the colic and vomiting described by his pediatrician he gained weight in the three weeks Mother was hospitalized. It was noted in the hospital that he slept little and fussed a great deal unless he was held.

Terry was described as an alert, active infant. From his baby book the following developmental landmarks were noted: he sat at four months; stood at six months; walked alone at one year; and said "Momma," "Daddy," and "Go" at eight months of age. At that time he also had severe flu with a high fever of several days' duration.

Mother's attention was divided between Terry and her own ailing mother who died when Terry was four months old. Thus, Mother took care of Terry all night and nursed her mother all of the rest of the time. Brother helped hire a practical nurse for a few months until their mother's death, but insisted that the nurse care for Terry and that Mother care for their mother until her death. Shortly thereafter brother moved out, Father was almost never at home, so that Mother had to care for Terry alone. Her suggestion to Father that she needed help to recover was met with scepticism despite Mother's obvious weariness, weight loss, and depression. A month later her lover, Terry's natural father, was killed in an auto accident. Mother has little recall for the next six months.

The pediatrician's record indicates Terry's continued normal physical development with increased complaints by Mother of his sleeplessness and crying at night. Mother had only their pediatrician to turn to and angrily rejected him when he failed to help with Terry's night time behavior and failed to recognize its effect on Mother. Finally he suggested that elixir of phenobarbital be given at bedtime. When in desperation Mother did try it, Terry became wild and uncontrollable so that she abandoned any further attempts at bedtime sedation.

During Terry's second year of life he became very agile and was fearless on play apparatus. At night he would get out of his crib every few minutes and come to his mother's bedroom unless she rocked him for several hours until he fell asleep.

At 13 months of age he pried open the cover to a sand box, crawled in, and was trapped inside. His cries were not heard by Mother until about an hour later when in her frantic search she found him crying in terror. Thereafter Terry was even more sleepless. On several occasions on the playground he was hurt by older children. Mother usually did not hear his first cries and he became increasingly fearful of all children and would not play with them, even in his own back yard.

During the third year of life Terry began to prowl at night and became very proficient at taking appliances apart. He was especially fascinated by the hot water heater and the clothes washer. These activities were frightening to Mother since she was alone with him. She found that spanking had no effect on him. During the days he became the neighborhood nuisance and would wander away from home and dismantle appliances, turn off hot water heaters in garages, and dismantle toys he found lying around.

At age 2½ to 3, Mother's oldest brother had another reversal of fortune and came to live with her. He would often take care of Terry during the days. When Terry became increasingly frightened of play equipment Mother's inquiries revealed that neighbors had noticed her brother forcing Terry to swing and to use the slides and spanking him severely if he wandered off. He also became very fearful of riding in an auto, her brother's mode of transport to the playground. At this time his speech which had consisted of short sentences, stopped, and he ceased answering the telephone and doorbell which had previously been a great delight to him.

Bowel training had been fairly successful. To stop his nocturnal prowling, Brother and Father insisted on tying Terry in bed, which may have accounted for his continued nocturnal enuresis.

After Mother got rid of her brother, Terry made no effort to talk and made his wants known by sign language. He would often wander at night and take the sink, toilet, or refrigerator apart. Mother would keep watching and halting Terry's destructiveness until she fell asleep from sheer exhaustion.

Against her pediatrician's advice, Mother took Terry to a nearby university speech clinic when he was 3½ years old. They diagnosed Terry as deaf, but Mother was certain this was not so. She then took him to a famous pediatric clinic in a large eastern city where a complete physical and neurological examination and E.E.G. yielded no positive findings. They made a tentative diagnosis of congenital cerebral arrest and suggested a day school for brain-damaged children. This school felt Terry was unlike any of the other children enrolled. From their report it was clear they could help him learn to say words clearly if they spent time with him. His great manual dexterity and agility was noted, as was his alertness and capacity to do exactly the opposite of the task requested of him. They also noted with dismay his great facility for taking the toilets and appliances apart if not watched. He learned to say a few words on demand, but there was no spontaneous speech.

At about age 4½ Mother found Terry tied to a tree, being flogged with ropes by neighborhood children whose wheel toys Terry often dismantled. His fear of children increased and often Mother would find him miles away from home playing in a creek bed alone. Mother's older brother visited often and made light of Mother's concerns and efforts to find help for Terry.

Brother insisted that only severe beatings were needed to straighten him out. Father was still rarely at home and seemed unaware that Terry was not normal.

Between ages 4 and 5 Mother tried to stop Terry's grabbing food at the table by hitting his hands and after a while he refused to use his hands to eat. The pediatrician advised a period of starvation. This did not work, and finally Mother resorted to spoon feeding him. After about five months he began to use his hands and for the first time learned to use utensils for eating. During this time Terry often played in his neighbor's car and on one occasion he released the brake and the car rolled down the driveway into the street. On another occasion Mother found him screaming as a neighbor in desperation was closing the car door on his fingers in an attempt to teach him to stay out of the car.

Shortly after this event the Clinic for Organically Disturbed Children suggested further study at a well-known speech clinic. There they diagnosed Terry's difficulties as emotional and told Mother she was responsible for his troubles, that she was bad for Terry, and suggested a residential treatment center for him. During these years Mother was depressed and desperate. Shortly before Terry was 5, Mother had a bad fall and broke her right arm. Father felt they could not afford a housekeeper so that Mother had to try to care for the hyperactive, sleepless child alone. Father was still away most of the time during the week and often on weekends.

When Terry was 5½ years old the parents agreed to place him in the residential treatment center, despite the fact they could not visit him for two months until he was "adjusted to the setting." When Terry was told of the plans a few weeks before the placement he refused any physical contact with either parent, despite his previous pleasure in hugging and being hugged. Mother hoped that with Terry in school she might have the recommended surgery for her increasing deafness. Father, however, felt they could not afford both the surgery and the residential treatment. At this time also Mother was depressed due to litigation over her mother's estate begun by cousins which resulted in her brothers acquiring all the property. Even the heirlooms left to her in her mother's will were sold by her brothers.

Between ages 5½ and 7 Terry was in the eastern residential center. From their report we learned that he refused to use his hands except to take apart toilets and appliances, would not eat unless fed, and withdrew from contact with pupils, teachers, and aides. He refused to remain in the same room or outdoor area with his therapist. A change of therapists did not alter this situation. Just before he was 7 the school wrote to the parents that they were unable to help Terry and requested his prompt removal because he was so destructive.

Back at home Terry would not use his hands at all except in taking apart appliances or plumbing. He was fearful of all adults except his parents and would not enter the car. Mother felt this was because he feared being taken away from home again. For six months he had to be spoon fed. Mother was again very depressed and sought psychiatric help for Terry. Dexedrine did not alter his behavior and anterior pituitary hormone was tried with little effect. He was again taken to the speech clinic where he began to say a few words, again in parrot fashion.

During the last half of Terry's 7th year Mother had surgery for her deafness. The operation was successful, but a cold complicated the healing and resulted in continued drainage. This occurred because she was called out to come to her younger brother's aid. Thinking it emergent she went out on a very cold, wet night only to find he'd quarreled with a girlfriend and needed her advice. The drainage continued as Terry's hyperactivity gave Mother little sleep at night. A housekeeper was finally hired to help out but was unable to keep an eye on Terry or to stop his destructive activities. Thus, Mother was again very physically tired and depressed. Her hearing was becoming worse, and Terry was no better. Mother felt angry at Father for his lack of understanding and help during these troubled times and contemplated divorce.

Father, during this year after Terry's return from the residential center, had spent much more time at home with Mother and Terry. He found himself very depressed also because he could not manage Terry, comfort his wife, or find any solution to getting help for Terry. Finally, on a friend's recommendation, Terry was taken to a neurologist who placed him on Dilantin. In retrospect the doses seemed inadequate for his age and size and had no effect at all on Terry's sleeping or other behavior.

It was thus in desperation that the parents brought Terry to us for inpatient evaluation shortly after his 8th birthday. Father had been transferred to the West Coast to head a division of the laboratories and had been told by his associates of the clinic. After their previous experiences they tried to obtain information about the clinic from various physicians in the area. The only consistent report they obtained was that the staff was not reluctant to work with very disturbed children and that they encouraged parent participation not only in terms of frequent visits and taking the child home for weekends, but also participation in the treatment process.

THE FIRST YEAR OF WORK WITH TERRY AND PARENTS

Initial Phase on the Ward

During the eight days of evaluation Terry was quite tense, would not engage in any activities in the play room and seemed very frightened whenever he lost sight of his mother. On the introductory visit to the ward Terry clung to his mother and would not be separated to be introduced to staff or children. After the evaluation when the decision to try Terry on the ward was made, Terry would not listen to any reassurances of weekends at home and daily ward visits, he screamed when Mother left, could not be consoled and had to be secluded with a nurse because of his continual wailing. After a sleepless night Terry began a frenzy of destructive activities. He tried to jam the toilets, to get into the ward kitchen where he turned on all the gas jets and in a twinkling had the pins out of the refrigerator door hinges. It almost appeared as if the frantic destructive activities gave Terry some relief from anxiety.

Despite repeated visits by Mother he still was very anxious, slept little, ate with his hands, and tried to escape from the ward whenever the door was opened. He could not be engaged in any ward or school activity and he kept all staff members at a distance. Each successful foray into the kitchen or bathroom, with destruction of some equipment and angry response by staff members, brought a sly smile to his face.

A very aggressive four-year-old girl kicked and scratched Terry when he wandered near, and thereafter he appeared terrified of her.

During the fourth month on the ward a new evening nurse began to take Terry with her on her rounds and got him to accompany her as she performed various chores since his wailing and sleepless wandering disturbed others. When she went into the chart room to do her charting he'd leaf through magazines and when she'd drink coffee, Terry would drink milk or fruit juices which he'd never touch during the day. Despite their spending time in the ward kitchen, he did not dismantle the equipment when with her. To avoid the night nurse with whom he did not get along, he readily went to bed and was quiet just before the evening nurse went off duty. On his evening nurse's day off he wailed and hit his head on the bed; the substitute nurses could do nothing with him. Often he required physical restraint, holding by an aide, until he fell asleep.

Psychotherapy during the First Year with Terry

Terry's first therapist, a young male trainee in child psychiatry, was unable to make any contact with him. The three times weekly playroom hours were painful for both. Terry would have to be forcibly led to the playroom and once there he kicked, scratched, and spit at the therapist, wailing all the time. It semed clear that both were frightened of each other and their own feelings. The therapist's efforts at interpretive behavior and comments without any clear response left him feeling ineffectual. During supervision the efforts were to help the therapist find somewhere to take hold, some way to engage this severely traumatized and frightened boy. During the year there was some reduction of the violence of the interaction, and Terry appeared pleased to see his therapist but would not permit any closeness. When physical restraint was necessary, the therapist found it difficult to gauge when Terry was relaxed so he could let him go. Because it was difficult for this therapist to learn to be playful himself, early in his learning, Terry was not engaged through play. Because of staffing problems in the inpatient unit I was unable to begin to work with Terry until the following year.

Terry and His Teacher

One other person on the staff had some impact on Terry during his first year: his teacher. She was an elderly woman, competent and kindly but a "no nonsense" kind of person. She dealt with all the disturbed children in the same way. She believed in their learning capabilities and was determined, despite their behavior difficulties, that they would in time learn something. She spent 15 to 20 minutes a day with Terry on pre-primer activities. During the first four months he screamed, took off all of his clothes and spit and hit out at her whenever she introduced anything. With the help of nurse's aides he was restrained, and when he quieted down she would try again. He gave no indication that he understood any of the material presented, but the teacher's persistence and her warm welcoming smile and words each day gradually reduced the number and intensity of Terry's tantrums and in their stead there came a very precise negativism. It became very clear that Terry understood directions very well since he always made exactly the wrong choices. The teacher accepted this kind of involvement as a meaningful engagement and an indication of his intelligence and capacity for learning.

Toward the end of the first year Terry also made contact with a very large and active female attendant who would rough house with him in the play yard and the park. At first he avoided these contacts and struck out at her, but in a short time his eyes would gleam and he'd giggle quietly as she tickled or chased him and rolled him on the grass.

On weekends at home throughout this year, he continued his sleeplessness and his nocturnal wandering and destructiveness. He seemed more relaxed on Sunday nights but toward the end of the year resisted returning to the ward on Monday mornings. He would sometimes jam the car door locks and once darted from the car when Mother parked it at the hospital. He ran away from her and had to be found by the police. Terry learned the geography of the city so precisely that on the frequent drives with the family, if they came from any direction to a street that led to the hospital, even though 5 to 10 miles away, he'd begin to wail.

Initial Therapeutic Efforts with Mother

During the first year with another therapist Mother was constantly on the defensive, having been told previously that Terry's problems were all her fault. Thus, any questions about Terry, or about Mother's reaction to the ward program, etc. led to angry denial that anything in her past life or relations with Father had in any way affected Terry. Much of the historical data previously reported was gathered in the last few years of therapeutic work when some trust had been built up. This extreme sensitivity to any exploration or data gathering made her first therapist very defensive since his comments were taken as criticism. At the same time, since Terry made very little progress, Mother's doubts about the effectiveness of the treatment program, her disparaging comments about the reputation of the children's service, and her questioning of the treatment philosophy were difficult for the therapist so that the underlying anxiety, fear and concern were not recognized. In desperation after a bad weekend with Terry, Mother asked a nurse for suggestions. The therapist, alerted by the nurse, also attempted to suggest ways of dealing with Terry. These comments were always received with a disdainful sniff so that it became difficult to persist beyond the defensiveness to discuss the actual sequences of events that led to temper outbursts and destructiveness. Thus by the end of the first year Mother had been only very slowly engaged in therapeutic work and was still very defensive and fearful of being blamed for Terry's illness.

Father's First Year in Psychotherapy

During this period Father was engaged in therapeutic work by a more experienced trainee. He quickly recognized Father's very poor self-image and his feelings of not being very effective in any area except in his profession. Thus Father was helped to begin some historical reconstruction, despite his certainty that there were no marital problems, that Terry's difficulties must be organic, and that his sexual life was ideal despite the surgical and x-ray scarring of the abdomen which made physical contact painful for him. Father regarded his therapist as a warm and friendly person from whom he could receive some help and understanding.

Despite Terry's lack of progress, Father felt hopeful. Besides he was not sure that organic problems could be helped. When his relatives prodded him, he would hesitatingly raise the question of the worthwhileness of the continued expenditure of money for treatment.

THE SECOND YEAR OF PSYCHOTHERAPEUTIC WORK

When I took over the work with Terry and his parents I felt that this 9 year old who created such havoc on the ward and off was a major therapeutic challenge. In retrospect the feeling of omnipotence was reflected in my conviction that I could help this obviously bright boy and his intelligent parents. I did not comprehend the meaning of such belief in one's own magic until several years and many scars later.

Work with Terry

My first few efforts to take Terry to the playroom were very difficult. Terry ran away from me; he hid under beds refusing to accompany me to the playroom, leaving me feeling helpless and inadequate in the face of the ward staff and other fellow staff members and trainees. Once in the playroom—when we did get there—Terry spit, kicked, knocked over toys and overturned the dollhouse. He made such a shambles of the room that I had to cut our sessions down to ½ an hour so I could clean up in the remaining 20 minutes after a perilous return trip to the ward. About six weeks later it seemed clear to me that our engagement would have to occur in a setting where there were fewer objects to destroy and where I had more control over the environment. I also in part wanted to avoid the hazards of the trip from the ward to the playroom and back, especially since Terry had, on one occasion, jammed the elevator so that we were stuck for ½ an hour. The Institute Director had then asked to see me to have me explain my poor control over a nine-year-old patient. In response to my detailed historical account of the severity of Terry's problems, he nodded with understanding but said emphatically that he didn't want the elevators jammed again.

Thus, I began to see Terry on the ward in a side room used for isolation for contagious illnesses. Besides the bed and table and chairs I brought in clay, paper, and crayons. Terry and I met here for the next four months, three to four times a week for as long as I had energy each session. In this bare room I learned to protect my shins from Terry's kicks, to hold him from behind with both arms and legs when he attacked me or tried to overturn the bed and table, and to anticipate his sudden charges to escape from the room or to fling a chair at me. I found that under these circumstances I could not only restrain Terry more easily, but because I got hurt less, and there was less to be destroyed, I felt less retaliatory and revengeful when I held him. Thus I could tune in to his state of muscular tension and relaxation so that I could talk to him more meaningfully of my awareness of his physical state and how I hoped he'd discharge some of his anger in pounding the clay. During the ensuing weeks I also became attuned to his facial expressions, muscular tensions and half smiling grimace which frequently preceded a tantrum. At such moments I would quickly restrain him since I learned early never to be more than a step from his side.

As I became more prompt, skillful and gentle in my restraints, Terry seemed to be less violent in his explosions. Either I became more attuned to all the non-verbal signs of tension which led to a tantrum or Terry became more obvious in his signals. During the long periods of restraint, or when we sat and looked at each other, or when I tried to help Terry color with crayons but prevented his biting and swallowing them, I kept a constant stream of comment going. I had learned in several other psychotherapeutic efforts with assaultive, destructive, psychotic children that my repeated comments about how they appeared to me seemed to be heard. Thus I commented as signs of tension occurred which were revealed by facial expression, vascular changes, or changes in respiration or muscle tone. I felt that this led to my being more attuned to Terry. Usually some increased relaxation on Terry's part followed so that my comments could then shift to encouraging play activities that could be undertaken by the patient alone or in cooperation with me. In time as I held him and talked to him in a free associative way Terry would begin to relax and lean against me. I learned not to comment on his leaning and finally cuddling against me, for when I did, he would stiffen and struggle. When he did relax and cuddle I'd talk about coloring or making clay balls or long clay snakes which at times he would seem to enjoy doing. Toward the end of this four-month period Terry began to reach for the crayons and fill page after page with heavy masses of black or red crayon. His intensive concentration and facial relaxation during these coloring periods led me to speculate about his feelings of satisfaction and pleasure as he colored. These comments usually resulted in his ceasing his activity and sitting looking sullenly at me. I finally became aware that these comments were taken as demands or intrusions on his activities. When I described what he was doing, rather than how I thought he was feeling, he would continue with unabated vigor. Slowly we learned to work together, and Terry began to look pleased when I approached.

Second Year on the Ward

Terry continued his attempts to avoid the staff and escape their notice so he could dismantle a sink, stuff the toilet, take a lock apart or sneak into the kitchen and dismantle the electric range and refrigerator. When restrained or closely watched he might bang his head, kick out at people or emit an ear-piercing scream for many minutes. The last was a new activity which disturbed staff so much they would leave him alone in the activity room. When he was thwarted or discovered in some dismantling activity, he would defecate on the floor of the isolation room where he'd been placed for a few minutes so the mess of an overflowing toilet could be cleaned up. Such defecation occurred despite his supervised toileting when he would regularly urinate and move his bowels.

When his parents visited on the ward and ignored him or especially when Father came for an appointment and only briefly acknowledged Terry before leaving, Terry would smear feces over the walls of the dormitory and throw feces at other children. Only one nurse could stop this activity and only the evening nurse could engage him in a friendly interaction.

Once, early during the second year, while he appeared quiet and ostensibly was coloring in the day room with other children and staff, he quickly became agitated in his movements and squealed. Suddenly he screamed, and when he turned around, blood was streaming from his penis where he had cut himself with a sharp piece of metal just behind the foreskin. The surgical resident, noting that the cut had been well washed, simply put a bandaid over it. Mother was very upset when told. Father replied, "He does such strange things," in a very quiet, restrained voice.

During this same period on outings in the clinic station wagon, he managed "unnoticed," to drop shoes, socks, belts, even trousers out of the window, usually never to be recovered. The staff frequently had to ask Mother to replace the shoes, belts and clothes. Mother in turn expressed anger and dismay that he could not be watched more closely, despite her own similar experiences.

An attendant noted that when Terry smeared feces on the wall and was required by the presence of a staff member to clean the wall with soap and water, he appeared to enjoy the activity and did a thorough job.

Another rather frightening activity began to occur on the ward and on weekends home. Terry would steal matches and light the contents of waste baskets. Although matches were carefully watched, he usually found a pack and set fire to a waste basket. This was frequently used as a diversion so that he could sneak into the kitchen to get at the stove or refrigerator. When staff and Mother began to require him to get some water in a pitcher to put the fire out, there was some reduction of this activity.

During the second year a boy his size and a year older, ten, was admitted to the ward. This boy enjoyed using the beds in the dormitory as trampolines and would bounce on the beds and bound from one to the other with great abandon. After watching this uninhibited play for several weeks, Terry began to join him. At first he was rather inhibited and restricted in his movements but after a week he too began to bounce and bound from bed to bed following Alex with a wide grin on his face. This was the most pleasure anyone had noted on his face during his year and a half on the ward. After about six weeks and a half dozen broken bed springs the housekeeper forbade such activity. Efforts to transfer these mutually pleasurable activities to several large inflated truck innertubes failed and both boys withdrew. Terry resumed his teasing dismantling of appliances and stopping up of toilets. The staff seemed to resent the interference of the housekeeping department's "reasonable demands" but could not openly talk about their feelings to the boys. Not until six months later was there an open discussion about the relative costs of repairing bedsprings vs. flooded toilets, dismantled appliances and broken locks that Terry so easily took apart with a hairpin, paper clip, etc.

Toward the end of the year Terry began an activity which caused all staff and faculty a good deal of distress. He would sneak up behind various individuals and flip their eyeglasses off their heads. Mother then began to complain about the expense of repairing glasses. At this time he did not touch his parents' eye glasses or mine.

In school he settled down to doing pre-primer work with evident satisfaction and could be trusted to sharpen pencils, sort out crayons, always turning to his teacher for words of approval.

Terry in Occupational Therapy

A fascinating phenomenon began to occur in occupational therapy. The male O.T. worker was an O.T. student, a paraplegic, who could control his hands and arms well enough to operate his electric wheel chair and to demonstrate how to use tools or materials. This man was very vulnerable to the abrupt and sometimes hostile movement of disturbed children, but Terry did his most effective work under his guidance. Terry very proudly exhibited the clay ash trays, book ends, etc. he made while this O.T. student worked with him. While he continued to enjoy O.T. subsequent to the student's departure, he was less cooperative and less involved, although each completed piece was proudly exhibited to his favorite ward staff, the teacher and his artistic mother. One of the ceramic ash trays he made during this period has survived all his destructive tearing apart and demolishing of objects of his room at home.

Play Therapy with Terry—Last Six Months of the First Year

During this half year Terry came to our sessions eagerly and began to pound clay with vigor and used the crayons to fill squares on the page with solid colors. He worked with great energy and my spoken comments about what he was doing were apparently heard. He often left a solidly colored page with me after such a half hour. On several occasions as I vocalized "bang, bang" loudly to accompany his vigorous pounding of large balls of clay he looked at me and smiled. At the end of each interview he not only helped me clean up but, despite the fact our playroom was on the ward, he took my hand as I walked with him to the activity room.

During that year, Terry began to demonstrate warmth toward his therapist and greeted him with enthusiasm when he saw him on the ward and looked hurt and disappointed when the therapist did not on each arrival on the ward take Terry into the playroom. The therapist had several other patients on the ward. There was some obvious rivalry with one of them, a very sick, anorexic girl. On several occasions Terry would intrude himself between the therapist and this girl when the therapist sat at her bedside.

Psychotherapy with Father

Father had to make a transfer to the author from his previous therapist with whom he had developed a good relationship. He tended to look at his previous therapist as a helper and supporter, especially in relation to a variety of work problems, and was just beginning to examine some of his relationships with his wife and with Terry when it was time for his therapist to leave and for the new therapist to take over. For a number of months Father expressed a feeling of loss and described his difficulties in relating to a new person. With the therapist's help it finally became clear that part of Father's anxiety had to do with the fact that all members of the family were being seen by the same therapist. This meant to Father that Mother, an extremely bright and verbal woman and accomplished in many ways, would of necessity become the therapist's favorite. He also had some anxiety that because the therapist was working with Terry that some of Terry's destructive and aggressive behavior would so frustrate the therapist that he would take it out on Father, blaming him for Terry's illness and his present behavior but especially for the fact that Father was not very skillful at restraining Terry's destructive behavior when Terry was at home.

Father began to participate more actively in this therapeutic relationship when he had some bothersome work problems. These concerned the development of a new laboratory to which he was the senior consultant. Disagreement occurred between Father and several of the younger physicists in the organization as well as the potential director of that laboratory. They felt strongly that Father was being arbitrary in his decisions and recommendations rather than heeding advice of people who were likely to be working there. Father, on the other hand, knew that none of these men had had the particular experiences in high energy physics that he had had, and therefore felt compelled to go ahead with the recommendations he had made. He was, however, tremendously uneasy because these colleagues disliked him so much and talked about him as a tyrant and autocrat. As these events were put into the context of previous experiences Father had had, he was able to recognize his own great reluctance to become authoritative rather than authoritarian, i.e., use his knowledge without being dictatorial. His need to be liked, even at the risk of not being accurate or effective in the particular job, had become clear to him. With some help from the therapist he finally was able to get another colleague who was equally experienced to look at the recommendations he had made for this laboratory and in a meeting with his colleagues these differences were thrashed out. Most of Father's recommendations were sustained.

Toward the end of that year, Father was beginning to relate to the therapist and for the first time began to talk about his own childhood. His feelings of inadequacy as a child because of the amount of time he spent in the hospital for surgery and radiation resulted in his not believing himself to be effective or potent except in the intellectual sphere. After one weekend, when Terry had been especially difficult to deal with and Father had to literally sit on him to keep him from destroying some of the furniture in his room, Father expressed some of his anxiety that he was so upset with Terry that he might actually choke him to death while he was holding him. In the same hour, Father came to recognize that although he felt that his arms and legs were extremely weak and puny, in reality he was a fairly strong man who exercised regularly to keep fit and who could control Terry if he were not so immobilized by his anxieties.

Therapy with Mother

Mother also had to change therapists. At first she was resistant to the idea of seeing someone new and angry that she had to reiterate some of the information that she had given to the first therapist. Her caustic comments about the poor ward setting and Terry's lack of progress seemed aimed at making the therapist uneasy. After a time the therapist could readily admit that there were indeed some shortcomings to the ward setting and that the progress with Terry had not been at all remarkable or pleasing to anybody on the staff. Certainly his burden to his parents, especially Mother, during weekends at home had not been reduced. These were issues which we recognized and we felt very strongly that none of our hopes for rapid change in Terry had been realized. Mother then turned to the fact that the therapist was also seeing Father and that being a man he couldn't help but identify with a man's point of view. She then went on to list her many grievances against Father, and his complete insensitivity to her needs throughout their marriage, especially after Terry was born. She did not, however, talk about their sexual relationship until the following year. She described in great detail the effects of her draining ear in reducing her hearing and Father's refusal to give her any household help at times when she was physically exhausted from trying to manage such an active and destructive child by herself, day and night, especially over the many weeks when Father was not at home at all. She described with great bitterness the attitudes of a number of professionals who had blamed her for Terry's illness and her anger in turn in blaming Father.

The therapist rather empathically inquired why there needed to be any blame of anybody under such difficult circumstances. In our experience people usually did all they could in terms of their own understanding and capacity to recognize particular needs. It was difficult for me to blame either Mother or Father but we did have a need to understand the events that occurred. Together we needed to analyze how the work with Terry and his parents currently could reverse the previous experience. At this point, Mother became very angry. She refused to acknowledge that Father was in any way not to be blamed for his lack of sensitivity and awareness and his use of her as a psychological and emotional crutch. At the same time, she very clearly spelled out how destructive her relationship with her brother had been! She described that she was accustomed to relationships with both men and women in which she was exploited and taken advantage of and in which nobody recognized her own needs. Mother was aware that there had been certain moments when, in fact, she could have asserted her own needs, probably getting Father to listen. However, she had the overwhelming need to have Father understand her and do what was necessary for her without making explicit what it was she needed and why. A recurrent theme about Mother's hearing troubles began and centered around the fact that Father would never spend the money on her to have her hearing corrected because he never felt that this was a high priority item despite the fact that, as her hearing deteriorated, he could not make himself understood. When questioned about this in terms of being able to get a loan of some kind, Mother became very angry, saying that this was Father's job and not hers. Mother then described a period when Terry was previously in the inpatient setting and she had been able to sell some of her art work. Each time she would begin to save enough money so that she could begin to plan for ear surgery, something would happen in Father's family that would require the money much more urgently. When again questioned about why she felt that she had to give her money for his family rather than asserting her priority to be able to hear better, Mother again became very angry and said that I simply did not understand.

Underneath the angry tone as she talked about these events was almost an anguished cry. I repeatedly sensed the amount of sadness beneath the bitterness and the very childlike cry for both understanding and help. Mother felt terribly attacked whenever my inquiries led in the direction of exploring her own feelings and understanding her motivations for her behavior. Inevitably she would feel she was being attacked and criticized as the person to blame for Terry's illness and perhaps even the person to blame for the marital problems. When on one occasion these issues were raised by Mother, the therapist gently questioned whether or not in fact Mother wasn't saying that she knew that Father depended on her a great deal, and that he had married her because of her great strength and capacity for managing life events. Also perhaps, had she really wanted things more explicitly, clearly, emphatically for herself or Terry she might have managed most of the family monies and might have also been able to get most of what she wanted from Father by taking a very clear and firm stand. (Mother vigorously denied this and hostilely attacked the therapist.) Using a bitter caustic tone of voice, she once again accused the therapist of not understanding her and blaming her for all the events that had occurred. No matter how many times the therapist tried to restate what he had said and what his meaning was, there was no apparent increased understanding on the part of Mother.

Toward the end of that year, the relationship between Mother and the therapist was friendly but cool and the antagonism was very close to the surface. Thus, the end of the second year could be said to be also the end of the introductory period of work with Terry's mother and father.

THIRD PERIOD OF WORK

The third period of work which I have labeled, "Terry's Destructiveness," continued for about three years. Omitting the voluminous detailed therapeutic work with Terry, Mother and Father, I will describe some of the highlights and crucial elements within the therapeutic work. As the third year of work began, Terry became terribly destructive at home. He frequently overturned tables and chairs and on several occasions he smashed furniture. Terry's parents were especially upset when he took a kitchen knife and slashed the paintings his mother had done when he was a child.

Terry, now 10 years old, was a very large boy for his age. When Mother or Father would try to stop his destructive actions, he would shake them off and push them away—although never striking them. During one of these tussles, however, he managed to push Father so hard that he fell over a footstool and banged his head severely. Terry appeared very frightened. Mother was both frightened and angry. In Terry's fright he became more wild, smashing furniture using the footstool as a weapon. Mother, a very large and powerfully built woman, finally mobilized herself and was able to contain Terry, holding his arms and sitting on him until he quieted down. In my effort to reconstruct the events, I asked Mother why she had not intervened earlier to quiet Terry, hopefully avoiding such an upsetting event. Mother angrily retorted that Father would never take a stand with Terry until either she forced him to or until Terry got very upset and literally began tearing things apart. Although it was Mother who spotted the early signs that Terry was upset, she felt that Father should be the one responsible for Terry's actions while he was at home and she wanted him to heed her early warnings that Terry was upset and intervene then. After all, why should she still have to carry this burden after so many years? When another effort was made to look at the critical issue—the restraint of Terry from developing the kind of excitement that occurred when he began to break things, making it harder to restrain him and cool him down— Mother would hear none of it. She was obviously angry and at the same time her deafness began to be obvious.

It seems as if the therapeutic work had exacerbated the parents' conflicts with each other by bringing these into the open and altering the equilibrium based on covert conflicts which were never discussed.

The hearing problem was a recurrent issue in therapy for the next seven years. At times it was clear Mother was not hearing what the therapist was saying. When the therapist tried to inquire about a sequence of events, there seemed to be a definite relationship between Mother's lack of hearing and her feelings of self-blame coupled with extreme anger and hurt.

During the first few months of this period very little destructive behavior took place on the ward. However, destructive behavior gradually began to accelerate. Terry would overturn waste baskets with a malicious smile. He tore up papers that were lying around and tore books out of people's hands. He began to light fires again and stuffed the toilets, broke appliances, and jammed the locks as before. It was only as these events became more chronic that we inquired in great detail about what was happening in the home situation. Mother revealed that Father had again agreed to work away from his base office in northern California, spending most of his week in southern California away from home. This sometimes included weekends if there were emergency projects, leaving Mother solely responsible for Terry when he was at home.

Mother's anger at Father was so great that she did not bring this up in the therapeutic sessions for a long time. Neither did Father, who kept his regular mid-week appointment, mention that he had a shift in job assignment. When this was brought up with him, he simply stated that he was not relieved of his responsibility to the Bay Area base but that he had been asked to spend most of his time in the Los Angeles office in order to help rectify some problems that required his particular expertise. When I inquired about its implications for the whole family, he looked rather blankly at me and asked what I was getting at. I pointed out that there seemed to me to be a clear connection between Terry's increasing amount of destructiveness and anger, his wife's feelings of having been deserted, and the change in his job situation which removed him from the family at a rather critical time in the family's effort to survive. Father looked pained and said that although he knew what I was talking about, he wasn't really sure that he was that important. We then examined some of Terry's behavior when Father was at home and the fact that Mother could not go to sleep at all when she was alone with Terry on the weekends Father was away. Father mused that this would certainly be so because when he was at home they took turns until Terry was actually fast asleep. They needed to be certain that Terry did not get up, wander about, and break up one of the appliances. When I raised the issue of hiring someone to stay with Mother during these weekends, there was obvious reluctance on Father's part because of the additional financial burden. For the first time, Father mentioned the serious problems presented by his mother who was in her seventies, an invalid with severe arthritis, who had only her Social Security to pay for her care. As the only son in the family, Father felt that he had major responsibility for her.

The ward staff became increasingly concerned because Terry was becoming very effective in flooding the tub in the side room; when the flood occurred he used the diversion either to break up some furniture or to get into the kitchen to the appliances, especially his favorite, the electric stove. He would jam the controls or set some flammable objects on the burners and turn them on. At this point, the staff began to consider whether they could keep Terry in the hospital. Both parents became alarmed at the thought that the staff might not keep Terry and felt that in many ways we were retaliating against them because of their own helplessness in dealing with Terry at home. Father especially expressed guilty feelings saying that perhaps it was he who had started this whole cycle by his ignorance of the implications of taking another job assignment away from home although he had never before questioned temporary reassignment of work.

Therapy with Terry

During this year Terry was seen three times a week as before but time periods varied. He began by tearing paper on my desk until he was restrained. He then went through a phase of dashing into the office and making a grab for the window shade, trying to tear it off. He usually overturned the waste basket. If the door to the office was left unguarded, he would, with a teasing, taunting smile, run out. In order to prevent Terry from destroying the materials on my desk, tearing the books or window shades, or dashing into the office and lashing out at the waste basket with his foot, it became necessary for me to hold his hand very tightly. Thus we walked into the office slowly, hand-in-hand, making sure that he could not disengage himself from me as I closed the door. On one occasion I was distracted by a phone call after we had been in the office about fifteen minutes. Terry had begun to settle down and look at one of the magazines that I had in the office for him which he could tear if he wanted to, although he usually riffled through the pages and picked out particular pictures to look at for long periods of time. These were usually pictures of families with small children. When I could not immediately free myself from the phone conversation, Terry sprang up from his chair, rushed to the window and tore the window blind from the roller. I was extremely angry both with myself for not having said to the person on the phone that I would return his call later and at Terry for the destruction. I held him with both arms; I shook him and told him how angry I was at him and how angry I was at myself for not cutting my phone conversation short. However, I was not going to permit him to destroy things and he and I were going to stay in the office and fix the window blind no matter how long it took.

He looked very angry at first and shook his head saying "n,n,n." Together we went out to the nurses' station where we were able to get a large stapler. We went back to the office, put the window shade roller on the floor and with a screw driver took out the old staples and tacks. I showed Terry how to hold the blind against the roller so that we could staple it. Our first effort was not very successful because I had not recognized how hard the wood was and the staples did not go in very far. We took out the row of staples and started again. With greater pressure on the stapler the staples were placed fairly close together and went all the way in. Terry watched me very carefully and toward the end I asked him if he wanted to put a couple of staples in while I held the window shade. At this he nodded his head and I held the window shade by its edges, giving him ample room to staple. He then used the stapler exactly as I had done with a great deal of skill and dexterity and put in the last half dozen staples. It then became necessary to rewind the spring on the roller and we utilized a can opener to do this. Terry was skillful in pushing the little cam that held the spring in place so that we could wind it steadily. We finally replaced it and rolled it up and down several times to see that it was functioning properly. By that time, Terry had become very interested in the process. I complimented him on his skills and patience and reminded him that I did not want him to tear at the window shade again. From that hour on, Terry made a number of abortive teasing gestures toward the window shade when he came into the office. He had numerous opportunities to dash away from me and tear down the window shade but he never did. In retrospect, with such an experience behind us, we could have built upon it in a number of other areas but it took some repetitive learning on my part to utilize this kind of experience in a way which might make it extend to other areas of our therapeutic work together.

During this third year the ward staff became very vigilant; someone was assigned to be with Terry most of the time so that he could not wreak havoc on the ward. If that person was his favorite aide, Terry by-and-large would play and be involved in activities and not become terribly difficult. If she were gone and one of the other aides who was frightened of Terry was placed in charge, he would frequently get into difficulty and it began to take two people to handle him. It finally became necessary to have his favorite aide work the five days of the week that Terry was in the hospital with weekends off rather than her previous staggered shift. Several scuffles with his parents took place around his destructive and aggressive behavior at home; however, there were no scuffles on the ward itself. Whenever someone grabbed Terry to hold him because he had been destructive, he usually quieted down, acting very frightened, as if he were about to be struck, and retreated from the adults who were with him. On several occasions such a retreat was felt by the staff to mean that Terry was now repentant and that he would not become destructive again, only to realize that when they took their eyes off him, he had darted away and repeated the very act for which they had restrained him. He demanded constant surveillance which made it very difficult for the staff since there were several other children who were equally destructive and especially self-destructive who also required a great deal of staff time and attention.

FOURTH YEAR OF TREATMENT

During the fourth year of treatment Terry continued much of his destructive activity at home and some of it on the ward although not at the same pace as during the previous year. Although much more manageable on the ward, he was destructive at home even though Father had returned full time to his executive position in the Bay Area. Father still had great difficulty in tuning in to Terry's moods and his potential for destructive behavior. Mother was still reluctant to be the one who restrained Terry promptly. When she asked Father to restrain Terry there was usually a lag between her first observation of the signs of Terry's destructiveness and the request of Father that he act. Thus Father's usually late restraint seemed a signal for increased destructive, hyperactive behavior. During this period, both parents felt terribly upset about their inability to control him at home and were to some extent disturbed by the fact that he was doing much better on the ward.

Therapy with Terry

Terry was often reluctant to go to the office now and wanted to stay on the ward in the day room. It was almost as if the numerous temptations in the office, especially the papers and folders on my desk, the waste basket, and the phone book from which he repeatedly attempted to tear pages were still very tempting to him. The few times that he did go to the office with me, he sat rather pensively and colored in the old way but half-heartedly, without his previous energy and obvious pleasure.

Toward the middle of that year, Terry had severe flu which was followed within a few weeks by mumps. During this period, I spent my time with Terry at his bedside. I would read to him aloud from fairy tale books with Terry turning the pages appropriately, almost as if he were reading with me as young children do, always turning the page at the correct moment. He was very responsive to my visits, welcoming me with a warm smile and obviously regretful when I had to leave. Each time I came to the ward he looked toward me eagerly so that I always made a point of stopping at his bedside, at least for a few moments, to chat with him. On several occasions during my brief visits when other members of the staff were busy, he searched for the fairy tale book at his bedside in an attempt to engage me to stay with him and become involved as I did during our longer times together. During his illnesses there was the same soft quality which many of us had seen in Terry during the period shortly after his admission. On a number of occasions he cuddled comfortably close to me and actually put his head on my shoulder while I read. After he had recovered from the mumps, Terry then began to want to come to the office. He would leaf through the picture books which were there for him. Occasionally he would look at the telephone book and go through the Yellow Pages with some minimal, rarely successful efforts to tear pages out. Usually a word from me when I noticed the impulse checked him from doing this. I had begun to comment about the increased anxiety and tension that I saw in him when he was tempted to do something destructive and such comments seemed to be helpful to him. A pattern began to emerge which was later confirmed by close observation and repeated opportunities to see the sequence. That sequence was one of coming into the office, being very happy to be there, obviously delighted at the opportunity to get his story books out and have them read to him. Later there was often some indifferent coloring or working with clay. He constantly glanced up at me to see whether or not I was closely observing him. Then he frequently presented me with another picture book, all of which were at the third or fourth grade level. During the reading, he would pull his chair close to mine and lean against me as we went through the book. At some point during these rather close and warm moments Terry would become tense and anxious.

When I was aware of this and could say he felt tense to me, we could move apart and stop reading. Terry would relax and the reading would go on until the end of our hour. When I was not aware of the beginning tension in his muscles, Terry would become increasingly tense and finally would jump up excitedly and tear at papers on the desk. As the tuning in on my part became more and more acute, the destructive part of the behavior was limited more and more.

Toward the end of that year whenever I saw Terry on the ward he would take my arm and walk with me to the office where I usually saw him. If it was not his time to see me, he looked very sad that he could not come in. Subsequently Terry would wander around the ward looking lonely and desolate. When his affect went unnoticed by staff who could engage him, he would frequently become involved in some destructive act. The quality of openness and softness which I had previously described was still there and noted by most of the ward staff and other faculty.

At first, when I took brief vacations or was ill, Terry reacted to my absence with temporary withdrawal. He would ignore me when I came on the ward, would not come to the office and would "look through" me when I sat with him in the day room and tried to read to him. He made no immediate response to my comments that he thought my absence, which I usually prepared him for, meant I was not coming back or that I did not care about him and did not want to be with him. However, toward the end of that year, an illness which kept me from the ward for about a week was not followed by the usual total withdrawal. When I did come back, Terry smiled at me with real pleasure and bounced up to come with me to the office where we went through the usual ritual. It was during one of these weeks that I noted for the first time, though I had some feeling that perhaps it had been present before without my clearly noting it, that as I read gutteral noises were coming from Terry which were so soft that one could easily miss them. The intonations of these gutteral sounds which came through his throat without much lip movement had some of the intonations that I used in the reading. I usually read each of the stories as dramatically as I could, using different voices for each of the characters. On several occasions when I forgot which voice I had used for the character before, Terry would stop me with a vigorous shake of his head, indicating that I was not now in character. I would then try to recapture the former voice and he would look relaxed again, smiling and pleased.

Therapy with Mother

During this year, Mother was feeling very anxious and angry. Her hearing had suddenly become worse and she was again contemplating surgery.

While Terry was on the ward each day she worked hard on her paintings, entering them in local art shows. A local dealer was handling her paintings for her and they were beginning to sell. While she expressed her pleasure and pride, she said she was still not sure that the money she saved would be used for her surgery. This brought about a recapitulation of the old complaint. She also began to talk, with anger and hurt feelings, about the many needs Father indicated they had for money. These especially had to do with the fact that Father's mother required nursing home care or nursing care within her own home and Father felt that he was the one who would have to supply the funds for this. Although very angry with Father, Mother did not have the courage to confront him with the fact that there were other family members who might contribute. Thus, most sessions were a repetitious expression of her feelings about being terribly isolated, her loss of hearing and her need for surgery—wondering whether or not her husband would permit her to use the money that she was currently earning for her own surgery.

Therapy with Father

During this year Father was very passive in his sessions, saying he had little to talk about. Things were going well at work. He was running the office efficiently and had begun a number of potentially successful research projects for which he was given more space and personnel. He was increasingly reluctant to discuss his relationship with his wife and the details of Terry's destructive behavior at home. Any effort on my part to lead him through a sequence of Terry's behavior at home would elicit from Father vagueness and declarations that he really did not know what was happening. When he became aware of the moment of onset of Terry's destructive acts, the problems seemed to exacerbate and Terry became even more violent and destructive although Father could somehow manage to restrain him from doing further damage. It was during this year that I tried to meet with both parents together in an effort to clarify the issue of Mother's surgery and Father's concerns about it.

During these hours, Mother and Father looked at each other with both hostility and bitterness. Father reacted to Mother's accusations that he really did not care about her, and was not concerned whether or not she could ever hear well again, with protests, but withdrew into a shell and said very little. On two occasions he reiterated his sense of responsibility toward his mother who had provided him with an education. He felt that somebody had to take care of her and he believed it was his responsibility. When we tried to delineate the actual income and expense of ward inpatient costs and what this left to manage the payments on the very lovely home they had bought, food costs, etc. and how much might be left from Mother's own savings for her own surgery, things began to blur again. It was very difficult for Father, despite his mathematical precision in other areas, to sit down and literally draw up a budget. Mother was totally unwilling to participate in planning a budget saying that she handled none of the family finances. This turned out to be untrue, since in fact she paid all the bills and was the one most informed about the actual expenditures of the family. She was also the only one who knew how much money she was now able to put away for her own surgery. It became clear again that Mother wanted Father to put her first and recognize her desperate need. During one of these hours, Mother hostilely pounced on Father after a particularly difficult siege with Terry at home because he would not notice when Terry began to look anxious and tense and waited for the first destructive act before intervening. In our discussion about what the first signs of tension and anxiety were, Father looked bewildered because these were signs that he was unable to recognize. In our discussions together we tried to utilize Mother's being attuned to Terry as a way of helping Father to become engaged with Terry prior to his destructive acts. Mother was still very reluctant to help alert Father to Terry's tension. We ended the joint sessions when it became clear that Father and Mother were using them in a very hostile and destructive way toward each other. It seemed as if they were not ready to face their mutual problems and to look at possible collaborative solutions.

Ward Activities—Fourth Year of Treatment

On the ward during this period, Terry was able to go out to the park with his particular nurse's aide and occasionally engaged in many activities with normal children. His agility on the slides and swings and his beginning agility on the swinging bars and rings gave him a sense of real accomplishment. The nurse's aide described how pleased he looked with himself when he could execute a new movement on the swinging bar and was now able to pull himself up and turn a somersault on the rings without any trouble. She described how often Terry emulated other children and the ways in which he would take his turn on the slides, the swings and other play apparatus. It was clear that his greatest pleasure came from emulating some of the youngsters who were working out on the rings. He would spend considerable time trying to duplicate their maneuvers—with obvious delight when he succeeded—but with no great sense of frustration when he didn't because he would continue these activities over and over again each day until he became much more adept and facile at the particular exercise. It also became clear to the nursing staff that many of Terry's destructive acts occurred at those moments on the ward when the adult who was with Terry became absorbed in something else or was not alert to what Terry seemed to be wanting to do. Terry would dash off and turn over a waste basket, flood the toilet, or, if he had matches, set a waste basket on fire.

FIFTH YEAR OF TREATMENT

During the fifth year of treatment, Terry's destruction was still occurring frequently at home and made his stay at home a constant anxiety for both parents. They, however, did not miss any opportunities to take him home and would not accede to my and staff members' suggestion that it was possible for him to stay an occasional weekend on the ward so that both parents could get away together for a holiday. While Father thought this was a reasonable idea and looked very eager, Mother disdainfully sniffed and said that Terry came first and she wouldn't think of not taking him home because he would then feel rejected and they would have even more trouble the following weekend.

This was one of the many times that the question of who came first to whom was raised. Mother wanted to come first to Father ahead of his mother and to be considered important enough to receive her needed ear surgery. Father wanted to come first to Mother ahead of Terry, and have some of his needs met. In various ways, the drama of who comes first was played out to the inevitable disappointment of the one who hoped for some consideration at a particular moment.

During this year Father again had some intermittent work to do in Southern California, supervising the opening of a new lab and helping train the new director and some of the personnel. In talking with both parents it was not clear to me whether Father opted for the weekends down south as a means of escaping from a tense and difficult situation at home or whether in fact the work demanded it. When I raised this question with Father, he looked rather sheepish and said he did not dare bring work home over the weekend because Terry would destroy it. There was never any time to work anyway because his time was occupied with keeping track of Terry to prevent destructive behavior. He used these weekends away from home to complete paperwork he could not get done at his office. Mother expressed bitterness that Father would occasionally bring work home and then try to isolate himself from Terry and their problems so that he could get some work done. Only in recent months had Father become resigned to the fact that when he was at home he had to be with Terry and Mother.

The Work with Terry

During the fifth year two notable points occurred in the therapeutic work with Terry. The first centered around the need for dental work. Over the years Terry had needed a good deal of dental work which the parents felt they could not get done because he was so violent in the dentist's chair. On one occasion, two years after he came to the hospital, because of urgent need for dental work Terry was given some medication and anesthetized early in the morning so the dentist at the clinic could fill some very deep cavities. When Terry came out of the anesthesia he was withdrawn, frightened and unreachable. Despite weeks of preparatory discussion, he avoided his favorite nursing aide and me for some weeks thereafter.

When, during this fifth year, more dental work was definitely needed, we began a new process of preparing him for it. We showed Terry pictures of teeth, helped him look in the mirror at the particular teeth that needed to be filled, walked with him down to the dentist's office and sat with him there while the dentist worked on other patients, sometimes children. At the same time the dentist talked to Terry in reassuring tones. Thus, many of our therapeutic hours were spent in the dentist's office. Terry looked forward to the visits and the opportunity to examine the variety of instruments in the case, which obviously fascinated him. On numerous occasions the dentist let him use one of his laboratory drills to drill into some wood and into soap so Terry would acquire a familiarity with the sound of the instrument. When we thought Terry felt sufficiently easy about the whole situation we arranged an appointment which Terry was informed about some weeks in advance. We continued our visits to the dentist's office, talking about what was going to be done and which teeth would be fixed. Terry permitted himself on a preliminary visit to sit quietly in the dental chair while the dentist carefully examined his teeth and planned the work. The dentist wisely gave Terry something to hold in his hand during the examination. Thus, he had a dental scraping tool and soapstone which he could dig away at during this time.

When the time came for Terry's dental appointment I went down with Terry to the dentist. He sat quietly while the dentist infiltrated the areas with novocaine. Terry then sat through the next hour without any obvious discomfort or anxiety while the dentist prepared the teeth and filled them. When I commented at what a great job he had done in the dentist chair and how pleased I was that he was able to sit quietly and permit the dental work to be done, Terry grinned widely at me. After the dental work was completed, Terry still wanted to go down to the dentist's office. Occasionally we did, and the dentist again permitted Terry to work with one of his drills or scrapers. Both parents were delighted that the dental work could be done this time without general anesthesia and with Terry's full cooperation.

Another crisis occurred shortly after mid-year. Terry had had a succession of incidents of sore throat and runny nose. The pediatrician who had looked after him for some time felt that his tonsils which were now meeting in the mid-line needed to come out. Both parents, the ward staff, and I were apprehensive about a tonsilectomy. We obtained a consultation at University Hospital whose E.N.T. department agreed it was high time Terry's tonsils be taken out. They were, however, quite anxious about the idea of operating on a youngster like Terry who might struggle and fight against the anesthesia. Fairly recently some anesthetic deaths had occurred because youngsters were so anxious about a tonsilectomy. They were understandably reluctant to operate on Terry. I felt that if we went through a process similar to that prior to Terry's dental work it might not be quite as difficult as everyone thought. One of the concessions we were able to get from the E.N.T. surgeons was that the surgery might be done in our own operating amphitheater with their instruments and their nurses. My reasoning was that it would be much more difficult to take Terry to the University Hospital where he would have to spend a night in a strange ward to be prepared for surgery by unfamiliar people whom he could not trust.

When the ear, nose and throat surgeons did agree to do the surgery in our own hospital amphitheater, I began a series of explorations with Terry into the surgical suite. We began this by simply walking into the surgical suite after an operation had been done to view the various instruments. Again, Terry was very curious about the instruments, these primarily being neuro-surgical instruments. I was able to show him through drawings and pictures what his tonsils looked like and why they needed to come out. He appeared rather indifferent to this part of our effort but he seemed to hear my comments and those of his favorite nurse's aide that his colds and sore throats would be better if we could get his tonsils out. I obtained permission from the neurosurgeons who used the amphitheater to take out some of the old instruments for Terry to play with. Thus, under my close supervision, he used scissors, scrapers, various bone drills, and probes on cardboard that we brought with us each time. He began to look at the surgical amphitheater as a place he could explore and he became very familiar with every part of it. On one occasion we visited the amphitheater when surgery was in progress. We walked up to the viewing platform above the amphitheater and sat quietly while the surgeons were at work. Terry was obviously interested, literally not moving during the two and one-half hour operation. Because I felt that this was so critical, I cancelled several appointments so that we could spend the entire time together. To prepare Terry for the anesthesia, an anesthetist who was most effective with children brought over a number of balloons for Terry to learn to blow up and to inhale from. He practiced this. I commented to Terry that if he were to blow these up and then let them come back into his throat he would learn how to take the anesthesia which would put him to sleep so he would feel no pain during surgery. While it was not clear whether Terry understood all of this, he played with the balloons first by filling them with water and squirting them out and then slowly blowing them up and inhaling the air. He was especially pleased with those balloons that were Mickey Mouse figures and he was eager to blow each one up to see what kind of a figure it was. Again, we spent most of our therapeutic time in the surgical suite.

Mother explained that one of the anxieties from Terry's previous encounter with surgery was his fear of the people in masks whom he did not know. I therefore asked the surgeons that I and his nurse's aide be present at the induction of anesthesia without a mask so that Terry would know we were there. We could then hold his hands. Several actual operations seen from the viewing room permitted Terry to observe surgeons with their masks off and then on and then taken off again after the surgery was over. When the surgery was finally scheduled, Terry seemed quite uneasy about the premedication. He complained loudly when he received his hypodermic injection but appeared fairly relaxed otherwise. He slept well that night and took the necessary premedication in the morning without any protest. When he was wheeled to the operating suite with the attendant and the nurse and I on either side of him there were no signs of great anxiety although there was a bead of sweat on his upper lip indicating some apprehension. The E.N.T. surgeon who was going to do the surgery had met Terry on a number of occasions, talked with him and sat quietly with me during some short periods with Terry so that Terry knew who he was. It was he and the anesthetist who approached Terry in the pre-operatory room and they talked to Terry until he appeared quite relaxed. Terry blew the balloon up and inhaled just as he had done in practice. He made very little protest when the gas anesthesia was introduced except to indicate that it did not smell or feel right and within a short time he was asleep. The tonsilectomy proceeded without any further difficulty. His nurse's aide and I were able to stay with him during the recovery period and when he came out of the anesthesia we were both there. While his throat hurt a great deal—which we had also prepared him for—he seemed very pleased that we were there and held out his hands to us. We again remarked at the superb job he had done in letting himself be anesthetized and have his tonsils taken out; he grinned wanly. Fortunately, one of the foods that Terry liked the most was ice cream. Since this was one of the foods he was permitted to have shortly after his surgery, he gulped large quantities of it. Even after he had fully recovered he still demanded ice cream in huge portions at every meal as if this were now his right.

However, this wore off after a time and he began to eat other foods even though he still preferred ice cream as desert.

It was of interest to the nursing staff and to the faculty that during Terry's period of recovery from the tonsilectomy, while he still had some pain and discomfort, Terry was friendly and warm with all of us. He did not go home on that weekend, was relaxed on the ward, and stayed in bed. He eagerly welcomed a visit from me during the weekend and pushed the fairy tale book in my hands so that I would read to him.

Terry's Behavior on the Ward

The fact that during this year Terry was able to have both dental work done and a tonsilectomy performed seemed extremely reassuring to most of the ward staff who had anticipated massive difficulties. Terry, too, subsequent to each of these procedures behaved as though he realized that our efforts were really to help him. He was much less destructive, and his play with his nurse both on the ward and in the park had a much more joyful and free quality than we had ever seen before.

The nursing staff began having increasing difficulty with Mother. Each time Mother brought Terry from home after a weekend, she looked completely exhausted, was impatient with the nurses and was obviously in a hurry to return Terry to the ward so that she would have an opportunity to recuperate and get some sleep. Even though she would report a terrible weekend at home, she clearly wanted no help from the nurses in examining the details of the weekend so that together they might consider how Terry might be better handled in the home setting and on the ward. She was quite contemptuous of the nurse's aide who handled Terry with obvious skill and ease. Mother appeared to want to hear that Terry had been equally destructive and difficult on the ward. When these comments were not forthcoming, she appeared angry and hostile.

Therapy with Mother

During this year there was a recurrent theme which the therapist found extremely difficult to work with. Mother rehearsed the history of her relationships with various mental health professionals and others who blamed her for Terry's difficulty. She would then look very directly and accusingly at me and say there seemed to be no way out for her except to kill Terry and commit suicide herself. When I tried to understand some of the elements of her feelings, Mother expressed her view that Terry was not very much better despite the successes in having both a tonsilectomy and dental work done and the fact that he was more relaxed and open on the ward. His behavior at home precluded his remaining at home and he was certainly no closer to talking or learning, thus becoming an effective human being. Since everyone blamed her for Terry's plight, she felt that there was no other way except to remove both of them from this terrible world in which they lived. Underneath this recurrent angry tirade and the statement of suicide and killing Terry was an obvious plea for reassurance that Terry would indeed become well. Mother desperately seemed to want a guarantee from the therapist and from the ward personnel that they saw something in Terry that she did not which would indicate that he was making progress and at some time in the next few years, he would be able to come home and live "a normal life."

The therapist felt very much on the spot when these recurrent hopeless statements and the implied questions came up. He sought some help in supervision in trying to deal with them. The reality was that we could not guarantee anything and that Mother was partly correct that no major changes had occurred in Terry which indicated that he would be able to take his place in society, even at a minimally functioning level. What became clear in supervision was that both the accusation and Mother's plea were difficult for the therapist to understand and deal with. On the one hand, he felt the burden of the possibility that Mother might carry out her threat. On the other hand, he felt that he could not guarantee what she wanted and felt caught in a double bind. What was difficult to understand under these circumstances was Mother's overwhelming sense of helplessness, her feeling of impotence, and her desire that someone else take over for her and in fact take care of her and all her problems. It was also difficult to be empathic and warmly supportive of Mother when she talked about suicide and killing Terry with the ferocity that she usually did or when she angrily blamed the staff and the ward milieu for the lack of progress with Terry. In this dilemma, it was almost impossible for the therapist to extract himself from the hostile, destructive aspects of Mother's threats and comments and deal with her underlying feelings—recognizing Mother's tremendous discouragement, the validity of her feelings—and at the same time, indicate our commitment to continue our work with Terry toward at least some limited objectives.

On one occasion Mother repeated in sequence the statement that it looked as if her savings would again be used by her husband to help support his ailing mother and that the deaths of Terry and herself seemed the only way to rid the world of their burden. She then immediately bitterly denounced the work of the faculty and staff of the clinic.

The therapist softly commented that he could understand most of the feelings she was talking about and felt very badly that he had not been able to be more helpful. He felt especially regretful that he had not been able to help Mother deal with a number of her personal problems with Father—especially her need for corrective surgery for her hearing loss— so that she might feel more worthwhile and recognize that she had an important place in the world whether Terry made it or not. Mother's first reaction was a total rejection of these comments with a very hostile, "How would you know how it feels if you haven't been in my shoes?" The therapist sat quietly waiting; Mother became tearful and rather quietly responded with, "I suppose you really do know something of what it feels like, because you have been with Terry over and over again and you have really withstood all kinds of anger and hate that I feel inside of me without throwing me out so that maybe you really mean it." Toward the end of this year these recurrent comments of Mother's occurred with much less force and she became more open to discussing the issues of her surgery and the need for taking care of herself. On one occasion the therapist made a suggestion about Mother's prompt intervention with Terry when he looked anxious when she was home alone with him. She was able to say, with a very warm and friendly smile, "I know exactly what you are saying and I'm trying to do it more and more; last weekend when I did spot that terrified flicker in his eye and put an arm around him, things did settle down."

It was also toward the end of this year that Mother began to talk about her relationships with other people in the community—especially the man and woman who ran the art studio that handled her paintings. She had developed a very warm and friendly relationship with both. She felt they supported her in her efforts to paint and they encouraged her and believed that her talent was beginning to take form. She also described her relationship with one of her students—a man in his early forties—in the art class she had helped to develop in the studio. She felt many kindred feelings toward this man; like her, he had had a very difficult time as a child and adolescent and then, a difficult marriage. He was now trying to become more creative as a means of dealing with some of his own frustrations. She described his obvious talent, his moroseness, depression and alcoholism, and with a wry smile and half-chuckle said she had often thought about alcoholism as a way out. However, she knew that once she started she would be stuck because nobody could drink and keep track of Terry at the same time. As she described her relationship with this man she kept looking at the therapist. At first the therapist felt this was a glance to see whether or not there was disapproval of this relationship and only in retrospect during the following year did it become clear that there was some hope on Mother's part that the therapist would be jealous of the developing relationship.

Toward the end of the year, Mother had come to a decision that Father's mother's need for financal help did not exceed her own need for inner ear surgery. She began to prepare for her operation by sending checks to the surgeon for him to accumulate until his fee was paid off. She said she would then pay off the hospital fees in the same way so that in fact she would not have the money in her savings account. This positive move on Mother's part reflected an increased sense of accomplishment in her teaching of art. She found herself in a mothering role with a number of the young students in her art class who responded very positively to her approaches and who manifested the effect of her teaching methods by the improvements in their painting.

Father's Therapy

During this year Father continued to talk about the need to take care of his mother. He talked of the desperate situation at home with his wife angry at him because they could not afford to care for his mother and pay for his wife's surgery at the same time and face the current costs of Terry's treatments and destructiveness. For the first time—toward the middle of that year—Father was able to describe the way his salary was apportioned and how it was paid out. It turned out that about 30% of his salary (after taxes) was invested in company shares which would permit him a good income on retirement. This led to a discussion about priorities in terms of his wife's need for surgery and the need for a very comfortable retirement salary. The question of whether he could turn in some shares—permitting both the care of his mother and his wife's surgery without scrapping the entire investment program—was raised. Father was obviously shaken by this idea and rejected it vehemently. Later, he began to examine his need for security and the various ways in which he had provided for the future security of himself and his family. When we talked about the company's retirement plan, it turned out that it was a good one but Father felt that, alone, it might be insufficient with the continuing expenses of Terry's care which he correctly felt would go on for many years.

It was only toward the end of the year after numerous discussions about finances, low interest loans, etc., that Father would even begin to discuss the possibility that both of his sisters might pitch in to help out with the care of his mother. At that time, he talked only in a fragmentary way about his sisters' capacity to help. He finally began to talk about his oldest sister. She was married to an extremely wealthy man who was several times a millionaire. The care of their mother was a topic that this sister had brought up a number of times. She said she would be willing to undertake the total financial cost since she too felt obligated and it was no financial burden for her. Father felt very strongly that he could not permit this. This issue was examined in great detail and it became clear that the care of his mother represented to Father a masculine strength which he could not relinquish and that if his sister took care of his mother, he would somehow have failed again as a man to do what was necessary as the head of the household. Again and again, the realities and the issues related to Father's need of proving his masculinity were reexamined. The whole question of priorities was slowly considered. Would Father not feel much more like a man if he could really help his wife out in her surgery so that she felt that he was concerned about her and was responsive as a husband? Would that not make him feel better? Father had never considered this a critical issue. As he began to talk about the possibility of surgery for Mother, he also began to talk about the possibility of corrective surgery for himself. This surgery was to correct the painful scars and contractures in his abdomen to reduce the tenderness from pressure. It seemed that once he could realistically consider his wife's needs with some tenderness, he could then begin to consider his own needs more objectively.

CONTINUATION OF COUNTERTRANSFERENCE PROBLEMS

During the following year, the seventh, elements of countertransference issues became clear in the therapeutic work with each member of the family.

Work with Terry

Terry's treatment during this year was focused on setting of limits within therapeutic hours as well as on the ward. He was not terribly destructive except for occasional outbreaks when he would rush up behind people and flip their eye glasses off, sometimes breaking them. It was interesting that, despite the staff's anger and Mother's anger at paying for broken lenses, it was not until the therapist had his glasses knocked off that he became thoroughly involved in the efforts to deal with Terry about this problem. On one occasion as they were walking into the office, Terry suddenly stepped behind the therapist and flipped his eye glasses off. The therapist bent quickly and recovered them before they broke. However, he was extremly angry. The degree of narcissistic hurt from Terry's action was not clear until later. The therapist grabbed Terry and brought him into the office; Terry was obviously frightened. The therapist held Terry very tightly, shook him and spoke angrily about the fact that he had knocked the therapist's glasses off and it was with some difficulty that he contained himself and did not retaliate by striking out at Terry. It was clear that Terry understood exactly what was being said because he looked increasingly apprehensive, his eyes darting around the room toward the door as if seeking a place to escape. However, he was held very firmly by the therapist who on occasion emphasized his anger by giving him a hard shake. At this point, Terry would whimper and the therapist would go on ventilating his anger.

After about ten to fifteen minutes of the therapist's expressing his full feeling toward Terry, Terry appeared somewhat sheepish as if he had not meant to make the therapist quite this angry. It was at this point that the therapist decided to state unequivocally that he was going to do all he could to halt Terry's destructive behavior, even if he guessed wrong sometimes and Terry was actually not going to do something destructive when the therapist intervened. Thus, in various ways, the therapist made explicit his determination to prevent Terry from any kind of destructive act if he could anticipate Terry's actions. Terry did not make another attempt to flip the therapist's glasses from his face although on rare occasions, it did occur with other staff members. The therapist continued to be vigilant with Terry in and out of his office, in the day room and on the ward. He hoped his prompt actions would serve to help the ward staff feel easier about intervening.

As the therapist began to read into Terry's actions a variety of potentials for destructive behavior, he began to limit some of his previously permitted behavior. Perhaps the climax of this occurred when the therapist tried to make clear to Terry that he could tear or bend the pictures in the *Life* or *Look* magazines that were brought there for him but he could not tear the telephone book. With his usual alertness, Terry began to test the limits. He would grab at a page of the telephone book and just gently pull at it so that there was a guarter-of-an-inch tear. The therapist soon learned to stop this immediately because if he did not, the whole page would come out. When this behavior was limited over and over again, Terry then began to fold the pages in half, looking at the therapist, waiting for a reaction. The therapist then understood that Terry was asking for further limit-setting and said that that too could not be done since it literally ruined the page, especially if several of them were folded back making it difficult to use the telephone book.

Terry then began a series of teasing maneuvers which are best characterized as very minute destructive acts. Each one of these could have been ignored but taken in context, each one appeared as if it were a request that the therapist be attentive to what was going on. Thus, on one occasion, Terry walked into the therapist's office, sat down in the therapist's chair where he usually sat and noted a brand new desk blotter which had just been obtained to cover the entire badly marred desk top. With a quick glance at the therapist, Terry picked up a ball point pen and made a little dot on it. The therapist waited and Terry made another couple of dots. At this point the therapist intervened, pointing out that here was a nice brand new blotter

and Terry had to test whether or not he could spoil the whole thing, perhaps by not only scribbling on it but by tearing through it with the ball
point pen. Terry was then told that this was not going to be permitted, and
he was not to touch the blotter. Terry looked terribly offended and squealed
in a high squeaky voice as if he were very angry at the therapist. However,
when the noise produced no result, and the therapist said that he was
prepared to be wrong once in a while—and maybe he was wrong this time—
but that he could not let Terry continue to do something which might
eventually lead to destructive behavior.

Terry then abandoned these efforts and turned to other kinds of play
which were beginning to take shape for the first time. He began to leaf
through the magazines that were for him, turning pages in series of twos,
threes, fours and five pages at a time. It was some time before the therapist
caught on to this and could quickly recognize how many pages Terry was
turning and in response enunciate that he was now picking up and turning
two pages or four pages or whatever the sequence was. Terry smiled and
appeared pleased at this interaction and responsiveness to his behavior.

Toward the end of that year, Terry tested the therapist several times. This
seemed like Terry's final effort. Terry looked nonchalantly at the floor while
he held the telephone book in his lap and very gently creased a tiny corner
of a page as he was turning it. The therapist commented that he knew that
Terry's desire was to tear the page and he would not even allow him to turn
the corner of the page, either to tear it off or just to bend it over because
he felt that this would only lead Terry to destructive behavior. Terry
screeched loudly and angrily. He continued screeching for several minutes
while the therapist sat by calmly. On several other occasions, Terry tested
out the very same maneuver, and each time he was stopped and told he
could not even turn over the corner of the page and crease it. Terry then
picked the minutest edge of the corner of the page and started to tear it. The
therapist repeated in a very loud and clear voice that he was to stop. Terry
again looked angry and screeched loudly with obvious indignation. The same
sequence occurred with Terry screeching and the therapist reaffirming that
he felt such actions were only the beginning of his destructive behavior and
that this could not be permitted.

Subsequent to these experiences Terry began to use word-like gutteral
sounds; they began with the sequence of Terry taking two magazine pages
at a time, turning them for several sequences, and then grabbing three pages
and turning three pages as he worked his way up the sequence to five pages
at a time. As the therapist would say "You have got three pages and you
are turning three pages, another three pages, another three pages, another
three pages," there were some gutteral sounds that sounded like "tee" and

"ages." The therapist took the sounds to be an effort on Terry's part to repeat what the therapist had just said. Thus began the efforts on Terry's part toward communicative speech. Similar sequences were seen in a variety of interactions in school, on the ward, and with the therapist, but never at home with his parents.

The countertransference aspects of therapeutic work seemed to stem from the difficulty in obtaining any real satisfaction through observing progress in therapy. It became vividly focused as the therapist felt that at last he was immune to Terry's attacks, such as Terry's efforts to break other people's glasses. When he found that he was not immune and Terry actually did knock his glasses off, there was a tremendous overreaction and rage at Terry for his behavior and a desire to retaliate. It was only as his feelings toward Terry were verbalized that it became clear to the therapist that he was overreacting, as he had not felt nearly as angry when Terry had broken the glasses of some colleagues on the ward. The therapist had felt a special omnipotence—an immunity to Terry's behavior. He was angry and felt helpless because he had been unable to help Terry improve sufficiently so that Mother and Father would feel less troubled. He was also concerned that his colleagues, the nursing staff, and the Director of the Children's Service were constantly evaluating the capacity of the staff to handle Terry and there remained the desire to be the great therapist who could cure Terry and the hope that Terry would be able to live a less frantic, anxious and terrified life.

Therapeutic Work with Father

Countertransference problems which occurred in the work with Father became clearer as he began to talk of his own need for surgery. It was then that Father's self-assertion was examined as it arose in his relationship with Mother. It was easier to assert his needs despite the fact that her need for ear surgery was essential whereas Father's surgery was elective. Although Father said he could completely understand the therapist's comments he appeared rather shaken when the therapist pointed out that despite Father's need for surgery so that he could live with less chronic tenderness and pain, perhaps the greater issue was his capacity to understand his wife's needs, and as a husband, be sensitive to these. As Father began to retreat from such explorations of his own need for surgery, it became very evident to the therapist that he was identifying with Mother and clearly saw the Father in the role of the non-feeling, self-centered husband and Father—a role familiar to the therapist out of his own experiences. As the therapist became aware of Father's retreat, he became more involved in an effort to help Father establish some priorities and examine means by which both surgeries could be accomplished. After another detailed examination of

Father's finances, Father was encouraged to inquire about what the cost of the operation might be. As Father began his inquiries, he appeared much brighter and seemed much more in tune with the various problems of the household. During this same period he was at home more with Terry and seemed able to more quickly sense the onset of destructive tensions. This awareness helped him to stop Terry more quickly without having to depend upon Mother's direction. During the latter part of this year, Father began to describe his impatient feelings whenever he needed something but had to wait for it. A tremendous amount of anger was always generated under such conditions. He then described a number of childhood situations in which he was thwarted in a desire for something—usually by his older sister or a cousin—and he developed a murderous rage toward them which frightened him. If he screamed his Mother would come in and usually give Father whatever he wanted. Father now guessed this was because he was usually either recovering from surgery or just about ready to be hospitalized again.

In a moment of insight Father was able to place some of his work experience into the context of his feelings. Finding that opposition to his ideas made him very angry—a feeling which he could not express to any of his colleagues—he felt immobilized and anxious. He was then unable to integrate the data which were usually at hand to help him bring about rational agreements and decisions. Thus, Father's insight into a variety of his interactions with colleagues, some of his friends, and with his wife increased. The latter remained in many ways obscured by his many feelings of guilt so he was only able to begin to examine a few of these interactions.

When he was derisively challenged by his wife about his lack of acuteness in understanding certain issues and problems or his failure to recognize the beginnings of difficulties with Terry, Father found himself so immobilized by anger that he literally could not be effective with Terry or find any rational way of describing his feelings to his wife. Even more troubling was the lack of awareness of a conscious basis for some of his behavior and decisions. In a circular fashion, Mother's utter contempt for his decisions and actions led to further anger and immobilization with other irrational consequences. As Father became more attuned to Terry and could intervene more promptly (despite the fact that this permitted Mother to be freer in the house and later on to engage in other activities away from home) it was difficult for Mother to acknowledge that Father was increasingly effective with Terry.

Work with Mother

During this seventh year of treatment, the countertransference problems with Mother became clearly centered around certain themes. When Mother heard Father talk about his surgical needs, she felt so angered and helpless that she almost abandoned her own plans, trying to recover the prepayments to her surgeon to give to Father for his needs in a perverse kind of revenge. Mother was mostly angry and hurt because Father could not even acknowledge Mother's right to hear. Father's hoarse, low voice was difficult for Mother to hear so there was little in the way of talking at home.

Another recurrent theme had to do with hearing aids. The therapist expressed his hope that while Mother was saving toward her surgery, she might at least explore the possibility of obtaining one of the newer hearing aids so that she would not feel quite as helpless and isolated from others. Mother became furious each time this issue was raised. She would reiterate the fact that she had tried her own mother's hearing aid and found it awful; it made so much noise that not being able to hear was a greater blessing than the noise in the hearing aid. When I mentioned that this had occurred some twenty years ago and better hearing aids had been developed, she would begin to fume. In biting tones she denounced the therapist for taking her husband's side and said he was only concerned with appeasement and not the cure of Mother's deafness. It was only toward the middle of the year that Mother began to acknowledge the therapist's sincerity in his desire that Mother at least have some temporary surcease from the agony of not being able to hear very much and that she had a right to both a hearing aid and the surgery. Although Mother began to understand more fully what the therapist was talking about, she could never go to the hearing center to try the various hearing aids and be fitted for one. Both Mother's audiologist and ear, nose and throat surgeon had strongly urged her to try a hearing aid since the drainage in her ear was such that it precluded immediate surgery. Nevertheless, Mother felt that such a temporary solution would only lead to Father's not being at all concerned with her surgery and again Mother would find herself short-changed, having to give way to someone else's need instead of having her own needs met.

A third theme recurred during this year. The therapist originally had some inklings about this but chose to ignore it when Mother began to frequently talk about her warm feelings for some of the students whom she taught. Each time she mentioned this, she looked directly at the therapist for his reaction. She finally made it clear to the therapist that she was hoping to evoke a feeling of jealousy. She also commented that the therapist's artistic capacities could be extended if he would learn to paint. The therapist listened each time but made no comments. It was only when Mother began to shower the therapist with a variety of gifts that it became clear to him that there were several themes involved. One was her hope that the therapist cared about her as an adult woman, perhaps was even attracted sexually and that he cared about her as a man who understood her problems and would consider her needs primary as if she were a very small child whose parent would take care of her. The countertransference issues became clearer as the therapist found himself uneasy in the face of Mother's unstated demands and coquettish behavior. He also found himself extremely reluctant to deal with the paternal-maternal and the sexual themes. On one occasion Mother bought a very attractive dress which was something she rarely did since she made her own clothes. She walked into the office with a model's gait and as she sat down, said in a rather provocative tone: "I hope you noticed my new dress. What do you think of it?" The therapist said that he thought it was extremely attractive and that Mother looked very nice in it. Mother began to glow and flush. The therapist was then able to continue to say that he thought Mother was a very attractive woman to whom he felt attracted and that he had a great many warm feelings for her which he hoped would aid and not hinder their therapeutic work. At the end of this statement Mother was not only flushed but she was clearly angry and hurt. It took a number of sessions to bring all of these feelings into focus. It was clear that Mother was aware that she was attracted to the therapist and that he had many warm feelings for her and was concerned with being helpful to her. She commented that this awareness made it easier for her to work with the therapist and to persist in it. Somehow Mother could not accept the fact that there was an amalgam of feelings—both adult and child-like—within her. This theme became clearer one day when the therapist came in with a very bad cold and Mother very solicitously gave him some Kleenex and advised him about some medication. The therapist laughingly asked whether this was an adult feeling of attraction or whether it was a natural motherly feeling trying to help someone that she cared about who needed her as a child or at least as a helpless adult. Somehow this analogy seemed to clarify a number of things for Mother who began to rather humorously describe the fact that if she could understand the distinctions she guessed they need not stand in the way of both kinds of feelings.

THE EIGHTH YEAR OF THERAPY

The eighth year of treatment which led to outpatient work was a continuation of most of the processes described in the seventh year. However, there was a great deal more freedom on the part of Mother and Father with the therapist and more exploration into some early feelings, permitting both parents to relate in a much more unambivalent way to the therapist.

Work with Terry

Work with Terry during this year primarily consisted of the therapist putting into words the variety of behaviors which Terry manifested. Terry continued to make more and more clearly enunciated grunts and noises which to the therapist seemed related to words. Thus, the words no and yes—which became "nyaa" and "yaa"—came out in a kind of laughing, teasing way whenever the therapist would ask Terry about whether he had correctly guessed the number of pages Terry wanted to turn or had understood what Terry wanted when he was looking around for another crayon for his coloring. Terry also began to hum several recognizable songs from school music classes while he rocked in the therapist's swivel chair. During this time there were occasional destructive behaviors on the ward but they became increasingly rare; his teacher reported with a great deal of enthusiasm her perception of Terry's pleasure in doing school work and the occasional words she thought she heard but could never be totally sure of. Most clearly Terry was able to say "Hi" with a great explosive "H" sound and a very clear "No" when he did not want to do something. Other words were less clear.

Terry's Behavior on the Ward

The nurses and nurse's aides who had begun to work with him effectively were delighted to work with the teasing friendly Terry rather than the previously destructive boy. By this time, Terry was a large six foot sixteen-year-old who towered over his nurses and therapist. He was extremely agile and loved to go to the park to play on the rings and swings. It remained evident that Terry had some anxiety about using his hands in a more integrative way because he would never return a baseball thrown his way or bounce a basketball even when his nurse tried to help him. Somehow his hands seemed completely ineffectual and he was unable to play catch, learn how to bounce a basketball or shoot at the basket. His behavior at home became much less destructive. Weeks went by without any destructive activity either on the ward or at home, although he still needed to be closely watched. At home Father had begun to garden and Terry became interested in being with him. Terry seemed to enjoy helping his Father in these activities. Mother was also able to get Terry's cooperation and help when she needed to size canvas to ready it for painting. Thus, both parents felt somewhat more encouraged about Terry's behavior, despite the fact that his speech consisted of three or four very badly enunciated words. The rest of his speech was totally garbled and meaningless to most listeners but it became evident to all that Terry could hear, understand and carry out directions without any confusion. Once both Terry and the therapist discovered that a leaky water pipe in the office had wet a number of the therapist's books and journals. He asked Terry to help him move the bookcase so that the plumber could get to the water pipe, which Terry did. He then requested Terry's help in opening the books and journals and spreading them out to dry. Terry was not only cooperative but fascinated by the opportunity to emulate the therapist's actions as he carefully opened each of the volumes so that they could be exposed to the sun. Terry would stand the books on their end, open them and then ruffle the pages in such a way as to produce the greatest amount of surface volume for exposure to the sun. Terry did a much more thorough job than the therapist.

The Therapeutic Work with Father

Father continued to talk about the need for his surgery and explored various avenues for getting it done. He was also able to begin to talk to Mother about his feelings that she really had priority; however, it was obvious as he described these conversations that there were still some feelings of hurt because he did not come first. He expressed conflicting feelings: on the one hand he felt he ought to be first and the favored one and on the other hand he was convinced that no one but Mother could stand him or would want to be with him. Exploration of these feelings led to a host of early memories relating to his mother and his siblings.

Toward the end of that year, Father's capacity to deal with Terry was fairly good. He was able to be more firm with Terry despite the fact that Terry now towered over him. He was willing to discuss with the therapist— and to practice with him—some ways of working with Terry in the house so that he would not feel that he would have to watch Terry constantly but could be involved in doing a variety of activities with him. Since Father had great difficulty in finding things he and Terry could do together, the therapist and Father drew up an inventory of the repairs needed around the house. With the help of the nurse's aide who had worked closely with Terry there was a joint discussion about how Terry might be involved in each of these activities. We focused on giving Terry increased responsibility as he began to demonstrate his interest and capacity for sustained involvement and his understanding of what the task actually was. Thus, together they undertook some woodwork projects—an effort to repair some of Terry's damage to the furniture at home. They also worked at putting together some furniture that came to them in knocked-down cartons and had to be glued together in order to be made functional. One of their first major projects was the building of a very large easel for Mother to use for painting since hers would only permit 2′ by 3′ canvases and Mother was moving in the direction of larger canvases and needed an easel that could be expanded. Father was very pleased when the easel was completed and delighted with the fact that Terry and he had been able to work together to get it done and that Terry had helped a great deal with it. Terry had become especially adept with the hand drill and the screwdriver so Father was relieved of much of the physical work with his hands which he found arduous and painful. Encouraged by their success, Father and Terry carried out a number of other projects together.

Several times during their initial project Father became helpless when Terry refused to work or cooperate and became negativistic. During his therapeutic hours, Father was coached in terms of how his voice sounded to Terry and he was asked to actually try to imitate the way in which he talked to Terry. It became clear that Father would only become firm with Terry when he was actually afraid that Terry was going to be destructive. As Father imitated his comments to Terry the therapist asked permission to imitate Father's voice as closely as he could and then asked Father whether the voice as he heard it was accurate. When Father said it sounded like his voice, he was asked if that tone of voice would help Terry to stop his obstructive behavior and begin working cooperatively with him again. Father then practiced using a much firmer voice until both he and the therapist were satisfied that his tone of voice was resolute and firm and that Father sounded like he indeed meant what he said. Subsequent to these practice sessions, work on home projects went on with only occasional interruptions when Terry would get tired or distracted by something else or when Father would miss Terry's signals which indicated that he would like to do the job that Father was doing. Within several months, Father became attuned to Terry's non-verbal cues and was able to state these out loud as questions and to obtain a very clear response from Terry in terms of a garbled "yes" or "no" which sounded like "yeh" or "naa." When these moments occurred Father would proudly report his capacity to deal with Terry and his feeling that he was now able to do that which his wife said he could never do. He was also pleased that this permitted his wife to leave the home and go to the studio to paint or sometimes to paint at home without being interrupted.

Ward Behavior

During this eighth year Terry continued to be only rarely destructive on the ward. He worked at a consistently high level in school, doing much of the fourth grade level written work. He seemed to enjoy his teacher's praise and interacted easily with nursing personnel who helped in the classroom. There was almost no destructive behavior in the classroom itself. In Occupational Therapy he continued to tease, depending on who the occupational therapist might be who was working nearby. He usually had to test each

new occupational therapist or student with a variety of teasing, and sometimes destructive acts with the O.T. materials, until they learned from the
chief occupational therapist the kind of firmness that was required to get
Terry to carry out his projects and to carry them out effectively.

During this period he lost very few items of clothing while on trips; however, if his nurse's aide was not with him or if she were preoccupied, he
might very quickly dispose of a pair of gym shoes, sweater or a shirt as if
to remind the staff that he still needed constant vigilance. The eating problems, pervasive during previous years, were less difficult since he used utensils well. The problem now was that he was growing so rapidly in stature
that he became gluttonous and would snatch food from other children's
plates despite the fact that he knew he could have all the second helpings
that he wanted. A mute boy of his age was his frequent victim. This boy
would scream and flap his hands in frustration if Terry took some of the
food from his plate. Terry also ate voraciously at home.

Toward the last quarter of the eighth year Terry's parents, the therapist
and members of the nursing staff sat down together to consider the possibility of outpatient treatment. The primary reason was Terry's size; he had
gotten so large that the children's ward no longer seemed to be a good
place for him. Secondly, there seemed some possibility of his being able to
get along in a special class within the community. And thirdly, with his
parents' greater ability to handle him at home, he presented fewer problems.
Mother's greatest concern, of course, was that with Terry at home she might
not have the time to paint.

Thus, numerous efforts were made by the ward nurses, the teacher and
the therapist to prepare Terry for outpatient treatment. Contacts were made
with one of the local special education classes where they felt Terry might
fit in; however, the question remained whether or not his "testing" of them
would be too difficult to work with for long periods of time. A final plan
was decided upon whereby Terry would attend school half days—part of
which would be a planned speech program—and would spend the other half
day with a young special education teacher from a nearby teachers' college.
They would engage in a variety of physical activities as well as work on
projects in carpentry and woodworking in which Terry had already developed some skills.

OUTPATIENT WORK

Work with Terry

During the ninth year, Terry was seen twice a week. He was usually
brought in by Mother, but if Father came home early from work on
Friday, he brought Terry. There was a continued effort on his part to make

sounds approximating speech. He took a particular delight in rocking in the therapist's swivel chair and making sounds which the therapist guessed were certain words. Terry reacted with a great deal of laughter, shaking his head and saying "nnn" if the therapist's guesses were wrong and "yah, yah, yah" if they were right. He occasionally made efforts at reminding the therapist that he could be destructive by reaching for the telephone book; when he was stopped from bending the edge of the telephone page, he smiled and immediately began coloring with crayons and humming. He came eagerly to the sessions with his parents and was very happy to see his nurse's aide. On occasion he was brought to the ward by the special education student; Terry completely ignored him while they were there because he so thoroughly enjoyed spending time with members of the ward staff. He looked very happy, alert, and was obviously making sounds.

Toward the end of the ninth year the special education student brought him to the park on an occasional outing with some of the ward children which he obviously enjoyed. Another remarkable event was reported by Mother about this same time. Terry and the special education student were home alone when the doorbell rang; a man came to the door and asked if they needed to have any cleaning done. Apparently, as reported by the cleaning man when later questioned by the student and Mother, Terry very clearly replied, "No thank you. We don't need to have any cleaning done." This was the only evidence of clear, articulate speech except for the "Hi" which he uttered on meeting the therapist and other familiar people.

Toward the end of the ninth year, Mother heard of a new school which taught psychotic children to speak through a new method. Mother went to visit the school and was impressed with the head of the school's forcible presentation of the successes they had had. While she did not see any dramatic results occurring in the various classrooms and in the one-to-one efforts at helping children to speak, her personal desire to see Terry use communicative language was so great that she immediately came back to discuss plans which she and Father had made to have Terry attend this school full time. The therapist investigated the new school as best he could and from his investigations could not hold out the same hope that Mother had. He found that some of the mute patients who had been previously seen at the clinic had not made great progress in this setting. Some of us who had met with the director also shared the feeling that some of the methods used tended *Oh my!* to be coercive and therefore tended to turn the youngsters off. These findings were presented to Mother with a very strong recommendation that the current outpatient program be continued rather than risking the problems that might occur by transferring Terry to a new school and involving him in a setting where he would know no one and where he might react to the coercion that we had seen with adverse and destructive behavior. However,

Mother was determined that Terry should have this opportunity. She came back to report further that if Terry did go to this school the director asked that neither Terry nor his parents be involved in our outpatient work because he felt this might interfere with the school's effort which was quite different from ours. The director had little confidence in psychotherapeutic efforts. Thus, toward the end of the ninth year, Terry discontinued his work with us and began to attend this school for emotionally disturbed children which focused on the acquisition and use of speech.

Work with Mother

Much of the early part of the ninth year was spent with Mother around her indecision whether she should go ahead and have her surgery since she had already paid for it. At this time she did not feel safe enough with Terry at home to undergo surgery and then come home for convalescence unless Father could take some vacation or leave time. This was an issue which was broached with Father and about which he had mixed feelings since he was directing some rather urgent high priority programs. However, he did feel that the volume of work would be reduced toward the end of the year and he might then be able to take time enough away from work to be at home during Mother's recuperation. We talked again about Mother's acquiring a hearing aid during the interim so that she would be able to hear Terry and her husband and more fully communicate with her painting students.

We also began to understand why, in the therapeutic hours, there were moments when she felt she could not hear and other moments when she heard very well by examining the differences in "feeling" state. It became evident to the therapist, and some months later to Mother, that Mother heard very well when she was talking about events or problems which had little emotional impact for her. Thus, when she talked about her work with her painting students she responded quite directly to the therapist's comments and seemed to hear well. When she described Terry's successful adaptation to home and to the half-day at school, she also seemed to hear well. However, when she talked about how difficult it was to get Father to accede to taking a vacation so that she could get her ear surgery done, it was almost impossible for her to hear the therapist's comments no matter how loudly he spoke. Whenever the issue of the hearing aid was discussed, Mother also experienced great difficulty in hearing the therapist.

There was a brief period when Mother's oldest brother was again in difficulty and came to her for advice. Mother matter-of-factly told him that she really didn't have any advice for him and suggested he seek professional help. Father also was able to back her up at this time. Brother, although angry that Mother was not her usual supportive self, did go away and did not become a burden as previously by moving in with them. Although he made light of Terry's progress, it was evident from a few of his comments that he was impressed with the fact that Terry seemed relaxed, was learning and was actually working on a number of building projects.

During one of the therapeutic hours, toward the middle of the ninth year, there was a rapid shift from Mother's being able to hear very clearly to not being able to hear at all. During that hour she described how pleased she was that she had won prizes at one of the exhibitions for several of her paintings and had sold them at excellent prices. During another part of the hour, the question was again raised about whether it was still not worthwhile for Mother to have some hearing tests and to try some of the hearing aids, especially since she had complained that one of the problems in her individual instruction and in classroom instruction with her painting students was that she sometimes did not hear clearly what was being said and thus did not respond as promptly and as precisely to the questions as she could. The therapist's comments at that point were not heard at all and the therapist finally resorted to writing them out. He had never done this before. Mother became very angry and upset and the therapist's efforts to help her verbalize her feelings to see if it might not reduce her tension and alter her hearing came to naught. Mother could only state over and over again that any substitute for the operation would mean that she was doomed for the rest of her life to a hearing aid.

During the latter part of the therapeutic work that year the issue of the new school came up. Mother reported her intensive investigation of the school and her conversations with the director. She discussed her reluctance to discontinue work with us but felt it was important for Terry to have every opportunity. When the issue of possible failure and its implications for Terry's regression were raised, Mother became very angry. She felt that we had not really done very much for Terry despite his more integrative behavior, his use of a few words and his capacity to work at things with a much longer attention span. She said with a flip of her long hair, "Really the only thing you have accomplished in these last years is that you helped him learn to tie his shoes." Mother was referring to an event that occurred during the eighth year of treatment with Terry. He had previously refused to learn how to tie his shoes and on one occasion had plopped his untied shoe into the lap of the therapist for him to tie. The therapist looked at this big, dexterous six-footer who wanted somebody else to tie his shoe and was determined that they would spend that hour—or as long as was necessary—until Terry could tie his own shoes. Lo and behold, toward the end of that hour he was able to tie his shoes perfectly well. He followed the therapist's step-by-step demonstration and practiced assiduously. He learned to tie bow knots on various objects in the room as well as to tie his shoes. At the time Mother reacted with pleasure but on subsequent occasions had commented that this was really the major achievement of the children's service.

Work with Father

Father, during the ninth year, talked a good deal about his need for surgery. He felt he would enjoy sexual relationships more as would his wife. In reply to my query, he said they had never talked about sexual matters. Father felt that he really did deserve that kind of opportunity. He began to explore rather intensively with one of the plastic surgeons the cost of the operation. He went into a detailed evaluation of the surgery—its cost, time in the hospital, time at home, and time away from work—and evaluated the drain on Mother during his period of convalescence at home.

End of Outpatient Work

Thus, at the end of the ninth year of treatment Terry and his parents were discharged from outpatient treatment. We said that we would be willing to continue treatment at any time if I had the time available.

SUBSEQUENT OUTPATIENT CONTACTS

Two and a half months later, the parents came to us extremely disturbed. The situation in the special school had deteriorated quickly and the parents had been told by the director that he did not want Terry in the school. Terry had reacted to the coercive aspect of the speech training with a massive amount of destructiveness and assaultive behavior at home. The parents had hoped against hope that perhaps this would cease after a short time and continued to work with Terry at home. Fortunately I could see the family promptly.

Terry appeared gaunt, frightened and walked with an apparent uneasiness. His eyes lit up when he saw me and he pushed past me to get to the office. Once there he sat in my chair, rocked quietly and hummed in a toneless voice. As I sat quietly with him he visibly relaxed and his head dropped to one side. Toward the end of the hour a smile appeared. I gently said "Hi." Terry replied with a broad smile, "H," "H," "Hi."

Work with Terry—End of Tenth Year

I saw Terry twice a week for the next 5 months. Each hour he greeted me with "Hi" and spent his time drawing nonobjective masses of black, red and blue with his crayons, the black color predominating. While he continued to say "Hi" and "No," he attempted no other speech. Several times I hummed or sang songs that he had sung from his school readers; he would smile but made no effort to sing with me, or to make any other sounds. There was no destructive behavior on the ward with his favorite nurse's aide and he was relaxed while waiting for his mother to see me. But at home his destructive behavior persisted.

Work with Mother—Tenth Year

Mother was distraught when she came in to resume therapy. She expected me to say "I told you so." Instead I talked about my feeling that Mother's decision had been a very tough one and she'd been brave to go against advice and could not be faulted for wanting the best treatment and hopefully the best results for Terry. I made it clear that I accepted and respected her decision. She tearfully mentioned the forceful methods they used to get children to talk. We would now call it "aversive conditioning." She said these methods had not been clear to her until she saw how Terry reacted to them. The director, although a burly man, was unable to restrain or contain Terry when he swiftly moved to break something. His destructiveness at the school had increased from day to day. Finally they could not contain him at all.

Now at home they were back to a constant watchfulness. Terry was again sleepless; he would get up and try to find matches to burn paper or would wreck some piece of furniture or sneak into the kitchen to dismantle appliances.

Although Mother's anxiety level was great and she had had no time to herself during the week after Terry had left the school, her hearing was fairly good. Mother was able to find another college student to help care for Terry during the days but he was unable to establish a trusting relationship.

After about two months Mother called me at 2:00 A.M. In a panicky voice she said Terry had been terribly excited all evening, would not go to bed and tried to hit her several times. She was scared and didn't know what to do. I dressed and drove to their house a few minutes away. Mother answered my ring, Terry right behind her pawing at her. Mother was dressed in a sheer silk nightgown and equally sheer robe, both torn. (I later learned that this was her usual bedtime attire, despite the fact that she had to handle Terry at night and that for the last five or six years he had become a tall, well developed and sexually mature adolescent.)

I spoke firmly to Terry and tried to lead him by the arm back to his bedroom. Terry resisted at first and refused to budge. Knowing I could not budge him against his will, I talked to him in a firm, but calm voice. I told him I knew he was excited and mad and it was hard for him to relax. After a bit he yielded to my tug and led me to his bedroom. We sat for 15 or 20 minutes together on the side of the bed. I continued talking to him and finally he yawned. I suggested he lie down; when he did I covered him with his blankets and remained sitting next to him with my hand on his. By this time his heart rate had come down from 130 to 70 per minute and his respiration was slow and even. The flush on his face and the dilated eyes were gone and in about 20 minutes he was dozing lightly.

I went to talk with Mother who had changed into a dress. Father had been called out of town for a one day consultation. During the last two months it had been obvious that Terry became excited each night and both she and her husband had a difficult time getting him to sleep. That night he wanted to touch her breast and when she rebuffed him he slapped out at her and became increasingly wild, grabbing at her and tearing her clothes.

When I next saw Mother we discussed the evening and I flatly said that she must begin wearing both opaque pajamas and an opaque robe at night. Better yet, she ought not to change until Terry was in bed. We then discussed the naturalness of Terry's sexual feelings and his excitement. Mother shook her head, wondering why she'd been so dense since she had observed his interest in her breasts but had somehow felt she didn't need to change her 20 year pattern of bedtime attire.

With my help Mother found a hospital aide who could sleep in Terry's room and help out at night. He was a warm middle-aged man who could get Terry to bed and to sleep so that everyone could usually get a good night's sleep.

The daytime destruction continued unabated. Toward the end of the five months, after an appointment at the clinic, Mother and Terry were walking down the steep hill near the clinic where Mother parked her car. Mother slipped on the slick sidewalk, fell, and skinned her entire leg and side. She screamed in pain. Startled, Terry began to scream and in his fright he pummelled Mother. When she regained her feet he ran away from her and she returned to the clinic to phone for the police to look for him. They found him in the park nearby where he usually went from the ward with his aide. For Mother this was the last straw. She subsequently joined Father in requesting a referral to a nearby state hospital.

Work with Father

Father's early therapeutic hours were also centered around the difficulties with Terry since he entered the local school. After the first week his parents began to recognize that Terry was extremely tense and apprehensive. Father's anxiety was so great about communicating his observations to Mother that he felt that he'd better remain silent since Mother was obviously also upset. Thus the parents did not talk very much until Terry's destructiveness and assaultiveness became such a concern that they began to visit the school. They then became aware of his increased destructiveness there and the fact that the director's methods seemed not to be working with Terry at all.

On return to a home program and beginning outpatient work with us again, Father was terribly discouraged. He felt they had missed the opportunity to capitalize on Terry's integration and his efforts to communicate more effectively and become a useful member of the family. Father became panicky after the first month of return to treatment; Terry again began to set fires at home and Father felt there was some chance that they would not be able to catch Terry's firesetting in time and that their whole house might burn down. He also found Terry much more difficult to handle physically and found that his previously effective interventions no longer seemed to stop Terry. His verbal "No" or his efforts to stop Terry physically now resulted in an increased amount of destructive behavior with some assaultiveness. During one interview, Father described in detail how Terry, when stopped, would now begin to push Father away. Father felt helpless in the face of this large six foot, two inch youngster and would try to appease him as he had when Terry was smaller. This was not at all helpful to Terry but Father felt that he had no way to stop Terry at this point. When Mother suffered the attack from Terry at night, Father recognized the kind of sexual impulses that Terry was having but felt that he could not deal with these and withdrew from any discussions with his wife or Terry about them.

Subsequent to Mother's fall, and Terry's pummeling her and running away, Father became increasingly discouraged, feeling Terry might become much more destructive and assaultive at home. He began to explore with the therapist the possibilities of state hospitalization. On one occasion Father tried to keep Terry from breaking up a chair in Terry's room. Terry pushed Father so hard that he fell down and as he scrambled to get up, Terry kicked at him. Father felt terrified and again expressed his conviction that neither he nor Mother could handle Terry at home. Following these events Mother and Father discussed with the therapist the possibility of state hospital care and were given some help in referral to the nearest state hospital. They made a trip there with Terry and described their problems.

State Hospital Care for Terry

Terry was hospitalized on a trial basis to enable the staff to evaluate his need for hospitalization. On the ward of the state hospital, Terry became increasingly destructive and difficult to handle. The parents visited Terry several times a week and tried to take him home for a weekend. It proved to be so difficult that the parents agreed with the hospital staff to leave him in the hospital for a period of several months before they tried another home visit. Over the next several months, both parents came in to visit the therapist, to discuss their problems with Terry, and some of their problems with each other. They seemed more relaxed at this point and could discuss some of their difficulties in containing Terry and the amount of anguish and terror they felt when Terry became destructive at home. Together, therapist and parents considered how Terry might be dealt with during weekends at home and the possibility that they might be able to get the hospital aide to come in for some weekends. Thus they might not have to wear themselves out in their vigilant surveillance of all Terry's activities. After the parents tried this for several weekends successfully, the therapist then suggested that perhaps they might bring Terry in for an interview each Friday evening when they brought him home.

During these interviews Terry was relaxed with the therapist but he looked increasingly vague, and it was much more difficult to engage him in eye contact. He did not respond to the therapist's comments about the feelings which seemed to be emerging in him and his friendly "Hi" only could occasionally be elicited from him and became more infrequent. The parents also commented that as the weeks passed, Terry seemed to become much more fearful although he was always happy to see them when they arrived. Terry was so apprehensive about returning to the hospital that Mother and Father were tempted to limit their visits with him to the hospital grounds rather than bringing him home and becoming involved in the struggle to take him back. They were fearful that he might even jump out of the car on the return trip.

The state hospital staff decided to institute electric shock treatment; they suggested to the parents that the weekends at home be discontinued because of Terry's increased apprehension and his destructiveness on the ward upon his return to the hospital.

Continued Work with Parents

The therapist continued to see each of the parents individually for another three months during which time Mother made plans for her surgery and Father began to consider when he might have his surgical work done. Mother did have her surgery during this period and the result was a moderate increase in her ability to hear. She was extremely careful about conserving her energy; after the surgical wounds had healed she was told to resume all of her activities, again teaching painting. Since Terry was no longer being seen as a patient, it was decided we would discontinue our work together.

The therapist wanted to keep in close contact with the family and hear about Terry's stay on the hospital ward and began some monthly telephone follow-up with the family.

Despite the variety of electric shock treatments and the use of each new psychotropic agent as it was introduced in the hospital, Terry continued to be difficult to deal with, and spent much of his time in restraints or in isolation. The parents recognized that the hospital staff had very little individual time to give him and that his developing relationships with numerous staff members were always cut off by that staff member either leaving hospital employment for another job or being transferred to another ward. They made several efforts to bring Terry home for long weekends or on holidays or his birthday and these seemed to work out fairly well. However, they had to be extremely vigilant that Terry did not again become destructive. By and large, these weekends became more successful and Terry's behavior was more subdued. During a number of these weekends the therapist visited Terry at his home. Terry was always pleased to see the therapist and appeared excited that he was there. He wanted the therapist to sit down and stay for a while and showed his pleasure by serving him tea and saying, "Hi, Hi, Hi" over and over again.

During these visits and other contacts with both parents, it appeared that the parents were more relaxed with each other and could make humorous comments to each other. During one visit home Father mentioned he'd finally had his surgery and was pleased at the reduction of discomfort. In none of these visits to the home to see Terry and his parents was there evidence of the previous anger between them.

In our last contact with the family, Terry was still in the state hospital and somewhat subdued. The parents reported that he is still extremely alert whenever they visit him. However, since the use of phenothiazines, Terry's anxiety appeared less but his previous alertness was also decreased. However, they understood the needs of the hospital staff to reduce Terry's destructiveness on the ward.

DISCUSSION

Evaluation Lessons

What have we learned from this unsuccessful effort in psychotherapy with a psychotic youngster and his parents? Perhaps the most obvious lesson from this early experience of the Children's Service is the need for more careful evaluation of factors indicating good versus poor prognosis.

From this study and others, we see that a careful history usually helps delineate the relationships and events during the first few months to two years of life which are predictive of severe and continuous conflicts and which are not easily resolved (1). The impact of several critical factors is seen clearly in this case. Interpersonal factors include Mother's depression and the severe ongoing conflicts between parents. Related traumatic life events, such as Mother's hysterectomy, her subsequent post partum illness, and the deaths of Mother's mother and friend, greatly aggravated the previous conflicts. The genetic factors of Terry's vitality and physical resiliency from birth on gave a particular direction to Terry's illness; the symptoms in their final form were predictive of poor psychotherapeutic results.

We also have begun to note more clearly during our evaluations the signs of severe and prolonged intra- and interpersonal conflicts in parents which predict the need for long term intensive psychotherapy. Indications are that simultaneous psychotherapy with child and both parents will not cause changes rapidly enough to significantly alter the child's severe disturbance. Thus, more effective and individuated living for the child appears unlikely to result from the total therapeutic efforts.

The age of onset of the severe illness, the duration and severity of the child's illness, and severity and duration of parental conflicts are all important indicators of prognosis. Elsewhere, we've also seen that factors of parental age, vitality and effectiveness in other areas of living also affect prognosis (4).

In our patient there was almost eight years of severe disturbance, six of these with mutism. It would seem unlikely, in light of our subsequent investigations and those of our colleagues in other settings, that the reversal of these conflicts or even their reduction to allow Terry to live more independently outside a hospital setting would be possible. However, we actually had been clearly successful at helping Terry's socialization and more adaptive living at home.

In this instance, Mother's interaction with Terry from birth to eight months of age was interrupted by a number of extremely traumatic events for her. The mothering relationship was seriously interfered with during these eight months, and the attachment so necessary for development of relationships and ego processes in all subsequent phases of infancy and childhood was tenuous at best. In this extremely vigorous and strong infant the symptoms of sleeplessness, sleep reversal, and constant crying did not lead to the infant's "giving-up" as in instances described by Spitz "on anaclitic depression" (2, 3).

Terry, very early, seemed to react to his whole variety of interpersonal deprivations including the indifferent caretaking of a nurse for the first five or six months of his life by screaming and restlessness during the nights. This behavior forced Mother and Father (but mostly Mother) to carry him about in order to reduce the amount of crying and sleeplessness. The sleeplessness and restlessness became a pattern for him as he grew older. To this pattern was added the variety of traumata which resulted from inter-actions with other caretakers. Mother's brother, in particular, with his unusually harsh behavior toward Terry, led to Terry's fear of people and to a diminution of speech until he finally became mute around age two. The many traumata that he experienced with neighborhood children and adults increased Terry's fear of human beings, especially terror of children, and resulted in social isolation. This degree of isolation is also predictive of poor prognosis.

Impact of Maternal Depression on Infant and Child

Mother's depression was not only massive during Terry's first eight months of life but continuous to a lesser degree for the next seven years. Although Terry was out of the home for a year and a half in an inpatient setting, Mother's depression served early to reinforce his withdrawal, isola-tion and survival behavior. By survival behavior, I'm referring to sleepless-ness, prowling, investigativeness and skillful dismantling of machinery, later to be regarded as destructive behavior. Such behavior had interpersonal sequelae of bringing attention to Terry in often harsh as well as integrative aspects of ego mastery.

From the data which slowly evolved through the therapeutic work, it seems likely that Mother's guilt about her love affair and pregnancy, coupled with guilt about her early anger toward Father's lack of awareness of her needs, permission for her hysterectomy and second thoughts about the via-bility of the marriage, were factors which increased her depression and reduced her capacity to assert herself on behalf of her child and herself. Mother's ongoing depression and severe conflicts about asserting her own needs, her massive helplessness in the face of mounting requirements to have help for Terry, her desire for surgery for her deafness, and the fact that she felt blamed by certain family members and professionals for Terry's condition all added to her inability to assess and deal with situations more effectively. Certainly, the professional people she had consulted were not very helpful to her at times of her greatest need.

Father's Role

Father also had severe conflicts about himself as a man, a husband, and a father. He sought to avoid contact with his difficult son and his constantly critical wife. In turn he put his own family's concerns, especially help for his ailing mother, to whom he was still the all important child, ahead of his wife's needs, causing recurrent conflict within the family. Unresolved conflicts within and between Terry's parents over many years also is evidence that the prognosis for treatment was not good.

Frequency of Countertransference Problems

We now recognize that the countertransference problems which were manifested early and then sporadically in our treatment frequently occur in work with very sick children and their parents. They stem not only from the unresolved problems within the therapist but also from the variety of situations within the ward setting itself which seems to augment these problems, especially the therapist's need to be successful with very difficult cases. In Terry's case, the need to omnipotently cure very sick children who, on careful analysis, have a poor prognosis was shared by ward personnel.

Results of Early Therapy as an Indicator of Prognosis

Thus, the treatment early in the therapeutic work on the Children's Service was not undertaken within the framework of our later understanding about indicators of prognosis. More recently, we utilize our therapeutic approach for a specified period. Periodic assessments help us determine whether changes that have occurred are in the direction of greater integration of child and parents. The time invested needs to lead to improvement or evidence of beginning changes in child's and parents' conflicts. Such clinical research efforts lead to greater awareness on the part of all faculty and ward staff. Constant examination of details of treatment and frequent assessment enable the staff to deal with other seriously psychotic children more effectively. Such evaluation has also led to concentrating our therapeutic work on young children and their parents. Not only is this effort designed to assure more favorable prognosis, but also to provide data, from more successful efforts, to alter our program and therapeutic work so that more disturbed and older children may be worked with more effectively.

ISSUES IN THERAPEUTIC WORK WITH PARENTS

Early in our therapeutic work with parents, we engaged them in as frequent therapeutic sessions as possible. Usually the father was the most difficult to engage and had more difficulty in freeing time for therapy. Mothers were seen as in this instance more frequently, usually twice as often as the father. However, rarely were both parents seen as frequently as the child, three and when possible, four times a week. More recently, we have recognized such disparity in the intensity of therapeutic work as a possible critical factor in effectiveness of our efforts at simultaneous therapeutic work in help-ing resolve both intra- and interpersonal conflicts in the family members.

Parental Projection onto the Therapist

Other issues have gradually asserted themselves in therapeutic work with parents. Among these is the frequent projection onto the therapist of a magical capacity to both fulfill their own needs as conflicted human beings and to magically cure the child who is a source of such distress and often continued conflict between the parents. The therapist, early in his experience, is both unaware of these projections and unclear about how these unconscious projections fit into his own countertransference problems and obstruct the early phases of therapeutic work.

Mother's hunger for satisfying relationships which were close and nurtur-antly sensitive to her nonverbal cues were not recognized early. Only as Mother could trust the therapist could she more openly express these feelings and come to understand them. The therapist early was overwhelmed by the bitter anger, the need and refusal of Mother to assert herself.

Similarly, Father's passivity and his understandable first priority—to satisfy his needs and his mother's—rather than to attend to the pressing needs of his own immediate family, reverberated with some of the therapist's personal experience. This made it difficult for him to perceive and separate out the elements of these conflicts and to deal with them in a nonthreatening way with Father.

Role of Somatic Problems in Parents

Physical disabilities—Mother's deafness and Father's congenital tumor and resulting surgical and X-ray traumata—and their impact on each parent also presented therapeutic obstacles and opportunities which the therapist did not recognize. Father's unawareness of his inadequacy as a sexual partner and his unwillingness to look at the fact that his sterility meant that his son was not his, could not be analyzed until Father was ready to consider his own past physical problems and the resulting altered view he had had of him-self since childhood. Even then it was difficult to bring the resulting conflicts into focus.

The fact that neither Mother's husband nor her family responded to her problem of deafness with any empathy or understanding contributed to Mother's defensiveness, bitterness, and unwillingness to compromise and try using a hearing aide for temporary relief.

Both Mother and Father needed to live through and, from past experience with others, to defend themselves from a genuine concern by another. They could not accept a concerned person's interest in their welfare rather than exploitation of each of them for the purpose of gratifying narcissistic needs, a concerned, but nonjudgmental individual who would try to help each of them. Inherent in this process is the effort to help each individual actually to try, and then after repeated efforts, to become effective in their dealing with previously avoided conflict areas.

Competency of Parents—Rational vs. Unconscious Processes

Another lesson that the therapist learned was that his early and conscious admiration for Mother's and Father's capacities and their integrative behavior made it more difficult to simultaneously understand and help with the many areas of dysfunctional behavior. Thus, Mother's artistic capabilities, her sensitivity to a variety of interpersonal situations, her sensitivity to the therapist's unconscious and nonverbal cues, along with Father's extraordinary competence as a physicist and his major contributions in research, made it difficult at first to hear their pleas for help. It was some time before these effective adults could be viewed as people who needed major help in other areas of their functioning.

Impact on Therapist of Overwhelming Conflict within the Family

The therapist gradually began to recognize the enormity of the parents' unconscious conflicts and the developmental implications of the unmet needs in each of them. For some time, the therapist's angry helplessness in reaction to Mother's anger and bitterness towards the ward setting, the helping personnel and the therapist made therapeutic work difficult. Father's avoidance of family problems by absenting himself from home and his use of therapy to resolve only work problems were also difficult to handle therapeutically. As often occurs early in psychotherapeutic work, such conflicts in patients await the therapist's working through similar but less severe conflicts either in his own personal therapeutic work or as the result of honest exploration of these problems with a sensitive and able supervisor (5).

Thus, some resolution of a therapist's conflicts in nuclear areas stemming from his childhood experiences permits greater understanding of and empathy with his patients. His own reduced defensiveness and greater understanding of his patients' defensive behavior permits more precise and gentle interpretive behavior and comments. Thus, slowly the patients are more involved in a therapeutic alliance to help reduce their own conflicts. Mother's anger, desperation and suicidal feelings, Father's passivity and more open indications of his need to be taken care of could only be dealt with as both the present realities and the conflicts from early childhood could be understood and gently commented on.

In this case as in many others, parental conflicts may be so great that the therapist despairs of being helpful. He requires constant aid in learning to become aware of the nonverbal cues so he can begin to work with his patients in areas where conflicts are less acute and begin to establish the therapeutic relationship. The therapist especially needs help with the feelings that he alone must be able to meet the parents' and child's many needs. In work with psychotic children and parents, there is only a short step from feeling omnipotent to feeling overwhelmed.

Problems in Work with Terry

With Terry, early problems were centered around the therapist's omnipotent need to be effective. Difficulties arose in effecting collaboration with other members of the staff to work through Terry's destructiveness, unpredictable firesetting, and jamming of locks and appliances. It slowly became clear that limits must be set. It later became clear in supervision that the therapist admired Terry's dexterity and facility for taking apart locks, refrigerators, stoves, etc. Still later he recognized that part of himself that identified with Terry's skillful evasion of detection and continued destructiveness despite the vigilance of ward personnel. Terry's successful defiance of all authority unconsciously pleased the therapist and as these issues were clarified by the therapist, he became more aware of how Terry needed to be helped.

The therapist gradually became aware that he needed to recognize early manifestations of Terry's destructive behavior. This was a difficult task because it demanded continuous vigilance and prompt action to have any impact on Terry's behavior. It was easier to ignore these manifestations and continue to work in other ways rather than to try to attend perceptively to the signs of incipient destructiveness. Only after the therapist had experienced in several situations that close attention to nonverbal details of incipient destructive behavior could sometimes lead to effective intervention did he move forward. The therapist's repeated efforts led to more integrated behavior on Terry's part. Therapeutic work progressed, in this case leading to beginning vocalization, attempted verbalization, as well as much more integrative play.

When he and Terry worked together to fix the window shade that Terry had torn in a destructive moment, only restitution of destructive behavior was the therapist's goal. At that time he did not recognize Terry's integrative efforts as a step toward mutual activities that might involve Terry's most competent and effective ego functions. Terry's great perceptiveness, dexterity, and capacity for working with tools, and, as illustrated by the window blind incident, his capacity to follow through and complete a task

Yet T. had been good in OT before that!

as soon as it was made clear to him what was expected were not reviewed or capitalized on. In retrospect, the therapist should have involved himself with more integrative aspects of Terry's behavior and used this opportunity to begin a new phase of work with Terry. He viewed Terry's behavior as a single incident in their work rather than recognizing the opportunity to begin a new phase. In subsequent therapy situations, the therapist has used such instances to initiate a new phase of work, using intact ego functions as a way to introduce speech, enhance closeness or playfulness, strengthen the therapeutic relationship or motivate learning in other areas.

Collaborative Issues

Another aspect of learning had to do with the collaborative aspects of therapeutic work, which are critical in helping a destructive and self-destructive child to learn self-control. It is clear that the therapist as a collaborator with the ward staff became fully involved with them only after he himself had become a victim of Terry's destructive behavior when Terry knocked his eye glasses to the floor. Prior to this incident, the therapist's primary concern was to contain Terry's behavior in his own office. This had some major therapeutic impact; however, there was little transfer to the ward setting or to enhancing the therapeutic work of ward personnel. The reciprocal kind of influence that might have occurred if each of the staff members who were therapeutically engaged with Terry had collaborated more effectively was not implemented early. Each of us had a difficult enough job to do in our own work. Thus, the attention to minute detail which is necessary in every aspect of the work did not take place early.

Several instances indicated that, when the therapist was determined to bring about some particular change, like helping Terry tie his shoes or insisting he use a tissue rather than his sleeve when he had a cold, the objective was reached. Within a relatively short time these therapeutic sessions resulted in Terry's becoming more independent and more socially adapted in his behavior. Retrospectively, in each instance, there was an awareness on the therapist's part that Terry could at that particular moment become engaged in a more integrative therapeutic process of learning and his behavior could be altered.

The necessary collaboration around details of moment-to-moment living seemed critical with Terry and have been as critical with other psychotic children. To bring about a slow but consistent change in behavior requires open collaboration between the therapist and other therapeutic personnel in the ward milieu, through honest communication, mutual self-awareness and clarity about the total process. Only later, when better collaboration did occur, was the anger of ward personnel toward the therapist for not being more helpful to the staff brought into the open. Results for close collaboration helped Terry in every aspect of his learning and his relationships to others.

Lessons in Milieu Therapy

The philosophy inherent in most milieu therapy but especially on the Children's Service is that each person who works with child or parents has a potential therapeutic effect on them. Thus nurses, aides, teachers, and occupational therapists are vitally important members of the therapeutic team. The integration of that team into open, communicating, task-oriented collaborators is essential for therapeutic effectiveness.

Some of the obstacles to communication and collaboration have been noted. The need has become clear for collaborators to know each other well over time so that they work together less ambivalently. The all-too-frequent rivalries between individuals and helping professions are destructive to the mutual effort.

In the last decade, milieu therapy has begun to move in the direction of parent involvement. The milieu philosophy is enlarged from full therapeutic collaboration of staff on behalf of a child and family to include the parents as collaborators. Thus, parents not only collaborate in discussing ward and home management problems with milieu staff but also begin to work with their child, or first with other children, under staff direction. In this process the parent observes and learns how others work with children and specifically their child. They also identify with these staff members. Thus, slowly they identify with their attitudes and use the methods they note to be most effective with a child. Members of the milieu staff develop special relationships with parents which make discussion of management problems easier. Parent involvement also permits staff to work in the home with the parents around particularly difficult problems of management.

In our experience parent collaboration with sensitive and skilled staff members may make the difference in the therapeutic work which helps the parents to live more easily with their child. In turn, each such step results in reduced conflict both in and between parents and their child. The total therapeutic effort is enhanced. We now view our early experiences and collaborative problems as necessary steps in development of a therapeutic milieu.

Learning from the Family

For this therapist, and I suspect for many others, one lesson learned from continuous long term work with a family is the necessity for developing the kind of "hovering" attentiveness described by Freud. Also acquired is the essential capacity for rapid intervention when needed. The therapist's behavior in providing models for identification to both parents and child in the therapeutic interaction and in the milieu has become increasingly important to this therapist. One can only understand the potential effectiveness of such interaction through prolonged work with a very sick child and his parents. The awareness of nuances of verbal and nonverbal behavior and their implications for understanding other kinds of feelings not expressed by the patient only become clear to the therapist through prolonged work and repeated opportunities. This provides repetition of particular behavior or moments of interaction that allow one to become aware of their possible meanings and the probable effects of verbal or nonverbal interpretation.

Problems of Simultaneous Therapeutic Work with Child and Parents

A therapist's capacity to work with both child and parents requires an increased amount of clarity. He learns not to over-identify with child or either parent. Certainly, that effort in itself leads to greater clarity within oneself about some of one's own unresolved feelings from childhood. One becomes more clear about personal needs to propitiate a parent when a particularly upset or discouraged parent—or both parents—vent their anger at the therapist in moments of crisis. At first, rather than helping them begin to analyze the events which have led to their present feelings, the therapist tries to be reasonable and helpful without understanding the issues. Early, therefore, the effort is often to reduce the force of the feeling. In almost no other therapeutic situation, except perhaps that with the acting-out adolescent, does the therapist feel under such great pressure. Only after prolonged work in simultaneous psychotherapy do the variety of elements that comprise this pressure become clear and understood by the therapist. He can then gradually work in the therapeutic situation to help child and parents work toward conflict reduction.

Such prolonged work with seriously disturbed children and their parents has indelible impact on a therapist, especially if he has been helped during the process by continuous supervision or personal therapeutic work. Efforts to understand himself and his patients with increased honesty and empathy lead to more effective work with other patients and hopefully greater and more rapid resolution of the conflicts in other children and parents so that they are more able to make decisions which permit integrative living.

For this therapist, the many experiences with Terry and Mother and Father have been critical learning opportunities which have contributed to his more effective work with many other families.

REFERENCES

1. BOWLBY, J. *Attachment and Loss. Vol. 1. Attachment.* New York: Basic Books, Inc., 1969.
2. SPITZ, S. A. Hospitalism: An Inquiry into the Genesis of Psychiatric Conditions in Early Childhood. *Psychoanalytic Study of the Child,* 1945, 1:53-74.
3. SPITZ, R. A. Anaclitic Depression. *Psychoanalytic Study of the Child,* 1946, 2:313-342.
4. SZUREK, S. A., and BERLIN, I. N. Elements of Psychotherapeutics with the Schizophrenic Child and His Parents. *Psychiatry,* 1956, 19:1-9.
5. SZUREK, S. A., and BERLIN, I. N. The Question of Therapy for the Trainee in the Psychiatric Training Program. *J. Amer. Acad. Child Psychiat.,* 1966, 5:155-166.

Index

158, 9 - Homer quotes
160 - secrets.
162 - depressing followup! 330

71 A. Meyer took Freud + Jung to task for being too biological.

224 - self-destructive - no app. pain

364)
366) not too Diff. to Rutter
368) - follow up results

379 - negativism

539 - an odd account (unrecognized) g a mother as a
therapist.

604 - Susselman, another th. who dresses like a dude to
play w. kids!
683 - insisting on fogiricacy even w. epileptic!
765 - parents at length as collaborators!
change